Dictionary of Literary Biography

Dictionary of Literary Biography Documentary Series

Dictionary of Literary Biography Yearbooks

1980 edited by Karen L. Rood, Jean W. Ross, and Richard Ziegfeld (1981)

1981 edited by Karen L. Rood, Jean W. Ross, and Richard Ziegfeld (1982)

1982 edited by Richard Ziegfeld; associate editors: Jean W. Ross and Lynne C. Zeigler (1983)

1983 edited by Mary Bruccoli and Jean W. Ross; associate editor Richard Ziegfeld (1984)

1984 edited by Jean W. Ross (1985)

1985 edited by Jean W. Ross (1986)

1986 edited by J. M. Brook (1987)

1987 edited by J. M. Brook (1988)

1988 edited by J. M. Brook (1989)

1989 edited by J. M. Brook (1990)

1990 edited by James W. Hipp (1991)

1991 edited by James W. Hipp (1992)

1992 edited by James W. Hipp (1993)

1993 edited by James W. Hipp, contributing editor George Garrett (1994)

1994 edited by James W. Hipp, contributing editor George Garrett (1995)

1995 edited by James W. Hipp, contributing editor George Garrett (1996)

1996 edited by Samuel W. Bruce and L. Kay Webster, contributing editor George Garrett (1997)

1997 edited by Matthew J. Bruccoli and George Garrett, with the assistance of L. Kay Webster (1998)

1998 edited by Matthew J. Bruccoli, contributing editor George Garrett, with the assistance of D. W. Thomas (1999)

1999 edited by Matthew J. Bruccoli, contributing editor George Garrett, with the assistance of D. W. Thomas (2000)

2000 edited by Matthew J. Bruccoli, contributing editor George Garrett, with the assistance of George Parker Anderson (2001)

Concise Series

Concise Dictionary of American Literary Biography, 7 volumes (1988-1999): *The New Consciousness, 1941-1968; Colonization to the American Renaissance, 1640-1865; Realism, Naturalism, and Local Color, 1865-1917; The Twenties, 1917-1929; The Age of Maturity, 1929-1941; Broadening Views, 1968-1988; Supplement: Modern Writers, 1900-1998.*

Concise Dictionary of British Literary Biography, 8 volumes (1991-1992): *Writers of the Middle Ages and Renaissance Before 1660; Writers of the Restoration and Eighteenth Century, 1660-1789; Writers of the Romantic Period, 1789-1832; Victorian Writers, 1832-1890; Late-Victorian and Edwardian Writers, 1890-1914; Modern Writers, 1914-1945; Writers After World War II, 1945-1960; Contemporary Writers, 1960 to Present.*

Concise Dictionary of World Literary Biography, 10 volumes projected (1999-   ): *Ancient Greek and Roman Writers; German Writers; African, Caribbean, and Latin American Writers; South Slavic and Eastern European Writers.*

Dictionary of Literary Biography® • Volume Two Hundred Fifty-Five

British Fantasy and Science-Fiction Writers, 1918–1960

Dictionary of Literary Biography® • Volume Two Hundred Fifty-Five

British Fantasy and Science-Fiction Writers, 1918–1960

Edited by
Darren Harris-Fain
Shawnee State University

A Bruccoli Clark Layman Book
The Gale Group
Detroit • San Francisco • London • Boston • Woodbridge, Conn.

Printed in the United States of America

The paper used in this publication meets the minimum requirements
of American National Standard for Information Sciences–Permanence
Paper for Printed Library Materials, ANSI Z39.48-1984. ∞™

Library of Congress Cataloging-in-Publication Data

British fantasy and science-fiction writers, 1918–1960 / edited by Darren Harris-Fain.
    p. cm.–(Dictionary of literary biography; v. 255)
"A Bruccoli Clark Layman book."
Includes bibliographical references (p.) and index.
ISBN 0-7876-5249-0 (alk. paper)
1. Fantasy fiction, English–Bio-bibliography–Dictionaries. 2. Science fiction, English–Bio-bibliography–Dictionaries. 3. English fiction–20th century–Bio-bibliography–Dictionaries. 4. Authors, English–20th century–Biography–Dictionaries. 5. English fiction–20th century–Dictionaries. 6. Fantasy fiction, English–Dictionaries. 7. Science fiction, English–Dictionaries. I. Harris-Fain, Darren. II. Series.

PR888.F3 B75 2002
823'.087609'003–dc21
[B]
                                            2002017152

For Julie and Elizabeth

Contents

Plan of the Series

. . . Almost the most prodigious asset of a country, and perhaps its most precious possession, is its native literary product—when that product is fine and noble and enduring.

Mark Twain*

The advisory board, the editors, and the publisher of the *Dictionary of Literary Biography* are joined in endorsing Mark Twain's declaration. The literature of a nation provides an inexhaustible resource of permanent worth. Our purpose is to make literature and its creators better understood and more accessible to students and the reading public, while satisfying the needs of teachers and researchers.

To meet these requirements, *literary biography* has been construed in terms of the author's achievement. The most important thing about a writer is his writing. Accordingly, the entries in *DLB* are career biographies, tracing the development of the author's canon and the evolution of his reputation.

The purpose of *DLB* is not only to provide reliable information in a usable format but also to place the figures in the larger perspective of literary history and to offer appraisals of their accomplishments by qualified scholars.

The publication plan for *DLB* resulted from two years of preparation. The project was proposed to Bruccoli Clark by Frederick G. Ruffner, president of the Gale Research Company, in November 1975. After specimen entries were prepared and typeset, an advisory board was formed to refine the entry format and develop the series rationale. In meetings held during 1976, the publisher, series editors, and advisory board approved the scheme for a comprehensive biographical dictionary of persons who contributed to literature. Editorial work on the first volume began in January 1977, and it was published in 1978. In order to make *DLB* more than a dictionary and to compile volumes that individually have claim to status as literary history, it was decided to organize volumes by topic, period, or

From an unpublished section of Mark Twain's autobiography, copyright by the Mark Twain Company

genre. Each of these freestanding volumes provides a biographical-bibliographical guide and overview for a particular area of literature. We are convinced that this organization—as opposed to a single alphabet method—constitutes a valuable innovation in the presentation of reference material. The volume plan necessarily requires many decisions for the placement and treatment of authors. Certain figures will be included in separate volumes, but with different entries emphasizing the aspect of his career appropriate to each volume. Ernest Hemingway, for example, is represented in *American Writers in Paris, 1920–1939* by an entry focusing on his expatriate apprenticeship; he is also in *American Novelists, 1910–1945* with an entry surveying his entire career, as well as in *American Short-Story Writers, 1910–1945, Second Series* with an entry concentrating on his short fiction. Each volume includes a cumulative index of the subject authors and articles.

Since 1981 the series has been further augmented by the *DLB Yearbooks,* which update published entries, add new entries to keep the *DLB* current with contemporary activity, and provide articles on literary history. There have also been nineteen *DLB Documentary Series* volumes which provide illustrations, facsimiles, and biographical and critical source materials for figures, works, or groups judged to have particular interest for students. In 1999 the *Documentary Series* was incorporated into the *DLB* volume numbering system beginning with *DLB 210: Ernest Hemingway.*

We define literature as the *intellectual commerce of a nation:* not merely as belles lettres but as that ample and complex process by which ideas are generated, shaped, and transmitted. *DLB* entries are not limited to "creative writers" but extend to other figures who in their time and in their way influenced the mind of a people. Thus the series encompasses historians, journalists, publishers, book collectors, and screenwriters. By this means readers of *DLB* may be aided to perceive literature not as cult scripture in the keeping of intellectual high priests but firmly positioned at the center of a nation's life.

DLB includes the major writers appropriate to each volume and those standing in the ranks behind them. Scholarly and critical counsel has been sought in deciding which minor figures to include and how full their entries should be. Wherever possible, useful references are made to figures who do not warrant separate entries.

Each *DLB* volume has an expert volume editor responsible for planning the volume, selecting the figures for inclusion, and assigning the entries. Volume editors are also responsible for preparing, where appropriate, appendices surveying the major periodicals and literary and intellectual movements for their volumes, as well as lists of further readings. Work on the series as a whole is coordinated at the Bruccoli Clark Layman editorial center in Columbia, South Carolina, where the editorial staff is responsible for accuracy and utility of the published volumes.

One feature that distinguishes *DLB* is the illustration policy—its concern with the iconography of literature. Just as an author is influenced by his surroundings, so is the reader's understanding of the author enhanced by a knowledge of his environment. Therefore *DLB* volumes include not only drawings, paintings, and photographs of authors, often depicting them at various stages in their careers, but also illustrations of their families and places where they lived. Title pages are regularly reproduced in facsimile along with dust jackets for modern authors. The dust jackets are a special feature of *DLB* because they often document better than anything else the way in which an author's work was perceived in its own time. Specimens of the writers' manuscripts and letters are included when feasible.

Samuel Johnson rightly decreed that "The chief glory of every people arises from its authors." The purpose of the *Dictionary of Literary Biography* is to compile literary history in the surest way available to us—by accurate and comprehensive treatment of the lives and work of those who contributed to it.

The *DLB* Advisory Board

Introduction

Even though the terms "fantasy" and "science fiction" as they are currently used are recent, the types of literature to which they refer date back to the origins of British literature in the case of fantasy and, following Brian W. Aldiss's widely accepted argument that Mary Shelley's *Frankenstein; or, the Modern Prometheus* (1818) is the first science-fiction novel, to the early nineteenth century in the case of science fiction. The two fictional subgenres are often discussed in conjunction for two reasons, one literary and one practical. The literary reason is that while fantasy deals with characters, situations, or worlds that have not existed and could not exist given natural laws, and while science fiction generally follows natural laws while extrapolating characters, situations, and worlds that do not exist but plausibly could, both subgenres deviate from the realistic depiction of the known world found in mimetic contemporary fiction or historical fiction. Both fantasy and science fiction, that is, are "fantastic," concerned with situations and settings that depart from the known world, as opposed to holding a mirror up to it. Aldiss has proposed the following distinction: if you come across a turtle, pick it up, and it's a real turtle, that's realism; if it's a real turtle and it talks to you, that's fantasy; and if it looks like a real turtle but on further inspection you find the words "Made in Japan" on its underside, that's science fiction.

The practical reason why fantasy and science fiction are often discussed together, along with dark fantasy or supernatural horror, is that while fairly clear genre boundaries exist, writers and readers frequently cross these boundaries. Thus, in fantastic fiction in Britain, one often finds authors who write both science fiction and fantasy, and certainly most readers consume both types of writing. Moreover, in the first few decades of the twentieth century, British fantasy and science-fiction readers and writers felt a need for both types. Given the rapid social and technological changes of the first half of the twentieth century, many turned to fantasy either as an escape from unpleasant realities or as a commentary on contemporary developments, and of course much of the appeal of science fiction lay in its depictions of possible futures, both optimistic and pessimistic.

Two years after the end of World War I–the war that, he predicted, would end all war–H. G. Wells published *The Outline of History* (1920). In contrast to the dark view of humanity's present circumstances and eventual fate presented in his scientific romances of the late 1890s and early 1900s, such as *The Time Machine* (1895), *The Island of Doctor Moreau* (1896), *The War of the Worlds* (1898), and *The First Men in the Moon* (1901), here Wells offers a view of humanity as the pinnacle of the evolutionary process and foresees a day of *Men Like Gods*–the title of his 1923 novel. Another vision of the human race's glorious future as Wells perceived it can be found in *The Shape of Things to Come* (1933), the basis of the 1936 motion picture *Things to Come*.

For Wells to prophesy such a grand future for humanity in the years between World War I and World War II required a visionary gift–or incredible naiveté. The 1920s were a time of great prosperity for many, but in Europe they were also a time of rebuilding from the so-called Great War and assorted political tensions. Also, the economic tensions that culminated in the stock-market crash of 1929, the ensuing Great Depression, and political upheavals that ushered in the rise of fascism in Europe hardly seemed to indicate progress, let alone steps toward humanity's glorious destiny. Thus, it is not surprising to find a fantasy title such as Sax Rohmer's *The Day the World Ended* (1930) in this interwar period.

Still, Wells was not alone in his vision, and many writers of fantasy and science fiction between the wars offered compelling imaginative portraits of worlds and times other than their own. For instance, David Lindsay's classic fantasy novel *A Voyage to Arcturus* (1920) presents a completely otherworldly setting in a combination of fantasy and science fiction, as does E. R. Eddison's *The Worm Ouroboros* (1922). Older writers, such as David Garnett and Eden Phillpotts, also continued to contribute to these forms.

As was the case in earlier British fantasy and science fiction, a host of lesser-known authors made their own small but significant contributions. Examples include E. V. Odle's *The Clockwork Man* (1923), in which a visitor from the future interacts with English villagers in the 1920s; Gerald Bullett's *Mr. Godly beside*

Himself (1924), about a man who, finding himself in Fairyland, tries to save it from extinction caused by the dominance of reason as opposed to imagination; the well-wrought fantasies of Margaret Irwin, such as *Still She Wished for Company* (1924) and *These Mortals* (1925); and Guy Dent's science-fiction novel *Emperor of the If* (1926), in which a scientist experiments with creating alternatives to human history.

One of the best-known fantasists of the twentieth century, Lord Dunsany, published some of his best work after 1918. His *The King of Elfland's Daughter* (1924) is representative of the direction in which fantasy was beginning to head. In contrast to much fantasy of the late nineteenth century, which showed the fantastic intruding into everyday life, Dunsany's book, like much later fantasy, deals primarily with other times—if not another world—and magical beings inspired by European folklore. Some decades later the Oxford don and fantasy writer J. R. R. Tolkien labeled the settings of such stories "secondary worlds."

Some modern fantasy, nonetheless, conforms to the older pattern of introducing the fantastic into the commonplace or else tries to combine the otherworldly and the everyday into a seamless whole. For instance, A. A. Milne's children's books *Winnie-the-Pooh* (1926) and *The House at Pooh Corner* (1928) make the child Christopher Robin a part of the world of talking animals. Intended for a much different audience but similar in its combination of the fantastic and the mundane, Virginia Woolf's *Orlando* (1928) features a protagonist who not only lives for centuries but also changes from a man into a woman. Another novel that uses the fantastic in the context of the everyday is John Collier's *His Monkey Wife; or, Married to a Chimp* (1930), the title of which gives a fair indication of the plot.

The 1920s were also significant in fantasy and science fiction because in this decade the pulp magazines, which had existed since the 1890s, began to become more specialized in content. While a popular magazine such as the British *Argosy* continued to publish all types of fiction, new magazines focused on subgenres such as romance fiction, adventure fiction, Western fiction—and, eventually, fantasy and science fiction. This phenomenon was largely an American one at first, but it soon spread to Britain. Moreover, American magazines such as *Amazing Stories, Astounding Science Fiction,* and *Weird Tales* were exported to Britain, and by the 1930s American magazine fiction, rather than the works of older writers such as Wells, was the model for many aspiring writers of fantasy and science fiction.

To be sure, despite the popularity and strong influence of the kinds of science fiction and fantasy published in the American magazines, the British tradition of the scientific romance remained strong between the

world wars. The distinction is an important one, as Brian M. Stableford argues in his landmark study *Scientific Romance in Britain, 1890–1950* (1985). According to Stableford, while American science fiction published in the pulp magazines of the period often featured heroes whose adventures led to happy endings, the British scientific romance tended to be darker in mood and to feature protagonists who were more fallible and less heroic. Moreover, the British scientific romance tended to emphasize theme and setting, as opposed to the plot-driven narratives that were generally found in American science-fiction magazines of the time. In particular, Stableford says, evolution and human beings' smallness in the great schemes of time and space are important threads in the scientific romance, as they are in the early fictions of Wells that helped to give this type of writing its name. In contrast, the future presented in American science fiction of the period was often not as distant as that in British speculative fiction, and space was often depicted as just another frontier to be conquered through competence and diligence.

One writer who continued the tradition of the scientific romance was S. Fowler Wright. His novel *Deluge* (1927), for instance, is about a catastrophic flood that isolates the inhabitants of southern England, while *The World Below* (1929) combines time travel with speculations about humanity's future reminiscent of Wells's *The Time Machine*. Writers such as Neil Bell, John Gloag, and John Taine offered additional approaches to the scientific romance.

Another writer in the scientific-romance mode was Olaf Stapledon. A major figure in the science fiction of the 1930s and 1940s, Stapledon presented a view of human evolution and humanity's future that was far grander than had ever been seen before and grander than that of most writers after him. *Last and First Men* (1930), for instance, traces the course of evolution twenty million years into the future through eighteen species of humanity, all of them fully and imaginatively rendered. *Star Maker* (1937), even more ambitious in scope, depicts a psychic journey through multiple universes filled with various types of life that culminates in a meeting with the dispassionate Star Maker, a god-like being who, driven by infinite fecundity and curiosity, continues to create world after world. Stapledon's science-fiction novels *Odd John* (1935) and *Sirius* (1944) also use evolution as a basis but are more modest in scale than *Last and First Men* and *Star Maker*. The protagonist of *Odd John* is a mutant superman, intellectually and psychically superior to those around him, while the title character of *Sirius* is a dog who is more intelligent than most humans. Both characters are destroyed by those who fear them, but they suggest that the human race may reach great heights of advancement. Like much science fiction, both novels challenge society's conventional notions by showing that they are rooted in unthinking custom and prejudice.

While the British tradition of the scientific romance continued after World War II and has still not vanished entirely, it had to compete with models of fantasy and science fiction that flourished in the specialized magazines, most of which either originated in the United States or were heavily influenced by magazines that did. At the same time, however, American science fiction changed after World War II as a consequence of the atomic bomb and the accompanying realization, present in science fiction since *Frankenstein,* that science could be a destructive force as well as a positive one. Other factors that helped to change American science fiction after World War II were the Cold War and a new generation of writers who were comfortable with the themes and conventions of modern mainstream literature. Consequently, even as the models of American speculative fiction became increasingly dominant among British writers of such fiction, those models were becoming closer to some of the characteristics of British scientific romance.

Certainly, a major preoccupation of the scientific romance and of American-style science fiction was the future and what it might hold; but it would be a mistake to say that all British speculative fiction of the mid twentieth century is concerned with the future per se. As the work of Stapledon shows, science fiction can also be set in the present. It is even possible, as some work of this period illustrates, to write science fiction about the past. For instance, each story in *If It Had Happened Otherwise* (1931), a collection edited by J. C. Squire and republished in the United States as *If; or, History Rewritten,* looks at an historical event and explores the possible consequences had the event turned out differently. Contributors to the volume include Hilaire Belloc, G. K. Chesterton, and André Maurois, and one of the best-known pieces is Sir Winston Churchill's "If Lee Had Not Won the Battle of Gettysburg" (1930). Though this contribution and some of the others are more essays than stories, the book is a seminal compilation of what is known in science fiction as alternate history—a thriving subcategory within the field.

Since science fiction is so closely associated in the popular mind with technology and the future, it may appear odd that a type of writing dealing with the past is considered science fiction; but two elements of alternate history help to qualify it as such. One is what critic Darko Suvin calls the *novum,* the introduction of an element that simultaneously produces "estrangement and cognition" in the reader. Here estrangement is induced by the different historical track, cognition through rec-

ognition of the historical background. The second element is extrapolation: just as most science fiction imagines some sort of change or set of changes in the future by extrapolating from present conditions or potential technologies, so writers of alternate histories extrapolate the effects that could have resulted in the present from a past event having transpired differently than it did.

Utopian literature, a predecessor and close cousin of science fiction, has existed in British literature since Sir Thomas More published the book that gave the genre its name in 1516. Such works, depicting societies that, if not ideal, were at any rate better than the society in which the author lived, proliferated in the centuries that followed; they particularly flourished in the nineteenth century and reached a culmination of sorts with Wells's *A Modern Utopia* (1905).

Wells's positive outlook, however, was not shared by all writers, and traditional utopianism was challenged by dystopianism. Most earlier utopias (the word *utopia* means "no place") were, strictly speaking, *eutopias* ("good places"); in contrast, the dystopia ("bad place") deals with the possibility of science not to improve life but to make it worse, of societies not working for the benefit of their citizens but for other, less pleasant ends. Certainly, some of the developments of the first half of the twentieth century supported a pessimistic reevaluation of the utopian vision.

The first major dystopia was published by a Soviet author, Evgeny Zamyatin. Although Zamyatin supported the socialist cause in Russia, he quickly became disenchanted with the direction of the new government, and his novel *My* pushes Soviet collectivism to a futuristic extreme to critique the damage totalitarianism inflicts on individuals. As if to confirm his fears, the novel, which he wrote in 1920, circulated only in manuscript in the Soviet Union for many years; it was first published in English translation as *We* in 1924, did not appear in Russian in its entirety until 1952, and was not published in the Soviet Union until 1989. As Mark R. Hillegas points out in *The Future as Nightmare: H. G. Wells and the Anti-Utopians* (1967), Zamyatin's work may have influenced Aldous Huxley's *Brave New World* (1932). One of the classic dystopian novels, *Brave New World* describes a future society that is completely controlled by a misguided scientific elite. Huxley offers a savage critique of such issues as class distinctions and eugenics in the context of this darkly imagined future.

The tone is also dark in Charles Williams's early novels, such as *War in Heaven* (1930) and *Descent into Hell* (1932). Williams found much to dislike about twentieth-century life on religious grounds, and his novels mix fantasy, adventure, and grand conflicts between good and evil. In this respect they have much in common with the works of Tolkien and C. S. Lewis, fellow members with Williams of an Oxford literary circle known as the Inklings.

While the darkness of Williams's novels stems from his metaphysical and theological concerns, the political landscape of the 1930s accounts for the bleak outlook of *Swastika Night* (1937), written by Katharine Burdekin under the pseudonym Murray Constantine. In this novel Burdekin imagines, at a time when many did not recognize the danger posed by Adolf Hitler and the National Socialist Party, the victory of the Third Reich over Europe. This theme became so common in science fiction that *The Encyclopedia of Science Fiction* (1993), edited by John Clute and Peter Nicholls, includes an entry titled "Hitler Wins"; the difference between most works in this category and Burdekin's is that they are alternate histories written well after the conclusion of World War II, while Burdekin's was composed before the war had begun.

Given the multitude of economic and political problems in Europe in the 1930s, it is not surprising that many British works of fantasy and science fiction, like many Hollywood movies of the decade, provided an escape from the present to other times and places. Thus, in James Hilton's *Lost Horizon* (1933), one of the last of the lost-race stories, an Englishman discovers the idyllic valley of Shangri-La; P. L. Travers's children's book *Mary Poppins* (1934) and its sequels are about a magical nanny who can make everything perfect; and another book for young readers, Tolkien's *The Hobbit; or, There and Back Again* (1937), describes the adventures of other races of people-like creatures in lands long ago and far away.

It is also common, however, to find in works of this period symbols, allegories, or other representations of contemporary tensions. Lewis, for example, produced some of his best work at this time. Predictably, given his orthodox Christian worldview, both his Space Trilogy—*Out of the Silent Planet* (1938), *Perelandra* (1943), and *That Hideous Strength* (1945)—and *The Screwtape Letters* (1942), which is a work of Christian apologetics and an often funny epistolary novel involving demons, deal with elemental conflicts between good and evil that were relevant not only to readers sharing Lewis's religious outlook but to all who were facing a war against fascism. Similarly, in T. H. White's books exploring the legends of King Arthur, Merlin, and the knights of the Round Table, beginning with *The Sword in the Stone* in 1938 and collected in *The Once and Future King* (1958), one sees many of the concerns of contemporary Britain played out through the adventures of the mythical former ruler. Even more allegorical is George Orwell's *Animal Farm* (1945), which combines elements of the traditional beast fable with a critique of the Russian Revolution of 1917 and the subsequent development of the Soviet Union under Vladimir Lenin and Joseph Stalin.

Science-fiction writers had been predicting the development of atomic weapons for decades when World War II ended in August 1945 with the dropping of atomic bombs on the Japanese cities of Hiroshima and Nagasaki by American airplanes. Wells died the following year; by the end of his life he had become a bitter man, predicting not a glorious future for humanity but its possible extinction at its own hands, either through nuclear weapons or through the sort of genocide exemplified by the Holocaust. The nuclear standoff between the United States and the Soviet Union naturally affected writers of fantasy and, especially, of science fiction, who produced many tales of catastrophe, mass destruction, and political domination in the wake of totalitarianism and the Bomb. For instance, in Mervyn Peake's fantastic Gormenghast trilogy—*Titus Groan* (1946), *Gormenghast* (1950), and *Titus Alone* (1959)—the young protagonist is able to discover his path in life only after maneuvering through the political machinations of those around him. Peake's work draws as heavily on the older conventions of Gothic fiction as on contemporary politics, but the abuse of power is certainly an important part of the trilogy.

A more obvious example of the impact of the war is Huxley's *Ape and Essence* (1948), one of many novels in this period to imagine the state of the world following a nuclear conflict. An expedition from New Zealand, which has been largely untouched by the fighting, discovers in Los Angeles that most of the small number of survivors have degenerated into almost subhuman brutes.

Descent into barbarism is a common element in the work of John Wyndham, a master of the catastrophe novel that flourished in postwar British science fiction. His books, such as *The Day of the Triffids* (1951) and *The Kraken Wakes* (1953), while not dealing specifically with the aftermath of a nuclear holocaust, depict humanity's efforts to survive and to rebuild civilization after disasters of various kinds.

Another example of the war's impact can be found in Orwell's *Nineteen Eighty-Four* (1949). Influenced by earlier dystopias such as Zamyatin's *My*, Huxley's *Brave New World*, and possibly Burdekin's *Swastika Night*, Orwell's nightmare vision of a future totalitarian state is nonetheless powerfully original in its depiction of the abuse of science to maintain control and in its portrayal of the deceptions of which governments are capable.

Though neither *Nineteen Eighty-Four* nor *Brave New World* was written specifically for an audience of science- fiction readers, both novels have had a considerable influence on the development of the genre and have been adopted as science fiction by many in the field. The labeling of such novels as science fiction has not, however, passed without controversy. Those who argue for the inclusion of *Brave New World* and *Nineteen Eighty-Four* in the science-fiction canon assume that the genre is defined by its content. Science fiction typically deals with current social and scientific trends extrapolated into the future; *Brave New World* and *Nineteen Eighty-Four* make such an extrapolation; therefore, both novels must be science fiction, whether or not their authors intended for them to be so categorized. Similar arguments are used by Aldiss to make the case for *Frankenstein* as the first science-fiction novel.

Others, however, contend that the factors determining whether or not a work is science fiction include authorial intent, publication venue, and—most nebulous of all—quality. According to their arguments, the science-fiction writers of the 1918–1960 period were those who consciously wrote in this mode and published in magazines devoted to it; since these considerations do not apply to authors such as Huxley and Orwell, they were not writing science fiction. Some make the claim that the works of authors such as Huxley and Orwell are simply better than anything writers of science fiction could produce. This position stems from the critical relegation of popular fiction—including science fiction and fantasy, but especially science fiction—to the realm of unoriginal hackwork. Thus, the argument goes, writers such as Huxley and Orwell could not have been writing science fiction, because they were writing literature. The assumption that "science fiction" and "literature" are mutually exclusive categories has been hotly contested by many in the science-fiction field.

This dispute is somewhat academic, but it has important practical consequences. The reputation of the now-canonical American author Kurt Vonnegut suffered early in his career because his novels resembled science fiction and his short stories appeared in science-fiction magazines; though the distinction between genre work and "literature" was never as sharp in British as in American fiction, the labeling of an author's output as science fiction in Great Britain in the mid twentieth century could place him (or, occasionally, her) in a literary "ghetto." Many writers who might have happily published in the genre magazines avoided doing so precisely because they were aware of the harm it could do to their reputations.

A writer who made a career of writing for science-fiction magazines, both British and American, was William F. Temple. His work is typical of much of the writing found in the magazines: if not highly literary, it is exciting and imaginative. An example is his novel *Four-Sided Triangle: A Romance* (1949), in which a love triangle is complicated by the cloning of the girl caught in the middle.

While Temple never became known outside the science-fiction audience, his friend and former roommate Arthur C. Clarke has had a different fate. Clarke established a reputation in science-fiction fandom in the late 1940s, when he was predicting the development of communications satellites and space flight decades before they were actually attempted. In 1953 he published one of the classics of science fiction, *Childhood's End,* in which an alien race takes control of human affairs not for evil purposes but to keep humanity from destroying itself before it can develop its intellectual and spiritual potential, a potential that is actualized as children rapidly evolve into cosmic beings that can unite with the Overmind, whose servants the aliens are. The novel is at once a Cold War warning and a Stapledonian tale of human evolution. This novel, and especially Clarke's collaboration with director Stanley Kubrick on the movie *2001: A Space Odyssey* (1969), made Clarke known to an audience much larger than writers such as Temple ever enjoyed.

Lewis and Tolkien were also interested in humanity's spiritual potential, but in a more traditional religious sense. Their values are apparent in *The Chronicles of Narnia* (1950–1956), Lewis's seven-volume fantasy series for young readers, and Tolkien's *The Lord of the Rings,* a long fantasy novel published in three volumes as *The Fellowship of the Ring* (1954), *The Two Towers* (1954), and *The Return of the King* (1955). Both are myth-like works that, through fantastic worlds, extol the virtues of integrity, courage, perseverance, and loyalty.

Loyalty is an appropriate word to describe the cottage industries that have evolved around both men. The multitalented Lewis was a literary scholar, an author of literature, and a tireless defender of what he described as "mere Christianity." Though his scholarly work is little read except by other academics, his fiction—especially the Space Trilogy and *The Chronicles of Narnia*—continues to sell well, and several of his books on the Christian faith are as popular with evangelical Protestants as John Bunyan's *The Pilgrim's Progress* (1678, 1684) was in earlier generations. And Tom Shippey, in a 2001 study of the Oxford philologist, has dubbed Tolkien "The Author of the Century"—not on the basis of his literary greatness, about which there is much dispute, but for the grandeur of his achievement and for his influence. The success of Tolkien's work reinvigorated fantasy as a modern literary genre and pushed it in the direction of medievalized secondary worlds populated by beings from European folklore, as well as by humans. By the end of the 1960s the three volumes of *The Lord of the Rings* were a phenomenon, ubiquitous especially on college campuses throughout the English-speaking world. Ever since, fantasy literature has been a booming business.

On the one hand, this has been a positive development, since the fantasy revival that Tolkien helped to initiate has not only fostered new work in the field but has also led profit-seeking publishers to bring earlier works back into print. On the other hand, some would claim that the overarching influence of Tolkien has resulted in too many lesser imitations, and that his narrative expansiveness has encouraged the expansion into trilogies and even longer series of stories that would be better if they were more concise. Additional criticisms of much modern fantasy in this epic vein concern its emphasis on masculine heroics and adventure and its simplistic dualism of good and evil.

Like Lewis and Tolkien, William Golding deals with values in his works; but he does so from a much different perspective. Though not science fiction—except, perhaps, in the sense that the young characters become isolated on an island as a result of a war that takes place in the near future—his *Lord of the Flies* (1954) shows how easily the veneer of civilization can be removed. Golding's *The Inheritors* (1955) also provides a critique of the weaknesses of civilization in its story of the defeat of a group of peaceful prehumans by a band of early Homo sapiens.

Other works dealing with the weaknesses of civilization in the 1950s were concerned with the possibility, if not the likelihood, of natural catastrophes and the self-destruction of the human race. Examples include the novels of Sam Youd, written under the pseudonym John Christopher and intended for younger readers; *The Black Cloud* (1957) by Fred Hoyle, who brings his expertise as Astronomer Royal to bear on a tale of the earth's contact with a sentient mass of interstellar matter; and Nevil Shute's *On the Beach* (1957), one of the best-known works about the aftermath of nuclear war.

Another development in fantasy and science fiction between 1918 and 1960 was their spread to media other than the printed page. Many movies and radio and television programs were adapted from previously published fantasy and science-fiction stories and novels, but much original work also appeared. Among the best of the latter were the television series written by Nigel Kneale in the 1950s and 1960s featuring the scientist Bernard Quatermass, who discovers evidence of the presence of aliens on earth. Like much science fiction of the Cold War 1950s, the shows reflect a strong sense of paranoia.

Movies, radio, and television were not the only media through which a broader audience was exposed to science fiction and fantasy between 1918 and 1960; the publishing of these genres changed substantially during the period. The specialty pulp magazines that dominated the field in the first half of the century were challenged by paperback books, which were introduced in their modern form in the late 1930s. The pulps died out by midcentury. Specialty magazines continued to be published, but in smaller numbers and typically in a digest format.

One substantial development in fantasy and science fiction that resulted from the replacement of magazines by paperback books was a shift from short fiction to longer works. While some paperbacks were anthologies of short stories, novels came to predominate in both fantasy and science fiction, a trend that has persisted to the present.

Some publishers saw a potential audience for fantasy and science fiction in hardcover. These publishers were divided into two categories: established firms taking a chance on work in the genres; and smaller presses, often started by fans, dedicated to reprinting the classics and occasionally supporting new work.

Fantasy and science fiction also began to make inroads into criticism and scholarship. In 1959 Kingsley Amis, the author of the critically acclaimed novel *Lucky Jim* (1954), was invited to deliver a series of lectures at Princeton University. Published the following year as *New Maps of Hell: A Survey of Science Fiction,* the lectures were a major step in raising the reputation of imaginative genre literature. Amis pointed out that science fiction is ideal for the purposes of social criticism and satire; he could have said the same about fantasy. Both subgenres experienced a revival of interest, both scholarly and popular, in the 1960s that has yet to diminish.

—Darren Harris-Fain

Acknowledgments

This book was produced by Bruccoli Clark Layman, Inc. Tracy Simmons Bitonti was the in-house editor, assisted by Philip B. Dematteis.

Production manager is Philip B. Dematteis.

Administrative support was provided by Ann M. Cheschi, Amber L. Coker, Linda Dalton Mullinax, and Angi Pleasant.

Accountant is Ann-Marie Holland.

Copyediting supervisor is Sally R. Evans. The copyediting staff includes Phyllis A. Avant, Brenda Carol Blanton, Melissa D. Hinton, Charles Loughlin, Rebecca Mayo, Nancy E. Smith, and Elizabeth Jo Ann Sumner. Freelance copyeditor is Jennie Williamson.

Editorial associates are Michael S. Allen, Michael S. Martin, and Pamela A. Warren.

Permissions editor is Jason Paddock.

Database manager is José A. Juarez.

Layout and graphics supervisor is Janet E. Hill. The graphics staff includes Karla Corley Brown and Zoe R. Cook.

Office manager is Kathy Lawler Merlette.

Photography supervisor is Paul Talbot. Photography editor is Scott Nemzek.

Digital photographic copy work was performed by Joseph M. Bruccoli.

Systems manager is Marie L. Parker.

Typesetting supervisor is Kathleen M. Flanagan. The typesetting staff includes Patricia Marie Flanagan, Mark J. McEwan, and Pamela D. Norton. Freelance typesetter is Wanda Adams.

Walter W. Ross did library research. He was assisted by Pamela A. Warren and the following librarians at the Thomas Cooper Library of the University of South Carolina: circulation department head Tucker Taylor; reference department head Virginia W. Weathers; Brette Barclay, Marilee Birchfield, Paul Cammarata, Gary Geer, Michael Macan, Tom Marcil, Rose Marshall, and Sharon Verba; interlibrary loan department head John Brunswick; and interlibrary loan staff Robert Arndt, Hayden Battle, Barry Bull, Jo Cottingham, Marna Hostetler, Marieum McClary, Erika Peake, and Nelson Rivera.

The editor would like to thank the contributors to this volume, as well as several other individuals who aided in the genesis and development of the book; among the latter are David Ketterer, Matthew McFall, and Jon Wynne-Tyson.

Dictionary of Literary Biography® • Volume Two Hundred Fifty-Five

British Fantasy and Science-Fiction Writers, 1918–1960

Dictionary of Literary Biography

Katharine Burdekin
(Murray Constantine)
(23 July 1896 – 10 August 1963)

Daphne Patai
University of Massachusetts Amherst

BOOKS: *Anna Colquhoun* (London: John Lane, 1922);
The Reasonable Hope (London: John Lane, 1924);
The Burning Ring (London: Butterworth, 1927); as Kay
    Burdekin (New York: Morrow, 1929);
The Children's Country, as Kay Burdekin (New York:
    Morrow, 1929);
The Rebel Passion, as Katherine Burdekin (London:
    Butterworth, 1929); as Kay Burdekin (New York:
    Morrow, 1929);
Quiet Ways, as Katherine Burdekin (London: Butter-
    worth, 1930);
The Devil, Poor Devil! as Murray Constantine (London:
    Boriswood, 1934; New York: Arno, 1978);
Proud Man, as Constantine (London: Boriswood, 1934);
    as Katharine Burdekin, with a foreword and after-
    word by Daphne Patai (New York: Feminist
    Press, 1993);
Swastika Night, as Constantine (London: Gollancz,
    1937); as Katharine Burdekin, with an introduc-
    tion by Patai (London: Lawrence & Wishart,
    1985; Old Westbury, N.Y.: Feminist Press,
    1985);
Venus in Scorpio: A Romance of Versailles, 1770–1793, by
    Burdekin, as Constantine, and Margaret Gold-
    smith (London: John Lane, 1940);
The End of This Day's Business, as Katharine Burdekin,
    with an afterword by Patai (New York: Feminist
    Press, 1989).

SELECTED PERIODICAL PUBLICATIONS–
UNCOLLECTED: "A Story: Poor Adam," as
    Katherine Burdekin, *Epilogue,* 2 (Summer 1936):
    139–144;

Katharine Burdekin

"Oranges and Lemons," as Murray Constantine, *Time
    and Tide* (14 May 1938): 671–673.

With the republication since 1985 of several of
her novels, Katharine Burdekin has emerged, in the
words of Gary K. Wolfe, as "the leading feminist utopian writer of her era, as well as one of the most
thoughtful and provocative sf [science-fiction] writers
of the 1930s." In both her published and unpublished

work Burdekin favored speculative fiction and fantasy, forms that allowed her the narrative strategies for elaborating critiques of her own society and exploring alternatives to it.

From the early 1930s until the mid 1980s Burdekin's identity as the author of the highly praised speculative fiction *Proud Man* (1934) and the remarkable dystopian novel *Swastika Night* (1937) was concealed from public view. Beginning in 1934, she published her work under the male pseudonym "Murray Constantine," evidently fearful that her decision to write against Adolf Hitler's Nazism—the most threatening political ideology of her time—would endanger her two young daughters in the event of a German invasion of England. So thoroughly did she cover her tracks and bind her publishers to secrecy that it took considerable effort by Daphne Patai, in the course of her biographical research, to persuade the original publishers of *Swastika Night* to disclose in 1981 that "Murray Constantine" was, in fact, Katharine Burdekin.

Though she produced twenty-four novels in a thirty-five-year period (a dozen of them left unpublished, along with poems, short stories, and plays), Burdekin's split identity—six novels published under her own name (sometimes misspelled as Katherine or given as Kay) between 1922 and 1930, and four published as Murray Constantine between 1934 and 1940—was thoroughly maintained during her lifetime and well beyond it. The pseudonymous novels brought her the greatest recognition, yet she never owned up to the pseudonym, nor did she ever attempt to weave together her two literary identities and claim them as the legacy of a single artist. More mysterious still, she ceased publishing altogether after 1940, though she kept on writing until she fell ill in 1955.

Burdekin was something of an alien presence in her own time, for she approached what scholars now call gender ideology from a perspective, and often in a vocabulary, that became current only with the second wave of the women's movement decades later. Her trenchant critique of fascism, in particular, presented in the pseudonymous novels Burdekin wrote during the 1930s, is constantly informed by her feminism, which allowed her to bring into focus the threat to civilization posed by exaggerated notions of masculinity.

Like other female writers of her generation, she did not call herself a feminist; her feminist viewpoint, however, is plain in almost all her work, even in a children's book she wrote for her own daughters. She read widely in the fields of history, religion, myth, legend, fairy tales, and fiction (including fantasy fiction), and all of these forms found their way into her own writing. She experimented with different literary structures; yet, her novels are clearly the work of one creative intelligence in the process of development. Above all she excelled in the creation of utopian fiction. The special vantage point afforded her by the imaginative leap into other "societies" resulted in her most important books: *Proud Man, Swastika Night,* and the posthumously published *End of This Day's Business* (1989). When *Proud Man* and *Swastika Night* first appeared, reviewers tended to miss the author's incisive critique of sexual politics. They did, however, on occasion note the feminist sympathies, which led some to suspect that "Murray Constantine" might be a woman.

Burdekin was born Katharine Penelope Cade in Spondon, Derbyshire, England, on 23 July 1896, the youngest of four children in an upper-middle-class family. In childhood she was called Penelope (though her nickname was Tommy because she was a tomboy). Her father, Charles James Cade, managed the family estate. Her mother, Mary Rowena Elizabeth Casterton Cade (formerly Smelt), a domineering presence, was a progressive woman whose formal schooling ended at age thirteen but who read voraciously.

Later the family moved to Cheltenham. There a governess educated the children at home until the two boys entered Cheltenham College as boarders, and the girls, at age eleven or twelve, went to Cheltenham Ladies' College as day students. Penelope attended from 1907 until 1913. At that time she told her parents that she wished, like her brothers, to attend Oxford, but they did not consent. Since a university education was not a possibility, she married instead, in May 1915; her husband was an Australian barrister named Beaufort Burdekin, who had attended Cheltenham College with one of her brothers. Family legend has it that she married simply for lack of other options.

After their honeymoon, her husband returned to France to serve in World War I, and Katharine Burdekin served as a nurse in a Voluntary Aid Detachment at an army hospital established on the Cheltenham Racecourse. This experience was eventually reflected in her sixth published novel, *Quiet Ways* (1930), which depicts her passionately antiwar convictions at the time.

Burdekin had two daughters: Katharine Jane, born in 1917, and Helen Eugenie, born in 1920. In August 1920 Burdekin traveled with her family and a nanny to Sydney, taking up residence in her mother-in-law's house. Australia is apparently where Burdekin started to write, and her first novel, *Anna Colquhoun,* was published in London in April 1922. The novel is a morality tale about a brilliant and tempestuous pianist who loses everything, including her beloved husband and musical career, on the path to moral regeneration. The annotation on the last page of the novel indicates that Burdekin wrote the book in Sydney between May and June in 1921, an early indication of her habits of writing quickly and revising rarely. She later destroyed a promised sequel to *Anna Colquhoun,* also written while in Sydney.

By June 1921 Burdekin had apparently separated from her husband, who took legal action for her return to the family domicile. He filed a second petition in 1923, but no evidence exists that a divorce was ever granted. Burdekin and her two daughters had meanwhile returned to England, in April 1922, and were living with her mother and sister in Cornwall, where they had settled after Burdekin's father's death in 1917.

In 1926 Burdekin met the woman who became her lifelong friend and companion and who, though she wished to remain unnamed, has been the source of much of the biographical information about Burdekin. The two women lived together from 1926 until Burdekin's death, caring for Burdekin's two daughters and later her companion's child as well. With the exception of a brief trip to Italy, once Burdekin had returned to England she did not leave the country for the remainder of her life. Moving from Cornwall, she and her companion lived for a time in Hampshire, Somerset, and Essex before finally settling in Suffolk in 1950. They often spent vacations in Cornwall, visiting her mother and sister. Three years older than Burdekin, her sister, Rowena Cade, became well known as the designer and builder of the Minack Theatre, an amphitheater built into a granite cliff at Porthcurno, near Land's End. Cade also served as the theater director for more than fifty years.

Burdekin spent the 1920s and 1930s writing, according to her companion, in a state close to possession. Novel followed novel rapidly. She would seldom discuss her plans for a book, but it was obvious when she was preparing to write, as her appetite dropped dramatically a few days prior to beginning a new project. During the time that she spent composing a novel, she remained absorbed in the work and inaccessible. It was like "being sick," her companion has said, and upon completion of a book Burdekin would plunge into a state of misery, as though the act of returning to the real world from a fictional one that she controlled was a difficult process. Long periods would follow in which she did no writing at all. Her companion has also said that Burdekin "was not in the accepted sense a *thinker,*" but rather, "she was a piece of cosmic blotting paper, or sponge, which some power squeezed, and out welled a strange confection!

. . . She never, in all the years I knew her, took longer than six weeks in writing any book." When not writing, her companion has said, she "really had very little connection with the writer. . . . the writer had very much the character of a visitant." Her companion also described Burdekin's process of composition, especially of her best work, as akin to "automatic writing." She did not consider her books important enough to work at them; rather, she simply took them for what they were.

Although Burdekin and her companion did not avoid social functions, they maintained quiet, private lives. They sometimes met other authors who wrote to Burdekin about one or another of her books. Radclyffe Hall, for example, wrote a letter of admiration in response to Burdekin's 1927 novel *The Burning Ring;* however, they did not meet until around 1930. Burdekin also heard from Hilda Doolittle (H.D.) after the publication of *Proud Man.* The poet later sent her several of her books, inscribed to "Murray Constantine," the name Burdekin signed in copies of her novels that she gave to H.D. Burdekin also corresponded with Havelock Ellis (as did H.D.; and Ellis's letters to H.D., discussing Murray Constantine and the importance of her work, are extant). They also knew such figures as Leonard and Virginia Woolf and Bertrand and Dora Russell. However, they were close to only a few, including the writers Norah James and Margaret Goldsmith, and Goldsmith's husband, the journalist Frederick Voigt.

Burdekin's second novel, *The Reasonable Hope* (1924), is a realistic exploration of a young man who is shell-shocked in World War I and of the bohemian artistic circle into which he is drawn. As in some of Burdekin's subsequent works, an important, if unnamed, theme of the novel is homosexuality. Her third book, *The Burning Ring,* represents Burdekin's first experiment with fantasy fiction. Its forty-year-old protagonist, an emotionally arrested sculptor, uses a magic ring to travel to three distinct historical periods (ancient Britain, the reign of Charles II, and the Elizabethan age), in each of which he has experiences that lead to his emotional growth. In the 20 January 1929 *New York Herald Tribune* Alice Beal Parsons considered this novel (which, in its original version, was twice the length of its published edition) to be "a new form. Just as *Orlando* might be called a novelized history of English literature, though it is many other things besides this, so *The Burning Ring* might be called a novelized outline of various aspects of history, though it is many other things besides this, notably a dramatization of the different phases of love through which the individual passes as he discovers progressively hero, friend and lover."

Burdekin wrote her single book for children in 1927 with the working title "St. John's Eve." It was published in the United States as *The Children's Country* (1929). It is a tale ahead of its time, challenging traditional gender roles in its account of the experiences of a boy and a girl in a fantasy land where preconceptions about gender do not exist. By means of a series of adventures and challenges, the young people break through the sex-role stereotypes of their real world.

According to her companion, Burdekin later came to think of her first novels as her "baby books." She believed her next novel, *The Rebel Passion* (1929), was the first of her mature works. Having experimented with the theme of androgyny in an earlier novel, a realistic bildungsroman about a young woman with a "masculine soul" ("Two in a Sack," withdrawn prior to publication but surviving in galley proofs dated 1928), Burdekin explored the same theme through a male protagonist and in the form of fantasy. Following the life of its narrator, the twelfth-century monk Giraldus of Glastonbury, who possesses the "understanding of a man and the soul of a woman," *The Rebel Passion* records visions of past and future, as cruelty is increasingly replaced by compassion or pity (the rebel passion). Like *The Burning Ring,* but far more extravagantly, the novel is a narrative spanning thousands of years and involving past, present, and future. Burdekin seems to have found such a vast sweep necessary in order to present her ideas effectively. As in most of her later novels, in *The Rebel Passion* Burdekin looks beyond the limitations of her own time, transcending the present to chart the future development of the species toward a genuine "humanity."

The reviewer for *The Times Literary Supplement* (*TLS*) (18 April 1929) noted the "oddly ascetic depreciation of the sex-instinct, often expressed by the phrase *man has the body of a beast,*" as well as Burdekin's apparent dislike of the non-Christian nations, which, Burdekin wrote, "have not a religion that teaches pity." The prospect of the future portrayed in the novel, stretching into the twenty-eighth century, includes the eventual development of a utopian society in some respects reminiscent of William Morris's *News from Nowhere* (1890).

Like writers as diverse as Samuel Taylor Coleridge and Virginia Woolf, Burdekin felt that artists are essentially androgynous. Her treatment of love recalls Plato's *Symposium,* in which love is presented as a quest for wholeness. Plato (or Aristophanes, his spokesman in the narration of the myth) describes an original complete being of three distinct types—male, female, and male-female—and in the myth each type, with the loss of its pristine completeness, is destined to seek eternally for its missing other half. In contrast, Burdekin keeps returning to the ideal of male and female complementing one another; she means a spiritual connection and compatibility that may occur in any two bodies, regardless of their biological sex. Her novels, as early as *The Reasonable Hope,* often include same-sex partners whose souls join together harmoniously, along with heterosexual couples whose relationship transcends sexual attraction. As in Charlotte Perkins Gilman's *Herland* (serialized in Gilman's journal *The Forerunner* in 1915, which, however, Burdekin is not likely to have known), Burdekin's vision of the future, projected in *The Rebel Passion,* specifically excludes sexuality, since the highest goal for each individual is a kind of completion that results in the ability to know God.

Burdekin distinguishes this aspiration from established religion. Nominally a member of the Church of England, Burdekin, though deeply spiritual, adhered to no theological doctrines and was a strong critic of ecclesiastical institutions. Related to her religious views are her ethics, especially the belief that using other people for the satisfaction of one's own appetites or desires is wrong, regardless of the sex of the partners. In *The Sociological Review* (October 1929) Patrick Geddes praised *The Rebel Passion* for its "ethico-social" focus, calling it "a notable contrast from the too simply mechanical, or at least mainly material, Utopias so much more characteristic of recent times."

Although philosophical ideas pervade her fiction, Burdekin's emphasis came to be increasingly on politics, above all on the conflict between fascism, the dangers of which she recognized early on, and communism, whose ideal of economic egalitarianism she viewed for years as the path through which humanity must pass on the way to maturity. She also focused with increasing passion on the politics of gender, specifically on the ways in which masculine and feminine identities are socialized into individuals, and on the harmful results of this process.

Burdekin was intensely responsive to the growing political crisis in Europe, which led her to be particularly prolific during the 1930s. Several of her outstanding speculative fictions, all written as "Murray Constantine," date from this period. The first of these is the satirical novel *Proud Man,* a kind of ethnographic report on the condition of England in the 1930s. It is narrated by a visitor from the future, a fully evolved being known as the Person, from whose mature perspective contemporary Britain appears to be peopled by "subhumans." This Person is telepathic, vegetarian, brown-skinned, entirely autonomous, androgynous, equipped to produce offspring through self-fertilization, and able to be completely still (a notable contrast to Burdekin's own habit of nervous gestures and constant motion). The Person understands the true relation of the self to the "not-self" and possesses a natural altruism requiring no instruction by external religious or ethical systems.

Throughout Burdekin's writing career, she experimented with a variety of narrative techniques. For the remote observer from a far future she drew on an especially useful example: *Last and First Men* (1930) by Olaf Stapledon, a writer who became an admirer of *Proud Man* and *Swastika Night*. But Burdekin decisively departs from Stapledon in her primary purpose, which is apparently to engage in a kind of "anthropology at home" (O. A. Oeser's phrase, coined in 1936). She accomplishes this intent by using an ironic and distanced first-person narrator as a perspective from which she can cast a cool and dispassionate eye on her own time and place—a frequent strategy in speculative fiction.

Forced to conform to the all-important worldly requirement of gender roles, the Person lives for a time in England first as a female, then as a male. Only a few exceptional characters in the novel recognize the narrator's unearthly qualities; most of the people the Person encounters try to assuage the discomfort caused them by a being who treats men with no deference and women with no contempt by simply categorizing this creature as homosexual.

This misapprehension is but one of a series of startling revelations of the "subhuman" condition. Burdekin highlighted these revelations by using italics to emphasize the oddness of many common terms and ideas. Just as she had offered a critique of war in the pacifist *Quiet Ways,* in *Proud Man* Burdekin sees armed conflict as the result of such subhuman qualities as envy, fear, greed, and the pursuit of glory. *War* is defined as a "large organized killing" whose attraction in part lies in the fact that it does not directly involve women. Similarly, a *soldier* is a "killing male." And men are depicted as being unable to bear for long the presence of those they despise, opting instead for those all-male institutions that bring men together into what Burdekin labels "homosexual packs," evident in boys' schools, sports teams, men's clubs, and, most particularly, the military.

Those whom Burdekin's narrator in *Proud Man* deems "subhumans" falsely believe themselves to be human beings, and this delusion is related to two significant ideas about their nature: "One is that it is fundamentally noble, and the other that it can never change. The first idea comforts them, while the second excuses them for their most grotesque actions, thus allaying, if very slightly, their feeling of guilt."

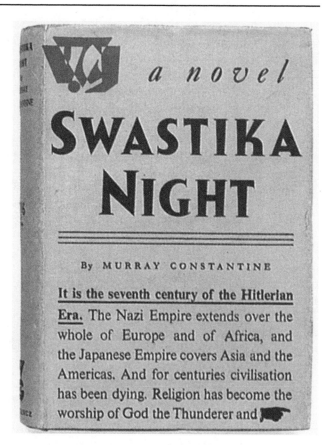

Dust jacket for Burdekin's 1937 novel, published under a male pseudonym to protect her daughters in case the Nazis invaded England

Related to this belief is what the Person calls "the subhuman concept of *privilege.*" In *Proud Man* and in her other utopian works, the author sees this concept as a significant factor in the problems behind social organization. In a passage that also illustrates Burdekin's recurring narrative technique of philosophical exposition, she argues:

> It is not very possible to explain privilege in any human way, as it is not a human thing. But as the subhumans believe that they are in some way *better* than animals, so they believe that some subhumans are, by reason of the colour of their skins, or their rearing, or their sex, *better* and more worthy than other subhumans of different colour, *class* and sex. This betterness entitles them to privilege. . . . A privilege of class divides a subhuman society horizontally, while a privilege of sex divides it vertically. Subhumans cannot apparently exist without their societies being divided, preferably in both these ways.

Burdekin's sophisticated understanding of gender, though she was writing decades before modern feminism offered the terminology to distinguish gender from sex, helped her to comprehend gender as a symbolic system with political implications. Anticipating Jacques Lacan's ideas about the phallus as signifier, Burdekin, in *Proud Man,* offered an analysis of its power: "The mere possession of a phallus . . . regardless of the *character* of the possessor, guaranteed a certain amount of civic power." Thus, "subhuman" males live with a constant fear of losing this power. Burdekin's narrator also attributes men's cultural contributions to anxieties caused by sex differences—anxieties that stem from "a deep root jealousy of the female's greater biological importance"—a theme that appears as well in Burdekin's short story "Poor Adam," published in *Epilogue* (Summer 1936). Science, writes Burdekin (who had obviously read Aldous Huxley's 1932 novel, *Brave New World,* and alludes to it in *Proud Man*), may eventually diminish or even render obsolete the biological importance of women. On the other hand, Burdekin's analysis in *Proud Man* of how men feel both fear and contempt for women does not leave women blameless for colluding in a system that oppresses them. This charge is another theme frequently found in Burdekin's work.

In *Proud Man* the Person both observes and participates, appearing in various episodes first as a woman and then as a man, conveying to the reader a remarkable awareness of a dynamic mostly taken for granted in Burdekin's time. "Unquestioned male dominance," in the narrator's view, has resulted in a severe limitation of the possibilities of life in the "subhuman" world.

Like Karen Horney, whose essays on feminine psychology could be found in English in the 1920s but were likely unknown to Burdekin, the author believes that male fear and jealousy of women's ability to bear life is behind the male imposition of a devalued social identity on women. Unlike Horney, however, Burdekin does not believe the phallus possesses any real superiority. Instead, the power of the phallus derives from its social significance. The psychological drive revealed by this insight eventually finds its culmination in the nightmarish vision of *Swastika Night,* in which pride in the phallus has become part of the central myth of a fascist society.

Despite the imperfections of *Proud Man*—in particular the weakness of its final episode, noted by many reviewers—critical response to the novel was often enthusiastic. In *The Listener* (30 May 1934) Edwin Muir called the novel "probably the most profound and sustained satire that has appeared in many years. It is a book which no intelligent reader can afford to miss." Philip Mairet (in *New English Weekly,* 24 May 1934) praised the novelist's grasp of "the movements of the soul" and of the "actual world-crisis as a psychic problem in human nature." He

concluded, "I know of no one who could thus combine the dynamic and personal view of life with the social and relative, and produce so objective a view of our total situation."

Burdekin's second "Murray Constantine" novel was the allegorical fiction *The Devil, Poor Devil!* (1934). This work is a sometimes clever but often hermetic satire on the problem of evil in the world, recounted through the adventures of the Devil and another figure called "the Independent" as these two take on human bodies. The *TLS* reviewer (6 December 1934) judged the novel a failure, commenting that "a book without human reality can scarcely begin to have metaphysical significance."

For the most part, Burdekin's works share certain major themes, with later novels often developing ideas suggested in earlier efforts. Thus, in *Proud Man* Burdekin had written that in the subhuman world, where conflict often comes from beliefs about "privilege," even when "privilege" is challenged in what subhumans call "revolution" the result is merely a "reversal of privilege" rather than its abolition. Such a reversal had first been envisioned in *Quiet Ways,* in which a conservative male character is shaken by the female protagonist's sufficiency and lack of attentiveness to men. Unnerved, this character has a premonition of future generations of women with such a sense of self-esteem. A similar vision—now sounded as a warning—can also be found in *Proud Man:*

> If women retain their biological importance, and become pleased with themselves from birth, and learn to associate power with the womb instead of with the phallus, a dominance of females over males is not only possible but likely. Their self-confidence, which would be rooted as deep as the old male jealousy, would cause in them a tremendous release of psychic power with which the males would be unable to cope. Naturally a female dominance would make the race no happier, nor bring it a whit nearer to humanity. The privilege would merely be reversed, and possibly it would be more oppressive and more cruel.

This vision—in some respects particularly appropriate in the new millennium, a time when feminism has resulted not only in many benefits to women but also in significant excesses as well as in distortions in the relations between the sexes in the English-speaking world—is expanded into a major theme in what may have been Burdekin's next novel, *The End of This Day's Business.* Left in typescript among her papers, *The End of This Day's Business* was only published in 1989—more than twenty-five years after Burdekin's death—as a result of Patai's research and correspondence with the author's heirs. Textual and other evidence suggests that this book was composed in 1935, before *Swastika Night* (which a letter of Burdekin's to Victor Gollancz reveals was written in 1936). The two novels are clearly a pair, one imagining a female-dominant society four thousand years in the future, the other a male-dominant Europe seven hundred years after the victory of Nazism. Though the former is in many respects utopian, while the latter is clearly dystopian, the female world of *The End of This Day's Business* also has its dystopian side, which is in keeping with Burdekin's suspicion of "reversals of privilege" that fail to challenge the underlying principle of domination. But the differences between the two novels are as revealing as their similarities.

The End of This Day's Business deals not only with the future but also with the past, as do Burdekin's other utopian works. Its most significant aspect, however, is its reversal of sex roles. In this world, four thousand years in the future, women govern peacefully, but to do so, they have had to dominate the men. These men, separate and unequal, live in a trivially pleasant world in which their physical prowess and sexual appetites are granted abundant opportunities. But they have no significant contribution to make. The men are, furthermore, denied knowledge of women's rites and their secret language (Latin, the sole tongue in which books survive). Isolated by women's silence, cowed by female rationality and calm superiority, knowing only their mothers but not the identity of their fathers, men are deprived of history and thus of the knowledge of their past achievements and status.

The main development of *The End of This Day's Business* involves the slow realization by the protagonist, Grania, that her society has reversed the problems created by male dominance without moving beyond its pattern. Instead of being motivated by the fear of male dominance, however justified, Grania comes to believe that her society must transcend this pattern. As before, Burdekin criticizes the culpability of women in helping to transmit unequal power, for it is they above all who inculcate belief systems in their children: "If the Mother brings up the boy to regard her as inferior to himself, men rule. If she brings him up to regard himself as inferior, women rule."

Indulging her penchant for long disquisitions, Burdekin offers in *The End of This Day's Business* a detailed history of her own time from the perspective of a far-future age. In 1935 she still held out hope for the Soviet Union, and in general she sympathized with the communist ideal of an equal society. In this "history" she describes the ideological and political conflict between communism and fascism in the first part of the twentieth century. Many other writers who opposed fascism during this period lashed out at politics in general, but Burdekin distinguishes between fascism, which she saw as extremely dangerous, and other political ideologies. She was critical, too, of European nationalism, and in *The End of This Day's Business* she defines *patriotism* as a "morbid growth" on one's natural love of country. It is a "mental disease," she writes, of which ten million men died in World War I.

An unpublished 1935 novel, "Snakes and Ladders," examines how a girl comes to have a sense of worth as a female, a sense quite unlike that found in patriarchal societies in which, as noted in *Proud Man,* women are ultimately of value only as producers of replacement males. In *Proud Man* Burdekin also expresses her concern with the profound psychological effects on women artists of the low regard in which they have been held. The character of Leonora in *Proud Man* is a writer, despondent that after twelve years and five publishers she has yet to make a name for herself. Through Leonora, Burdekin addresses the supposedly lesser talent of women. Burdekin herself was in the twelfth year of her career when *Proud Man* was published, and it was released by Boriswood, her fourth publisher. Thus, one is tempted to view as autobiographical the scene in which Leonora argues about the inferiority of women and vents her anger at a famous artist who echoes Charles Tansley's words in Woolf's *To the Lighthouse* (1927), "because he's one of these men who think women can't do anything at all, can't write, can't paint, can't make music. You have no idea what a handicap it is to a woman who wants to write or paint, the knowing that she is expected to fail, and that men want her to fail, not for any reason except that she is a woman."

An extreme form of such androcentric assumptions is played out in *Swastika Night*. This violently antifascist novel was first published in 1937 by Gollancz. Fewer than one thousand copies were sold at the time, but critical praise for the novel, and perhaps also its prescience about fascism, moved Gollancz to republish the book in 1940 as a Left Book Club selection. It was one of the few works of fiction ever selected for the club, which had been founded in 1936 by Gollancz, political campaigner John Strachey, and political-science professor Harold Laski to disseminate and promote left-wing ideas and values. With nearly nineteen thousand copies in this edition sold, *Swastika Night* was Burdekin's most widely read book.

Contemporaneous response was mostly positive, although—perhaps not surprisingly—many of the reviewers missed the crucial focus on Nazism as a form of hypertrophied masculinity. Evelyn Waugh wrote that *Swastika Night* "is better as social criticism than as fiction, but it is a very readable book" (*Night and Day,* 8 July 1937), and Tullis Clare described the novel as "ingenious" and "a subtle, brilliant commentary on the European line of civilization's progress" (*Time and Tide*, 28 June 1937). Decades later, Andy Croft, in *Red Letter Days: British Fiction in the 1930s* (1990), judged *Swastika Night* to be "the most original of all the many antifascist dystopias of the late 1930s."

Many details from *Swastika Night* appear to have been borrowed by George Orwell in his later *Nineteen Eighty-Four* (1949), several elements of which were also inspired by Evgeny Zamyatin's 1924 novel *We*. Orwell's first publisher was Gollancz, and his *The Road to Wigan Pier* (1937) had also been a selection of the Left Book Club. Orwell's friend Geoffrey Gorer wrote to the editor of *Time and Tide* (12 February 1938), calling readers' attention to *Swastika Night*, which he identified as belonging "in the group of prophetic novels of which *Brave New World* is the most notorious example, but it seems to me far more probable, moving, and better written than any other of the group." Gilbert Bonifas in *Notes and Queries* (March 1987) reported receiving a letter from Gorer confirming that he in all likelihood lent or gave a copy of *Swastika Night* to Orwell. But the strongest evidence of the influence of Burdekin's novel on *Nineteen Eighty-Four* remains the many textual similarities.

Swastika Night depicts the seventh century of the Hitlerian millennium. The German and Japanese empires that govern the globe are both militaristic but cannot afford to remain in a state of war. The Nazis have attempted to make their mythic history into an official reality by systematically destroying virtually all of the books, records, and monuments of the past. Hitler is worshiped as a god, and women are imprisoned in fenced compounds that make Margaret Atwood's dystopian *The Handmaid's Tale* (1985), which resembles *Swastika Night* in several ways, seem almost pleasant. This "Reduction of Women" serves to reinforce the patriarchal authority of the Nazis, expressed in the complete power men have over women, including the right to rape. Women are primarily vehicles for reproduction, although they are at times used also to satisfy such male lust for females as has managed to survive in the homosexual Nazi society envisioned by Burdekin. Even reproduction, however, has been affected by this "Reduction of Women"—as if biology itself were in revolt against male rule—and, since fewer girls are being born, the future of the Nazi empire is threatened. The novel tells the story of an Englishman who acquires the only extant copy of an actual history of the world and then struggles to protect and pass on this book.

By the time she began writing *Swastika Night*, Burdekin had largely overcome the xenophobia occasionally surfacing in her earlier work, though her later fiction suggests that she continued to believe in distinct national character types. She did not hold the Germans responsible for Hitler, and she did not see Germany as a unique case. The real target of her criticism was the political values that she saw as linked to patriarchy, which, when taken to extremes, led to expressions of fascism such as militarism, notions of racial superiority, and what Burdekin labels the "cult of masculinity." While fully aware of the historical shifts that had occurred in the early and mid 1930s, Burdekin in *Swastika Night* judges National Socialist policies against Jews, women, and political opponents in the light of her earlier analyses of the gender hierarchy. It was a theme she could not let go of until, to her relief, war broke out in 1939.

In *The End of This Day's Business* the female society of the future has established its own laws and customs. In certain ways these resemble the Hitlerian norms of *Swastika Night*. In both books marriage has been abolished, and the sexes live separately. Children live with only one parent, and socialization in gender norms begins at an early age and is unrelenting. But the contexts that inform these social structures differ enormously. In the female utopia, no cult of violence is practiced, and the women do not enjoy their domination over the opposite sex. *Swastika Night*, by contrast, recounts in chilling detail the pervasiveness of these traits in the fascist dystopia of the future.

While Burdekin's earlier works already demonstrated an awareness of problems related to gender ideology, Hitler's rise to power apparently increased her sense of the extraordinary dangers represented by traditional ideas about masculinity. To a feminist observer of events taking place in Nazi Germany (as well as in Benito Mussolini's Italy before that), the ways in which fascist thought represented gender must have been clear. Nazi proclamations about the lives and duties of women certainly were. In *Women and a Changing Civilisation* (1934) Winifred Holtby also issued a warning about how fascism in both England and Germany attacked reason. But Burdekin's real insight was understanding that the several elements of Nazi policy constituted a single ideology. She believed that the elevation of motherhood, which was an important element in Nazi ideology, could easily lead to the reduction of women to mere animals suitable only for breeding. In both the elevation of motherhood and the degradation of women as mere breeders, women are reduced to agents of biology, and Burdekin connected this diminution to the standard practices of patriarchy. In *Three Guineas* (1938), published a year after *Swastika Night*, Virginia Woolf also associated the tyranny of fascism with the masculinist values of patriarchal society. Postwar studies of fascism by scholars such as Maria-Antonietta Macciocchi and Klaus Theweleit have further corroborated this connection.

Like many other pacifists of the World War I era, Burdekin abandoned pacifism in the face of the threat represented by Hitler. While many people at the time failed to take Nazism seriously or to realize the dangers it posed, Burdekin observed it carefully, especially its rituals and ideology, and connected these to the patterns of traditional patriarchy she had traced in her novels. At least six years before it happened, she was also able to imagine the Nazi attempt to exterminate the Jews: it is mentioned in *The End of This Day's Business* and dealt with more explicitly in *Swastika Night*.

Burdekin seems also to have been preoccupied at this time with attempting to understand how such a phenomenon as National Socialism could ever have arisen. In the unpublished novel "Children of Jacob" she made another effort to explain this historical puzzle. Inspired as so much of her fiction was by recent events—in this case the aftermath of the German annexation of Austria in March 1938—this book represents an even greater imaginative leap than *Swastika Night*. The English protagonist of the novel, finding himself in Vienna in March 1938, witnesses a group of Nazi youths mocking an elderly Jew forced to wash the sidewalk, an incident drawn from the British press. The protagonist is thrown into a crisis in which he sees himself, in various incarnations, reliving the history of patriarchy with its attendant traditions of power, from biblical times to its end far in the future. Burdekin locates the source of this tradition in Jacob's theft of Esau's birthright. This theft is the original act of violence performed out of a desire for power and in willful disrespect for their mother, Rebekah, who, enraged at men's disdain of women, condones an everlasting hatred among the races of men until such time as they might learn to love and respect women.

Several other unpublished novels exist in which Burdekin continued her exploration of political themes through futuristic scenarios. "No Compromise," written in the mid 1930s, foresees a near-future England where communists and fascists are locked in battle. Though the dialogues between the fascist and the communist protagonists are often simplistic and pamphlet-like, the novel is noteworthy for Burdekin's characteristic touch: her broadening of the definition of politics to include gender. "Joy in Heaven," composed soon after World War II had ended, portrays Hitler, after his death, gradually coming to grips with his actions. Strangely, this novel, though written after the revelations about the death camps, focuses not on the Holocaust but

Dust jacket for Burdekin's novel, posthumously published in 1989, about a matriarchal society of the future

instead on some lesser cruelties perpetrated early in Hitler's career.

Other novelists in the years after the end of World War II tried to visualize a world in which Hitler and Nazism had been victorious. Philip K. Dick's *The Man in the High Castle* (1962) is perhaps the most notable example. In another, distinctly feminist vein, Suzy McKee Charnas's *Walk to the End of the World* (1974) also resembles *Swastika Night* in its depiction of a phallocratic society in which women are enslaved. But even in this broader context, Burdekin remains unusual in her prophetic ability to follow the logic of Nazi ideology before it had played itself out and its horrific effects had become apparent.

Burdekin was tall (five feet and ten inches), slender, and athletic, as are many of her heroines. She loved horses and fast cars. She also suffered from migraines and depression, the worst bout of which occurred in the autumn of 1938, following the Munich Conference, when she feared that England would capitulate to Hitler. Trying to help her friend, Margaret Goldsmith gave Burdekin her many research notes on Marie Antoinette. Burdekin turned this research into an historical novel titled *Venus in Scorpio: A Romance of Versailles, 1770–1793* (1940), which lists both Goldsmith and Murray Constantine as authors. Unlike most historical novels dealing with this period, *Venus in Scorpio* focuses on the intense friendship between Marie Antoinette and one of her ladies-in-waiting, Princess Marie de Lamballe. The novel was Burdekin's last published book and the only one not inspired by her own ideas.

Burdekin did not write fiction during World War II. She spent more than two years working in a shoe factory, quitting when health problems intervened. She liked her contacts with working people and seems to have enjoyed the manual labor. She disliked not earning her way, part of the reason she wanted her books to be successful. After the war she resumed writing, but the bombing of Hiroshima and Nagasaki profoundly affected her outlook. Certainly a significant difference exists between the passion of her political novels of the 1930s and the handful of unpublished works of the late 1940s and early 1950s—perhaps resulting from her ill health, or from her fatigue and the inability to sustain the indignation that had inspired her work earlier, or perhaps simply from having moved into a different stage of life. These late novels are no less feminist, but they focus more on spiritual matters than on politics. Religion, mysticism, and spiritual evolution, concerns appearing occasionally in Burdekin's earlier novels, later became central. Her explorations of the theme of reincarnation date from this period, as does a curious sequel to Radclyffe Hall's *The Well of Loneliness* (1928), a novel titled "The Stars Shine in Daylight," which picks up precisely where Hall's book ends. Burdekin did not try to publish any of these later works.

An aneurysm in 1955 almost killed Burdekin, but after four months in the hospital she returned home to Suffolk. She was bedridden until she died of congestive heart failure on 10 August 1963. Her last work, written in 1956, is the unpublished novel "Dolly," a pleasant fantasy set on a riverbank bordering heaven, where a diverse group of travelers arrives from a variety of the societies of the world. None of them are able to cross into heaven as long as they harbor earthly prejudices, however unconscious those may be. Education and culture are no excuse: hatred and contempt for anyone keep a person from crossing the rivers into heaven. "Dolly" is not the only one of Burdekin's after-death scenarios. Like the others, it is a broad commentary on human types and human destiny. Burdekin confessed that she liked it, along

with *The Rebel Passion* and *Proud Man,* which she considered her important books.

It is a challenge to determine influences on Burdekin's work since her reading was both extensive and eclectic. What is clear is that she enjoyed books dealing with time travel and time warps. One of these was Ford Madox Ford's *Ladies Whose Bright Eyes* (1911), which appears to be a model for the time travel found in both *The Burning Ring* and "Children of Jacob." Another personal favorite was Margaret Irwin's novel *Still She Wished for Company* (1924). Burdekin's time warps, however, differ from those of Irwin, who depicts past, present, and future blending together, a merging that suggests a static view of time. By contrast, Burdekin's millennia-spanning novels attempt to examine how humans have developed, in particular morally, within the context of history. This paramount concern is also apparent in Burdekin's unpublished novel "Father to the Man," written after World War II, which again employs a time warp.

While some reviewers in her own time responded positively to the moral urgency of Burdekin's writing, with its frequent didactic turns, others found her work unconvincing. Even *Swastika Night* was judged by E. B. C. Jones, a reviewer who entirely overlooked its critique of masculinity, to be "a very immature work" (*The Spectator,* 13 August 1937), and Kenneth MacPherson in *Life and Letters Today* (1937) considered the novel to be "not deeply thoughtful nor politically valid," concluding, "Politics are for newspapers or history; to-morrow comes always the unforeseen." Since the 1970s the rise of a reading public interested in earlier feminist writers has created a market for Burdekin's work, and the Feminist Press editions of three of her novels seem finally to have found an appreciative audience. Another group of modern readers, those interested in science fiction and fantasy and especially in women's contributions to these genres, is also responsive to her work.

Burdekin wrote in what has come to be dismissed as a romantic mode of artistic creation: intuitive, unrevised, and often uneven. This mode gives some of her work a naive, even child-like quality, while at other turns (often in the same work) her writing is subtle and incisive. In all her speculative fiction, her use of lengthy monologues and dialogues about politics and history allowed her to make a coherent argument. Thinking about the vast complexities of continuity and change required a moral imagination; writing about these issues required the ability to vivify them. Though she needed the narrative possibilities of time travel and utopian speculation as a scaffolding for her explorations of the European landscape of her own day, Katharine Burdekin's great strength as an author lay, in the end, not in fantasy (which served her merely as a tool) but in her ability to draw back from the givens of her own time and place so that she might truly attend to their ageless implications.

References:

Raffaella Baccolini, "'It's Not in the Womb that the Damage is Done': Memory, Desire, and the Construction of Gender in Katharine Burdekin's *Swastika Night*," in *Le Trasformazioni del narrare*, edited by Erina Siciliani (Fasano di Brindisi: Schena, 1995), pp. 293–309;

Andy Croft, *Red Letter Days: British Fiction in the 1930s* (London: Lawrence & Wishart, 1990);

Robert Crossley, "Dystopian Nights," *Science-Fiction Studies*, 41 (March 1987): 93–98;

Vita Fortunati and Raymond Trousson, eds., *Dictionary of Literary Utopias* (Paris: Honoré Champion Editeur, 2000), pp. 198–199; 507–508; 591–592;

Sarah Lefanu, *Feminism and Science Fiction* (Bloomington: Indiana University Press, 1989), pp. 71–73;

George McKay, "Metapropaganda: Self-Reading Dystopian Fiction: Burdekin's *Swastika Night* and Orwell's *Nineteen Eighty-Four*," *Science-Fiction Studies*, 64 (November 1994): 302–314;

Carlo Pagetti, "In the Year of Our Lord Hitler 720: Katharine Burdekin's *Swastika Night*," *Science-Fiction Studies*, 52 (November 1990): 360–369;

Daphne Patai, "Imagining Reality: The Utopian Fiction of Katharine Burdekin," in *Rediscovering Forgotten Radicals: British Women Writers 1889–1939*, edited by Patai and Angela Ingram (Chapel Hill: University of North Carolina Press, 1994), pp. 226–243;

Patai, "Orwell's Despair, Burdekin's Hope: Gender and Power in Dystopia," *Women's Studies International Forum*, 7, no. 2 (1984): 85–96;

Elizabeth Russell, "The Loss of the Feminine Principle in Charlotte Haldane's *Man's World* and Katherine Burdekin's *Swastika Night*," in *Where No Man Has Gone Before: Women and Science Fiction*, edited by Lucie Armitt (London: Routledge, 1991), pp. 15–28;

Gary K. Wolfe, review of Burdekin's *Proud Man, Locus* (March 1994): 27.

Papers:

Typescripts and manuscripts are held by Katharine Burdekin's literary executor.

John Christopher
(Sam Youd)
(16 April 1922 –)

John R. Pfeiffer
Central Michigan University

BOOKS: *The Winter Swan,* as Christopher Youd (London: Dobson, 1949);

Babel Itself, as Samuel Youd (London: Cassell, 1951);

Brave Conquerors, as Youd (London: Cassell, 1952);

Crown and Anchor, as Youd (London: Cassell, 1953);

A Palace of Strangers, as Youd (London: Cassell, 1954);

The Twenty-Second Century, as John Christopher (London: Grayson & Grayson, 1954; New York: Lancer, 1962);

The Year of the Comet, as Christopher (London: Joseph, 1955); republished as *Planet in Peril* (New York: Avon, 1959);

Holly Ash, as Youd (London: Cassell, 1955); republished as *The Opportunist* (New York: Harper, 1955);

Malleson at Melbourne, as William Godfrey (London: Museum Press, 1956);

Giant's Arrow, as Anthony Rye (London: Gollancz, 1956); as Samuel Youd (New York: Simon & Schuster, 1960);

The Death of Grass, as Christopher (London: Joseph, 1956); republished as *No Blade of Grass* (New York: Simon & Schuster, 1957);

The Friendly Game, as Godfrey (London: Joseph, 1957);

Dust and the Curious Boy, as Peter Graaf (London: Joseph, 1957); republished as *Give the Devil His Due* (New York: M. S. Mill/Morrow, 1957);

Daughter Fair, as Graaf (London: Joseph, 1958; New York: Simon & Schuster, 1958);

Felix Walking, as Hilary Ford (London: Eyre & Spottiswoode, 1958; New York: Simon & Schuster, 1958);

The Caves of Night, as Christopher (London: Eyre & Spottiswoode, 1958; New York: Simon & Schuster, 1958);

A Scent of White Poppies, as Christopher (London: Eyre & Spottiswoode, 1959; New York: Simon & Schuster, 1959);

The Sapphire Conference, as Graaf (London: Joseph, 1959; New York: Washburn, 1959);

Felix Running, as Ford (London: Eyre & Spottiswoode, 1959);

The Long Voyage, as Christopher (London: Eyre & Spottiswoode, 1960); republished as *The White Voyage* (New York: Simon & Schuster, 1961);

The Choice, as Youd (New York: Simon & Schuster, 1961); republished as *The Burning Bird* (London: Longmans, 1964);

Messages of Love, as Youd (New York: Simon & Schuster, 1961; London: Longmans, 1962);

The World in Winter, as Christopher (London: Eyre & Spottiswoode, 1962); republished as *The Long Winter* (New York: Simon & Schuster, 1962);

The Gull's Kiss, as Graaf (London: Davies, 1962);

The Summers at Accorn, as Youd (London: Longmans, 1963);

Cloud on Silver, as Christopher (London: Hodder & Stoughton, 1964); republished as *Sweeney's Island* (New York: Simon & Schuster, 1964);

Bella on the Roof, as Ford (London: Longmans, 1965);

The Possessors, as Christopher (London: Hodder & Stoughton, 1965; New York: Simon & Schuster, 1965);

A Wrinkle in the Skin, as Christopher (London: Hodder & Stoughton, 1965); republished as *The Ragged Edge* (New York: Simon & Schuster, 1966);

Patchwork of Death, as Peter Nichols (New York: Holt, Rinehart & Winston, 1965; London: Hale, 1967);

The Little People, as Christopher (New York: Simon & Schuster, 1967; London: Hodder & Stoughton, 1967);

The White Mountains, as Christopher (London: Hamilton, 1967; New York: Macmillan, 1967);

The City of Gold and Lead, as Christopher (London: Hamilton, 1967; New York: Macmillan, 1967);

The Practice, as Stanley Winchester (London: W. H. Allen, 1967; New York: Putnam, 1967);

John Christopher (Sam Youd) (photograph by Sally Chandler; courtesy of the author)

Men with Knives, as Winchester (London: W. H. Allen, 1968); republished as *A Man With a Knife* (New York: Putnam, 1968);

The Pool of Fire, as Christopher (London: Hamilton, 1968; New York: Macmillan, 1968);

Pendulum, as Christopher (London: Hodder & Stoughton, 1968; New York: Simon & Schuster, 1968);

The Lotus Caves, as Christopher (London: Hamilton, 1969; New York: Macmillan, 1969);

The Helpers, as Winchester (London: W. H. Allen, 1970; New York: Putnam, 1970);

The Guardians, as Christopher (London: Hamilton, 1970; New York: Macmillan, 1970);

The Prince in Waiting, as Christopher (London: Hamilton, 1970; New York: Macmillan, 1970);

Beyond the Burning Lands, as Christopher (London: Hamilton, 1971; New York: Collier/Macmillan, 1971);

The Sword of the Spirits, as Christopher (London: Hamilton, 1972; New York: Macmillan, 1972);

In the Beginning, as Christopher (London: Longman, 1972); revised as *Dom and Va* (London: Hamilton, 1973; New York: Macmillan, 1973);

A Figure in Grey, as Ford (Tadworth, U.K.: World's Work, 1973);

Ten Per Cent of Your Life, as Winchester (London: W. H. Allen, 1973);

Wild Jack, as Christopher (London: Hamilton, 1974; New York: Macmillan, 1974);

Sarnia, as Ford (London: Hamilton, 1974; Garden City, N.Y.: Doubleday, 1974);

Castle Malindine, as Ford (London: Hamilton, 1975; New York: Harper & Row, 1975);

A Bride for Bedivere, as Ford (London: Hamilton, 1976; New York: Harper & Row, 1977);

Empty World, as Christopher (London: Hamilton, 1977; New York: Dutton, 1978);

Fireball, as Christopher (London: Gollancz, 1981; New York: Dutton, 1981);

New Found Land, as Christopher (London: Gollancz, 1983; New York: Dutton, 1983);

Dragon Dance, as Christopher (London: Viking Kestrel, 1986; New York: Dutton, 1986);

When the Tripods Came, as Christopher (London: Viking Kestrel, 1988; New York: Dutton, 1988);

A Dusk of Demons, as Christopher (London: Hamilton, 1993; New York: Macmillan, 1994).

OTHER: "Of Polymuf Stock," in *Young Winter's Tales 2,* edited by Marion Rous Hodgkin (London: Macmillan, 1970), pp. 130–147;

"Summer's Lease," in *The Best of British SF 1,* edited by Mike Ashley (London: Futura, 1977), pp. 325–328;

"Paths," in *Hundreds and Hundreds,* edited by Peter Dickinson (London: Puffin, 1984);

"Dancing Bear," in *Guardian Angels,* edited by Stephanie Nettell (Harmondsworth, U.K.: Viking Kestrel, 1987), pp. 41–55;

"C. S. Youd," *Something about the Author Autobiography Series,* volume 6 (Detroit: Gale, 1988), pp. 297–312.

SELECTED PERIODICAL PUBLICATIONS–
UNCOLLECTED (as John Christopher unless otherwise noted): "For Love of Country," as Christopher Youd, *Lilliput* (1939);

"Dreamer," *Weird Tales* (March 1941): 65;

"Impetus," *Zenith,* 4 (February 1942): 60–66;

"Socrates," *Galaxy,* 1 (March 1951): 84–97;

"Man of Destiny," *Galaxy,* 2 (May 1951): 124–132;

"Resurrection," *Science Fantasy,* 2 (Spring 1952): 4–42; republished as "A World of Slaves," *Satellite Science Fiction,* 3 (March 1959): 4–24;

"Aristotle, an Ironic Tale," *Science Fiction Quarterly,* 1 (February 1953): 105–114;

"Relativity," *Space Science Fiction,* 1 (February 1953): 115–119;

"The Drop," *Galaxy,* 5 (March 1953): 112–130;

"Planet of Change," *Authentic,* 36 (August 1953): 20–35;

"Rocket to Freedom," *Imagination Science Fiction,* 5 (February 1954): 72–82;

"Escape Route," *New Worlds,* 8 (June 1954): 61–69;

"The Name of this City," *Worlds of If,* 4 (October 1954): 62–73;

"Winter Boy, Summer Girl," *Fantastic* (October 1954); republished as "Summer's Lease," *Argosy,* 20 (July 1959);

"Vacation," *Worlds of If,* 4 (November 1954): 98–103, 117;

"Talent for the Future," *Fantastic Universe,* 11 (December 1954): 47–55;

"Conspiracy," *Authentic,* 53 (January 1955): 43–64;

"Manna," *New Worlds,* 33 (March 1955): 46–60;

"Mistaken Identity," *Evening Standard* (14 December 1955): 19;

"The Decline and Fall of the Bug-Eyed Monster," *Fantasy and Science Fiction,* 11 (October 1956): 74–76;

"The Gardener," *Tales of the Frightened,* 1 (Spring 1957): 116–121;

"The Noon's Repose," *Infinity,* 2 (April 1957): 68–77;

"Doom over Kareeta," *Satellite,* 2 (October 1957): 112–121;

"Science and Anti-Science," *Fantastic Universe,* 9 (June 1958): 101–103;

"A Few Kindred Spirits," *Fantasy and Science Fiction,* 29 (November 1965): 119–128;

"Ringing Tone," *Escapade* (June 1966);

"A Ticket in the Raffle," *Writer,* 79 (June 1966): 13–15;

"Rendezvous," *Playboy,* 13 (September 1966): 123, 148, 230;

"Communication Problem," *Argosy,* 27 (November 1966): 35–40;

"Legacy of Love," *Argosy,* 27 (May 1967): 93–101;

"The Long Night," *Argosy,* 28 (September 1967): 2–17;

"Not What-If but How-He," *Writer,* 81 (November 1968): 15–17, 45;

"A Cry of Children," *Argosy,* 31 (October 1970): 106–124;

"The Island of Bright Birds," *Ellery Queen's Mystery Magazine,* 59 (February 1972): 109–118;

"Specimen," *Fantasy and Science Fiction,* 35 (December 1972): 151–158;

"The Very Beautiful Swan," *Cricket* (April 1974): 38–42;

"Notes on Joy," *Encounter,* 34 (April 1987): 41–43;

"A Journey South," *Interzone,* 44 (February 1991): 41–60;

Bad Dream, Spectrum SF, 4 (November 2000): 4–52; 5 (February 2001): 40–106; 6 (May–July 2001): 84–146.

Sam Youd distinguished himself as a writer of science fiction, first for the general reader and then for young adults, under the pseudonym John Christopher. Although he has several other pseudonyms–Hilary Ford, William Godfrey, Peter Graaf, Peter Nichols, Anthony Rye, and Stanley Winchester–the "John Christopher" name is on almost all of his science fiction. Productive, critically successful, and popular for more than half a century, he ranks among the top British science-fiction writers of the modern era. His short stories have appeared in the premier science-fiction venues, including *Fantasy and Science Fiction, Playboy,* and the best-of-the-year anthologies. His 1956 novel *The Death of Grass* (filmed in 1970) is a minor science-fiction classic. His young-adult science fiction is even more significant, especially the critically acclaimed Sword trilogy and the Tripods trilogy, on which the 1980s British Broadcasting Corporation (BBC) television series *Tripods* was based.

No significant writer of science fiction has explored more prolifically the fictional postcatastrophe behavior of people than Youd. The concern with how humans handle the stress of radical change and the loss of civilization and culture dominates the speculative fiction he has written for general audiences and forms the background for most of his young-adult works. His stories are also fascinating when they are read as analyses of how civilization and culture are acquired. Youd wrote science fiction successfully from the beginning of his career but was uneasy with many of the tropes of the genre, especially a futurism that included the possibility of humanity coming into significant contact with sentient alien species. Moreover, he often preferred, instead of extrapolation of technologically advanced human futures, to construct devolved scenarios of human history. The fictive postcatastrophe-descent-to-savagery or regression-to-a-simpler-civilization narrative comfortably accommodated Youd's disposition.

His general science-fiction novels present ecocatastrophe or the collapse of government, setting a stage upon which to analyze the behavior of humans in populations that will have to survive as small groups that become tribal. His young-adult novels use postcatastrophe settings that exhibit a markedly different interest. In them is addressed the conflict of the individual with society, of reason with feeling, of personal morality with public and popular morality, and of tradition and custom with progress and change. They are not significantly more optimistic; Youd refuses to talk down to children and young-adult readers. In his art and themes he is motivated by his singular admiration for Jane Austen. The idea of a transformation of Austen's drawing rooms to Youd's postcatastrophe landscapes suggests the juxtaposition of civilization and savagery that elucidates much of Christopher's fictional world.

Youd was born on 16 April 1922 in Knowsley, Lancashire, England, a suburb of Liverpool, the only child of Sam and Harriet Youd. His parents had little education but were superior in native intelligence. His father was a wire drawer who also served in the army. He had met Youd's mother while serving as a gunner. Youd's mother, Harriet, maiden name Hawkins, was the youngest of twenty-one children (by two wives) of an Irish peasant farmer. She went into domestic service and rose eventually to the rank of cook-housekeeper with titled families. She had three children by earlier marriages. Married to Youd's father in 1919, she had a stillborn boy in 1920; Youd assumes his parents regarded him as a replacement for that child, who was to have been called James.

Youd lived at Lime Grove Cottages, Liverpool Road, Knowsley (or Huyton as boundaries changed), from birth to 1932. His first school was Huyton-cum-Roby C. of E. (Church of England), where he gained a scholarship to Prescot Grammar School. In the middle of the first term the family moved two hundred miles south to Eastleigh, Hampshire, a factory town near Southampton, and Youd was transferred to Peter Symonds School, Winchester—then a minor but aspiring English public school. Youd wrote in a 1994/1995 personal letter that he "spent an undistinguished six years there, getting a School Certificate at 14 but miserably failing Higher Schools at 16." In 1938 he went to work in a local government office. In April 1939 he

started the science-fiction fanzine *The Fantast,* which he edited until 1942, beginning his apprenticeship like Ray Bradbury, who started the fanzine *Futuria Fantasia* in his early years.

His first published story, "For Love of Country" (*Lilliput,* 1939), appearing under the name Christopher Youd, was not science fiction but exhibits one of his signature plots, about an Anglophile German bomber pilot turning away from his urban target to drop his bombs in open country but in fact demolishing a camouflaged factory. Youd's daily train to work passed such a factory and inspired the story. He was paid £10 for the story, equal to ten times his weekly wage, and he used it to buy a decent portable typewriter. His undertakings in science fiction began when he wrote letters to the editors of *Astounding, The Futurian* (a fanzine), *Tales of Wonder, Weird Tales,* and *Zenith* (another fanzine) between 1938 and 1942. "John Christopher's" first creative piece published in the United States was in the March 1941 issue of *Weird Tales,* a mediocre sonnet titled "Dreamer."

In February 1942 Youd enlisted in the Royal Signals. That same month the fanzine *Zenith* published his first science-fiction story, "Impetus," about three futures and alternative fates of Clive Hamilton, each depending on how much more or less true to himself and the good of humanity he remains. Rereading the story in his seventies, Youd in a personal letter pronounced it "callow."

During World War II he was stationed on Gibraltar for a year beginning in the summer of 1942. Then, after a brief tour in North Africa, he served in Sicily and Italy until the end of the war. Afterward he was stationed for a time in Austria. In 1946 he married Joyce Fairbairn, who worked in scientific research and then in science journalism. From this marriage came five children: Nicholas in 1951, Rose in 1953, Liz in 1955, Sheila in 1957, and Margret in 1959.

After demobilization at the end of 1946, Youd lived in London: first in South Kensington, and later in West Dulwich. He had an office job from 1949 to 1958 working in and eventually heading the Industrial Diamond Information Bureau of the Diamond Corporation. Evenings and weekends he devoted to writing, but he allowed himself an evening a week off, which he spent at the science-fiction pub—first the White Horse in Fetter Lane, later the Globe in Hatton Garden. There he socialized with writers such as Arthur C. Clarke, William F. Temple, John Wyndham, and Joy Gresham (later the wife of C. S. Lewis).

Writing in his spare time, Youd won a Rockefeller Foundation Atlantic Award (1946–1948) on the basis of a draft chapter from his novel *The Winter Swan.* Appearing in 1949, the novel utilizes fantasy to tell the story of Rosemary Sedgwick, who is reincarnated in the consciousnesses of people she knew during life. The story

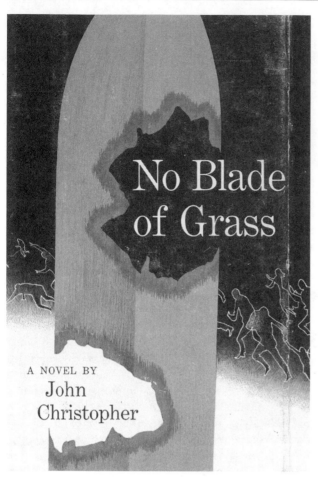

*Dust jacket for the U.S. edition of Christopher's 1956 novel,
about the survivors of a worldwide famine
(Bruccoli Clark Layman Collection)*

begins at her death at sixty-six and ends in her youth, revealing a haunting woman who all her life refused to surrender to emotions. Of additional interest in *The Winter Swan* is the mention of bubble spheres built by "clever scientific men. . . . Perhaps they would yet learn to build transparent, floating bubbles in which each man might ride the storm, secure and defiant." Youd later used such a device in his first deliberately science-fiction novel, *The Year of the Comet* (1955).

Four of the uncollected stories of the 1949–1954 period are notable. "Socrates" (*Galaxy,* March 1951) is about one survivor of a litter of five mutated dogs that are highly intelligent and psychic. The unnamed narrator tells of trying to buy the dog from Jennings, a cruel caretaker who knows the dog may bear some intelligence but wants to exploit it in a show-business act and enforces Socrates' training with a whip. Socrates, who learns to talk, can accept the narrator's friendship and an invitation to be educated but persists in canine loyalty to the cruel Jennings. Socrates dies trying to save Jennings from drowning. In an epilogue the narrator

mourns the lost achievements that Socrates, less than a year old at death, might have reached but reflects that his own ordinary dog, Tess, with whom Socrates romped in the fields, is pregnant and perhaps may deliver mutant puppies. "Socrates" was reprinted at least five times in prestigious anthologies. A mordant message of the story is that the deep-seated instinct in the dog species for faithfulness to a master might block the species from reaching a higher status in nature.

"Man of Destiny" (*Galaxy,* May 1951) features Theodore Pike, who is marooned in another solar system. The people are primitive but almost preternaturally peaceful. Pike imagines that he has become their god; but toward the end of the first year he is there, the people save him from the foolishness of trying to ride out an annual high tide. He dies after twenty years of a contented life, afraid only that Earthmen might come and disturb this peaceful species.

"Resurrection" (*Science Fantasy,* Spring 1952) anticipates Youd's successful young-adult Tripods novels in the late 1960s. The story is set in a postcatastrophe North America about one hundred years in the future, when Stanley Liggard awakes from suspended animation to an Earth dominated by a "Brain," an artificial intelligence made by humans and encapsuled at the top of three fifty-foot mechanical legs. The Brain has reduced the population of Earth to two million and made tortured playthings of the survivors, all of whom must live rurally so that no big cities can hide the elaborate technology that humans would need to defeat the Brain. The Brain is finally killed by a nuclear bomb carried by a man named Luthor on his own body, while Luthor's daughter, Patience, and Stanley survive to live in the newly unburdened world. In the novel, machine technology has enslaved humanity. The solution may be to return to a technologically simpler civilization.

In the poignant "Winter Boy, Summer Girl" (*Fantastic,* October 1954) Ronnie is a "winter person" living in a civilization that puts the great majority of the population into hibernation for the winters. He sees Jill, a "summer person," in her hibernating sleep and falls in love with her. She then watches over him as he hibernates in the summer. In love, he tries to stay awake with her the next summer, but he hates the world of crowded millions. She then stays awake with him for the winter, but is lonely and frightened in the peopleless world. Their love is doomed. In the final scene he is looking at her hibernating body, knowing that he loves her but will never be able to be with her. Youd revisited the hibernation/suspended-animation premise with a far more sinister meaning in his novel *Bad Dream* (2001).

Most of the short stories from this early period are included in Youd's only short-story collection, *The Twenty-Second Century* (1954). It is divided into three sections. The title section features stories centering upon a character named Max Larkin and projecting a postcapitalism/socialism managerial society. Section two, "The Light Fantastic," expresses Youd's ambivalent feelings toward science fiction. For example, many time-travel narratives display a fatuous optimism, while Youd's stories with this premise almost invariably yield perverse effects for their protagonists. Section three, "The Old Way Home," reflects Youd's then-active interest in religion, especially Roman Catholicism.

Six of these stories, each of which has been reprinted at least four times, are especially remarkable. In "Christmas Roses" (*Astounding,* February 1949) Joe Davis, a rocket-ship crewman on rounds from Earth to local planets and moons, becomes permanently grounded on Earth's moon because further space travel will kill him. He has just brought roses from Earth for Old Hans, who had suffered a similar fate forty years before, at age thirty. In "Balance" (*New Worlds,* Spring 1951) Max Larkin, the hero of the six managerial stories in *The Twenty-Second Century,* kills a beautiful woman supergenius to maintain the balance of power in the world. Larkin is an old man, a conservative in a technologically advanced world who likes trains, unpaved earth, old wine, and books printed on paper.

"Mister Kowtshook" (*Avon Science Fiction and Fantasy Reader,* 1953) tells of a strange man, an alien in fact, who joins a circus for a time and makes everybody happy until he is arrested by agents from his alien species as a criminal of some sort, although his crime is not revealed. The clown Mike Cinnabon, who tells the story, is impressed by the power of the aliens but repulsed by a culture that would find Mr. Kowtshook a criminal. In "Blemish" (*Authentic,* November 1953) a future dystopian Earth similar to that depicted in Aldous Huxley's *Brave New World* (1932) is reprieved from extermination by the galactic authority because of a single isolated community that still cherishes individualism and spiritual values.

In "The New Wine," first published in *The Twenty-Second Century,* Harl goes on a time-dilation starship trip, leaving his fiancée, Ellen, behind. She is part of a project that will turn all human children and animals into telepaths. One hundred years later by Earth time, Harl returns and discovers that not only Ellen but also virtually everyone else is dead. A lone survivor born just before the telepathic irradiation effect tells Harl and the others that people's minds were just too nasty for themselves or others to handle. As a result, all telepaths committed suicide. The telepaths had no children, and the two women on the spaceship crew, presumably still normal, are in their fifties and too old to have children, so the human race will become extinct. "Weapon," also first published in *The Twenty-Second Cen-*

tury, tells a story in which precognitive science is perfected by the military in 1954 to predict the weaponry of one hundred years hence. The weapon predicted is the crossbow, indicating that a major catastrophe to high-tech civilization will occur, reducing humanity to a medieval technology.

Between *The Winter Swan* and *The Year of the Comet,* Youd published four non-science-fiction novels: *Babel Itself* (1951), *Brave Conquerors* (1952), *Crown and Anchor* (1953), and *A Palace of Strangers* (1954). They did not do well. *The Year of the Comet* features Charles Grayner, a twenty-first-century diamond physicist with latent managerial instincts who is caught up in the struggle for control and development of diamond refraction physics to produce batteries and heat rays from the sun, a military advantage desired by the multinational conglomerates that have replaced capitalist and socialist governments. In the not-too-sturdily-erected background for the novel, astronomical observations reveal that a comet is on course to pass Earth closely. The story is a symbolic warning tale, with Earth still threatened in the end. At the end of the story Charles is working successfully on a diamond battery-laser for the Cometeers, the religious catastrophists who watch the incoming comet and expect doom. Charles and his love interest, Sara, do find happiness, however. A central intelligence for the novel is furnished by Hiram Dinkuhl, a cynical television owner/manager and entrepreneur who is the single trustworthy confidant for Charles throughout a story moved by repeated deceptions from all sides. Dinkuhl finally concludes that religious revelation, rather than extinguishing hope, actually is hope.

The Death of Grass was Youd's tenth novel and his first significant financial success. It brought him major critical and popular acclaim. Damon Knight noted in his review of the novel in the October 1957 issue of *Infinity* that Youd had told this postcatastrophe story better than anyone had before him. The novel ran as a seven-part serial in *The Saturday Evening Post* in 1957, which was the first wide exposure for "John Christopher," and it was made into a motion picture in 1970 titled *No Blade of Grass.* It is built upon the story of two brothers and their connected fate in a postcatastrophe England. John Beverley is a city man and an architect. David Beverley chose the country and the family farm, Blind Gill, which by extraordinary geological formations was fortified against virtually all intrusion and could be entered only through a bottleneck pass that would allow a few defenders to hold off an army of invaders. When a disease attacks the grasses—first in the Far East and gradually over the whole planet, including the British Isles—famine and the resulting panic, especially in the population centers, drive John,

Dust jacket for Christopher's 1967 novel, the first volume of his Tripods trilogy, in which three boys resist mind control by the aliens who have invaded Earth (courtesy of the author)

with his family and a few close friends, to seek shelter with David. Their journey, during which they acquire allies and companions, including the gunsmith and gunman Pirrie, is a descent into savagery for those who survive. John and his wife, Ann, learn to kill, taught by Pirrie. Killing to survive extends ultimately to the killing of David, presumably by Pirrie, who himself dies in the battle to secure the farm as a stronghold against other famine-panicked survivors who have also descended to brutal behavior, exhibiting a spectrum of pathological personalities that tend to be concealed or only minor when the veneer of civilization is in place. *The Death of Grass* was the first of four postcatastrophe Christopher novels for adults that examine the behavior of individuals in a society of radically reduced population and simplified civilization. It was a runner-up to J. R. R. Tolkien's *The Lord of the Rings* (1954–1955) for the International Fantasy Award in 1957 and went through at least twenty-five printings. On 14 January

2002, under the headline "Apocalypse Then: A Message for 2K2," it was the subject of a feature in the *Washington Post* pointing up its relevance to the terrorist attacks in America on 11 September 2001.

Meanwhile, Youd published thirteen non-science-fiction novels under his various pseudonyms between 1956 and 1961. Early in 1958 he finally quit his job and began to write full time. The family left London and spent time in 1958 and 1959 in Switzerland and Ireland, both of which supplied Christopher with settings for later novels. In these years the only non-science-fiction novels under the John Christopher pseudonym were published: *The Caves of Night* (1958), *A Scent of White Poppies* (1959), and *The Long Voyage* (1960). *The Caves of Night* and *The Long Voyage* especially exhibit Youd's particular talent and preference for exploring the dynamics of a group of characters forced into a physically tight space and experiencing a life-threatening event. The settings of an underground cave system in *The Caves of Night* and an Arctic shipwreck in *The Long Voyage* were ideal for his purposes.

In *The World in Winter* (1962) a new ice age reduces Britain to a fraction of its population. The story has British survivors going to Nigeria to become second-class citizens and menials. Eventually, Nigeria sends an expedition to take London from the remaining British survivors and occupy it, but the Nigerians are defeated in a struggle involving the protagonist of the novel, the British Andrew Leedon, who has been befriended by Abonitu, a Nigerian television director. Abonitu, sent to film the occupation effort, inadvertently takes over the military task. Andrew, accompanying him as a technician, is the instrument of the undoing of the expedition. Andrew subverts the African force by disconnecting the television searchlights so that the British survivors can defeat the Africans. The London forces also keep the captured fleet of African hovercraft, which will give them good defenses, in spite of the cold, to last a few years and see whether London can live again in an arctic climate. Especially noteworthy are the descriptions of the desperate and selfish behavior of people as worldwide temperatures drop and the poignant observation of the imminent threat to books in libraries, which the freezing mobs will use for fuel, conveying a keen sense of the vulnerability of high culture when technology is overloaded and fails.

Published in the same year under the pseudonym Peter Graaf was the non-science-fiction work *The Gull's Kiss* (1962), a spy-thriller psychodrama that Youd feels is one of his best novels. With its failure to do well, and the weak reception the following year of *The Summers at Accorn* (1963), he felt he had to put aside hopes of being regarded as a serious writer.

The next Christopher work, *Cloud on Silver,* appeared in 1964. It is another psychological adventure yarn, with science-fiction elements, in which a wealthy man, Sweeney, takes a group of people to a South Sea island, perhaps to observe their descent into savagery. Youd wrote the story in reactive opposition to William Golding's *Lord of the Flies* (1954).

The following year three important works appeared. The plot of *The Possessors* (1965) is fragile in logic but sturdier in its dramatization of a small group of people on holiday, isolated in a snowbound Swiss chalet, who are attacked by body-snatching alien beings who have lain sporelike in the ancient ice until a glacial shift has released them. The interest of the story is generated by the able representation of the various victims, children and adults, under the stress of sensationally bad weather and the attack of the spore-aliens, who take over the bodies of the humans one by one. Four people survive when the aliens are defeated by burning the chalet down with all the "possessed" people trapped inside. Because they think that no one will believe them, the survivors agree not to talk to authorities about the fact that extraterrestrial creatures caused the tragedy. The novel went to at least seven printings.

A small group of survivors is again the focus of *A Wrinkle in the Skin* (1965), which some think is his best adult science-fiction work. During a summer in the 1960s new mountain-building geological events kill most of humanity. Matt and Billy, among others, survive on the Channel island of Guernsey, where Youd had been living since 1959. The devastation on the British mainland is dramatized when Matt travels with Billy to search for Matt's daughter, Jane. They travel across the now-dry seabed, where they find a psychotic captain of a grounded ocean freighter living on his ship's supplies and watching cartoons and old movies with an emergency generator. Later, they meet April and Laurence and their group of local survivors, who take them in. There is the beginning of a relationship between April and Matt, but he abandons it to continue his search for his daughter. Billy travels with him. Eventually Matt discovers that the area where Jane was living has been submerged by a new stretch of sea. He gives up his search and begins a return to April, nursing a sick Billy and even carrying the boy for a couple of days. He reaches April's old camp, only to find the people gone. He returns to the Channel Islands, where he finds April and Laurence at last and a new and more real chance of happiness.

A Wrinkle in the Skin exhibits Youd's art of telling the postcatastrophe story in all of its important elements. His surviving characters are a combination of vulnerability and competence. They also become the central intelligence and the explainers of the state of things. Typical of Youd's sympathetic central characters, Matt does not interfere with the brutal behavior of Miller, the leader of one of the survivor groups that they encounter. Geological forces are a significant element in *A Wrinkle in the Skin,* yet the geologist character survives only long enough to let readers remember that a science of geology exists. For Youd's British audience the loss of the ever-present and close sea, making Britain no longer an island country, would have a major meaning.

Regardless of how coherent it is, Youd's theory of postcatastrophe behavior is the result of no systematic research. His reference to an article in *The Lancet* on the psychological effects of an earthquake on South Island, of the Kopje quake, and of the bombings at Dresden and Hiroshima, he says, was purely serendipitous. Even so, a whole page of the novel is devoted to the psychosis of postcatastrophe behavior. A major premise is that when purpose in life is gone, the sanest people become aberrant. The island survivors are more resilient than mainland survivors because they are used to being psychologically and practically independent of the larger civilization of the mainlands. The relatively happy ending of *A Wrinkle in the Skin,* along with the hope that is allowed at the end of Youd's other postcatastrophe books, demonstrates his desire to limit in his readers the feeling of massive loss with a story of grief endured and transcended.

Youd's third science-fiction piece of 1965 was "A Few Kindred Spirits" (*Fantasy and Science Fiction,* November 1965), which comically utilizes the reincarnation trope he employed in *The Winter Swan.* In this work homosexual men, mostly writers, are reincarnated first as homosexual dogs and eventually as homosexual budgerigars. The story was reprinted in *The Best of Fantasy and Science Fiction* for the year.

Youd's only novel for 1966 (published a year later) was *The Little People;* it is a yarn with science-fiction elements. Bridget Chauncey inherits a backwater Irish castle that she turns into a vacation place, only to discover that her uncle Seamus had inherited the fruits of a bizarre Nazi research experiment, planned originally to secure immortality for the Führer, which had resulted in the creation of people no more than a foot high, whom Seamus used as playthings. The little people have some psychic power to magnify human emotional tendencies. They are discovered by the vacationing boarders, who plan to show them to the world with the attendant pain such sideshow exposure would create. However, the little people telepathically conjure dreams in the boarders, causing them to experience their deepest fears and hopes. Afterward, Bridget decides not to marry her fiancé, about whom she has

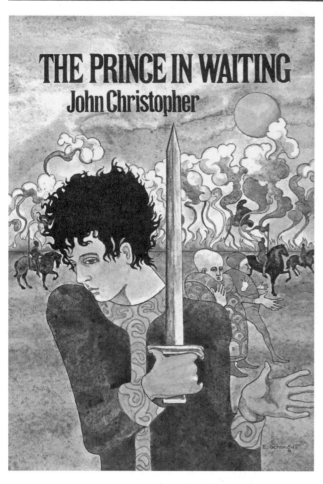

Dust jacket for Christopher's 1970 novel, the first volume in his
Sword trilogy, set in a post-catastrophe twenty-third century
in which technology has regressed to medieval levels
(courtesy of the author)

been ambivalent, and abandons the place to the little people, who will die off without breeding.

One more postcatastrophe novel, *Pendulum* (1968), completes the inventory of early Christopher science-fiction novels for a general audience. A social revolution puts a younger and brutal generation in power in Britain (the rest of the world is only vaguely implicated). The story starts with the rise of violence as a permissive socialist economy fails, in part because of the loss of the old virtues of honest work and fair pay in favor of a program that is too weak in leadership to protect itself from its inherent weaknesses as an economic reward system. Following the lives of Rod, an honest builder-developer, and his family, the story is of a civilization that descends to near anarchy where only the "Yobs" ("backward boys") hold power in the metropolitan areas of England. Their misrule is demonstrated in the vile ways Rod's family is treated. Their "Commander" humiliates Rod but spares him because Rod's wife,

Hilda, reminds him of his mother. But he is overthrown and killed by one of his lieutenants, Ape, who rapes Rod's sister-in-law Jane. Rod escapes with two of his children, Peter and Linda, after Hilda dies of cancer. At the same time, the rise of the puritanical Robeys occurs, with Rod's brother-in-law Martin's psychotic transformation as an illustration of its progress. The Yobs' abuse of power allows the Robeys to seize it and restore law and order but under a repressive regime. The Robeys are in power, and Rod, despite his brother being a senior official, is condemned to hard labor under them; his children are taken away to be brainwashed. Linda and her lover, Micky, crippled by Ape during an attempt to save her, survive, though in desperate poverty. The outlook is bleak. Only Jane's coming child, conceived in rape, offers hope for the future.

In 1967 Youd embarked upon two ambitious writing ventures. The less successful one, only revealed to the public in 2001, resulted in publication of four novels, three of them about the medical profession, as Stanley Winchester: *The Practice* (1967), *Men with Knives* (1968), *The Helpers* (1970), and *Ten Per Cent of Your Life* (1973). In the second of the ventures Youd began to write novels for young adult readers. They brought him new critical recognition and a financial return that managed to maintain his large family. In all he has written fifteen, comprising three trilogies and six single works. In 1967 and 1968 the Tripods trilogy appeared. Hamish Hamilton had offered Youd a commission to write a science-fiction story for boys. He refused the commission but wrote *The White Mountains* (1967). His American agent showed the manuscript to Macmillan in the United States; Macmillan liked the first chapter of the book but wanted a complete rewriting. Youd reluctantly studied Macmillan's detailed criticisms and found them valid. He rewrote it, coming to understand as he did so that writing a story for young adults was not as easy as he had thought. He also had to rewrite *The City of Gold and Lead* (1967). The third book of the trilogy, *The Pool of Fire* (1968), needed no rewriting. The trilogy is by far the most successful of the Christopher works. For much of this success he credits his American editor at Macmillan, Susan Hirschman, and his United Kingdom editor at Hamilton, Julia Macrae.

The White Mountains introduces Will Parker; Henry Parker, his cousin; and the French youth Jean Paul, who is called "Beanpole" both for his lanky body and for the early mishearing of his French name by Will and Henry. An invasion by aliens, which the humans call "Tripods," has reduced the human population to a tiny percentage of its twentieth-century number. When humans reach adolescence, the aliens fit them with metal skullcaps—a process called "capping"—that control parts of the brain and make them docile and slave-like for life. The thirteen-year-old boys journey to France and then south to escape capping by the Tripods, who hold the surviving population in thrall—using, in addition to capping, the imposition of a medieval hierarchical social structure. The adventures of the three boys consist of their being tracked and chased by the Tripods, vehicles that consist of a pod about twenty feet in diameter that is fitted with three articulated legs fifty feet long as well as a flexible tentacle that reaches down from the belly of the pod to strike and ensnare its prey.

The boys' destination is the "White Mountains," the Swiss Alps, where the Tripods, since they originated on a flat marshy planet, are severely disadvantaged and where the boys join rebel humans in their hideaways in a mountain formerly tunneled for railways. The purpose of the Tripods is not at first clear. The three boys believe that humans will finally prevail, even though the technological superiority of the aliens is manifestly overwhelming. Personal freedom is the basic and critical consideration.

In the first book there is no description of the aliens themselves, only their vehicles; even Youd did not know what was inside the Tripods. He later realized that he had unconsciously borrowed the concept from H. G. Wells, and he set about creating what might be more likely users of such vehicles than Wells's Martians.

In *The City of Gold and Lead* Will, Beanpole, and a new character, Fritz, having been trained for months at the underground hideout in the White Mountains, are sent by the sixty-year-old rebel leader to the athletic games staged by the Tripods to identify the physically best humans. Fritz and Will are among the winners of these contests and are taken into the aliens' domed city, the City of Gold and Lead. They must be strong to withstand slavery in the leaden super-gravity that the aliens have created; it usually kills the strongest within two years. In the city Fritz and Will learn that the Tripods are beings called Skloodzi but always referred to as the Masters, who come from another star and have conquered many other planets, going in ships that have faster-than-light drives. They also have faster-than-light means of communication with their home planet, and they await machinery that they have ordered by message that will transform Earth's atmosphere into one suited for them, thus dooming not only humanity but virtually all the native Earth species.

The Masters, Will and Fritz (and the readers) discover, are conical in shape, about twelve feet tall, five feet in circumference at the base, with three tentacles and three feet, and with a face with three eyes. The nose speaks and breathes above the mouth. They travel by spinning on their three legs. They reproduce by parthenogenesis, are flesh and blood, and are addicted to a kind of gaseous recreational drug; they require a green, moist atmosphere poisonous to humans, as well as a heavier gravity than humans. They read, write, and clearly possess a powerful science. They have individual characters: some are sadistic, and some are kind— but only relatively. Like butterfly collectors they mount macabre exhibitions of beautiful human girls.

When the boys need to escape the city, Fritz, who has been badly beaten by his sadistic master, selflessly helps Will get out by means of a river that flows through the city and out into the surrounding country. Beanpole, having waited with dog-like loyalty, fishes out the nearly dead Will. Together they make it back to the White Mountains with valuable information about the Masters, including specimens of their air and food. Fritz seems left for dead—another reason to seek retribution upon the aliens.

But Fritz survives to help the rebel humans mount a successful counterattack in *The Pool of Fire,* the story of the defeat of the Masters by the destruction of their three cities on earth. The final attack is made with hot-air balloons carrying bombs over the last of the alien cities, situated on the Panama Canal. After the victory, the old nations reemerge, resuming their ancient political divisions, with all the potential conflicts these have always brought. In fact, humanity has learned almost nothing from the occupation of the Masters. The resolution of Will, Fritz, and Beanpole to work for peaceful international relations does not leave one hopeful of success.

Each volume of the trilogy sold nearly twenty printings. The trilogy was a runner-up for the Guardian Award in 1969 and received the George G. Stone Center for Children's Books Recognition of Merit Award in 1977. The first two volumes were the bases for BBC television series in the fall seasons of 1984 and 1985. The television production of the Tripods story took several liberties with the details of the novels, however. Reviews of the series were generally complimentary, but it was canceled before the third season. This production remains available on videocassette.

The commercial success of the Tripods books was continued in most of Youd's later science-fiction books for younger readers. *The Lotus Caves* (1969) is about two boys in a lunar colony who out of boredom break the settlement rules by taking out a lunar crawler without authorization. They investigate a long-deserted outpost, where they find a diary of Andrew Thurgood, one of the early colonists, with improbable but tantalizing references to seeing a flowering plant among the dead rocks of the moon. Following his grid references, they fall into a crevasse and

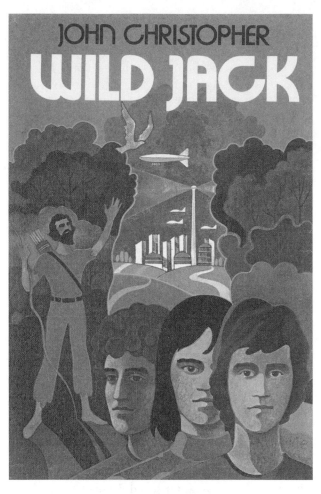

*Dust jacket for Christopher's 1974 novel, in which social chaos
results from the exhaustion of natural resources
in the early twenty-first century*

ity of the satellite to survey the surface of the moon so thoroughly as to track Marty and Steve, as contemporary satellites could easily do.

Youd's most honored novel is *The Guardians* (1970), a young-adult dystopian tale that presents Robin "Rob" Randall, born on 17 August 2038 in the Fulham sector of Greater London. The future England in which he lives has evolved into what appears to be a severe cultural bifurcation: between urban people, who live on preserved food and watch games and "holovision," and a much smaller population of aristocrats living on grand estates with many servants, enjoying a more attractive life of natural food and personal participation in competitive sports—all with a nineteenth-century aura. In 2052, at age fourteen, following the mysterious death of his father, Rob leaves the city "Conurb" and escapes to the "County." His escape is made successful when Mike Gifford befriends him. Rob becomes a part of the Gifford family, passed off as the nephew of Mike's mother, and is given the privileges of the gentry. At school, Rob learns that Mike and his friends plan a rebellion to overturn the static culture of the County. They feel that it is too steeped in custom and controlled by an elite group with a hidden agenda. Rob refuses to be associated with the rebels. The rebellion is begun and quickly quashed with surreptitiously ready guns and helicopters by the "Guardians," who deal with dissenters by a brain operation that removes their power to rebel, similar to the "capped" adults in the Tripods stories. Rob learns that the Guardians have known almost from the first his real identity as an escapee from the Conurb. He is invited to join the ranks of the Guardians, but he finds he cannot tolerate their illiberality and ruthlessness. In the end he joins Mike and the rebels by returning to the Conurb to carry on the rebellion in the city, against staggering odds.

Comparison can be made to George Orwell's *Nineteen Eighty-Four* (1949), especially in the "Uncle" of the holovision for the Conurb populations, recalling Orwell's "Big Brother." There is as well an Orwellian war in China, to which incorrigibles from both populations are sent. The Guardians manage both the Conurb and County populations to keep in place political cultures that suppress radical thinking and action. What is being guarded, then, is actually a repressive status quo. The novel has reached at least twenty printings and received the Christopher Award in 1970 and the Guardian Award for children's fiction in 1971. *The Guardians* was translated into German as *Die Wächter,* which won the German Children's Book Prize in 1976, and the story has been televised in Germany.

Between November 1970 and March 1972 Youd published the three novels of the Sword trilogy. *The*

through the surface of the moon to a vast multiplex of caves, blossoming with life. They also find a still youthful Thurgood, who explains that the Plant, seeded here long ago from a distant galaxy, can not only give them wonderful food but also provide practically anything they might desire. But Thurgood worships the Plant as a god, and they realize that the food the Plant supplies has been responsible for this devotion and will bring them to a similar slave-like condition. They trick Thurgood into revealing a possible way out, and take it while they are still capable of independent thought. Thurgood goes back to his Plant-God; the boys for their part decide to accept punishment when they get back to the base, rather than reveal the existence of the Plant, which, powerful in its own sphere, would be destroyed by human technology. As usual in Youd's stories, time is marked fairly exactly. The 1969 information about the moon is still accurate except for the limits placed on the abil-

Prince in Waiting (1970) is a tale set in a postcatastrophe southern England, wherein the general level of technology for the average person is medieval. In a construction Youd uses in other young-adult futuristic novels, a monastically styled order of Seers preserves and can use the high science and technology reached before civilization was destroyed. The Seers guide the life of Luke Perry, the hero of the trilogy, whom they have chosen to lead culture back to a state where it can try again to make responsible use of the advantages of advanced science and technology. This agenda of hope for return to a past greatness of technology with a new social enlightenment is never so explicitly present in the adult postcatastrophe Christopher novels.

Luke is the son of Robert, a common soldier who was promoted to Captain for bravery and who, through the furtive manipulation of the Seers, becomes the Prince of Winchester—making the younger of his two sons, Luke, born of a second wife for whom he divorced his first, the "Prince in Waiting." Luke validates himself as the Seers' choice by defeating the other young captains against considerable odds. After his victory and a special benediction by the "spirits" (a device of the Seers), Luke has a happy summer, but in the winter his mother is murdered through a plot originating with Robert's first wife, Mary, mother of Luke's halfbrother, Peter. Mary is tried and executed. Prince Robert, who had previously made his mark by conquering two neighbouring towns, is reduced to grieving inactivity. When he finally rouses himself from torpor, he is tricked by another Prince, Jeremy of Romsey, who kills him and captures the defenseless town. Winchester is only recovered through Peter, who is married to a Christian, revealing a secret Christian tunnel through which the despairing army can gain admission to their lost stronghold. In return he demands the succession to the princedom, and the army grants it. The Seer Ezzard, fearful that Luke's life is now at risk, engineers his escape to a sanctuary under Stonehenge, where he learns that the men who preserve the science and technology of the precatastrophe world have plans for him to be the military leader who brings about conditions for the restoration of a high-tech civilization. The previous civilization fell by a combination of geological upheavals and freakishly increased solar radiation. Conspicuously in this story, as in most of Youd's adult postcatastrophe stories, the fall of humanity has not been caused by cultural incompetence.

Even so, this work, more than Youd's other stories for young adults, presents human culture in its most morally complicated and violent transformations. The stories are a far cry from the Bobbsey Twins and the Hardy Boys.

Beyond the Burning Lands (1971) brings Luke back to Winchester from the Seers' Sanctuary at the invitation of Peter, acting under the influence of his wife, Ann. Luke is cheered and welcomed by old friends and retainers, including the dwarf armorer, Rudi, whose son, Hans, Luke agrees to take with him on an expedition beyond the burning lands, a geologically volcanic region that separates southern from northern England. The expedition leaves, but only after Ann drowns in her bath, apparently accidentally, together with a child in her womb, and Peter names his brother again as Prince-in-Waiting. The expedition beyond the burning lands is guided by Yews the peddler, who came from Klan Gothlen, a "Wilsh" city-state northwest of the burning lands ruled by a Cymru or king. The group crosses the volcanic surface, protecting their horses' hooves with wetted leather boots, and they find mutated animals that in the south would have been destroyed. In Klan Gothlen, the people do not abide by a genetic caste system, as in Luke's homeland. In this land it seems that, without the interference of the Seers, natural talent from polymufs (humans with visible mutations) and dwarves, as well as normal humans, has been allowed to emerge and prosper. At the Cymru's court they watch an animated cartoon, a remnant of a dead civilization, as in *A Wrinkle in the Skin* when the psychotic ocean freighter captain watches movies from his ship's library after civilization is gone.

Later they participate in a hunt, heavily managed so that there is no danger to the hunters who wait. The game is pre-caught and released within the hunters' range to be shot with crossbows. Even gravid sows are game, violating the rules of Luke's culture. The Klan Gothlen inhabitants' total acceptance of mutated people and animals is also an assault upon Luke's morality. The Klan Gothlen culture is a fictional extrapolation of tendencies in Welsh culture, which include a love of colors and music. The burning lands separate two cultures, each of which can disgust or outrage the other, although Luke's is easily the more conservative and puritan.

Meanwhile, Luke meets the incomparably beautiful Blodwen, Cymru's daughter, who is betrothed to him by the ruler. Her beauty transcends both cultures, matched by a spirit that bows to no man. Luke's character is illustrated when he kills a Bayemot—a whale-sized sluglike creature—in a near-suicidal attack with a long dagger. By his own analysis he was not brave but angry, foolhardy, and ultimately lucky.

Although Blodwen is betrothed to him, Luke elects to leave her and return to Winchester. On the way, he is captured by matriarchal tree people, who plan to roast him on a spit. Hans, the dwarf warrior, helps him escape, setting the tree dwellers' village afire.

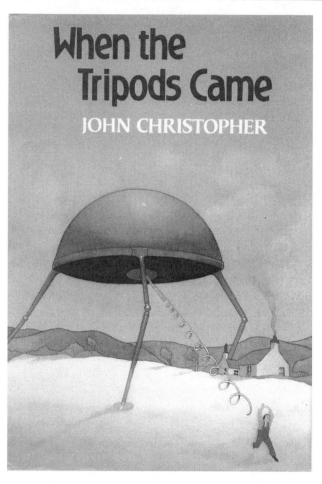

Dust jacket for Christopher's 1988 prequel to his Tripods trilogy, in which aliens invade Earth

Luke and Hans return to Winchester to find that Luke has been, in absentia, unjustly condemned to death for complicity in Ezzard's plot to kill Ann and secure the succession for his protégé. But Luke challenges Peter to a swordfight and kills him with his induction-hardened "Sword of the Spirits." The book ends with Luke as Prince of Winchester, contemplating the loss of his family, and particularly of his dead brother.

In the last book of the trilogy, *The Sword of the Spirits* (1972), Blodwen comes to Winchester to see the home of her prospective husband, but falls in love with Luke's friend Edmund. The city is split between two factions, and the other Captains depose Luke and send him into exile. He gets a new army from the Wilsh and, armed with primitive machine guns by the Seers, they overwhelm the southern armies and are poised to retake Winchester when Luke is shamed by the courage and self-sacrifice of his fellow townsmen and withdraws. Cymru designates him as his successor. He rules the northern kingdom, where the miracles of twentieth-century science and technology are

resurrected. The Wilsh will eventually conquer all of Britain; however, Luke does not care. He has lost the love of Blodwen, cannot love another woman, and will not have a son. He has been shamed by the Christian-inspired and self-sacrificial defiance of his former friends.

The trilogy has many meanings. It is about the end of the tyranny of monarchy and the rise of democracy. It is also about the balance of individual talent, strength, and ambition with success, failure, and grief. It received some of the highest praise of all Youd's books.

An interlude work of this period in Youd's writing career was *In the Beginning* (1972), a graded reading text for reader education programs. It was successful and was rewritten as the young-adult novelette *Dom and Va* (1973). It begins:

> Five hundred thousand years ago or thereabouts, in Africa, two different kinds of early man lived and died and left their bones, which scientists find today in the Olduvai Gorge. One race had no tools but had weapons—weapons made from the bones of the antelope, whose flesh they ate. They were hunters and fighters: killers by nature. The other race learned how to make tools out of stones. They were gentler and weaker than the hunters.
>
> When the climate changed and the two races met at last, and fought for existence, there could be no doubt which must win.

The arrival of an ice age, as in one of the adult Christopher novels, precipitates a migration of peoples, bringing them into violent and fateful confrontation. Dom's northern tribe of hunters defeats Va's southern tribe and forces Dom and Va into a marriage of convenience, in which, despite Dom's protection of her and eventual acceptance of her moral superiority, Va continues to reject him. Va nevertheless becomes pregnant; she teaches Dom to build a hut; and baby Kin is born. Outsiders attack Va and the baby after Dom has left them to hunt for game. But he returns in time to fight and defeat the outsiders with Va's help. Va then forgives Dom for killing her parents and loves him for himself as well as a protector of her and Kin. Others join them where they live, and a village begins. Mere survival is transformed into the beginning of high human culture when the race of hunters and the race of artisans and builders combine in friendship and love, especially in families. This meaning is present as a significant subtext in most of the Christopher works. This book, unusually, had only one printing; Youd maintains that it was "strangled at birth" by feminist librarians who took offense at the promotion of sexual bonding.

Almost two years later, after two short stories and a Hilary Ford novel, *A Figure in Grey* (1973), another young-adult novel by Christopher appeared, called *Wild Jack* (1974). In it a societal breakdown has occurred because of the loss of coal and oil in the early twenty-first century, causing war and a rebellion of the hungry, resulting in mass death. A few survive by exploiting a knowledge of nuclear energy. While his parents are away, Clive Anderson is arrested in postbreakdown London on a trumped-up charge of bad citizenship and sent to a punishment island. From there—with two friends, Kelly the American and Sunyo the Japanese—he escapes in a plastic boat to the Outlands forest. It turns out to be inhabited by people led by a Robin Hood–like commander who teaches Clive the meaning of freedom, which he almost forfeits, except that they rescue him after he returns to Southampton. The story effectively uses many parts of the Robin Hood tale, such as when Clive is forced into a balancing test on a rope footbridge, reminiscent of meeting an honorable adversary on a log bridge. Wild Jack is a rebel hero figure epitomizing Youd's message for young readers in support of the absolute value of personal political freedom.

During the next three years Youd published three relatively successful modern-Gothic Hilary Ford novels, including *Sarnia* (1974), *Castle Malindine* (1975), and *A Bride for Bedivere* (1976). In 1976 he spent some months in Dublin, after which he took up residence in Rye in June 1977. That year the eerily moving *Empty World* appeared. In this novel a plague kills almost everybody, leaving a handful alive in England. Eventually Neil Miller finds two women, Lucy and Billie. When Neil and Lucy fall in love, Billie is too possessive to allow Lucy a peaceable relationship with Neil. In her brooding jealousy Billie tries to kill Neil, but she is thwarted. Although Neil and Lucy could leave her to be alone forever, they do not. The story is reminiscent of the 1959 movie *The World, the Flesh and the Devil*, based upon M. P. Shiel's *The Purple Cloud* (1901). The novel, with its focus upon only three characters, is wonderfully evocative of the loneliness of a peopleless, postdisaster world, thus making an interesting irony when the narrative suggests, as the lonely protagonists enter a deserted bookstore, that science fiction presents "hundreds and hundreds of exciting futures for the human race." Youd has reported that he was impressed by George R. Stewart's *Earth Abides* (1949), one of the most celebrated of post-disaster narratives. *Empty World* is particularly reminiscent of it. The novel appeared in at least nine printings and was televised, like *The Guardians,* in a German-language version.

Although his writings had been published in the United States since the 1940s, Youd did not visit America until 1978, traveling through New York, San Francisco, Dallas, Boston, and Virginia. His divorce from his first wife was final in July 1979. His second marriage was to Jessica Valerie Ball on 24 December 1980. (Jessica had a granddaughter, Charlotte Louise de Putron, to whom some of Youd's young-adult books are dedicated. She was killed in an automobile accident in April 1992 at age twenty.)

Youd published the Fireball trilogy between 1981 and 1986. In the first volume, *Fireball* (1981), Simon, a British youth, and Brad, his American cousin, enter a parallel universe wherein a twentieth-century England remains at a medieval level of technology because the Roman Empire has endured into modern times, although at the cost of the technological progress that has taken place in the universe they left behind. Conveniently, Brad has an extraordinary memory and a nearly encyclopedic general knowledge of things, so that the two boys precipitate significant culture shock and politically threatening changes in the world they have entered. After thus becoming personae non gratae, they set sail for the New World and New England, where their initial contact is with the Algonquin Indians.

New Found Land (1983) begins with the experiences of Brad and Simon with the Algonquins. The boys are detained against their wills with their Latin friends Curtius, a soldier, and Bos, a gladiator, but escape via a raft journey south on the Atlantic Ocean. Lost on the raft, they are picked up by Vikings who live on Nantucket Island and at first treat them well. These Vikings have been in place for nearly a thousand years; therefore, according to the story, they are culturally tired and even corrupt. It turns out that they practice human sacrifice, which the four learn just in time to escape and travel on with a Viking woman, Lundiga, who falls for Brad and tags along. They go by way of the Southwest, where they encounter an Incan-Aztec hybrid culture and make money by becoming professional athletes playing a form of lacrosse/jai alai/basketball on a team that includes the two Romans, Curtius and Bos, and Lundiga, whose skill is that of a man. She illustrates Youd's understanding that men and women can be physical as well as intellectual equals. *New Found Land* received the Parents' Choice Award for literature from the Parents' Choice Foundation in 1983.

The trilogy finishes with *Dragon Dance* (1986), in which Brad and Simon leave the west coast of the North American continent and travel to a parallel-world China, where they experience a nation dominated by a form of logical magic. They spend time in a mountain monastery with a seemingly young girl who turns out to be ancient in age. Later they participate on opposite sides of a battle wherein Brad's reinvented airplanes defeat Simon's magical kites, and the old

Christopher in 1984

monk from the monastery is identified as an alternate-world Roger Bacon. The boys are presented with an option to return to their own dimension, but Brad opts for new adventures, and Simon, though homesick, elects to go with him.

Youd and his wife remained in Rye until 1986. From early 1986 to early 1989 they lived again in Guernsey, after which they resumed residence in Rye. In 1987 Youd published "Dancing Bear" in the anthology *Guardian Angels,* a collection of fifteen new stories by winners of the *Guardian* Children's Fiction Award. Not science fiction but set in ancient Roman Britain, the story is of the Roman soldier Ursus (bear), who, by taking refuge in an abbey, survives his father and evil half-brother in an onslaught of barbarians. When he enjoys victory and the plunder of the barbarians, he realizes, in his fifties, that his victory is temporary and that the people he rules are not tough enough to found a new nation and a new "City." He decides not to be a king, at least in his heart, even if he must be in body. He is too old to play or dance, or be the founder of another national myth.

The success in print and media of the Tripods story might have made the publication of *When the Tripods Came* (1988) welcome, but it sold only a few printings on its own (it continues in print as part of a boxed set with the Tripods trilogy). It is a prequel to the trilogy, with different characters, including first-person narrator Laurie Cordray. After the Masters' initial invasion, some of the characters eventually reach the mountains to set up the resistance movement that will later attack and destroy the aliens but only after the aliens have held Earth for several generations.

With the exception of *When the Tripods Came,* Youd did not publish another novel until *A Dusk of Demons* (1993), which is reminiscent of the Sword trilogy. It is the story of Ben, the son of a dead "Master" in a postcatastrophe world. This time the catastrophe has been a failure of moral culture in a massive abuse of drugs of all kinds, causing the collapse of the machinery that fed the masses, resulting in the deaths of millions. The surviving world has only one-thousandth the population of the past. The cultures that emerge are opposites: one is antimachine and one, as in the Sword trilogy, secretly preserves technology and manipulates the politics of the antimachine culture to restore a high-technological world. Ben becomes the pawn in the conflict of the machine culture over whether to leave the antimachinists in a "Demon"-ruled state of submissive superstition or to change the protocol by freeing them of the Demons (holographic projections) and returning the benefits of technology to the whole of the population. The side of technology is in the ascendency as the tale ends. The story includes Ben's excursion through a carnival side-show of freaks, an episode similar to Bradbury's in his *Something Wicked This Way Comes* (1962); but where Bradbury used the carnival freaks to symbolize the adolescent boy's coming to grips with his own weirdness, Youd's Ben is fascinated by and capable of seeing through the mummery of the freak-show exhibits.

Youd's characters are much more consciously analytical than one expects children to be. Moreover, his young characters perceive accurately the goodness and badness of people. Perhaps this perceptiveness is unrealistic, but it is a modeling myth to encourage young readers to see what is really before them, to see through unworthy illusions.

Youd's life at the end of the 1990s was somewhat disorganized as a result of the long illness of his wife, Jessica; she died on 31 October 2001. These years, however, were especially successful ones for him professionally. Two websites devoted to the Tripods, and one called "The John Christopher Cavern," established by Terry Jenkins, were started. In August 2001, after a long option period, Disney Studios (Touchstone) bought the rights to *Tripods*. The March 2001 issue of *Interzone* was a special number, titled "A Celebration of John Christopher," featuring an extended interview with Paul Brazier. And the May–July 2001 issue of *Spectrum SF* published the last chapters of its serialization of his latest novel, *Bad Dream*.

The novel is a "dystopia postponed" story with the premise that a multi-state world is better than a global federation–though only just barely, because among the elements of the narrative is the persistent psychotic nationalism of the Neo-Nazis. England and Germany are the settings for this tale of a provisionally successful revolt of British nationalists against the federation of European states that has come into being by about 2020. By an oscillation of its own political agenda, America is supportive of a new British independence. More sinister is the sub-story of a plot to combine virtual reality with a form of suspended animation to put workers into a form of hibernation when demand for their labor is down. *Bad Dream* warns against the rise of an uncheckable centralized government. The reason humans fight to preserve individual freedom is represented in the family love and loyalty of Caucasian Briton Michael Frodsham and African-American Lucy Jones, who literally disappear into the night at the end of the novel, with Lucy anticipating pregnancy.

The list of subjects not present in Youd's science fiction is a reflection of his reservations about the genre. There are no supermen, no artificial intelligence, no important new technology, few aliens (with the exception of the Plant of *The Lotus Caves* and the Skloodzi of the Tripods trilogy), and no utopias. Ultimately Youd's contribution to the body of popular writing is his achievements in the speculative-fiction genre. Among Youd titles in print or scheduled for republication are *Year of the Comet, The Possessors, Wrinkle in the Skin, The Little People,* and *The Tripods,* along with a new volume of previously uncollected short fiction. His best-known works will likely remain *The Death of Grass,* the Tripods trilogy, and the Sword trilogy.

Interviews:

John Gough, "An Interview with John Christopher," *Literature in Education,* 15 (Summer 1984): 93–102;

Colin Brockhurst, "Luck, Stamina and Gusting Peacocks: Sam Youd (John Christopher) Interviewed in January 1999," *Circus,* 8 (August 1999): 34–38;

Paul Brazier, "'A Lot of Fun Trying . . . ' Interview with John Christopher," *Interzone,* 165, special Christopher issue (March 2001): 14–28.

Bibliography:

Phil Stephensen-Payne, *Christopher Samuel Youd: Master of All Genres,* second revised edition (Leeds: Galactic Central, 1990).

References:

K. V. Bailey, "Masters, Slaves, and Rebels: Dystopia as Defined and Defied by John Christopher," in *Science Fiction for Young Readers,* edited by C. W. Sullivan III (Westport, Conn. & London: Greenwood Press, 1993), pp. 97–112;

Colin Brockhurst, "The Shattered Worlds of John Christopher," *Circus,* 8 (August 1999): 31–33;

Hugh and Maureen Crago, "John Christopher: An Assessment with Reservations," *Children's Book Review,* 1 (June 1971): 77–79;

Sam Moskowitz, *Seekers of Tomorrow: Masters of Modern Science Fiction* (New York: Ballantine, 1967);

Chris Orton, "*The Tripods:* A Trilogy in Two Parts," *Circus,* 8 (August 1999);

Orton, "*The Tripods'* Richard Bates Interview: *The Avengers* and *Tripods* Producer Talks to Chris Orton," *Circus,* 8 (August 1999);

T. A. Shippey, "*No Blade of Grass,*" in *Survey of Science Fiction Literature,* volume 4, edited by Frank N. Magill (Englewood Cliffs, N.J.: Salem Press, 1983), pp. 1541–1544;

John Rowe Townsend, "John Christopher," in his *A Sense of Story: Essays on Contemporary Writers for Children* (Philadelphia: Lippincott, 1971), pp. 48–56.

Papers:

A fair collection of John Christopher's papers is held in family archives.

John Collier

(3 May 1901 – 6 April 1980)

Betty Richardson
Southern Illinois University at Edwardsville

See also the Collier entry in *DLB 77: British Mystery Writers, 1920–1939.*

BOOKS: *His Monkey Wife; or, Married to a Chimp* (London: Davies, 1930; New York: Appleton, 1931);
Gemini (London: Ulysses, 1931);
No Traveller Returns (London: White Owl Press, 1931);
An Epistle to a Friend (London: Ulysses, 1932);
Green Thoughts (London: William Jackson, 1932);
Just the Other Day: An Informal History of Great Britain Since the War, by Collier and Iain Lang (London: Hamilton, 1932; New York & London: Harper, 1932);
Tom's A-Cold: A Tale (London: Macmillan, 1933); republished as *Full Circle: A Tale* (New York: Appleton, 1933);
Defy the Foul Fiend; or, The Misadventures of a Heart (London: Macmillan, 1934; New York: Knopf, 1934);
The Devil and All (London: Nonesuch, 1934);
Variation on a Theme (London: Grayson & Grayson, 1935);
Witch's Money (New York: Viking, 1940);
Presenting Moonshine (New York: Viking, 1941; London: Macmillan, 1941);
Wet Saturday: A Play Adapted from the New Yorker Short Story (Boston: One Act, 1941);
The Touch of Nutmeg, and More Unlikely Stories (New York: Readers Club, 1943); republished as *Green Thoughts and Other Strange Tales* (New York: Editions for the Armed Services, 1945);
Fancies and Goodnights (Garden City, N.Y.: Doubleday, 1951); abridged as *Of Demons and Darkness* (London: Transworld, 1965);
Pictures in the Fire (London: Hart-Davis, 1958);
The John Collier Reader (New York: Knopf, 1972; London: Souvenir, 1975); abridged as *The Best of John Collier* (New York: Simon & Schuster, 1975);
Milton's Paradise Lost: Screenplay for Cinema of the Mind (New York: Knopf, 1973).

John Collier

PRODUCED SCRIPTS: *Sylvia Scarlett,* motion picture, adapted by Collier, Gladys Unger, and Mortimer Offner from Compton MacKenzie's novel, RKO, 1936;
Elephant Boy, motion picture, adapted by Collier, Akos Tolnay, and Marcia De Silva from Rudyard Kipling's novel *Toomai of the Elephants,* United Artists, 1937;
Her Cardboard Lover, motion picture, adapted by Collier, Jacques Deval, Anthony Veiller, and William H. Wright from Valerie Wyngate and P. G. Wodehouse's adaptation of Deval's play *Dans sa candeur naive,* M-G-M, 1942;
Deception, motion picture, adapted by Collier and Joseph Than from Louis Verneuil's play *Monsieur Lambertheir,* Warner Bros., 1946;

Roseanna McCoy, motion picture, adapted by Collier from Alberta Hannum's novel, Samuel Goldwyn, 1949;

The Story of Three Loves, motion picture, adapted by Collier, Jan Lustig, and George Froeschel from stories by Jacques Maret, Arnold Philips, and Ladislao Vajda, M-G-M, 1953;

I Am a Camera, motion picture, adapted by Collier from Christopher Isherwood's *Berlin Stories* and John Van Druten's play *Romulus,* 1955;

The War Lord, motion picture, adapted by Collier and Millard Kaufman from Leslie Stevens's play *The Lovers,* Universal, 1965.

OTHER: John Aubrey, *The Scandal and Credulities of John Aubrey,* edited by Collier (London: Davies, 1931; New York: Appleton, 1931);

"Please Excuse Me, Comrade," in *Ten Contemporaries: Notes Toward Their Definitive Bibliography,* second series, edited by John Gawsworth (London: Joiner & Steele, 1933), pp. 109–117.

SELECTED PERIODICAL PUBLICATIONS–
UNCOLLECTED: "Things Seen," *Dial,* 86 (July 1929): 591–696;

"Insincerity," *New Yorker,* 9 (22 July 1933): 13–15;

"Simply Appalling," *New Yorker,* 9 (4 November 1933): 15–16;

"Perfect Murder," *New Yorker,* 10 (24 March 1934): 17–18;

"Faults on Both Sides," *New Yorker,* 10 (21 July 1934): 25–26;

"The Gables Mystery," *New Yorker,* 10 (28 July 1934): 15–16;

"Deferred Payment," *Collier's,* 105 (27 April 1940): 12;

"Meeting of Relations," *Yale Review,* 31 (December 1941): 430–432;

"None Are So Blind," *New Yorker,* 32 (31 March 1956): 29–34;

"The Dog That Came to the Funeral," *Ellery Queen's Mystery Magazine,* 32 (December 1957): 96–104;

"Anniversary Gift," *Ellery Queen's Mystery Magazine,* 33 (April 1959): 50–61.

John Collier wrote more than one hundred short stories, three novels, eight produced movie scripts, a volume of poetry, a modernized dramatic version of John Milton's *Paradise Lost* (1667), and a social history of England in the 1920s, along with many reviews and other minor works; but he is best known for his fantasies. His talent has been compared with that of Lord Dunsany, S. J. Perelman, Anatole France, Sax Rohmer, James Branch Cabell, and–to Collier's dismay–H. H. Munro (Saki). In an unpublished, undated letter to Betty Richardson in which he offered comments to be published in her study of Collier, science-fiction writer Ray Bradbury described Collier as a combination of W. Somerset Maugham, Rudyard Kipling, and Evelyn Waugh. The many comparisons point to the difficulty of describing Collier's distinctive style, especially in his stories, which are cool, economical, and witty. As noted motion-picture writer and longtime friend Paul Jarrico observed in a 13 April 1980 memorial speech, Collier wrote with infinite effort to create a style that seems effortless. By many, he is considered a writer's writer.

John Henry Noyes Collier was born in London on 3 May 1901, son of John George and Emily Mary Noyes Collier. He had one sister, Kathleen Marx Collier. His father was one of seventeen children; family finances did not allow a gentleman's formal education, and he took work as a clerk. He, in turn, could provide little money for his son's education, and young John Collier, apart from a brief period at preparatory school, was educated at home. He began reading Hans Christian Andersen fairy tales at three; these began a lifelong interest in myth and legend that was further stimulated when, in his teens, he discovered James Frazer's *The Golden Bough* (1890–1915). An uncle, Vincent Collier, himself a minor novelist, introduced the boy to seventeenth- and eighteenth-century literature. Collier particularly admired Jonathan Swift, and an eighteenth-century satirist's view of life became his own. From his first work to his version of *Paradise Lost,* Collier saw humans, flawed but with potential, everywhere contaminated by narrow creeds, institutions, coteries, vanities, and careers.

Assisted by his father, Collier found lodgings in London and by the early 1920s had begun working as a short-story writer, journalist, and reviewer. He became poetry editor of *Time and Tide* during the 1920s and 1930s, and he won a poetry award from *This Quarter* in 1932 after publication of his poetry collection, *Gemini* (1931). His excitement with the intellectual ferment of London in the 1920s is evident in *Just the Other Day: An Informal History of Great Britain Since the War* (1932), written with Iain Lang. By the end of the decade he had written *His Monkey Wife; or, Married to a Chimp* (1930), the fantasy that first made his reputation.

His Monkey Wife is the last among light early-twentieth-century fantasies that include G. K. Chesterton's *The Man Who Was Thursday* (1908), Max Beerbohm's *Zuleika Dobson* (1911), and Virginia Woolf's *Orlando* (1928). Collier's book, however, appeared immediately after the economic crash and the start of the Great Depression in 1929, when the tone of the literary and intellectual world darkened. While his

Dust jacket for Collier's 1951 short-story collection

novel was well received, it did not achieve the fame of the earlier fantasies.

His Monkey Wife is the story of Albert Fatigay, who abandons his relatively simple missionary life in Africa for the jungles of urban London. Fatigay adores a fashionable London girl, Amy Flint; he is unaware that his pet chimpanzee, Emily, has long loved him. Emily, of course, cannot speak, but, unknown to Fatigay, she has taught herself to read and has studied the advanced works of Woolf and George Bernard Shaw. She is a serious intellectual; she fervently admires the suffragettes Emmeline, Christabel, and Sylvia Pankhurst, and, upon arriving in England, immediately seeks out the British Museum in order to study Charles Darwin's *The Origin of Species* (1859). Her principles are real, as contrasted with the denizens of London such as Amy, whose advanced thought is an excuse for self-serving behavior. Inevitably, Fatigay suffers at Amy's hands, is reduced to the gutter, and is rescued by Emily, who has become a successful dancer, complete with elegant home and chauffeur-driven car. After all, in Collier's London, men, whether scholars at the British Museum or music-hall patrons, are content if a woman is silent and sensual; since they do not take women seriously, they overlook details such as Emily's species. Finally, Fatigay and Emily return to Africa; the marriage into which Emily has tricked Fatigay to save him from Amy is presumably consummated, since the novel ends as they retire and Emily reaches out a prehensile foot to put out their candle. This ending caused protests, but the novel creates much sympathy with the fully evolved Emily; it is the people around her who act like monkeys.

Much in this novel echoes, without Swift's bitterness, the contrast between Gulliver and the rational Houyhnhnms in *Gulliver's Travels* (1726). Collier's style, however, is playful; he borrows heavily from Joseph Conrad, parodies the style of Thomas De Quincey when Fatigay is turned penniless into the streets, and otherwise sustains the light and artificial tone by literary borrowings throughout. (Emily's name is borrowed from one of the Brontës.) The contrast between urban stupidity and pastoral calm (although Collier's Africa is hardly idyllic, since it contains humans) reflects a lasting theme; that contrast is the subject of his single volume of poetry, *Gemini,* in which the twins of the zodiac are personified as twin elements of the author's character, the rough man of nature and the citified dandy.

Collier's second novel, *Tom's A-Cold: A Tale* (1933), published in the United States as *Full Circle: A Tale,* is a different kind of fantasy, grim and sober, part of a tradition of apocalyptic literature that began in the 1870s. Apocalyptic novels of the period include Erskine Childers's *The Riddle of the Sands* (1903), Saki's *When William Came* (1914), and H. G. Wells's *The War of the Worlds* (1898) and *The War in the Air* (1908). Usually, this literature shows an England destroyed by alien forces, but in Collier's novel, set in Hampshire in 1995, England has been destroyed by its own vices—greed, laziness, and an overwhelming bureaucracy crippled by its own committees and red tape. Only a few old men, such as the father of the hero, Harry, survive to pass down the finest values of the past and to warn against repeating past errors.

Harry, a natural leader reminiscent of William Shakespeare's Prince Hal, shows the good that can happen when genuine aristocrats compassionately lead the workers, as Benjamin Disraeli and his Young England movement had urged in the previous century. Harry's tribe is relatively comfortable, but it must disguise its prosperity when members raid other tribes to secure women to avoid inbreeding and fighting over the tribe's few women among the young men. The raids offer Collier a chance to portray other forms of tribal life, including those resembling the lives of the Yahoos in *Gulliver's Travels*. The conflict in the novel is between Harry and his family, on the one hand, and on the other, a popular, charismatic leader and his egocentric and sadistic assistant, who embody the greed, lust, and laziness that earlier destroyed England. The thwarted love affair between Harry and a kidnapped girl leads to the violent ending of the novel. The strength of the book lies in its descriptive passages, but it lacks Collier's characteristic wit, and like most utopian or dystopian fiction, it is slowed by lengthy discussions of power and leadership.

By the time he published his third and last novel, *Defy the Foul Fiend; or, The Misadventures of a Heart* (1934), an imitation eighteenth-century picaresque work that is not a fantasy, Collier was publishing the short stories for which he is best known. He began writing them in 1926, later saying that the ideas just came to him. Doubtless, this ease was because he viewed events and ideas with an eye uninhibited by convention.

His first collection, *The Devil and All,* also appeared in 1934, although individually bound stories were published as chapbooks, including *No Traveller Returns* (1931), *Green Thoughts* (1932), and *Variation on a Theme* (1935). *Green Thoughts*, in which a self-righteous, wealthy man falls victim to a carnivorous orchid, was the first to be anthologized; written in 1926, the story was included in Dashiell Hammett's 1931 collection *Creeps by Night,* shortly after its initial appearance in *Harper's Monthly Magazine* and the *London Mercury* in May of the same year.

During the 1930s Collier left the home he owned in England, Wilcote Manor, and traveled first to France, where he lived briefly at Antibes and Cassis. In France he saw a boat he wanted to buy; at the recommendation of English novelist Hugh Walpole, Collier then left for Hollywood to earn the money to buy the boat. He arrived in Hollywood on 16 May 1935, under contract to RKO Radio Pictures. Collier wrote eight scripts for movies actually produced and did the first draft of *The African Queen* (1951). He also wrote stage plays, including one-act plays titled "The Old Woman" (adapted from Andre de Lorde's short story "The Needle") and "The Mask" (adapted from "Behind the Mask," a short story by H. M. Harwood and Tennyson Jesse). These were part of a program called *Horror Tonight: Masterpieces of the Macabre,* produced at the Belasco Theatre in Los Angeles in June and July 1943.

Although Collier worked on stories throughout his career, many of his major stories were written between 1937 and 1939. Most of them appeared originally in such magazines and journals as *The New Yorker* (which published at least twenty-eight between 1933 and 1958), *Playboy, Collier's, Harper's Bazaar, Harper's Magazine, Esquire, The Magazine of Fantasy and Science Fiction,* and *Ellery Queen's Mystery Magazine.* Fantasies among these stories generally take three forms: animal fables, rewritings of fairy tales or myths, and variations on the Faust theme of the man who sells his soul to the devil.

Variation on a Theme exemplifies Collier's early animal fables. It is a satiric treatment of the state of modern art, with its fashions and self-serving critics. The human hero is Grantly, a mannered writer of great delicacy and refinement who longs to be popular. At the zoo, he meets the caged Ernest Simpson, a gorilla who has also written a novel, but Simpson's novel represents the art of grunts, moans, and passionate women. (The treatment of the Ernest Hemingway school of fiction is obvious.) Grantly befriends the gorilla, who lustfully and successfully assaults Grantly's wife and who, hearing that fine style is coming back, substitutes his own novel for Grantly's so that Grantly's mannered work is submitted under Simpson's name. Then, at a party, Simpson lays the same lustful hands on the fiancée of a leading critic, who thereupon swears to condemn anything written by Simpson, whatever its merits. Moreover, in the oppressive political climate of the 1930s, Simpson is also assaulted by political thugs and tried for libel, sedition, and other crimes, while his book, printed under Grantly's name, is successful. Grantly becomes a fashionable favorite; Simpson ends behind bars again, this time those of a prison cell.

"Gavin O'Leary" (1938) is another such tale, this time showing the effect of Collier's Hollywood years. Gavin begins as a simple flea, but he takes on the characteristics of the various creatures whose blood he sucks. One victim after another inevitably leads him to Hollywood, a bloodsucker's natural habitat. Finally, Gavin becomes perhaps the only fictional hero to be a homosexual flea garbed in purple evening clothes. His success, however, is threatened by guardians of public morality and self-proclaimed patriots. Gavin ends as he begins, sucking on the flesh of an innocent country girl, but since she too is about to become a star, the outcome is inevitable; they will both spend their lives adoring her. Other animal stories of this type include "Mary" (1939), about a narcissistic star who is a pig; "The Dog That Came to the Funeral" (1957), in which the dog may or may not be someone's reincarnated husband; and "The Invisible

Dust jacket for Collier's 1973 modernized dramatization of John Milton's 1667 epic poem

Dove Dancer of Strathpheen Island" (1939), an eerie story of nature pitted against acquisitiveness.

"The Devil George and Rose" (1934) typifies Collier's early retelling of myth and fairy tale. Rose is associated with Persephone who, abducted by Hades, is sought by her mother, Demeter, and allowed to return to earth for half of every year. Rose, a twentieth-century girl, represents vital life forces; she is sent to hell by accident, but her natural vitality defeats the forces of hell. Collier's hell, however, is not traditional; like that of Shaw in *Back to Methuselah* (1921), it is a hell of popular entertainment and middle-class values, where inhabitants suffer everything from pornography to keeping up with the neighbors. Collier's satiric point, like Shaw's, is that modern life is far grimmer a fate than the hellfire envisioned by earlier ages.

"Sleeping Beauty" (1937), a retelling of the fairy story, represents the same satiric values but reflects Collier's American experiences. Its English hero, Edward Laxton, owns the perfect English estate and seeks the ideal wife. He demands absolute perfection and naturally finds it in no living woman. Trapped by automobile troubles in a small Arkansas town, he sees the sleeping beauty; in this twentieth-century version, she has been put to sleep not by a wicked fairy but by

a hormone disorder. Laxton, despite problems with blackmailers and the law, takes her home, never dreaming that, awakened by the miracles of modern medicine, she will have a mind of her own. She does, and it is rustic, profane, tasteless, and adulterous. Still craving the ideal woman, Laxton deprives her of her medicine and thus, in Collier's feminist retelling, re-creates all that a man could desire of a "perfect" woman: she is beautiful and unconscious. Other stories of this type include "The Frog Prince" (1938), in which modern medicine effects a spectacular sex change; "Three Bears Cottage" (1941), in which the inhabitants are reduced by togetherness to murdering each other; and "Bottle Party" (1941), which features an exceptionally tricky jinni in a bottle.

Collier's Faust tales include "Halfway to Hell" (1934) and "Pictures in the Fire" (1937). In the first, Louis Thurlow, a dandy, considers suicide because of an unhappy love affair. He poisons himself, thereupon discovering that life after death is an eternity of head colds, subway mobs, and fashionable vices. He tricks the devil, returns to Earth, rethinks the question of love, and flees from England. Similarly, "Pictures in the Fire" repeats the theme but shows the effects of Hollywood on Collier. The hero in this tale is an unsuccessful writer who sells his soul to the devil for money. The devil, in turn, wants to become a major Hollywood producer, a job for which he is temperamentally well suited. The devil's ego, however, is no match for that of an ambitious actress, whose demands bankrupt hell. Totally rattled, the devil does not pick up his option on the writer, who, having won the Faustian bargain, retreats to Malibu. Collier set other stories in hell, including "Fallen Star" (1938), in which hell again is the world of popular entertainment, and "After the Ball" (1933), with its singularly inept devil.

In many other stories, more often crime stories than fantasies, Collier satirizes marriage, parenthood, and the greed and self-serving qualities of professional men—physicians, attorneys, clergymen, and intellectuals. One of his most perfect fantasies is of this type. "Evening Primrose" (1941) takes place in a department store—the Valhalla, of course, of a consumer society. The story is in the form of a written narrative by a poet who has tried to escape the real world by hiding in the store, only to find it populated by acquisitive people who pose as mannequins by daylight; by night, they emerge to grab what they want. Happy to sacrifice all human emotions—love, pity, integrity—for the sake of consumer goods, these denizens have their own pecking order and police. The primary duty of the latter is to suppress any rebellion against this materialistic society. The police do so by turning people into mannequins. The poet, whose story is recorded on a pad of paper, tries to rescue a young girl who is about to be turned into a mannequin; wandering through the store as a lost child, she was captured and used as a servant for many years because she did not fit in. She is condemned to death when she falls in love with a store employee. The story ends as the poet begins his rescue. Presumably, his attempt fails; the pad of paper has been purchased by Miss Sadie Brodribb, and the story is thus revealed to the world.

Collier lived in Hollywood much of the time until 1954, when he left for London to do the script for *I Am a Camera* (1955). Oppressed by the atmosphere of intimidation during the Joseph McCarthy era, he did not return to Hollywood for many years; while not himself blacklisted and certainly not intellectually inclined to be a committed party member of any sort, he felt great sympathy for McCarthy victims and believed that the FBI was keeping a file on him. He went to Mexico, where he married for the third time on 25 May 1954; previous marriages to Shirley Lee Palmer, in 1936, and Margaret Eke, in 1945, had ended in divorce. His third wife, Harriet Hess Collier, survived him; they had one son, John G. S. Collier, born in Nice, France, on 18 May 1958. The family traveled extensively, but in 1955 Collier bought

Domaine du Blanchissage in Grasse, France, which Collier considered his home until the 1970s. His stories were collected repeatedly; the most important collections are *Fancies and Goodnights* (1951) and *The John Collier Reader* (1972), which was republished in paperback, without the text of *His Monkey Wife*, as *The Best of John Collier* (1975). These collections overlap but are not identical.

Although Collier continued writing, his major work was done by 1955; the exception is his retelling of *Paradise Lost*, the final long fantasy by which he hoped to be remembered. After returning to the United States in 1979 to live first in Santa Monica and then in Pacific Palisades, California, he continued revising this project as a movie script until his death from a stroke on 6 April 1980.

Milton's Paradise Lost: Screenplay for Cinema of the Mind, a version published in book form in 1973, was actually intended for stage or screen presentation. Collier believed that an outraged review by John Updike in *The New Yorker* on 10 August 1973 ended all interest, while the publisher's retitling from Collier's original "Paradise Lost: Made into a Picture for the Mind's Eye" and the use of white-on-black pages and ornate graphics offended its author. Collier realized that tampering with Milton might be considered sacrilegious, and that establishment critics would not take a movie version of Milton seriously; but he regarded motion pictures as a valuable communications medium and sought to make a modern version of humanity's fall accessible to a popular audience, much as an earlier age had recounted moral and religious truths through stained-glass windows and holiday pageants. Collier's version is at once a psychological drama, an adventure story, and a vitalist play in the tradition of Henri Bergson or Shaw.

In Collier's view Adam, Eve, Satan, and Raphael are engaged in an adventure. Satan and Eve, not God and Adam, are Collier's protagonists. To Collier, Western theology has reduced God to a tyrannical parent who, drunk with power, introduces evil into the world merely to maintain the status quo; God, in Collier's work, has the mind of a high-level bureaucrat. His angels are his administrative assistants whose function is to stop change. In psychological terms God stands for the human desire for stability and fear of change, which, for Collier as for Shaw, creates a hell, not heaven. Collier's Satan is any radical or rebel; he is the creative artist, introducing magic and disorder into the universe, but as an artist he is also spiteful and vain, jealous of his own creative powers.

Eve is the hero. Like many of Collier's other fully autonomous female figures, she represents life-giving qualities; Collier saw her as essentially sensual, a point particularly criticized by Updike. As a dreamer, she cannot but question God's status quo, especially when she is punished for the evil that God himself created; as a woman, she is offended when patronized by Adam and the angel Raphael. Satan offers her a way to realize her dreams, but God condemns her, Adam chastises her, and Satan views her with the eye of a collector of beautiful objects. She is left with an outraged sense of the injustice of the universe, an injustice that can be mitigated, she realizes, only by her own ability to create life and joy. In short, Collier transforms Milton's epic into an attack on the raw power that Western civilization has confused with deity and that, as he makes clear in the text, is responsible for such outrages as the Holocaust, Hiroshima and Nagasaki, and the napalming of innocents in Vietnam, all made vivid through Collier's use of spectacular visual effects.

Updike was one of the few established writers to respond negatively to Collier's work. Professional writers expressing admiration for Collier in reviews, prefaces, articles, talks, or correspondence have included Edith and Osbert Sitwell, Wyndham Lewis, C. S. Forster, Roald Dahl, Anthony Burgess, Frederik Pohl, Paul Theroux, Christopher Isherwood, Jarrico, and Bradbury. Collier's popular appeal was apparent when, in 1952, he received a Mystery Writers of America award for *Fancies and Goodnights*. His name is not a household word, surely in part because of his profound distaste for self-serving personal publicity. During his long lifetime, he apparently gave only two interviews, with Tom Milne and Betty Richardson. Yet, there seems no question that his reputation will be fostered by professional writers and by readers everywhere who value the art of well-crafted fiction.

Bibliography:

L. W. Currey, *Science Fiction and Fantasy Authors: A Bibliography of First Printings of Their Fiction and Selected Nonfiction* (Boston: G. K. Hall, 1979), pp. 121–122.

References:

John J. Kessel, "John Collier," in *Supernatural Fiction Writers: Fantasy and Horror,* edited by E. F. Bleiler (New York: Scribners, 1985), pp. 577–583;

Matthew McFall, "John Collier (1901–1980): Life and Works," dissertation, University of Oxford, 1998;

Tom Milne, "The Elusive John Collier," *Sight and Sound,* 45 (Spring 1976): 104–108;

Betty Richardson, *John Collier* (Boston: G. K. Hall, 1983);

Paul Theroux, "*His Monkey Wife,*" in his *Sunrise with Seamonsters: A Paul Theroux Reader* (Boston: Houghton Mifflin, 1985), pp. 303–308.

Papers:

Collections of John Collier's papers, including unpublished and unproduced movie treatments and scripts, are held by the Harry Ransom Humanities Research Center, University of Texas at Austin; the University of Iowa; by Collier's son, John G. S. Collier; and by Matthew McFall, Oxford, England.

Roald Dahl

(13 September 1916 – 23 November 1990)

Robert Carrick

See also the Dahl entry in *DLB 139: British Short-Fiction Writers, 1945–1980.*

BOOKS: *The Gremlins: From the Walt Disney Production. A Royal Air Force Story by Flight Lieutenant Roald Dahl* (New York: Random House, 1943; London: Collins, 1944);

Over to You: Ten Stories of Flyers and Flying (New York: Reynal & Hitchcock, 1946; London: Hamilton, 1946);

Some Time Never: A Fable for Supermen (New York: Scribners, 1948); republished as *Sometime Never: A Fable for Supermen* (London: Collins, 1949);

Someone Like You (New York: Knopf, 1953; London: Secker & Warburg, 1954); revised and expanded (London: Joseph, 1961);

Kiss Kiss (New York: Knopf, 1960; London: Joseph, 1960);

James and the Giant Peach (New York: Knopf, 1961; London: Allen & Unwin, 1967);

Charlie and the Chocolate Factory (New York: Knopf, 1964; London: Allen & Unwin, 1967);

The Magic Finger (New York: Harper & Row, 1966; London: Allen & Unwin, 1968);

Twenty-Nine Kisses from Roald Dahl (London: Joseph, 1969)—comprises *Someone Like You* and *Kiss Kiss;*

Fantastic Mr. Fox (New York: Knopf, 1970; London: Allen & Unwin, 1970);

Charlie and the Great Glass Elevator (New York: Knopf, 1972; London: Allen & Unwin, 1973);

Switch Bitch (New York: Knopf, 1974; London: Joseph, 1974);

Danny, the Champion of the World (New York: Knopf, 1975; London: Cape, 1975);

The Wonderful Story of Henry Sugar and Six More (London: Cape, 1977; New York: Knopf, 1977);

The Best of Roald Dahl (New York: Vintage, 1978; London: Joseph, 1983);

The Enormous Crocodile (New York: Knopf, 1978; London: Cape, 1978);

Roald Dahl (photograph © 1990 Horst Tappe)

My Uncle Oswald (London: Joseph, 1979; New York: Knopf, 1980);

Roald Dahl's Tales of the Unexpected (London: Joseph, 1979; New York: Vintage, 1979);

More Roald Dahl Tales of the Unexpected (London: Joseph, 1980);

A Roald Dahl Selection: Nine Short Stories, edited by Roy Blatchford (Harlow, U.K.: Longman, in association with Joseph, 1980);

The Twits (London: Cape, 1980; New York: Knopf, 1981);

George's Marvellous Medicine (London: Cape, 1981; New York: Knopf, 1982);

The BFG (New York: Farrar, Straus & Giroux, 1982; London: Cape, 1982);

Roald Dahl's Revolting Rhymes (London: Cape, 1982; New York: Knopf, 1983);

The Witches (New York: Farrar, Straus & Giroux, 1983; London: Cape, 1983);

Roald Dahl's Dirty Beasts (New York: Farrar, Straus & Giroux, 1983; London: Cape, 1983);

Boy: Tales of Childhood (New York: Farrar, Straus & Giroux, 1984; London: Cape, 1984);

The Giraffe and the Pelly and Me (New York: Farrar, Straus & Giroux, 1985; London: Cape, 1985);

Going Solo (London: Cape, 1986; New York: Farrar, Straus & Giroux, 1986);

Two Fables (Harmondsworth, U.K.: Viking, 1986; New York: Farrar, Straus & Giroux, 1987);

A Second Roald Dahl Selection: Eight Short Stories, edited by Hélène Fawcett (Harlow, U.K.: Longman, 1987);

Matilda (New York: Viking Kestrel, 1988; London: Cape, 1988);

Ah, Sweet Mystery of Life: The Country Stories of Roald Dahl (London: Joseph, 1989; New York: Knopf, 1990);

Rhyme Stew (London: Cape, 1989; New York: Viking, 1990);

Esio Trot (London: Cape, 1990; New York: Viking, 1990);

The Minpins (London: Cape, 1991; New York: Viking, 1991);

Roald Dahl's Guide to Railway Safety (N.p.: British Railways Board, 1991);

The Vicar of Nibbleswicke (London: Century, 1991; New York: Viking, 1992);

The Dahl Diary 1992 (London: Puffin, 1991);

Memories with Food at Gipsy House, by Dahl and Felicity Dahl (London: Viking, 1991);

My Year (London: Cape, 1993; New York: Viking, 1994);

The Roald Dahl Diary 1997 (London: Puffin, 1996);

The Mildenhall Treasure (London: Cape, 1999).

Collections: *The Collected Short Stories of Roald Dahl* (London: Joseph, 1991; New York: Penguin, 1991);

The Roald Dahl Treasury (New York: Viking, 1997).

PLAY PRODUCTION: *The Honeys,* New York City, Longacre, May 1955.

PRODUCED SCRIPTS: *You Only Live Twice,* motion picture, adapted by Dahl and Harold Jack Bloom from Ian Fleming's novel, United Artists, 1967;

Chitty Chitty Bang Bang, motion picture, by Dahl, Ken Hughes, and Richard Maibaum, from Ian Fleming's novel, United Artists, 1968;

The Night Digger, motion picture, adapted by Dahl from Joy Cowley's *Nest in a Falling Tree,* M-G-M, 1970;

Willy Wonka & the Chocolate Factory, motion picture, adapted by Dahl and David Seltzer from Dahl's *Charlie and the Chocolate Factory,* Paramount, 1971.

OTHER: *Roald Dahl's Book of Ghost Stories,* edited by Dahl (London: Cape, 1983; New York: Farrar, Straus & Giroux, 1983).

SELECTED PERIODICAL PUBLICATION—UNCOLLECTED: "Writing Children's Books," *The Writer* (August 1976): 18–19.

Roald Dahl was one of the most successful writers of children's books ever, both in terms of copies sold and money made. Ten months before his death, the five top-selling children's books in Britain were ones he had written. In 1989 more than 2,300,000 copies of his books were sold in Great Britain alone. His last full-length book, *Matilda* (1988), broke all records for juvenile sales: 500,000 copies in paperback during the first six months after it appeared. Although most of his literary reputation—and his considerable fortune—derived from the writing of children's books, he did not begin doing so until he was more than forty. Even then, it was not a deliberate move. That he became a writer at all was, by his own account, fortuitous.

After beginning his writing career with stories based on his Royal Air Force (RAF) experiences and with an unsuccessful apocalyptic novel, *Some Time Never: A Fable for Supermen* (1948), he turned to the sort of tingly and clever dark fantasy that appealed to sophisticated American readers. These stories appeared in such magazines as *The New Yorker, Town and Country, Playboy,* and *Esquire.* Even after he discovered his talent for writing children's books he was able to return at will to the short stories of cool horror that delighted adults. It must be said, however, that his children's books were sometimes more horrific or fantastic than the stories for their parents.

Roald Dahl was born in Llandaff, South Wales, on 13 September 1916 to Harald and Sofie (Hesselberg) Dahl, Norwegian immigrants. He was the middle child of five, and the only boy; he also had two half siblings from his father's first marriage. Despite growing up without a father, who died when the boy was four years old, Dahl believed that he had a normal, happy childhood, as is evident from his reminiscences in *Boy: Tales of Childhood* (1984), the first of his autobiographical books. He first attended St. Peter's School in Weston-super-Mare (1925 to 1929), then Repton in Derby (1929 to 1932). Except for his increasing excellence at sports, as he grew to within an inch or two of his eventual height of six feet six inches, he did not enjoy his time at either school and did not excel academically. His mother offered to pay for his education at either Oxford or Cambridge, but Dahl had had enough of school and declined.

At that time, hundreds of graduates from the English public school system applied every year for the few openings available as Eastern Staff trainees in the Shell Oil Company. To the astonishment of his housemaster at Repton, Dahl was selected to fill one of the positions. After two years in England, he was sent to Dar es Salaam in what was then Tanganyika, where he spent two years selling and promoting Shell products, more or less on his own, and clearly developing the self-reliance that characterized his later years. His second volume of autobiography, *Going Solo* (1986), depicts a contented bachelor with his foot firmly planted on the Shell corporate ladder, with every likelihood of his ascending but for Great Britain's entry into World War II. When his country declared war, Dahl obtained his release from Shell, drove to Nairobi, and enlisted in the RAF.

Some idea of just how perilous an occupation that was in those early days of the war is conveyed by Dahl in *Going Solo* when he mentions that thirteen of the fifteen pilot trainees he began with in Nairobi were killed in combat within two years. After eight months of flight training in Kenya and Iraq, Dahl crashed his Gladiator fighter en route to joining his squadron in the Western Desert. The resultant head and back injuries put him in an Alexandria hospital for five months and caused recurrent problems throughout his life. When he was released from the hospital, Dahl rejoined his squadron, which had been posted to Greece to fly Hurricanes against far superior numbers of German, Italian, and Vichy French aircraft. He only lasted about three months in combat, in Greece and Palestine, before the effects of the injuries he sustained in his crash caused him to be invalided out of active duty in June 1941. It was a hectic three months, however, sometimes involving several combat sorties on the same day.

Out of the shooting war, Dahl was sent to Washington, D.C., as assistant air attaché and, Jeremy Treglown strongly suggests in *Roald Dahl: A Biography* (1994), a kind of casual spy for the British government. Early during his tour in Washington, Dahl wrote, on his own time, an account of the "gremlins," imaginary demons the RAF personnel blamed for anything that went wrong with their aircraft. Someone in the British embassy had Hollywood connections, and the story was brought to the attention of Walt Disney, "who immediately wanted to buy it," Dahl recalled in an interview with Christopher Sykes conducted shortly before he died and reported in the *Times* (London) on 30 November 1990; "It had no literary merit, but it was my first published story."

Dahl at Repton School in Derby

It was published as *The Gremlins: From the Walt Disney Production. A Royal Air Force Story by Flight Lieutenant Roald Dahl* (1943). Certainly this work qualifies as a fantasy, thanks to its eponymous troublemakers, and it could be argued that it was Dahl's first children's book; however, it bears little resemblance to his later children's books and would perhaps be better remembered as the text for a Disney picture book, given Dahl's own assessment of its quality. At the time, it did not inspire him to further literary efforts.

Shortly after the Disney encounter, however, Dahl met English novelist C. S. Forester, who was also assigned to the American capital in a liaison capacity. Forester was intrigued by Dahl's recounting of his near-fatal fighter plane crash in the North African desert and asked the young air attaché to write it down for possible propaganda use. Dahl did so, and Forester, impressed with the vividness of the account, sent it to the then-prestigious American magazine *The Saturday Evening Post*. Ten days later an incredulous Dahl found himself in receipt of a check for $1,000 in payment for the piece. "If writing's as easy as that," he later recalled thinking, in a 1980 interview with Sarah Crichton, "I'll just have to do more of it." He continued to write primarily about RAF pilots, and many of the stories were fictionalized accounts of his own experiences and observations. The stories were welcomed by some of the better American periodicals, primarily *The New Yorker*, one of the most sophisticated general-interest magazines of the time.

Title page for the 1944 British edition of Dahl's first book, published in the United States the previous year, about the imaginary demons that pilots blamed for causing mechanical problems in their airplanes

Over To You: Ten Stories of Flyers and Flying (1946) collects these stories, only one of which is unmistakably speculative fiction. In the story "They Shall Not Grow Old" there is a time slip: a pilot is missing for two days, according to his comrades, and presumed shot down, while by his reckoning his flight lasted precisely one hour and five minutes. Later, at the exact moment of another flyer's death, the pilot remembers that during his mysterious absence he went through a prolonged and detailed near-death experience. When he later plunges to his own death, he does so calmly, serene in the belief that he is on his way to the Elysian Fields seen during the near-death experience. It is a much more polished story than one would expect from a relatively inexperienced writer; a notable aspect of this piece, also seen in several of the other stories in the book, is the clear influence of Ernest Hemingway on the young writer's style.

Another story in this volume may be read as dark fantasy or crime fiction, but it is certainly horrific. "An African Story" is the tale of two reclusive white men living in isolation in the Kenyan highlands sometime before the advent of World War II. The relationship is one of master and slave, although the reader never learns why except, possibly, that the "slave" is obviously mentally defective and therefore easily dominated. When the "master" discovers that a deadly black mamba snake is milking his cow every night, he devises a plan for murdering the slave in retaliation for killing the master's dog, with no fear of becoming implicated. He sets the slave up to be bitten by the snake, and the man dies horribly. The idea of a snake that not only steals milk but is also the weapon in a murder is a difficult one to accept, but with his ability to persuade the reader that the most outlandish events can and do take place—a talent he displays often in his work—Dahl makes it seem entirely plausible.

Dahl continued to write and sell stories, in the United States only, while working on his first novel, *Some Time Never*. The book, published in 1948 in the United States and in 1949 in England, is science fiction or fantasy of the apocalyptic variety: it begins with the Battle of Britain and finishes with the end of human civilization following World War III. In it the author resurrects the gremlins, and in their leader one may see the prototype of Willy Wonka, one of the few good things to come from the book. It was neither a critical nor a commercial success. Treglown comments, "The book can't decide whether it is for adults or for children, and the resulting clashes of tone are bizarre." At the same time, while Dahl was living at his mother's house in Great Missenden, England, he was working on another novel tentatively titled "Claud's Dog," which never came to fruition, though material intended for it was later published as four short stories.

In 1953 Dahl married American actress Patricia Neal, with whom he ultimately had five children: Olivia, Theo, Tess, Ophelia, and Lucy. The same year, with the publication of the eighteen-story collection *Someone Like You,* Dahl began to attract serious critical consideration. The *Time* magazine review of the book (28 December 1953) was titled "British O. Henry," and the reviewer found Dahl to be "an adroit craftsman who knows how to make the unlikely seem probable." *The Times Literary Supplement* (*TLS*) (11 June 1954) commented that the book had "real narrative ingenuity" but noted the presence of "morbidity and a certain irresponsible cruelty." Apart from the word "irresponsible," Dahl would have concurred, since his more memorable stories are about morbidity and especially cruelty. Even in his books for children, as he says in "Writing Children's Books" (1976), he believed "They love being spooked. . . . They love seeing the villain meet a grisly death." But his cruelty is seldom gratuitous; it is used to establish a character's despicable nature, and it is usually repaid in kind or worse. The book was generally well received and sold seven thousand copies in the United States in a few months—a major accomplishment for a book of short stories at that time and one that Alfred Knopf told Dahl he thought was a record.

Nine of the stories in *Someone Like You* can be considered speculative fiction, mostly in the dark fantasy or horror subgenre. In "Man from the South" a rich old man bets a young sailor that the youngster cannot make his cigarette lighter ignite ten consecutive times. The terms of the bet are that if the sailor wins, he gets the old man's Cadillac; if the old man wins, he gets to chop off the sailor's little finger. Dahl skillfully builds the tension through the business of locating a cleaver, fastening the sailor's hand to a table, and igniting the wick successfully on the first eight attempts. The old man's companion arrives and immediately puts a stop to the proceedings, telling the group that the old man has nothing with which to bet, as she won it all from him over the years; then she reaches for the keys to the Cadillac. In the final sentence, the narrator says, "I can see it now, that hand of hers; it had only one finger on it, and a thumb."

In "Poison" readers quickly realize something is terribly wrong and soon discover that the "something" is a deadly snake in bed with one of the characters. Although the horror element is intensely effective in this piece, it has nothing to do with the theme, which is that a person in mortal danger will accept succor from a savior he despises but, once safe, will revert to type or worse.

The other speculative-fiction stories in the book are "The Soldier" (war-induced, murderous madness); "Dip in the Pool" (a schemer unwittingly puts his life in the hands of an imbecile); "The Wish" (a child's horror fantasy comes true); "The Sound Machine" (a man discovers that plants can feel pain); "The Great Automatic Grammatisator" (a computer genius and amateur writer invents a story-writing machine); "The Ratcatcher" (the title character takes on all the attributes of a rat); and "Rummins" (a body is found in a hayrick). The other pieces in the book are equally rewarding to read—in fact, they include some of Dahl's best stories—but they are not, strictly speaking, speculative fiction.

Kiss Kiss (1960) is a collection of stories, most of which were published previously in American magazines. It was a popular success on both sides of the Atlantic, selling twenty thousand copies (astounding for a book of short stories) in England within a few years. A critic for *TLS* (28 October 1960) commented that in this volume "Mr. Dahl's macabre realism stretches the intellectual nerve almost beyond bearing" and that the author is "a social satirist and a moralist at work behind the entertaining fantast." The reviewer found many of the stories to be on a par with the early work of Angus Wilson.

Again, about half of the stories in this book are speculative fiction. In "The Landlady" the reader comes to the chilling realization that the kindly old lady is not only a murderess but also a taxidermist. Much of the horror in "William and Mary" comes from the description of the removal from his skull of a dead man's still-living brain, which Dahl records in clinical detail. The real shock, however, Dahl characteristically saves until the end, when the man's long-suffering wife, about to take charge of the fully functioning brain, says, "from now on, my pet, you're going to do just exactly what Mary tells you. . . . So don't be a naughty boy. . . . Naughty boys are liable to get punished most severely nowadays, you ought to know that." According to Treglown, this story created some difficulty because of the similarity of the subject matter to that of Curt Siodmak's 1943 novel, *Donovan's Brain*. In "The Way Up to Heaven" another tormented wife leaves her husband trapped in the elevator in their house while she flies off to Paris for six weeks. This story is typical of those *The New Yorker* was buying and publishing in the 1950s and 1960s: a simple plot with carefully layered character delineation, in this case stressing the wife's nervousness and timidity and the husband's subtle cruelty.

In "Royal Jelly" a sickly baby girl is given large doses of the substance bees use to feed their larvae and, rather predictably, appears to be turning into a bee; the surprise is that the father, who already has become more bee than man, took massive quantities of the stuff in order to sire her. "Pig," an unsuccessful attempt at a kind of black humor, foreshadows some of Dahl's crueler children's books, with the young hero, in a kind of trance, finding himself in a slaughterhouse for pigs and sharing their fate. Two other pieces in the book are examples of humorous horror, one of the most difficult forms of speculative fiction to write convincingly—successful because the horror is that of the cheater hoist by his own petard, a solid vicarious pleasure for most readers. In "Parson's Pleasure" a con man sees a fortune evaporate as a swindle backfires, and in "Mrs. Bixby and the Colonel's Coat" an adulteress loses the wages of her sinning by being too clever.

Dahl's first bona fide children's book, *James and the Giant Peach*, enjoyed a modest success in the United States when published there in 1961, but Dahl could not find a British publisher. Indeed, the book includes many of the elements that drew disapproval from parents, teachers, librarians, and critics of children's literature, especially in England, for years to come: child abuse, violence (including the messy demise of several adults), unspeakable practices (such as eating "earwigs cooked in slime"), and the apparent promulgation of the philosophy that it is a wise child who regards adults with suspicion until they have proved that they are

Dust jacket for Dahl's 1960 short-story collection

trustworthy. After the book was finally published in England in 1967, Michel Simeon, reviewing it for *TLS* (14 December 1967), found it to be "robust, entertaining and funny" and its violence "no worse than *Alice*, Lear and most fairy tales." But that was after *Charlie and the Chocolate Factory* had turned the children's book establishment upside down.

Charlie and the Chocolate Factory was an instant success in the United States when it was published there in 1964, selling out its first printing of ten thousand copies within a month. The book is simple in plot, full of violence and corny humor, and decidedly bizarre; many critics, lay as well as professional, abhorred it, and many still do. However, children everywhere adore it, and the very things that their elders object to are the things they most like about it. All of the characters except Charlie and his parents are grotesques, even Willy Wonka. Of the five children who win the coveted visit to the chocolate factory, all except Charlie come to gruesome ends, and even though Willy resurrects them at the end, Dahl's delighted readers have no way of knowing that at the time. In a way, however, it is unfair that Dahl should have been so castigated for pandering to children's basic instincts in this particular book, because its moral is clear. Nasty character traits (selfishness, greed, addiction to television, and laziness) are punished, and admirable ones (honesty and devotion to family) are rewarded. This book is unquestionably Dahl's seminal work of juvenile fiction and still the one most associated with his name. A popular motion-picture version, *Willy Wonka & the Chocolate Factory,* was released in 1971 and is still shown occasionally on television.

After two short children's books, *The Magic Finger* (1966) and *Fantastic Mr. Fox* (1970), Dahl wrote *Charlie and the Great Glass Elevator* (1972), a sequel to *Charlie and the Chocolate Factory*. The second book is considerably more complex than the first. The first book had to do with seeing to it that Charlie got one of the five magic tickets to visit the chocolate factory and that he was the eventual winner of the special present. The second involves nothing less than saving the Earth from invasion by the Vermicious Knids (shapeshifters from the planet Vermes, "the most brutal, vindictive, venomous, murderous beasts in the entire univere") and rescuing a Commuter Capsule that travels between Earth and a Space Hotel. Also dealt with in the second book is the entirely separate crisis of retrieving Charlie's grandparents from overdoses of the age-altering vitamin, Wonka-Vite. The American president and his cabinet play an important (and hilarious) role in the story, supplying much burlesque humor.

There is less violence in this book—at least toward human beings—than in most of Dahl's juvenile works, and without being too didactic, he establishes some good moral guidelines, such as staying away from the medicine chest and learning to recognize the characteristics of dishonest politicians. There is some wacky poetry in the form of couplets, limericks, and even epic verse of a sort. Dahl also gives his young readers some of Willy Wonka's philosophy to ponder: "It was an unhappy truth, he told himself, that nearly all people in the world behave badly when there is something really big at stake. Money is the thing they fight over most." Although there is a lot of tomfoolery regarding the mechanics of the magical elevator, Dahl includes some hard science data, as when explaining, in simple but accurate terms, what happens when a space capsule reenters the atmosphere.

The collection *Switch Bitch,* published in 1974, consists of four novelettes, all previously published in *Playboy.* Two of the stories are speculative fiction. "The Visitor," nearly a novella in length, introduces readers to Uncle Oswald, hero of "Bitch" and the 1979 Dahl novel, *My Uncle Oswald.* "The Visitor" is a character study of a likeable rogue—likable, that is, except for his satyric and singleminded lusting after women. One must commiserate with him in this story in any case. True, he does not fight off the advances of one of his host's women in his dark bedroom, but he is the victim of a Byzantine plot for revenge engineered by that same host, who seems to have orchestrated the entire affair. The host's attempt to infect Oswald with an incurable strain of leprosy through this encounter is as dark as fantasy gets, especially when it occurs in the opulence of a modern *Arabian Nights* setting.

"Bitch," which deals with the discovery of an aphrodisiacal perfume, was the subject of some adverse criticism for its sexist theme, particularly for two instances of women responding positively to what are technically acts of rape. It can be argued, however, that such criticism takes the incidents out of context. One arose from an experiment in which the victim knew that sexual assault was one of the risks, and the other was an accident in which Uncle Oswald is overcome by the perfume instead of the iniquitous politician whom it was intended to embarrass. Both incidents, of course, are intended to be black humor. In any case, most reviewers, especially in the United States, felt that the story was an amusing sex spoof.

Danny, the Champion of the World, published in 1975 as a children's book, is an expansion of a story titled "The Champion of the World" published some fifteen years earlier in *The New Yorker* and then in Dahl's collection *Kiss Kiss.* The story version is certainly adult—there is no Danny or any other young principal—but the book, though definitely a juvenile, differs greatly from the other children's books published by the author. It is a much gentler story, featuring some adults who are

neither freaks nor monsters, and it even centers on a loving relationship between father and son. The father is portrayed in a positive way, and the doctor, the policeman, and most of the townspeople are shown as characters the juvenile readers should love and respect. Only the nasty Mr. Hazell and his henchmen are depicted with the vitriol used for most adults in Dahl's other children's books. All story elements are well realized, but the enormous haul in poached pheasants from the villains' scheme and its subsequent unraveling calls for a generous helping of the suspension of the reader's disbelief.

Three of the seven pieces in *The Wonderful Story of Henry Sugar and Six More* (1977) are speculative fiction. Two of those stories, "The Boy Who Talked with Animals" and "The Swan," are unexceptional fantasies involving anthropomorphized animals, but the third, the title novella, is substantial. It follows the protagonist from unfocused youth through prosperity, which becomes meaningless, to philanthropy, from which he attains a state of grace. The construction is unusual, including a complete short story describing the protagonist's acquisition of his telepathic ability within a recounting of the protagonist's life history, which is itself included in the body of the novella.

The Enormous Crocodile (1978) brought Dahl together with illustrator Quentin Blake for the beginning of a long and successful collaboration. It is another of Dahl's scary tales that makes young readers squirm with delighted horror as the wicked reptile zeroes in on his choice of edible prey: children. As Treglown says, "It would be hard not to like *The Enormous Crocodile,* which has a simple, cumulative plot, exciting in its threat to the children whom the crocodile is determined to eat and funny in his simple, repeatedly thwarted stratagems for doing so." There is also more of Dahl's verse, which is delightful to adults as well as children.

In 1979 Dahl published *My Uncle Oswald,* his only novel—a realistic fantasy—aimed at an adult audience. For American reviewers it was "a romp" (*New York Magazine*), "titillating" (*Booklist*), and "a masterfully ribald tale" (*Hartford Courant*); for the British establishment, it was a bit past the mark. Sylvia Clayton wrote in *TLS* (23 November 1979) that it was "a pity" Dahl "has spent so much labour on this lumbering comedy." The story expands the adventures of the narrator's Uncle Oswald, introduced first to readers of *Playboy* and then to general readership in his collection *Switch Bitch.* Basically, the plot is that Oswald acquires a powerful African aphrodisiac, a beautiful seductress, and, through them, the sperm of rich, royal, and famous men to be frozen and sold to the highest bidders among ambitious females. Whether one approves of the plot or not, many of the lines and the described scenes are at least

Publicity still for the 1971 movie Willy Wonka and the Chocolate Factory, *adapted by Dahl and David Seltzer from Dahl's 1964 children's book* Charlie and the Chocolate Factory *(Paramount Pictures)*

amusing to anyone having read far enough to encounter them and considerably funnier to readers more appreciative of the blatantly bawdy. The scheme collapses on Uncle Oswald at the end, but the character retains the sympathy of readers not put off by mild eroticism.

The length of *The Twits* (1980) is about 8,500 words—less than the average novelette. It is arguably the author's most distasteful book, both textually and pictorially (the illustrations are by Blake). Even youngsters appear not to have taken to it with the usual enthusiasm they have for most of the rest of Dahl's juvenile work. There are no sympathetic humans in this book—the only Dahl book about which that can be said—the "heroes" being the monkey family imprisoned by the Twits and their savior, the Roly-Poly bird. The only humans are Mr. and Mrs. Twit, people with no redeeming characteristics to offset their revolting personalities and behavior.

George's Marvellous Medicine (1981) is like *The Twits* in more ways than one. First, though published as a book, it is only a novelette in length (about 12,250 words). Second, it does not have the same literary merit

of Dahl's better-selling books. Third, it is gratuitously nasty. Unlike James, Charlie, and Danny in Dahl's previous children's books, George is a sadistic, potentially murderous little brute who does not have the slightest hesitation in giving to his grandmother a concoction containing many noxious ingredients, most of which would have killed her in agony in real life. Admittedly, she is no Mary Poppins, but she is a helpless old woman, and she is George's grandma. Children may have loved it, but this book was approved of by few adults, and certainly not those who were already critical of unseemly material in some of his previous works for juveniles.

The BFG (1982) met with much more success. It is a simple story. There are ten giants in Giant Country: nine bad giants who gobble up human "beans" every night, and the Big Friendly Giant (BFG) who provides humans with dreams. A little girl named Sophie wakes up in the middle of the night, looks out a window, and sees the BFG. He kidnaps her because she has seen him and he is afraid she will tell someone, which will lead to a giant hunt and the possibility of his being locked up in a zoo. When Sophie learns that the bad giants eat people—children by choice—every night, she persuades the BFG to take her to London so she can inform the queen of this terrible state of affairs. He does so, and with the help of one of his dreams, the queen is convinced. She calls out the Royal Army and the Royal Air Force, has them capture the bad giants with the indispensable help of Sophie and the BFG, and puts them in a deep pit, where they will remain forever. Sophie and the BFG are showered with honors and gifts. The queen has a house built for the BFG next to her castle, where he takes up writing and produces *The BFG.* Sophie gets her own cottage next door.

Dahl uses several devices effectively in this book. Foremost among these is his extensive use of made-up language. He uses invented words in all his books, but not nearly to the extent that they are used in this story, and they are the kind of words that will make his young readers giggle, often because of their naughty or nasty implications. The bad giants are given appropriate names such as Childchewer and Bloodbottler, and they are *whiffsy, disgusterous, rotsome,* and *sickable* and should be *dispunged* from the face of the Earth. The only vegetable grown in Giant Land, the *snozzcumber,* is totally *foulsome* and *scrotty, maggotwise.* Even a five-year-old can tell that *uckyslush* is opposite of *scrumdiddlyumptious.* But the term that undoubtedly breaks up new readers the most, year after year, is *whizzpopper;* that is to say, flatus. Whether one approves of such material in children's books or not, it must be admitted that Dahl handles it with relative decorum.

Another device that pleased Dahl's audience was the BFG's ungrammatical and word-garbling manner of speaking, as in "Your Majester . . . I is your humbug servant." Dahl uses puns, malapropisms, onomatopoeia, and spoonerisms, all forms of humor that generally appeal more to the young (or young at heart) than to their elders. He also includes his tested and proven device of having a small, mistreated hero or heroine in the clutches of hateful grownups. In this book the latter are not actually introduced, but they are definitely there, lurking in the background. Dahl rarely preached in his children's books, correctly realizing that it was one of the surest ways to turn the kids off, but in *The BFG* he makes the point briefly that "Human beans is the only animals that is killing their own kind."

Between two books of his juvenile-oriented verse—*Roald Dahl's Revolting Rhymes* (1982), which Treglown called "as comically ruthless as anything Dahl wrote," and *Roald Dahl's Dirty Beasts* (1983)—Dahl published *The Witches* (1983). It is a piece with which he was well satisfied, and he was therefore all the more vituperative when the 1990 movie version did not meet his expectations. "It is utterly *appalling,*" a writer for *The Times* (London) quoted him as saying in an article pub-

lished on 27 February 1990; "They've gone completely for the adult market. I wanted them to remove my name from the credits, but they wouldn't." Dahl's opinion notwithstanding, the Nicolas Rocg movie was favorably reviewed, with one well-distributed caveat advising parents not to allow children under the age of eight to see it, so frightening were its special effects. Much of the background of the story was based on Dahl's own life. The important character of the narrator's grandmother was modeled on Sofie Dahl, and the narrator's history up to the age of seven was clearly Dahl's own, as described in his autobiographical *Boy: Tales of Childhood.*

The Witches begins with a convention of witches held at the Bornemouth hotel where the young hero and his convalescent grandmother are staying. The lad inadvertently overhears their plan to wipe out the world's children after turning them into mice by means of "Formula 86 Delayed Action Mouse-Maker." The witches catch the boy and turn him into a mouse, with the immediate view of luring him into a mousetrap. He escapes, purloins a vial of Formula 86, gets it into their banquet soup, and turns them into mice that are exterminated by waiters, patrons, and assorted mice-haters.

In a departure from his usual all-problem-solving finish, Dahl reveals that the hero's conversion into a mouse is irreversible but makes good use of the opportunity to inject a moral with which not even his strongest critics could quarrel. "My darling, are you sure you don't mind being a mouse for the rest of your life?" his grandmother asks. "I don't mind at all," the boy replies; "It doesn't matter who you are or what you look like so long as somebody loves you." The coda shows the boy and his indefatigable grandmother planning to travel the world, turning witches into mice and then exterminating them.

Between the two halves of Dahl's autobiography, *Boy: Tales of Childhood* and *Going Solo,* the relatively minor *The Giraffe and the Pelly and Me* (1985) appeared. Perhaps because it is a gentler book than most of his other works for children, it did not attract as much interest or criticism.

In 1986 Dahl published a thin book composed of two short stories. As such it is a minor work but could still be considered a tour de force, with appeal to adults and youngsters alike. "The Princess and the Poacher" is a fable or a fairy tale basically about the frog who is turned into a prince, except that this frog is an extremely ugly young man from a poor family. He refuses to follow his father's trade of basket-weaving or even to collect from the river bank the willows essential to the craft. He has lustful thoughts about females, and he takes up poaching, going so far as to do so in the king's own forest. One day, while he is in the king's wood about to steal a deer, he risks his life to save the

Dahl's second wife, Felicity Crosland Dahl (from Jeremy Treglown, Roald Dahl: A Biography, 1994)

royal princess from death or mutilation by a wild boar, a feat the king witnesses. Overcome with gratitude, the king not only makes the lad a count, with a mansion, servants, a lavish wardrobe, and a generous income but also endows him with the right to ravish any female in the kingdom and forbids any of his subjects to interfere with that right upon pain of death. It might be felt that Dahl goes a bit overboard on that point, but in a way, it helps him round off the young man's character, and it definitely gives him the chance to quote a moral. The king has already stated one moral for his young readers, which is that no person is responsible for the appearance nature gave him. Now, when the new count shows no interest in availing himself of the favors of the ladies, to which the king has granted him full access, the king says that this situation is the old story of the forbidden fruit: make it easy to get, and the desire goes. Presently, the count becomes morose, telling the king that no one likes him because of his sexual prerogative, even though he does not take

advantage of it; whereupon the princess says she not only likes him but loves him. This exchange sets up the typical fairy tale ending, makes the king happy, and presumably gives the people cause to form a new and higher opinion of the count.

The companion piece, "Princess Mammalia," is a near-perfect example of a Dahl children's story. The title princess succumbs to the dreadful disease of vanity and, in one short year, goes from being a plain, gentle girl loved by all to a beautiful femme fatale unmoved by seeing men castrated and killed to protect her from their advances, real or potential. "As we all know," Dahl points out to his readers, "power, with all its subtle facts, is a voracious bedfellow. The more one has, the more one wants. There is no such thing as getting enough of it."

As the eldest of seven children, all girls, Princess Mammalia is already next in line for the crown, but so self-centered has she become that she schemes to devise a way to do in her father to attain the throne sooner.

One day an old beggar, who says to her that he is "on the side of the righteous," tells her that the only way in the world "to dispose of an enemy" without being caught is by means of undetectable poisoned oysters. For her eighteenth birthday, the princess asks to begin the meal with oysters and, when they have been set out, surreptitiously doctors the king's portion. When the king inspects the dining hall, prior to the admittance of the guests, he observes that the largest, choicest oysters have been put upon his plate, as is the custom. He informs the butler that in honor of her birthday, the princess should have the best, and he has the servant switch the two plates. That night the princess is taken violently ill and fails to evacuate the poisoned bivalves in time to save her rotten life. The next morning, the grieving king tells his valet to burn the false beard and beggar's rags because "We can't have fancy-dress parties while the court is in mourning."

Rhyme Stew (1989) was the best-selling children's book in England at Christmas 1989, but it was verse, not prose. *Esio Trot* (1990), *The Minpins* (1991), and *The Vicar of Nibbleswicke* (1991) were all pleasant little tales and were well received and favorably, if briefly, reviewed, but they were stories, not books, none of them even approaching novel length. Dahl's last full-length book was another matter altogether.

Treglown refers to *Matilda* as Dahl's "last substantial book" and considers it one of his best. As usually happened with Dahl's books for children, not all reviewers agreed. Claire Tomalin, commenting on the Treglown biography in the *New York Review* (9 June 1994), stated that, of Dahl's books for children, "*Matilda* is a particularly crude and unpleasant example, which I would not willingly read aloud to any child myself." Certainly "crude and unpleasant" are among the mildest terms to describe the behavior of Matilda's parents and the awful and frightening school headmistress, Miss Trunchbull, but the book provides positive messages for children, such as Dahl's strong recommendation that they read more books and watch less television.

The story is a simple one, although there are two distinct plotlines: Matilda's growing alienation from her family, and the relationship and gradually revealed history of Matilda's teacher, Miss Honey, and Miss Trunchbull. The latter ends happily by anyone's standards, but the ending of the former is controversial. Most young readers probably think that Matilda's final separation from her dreadful family is a blessing; parents, understandably, may not care for the message such a resolution might send.

Dahl was admitted to the hospital on 12 November 1990, having been previously diagnosed with a form of leukemia. He died on 23 November 1990 and was buried in the parish churchyard of Great Missenden, England, his home for more than thirty-five years.

Dahl's continued popularity with his young audience seems assured for the foreseeable future. In the first weekend following its release in April 1996, *James and the Giant Peach*, a Disney motion picture combining live action with animation, was second at the box office in the United States. *Matilda*, a live-action motion picture by TriStar, was rated first in America on its initial weekend in August 1996. *The BFG* was an animated feature in 1989 and has also become a comic strip in *The Sunday Mail*. Plans for a live movie version have not materialized.

"Dahl's books," wrote David Gritten in a 15 April 1995 *Los Angeles Times* article, "now sell in the millions worldwide. Proportionately, he is less popular in America, but in many countries he is by far the preeminent children's author. A recent survey of 8,000 British children ages 10 to 14 named him their favorite writer; an astonishing seven Dahl books were on the ten favorite books among this group." It is entirely possible that Roald Dahl's fantasy books for children will enjoy a multigenerational success akin to that of the writings of A. A. Milne, E. B. White, and Dr. Seuss. His stories for adults also contribute to his place in the fantasy tradition: Ben Indick commented in *The Penquin Encyclopedia of Horror and the Supernatural* (1986) that in Dahl's stories, "the strain of fantastic satire developed by Saki and John Collier is continued with brilliance and a delightful, often chilling malice."

Interviews:

Sarah Crichton, "PW Interviews: Roald Dahl," *Publishers Weekly,* 217 (6 June 1980): 10–11;

Christopher Sykes, "Unexpected to the Very End," (London) *Times,* 30 November 1990, p. 18.

Biographies:

Barry Farrell, *Pat and Roald* (New York: Random House, 1969; London: Hutchinson, 1970);

Jeremy Treglown, *Roald Dahl: A Biography* (New York: Farrar, Straus & Giroux, 1994; London: Faber & Faber, 1994).

References:

Alan Warren, *Roald Dahl* (Mercer Island, Wash.: Starmont, 1988); revised and expanded as *Roald Dahl: From The Gremlins to The Chocolate Factory,* edited by Dale Salwak and Daryl F. Mallett (San Bernardino, Cal.: Borgo Press, 1994);

Warren, "Roald Dahl: Nasty, Nasty," in *Discovering Modern Horror Fiction,* 1, edited by Darrel Schweitzer (Mercer Island, Wash.: Starmont, 1985), pp. 120–128;

Mark I. West, *Roald Dahl* (New York: Twayne, 1992).

Walter de la Mare

(25 April 1873 – 22 June 1956)

Darren Harris-Fain
Shawnee State University

See also the de la Mare entries in *DLB 19: British Poets, 1880–1914; DLB 153: Late-Victorian and Edwardian British Novelists, First Series;* and *DLB 162: British Short-Fiction Writers, 1915–1945.*

BOOKS: *Songs of Childhood,* as Walter Ramal (London, New York & Bombay: Longmans, Green, 1902);

Henry Brocken: His Travels and Adventures in the Rich, Strange, Scarce-Imaginable Regions of Romance (London: Murray, 1904; New York: Knopf, 1924);

Poems (London: Murray, 1906);

The Return (London: Arnold, 1910; New York & London: Putnam, 1911; revised, London: Collins, 1922; revised, London: Faber & Faber, 1945);

The Three Mulla-Mulgars (London: Duckworth, 1910; New York: Knopf, 1919); republished as *The Three Royal Monkeys; or, The Three Mulla-Mulgars* (London: Faber & Faber, 1935); republished as *The Three Royal Monkeys* (New York: Knopf, 1948);

The Listeners, and Other Poems (London: Constable, 1912; New York: Holt, 1916);

A Child's Day: A Book of Rhymes (London: Constable, 1912);

Peacock Pie: A Book of Rhymes (London: Constable, 1913; New York: Holt, 1917);

The Sunken Garden, and Other Poems (London: Beaumont, 1917); republished as *The Sunken Garden, and Other Verses* (Birmingham: Birmingham School of Printing, 1931);

Motley, and Other Poems (London: Constable, 1918; New York: Holt, 1918);

Flora (London: Heinemann, 1919);

Rupert Brooke and the Intellectual Imagination: A Lecture (London: Sidgwick & Jackson, 1919; New York: Harcourt, Brace & Howe, 1920);

Poems, 1901 to 1918, 2 volumes (London: Constable, 1920); republished as *Collected Poems, 1901–1918* (New York: Holt, 1920);

Story and Rhyme (London & Toronto: Dent / New York: Dutton, 1921);

Walter de la Mare

Memoirs of a Midget (London, Glasgow, Melbourne & Auckland: Collins, 1921; New York: Knopf, 1922);

Crossings: A Fairy Play, music by C. Armstrong Gibbs (London: Beaumont, 1921; New York: Knopf, 1923);

The Veil, and Other Poems (London, Bombay & Sydney: Constable, 1921; New York: Holt, 1922);

Down-Adown-Derry: A Book of Fairy Poems (London: Constable, 1922; New York: Holt, 1922);

Lispet, Lispett and Vaine (London: Morland, 1923);

Thus Her Tale: A Poem (Edinburgh: Porpoise, 1923);

The Riddle and Other Stories (London: Selwyn & Blount, 1923); republished as *The Riddle, and Other Tales* (New York: Knopf, 1923);

A Ballad of Christmas (London: Selwyn & Blount, 1924);

Ding Dong Bell (London: Selwyn & Blount, 1924; New York: Knopf, 1924; enlarged edition, London: Faber & Faber, 1936);

Broomsticks, and Other Tales (London: Constable, 1925; New York: Knopf, 1925);

Miss Jemima (Oxford: Blackwell, 1925; Poughkeepsie, N.Y.: Artists and Writers Guild, 1935);

The Connoisseur, and Other Stories (London, Glasgow, Sydney & Auckland: Collins, 1926; New York: Knopf, 1926);

St. Andrews: Two Poems, by de la Mare and Rudyard Kipling (London: A. & C. Black, 1926);

Selected Poems (New York: Holt, 1927);

Old Joe (Oxford: Blackwell, 1927);

Stuff and Nonsense, and So On (London: Constable, 1927; New York: Holt, 1927);

Told Again: Traditional Tales (Oxford: Blackwell, 1927); republished as *Told Again: Old Tales Told Again* (New York: Knopf, 1927);

Alone (London: Faber & Gwyer, 1927);

Lucy (Oxford: Blackwell, 1927);

At First Sight: A Novel (New York: Crosby Gaige, 1928);

Self to Self (London: Faber & Gwyer, 1928);

The Captive, and Other Poems (New York: Bowling Green Press, 1928);

A Snowdrop (London: Faber & Faber, 1929);

Stories from the Bible (London: Faber & Gwyer, 1929; New York: Cosmopolitan, 1929);

News (London: Faber & Faber, 1930);

Poems for Children (London: Constable, 1930; New York: Holt, 1930);

On the Edge: Short Stories (London: Faber & Faber, 1930); republished as *On the Edge* (New York: Knopf, 1931);

Two Poems (Bristol: Henry Hill, 1931);

Seven Short Stories (London: Faber & Faber, 1931);

To Lucy (London: Faber & Faber, 1931);

The Printing of Poetry (Cambridge: Cambridge University Press, 1931);

The Dutch Cheese (New York: Knopf, 1931);

Lewis Carroll (London: Faber & Faber, 1932);

The Fleeting, and Other Poems (London: Constable, 1933; New York: Knopf, 1933);

The Lord Fish (London: Faber & Faber, 1933);

The Walter de la Mare Omnibus (London: Collins, 1933);

A Froward Child (London: Faber & Faber, 1934);

Poetry in Prose (London: Milford, 1935; New York: Oxford University Press, 1937);

Poems, 1919 to 1934 (London: Constable, 1935; New York: Holt, 1936);

The Nap, and Other Stories (London & Edinburgh: Thomas Nelson, 1936);

The Wind Blows Over (London: Faber & Faber, 1936; New York: Macmillan, 1936);

This Year: Next Year (London: Faber & Faber, 1937; New York: Holt, 1937);

Stories, Essays and Poems, edited by Mildred M. Bozman (London: Dent, 1938);

An Introduction to Everyman (London: Dent, 1938);

Memory, and Other Poems (London: Constable, 1938; New York: Holt, 1938);

Two Poems by Walter de la Mare and—but!—Arthur Rogers (Newcastle: Privately printed, 1938);

Haunted (London: Linden, 1939);

Pleasures and Speculations (London: Faber & Faber, 1940);

Collected Poems (New York: Holt, 1941; London: Faber & Faber, 1942);

The Picnic, and Other Stories (London: Faber & Faber, 1941);

Bells & Grass: A Book of Rhymes (London: Faber & Faber, 1941); republished as *Bells and Grass* (New York: Viking, 1942);

Mr. Bumps and His Monkey (Chicago & Philadelphia: Winston, 1942);

Time Passes, and Other Poems (London: Faber & Faber, 1942);

The Old Lion, and Other Stories (London: Faber & Faber, 1942);

Best Stories of Walter de la Mare (London: Faber & Faber, 1942);

The Magic Jacket, and Other Stories (London: Faber & Faber, 1943); republished as *The Magic Jacket* (New York: Knopf, 1962);

Collected Rhymes & Verses (London: Faber & Faber, 1944); republished as *Rhymes and Verses: Collected Poems for Children* (New York: Holt, 1947);

The Scarecrow, and Other Stories (London: Faber & Faber, 1945);

The Burning-Glass, and Other Poems (London: Faber & Faber, 1945); republished as *The Burning-Glass and Other Poems, Including The Traveller* (New York: Viking, 1945);

The Dutch Cheese and Other Stories (London: Faber & Faber, 1946);

The Traveller (London: Faber & Faber, 1946);

Collected Stories for Children (London: Faber & Faber, 1947);

The Collected Tales, edited by Edward Wagenknecht (New York: Knopf, 1950);

Inward Companion: Poems (London: Faber & Faber, 1950);

Winged Chariot (London: Faber & Faber, 1951); republished in two volumes as *Winged Chariot, and Other*

Poems (New York: Viking, 1951), with volume 2 comprising *Inward Companion;*

Selected Stories and Verses (Harmondsworth: Penguin, 1952);

Private View (London: Faber & Faber, 1953);

O Lovely England, and Other Poems (London: Faber & Faber, 1953; New York: Viking, 1956);

The Winnowing Dream (London: Faber & Faber, 1954);

Selected Poems, edited by R. N. Green-Armytage (London: Faber & Faber, 1954);

A Beginning, and Other Stories (London: Faber & Faber, 1955);

Walter de la Mare: A Selection from His Writings, edited by Kenneth Hopkins (London: Faber & Faber, 1956);

Ghost Stories (London: Folio Society, 1956);

A Penny a Day (New York: Knopf, 1960);

A Choice of de la Mare's Verse, edited by W. H. Auden (London: Faber & Faber, 1963);

Complete Poems (London: Faber & Faber, 1969; New York: Knopf, 1970);

Eight Tales (Sauk City, Wis.: Arkham House, 1971).

OTHER: Philip Edward Thomas, *Collected Poems,* foreword by de la Mare (London: Selwyn & Blount, 1920);

Come Hither: A Collection of Rhymes and Poems for the Young of All Ages, edited by de la Mare (London: Constable, 1923; New York: Knopf, 1923);

Readings: Traditional Tales, compiled by de la Mare and Thomas Quayle (6 volumes, Oxford: Blackwell, 1925–1928; 1 volume, New York: Knopf, 1927);

William Shakespeare, *The Shakespeare Songs,* edited by Tucker Brooke, introduction by de la Mare (London: Dent, 1929);

Christina Rossetti, *Poems,* edited by de la Mare (London: Dent, 1929);

The Eighteen-Eighties: Essays by Fellows of the Royal Society of Literature, edited by de la Mare (Cambridge: Cambridge University Press, 1930);

Desert Islands and Robinson Crusoe, edited by de la Mare (London: Faber & Faber, 1930);

They Walk Again: An Anthology of Ghost Stories, edited by Colin de la Mare, introduction by Walter de la Mare (London: Faber & Faber, 1931);

Tom Tiddler's Ground: A Book of Poetry for the Junior and Middle Schools, edited by de la Mare (London & Glasgow: Collins' Clear-Type Press, 1931); republished as *Tom Tiddler's Ground: A Book of Poetry for Children* (London: Collins, 1932; New York: Knopf, 1962);

Charles Dickens, *The Cricket on the Hearth,* introduction by de la Mare (London: Golden Cockerel, 1933);

Shakespeare, *A Midsummer Night's Dream,* edited by C. Aldred, introduction by de la Mare (London: Macmillan, 1935);

Early One Morning in the Spring: Chapters on Children and on Childhood as It Is Revealed in Particular in Early Memories and in Early Writings, edited by de la Mare (London: Faber & Faber, 1939; New York: Macmillan, 1939);

Behold, This Dreamer! Of Reverie, Night, Sleep, Dream, Love-Dreams, Nightmare, Death, the Unconscious, the Imagination, Divination, the Artist, and Kindred Subjects, edited by de la Mare (London: Faber & Faber, 1939; New York: Knopf, 1939);

Animal Stories, edited and adapted by de la Mare (London: Faber & Faber, 1939; New York: Scribners, 1940);

Love, edited by de la Mare (London: Faber & Faber, 1943; New York: Morrow, 1946);

Nursery Rhymes for Certain Times, edited by Roger E. Ingpen, introduction by de la Mare (London: Faber & Faber, 1946);

Jean Baptiste Siméon, *Chardin (1699–1779),* introduction and notes by de la Mare (London: Faber & Faber, 1948);

Arthur Shepherd, *The Fiddlers,* words by de la Mare (South Hadley, Mass.: Valley Music, 1948);

Robin Humphrey Milford, *This Year: Next Year, A Song Cycle for Two-Part Choir (S.S.) and Piano,* words by de la Mare (London: Oxford University Press, 1948);

William B. Wordsworth, *Four Songs for High Voice with Pianoforte Accompaniment,* words by de la Mare and Robert Bridges (London: Lengnick, 1948);

Cecil Armstrong Gibbs, *In a Dream's Beguiling: Suite for Mezzo-Soprano Solo, or Semichorus, Women's Choir, S.S.A., String Orchestra, and Pianoforte,* words by de la Mare (London: Boosey, 1951).

Walter de la Mare is better known as a poet and a writer for children than as an author of fantasy or science fiction, but much of the fiction he wrote is fantastic in nature. Within fantasy and horror fiction he is widely considered a figure of considerable importance, even as his general literary reputation has declined since his death. His work is frequently described as neo-Romantic, and his evocations of nature and the past are often connected with the supernatural. As Doris Ross McCrosson points out in her 1966 study of de la Mare's career, much of his work is concerned with the roles of imagination and dreams and with the experiences of children, and fantastic fiction was central in his exploration of these concerns. She also notes how de la Mare, like many of the Victorian writers before him, employed realistic settings and characterization as a means of easing the reader into the supernatural events described in his fantasies: "De la Mare's settings are firmly anchored in reality, his characters are credible, and the situations in which they find themselves are easily possible. At least, this is so at the beginning of the tales; and, by the time de la Mare ventures into the incredible, the reader has, in Coleridge's phrase, willingly suspended disbelief."

Moreover, for de la Mare the fantastic is not used merely for entertainment but also as a suggestion of a reality beyond that of the senses. G. K. Chesterton best summed up this quality in his 1932 *Fortnightly Review* essay on de la Mare: "The fairy-tales of de la Mare are not those of the Sceptic but of the Mystic. . . . de la Mare's world is not merely a world of illusion; it is in quite another sense a world of imagination. It is a real world of which the reality can only be represented to us by images." Though de la Mare resisted a systematic analysis of the nature of this world of imagination, he nonetheless attempted to convey a sense of its reality through his work. What makes for poor metaphysics makes for effective fiction and poetry, and the mysteriousness of the dimly glimpsed otherworlds he presents contributes to the impact they make on the reader.

Like many visionaries, de la Mare came from rather prosaic origins. He was born Walter John Delamare (he changed the name to de la Mare as a young adult, partly in tribute to his Huguenot ancestry) on 25 April 1873 in Charlton, Woolwich. His father, James Edward Delamare, was a clerk in the City, the financial district of London, and served as warden of the church where his brother, Abraham, was rector. The author's mother, Lucy Sophia Browning Delamare, was James's second wife and twenty-six years his junior. She was the daughter of a naval surgeon and a distant relative of Victorian poet Robert Browning. De la Mare was the sixth of seven children born to the couple.

De la Mare's father, sixty-one when the author was born, was forced by a bank regulation to retire four years later, and he had not saved enough money to provide complete educations for all of his children; moreover, he died soon after his retirement and his brother's death. Lucy Delamare then moved the family to London, where de la Mare was educated at St. Paul's Cathedral Choir School. There he founded the school magazine, *The Choristers' Journal,* at age sixteen. An avid reader and budding writer, he also composed a good portion of its contents. Because of his family's limited resources, instead of going to a university de la Mare began working in 1890, at age seventeen, as a bookkeeper in London for the

Dust jacket for the posthumously published 1971 collection of de la Mare's early stories of the supernatural

Anglo-American Oil Company, a division of Standard Oil. In the eighteen years he worked there, he also toiled on his creative efforts. His first publication came in 1895 with a story titled "Kismet" in *The Sketch*. After that he occasionally placed stories and poems (many, like "Kismet," under the pseudonym Walter Ramal) in various periodicals of the day, among them *The Cornhill* and *The Pall Mall Gazette*.

A few of these early stories were collected posthumously in 1971 as *Eight Tales* by the highly regarded American fantasy and horror publisher Arkham House. In these adult fictions, in contrast to de la Mare's fantasy for children, characters find themselves trapped in various states of stasis or transition between the natural and the supernatural without being able fully to experience a different realm of existence, as de la Mare's child protagonists often can. For instance, in "The Moon's Miracle" people are able to witness some sort of supernatural conflict happening on the moon. This glimpse into an unknown world lasts only one night, however, and, at any rate, the people can only observe from a great distance.

Another common theme of de la Mare's early stories, which carries over into his later work, is the human capacity for evil. Just as the realm of the supernatural in de la Mare's fiction is not necessarily good, so human beings in his fiction have an innate tendency toward evil–a tendency present in children as well as adults. Nor does this theme appear only in de la Mare's fantastic narratives; it is equally apparent in his more realistic stories and novels. At the same time, though, in de la Mare's work human beings are not so cursed with a sense of original sin that they are incapable of goodness, and in his fiction the potential for human depravity is balanced by the potential for better things.

In 1899 de la Mare wed Constance Elfrida Ingpen, whom he met in the Esperanza Amateur Dramatic Club. The couple eventually had four children: Florence, Richard, Jinnie, and Colin. In 1899 de la Mare also began an association with J. B. Pinker, one of the best-known literary agents of the period. Pinker was instrumental in helping de la Mare to publish his poems and stories in various periodicals of the day.

In 1902 de la Mare published his first book, the collection of poems *Songs of Childhood,* under the pseudonym Walter Ramal. This book firmly fits into the tradition of British fantasy aimed at children but also capable of being read with pleasure by adults, a category ranging from Lewis Carroll's *Alice's Adventures in Wonderland* (1865) and *Through the Looking-Glass, and What Alice Found There* (1871) to Rudyard Kipling's *The Jungle Books* (1894, 1895) to E. Nesbit's early-twentieth-century fantasies, J. M. Barrie's play *Peter Pan* (1904), and Kenneth Grahame's *The Wind in the Willows* (1908).

In the poems that comprise *Songs of Childhood* and in much of his poetry in general–most notably in the collections *The Listeners, and Other Poems* (1912), *A Child's Day: A Book of Rhymes* (1912), *Peacock Pie: A Book of Rhymes* (1913), *Down-Adown-Derry: A Book of Fairy Poems* (1922), *Stuff and Nonsense, and So On* (1927), *Poems for Children* (1930), and *Bells & Grass: A Book of Rhymes* (1941)–de la Mare tends to focus on certain central concerns; dreams and travels are two of the major themes. Both of these themes, as employed in several of the poems, are related to the general question of true consciousness. Is the material world of the physical senses the only true world, or are there others? Are dreams, visions, or reveries possibly portals to other realms? If other worlds do exist, how can one approach them? Such questions are not so much stated directly as they are implied or suggested

by many of de la Mare's poems, and in those works that are specifically aimed at children there is often the suggestion–common in much fantasy for children or featuring young characters–that children may be more attuned to a numinous world than are their jaded adult counterparts. More broadly, for de la Mare these other realms that stand in contrast to the mundane world could also include a paradisiacal state of nature, a past nostalgically recalled, or both. However, in his poetry as well as in his fiction, the supernatural is not necessarily idyllic or benign; while the other world may indeed be fantastic, it can also be frightening. Also, the voyage to another realm of existence may be accomplished not through dream but through death.

Two years after the publication of *Songs of Childhood* de la Mare's first lengthy work of fiction, *Henry Brocken: His Travels and Adventures in the Rich, Strange, Scarce-Imaginable Regions of Romance* (1904), appeared under his own name. *Henry Brocken* is based on an intriguing premise: a young man steeped in the world of books undertakes a sort of *Wanderjahr,* possibly through daydreams, in which he meets a host of literary characters, including Bottom and Titania from William Shakespeare's *A Midsummer Night's Dream* (1600), Charlotte Brontë's Jane Eyre, and Edgar Allan Poe's Annabel Lee. Extremely well read, de la Mare alludes to a host of literary antecedents throughout his work, generally assuming a similar level of erudition on the part of his older readers.

Although the central concept of the novel is interesting, de la Mare does not develop the individual episodes linked together by the larger frame narrative to any great degree, and often the protagonist is more of an objective observer than a participant in the stories into which he enters. Moreover, while de la Mare sometimes compares and contrasts the various literary worlds through which Henry Brocken travels with his own mundane environment–as in the "Sleeping Beauty" section, where the somnolent community of Sleeping Beauty's brother, Prince Ennui, compares with Henry's own community, and in the *Gulliver's Travels* section, where Henry is as uncomfortable with the insularity of the Houyhnhnms as he is with that of his own world–in general, de la Mare does little with the differences between the fantastic and ordinary worlds of Henry's experience.

Critics generally consider *Henry Brocken* one of the author's lesser efforts, often noting that his attempts to capture the various styles of the writers whose literary worlds the protagonist visits generally fall short, and de la Mare later dismissed the novel as a failure. Although neither this book nor *Songs of*

Childhood sold well, de la Mare was well under way in what became a lengthy literary career.

His career was substantially aided in 1908, when he received a Civil List stipend of £200, thanks to the efforts of his friend Henry Newbolt, editor of *The Monthly Review;* the award encouraged de la Mare to leave the world of business and write full-time. Between 1909 and 1920 he also worked as a reader for Heinemann, and in 1915 he became the Royal Society Literature Chair of Fiction, became a director of the children's magazine *Chatterbox,* and was granted a Civil List pension of £100 a year. With these various sources of income and the sale of his publications, de la Mare was able to devote most of his attention to his writing for the remainder of his life.

One of de la Mare's best-known children's books is *The Three Mulla-Mulgars* (1910), which began as a series of stories he told aloud to his children—as did many of his works for younger readers. Told in the form of an animal fable, the story involves the journey of three royal monkeys, Thumma, Thimbulla, and Nod, to the mysterious Valley of Tishnar, where their father, Seelem, was born. There they hope to find their missing father (who had promised to return for his wife and sons) and receive recognition of their royal status. Along the way they experience various adventures, through which Nod, the youngest of the royal monkeys, matures to become the leader of his brothers, aided partly by the magical "wonderstone" their dying mother, Mutt-matutta, entrusts to him and partly by his imagination and his openness to experience. Humorous touches pervade the book, and Nod is closer to a trickster figure than a conventional hero, but the quest of the mulla-mulgars is treated seriously, almost in epic fashion.

Considerably different from the playful tone of *The Three Mulla-Mulgars* is de la Mare's novel *The Return* (1910), which has spiritual possession and personal identity as its subject. After falling asleep in a cemetery, Arthur Lawford finds that his appearance has changed to that of a Huguenot exile named Nicholas de Sabathier, who killed himself years ago, beside whose grave Lawford slept. This alteration results in the protagonist's rejection by those around him, including his family and friends. Isolated in a world that was once familiar to him, he embarks on a spiritual journey in search of his own identity: is he still the man he once was, or has he changed spiritually as well as physically? Is the eighteenth-century Huguenot taking over his soul as well as his body? Even after fighting against the intrusion of de Sabathier's spirit into his own soul, Lawford truly has changed and can no longer accept his conventional life of duty and routine. As in much of de la Mare's fantasy, the focus is

HENRY BROCKEN
HIS TRAVELS AND ADVENTURES IN THE RICH, STRANGE, SCARCE-IMAGINABLE REGIONS OF ROMANCE

BY WALTER J. DE LA MARE
("WALTER RAMAL")

LONDON
JOHN MURRAY, ALBEMARLE STREET, W.
1904

Title page for de la Mare's first lengthy work of fiction, in which a young man meets literary characters from the works of such authors as William Shakespeare, Charlotte Brontë, and Edgar Allan Poe (courtesy of The Lilly Library, Indiana University)

less on the supernatural phenomena and more on the psychological impact these phenomena exert on characters, as well as their metaphysical implications. The supernatural transformation that the protagonist undergoes is at one level a metaphor for the transformation of personality. A similar metaphor is employed in de la Mare's novel *Memoirs of a Midget* (1921), in which the protagonist's stature is more a symbol of her alienation from society than a focus of attention for its own sake.

One of de la Mare's best-known poems provides the title for *The Listeners, and Other Poems,* the book that, along with the children's poetry collection *Peacock Pie* the following year, first introduced him to a wide readership. "The Listeners," long a standard for young memorizers and reciters of poetry, is a narrative poem about a traveler who knocks on the door of a house. No one answers, but the spirits that dwell in the vacant house attentively listen to "that voice from the world of men." De la Mare's popularity led to an informal American lecture tour in late 1916 and early 1917; also while in the United States, he accepted the Howland Memorial Prize on behalf of his friend Rupert Brooke, who had died in World War I in 1915. De la Mare returned to England anxious to help in the war effort, and he spent the remainder of World War I working in the Food Controller's Office, organized to handle the food rationing made necessary by the war.

Memoirs of a Midget was his greatest novelistic success, both commercially and critically. Although the work–like his next and last novel, *At First Sight* (1928)–includes nothing of the fantastic, it is similar to much of de la Mare's fantastic fiction thematically, as it concerns a character who stands outside the stultifying norms of society and who matures to assert her own individuality. In addition, by telling the story from the perspective of his protagonist he effectively depicts a familiar world as foreign and strange, much as he does in his more fantastic works.

De la Mare's dramatic work for children, *Crossings* (1921), is subtitled "A Fairy Play." In it, a group of children fend for themselves in an isolated manor, though they are aided by a butcher, a baker, and a candlestick maker. The children also have dealings with a kind ghost and less-benevolent fairies. The play was written for and first produced at the Wick School, a preparatory school in Hove, early in 1919. While those who attended its premiere described the play as a success, it failed to fulfill de la Mare's hopes of a successful run in London, although a production including the well-known actress Ellen Terry in her last performance was produced to good reviews at the Lyric Theatre, Hammersmith, in November 1925.

In *The Riddle, and Other Stories* (1923), one of his most widely praised collections, de la Mare includes several of his short stories of the strange and the supernatural. Many of these deal with the nature of evil–such as "Seaton's Aunt," about an old woman whose wickedness, said Chesterton, "had an extension beyond this world." The horror of this particular story is compounded by the fact that the reader sees this woman through the eyes of her young nephew and his friend. Even though *The Riddle, and Other Stories* is not a book for young readers, children also figure prominently in the title story, which deals with the disappearance of seven siblings through an old chest in which they are told not to play; in "Out of the Deep," in which a child's suffering is connected to the mysterious powers that haunt the main character; and in the disturbing, realistic story "The Almond Tree." A young girl is also the protagonist of "The Looking

Glass," a distorted combination of Carroll's *Through the Looking-Glass, and What Alice Found There* and Frances Hodgson Burnett's *The Secret Garden* (1911). In "The Looking Glass" a girl named Alice, who has tuberculosis, is told that her garden is haunted. Alice accepts this statement, speculating that the garden might be like a spiritual looking glass. The idea that comes to her is that she is a spirit herself, in contrast with the delusion of the material world.

Perhaps one reason for the prominence of children in much of de la Mare's writing is that, like many of his adult characters, they are in a sense outsiders in their own world. Thus, their status as aliens enables them to see the oddness of a world that most people take for granted and at times to step beyond the boundaries of that world, either by defying its conventions or, as in de la Mare's fantasy, entering into other realms.

Ding Dong Bell (1924) includes the story "Winter," which serves as a good example of a typical quality in de la Mare's supernatural tales: an eerie atmosphere of strangeness, if not of horror. In this story the narrator, while in a cemetery, encounters a being not of this world. Although this figure comes "in human likeness," the narrator adds that it "was not of my kind, nor of my reality." The narrator observes this being with an almost objective fascination, while the entity looks at him "with unconcealed horror." Little happens in this story apart from this unusual meeting; what is important is the evocative description of the uncanny and the mood of the piece. Like "Winter," the other two stories in the collection, "Lichen" and "Benighted," take their titles from tombstone epitaphs, and all touch on the world beyond the grave in one fashion or another.

Broomsticks, and Other Tales (1925) collects several of de la Mare's short fantasies for children, many of which resemble fairy tales. For instance, in "Miss Jemima" an elderly woman relates to her granddaughter how, when she was a child, she was not only harassed by members of her aunt's household when she lived there but also was approached by a spirit that tried to lure her to her doom. The story presents the temptation to escape one evil for what is later revealed to be a greater one. Similarly, in "Alice's Godmother" Alice's centuries-old grandmother (apparently a witch) offers to share her secret of immortality, which Alice wisely rejects.

Lighter in tone, though still touching upon the supernatural, "Broomsticks" is about the hidden life of a cat, while a story such as "The Dutch Cheese," in which a young farmer tries to prevent a gang of fairies from luring his sister away, falls somewhere in between the seriousness of the supernatural threat and the farmer's comic efforts. Other stories in *Broomsticks, and Other Tales* are harder to classify. These include "Pigtails, Ltd.," in which a woman gathers a following of ten-year-old girls who remain ten during the woman's lifetime and die when she does; "The Thief," about a man who finds a magic egg; and "Lucy," in which a woman's lifelong imaginary friend briefly becomes visible toward the end of the woman's life.

Another collection for both adults and children is *The Lord Fish* (1933), which includes "Dick and the Beanstalk," a humorous sequel to the well-known folktale. Other stories in the volume are also in the fairy-tale mode, such as the title story, in which a young man encounters a woman magically transformed by the Lord Fish into a half-woman, half-fish creature; because she is beautiful, he naturally attempts to save her, with mixed results. In "A Penny a Day" a woman strikes a deal with someone she believes is a dwarf but instead is a brownie, by nature a benevolent creature.

Often in de la Mare's fantasy there is the sense that people are aware of the close connection between the natural and the supernatural in moments when, to borrow a phrase from "Mr. Kempe" in *The Connoisseur, and Other Stories* (1926), "the natural edges off into the unknown," but they are often afraid to recognize this connection. When people do, the consequences are frequently horrifying. For instance, in "All Hallows," also collected in *The Connoisseur, and Other Stories,* the narrator receives the suggestion that a crumbling cathedral is occupied by demonic powers, who are actually at work rebuilding the decaying structure. A further twist is the fact that these supernatural forces are no longer held at bay by the faith the declining cathedral symbolizes. In "The Creatures" the narrator learns of the existence of an unusual couple in a sort of rustic earthly paradise. The idea that these "creatures" may be otherworldly beings is discounted, but their mysteriousness remains intact and disturbing.

Among the best efforts collected in *On the Edge: Short Stories* (1930) are three ghost stories: "A Recluse," "Crewe," and the frequently reprinted "The Green Room." Like many of de la Mare's ghost stories, both "A Recluse" and "Crewe" concern the people who are haunted more than the otherworldly entities that are haunting them. "The Green Room" is about the ghost of a poet who committed suicide; the ghost haunts an old bookstore following the posthumous publication of a collection of her poems, but the young man to whom she appears pities her rather than fears her. As Forrest Reid notes

Dust jacket for the highly praised 1923 collection that includes several of de la Mare's stories of the strange and the supernatural, among them "Seaton's Aunt" and "Out of the Deep" (Bruccoli Clark Layman Collection)

in his 1929 critical study, the story adroitly expresses "a fragile, lingering, half-pathetic sense of the past."

De la Mare returns to the ghost story in several tales in *The Wind Blows Over* (1936). The best known of these is "A Revenant," which owes a substantial debt to the horror fiction of Edgar Allan Poe, whose spirit is the ghost of the title and to whom de la Mare was frequently compared during his career. Like "The Green Room" in *On the Edge,* the story comments obliquely on the depredations sometimes inflicted on the lives (or, in these stories, the afterlives) of writers. It concerns a lecturer on Poe who is visited by the spirit of the departed writer himself, with whom he converses following his public lecture. Though the ghost of Poe appears to this man more out of curiosity than malice, the lecturer is nonetheless stricken with fear when confronted by the dead man of whom he has so often spoken casually. In the process of their meeting, Poe seems more fully alive than the man who has devoted much of his life to studying him. Another ghost story in the book is "Strangers and Pilgrims," in which a stranger enlists the help of a church caretaker to find a particular grave—the stranger's.

Another story in *The Wind Blows Over,* "Physic," is more generally supernatural in character. A young girl constantly wants to pull the blinds because she sees frightening faces in the windows. While children can be just as blind to the presence of otherworldly forces as adults in de la Mare's fiction, and while he generally observed the longstanding fantasy trope that holds that they are more attuned to the marvelous than their elders, sometimes children do get glimpses of the supernatural. However, unlike much fantasy featuring child protagonists, the worlds they perceive are not always benignly magical.

De la Mare continued to work on his fiction throughout the 1930s, but during this decade he devoted more of his energies to his poetry and to the wide-ranging anthologies he collected. In particular, after the death of his wife in 1943, de la Mare continued to write original work but spent more of his time revising and republishing earlier work. It should be noted that while a casual glance at de la Mare's bibliography might give one the impression that many of his books, especially later ones, are merely collections of reprinted material arranged differently, such an impression would miss the fact that de la Mare frequently did revise his work for republication. This fact means that anyone interested in a particular work would do well to investigate its publishing history, as de la Mare might have revised it more than once over the course of his career. This situation is a nightmare for students and scholars, but it reveals just how seriously de la Mare considered the craft of fiction, much like the assiduous revisions of near contemporaries such as William Butler Yeats and W. H. Auden reveal their concern about the nature and identity of their poetic work.

Two later original works are long poems that, in their visionary nature, touch on the fantastic: *The Traveller* (1946) and *Winged Chariot* (1951). Both describe, in highly evocative if sometimes vague language, mythic journeys into dream-like, unreal realms, offering a metaphor for life as a journey. *The Traveller* is narrative in nature, in contrast to *Winged Chariot,* which is more lyric and contemplative.

One of de la Mare's last books, *A Beginning, and Other Stories* (1955), includes the late ghost story "Bad Company." More conventionally a work of horror fiction than most of his earlier ghost stories, "Bad Company" features a narrator lured from a subway by the ghost of an old man, who leads the narrator to the old man's corpse.

In his last years de la Mare also enjoyed the literary reputation he had earned over the course of a long career. Among the honors he received toward the end of his life were the Carnegie Medal, the Order of Merit, and several honorary degrees. Also, King George VI named him a Companion of Honour in 1948. De la Mare's activities were curtailed after he was injured in a fall in 1954, and he died at his home in Twickenham, Middlesex, on 22 June 1956. His ashes were interred at St. Paul's Cathedral in London.

Although de la Mare's life could be described as relatively uneventful, he not only created a voluminous and diverse body of work but also was active in British literary life during an exciting period and knew many important fellow authors. De la Mare's work in fantasy and horror is as individual as his poetry and children's books. Neither a realist nor a modernist, he instead fashioned his own literary identity. His fantastic fiction is carefully crafted in language, plot, and characterization, all of which contribute to his subtle, thoughtful treatment of such concerns as identity, death, and the supernatural. Widely admired if not extremely influential or imitated in the fields of fantasy and horror, Walter de la Mare created an important body of work in the history of fantastic literature, and his achievements remain a significant area of study and enjoyment for scholars and other readers.

Bibliographies:
Leonard Clark, "A Handlist of the Writings in Book Form (1902–53) of Walter de la Mare," *Studies in Bibliography,* 6 (1954): 192–217;
Edward Wagenknecht, "A List of Walter de la Mare's Contributions to the London *Times Literary Supplement,*" *Boston University Studies in English,* 1 (Winter 1955): 243–255;
Clark, "Addendum: A Checklist of Walter de la Mare," *Studies in Bibliography,* 8 (1956): 269–270;
Clark, *Walter de la Mare: A Checklist* (London: Cambridge University Press, 1956).

Biography:
Theresa Whistler, *Imagination of the Heart: The Life of Walter de la Mare* (London: Duckworth, 1993).

References:
John Atkins, *Walter de la Mare: An Exploration* (London: Temple, 1947);
Russell Brain, *Tea with Walter de la Mare* (London: Faber & Faber, 1957);

Julia Briggs, "On the Edge: Walter de la Mare," in her *Night Visitors: The Rise and Fall of the English Ghost Story* (London: Faber & Faber, 1977), pp. 182–195;

Lord David Cecil, "The Prose Tales of Walter de la Mare," in his *The Fine Art of Readings and Other Literary Studies* (New York: Bobbs-Merrill, 1957), pp. 219–232;

G. K. Chesterton, "Walter de la Mare," *Fortnightly Review*, new series, 138 (July 1932), pp. 47–53; republished in *The Common Man* (London: Sheed & Ward, 1950), pp. 206–213;

Henry Charles Duffin, *Walter de la Mare: A Study of His Poetry* (London: Sidgwick & Jackson, 1949);

Graham Greene, "Walter de la Mare's Short Stories," in his *Collected Essays* (New York: Viking, 1969), pp. 141–148;

Kenneth Hopkins, *Walter de la Mare,* revised edition (London: Longmans, Green, 1957);

Doris Ross McCrosson, *Walter de la Mare* (New York: Twayne, 1966);

R. L. Mégroz, *Walter de la Mare: A Biographical and Critical Study* (London: Hodder & Stoughton, 1924);

Peter Penzoldt, "Walter de la Mare," in his *The Supernatural in Fiction* (London: Nevill, 1952), pp. 203–227;

J. B. Priestley, "Mr. De la Mare," in his *Figures in Modern Literature* (London: John Lane–Bodley Head, 1924), pp. 31–54;

Forrest Reid, *Walter de la Mare: A Critical Study* (London: Faber & Faber, 1929);

Edward Wagenknecht, "News of Tishnar: Walter de la Mare," in his *Cavalcade of the English Novel: From Elizabeth to George VI* (New York: Holt, 1943), pp. 533–546;

Wagenknecht, *Seven Masters of Supernatural Fiction* (New York: Greenwood Press, 1991), pp. 121–149;

John H. Wills, "Architecture of Reality: The Short Stories of Walter de la Mare," *North Dakota Quarterly,* 32 (Autumn 1964): 85–92.

Papers:

The papers of Walter de la Mare are located at Temple University Libraries, Rare Book Department; the University of Chicago Library; the Syracuse University Library; and King's College, Cambridge.

Lord Dunsany
(Edward John Moreton Drax Plunkett, Baron Dunsany)
(24 July 1878 – 25 October 1957)

Darren Harris-Fain
Shawnee State University

See also the Dunsany entries in *DLB 10: Modern British Dramatists, 1900–1945; DLB 77: British Mystery Writers, 1920–1939; DLB 153: Late-Victorian and Edwardian British Novelists, First Series;* and *DLB 156: British Short-Fiction Writers, 1880–1914: The Romantic Tradition.*

BOOKS: *The Gods of Pegana* (London: Elkin Mathews, 1905; Boston: J. W. Luce, 1916);

Time and the Gods (London: Heinemann, 1906; Boston: J. W. Luce, 1913);

The Sword of Welleran and Other Stories (London: George Allen, 1908; Boston: J. W. Luce, 1916);

A Dreamer's Tales (London: George Allen, 1910; Boston: J. W. Luce, 1916);

Selections from the Writings of Lord Dunsany (Churchtown, Ireland: Cuala Press, 1912);

The Book of Wonder (London: Heinemann, 1912; Boston: J. W. Luce, 1913);

Five Plays (London: Richards, 1914; New York: Kennerley, 1914);

Fifty-One Tales (London: Elkin Mathews, 1915; New York: Kennerley, 1915);

Tales of Wonder (London: Elkin Mathews, 1916); republished as *The Last Book of Wonder* (Boston: J. W. Luce, 1916);

A Night at an Inn (New York: Sunwise Turn, 1916; London: Putnam, 1922);

Plays of Gods and Men (Dublin: Talbot Press, 1917; London: Unwin, 1917; Boston: J. W. Luce, 1917);

A Dreamer's Tales and Other Stories (New York: Boni & Liveright, 1917);

The Book of Wonder [with *Time and the Gods*] (New York: Boni & Liveright, 1918);

Tales of War (Boston: Little, Brown, 1918; Dublin: Talbot Press / London: Unwin, 1918);

Nowadays (Boston: Four Seas, 1918);

Unhappy Far-Off Things (Boston: Little, Brown, 1919; London: Elkin Mathews, 1919);

Edward John Moreton Drax Plunkett, Baron Dunsany

Tales of Three Hemispheres (Boston: J. W. Luce, 1919; London: Unwin, 1920);

If (London & New York: Putnam, 1921);

The Chronicles of Rodriguez (London & New York: Putnam, 1922); published as *Don Rodriguez: Chronicles of Shadow Valley* (New York & London: Putnam, 1922);

The Laughter of the Gods (London: Putnam, 1922);

Plays of Near and Far (London & New York: Putnam, 1922); expanded as *Plays of Near and Far (Including If)* (London & New York: Putnam, 1923);

King Argimenes and the Unknown Warrior (London & New York: Putnam, 1923);

The Glittering Gate (London & New York: Putnam, 1923);

The Lost Silk Hat (London & New York: Putnam, 1923);

The King of Elfland's Daughter (London & New York: Putnam, 1924);

Alexander and Three Small Plays (London & New York: Putnam, 1925);

Alexander (London & New York: Putnam, 1925);

The Charwoman's Shadow (London & New York: Putnam, 1926);

The Blessing of Pan (London & New York: Putnam, 1927);

Seven Modern Comedies (London & New York: Putnam, 1928);

Fifty Poems (London & New York: Putnam, 1929);

The Old Folk of the Centuries (London: Elkin Mathews & Marrot, 1930);

The Travel Tales of Mr. Joseph Jorkens (London & New York: Putnam, 1931);

Lord Adrian (Waltham Saint Lawrence, Berkshire: Golden Cockerel Press, 1933);

The Curse of the Wise Woman (London: Heinemann, 1933; New York & Toronto: Longmans, Green, 1933);

If I Were Dictator (London: Methuen, 1934);

Jorkens Remembers Africa (New York & Toronto: Longmans, Green, 1934); republished as *Mr. Jorkens Remembers Africa* (London & Toronto: Heinemann, 1934);

Building a Sentence (New York: Marchbanks Press, 1934?);

Mr. Faithful (New York, Los Angeles & London: S. French, 1935);

Up in the Hills (London & Toronto: Heinemann, 1935; New York: Putnam, 1936);

Rory and Bran (London & Toronto: Heinemann, 1936; New York: Putnam, 1937);

My Talks with Dean Spanley (London & Toronto: Heinemann, 1936; New York: Putnam, 1936);

My Ireland (London: Jarrolds, 1937; New York & London: Funk & Wagnalls, 1937);

Plays for Earth and Air (London & Toronto: Heinemann, 1937);

Patches of Sunlight (London & Toronto: Heinemann, 1938; New York: Reynal & Hitchcock, 1938);

Mirage Water (London: Putnam, 1938; Philadelphia: Dorrance, 1939);

The Story of Mona Sheehy (London & Toronto: Heinemann, 1939; New York & London: Harper, 1940);

Jorkens Has a Large Whiskey (London: Putnam, 1940);

War Poems (London: Hutchinson, 1941);

Wandering Songs (London: Hutchinson, 1943);

A Journey (London: Macdonald, 1944);

Guerrilla (London & Toronto: Heinemann, 1944; Indianapolis: Bobbs-Merrill, 1944);

While the Sirens Slept (London: Jarrolds, 1944);

The Donnellan Lectures (London & Toronto: Heinemann, 1945);

The Sirens Wake (London: Jarrolds, 1945);

The Year (London: Jarrolds, 1946);

A Glimpse from a Watch Tower: A Series of Essays on Man's Outlook in an Uncertain Future (London: Jarrolds, 1946);

The Fourth Book of Jorkens (London: Jarrolds, 1947; Sauk City, Wis.: Arkham House, 1948);

To Awaken Pegasus (Oxford: Ronald, 1949);

The Man Who Ate the Phoenix (London: Jarrolds, 1949);

The Strange Journey of Colonel Polders (London: Jarrolds, 1950);

Carcassonne (Boston: J. W. Luce, 1950);

The Last Revolution (London: Jarrolds, 1951);

His Fellow Men (London: Jarrolds, 1952);

The Little Tales of Smethers and Other Stories (London: Jarrolds, 1952);

Jorkens Borrows Another Whiskey (London: Joseph, 1954);

The Sword of Welleran and Other Tales of Enchantment (New York: Devin-Adair, 1954);

At the Edge of the World, edited by Lin Carter (New York: Ballantine, 1970);

Beyond the Fields We Know, edited by Carter (New York: Ballantine, 1972);

Gods, Men, and Ghosts: The Best Supernatural Fiction of Lord Dunsany, edited by E. F. Bleiler (New York: Dover, 1972);

Over the Hills and Far Away, edited by Carter (New York: Ballantine, 1974);

The Ghosts of the Heaviside Layer and Other Fantasms, edited by Darrell Schweitzer (Philadelphia: Owlswick, 1980);

An Enemy of Scotland Yard and Other Whodunits/Ein Feind vom Scotland Yard und andere Kurzkrimis, translations by Elisabeth Schnack (Munich: Deutscher Taschenbuch, 1985);

Verses Dedicatory: 18 Previously Unpublished Poems, edited by Carter (Upper Montclair, N.J.: Charnel House, 1985);

The Hashish Man and Other Stories (San Francisco: Manic D Press, 1996).

PLAY PRODUCTIONS: *The Glittering Gate,* Dublin, Abbey Theatre, 29 April 1909; London, Court Theatre, 6 June 1910;

King Argimenes and the Unknown Warrior, Dublin, Abbey Theatre, 26 January 1911; produced as *King Argimenes,* London, Court Theatre, 26 June 1911;

The Gods of the Mountain, London, Haymarket Theatre, 1 June 1911;

The Golden Doom, London, Haymarket Theatre, 19 November 1912;

The Lost Silk Hat, Manchester, Gaiety Theatre, 4 August 1913;

Frontispiece and title page for Dunsany's first book, a collection of short stories in which he begins the construction of the world of gods that appears in much of his subsequent fiction (courtesy of Special Collections, Thomas Cooper Library, University of South Carolina)

The Tents of the Arabs, Paris, Le Petit Theatre Anglais, April 1914; Liverpool, Playhouse, 19 September 1914;

A Night at an Inn, New York, Neighborhood Playhouse, 23 April 1916; London, Palace Theatre, 6 November 1917;

The Queen's Enemies, New York, Neighborhood Playhouse, 14 November 1916;

The Prince of Stamboul, Detroit, 1918;

The Laughter of the Gods, New York, Punch and Judy Theatre, 15 January 1919;

The Murderers, Indianapolis, Shubert Murat Theatre, 14 July 1919;

The Compromise of the King of the Golden Isles, New Haven, Yale University, 1919;

Fame and the Poet, Cambridge, Massachusetts, Harvard University, 1919; Leeds, Albert Hall, 8 February 1924;

A Good Bargain, St. Louis, Artists' Guild, 1920;

If, London, Ambassadors' Theatre, 30 May 1921;

Cheezo, London, Everyman Theatre, 15 November 1921;

Lord Adrian, Birmingham, Prince of Wales's Theatre, 12 November 1923;

His Sainted Grandmother, London, Fortune Theatre, 8 December 1926;

The Jest of Hahalaba, London, Playroom 6, 22 March 1927;

Mr. Faithful, London, Q Theatre, 22 August 1927.

OTHER: *Modern Anglo-Irish Verse: An Anthology Selected from the Work of Living Irish Poets,* edited by Dunsany (London: Nutt, 1914);

Francis Ledwidge, *Songs of the Fields,* introduction by Dunsany (London: Jenkins, 1916);

Ledwidge, *Songs of Peace,* edited by Dunsany (London: Jenkins, 1917);

Ledwidge, *Last Songs,* introduction by Dunsany (London: Jenkins, 1918);

Ledwidge, *The Complete Poems of Francis Ledwidge,* introduction by Dunsany (London: Jenkins, 1919; New York: Brentano's, 1919);

The Golden Book of Modern English Poetry, 1870–1920, edited by Thomas Caldwell, introduction by Dunsany (London & Toronto: Dent, 1922); expanded as *The Golden Book of Modern English Poetry, 1870–1930* (London: Dent, 1930);

Seamus MacCall, *Gods in Motley,* foreword by Dunsany (London: Constable, 1935);

Mary Lavin, *Tales from Bective Bridge,* introduction by Dunsany (London: Joseph, 1945);

George Meredith, *The Egoist,* introduction by Dunsany (London: Oxford University Press, 1947);

Mary Hamilton, *Green and Gold,* introduction by Dunsany (London: Wingate, 1948);

Annie Crone, *Bridie Steen,* introduction by Dunsany (London: Heinemann, 1949);

Judith Anne Dorothea Wentworth Blunt-Lytton, Baroness, *Drift of the Storm,* introduction by Dunsany (Oxford: Ronald, 1951);

Stanton A. Coblentz, *Time's Travellers,* introduction by Dunsany (London: Richards, 1954);

Arthur Machen, *The Hill of Dreams,* introduction by Dunsany (London: Richards, 1954).

TRANSLATIONS: *The Odes of Horace* (London & Toronto: Heinemann, 1947);

The Collected Works of Horace, translated by Dunsany and Michael Oakley (London: Dent, 1961; New York: Dutton, 1961).

SELECTED PERIODICAL PUBLICATIONS–UNCOLLECTED: "Romance," *Saturday Review* (London), 2796 (29 May 1909): 685–686;

"Romance and the Modern Stage," *National Review,* 341 (July 1911): 827–835;

"Helping the Fairies," *Strand Magazine,* 113 (May–June 1947): 28–31;

"The Story of Tse Gah," *Tomorrow,* 7 (December 1947): 19–20;

"The Dwarf Holóbolos and the Sword Hogbiter," *Collins for Boys and Girls,* 1 (July 1949): 9–16;

"Near the Back of Beyond," *Ellery Queen's Mystery Magazine,* 26 (November 1955): 30–42.

Lord Dunsany was an aristocrat, a soldier, a sportsman, an avid chess player, and an author. He wrote many things, both in terms of genre–poems, plays, stories, novels, and essays–and in quantity. Such a varied and prolific career was typical of many British writers between the world wars, but since that period Dunsany has been singled out for that portion of his vast output devoted to the fantastic.

He was born Edward John Moreton Drax Plunkett on 24 July 1878 near Regent's Park in London. His early upbringing, however, was that of the English country house–specifically Dunstall Priory near Sevenoaks in Kent. There he first developed the love of the countryside that he retained throughout his life. This fondness for the outdoors was further developed after his grandfather died; his father became the seventeenth Baron Dunsany in 1889, and the family began to divide its time between Dunstall Priory and Dunsany Castle, built in 1190 in County Meath, Ireland, northwest of Dublin. In Ireland he learned to hunt, and he continued to practice the sport for the rest of his life.

Travel was also part of the family heritage. On his mother's side of the family he was related to the flamboyant nineteenth-century explorer Sir Richard Burton, and Dunsany grew up among the many objects collected from around the world that filled his father's study. In adulthood Dunsany himself traveled extensively, and such experiences informed his mainstream books about the experiences of his fictional character Joseph Jorkens.

Dunsany's earliest education was provided at home by a governess, then at a boarding school in Kent. During this time he became acquainted with the works of writers such as the Brothers Grimm, Hans Christian Andersen, and Edgar Allan Poe, all naturally fertile ground for someone inclined to fantasy. At age twelve he began attending Cheam School, an English prep school, where he studied Greek and the Bible. From Cheam he went to Eton College in 1891.

Given his predilections, Dunsany naturally disliked much of his experience at Eton, one of the most prestigious public schools in Britain. He enjoyed the intellectual and artistic atmosphere of the school and launched himself into poetry there, but he also found the academic environment oppressive. His father withdrew him from Eton for another reason, however: to turn him into a soldier. In the late nineteenth century, decades prior to World War I, military life was as class-bound as other aspects of British society, and military training was often viewed as an appropriate accomplishment for aristocratic young men. Thus, Dunsany's father pulled him from Eton and sent him to the Royal Military Academy in Sandhurst. Dunsany proved an able pupil and rose to officer status. He served first with the Coldstream Guards on Gilbraltar, then in South Africa in the Boer War of 1899–1902; but his experience with actual warfare was limited, and he returned home in 1901.

In 1899 he became the eighteenth Baron Dunsany upon his father's death, and he claimed Dunstall Priory in Kent for his home, even though his uncle,

*Dunsany in the uniform of the Fifth Royal Inniskilling
Fusiliers during World War I*

Horace Plunkett, took over many of the family responsibilities since Dunsany was still in his early twenties. In 1904 he married Lady Beatrice Child-Villiers, daughter of the Earl and Countess of Jersey, and moved to Dunsany Castle. In 1906 their only child, Randal Arthur Henry, was born.

Dunsany occupied himself with domestic life, hunting, and writing, picking up his schoolboy hobby. Dunsany's claims about his writing appear contradictory when taken together. He typically claimed that he wrote only as an avocation, and only when he felt inspired to do so, but his voluminous output seems to belie this claim, even if one accepts his assertion that he wrote quickly. Yet, he sometimes took offense at the suggestion that, since he was a lord, he was merely dabbling in literature. He suggested that he was casual about his literary efforts, yet at the same time he asserted that he wanted to be taken seriously as a writer.

Dunsany's first mature literary efforts included poems and short stories, and his first book was a collection of stories, *The Gods of Pegana* (1905), the publication of which he financially supported. In this volume begins the construction of a fantastic secondary world that occupied much of his subsequent fiction. *The Gods of Pegana* details how this secondary world of assorted gods, the physical universe they create, and the human beings to which they are connected came to be. As a fictional mythology, it anticipates such later works as J. R. R. Tolkien's posthumously published *The Silmarillion* (1977) in its inventive alternatives to existing creation myths and to mundane human history.

The presence of such alternatives to existing religious beliefs begs the question as to Dunsany's motives. The author's own religious beliefs are a matter of some debate among critics and biographers, but most certainly he did not adhere to the conventional Christianity in which he was raised. Nor does it seem likely that in *The Gods of Pegana* he is seriously proposing that the gods described in the stories actually exist. In one way the stories could be read as allegories of the histories of religious faith, beginning with early humans granting divine status to natural forces. But if the book existed solely to convey such a focused thesis, why go to the trouble of presenting it in such elaborate fictional terms? Clearly, part of Dunsany's intent was not merely to express ideas but to create a convincing, interesting, and unworldly world. Dunsany not only reproduces several of the characteristics of traditional creation myths and legends but also mixes these elements with more-modern ideas, such as evolution and physics. In addition, while the subjects are definitely in religious territory, the attitudes conveyed about religious ideas and leaders are not always respectful or pious.

The stories in *The Gods of Pegana* also introduce a characteristic of much of Dunsany's fantasy: an elevated, deliberately antiquated style, akin to older English translations of ancient epics or literal translations of non-Western creation myths. The book opens:

Before there stood gods upon Olympus, or ever Allah was Allah, had wrought and rested Mana-Yood-Sushai.

There are in Pegana—Mung and Sish and Kib, and the maker of all small gods, who is Mana-Yood-Sushai. Moreover, we have a faith in Roon and Slid.

And it has been said of old that all things that have been were wrought by the small gods, excepting only Mana-Yood-Sushai, who made the gods, and hath thereafter rested.

As the materials of Dunsany's fantasy are often epic in nature if not always in scope, he apparently felt that such an approach was more appropriate than a more contemporary prose style. Additionally, while the text introduces a fictional cosmogony counter to that of the Judeo-Christian tradition, the language is reminiscent of the King James Version of the Bible, which Dunsany admitted was an enormous influence on his prose.

Dunsany continued to explore his invented fantasy realm in his next book, *Time and the Gods* (1906). The narrative nature of this collection is perhaps stronger than that of *The Gods of Pegana,* consisting as it does of stories that read like legends. There is also a greater thematic unity in this volume, with Time repeatedly emerging as a force greater than even the gods. Human beings, of course, are subject to the power of Time, as is nicely allegorized in the story "In the Land of Time," about a king who vainly attempts to vanquish Time. In response, Time throws years at the king's soldiers, rendering their knees stiff and their hair gray. In *Time and the Gods,* however, Time also overpowers Dunsany's fictional deities, as in Time's sacking of the gods' beloved city in the title story.

Both *The Gods of Pegana* and *Time and the Gods* were generally well received, opening periodical markets for his work and creating a demand for further fantasies. Dunsany's next collection, *The Sword of Welleran and Other Stories* (1908), continues his trend of writing loosely linked short stories and sketches centered around a fictional pantheon of gods and their relations with a fantastic human world. However, rather than merely repeating himself, Dunsany creates newly imagined stories and situations in this book.

For example, two of the stories—"The Sword of Welleran" and "The Fortress Unvanquishable, Save for Sacnoth"—are of a type new to Dunsany's career at this point: heroic fantasy. The latter features a heroic protagonist, Leothric, who undertakes a series of challenges, largely supernatural, to restore the land to its previously untainted state. He succeeds not only because of his bravery but also because he is armed with the magical sword Sacnoth. Again using a deliberately elevated style, Dunsany has his narrator relate the tale of the hero's exploits in language reminiscent of older epics such as *Beowulf.*

Another story from *The Sword of Welleran and Other Stories* is worth noting for its use of fantastic elements combined with commentary on human frailties, typical of much of Dunsany's fantasy. "The Kith of the Elf-Folk" is about a supernatural "Wild Thing" who, disenchanted with the world of magic, acquires a soul so that she can experience life with the human beings. Such an experience, however, is more disappointing than anything else, especially since she finds herself working in a factory, that frequent symbol of the industrial modern world opposed to the fantastic. Another noteworthy point about this story is its setting: rather than employing the orientalized locales of much of his fiction up to this point, "The Kith of the Elf-Folk" is set squarely in England.

In addition to writing stories, Dunsany was interested in the stage and befriended several of the most important Irish playwrights of the time, among them Lady Isabella Augusta Persse Gregory and William Butler Yeats. The latter encouraged Dunsany to write something for Dublin's Abbey Theatre, the most prominent center of Irish theatrical activity in the early twentieth century. The result was *The Glittering Gate* (1909), a one-act play that, like many of Dunsany's dramas, combines the realistic and the fantastic.

The "glittering gate" of the title is the fabled gate of heaven, but the surrounding landscape is composed of rocks and debris rather than clouds, and Saint Peter is nowhere to be seen. Two men, who in life had been burglars, approach the gate and find it locked, a cruel joke of the gods. The older man accepts the futility of trying to outmaneuver the gods, but the younger man attempts to pick the lock. He succeeds, only to be the victim of a crueler joke: there is only emptiness in heaven, accompanied by the gods' mocking laughter. Despite a small degree of scandal created by this suggestion of the emptiness of heaven, the play was generally well received.

Dunsany's next collection of stories was published in 1910. Its title, *A Dreamer's Tales,* is suggestive of the mood of most of the pieces, which tend to focus more on setting and feeling than on character and plot. Critics were not entirely dismissive in their estimation of the book. Many singled out "Idle Days on the Yann," about a dream-like river voyage inspired by the author's anticipated visit to Egypt, as one of Dunsany's most effective works. Central to this story is a feature often associated with science fiction, a "sense of wonder," and in *A Dreamer's Tales* Dunsany evokes this sense even in stories that are not overtly fantastic. For instance, in "The Beggars" the narrator is taught by the title characters to view "unromantic, dreary" London in a new light, even if the light is obscured by smoke: "Behold the smoke. The old coal-forests that have lain so long in the dark, and so long still, are dancing now and going back to the sun." Similarly, in "Blagdaross" a jumble of cast-off objects are imbued with life, and when one of them, an old rocking horse, is taken up by a young boy, the horse assumes something of its former glory. Such stories echo the sentiment expressed in his uncollected prose poem "Romance," published a year before *A Dreamer's Tales:* that the imagination, rather than being limited to the utterly fantastic, "has a way of touching quite common things."

Other stories in *A Dreamer's Tales* could easily be classified as horror or dark fantasy. Two related stories that fall into this category are "The Ghosts" and "Where the Tides Ebb and Flow." In the former the ghosts themselves do not depart substantially from conventional depictions of the departed, but what is striking about them are their companions, horrible creatures resembling dogs that embody the sins they committed while living. Similarly, in "Where the Tides Ebb and Flow" human sinfulness is incarnated, this time in the form of a corpse that is repeatedly unearthed by groups of evil men century after century.

As in *The Glittering Gate,* human hubris and the power of the gods are also central to Dunsany's 1911 play *The Gods of the Mountain,* first performed at the Haymarket Theatre in London. Seven beggars pretend to be gods, imitating the seven mountain gods rendered in jade in the village, but the joke is on them: the gods are real, and in turn they punish the beggars by transforming them into living, moving statues representing the false gods they pretended to be. Furthermore, other people, in punishment for their own transgressions, are forced to worship these false deities.

The Gods of the Mountain was a popular success and has been acclaimed by some critics as Dunsany's best play. A few months after its premiere, Frank Harris, writing for the *Academy,* said "It was far and away the most interesting dramatic experiment I have ever seen; for the first time in my life I understood how the terrible realism of the stage could be . . . used so as to make the unlikely probable and to clothe the fantastic with vivid life."

Another one-act play, *The Golden Doom* (1912), resembles much of Dunsany's fantastic fiction in its exotic orientalized setting and its elevated poetic language. Like his other fantastic plays up to this point, it too deals with human foibles and how the gods respond.

By 1912 Dunsany was sufficiently known to support the publication of a collection of his work, *Selections from the Writings of Lord Dunsany.* Yeats provided the preface of the book, another testament to Dunsany's growing reputation. For all of Yeats's admiration of Dunsany, however, he was not entirely uncritical; as he notes, "Not all of Dunsany's moods delight me, for he writes out of a careless abun-

dance"—a criticism of Dunsany that has been repeated more than once.

Also in 1912, Dunsany published another collection of fantastic stories, *The Book of Wonder.* Four years later he followed this volume with a similar collection, *Tales of Wonder* (1916), which was published in the United States as *The Last Book of Wonder.* Both books are similar to each other and different from Dunsany's previous collections in their use of humor, in particular a tone that somewhat mocks the seriousness of the high-fantasy tropes employed. At any rate, several of the stories are lighter rather than darker, as if the author is unable to treat such subjects seriously.

On a similar note, in 1912 Dunsany published two stories in the *Irish Review,* later collected in *Tales of Three Hemispheres* (1919), that cast a somewhat critical light on the enterprise of fantasy. They appear to be sequels to "Idle Days on the Yann." In "The Shop in Go-by Street" the narrator, in his efforts to return to the world he had visited before, finds a London shop where the back door is a portal to the fantastic realm. When he passes through it, however, he discovers his ruined boat. More time has passed in this realm, evidently, than in his own world. This experience, however, does not deter him from returning in "The Avenger of Perdóndaris." The shop in London takes him to this fantastic world again, but instead of returning to his own world through the same back door after assorted adventures, he chooses another door. He finds himself back in London—but not the London he originally left. First, he finds himself two thousand years in the future. Second, rather than becoming a futuristic city such as a science-fiction writer might envision, this London has instead reverted to a pastoral state. While such a world closely resembles Dunsany's own ideal, the narrator is tired of visiting what he calls "the Lands of Dream" and longs for "the fields we know."

This new tendency toward lightness in Dunsany's fantasy was later criticized by American horror writer H. P. Lovecraft, otherwise a great admirer of Dunsany's work. In a 15 November 1936 letter to fellow American fantasist Fritz Leiber, Lovecraft complained of Dunsany:

As he gained in age and sophistication, he lost in freshness and simplicity. He was ashamed to be uncritically naïve, and began to step aside from his tales and visibly smile at them even as they unfolded. Instead of remaining what the true fantastiste must be—a child in a child's world of dream—he became anxious to shew that he was really an adult good-naturedly pretending to be a child in a child's world. The hardening-up began to shew, I think, in *The Book of Wonder.* . . .

Lovecraft's interpretation, of course, is not the only possible one, either of Dunsany's motives or the nature of the "true fantastiste," and some readers would argue that these two collections add to Dunsany's accomplishment rather than marking the beginning of the end of his creative powers.

Moreover, these collections are not entirely light in tone. For instance, "The Distressing Tale of Thangrobrind the Jeweller" in *The Book of Wonder,* though not as distressing as the title suggests, involves some small-time crooks receiving their just punishment. Perhaps more disturbing is "The Coronation of Mr. Thomas Shap" in the same volume. A lowly clerk begins to imagine himself king of an imaginary land, and his mental life appeals to him so much more than his real one that he grows increasingly out of touch with reality, to the point that he must be institutionalized. The protagonist is actually happiest once he has completely succumbed to his fantasies.

"The City on Mallington Moor," collected in *Tales of Wonder,* also touches on the theme of illusion versus reality, along with Dunsany's more familiar theme of nature versus "civilization." The protagonist, weary of London life, has a vision of a better city, one closer to nature than the urban environment he knows. The vision vanishes, but for the man it was nonetheless real.

Tales of Wonder had been preceded in 1915 by *Fifty-One Tales,* a collection of short sketches and vignettes. *Fifty-One Tales,* though mostly composed of earlier-published works, is noteworthy for a few original stories, most of them quite short. As in *Time and the Gods,* some concern the nature of time. "The Raft-Builders," for instance, reads like a parable in which the writer's craft is compared to the building of rafts, and art is viewed as an effort to surpass the limitations of time. Even less subtly, "Nature and Time" is an allegory in which the two title concepts are personified and in which Dunsany returns to a favorite theme, the glories of nature and the blight of modern civilization. When Nature asks Time, "When will the fields come back and the grass for my children?" Time replies, "Soon, soon."

Dunsany strikes a similar note in *Fifty-One Tales* in "Prayer of the Flowers," in which the pagan god Pan comforts the personified flowers suffering from the pollution of the cities; he tells them, "Be patient a little, these things are not for long." This idea also emerges in a more realistic story, "The Workman," in which the ghost of a man who has died in an industrial accident says, "Why, yer bloomin' life 'ull go by like a wind . . . and yer 'ole silly civilization 'ull be tidied up in a few centuries."

Such stories embody a set of ideas that Dunsany had articulated earlier in a 1911 essay published in the *National Review* titled "Romance and the Modern Stage," in part a defense of his use of fantasy as a playwright. Thematically, the essay echoes William Wordsworth's 1807 poem "The World Is Too Much with Us," in which the speaker bemoans the distance of his civilization from nature and looks longingly back to an idealized past in which human beings enjoyed a closer communion both with nature and with the gods who animated nature. Similarly, Dunsany defends his dramas of gods and humanity by arguing that they are efforts to evoke such an idealized past, more pastoral than industrial.

In contrast to his evocative fantasy worlds, Dunsany, as an English peer with an Irish title, found himself caught up in the bitter politics of the day, as his unsuccessful bids for Parliament as a Conservative candidate early in the century attest. He did not involve himself extensively with Irish politics, however, beyond advocating a Unionist support of continued British control, and neither he nor his property were harmed in the political uprisings of the era, with the exception of what turned out to be a minor incident.

The year 1916 was particularly eventful for Dunsany. Following his mother's death he found himself in the uncomfortable position of suing his younger brother, Reginald, with whom he already had a strained relationship, over her estate, which left the two permanently estranged. Also, during the 1916 Easter Rebellion in Dublin, Dunsany as an officer of the Royal Inniskilling Fusiliers was attempting to assist another officer when he inadvertently led his men into enemy territory and received a minor facial wound. He was captured but came to no further harm, and he was released soon thereafter. Dunsany also saw action during World War I while in France in 1917. Later he served in the War Office in London, and after the Armistice he continued to serve with the Royal Inniskilling Fusiliers.

Dunsany's military experience stands in sharp contrast to how he normally spent his time. When not writing, attending to his duties as a landlord, or engaging in social and political reforms, he occupied himself with a variety of activities, including hunting at home and abroad in Africa, playing cricket, and playing chess, at which he excelled.

Sometimes Dunsany could make it appear that his literary efforts were offhand productions. For instance, he claimed to have written his 1916 one act play *A Night at an Inn* in one sitting in January 1912. Nevertheless, it was popular in its New York production. The plot concerns a conflict between a group of English ruffians and a group of

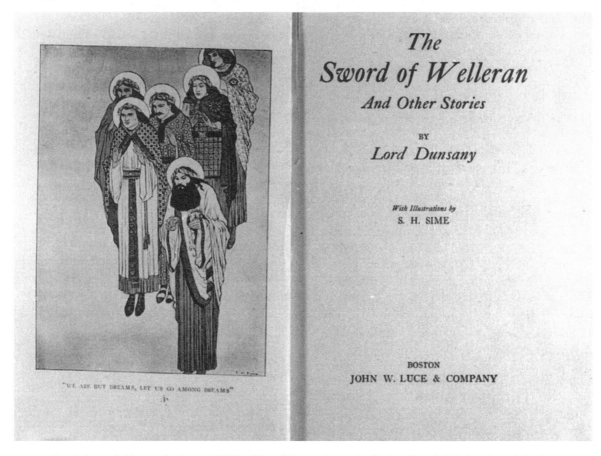

Frontispiece and title page for the 1916 U.S. edition of Dunsany's second collection of loosely linked stories and sketches.
The British edition appeared in 1908 (courtesy of Special Collections,
Thomas Cooper Library, University of South Carolina).

Indian priests and their idol, which turns out to be a god. Dunsany thus revives his stage effect of the living statue, originated in *The Gods of the Mountain*, and the play is also similar to his other fantastic dramas in its theme of human arrogance being rebuked by the greater power of the gods.

This theme is also part of Dunsany's 1919 play *The Laughter of the Gods*, which like *A Night at an Inn* debuted in the United States, where Dunsany was held in higher esteem as a dramatist than in England. In this play a king and his court receive a deserved comeuppance at the hands of the gods, though the actual story is not as serious as it sounds in summary. In fact, a contemporary review in *The Nation* praised the play as "robust and humorous, a humor that combines the intimacy of satire with the remoteness of irony."

The year 1919 also marked Dunsany's return to fantastic short fiction with the publication of *Tales of Three Hemispheres*. Among other works, Dunsany reprints "Idle Days on the Yann" and its sequels, "The Shop in Go-by Street" and "The Avenger of Perdóndaris." The volume was not well received, and

there is general critical consensus that by this time Dunsany had produced the short fantasies that secured his reputation in the field of fantastic literature, even though his career continued for decades later. It is worth noting, for instance, that later collections of Dunsany's fantasy–such as Lin Carter's *At the Edge of the World* (1970), *Beyond the Fields We Know* (1972), and *Over the Hills and Far Away* (1974), along with E. F. Bleiler's *Gods, Men, and Ghosts: The Best Supernatural Fiction of Lord Dunsany* (1972)–draw most of their stories from Dunsany's collections of the first and second decades of the twentieth century.

In his first autobiographical volume, *Patches of Sunlight* (1938), Dunsany himself seems to acknowledge a sense of frustration over the increasingly negative reception of his short stories and asserts that this decline pushed him into the writing of novels. Dunsany still had much to contribute to fantasy, both in his continued efforts for the stage and as he developed into a novelist. Furthermore, he sometimes introduced supernatural elements into otherwise realistic stories, such as those concerning his fictional

Joseph Jorkens, which developed an audience all their own from the 1930s to the 1950s.

Among Dunsany's dramatic efforts, his popular play *If* (1921), which ran for two hundred performances, is different from his others in subject and theme. Instead of dealing with human frailties contrasted with the ways of the gods, *If* involves a protagonist who, as a result of the intervention of a magician, finds himself the hero of a series of orientalized escapades. The ending of the play, however, does resemble similar moments in other fantastic dramas by Dunsany: the protagonist awakes, uncertain as to the reality of his adventures, and the play closes with the laughter of the magician, pleased with the results. Although the magician is not clearly presented as a god, he seems to be a figure of superior power toying with a weaker human being.

If owes a great deal to *The Thousand and One Nights,* as does Dunsany's first novel, *The Chronicles of Rodriguez* (1922). While the setting of the novel is Spain in its "Golden Age," the picaresque narrative is as indebted in its adventurous incidents to the Arabic classic as it is to influences closer to home, such as European romance and Miguel de Cervantes's *Don Quixote* (1605, 1615). The story concerns the oldest son of the Lord of the Valley of Arguento. When his father gives him a mandolin and a sword, as opposed to his father's realm, Don Rodriguez sets out on a series of adventures in search of a realm he can claim as his own.

Little of this plot extends beyond the conventions of adventure fiction until Don Rodriguez earns the trust of the King of Shadow Valley. At this point the narrative takes a sharp turn toward the fantastic. Permitted access to two magic windows, which look out upon the past and the future, Don Rodriguez views battles of the past and those to come. Neither panorama offers the worlds he thinks should exist, just as *Don Quixote* deflates romantic notions of chivalry. Don Rodriguez also befriends a magician, who enables him to travel to other planets. Such travel, however, is depicted in fantasy terms rather than those of science fiction.

Dunsany's next novel, *The King of Elfland's Daughter,* was published in 1924. It is set in a fictional medieval world that includes both human kingdoms and more fantastic realms, in particular Elfland. The story concerns a human prince, Alveric, in a kingdom that has as a neighbor the kingdom of Elfland. The daughter of the title is Lirazel, the princess of this realm, with whom Alveric falls in love after making his way through Elfland aided by a magic sword, given to him by a good witch. Lirazel reciprocates his feelings and returns with him to his kingdom, curious

about a world in which time passes rather than standing still. Despite their love, however, and the son they share, and despite the fascination that the inhabitants of Elfland typically have with the human world, she is miserable in the human world. Thus, when her father misses her and sends her a magic letter that, once read, returns her to her father's side, she is happy to go back to his magical kingdom. Realizing that his criticism of her failure to conform to the ways of humans helped to alienate her, the prince once more attempts to win her, although he finds the task much more difficult the second time. Much of the novel is given over to his efforts, aided by a ragtag band of comrades, and their adventures are described at great length and detail.

Finally, the couple is reunited–not through Alveric's efforts, but through the king of Elfland resolving the conflict, in part because his daughter misses her human family, in part because her son, Orion, misses her and has tired of the human world and its duties. Thus, the king simply merges Elfland and the human kingdom. The ending is not entirely happy, however, since the union of the human world and the fantastic world of Elfland marks the beginning of the end of the latter.

This last aspect of the plot of *The King of Elfland's Daughter* has been taken by many critics to be allegorical, signifying the loss of magic and enchantment as a result of the rise of a more mundane rationalistic worldview. In this reading of the novel, Dunsany is thought to be making a point common to his work: that the fantastic, though wonderful, cannot survive in the face of the modern world. In addition, it is noteworthy that the novel includes something found in other works of fantasy by Dunsany: a Christian opposition to the powers of faerie. In this work such opposition is safely contained, as later it is overthrown entirely in *The Blessing of Pan* (1927), but still Christianity is frequently equated with forces antagonistic to fantasy in Dunsany's fiction.

Even if critics do not fault the novel for its allegorical nature, some have claimed that Dunsany's second effort as a novelist fails in fictional terms. The descriptive and imaginative gifts that many have praised in his short fiction, these critics argue, do not serve him well in a longer form, and the book suffers from wordiness and excessive detail. In contrast, others assert that *The King of Elfland's Daughter* is among Dunsany's highest achievements.

Dunsany demonstrated greater control in his next novel, *The Charwoman's Shadow* (1926), partly because of its tighter plot. A young man, Ramon Alonzo, is apprenticed to a magician, and his kind heart is apparent not only from his desire to learn to

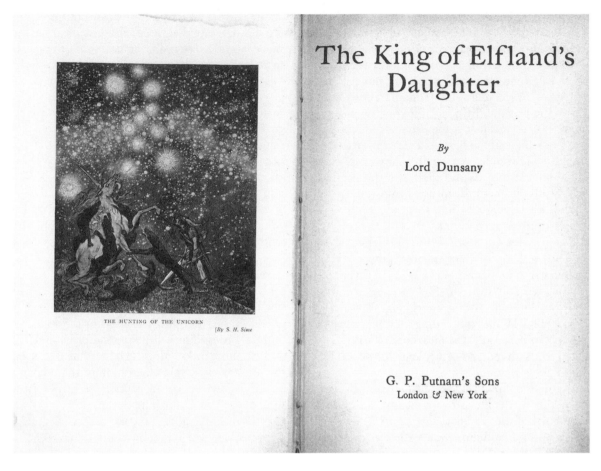

THE HUNTING OF THE UNICORN

[By S. H. Sime

The King of Elfland's Daughter

By

Lord Dunsany

G. P. Putnam's Sons
London & New York

*Frontispiece and title page for Dunsany's 1924 novel, about the love of a human prince and an elf princess
(Dacus Library, Winthrop University, Rock Hill, South Carolina)*

make gold for his sister's dowry (rather than for his own profit) but also from his desire to assist the wizard's charwoman, a woman hired to do domestic chores. She tells Ramon that, in exchange for immortality, as a young woman she had given away her shadow, whose loss she now laments. Besides the fact that she is now old and miserable and futilely wishes for death, Ramon learns another important reason for her grief: their shadows are not just shadows but constitute a part of their souls. This circumstance becomes more personal to Ramon when he too loses his shadow to the magician. The revelation about the nature of their shadows leads to the main part of the story, their concerted efforts to regain what they have lost.

The story becomes more interesting when Ramon makes the acquaintance of another magician, Raymond Lull, a character based on a real thirteenth-century mystic. Lull aids Ramon in mastering the magic words that open the casket in which the wizard keeps the shadows he has collected and that he uses for his own nefarious purposes. One of these shadows

is that of the old charwoman, but this shadow is still young and beautiful. Ramon falls in love with her shadow, and when the shadow is restored to the charwoman, she is transformed into the attractive young woman she was when she first gave it away. Of course, she and Ramon live happily ever after, and the powers of evil are banished.

The last play Dunsany wrote that included fantastic elements was *The Jest of Hahalaba* (1927). Once again he explores familiar dramatic territory, as the play involves a venal human being and how he is humbled by a deity. A theme similar to that of *The Jest of Hahalaba* informs Dunsany's next novel, *The Blessing of Pan* (1927), which also concerns the intrusion of the fantastic into the human world. In this work the intrusion comes in the form of Pan, who appears when Tommy Duffin, a farmer's son, begins playing the music of the goat-footed pastoral god. This occasion leads to a revival of the old pagan religion in Wolding, the village in Kent where the novel is set—an event much abhorred by the parish vicar, Elderick Anwrel. Just as in *The King of Elfland's Daugh-*

ter, in which a Christian element in the human realm objects to the magic of Elfland as dangerous, so too in this novel there is a conflict between two ancient religions, or to be more precise, two worldviews. The pagan faith, equated with nature, is presented more sympathetically, while the conventional Christianity represented by the vicar, while not depicted as evil, is related to the stultifying forces of civilization in the modern world. Anwrel tries to stop the new paganism, but in vain; his efforts are no match for the strength of the old new faith, which lures the inhabitants of Wolding to the old pagan places, and eventually he goes along with the crowd.

Dunsany's three-act play The Old Folk of the Centuries was not published until 1930, though it was written late in 1918. A witch's spell turns a Cockney boy into a butterfly. Rather than finding this situation a curse, however, the boy, once another spell has restored him to human form, convinces the witch to transform him into a butterfly again, explaining that its perceptions so transcend those of human beings that he would prefer to be returned to that state. Such a story is consistent with other Dunsany works in which the limitations of mundane human experiences are contrasted with a full openness to the wonders of nature or to the possibility of the supernatural.

The Blessing of Pan and The Old Folk of the Centuries are indicative of a new emphasis in Dunsany's work upon realistic, recognizable settings, even if many of the proceedings are fantastic or in various ways incredible. Another such work is The Curse of the Wise Woman (1933). While Dunsany had earlier avoided Irish settings and subjects in his fiction, for which he was often criticized by his contemporaries, he places this novel in a lavishly described contemporary Ireland whose beauty contrasts sharply with its religious and political divisions. The story may or may not be supernatural, depending on whether the protagonist, Mrs. Marlin, is a witch or merely a wise woman; but at any rate she successfully manages to prevent a British company from developing a peat bog in County Meath. Dunsany thus infuses politics into a novel that deals with contemporary concerns.

Also related to this trend toward the realistic and recognizable is The Travel Tales of Mr. Joseph Jorkens (1931), a collection of stories centered around the title character and his amazing exploits. Plied with whiskey, Jorkens willingly tells these tales at the Billiards Club. Most of the stories fall into the category of the tall tale, and the possibility is constantly raised that Jorkens may be lying, but many also border on the fantastic, such as his accounts of hunting unicorns or marrying mermaids. The jocular stories are uniformly entertaining and often rather funny, and the

popularity of the first volume led to other collections, including Jorkens Remembers Africa (1934), Jorkens Has a Large Whiskey (1940), The Fourth Book of Jorkens (1947), and Jorkens Borrows Another Whiskey (1954). Eventually Dunsany, ever prolific, composed 135 stories featuring Jorkens. Part of the popularity of these stories, besides their humor and imagination, stemmed from the fact that they were often based on Dunsany's own extensive travel experiences and thus bore an air of verisimilitude even when they played with the truth.

Dunsany rarely wrote anything resembling science fiction, but one story in The Travel Tales of Mr. Joseph Jorkens is worth noting in this regard. "Our Distant Cousins" concerns a trip to Mars in which the discoverer finds that the intelligent, human-like race he encounters does not rule the red planet but rather provides a horrible monster with its source of food, much like the Eloi are subject to the Morlocks in H. G. Wells's The Time Machine (1895). As with several of Dunsany's works of the 1930s, human beings are shown in a reduced light.

Another result of Dunsany's reading and extensive travels was his interest in non-Western religions. In particular, he was fascinated by the concept of reincarnation, especially for its fictional possibilities. One work to employ this religious belief in its narrative was My Talks with Dean Spanley (1936), a novelistic collection of stories about a man who recalls having lived as a dog in a former life. Whether the dean is recalling a past life or is simply intoxicated is left open, but his account makes the naturalness of life as a dog seem much preferable to life as a man.

My Talks with Dean Spanley, like the 1930 play The Old Folk of the Centuries, contrasts human and animal experience. So does Dunsany's radio play The Use of Man, published in Plays for Earth and Air (1937), although in a different sense. A man wonders why certain animals that seem to have no usefulness to human beings exist, which leads to a supernatural meeting of his spirit with the spirits of a collection of animals who similarly wonder, "What is the use of man?" Human beings are defended by the spirit of the dog, but the other animals are unconvinced until finally the mosquito, one of the creatures whose usefulness the man had questioned, asserts that humans are useful as food. In this story humans, rather than being granted dominion over the animals, are put into a much humbler place. So is the hunter in "Elephant Shooting," a story collected in Jorkens Has a Large Whiskey. While attempting to trap a wily elephant, the hunter finds himself caught by the elephant instead.

Other works in which Dunsany explores the relationship between humans and animals include his 1922 play Mr. Faithful, about a man who, needing

Dust jacket for Dunsany's 1951 novel, in which machines turn on their creators (courtesy of The Lilly Library, Indiana University)

work, takes a job as a watchdog, complete with canine actions; and the realistic *Rory and Bran* (1936), about a boy and his dog in Ireland. While neither work includes elements of the fantastic, they are still worth comparing to other Dunsany works that gauge human beings and their civilized ways by their relations with the natural world.

In 1938, at age sixty, Dunsany published the first volume of his autobiography, *Patches of Sunlight,* a volume which was followed by two more autobiographies, *While the Sirens Slept* (1944) and *The Sirens Wake* (1945). Although this volume is not a work of fantastic fiction, it is nonetheless important for scholars who seek a connection between the details of the author's life and the fiction that he wrote. For instance, in this book he cites several influences on the exotic settings of much of his fiction, including his father's stories about Egypt, his early reading of the Bible and Rudyard Kipling, his studies of ancient Greece and Rome, and his travels in northern and southern Africa.

Although *The Story of Mona Sheehy* (1939) is a realistic novel with a contemporary setting, it is noteworthy in Dunsany's canon as an antifantasy of sorts. An Irish girl believes that she is the child of fairies, but in fact she is the bastard offspring of a noblewoman and a farmer. Her mistaken assumptions about her origins create problems for her, as does the experience of working in a London advertising agency. While the story is considerably different from the fantasies for which the author is better known, the themes are similar: rural versus urban life, nature versus civilization, and simplicity versus sophistication.

During World War II Dunsany returned to Dunstall Priory in England as part of the Home Guard, hoping to assist if needed in capturing fallen German pilots or defending England against a possible invasion—neither of which happened, somewhat to Dunsany's disappointment at his inability to contribute something to the war effort. However, a threatened German invasion in 1941 forced Dunsany to flee Greece, where he and his wife had gone upon his appointment as Byron Chair of English Literature at the national university in Athens.

The Man Who Ate the Phoenix (1949) is one of Dunsany's later collections of short fiction. The title novella, like so many of Dunsany's stories, adroitly unites the realistic world of the present with a supernatural realm. In this case a man shoots what he believes to be a phoenix; however, the bird turns out to be an ordinary golden pheasant. Nonetheless, the experience renders the man open to the fantastic, as does his Irish heritage in general. Critics generally found "The Man Who Ate the Phoenix" a stronger work than the other stories in this book. A frequent remark was that by this point in his career Dunsany seemed to have exhausted his fictional resources and was merely repeating past successes but less effectively.

Dunsany returned to the theme of reincarnation in his 1950 novel *The Strange Journey of Colonel Polders,* although he develops the subject in much greater depth. The novel was published two years after India gained its independence from Great Britain, but its plot and characters are still rooted in the colonial experience, although Dunsany appears much more sympathetic to the East than the West. The latter is personified in the title character, a British officer who accepts colonialist notions of "the white man's burden" wholeheartedly. In the process, he runs afoul of a native religious leader, an adept.

From this point the plot echoes several other Dunsany fantasies in which a person is taught a valuable lesson at the hands of supernatural forces. In Colonel Polders's case the adept makes him experience a succession of lives through an accelerated cycle of repeated reincarnation, all of them animals ranging from large to small, from mammal to insect. Forced to see the world from a variety of different perspectives, the arrogant Westerner is led to adopt a humbler attitude toward others and his place in the great scheme of things. Moreover, as in *The Old Folk of the Centuries* and *My Talks with Dean Spanley,* he finds animal life to be much more pleasant than his regimented human existence.

Apart from his more mainstream works, Dunsany is typically known as a fantasist, and his anti-modern sentiments did not incline him much toward science fiction. One late novel, *The Last Revolution* (1951), however, stands on the border between fantasy and science fiction, even though its ideas continue to parallel the general nostalgia of his work. *The Last Revolution* follows a theme found in many other works of science fiction—namely, machines turning against those who created them, a theme with science-fiction roots that extend at least as far back as Mary Shelley's *Frankenstein* (1818) and fantastic roots that go even further back. In Dunsany's novel the story is not much different: machines of various kinds assume life and sentience and turn on their human makers. Despite its conventionality within the context of science fiction, however, the novel is noteworthy within Dunsany's work for its elaboration of an important personal theme—the loss of a better way of life under the steamroller of "progress"—through a different type of story for the author.

Dunsany remained active until the end of his life, writing extensively and traveling often. He died at age seventy-nine of appendicitis on 25 October 1957, leaving behind a large body of uncollected work in addition to his dozens of published books.

Like the work of many other British fantasists of the first half of the twentieth century, Lord Dunsany's fantasy stories and plays serve both as an evocation of an earlier, more idyllic age and as a critique of the modern world. Such a world, informed by greed, machinery, and convention, is shown as ugly and lifeless, especially in contrast with the vivid fantasy realms of Dunsany's imagination. Yet, these worlds are not entirely benign, and individuals within these realms are just as capable of venality as their contemporary counterparts. In this way Dunsany's fantasy also critiques human nature in addition to modern life.

Letters:

Arthur C. Clarke and Lord Dunsany: A Correspondence, edited by Keith Allen Daniels (San Francisco: Anamnesis Press, 1998).

Interviews:

Clayton Hamilton, "Lord Dunsany: Personal Impressions," *Bookman* (New York), 50 (February 1920): 537–542;

Bertrand de La Salle, "Une Visite à Lord Dunsany," *Revue de Paris,* 8 (August 1956): 39–43.

Bibliography:

S. T. Joshi and Darrell Schweitzer, *Lord Dunsany: A Bibliography* (Metuchen, N.J. & London: Scarecrow Press, 1993).

Biographies:

Hazel Littlefield, *Lord Dunsany: King of Dreams—A Personal Portrait* (New York: Exposition Press, 1959);

Mark Amory, *Biography of Lord Dunsany* (London: Collins, 1972).

References:

Angelee S. Anderson, "Lord Dunsany: The Potency of Words and the Wonder of Things," *Mythlore* 15 (Autumn 1988): 10–12;

Mike Ashley, "Lord Dunsany," in his *Who's Who in Horror and Fantasy Fiction* (London: Elm Tree Books, 1977), pp. 70–72;

Edward Hale Bierstadt, *Dunsany the Dramatist* (Boston: Little, Brown, 1917; revised, 1919);

E. F. Bleiler, "Lord Dunsany," in his *The Guide to Supernatural Fiction* (Kent, Ohio: Kent State University Press, 1983), pp. 165–172;

Ernest A. Boyd, "Lord Dunsany—Fantastiste," in his *Appreciations and Depreciations: Irish Literary Studies* (London: Talbot Press, 1917), pp. 71–100;

William Chislett, "New Gods for Old," in his *Moderns and Near-Moderns* (New York: Grafton, 1928), pp. 171–188;

L. Sprague de Camp, "Two Men in One: Lord Dunsany," in his *Literary Swordsmen and Sorcerers: The Makers of Heroic Fantasy* (Sauk City, Wis.: Arkham House, 1976), pp. 48–63;

Max Duperray, "'The Land of Unlikely Events': L'Irlande de Lord Dunsany," *Etudes Irlandaises,* 4 (1975): 31–37;

Duperray, "Lord Dunsany Revisited," *Studies in Weird Fiction,* 13 (Summer 1993): 10–14;

Duperray, "Lord Dunsany: Sa place dans une eventuelle litterature fantastique," *Etudes Irlandaises,* 9 (December 1984): 81–88;

Grace Eckley, "The Short Fiction of Lord Dunsany," in *Survey of Modern Fantasy Literature,* 5 volumes, edited by Frank N. Magill (Englewood Cliffs, N.J.: Salem, 1983), pp. 1507–1510;

John Wilson Foster, "A Dreamer's Tales: The Stories of Lord Dunsany," in his *Fictions of the Irish Literary*

Revival: A Changeling Art (Syracuse, N.Y.: Syracuse University Press, 1987), pp. 291–298;

Martin Gardner, "Lord Dunsany," in *Supernatural Fiction Writers,* 2 volumes, edited by E. F. Bleiler (New York: Scribners, 1985), volume 1, pp. 471–478;

Josephine Hammond, "Wonder and the Playwright: Lord Dunsany," *Personalist* (January 1922): 5–30;

Vernon Hyles, "Lord Dunsany: The Geography of the Gods," in *More Real Than Reality: The Fantastic in Irish Literature and the Arts,* edited by Donald E. Morse and Csilla Bertha (Westport, Conn.: Greenwood Press, 1991), pp. 211–218;

Ben P. Indick, "Beyond the Fields: The Theatre of Lord Dunsany," *Studies in Weird Fiction,* 22 (Winter 1998): 1–13;

S. T. Joshi, "Lord Dunsany: The Career of a *Fantastiste,*" in his *The Weird Tale: Arthur Machen, Lord Dunsany, Algernon Blackwood, M. R. James, Ambrose Bierce, H. P. Lovecraft* (Austin: University of Texas Press, 1990), pp. 42–86;

Joshi, *Lord Dunsany: Master of the Anglo-Irish Imagination* (Westport, Conn.: Greenwood Press, 1995);

Ursula K. Le Guin, "From Elfland to Poughkeepsie," in her *The Language of the Night: Essays on Fantasy and Science Fiction,* edited by Susan Wood (New York: Putnam, 1979), pp. 83–96;

Jared C. Lobdell, "The Man Who Didn't Write Fantasy: Lord Dunsany and the Self-Deprecatory Tradition in English Light Fiction," *Extrapolation,* 35 (Spring 1994): 33–42;

H. P. Lovecraft, "Lord Dunsany and His Work," in his *Miscellaneous Writings,* edited by Joshi (Sauk City, Wis.: Arkham House, 1995), pp. 104–112;

Linda Pashka, "'Hunting for Allegories' in the Prose Fantasy of Lord Dunsany," *Studies in Weird Fiction,* 12 (Spring 1993): 19–24;

George Brandon Saul, "Strange Gods and Far Places: The Short Stories of Lord Dunsany," *Arizona Quarterly,* 19 (Autumn 1963): 197–210;

Darrell Schweitzer, *Pathways to Elfland: The Writings of Lord Dunsany* (Philadelphia: Owlswick, 1989);

Odell Shepard, "A Modern Myth-Maker," in his *The Joys of Forgetting: A Book of Bagatelles* (Boston: Houghton Mifflin, 1929), pp. 30–47;

Peter Tremayne, "Lord Dunsany (1878–1957)," in his *Irish Masters of Fantasy* (Postmarnock, Ireland: Wolfhound Press, 1979), pp. 205–210.

Papers:

A selection of Lord Dunsany's letters to Mary Lavin is housed in the manuscript collection of the library of the State University of New York at Binghamton.

E. R. Eddison

(24 November 1882 – 18 August 1945)

Darren Harris-Fain
Shawnee State University

BOOKS: *The Worm Ouroboros: A Romance* (London: Cape, 1922; New York: Boni, 1926);

Styrbiorn the Strong (London: Cape, 1926; New York: Boni, 1926);

Mistress of Mistresses: A Vision of Zimiamvia (London: Faber & Faber, 1935; New York: Dutton, 1935);

A Fish Dinner in Memison (New York: Dutton, 1941; New York & London: Ballantine, 1968);

The Mezentian Gate (Plaistow, U.K.: Curwen, 1958; New York: Ballantine, 1969).

Collection: *Zimiamvia: A Trilogy,* edited by Paul Edmund Thomas (New York: Dell, 1992).

OTHER: Philip Sidney Nairn, *Poems, Letters, and Memories of Philip Sidney Nairn,* edited by Eddison (London: Privately printed, 1916);

Snorri Sturluson, *Egil's Saga,* translated, with an introduction and notes, by Eddison (Cambridge: Cambridge University Press, 1930; New York: Greenwood Press, 1968).

Though not as prolific as many of his contemporaries in British fantasy between the wars, E. R. Eddison is routinely singled out as one of the most significant contributors to fantasy literature during this period on the strength of his first novel, *The Worm Ouroboros: A Romance* (1922), and his uncompleted Zimiamvia trilogy. His work was praised by writers as diverse as C. S. Lewis and H. P. Lovecraft, and he is regularly compared with near-contemporaries such as Lord Dunsany and J. R. R. Tolkien. Like Tolkien, Eddison created a secondary world that, despite its fantastic nature, comes to vibrant life for the reader. His creation of this world was, like Tolkien's, informed by his studies in northern European mythology and folklore—in particular the Icelandic sagas. Some critics have even suggested that, for all Tolkien's gifts and his importance in fantasy literature, Eddison is the greater talent. In a letter of 24 June 1957 to Caroline Everett regarding Eddison's influence on *The Lord of the Rings* (1954–1955), Tolkien himself said that, despite some

E. R. Eddison

reservations about Eddison's work and rejecting the idea of influence, he considered Eddison "the greatest and most convincing writer of 'invented worlds' that I have read."

Eric Rucker Eddison (some sources render it "Rücker") was born on 24 November 1882 in the village of Adel in Yorkshire, which has since become a suburb of Leeds; he had one brother, Colin Rucker Eddison. Their parents, Octavius and Helen (Rucker) Eddison, instilled in them a love of literature that especially manifested itself in "Ric's" childhood interests. For instance, he formed a lifelong friendship with Arthur Ransome, who later became a journalist and children's book author, and the two collaborated on puppet plays. Early on, however, Eddison seemed to realize that he would earn his living in a way other than through writing. Like many young men of his class at the time, he received a privileged education preparatory to a career in the civil service. As a student at Eton College, the most prestigious of England's public schools, Eddison wrote his first stories, in which he created Horius Parry, who later emerges as a villain in Eddison's Zimiamvia trilogy. Other youthful literary efforts presage his later composition of *The Worm Ouroboros* in their characters and events. In addition, while at Eton he discovered the Norse literary tradition. There he taught himself Icelandic in order to read the literature in the original language.

After Eton he attended Trinity College of Oxford University, and by the time he completed his education in 1905 he had mastered Greek, Latin, and French in addition to Icelandic. He read the works of ancient Greek poets Homer and Sappho, two admitted influences on his work—as was his later reading of Elizabethan prose and the contemporary novels of Joseph Conrad. In 1906 Eddison joined the Board of Trade in London. He began his career as a clerk and remained in the Board of Trade until his retirement in 1938, by which time he had worked his way to a position as deputy overseas comptroller. He also served for a time on the Council for Art and Industry. After his retirement he moved his family from London to Marlborough.

Little else is known of the other details of Eddison's life outside his literary career, except that in 1909 he married Winifred Grace Henderson, and the couple had one daughter, Jean Gudrun Rucker Eddison, later Latham. Several scholars have noted that Eddison's competent yet routine professional life and placid personal life were the calm surface beneath which stirred his more exciting imaginative life. Other commentators have added that this state of affairs correlates well with Eddison's rejection of the modern world around him.

Eddison's first foray into publication was a privately published collection of assorted writings by Philip Sidney Nairn, which Eddison edited in 1916 and in which he included a hundred-page memoir of his friend, a poet who died in World War I. The remainder of Eddison's literary work is of a quite different character, related either to Norse legend or purely fantastic worlds.

Eddison's first and best-known novel, *The Worm Ouroboros,* was published in 1922. The story is set in what Tolkien later termed a "secondary world"—that is, a fictional, fantastic realm—although the setting bears a strong resemblance to northern Europe in the days of the Vikings. However, *The Worm Ouroboros* is not an historical novel, since much of its content is imaginary rather than strictly realistic. In a 2 March 1933 letter to fellow writer E. Hoffman Price, Lovecraft said of the novel, "It weaves its own atmosphere, and lays down its own laws of reality."

This characteristic relates to the romantic nature of the novel. The world of *The Worm Ouroboros* is lavishly depicted, both in language and in imagery, and it is a world of splendor and spectacle. It is also a world of magic. Thus, the book is a romance, with its exotic setting and its elements of the supernatural. In many ways it is a continuation of the tradition of the fantasy romance as practiced in the late nineteenth century by William Morris. It should be noted, though, that Eddison does not romanticize his subject. As Lewis observes in his short essay "A Tribute to E. R. Eddison" (1958), Eddison employs a "precise blend of hardness and luxury, of lawless speculation and sharply realised detail, of the cynical and the magnanimous." The same could be said of the striking illustrations for the novel by Keith Henderson, Eddison's wife's brother, which assist in bringing the narrative to life.

The Worm Ouroboros is also romantic in its writing. Like that of Dunsany in much of his work, Eddison's style in *The Worm Ouroboros* and his other fantasies is deliberately archaic in diction, spelling, and construction. The vividly descriptive language is consciously elegant, emulating the elevated, often complex style appropriate to epic and common to the ornate scaldic poetry of Norse literature from the tenth century until its attempted revival by Snorri Sturluson in the thirteenth century. In addition, some commentators have suggested that Eddison's style, though unusual, is also indebted to the Elizabethan prose writers he read as a young man. Moreover, like Dunsany, Eddison believed that a more "mundane" style would clash with his tales of other worlds and times; a distinctive style, these writers thought, was best for a distinctive type of fiction. As Ursula K. Le Guin puts it in her essay "From Elfland to Poughkeepsie" (1973), "He really did write Elizabethan prose . . . . His style is totally artificial, but it is never faked. If you love language for its own sake he is irresistible."

While *The Worm Ouroboros* is a romance in its mode, it is also epic in its story, which involves great battles and noble warriors whose abilities often appear beyond human possibility. The story is somewhat Homeric in character—in his introduction to the 1952 Dutton edition Orville Prescott describes it as a modern *Iliad*—but more specifically, it resonates with overtones of northern European legend. The worldview of these characters parallels that of the heroes of Norse and Anglo-Saxon legend, as in *Beowulf*. It is a man's world, with a hierarchical system of clans and related loyalties—a world in which warriors strive to become heroes, seeking power for their lords and glory and fame for themselves.

The novel begins in a realistic setting, an English country house, with a realistic character, a man named Edward Lessingham; but soon things become strange. The house includes a magical Lotus Room that allows a person who sleeps there to travel to other worlds. Lessingham is thus transported to Mercury, but the reader soon realizes that this Mercury is a planet closer to myth than to science. Thus, Eddison introduces the narrative through a framing device that is somewhat awkward; however, this frame is quickly dropped—Lessingham becomes an unseen observer of events and is not mentioned past the second chapter—as the real action of the novel unfolds.

This action concerns the many kingdoms of Eddison's fictional Mercury, among them Goblinland, Impland, and Pixeyland, and especially Demonland and Witchland, whose conflict is the focus of the novel, along with the related quest of Lord Juss of Demonland. Lessingham arrives in Lord Juss's castle, where a delegation from King Gorice XI of Witchland has come asserting the rule of Witchland over Demonland and all the other kingdoms of this world. Lord Juss, insulted by this declaration along with the failure of Witchland to assist in his successful war against the Ghouls, refuses to bow down to King Gorice; and Lord Juss's brother, the equally aristocratic Goldry Bluszco, challenges King Gorice to individual combat and slays him. Thus begins the war between Witchland and Demonland.

Gorice's successor, King Gorice XII, vows revenge and turns to magic, calling forth the "worm" Ouroboros—a powerful dragon that, like its mythic namesake on Earth, devours its own tail. Witchland attacks the noble warriors of Demonland, and Goldry is missing at the end of the battle. Uncertain at first whether his brother has been killed or taken captive, Lord Juss learns in a dream that Goldry is held prisoner, in a magical state of enchantment, in Impland.

Accompanied by an impulsive aristocrat of his court, Brandoch Daha, Lord Juss sets off in search of his brother. However, he and Brandoch face several obstacles and dangers along the way. They have the good fortune to encounter Queen Sophonisba, who has resided on a mountain called Koshtra Belorn for more than two hundred years, ever youthful, since she was carried there by magic at age seventeen. There she tells the two journeyers that Goldry can be freed from his state of enchantment by a hippogriff, a mythological beast, part griffin, part horse, that is real in this world.

Dust jacket for Eddison's 1926 novel, about a Viking prince who tries to wrest the Swedish throne from his uncle

Lord Juss and Brandoch are distracted from their quest when the warriors of Witchland invade Demonland. Although the forces of Witchland devastate Lord Juss's land, his return prevents the enemy's victory. Once the threat has been laid to rest, Lord Juss again travels to Impland in search of his lost brother. This time he succeeds, and Goldry returns with him to Demonland and aids him in invading Witchland. The victory of Demonland is secured when King Gorice XII desperately attempts to stave off the Demon forces by using magic, only to be destroyed by it.

Even though the Demons are the heroes of *The Worm Ouroboros* and the Witches are the villains, it should be noted that the major players of both sides at least act out of the strength of their convictions. Thus, the warriors of Demonland relish their victory in part because their opponents were worthy foes. In contrast, Lord Gro, adviser to King Gorice XII, lacks such firm convictions. Having deserted his native Goblinland to serve Gorice, he again shifts allegiances once the forces of Witchland are in trouble, this time to the Demons. He does so not only to save his own skin but also because of his love for Lady Mevrian of Demonland, sister of Brandoch Daha. He ultimately pays for his treachery.

By the end of the novel, peace has been achieved. However, like Odysseus in Alfred Tennyson's poem "Ulysses," the victorious warriors are uncomfortable with such a peace, feeling fully alive only in the midst of conflict. Queen Sophonisba, who has joined their celebration, then offers to intercede with the gods and give the combatants the opportunity to relive the conflict. As they agree to a continuation of their adventures, they learn that the enemies whom they have killed have been magically returned to life, and the war resumes exactly where it began, with the arrival of King Gorice XI's delegation. The plot thus comes full circle.

The circular structure of the plot relates to the central symbol of the title of the book. In ancient Greek and Egyptian mythology, Ouroboros was a serpent (or "worm," to use a medieval term) depicted as simultaneously eating its own tail and being reborn from its own mouth. As such, the serpent symbolized circularity, eternity, and interrelatedness. Similarly, in Eddison's novel the warriors find themselves at the end where they were in the beginning, but the title suggests that this outcome is the nature of things, lest the reader believe that this conclusion points to the futility of their efforts and their lives. The dragon named Ouroboros plays only a minor role in the novel, but as a symbol it helps to define the work.

The Worm Ouroboros was warmly received by readers and critics alike—in part, no doubt, because of Eddison's affection for and ability with materials quite different from the realist or modernist novels of the day, even though readers in the early 1920s were doubtless reminded of the recent world war by Eddison's depictions of the carnage of battle. Among the admirers of the book was the American fantasist James Branch Cabell. Positive comments tended to focus on the imaginative qualities of the novel, with some readers admiring the style as well. Others noted flaws in the book, among them stylistic inconsistencies and plotting problems such as excessive complexity, digressions, slow pacing, and temporal gaps.

One other problem some readers have with the novel concerns the names Eddison employs. In his 1957 letter to Everett, for example, Tolkien wrote, "I thought his nomenclature slipshod and often inept." As Paul Edmund Thomas observes in his extensive introduction to the 1991 Dell edition of the novel, the reason behind the jumble of names as varied as Goldry Bluszco, Spitfire, Brandoch Daha, and Fax Fay Faz is that "many of the characters, episodes, and places of *Ouroboros* were born in Eddison's childhood, and even though he wrote the novel in his late thirties, he maintained the names that he had invented as a boy." This claim is supported by a piece of juvenilia found among Eddison's papers in the Bodleian Library at Oxford University: "The Book of Drawings," dated 1892, which includes fifty-nine drawings of assorted characters who appear thirty years later in *The Worm Ouroboros*.

In his next novel, *Styrbiorn the Strong* (1926), Eddison drew upon his extensive knowledge of Norse history and legend to create a fictionalized presentation of Viking life—in particular, the life and varied adventures of Styrbiorn Starki, the prince of Sweden who died in 983 trying to wrest the throne from his uncle. Although *Styrbiorn the Strong* did not receive the same amount of attention as *The Worm Ouroboros* in the 1920s, nor has it since, many who have read the book have been impressed by how Eddison brings a distant world that few know much about to life—again assisted by Henderson's illustrations.

Eddison's next book also resulted from his scholarship in Norse literature: a 1930 translation from the Icelandic of Sturluson's *Egil's Saga,* published by the Cambridge University Press. More historical literature than fantasy, *Egil's Saga* reports on the various blood feuds among families in Iceland a few centuries before the original composition of the book in the twelfth and thirteenth centuries. As with *Styrbiorn the Strong,* there is nothing supernatural or fantastic; although both books possess a sense of otherworldliness simply because of their subject matter, it is treated realistically in both.

Eddison's last three books make up a trilogy that, though uncompleted, cements his reputation in the history of fantasy literature and complements his achievement in *The Worm Ouroboros,* although the trilogy is considerably different in tone if similar in style. The Zimiamvia books are *Mistress of Mistresses: A Vision of Zimiamvia* (1935), *A Fish Dinner in Memison* (1941), and the posthumously published *The Mezentian Gate* (1958); the trilogy was also published in a 985-page omnibus edition as *Zimiamvia* in 1992.

The first published volume in the trilogy, *Mistress of Mistresses,* introduces readers to the fantasy realm of Zimiamvia. As is often the case in fantasy series, however, in his later books set in this world the author went back to an earlier period in the world's "history." Consequently, the events of *Mistress of Mistresses* occur later in the chronology of the trilogy than the events of the other two books. It is possible, though, for a reader to begin the trilogy with this volume with little confusion.

What confusion the reader does encounter coming to *Mistress of Mistresses* for the first time stems not from problems of chronology but rather from the complex plot and the fantastic strangeness of Eddison's fictional Zimiamvia, once more illustrated by Henderson. The reader familiar with *The Worm Ouroboros* will already have heard of Zimiamvia, which is briefly mentioned in that novel, but nothing there prepares the reader for its full-blown reality in this first book of the trilogy.

While the Vikings believed in Valhalla, a home in the gods' realm of Asgard set aside for slain warriors, the warriors of *The Worm Ouroboros* have as their equivalent Zimiamvia, described there as a place "the blessed souls do inhabit . . . of the dead that be departed, even they that were dead upon the earth and did great deeds when they were living." In Valhalla, it was believed, warriors fought by day and feasted by night; likewise, Zimiamvia is no peaceful, static otherworld. If anything, it resembles an altered yet recognizable version of Renaissance Europe. The comparisons with the Viking conception of Valhalla end there, however, since Zimiamvia possesses a substantiality lacking in most notions of an afterlife. In fact, Zimiamvia is presented as a secondary world as detailed as the Mercury of *The Worm Ouroboros*.

The convoluted plot of *Mistress of Mistresses* bears out the dynamic nature of Zimiamvia, further complicated by the fact that, as in *The Worm Ouroboros* to a lesser degree, characters undergo different incarnations. In *Mistress of Mistresses,* for instance, sometimes a single character experiences more than one incarnation, at times even simultaneously.

In addition, while the action of *The Worm Ouroboros* is almost entirely confined to Eddison's otherworldly Mercury, events in the trilogy are not limited to Zimiamvia. Instead, this particular alternate world is related to and interacts with the real world of the reader. Characters sometimes cross between the two realities, and there are other ways in which the inhabitants of each world show an awareness of the otherworld. For instance, the English the Zimiamvians speak strongly resembles the early modern English of the Elizabethan Age, and they occasionally employ Greek, Latin, Italian, and French. Furthermore, at times characters in Zimiamvia quote from literature of the classical and Renaissance periods.

While Edward Lessingham plays a relatively insignificant role in *The Worm Ouroboros,* he is much more important in *Mistress of Mistresses*—which might seem odd at first, since at the beginning of the novel he is dead. Before his death he managed to establish a kingdom of his own on an island north of Norway, and just before the Norwegian government arrived to put an end to the affair, he died peacefully. The novel opens with a friend sitting by the coffin and being joined by a woman who was Lessingham's companion.

After she speaks to the friend of Zimiamvia, the story cuts to this otherworld.

Zimiamvia, the reader comes to learn, is composed of three kingdoms, which in turn are composed of many small towns that function fairly independently. Apparently Zimiamvia resides in a portion of the same Mercury as the events of *The Worm Ouroboros,* and the three kingdoms are placed in a vertical column: Fingiswold in the north, Rerek in the middle, and Meszria in the south. All three are bounded by mountains, ocean, and another realm to the far north.

The story in Zimiamvia also begins with a death: that of King Mezentius, who had brought unity to the three kingdoms—a unity that is lost with his passing. Confusion reigns, both within the kingdoms and as to the matter of who will succeed him. He had two children by his wife (now deceased), Queen Rosma: the prince Styllis and the princess Antiope. He also had a son, named Barganax, with his beloved mistress, Amalie, the duchess of Memison. The late king's legitimate children are either unable or unwilling to assume power, and his viceroy in Rerek, Vicar Horius Parry, has designs on the throne. The vicar is aided by his nephew, the reborn Edward Lessingham, who appears as a young man and remembers little of his previous existence. This situation leads to a series of courtly intrigues as Lessingham aids his Zimiamvian uncle's machinations. In particular, Lessingham finds himself and the bastard Barganax in a relationship of conflict suffused with mutual respect for each other's abilities, similar to how the Demons regard their enemies, the Witches, in *The Worm Ouroboros*.

Lessingham, like the other main characters in the trilogy, is indeed blessed with abilities, in both his earthly and Zimiamvian guises. The English Lessingham is almost superhuman in his accomplishments, which range from warfare and politics to the arts and letters. In Zimiamvia, he truly is a superman. As L. Sprague de Camp explains, "He is the sword-and-sorcery hero *par excellence,* making most of the heroes of the genre look like oafs and simpletons. He is the man of the Renaissance squared. . . . he is (we may suppose) an idealization of his creator—the man the author would like to have been."

Lessingham's foil, Barganax, is also important in the other main story line of *Mistress of Mistresses,* a pair of romantic subplots involving him and Fiorinda on the one hand and Lessingham and Antiope, who later becomes queen with Lessingham as her manipulative regent, on the other. More significant than the love stories, perhaps, is what these characters embody, both in the world of the novel and in Eddison's philosophy. First, Fiorinda is an incarnation of the woman who meets the dead Lessingham's friend at the beginning of the book and speaks to him of Zimiamvia. In addition, both women (the same woman in two guises, actually) are avatars of a figure Eddison referred to as the Goddess. All women, Eddison explains, share in the nature of the Goddess, just as all men share in the nature of the God, but the degree to which women and men do so and are aware that they do so varies. In Fiorinda's case, she is fully the Goddess, incarnated in human form. Antiope is also an incarnation of the Goddess, but she is unaware of this fact—just as Barganax and Lessingham, both of them different manifestations of the God, do not truly realize their divinity. The two women stand in sharp contrast: the dark-haired Fiorinda is self-confident and manipulative, while the blonde Antiope is gentle and innocent.

In addition to these gods in human form are the demigods who populate *Mistress of Mistresses*. The most important are the aides and servants of the main characters. They have human roles to play, but they are also manifested as magicians, animals, or nature spirits at various times. One such figure, Doctor Vandermast, serves as Barganax's secretary and Fiorinda's tutor, but he is also a magician who plays a key role in the story; the Spinoza-quoting magician may also be an incarnation of Lessingham's human friend, a philosopher, at the beginning of the novel.

At any rate, Doctor Vandermast clearly has a connection to the mundane world. At one point there is a reference to one of his creations, a so-called House of Peace. From its description, it clearly resembles Lessingham's house, with its Lotus Room from which he launched himself to Mercury in *The Worm Ouroboros*. In Zimiamvia, Lessingham and Antiope come across Vandermast's House of Peace, which spurs their memories of their earthly existence: he as Edward Lessingham; she as his late wife, Mary.

Although the central characters are actually gods—for instance, conventional time holds no mastery over them, and some of the most confusing scenes in the novel involve extensive sequences that happen in the blink of an eye in "normal" time—they behave much like human beings, even if Eddison clearly presents them as larger than life even in their human mode. Also, in their human forms they can die, as some of them do as the plot twists and turns in its political mode. The reborn Lessingham in Zimiamvia is killed, for instance, only to be promised yet another incarnation.

The story in the next published book in the trilogy, *A Fish Dinner in Memison,* is less complex than that of the first, lacking the political intrigues of *Mistress of Mistresses,* but it, too, spans both the real world and the world of Zimiamvia. As a prequel to *Mistress of Mistresses,* it presents readers with background on some of the characters of the first novel. For instance, the courtship of Lessingham and his wife, Mary, is detailed, and one of the interesting things about this portion of the novel is Eddison's use of the modern English idiom, as opposed to the more antiquated style of his fantasies. King Mezentius, dead at the beginning of *Mistress of Mistresses,* is also featured in this novel.

The end of the book relates an extended dinner conversation, part of which involves what the participants would do if they were gods. In the process, Mezentius learns that he possesses godlike powers, and Fiorinda asks him to create a world unlike their own. He does so easily, making a world captured in miniature above their table. According to Fiorinda's specifications, it is a world of natural laws devoid of magic. In point of fact, it is the reader's world. In a mere half an hour over dinner in Zimiamvia, the familiar world of the reader passes through eons of prehistory and history up until the twentieth century, at which point King Mezentius and his son's lover, Fiorinda, inhabit it as human beings. As though the various incarnations and crossovers of *Mistress of Mistresses* were not enough to challenge the reader, in occupying this created world Mezentius and Fiorinda become none other than Edward and Mary Lessingham.

Although it is unlikely that Eddison had Hinduism in mind, a useful parallel to understand part of what Eddison is doing in this novel is to consider that in Hinduism, there are simultaneously many gods and one god, who presents himself as thousands of different gods. Similarly, Eddison seems to be suggesting that there are a variety of characters and at the same time only two, male and female, manifestations of the God and the Goddess.

A Fish Dinner in Memison is the most philosophical work in the Zimiamvia trilogy, but the last volume, *The Mezentian Gate,* comes close. The book was uncompleted at Eddison's death in 1945, but he had completely outlined the story and finished two-fifths of it before he died; his brother, Colin, and his friend George Rostrevor Hamilton finally assembled it for publication by Eddison's wife in unfinished form in 1958. The impetus behind it, Eddison claimed in his introduction to the work, was a "searching curiosity" about Zimiamvia, his own created world, and an effort to settle questions left unanswered in the earlier two volumes. Here he develops even more background on King Mezentius, taking readers back to his childhood and ahead to the events prior to his death. What he was unable to complete is present in an outline and notes.

What narrative exists in *The Mezentian Gate* focuses on King Mezentius. In *A Fish Dinner in Memison* he learns that he is no mere mortal but rather a god-like being, and in that novel such knowledge leads him to question the worth of all human enterprise. In this book he considers using his divine powers to destroy his world, including himself. However, his relationships with his lover and their son lead him away from such an action, and instead he chooses only his own death, with which *Mistress of Mistresses* begins, as he knowingly allows his wife to poison him. Even so, given his god-like status, death for King Mezentius is only temporary.

As with *The Worm Ouroboros,* the narrative structure of the Zimiamvia trilogy is circular. However, the trilogy does not repeat the notion of a closed circle of time found in Eddison's first novel. Instead, the trilogy begins chronologically with *A Fish Dinner in Memison* as King Mezentius realizes his true nature. Then the story continues into *The Mezentian Gate,* which culminates with his death and Lessingham's arrival–which is where the action of *Mistress of Mistresses* picks up. Thus, while the narrative of *The Worm Ouroboros* could be represented by a simple circle, that of the Zimiamvia trilogy is more like a Mobius strip.

Even though there is a fair amount of action in the Zimiamvia trilogy, it stands in contrast to *The Worm Ouroboros* in this regard as well. Eddison's first novel was primarily a heroic epic, filled with battles and other action, with little room for philosophical meditations. The Zimiamvia books, however, include a great deal of philosophical material and considerably less action and adventure, although this focus does not make them dull reading given the many intrigues of the trilogy. As Lin Carter puts it in his 1969 essay "The Men Who Invented Fantasy," *The Worm Ouroboros* "is Homeric; the trilogy is Machiavellian."

Some writers of fantasy and science fiction are primarily storytellers, while others use their stories as a way of addressing social, political, philosophical, or religious issues. In *The Worm Ouroboros* Eddison is primarily a storyteller, although one of his main concerns is present as well, a concern elaborated upon more fully in the Zimiamvia trilogy: the nature and importance of beauty. Eddison believed that beauty was independent of times and circumstances, whereas other value systems were contingent upon cultural factors. Furthermore, Eddison believed that beauty could be and should be valued for its own sake, apart from any notions of its utility.

Related to Eddison's regard for beauty as a value in and of itself is the subject of art and creativity. No doubt, part of what Eddison was trying to achieve through his elaborate style was a sense of language as beautiful for its own sake; the same could be said of his descriptions of his imaginary worlds. The artist is a creator, just as the word *poet* stems from the Greek term for "maker." Thus, the god-like creativity manifested in *A Fish Dinner at*

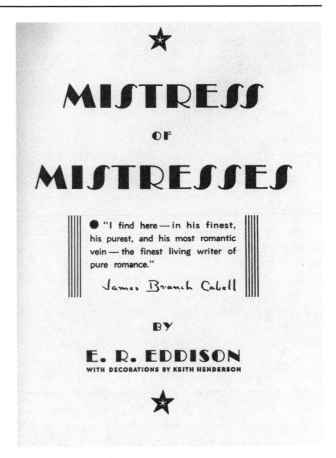

Dust jacket for Eddison's 1935 novel, the first volume of his trilogy about the alternate universe of Zimiamvia

Memison becomes a metaphor for creativity in general and perhaps artistic creativity in particular.

Similarly, just as the characters-cum-deities in *A Fish Dinner in Memison* contemplate the destruction of the worlds they consider making, similar to the temptation King Mezentius faces in *The Mezentian Gate,* so Eddison suggests that beauty, though a permanent source of value, lodges within an ever-changing physical world, most notably symbolized in his work by the image of the worm Ouroboros. In a way, Eddison's philosophy at this point is practically Platonic: though the world is transient, beauty is eternal. At times, in fact, Eddison comes close to Plato in suggesting that the world of experience is not only transient but also illusory, a mere shadow of a truer realm of being.

All of these abstruse philosophical concerns have a direct bearing on Eddison's status as a writer of fantasy. What he almost certainly strove for in his work was to tell interesting stories, which he accomplished rather well. As he explains to his brother, Colin, in the "Letter of Introduction" that he intended as a preface to *The Mezentian Gate:*

With our current distractions, political, social and economic, this story (in common with its predecessors) is as utterly unconcerned as it is with Stock Exchange procedure, the technicalities of aerodynamics, or the Theory of Vectors. Nor is it an allegory. Allegory, if persons have life, is a prostitution of their personalities, forcing them for an end other than their own. If they have not life, it is but a dressing up of argument in the puppetry of frigid make-believe. To me, the persons *are* the argument. And for the argument I am not fool enough to claim responsibility; for, stripped to its essentials, it is a great eternal commonplace, beside which, I am sometimes apt to think, nothing else really matters.

Such an assertion demonstrates another aspect of Eddison's work besides simple storytelling. It seems that in his fantasy novels he was attempting to convey in fictional terms a larger set of truths than those afforded by a close examination of human nature. At the same time, since his fictional worlds are divorced from more recognizable ones, he is liable to the same charge leveled at fantasy literature in general: that it is mere escapism, having nothing to do with "reality." Eddison's response to this charge might well be that in his fantasy novels he is concerned with a sense of reality beyond that of mere realism. On the other hand, such a stance could be taken as a retreat away from concrete matters of the here and now, and critics could easily assert that Eddison does what the German philosopher Friedrich Nietzsche accused Christianity of doing: avoiding more immediate problems by escaping into a belief in a "higher reality." Most readers of Eddison's fantasies do not go so far in analyzing his work, reading more for the fantasy and adventure elements, but the fact that such issues have been raised in the dialogue over Eddison's work points to the existence of something more substantial than those who dismiss fantasy as puerile entertainment care to acknowledge.

These elements in Eddison's work also help to account for the mixed responses it has generated even among his most ardent admirers. Christian fantasists Lewis and Tolkien, for instance, applauded Eddison's imaginative construction of alternate worlds while finding themselves uncomfortable with the nature of his fictional worldview. Other readers, if not sharing the same theological reservations, have found Eddison's apparent valorization of power disturbing. It should be noted, however, that Eddison is writing in the epic mode; his heroes are larger than life and occupy a sphere different from that of mere mortals, and they should not be taken as exemplars of human behavior.

At the same time, Eddison brings the stories that compose the Zimiamvia trilogy closer to human concerns in his treatment of the relationship between men and women. As Brian Attebury remarks in his discussion of the trilogy, "The Zimiamvian books are love stories more than they are tales of heroic adventure." Through a series of romantic relationships—each of which is a different manifestation of the relationship in Eddison's worldview of the God and the Goddess, Zeus and Aphrodite—Eddison portrays, as Attebury describes it, "a sense of balance, of equals meeting to the enrichment of both," an accomplishment, he notes, that is rare in fantasy literature.

Less enlightened by modern standards is Eddison's treatment of class and race. While occasionally his characters are not exclusively class-bound, his sympathies are definitely with the upper classes, both on Earth and in his fantasy worlds; his development of feudal societies practically seems favorable to such social systems. Not much discussion is accorded to the little men and women of his tales, nor are their losses in warfare portrayed as terribly significant. Despite the author's claim to his brother that his fiction should be considered as distinct from contemporary concerns, it is difficult not to think that Eddison uses Lessingham as an alter ego when the latter says such things as: "The vast majority of civilized mankind are, politically, a mongrel breed of sheep and monkey: the timidity, the herded idiocy, of the sheep; the cunning, the dissimulation, the ferocity, of the great ape."

Moreover, the English Lessingham's assertion covers only those he considers among "civilized mankind," which in Eddison's fiction presumably includes only those of European ancestry or its equivalent in Zimiamvia. Others fare less well, as illustrated by the occasional derogatory references to Jews and "half-niggers." Such things, along with the deliberately antiquated diction, contribute to the datedness of Eddison's work and give readers another reason to take offense at the worldview they find there.

Eddison died of a heart attack at age sixty-two on 18 August 1945 in Marlborough. Despite his recognition as an important figure in fantasy literature during his lifetime and into the period of writers such as Lewis and Tolkien—in the late 1940s he met both of them and corresponded with Lewis—Eddison never achieved the same larger readership of those writers or of some of his contemporaries. His reputation was revived somewhat in the late 1960s in the United States, as fantasy fiction—in the wake of the enormous popularity of Tolkien's *The Lord of the Rings,* particularly in the Ballantine paperback edition published in that decade as part of their Adult Fantasy series—became a profitable publishing category, causing publishers (most notably Ballantine) to begin seeking new works along similar lines and republishing older ones. Ballantine thus republished Eddison's four works of fantasy, though they sold nowhere near as well as the fantasies of Tolkien and his imitators. Eddison has remained a marginal figure in the mainstream literary tradition while continuing as a noteworthy if not popular one in fantasy literature. In fact, the very popularity of heroic fantasy resulting from the increased interest in it from the late 1960s onward may account for his lack of widespread popularity, as part of what made his work unusual is no longer so uncommon.

Those who continue to read Eddison persist in promoting and analyzing his work, admiring it for its distinctiveness. Such readers second Percy Hutchinson's assessment of Eddison in an 11 August 1935 review of *Mistress of Mistresses* in *The New York Times Book Review:* "Probably in every generation there will be an author moving in an orbit so individually his own as to defy all the measuring instruments of watchers of the literary skies. Such a one is E. R. Eddison." It is uncertain whether Walter Yust's prediction in the 26 June 1926 *Literary Review* that *The Worm Ouroboros* "will survive the century; . . . indeed a number of centuries" will come true; but it is likely that Eddison will be read and studied for some time to come.

References:

Brian Attebury, "The Zimiamvian Trilogy," in *Survey of Modern Fantasy Literature,* edited by Frank N. Magill (Englewood Cliffs, N.J.: Salem, 1983), pp. 2206–2213;

Lin Carter, "The Men Who Invented Fantasy," in his *Tolkien: A Look Behind* The Lord of the Rings (New York: Ballantine, 1969), pp. 134–151;

Don D'Ammassa, "Villains of Necessity: The Works of E. R. Eddison," in *Discovering Classic Fantasy Fiction: Essays on the Antecedents of Fantastic Literature,* edited by Darrell Schweitzer (San Bernardino, Cal.: Borgo, 1996), pp. 88–93;

L. Sprague de Camp, "Superman in a Bowler: E. R. Eddison," in his *Literary Swordsmen and Sorcerers:* *The Makers of Heroic Fantasy* (Sauk City, Wis.: Arkham House, 1976), pp. 114–134;

Verlyn Flieger, "The Man Who Loved Women: Aspects of the Feminine in Eddison's Zimiamvia," *Mythlore,* 13 (Spring 1987): 29–32;

Flieger, "The Ouroboros Principle: Time and Love in Zimiamvia," *Mythlore,* 15 (Summer 1989): 43–46;

G. Rostrevor Hamilton, "The Prose of E. R. Eddison," *English Studies, New Series,* 2 (London: Murray, 1949), pp. 43–53;

C. S. Lewis, "A Tribute to E. R. Eddison," in his *On Stories and Other Essays on Literature,* edited by Walter Hooper (New York: Harcourt Brace Jovanovich, 1982), p. 29;

C. N. Manlove, "Anaemic Fantasy: Morris, Dunsany, Eddison, Beagle," in his *The Impulse of Fantasy Literature* (Kent, Ohio: Kent State University Press, 1983), pp. 127–154;

Helmut W. Pesch, "The Sign of the Worm: Images of Death and Immortality in the Fiction of E. R. Eddison," in *Death and the Serpent: Immortality in Science Fiction and Fantasy,* edited by Carl B. Yoke and Donald M. Hassler (Westport, Conn.: Greenwood Press, 1985), pp. 91–101;

William M. Schulyer Jr., "E. R. Eddison's Metaphysics of the Hero," *New York Review of Science Fiction,* 31 (March 1991): 12–17;

Paul Edmund Thomas, Introduction, *The Worm Ouroboros* by E. R. Eddison, annotated by Thomas (New York: Dell, 1991), pp. xv–xlii;

Sharon Wilson, "The Doctrine of Organic Unity: E. R. Eddison and the Romance Tradition," *Extrapolation,* 25 (Spring 1984): 12–19.

Papers:

A collection of E. R. Eddison's letters, notes, and manuscripts is held by the Bodleian Library of Oxford University. Other manuscripts are located in the Local History Library at the Central Library of Leeds.

John Gawsworth
(Terence Ian Fytton Armstrong)
(29 June 1912 – 23 September 1970)

Steve Eng

BOOKS: *An Unterrestrial Pity: Being Contributions Towards a Biography of the Late Pinchbeck Lyre,* as Orpheus Scrannel (London: Blue Moon Press, 1931);

Confession: Verses (London: Twyn Barlwm Press, 1931);

Snowballs, as Scrannel (London: E. Lahr, 1931);

Fifteen Poems, Three Friends (London: Twyn Barlwm Press, 1931);

Above the River (London: Ulysses Bookshop, 1931);

Ten Contemporaries: Notes toward Their Definitive Bibliography (London: Benn, 1932; Folcroft, Pa.: Folcroft Library Editions, 1972);

Apes, Japes and Hitlerism: A Study and Bibliography of Wyndham Lewis (London: Unicorn Press, 1932);

Kingcup: Suite Sentimentale (London: Twyn Barlwm Press, 1932);

Lyrics to Kingcup (London: E. Lahr / Blue Moon Press, 1932);

Mishka and Madeleine: A Poem Sequence for Marcia (London: Twyn Barlwm Press, 1932);

The Personal Library of John Gawsworth (London: Bertram Rota, 1933);

The Twyn Barlwm Press, 1931–1932: A Record of the Venture and a List of Publications (London: Privately printed, 1933);

Ten Contemporaries: Notes toward Their Definitive Bibliography (Second Series) (London: Joiner & Steele, 1933);

Poems, 1930–1932 (London: Rich & Cowan, 1933); revised and enlarged as *Poems* (London: Richards, 1938);

Annotations on Some Minor Writings of "T. E. Lawrence," as "G" (London: E. Partridge, 1935);

The Flesh of Cypris: Poems (London: E. H. Samuel, 1936);

New Poems (London: Secker & Warburg, 1939);

The Mind of Man: Poems (London: Richards, 1940);

Marlow Hill: Poems (London: Richards, 1941);

Legacy to Love: Selected Poems, 1931–1941, volume 1 of *The Poetical Works of John Gawsworth* (London: Collins, 1943);

John Gawsworth (Terence Ian Fytton Armstrong)

The Crimson Thorn: Poems for Lovers, 1931–1941, volume 2 of *The Poetical Works of John Gawsworth* (Calcutta: Susil Gupta, 1945);

In English Fields: Poems from Books, 1931–1941, volume 3 of *The Poetical Works of John Gawsworth* (Calcutta: Susil Gupta, 1945);

Farewell to Youth, volume 4 of *The Poetical Works of John Gawsworth* (Calcutta: Susil Gupta, 1945);

Snow and Sand: Poems from the Mediterranean, 1942–1944, volume 5 of *The Poetical Works of John Gawsworth* (Calcutta: Susil Gupta, 1945);

Blow No Bugles: Poems from Two Wars, 1942–1945, volume 6 of *The Poetical Works of John Gawsworth* (Calcutta: Susil Gupta, 1945);

The Collected Poems of John Gawsworth (London: Sidgwick & Jackson, 1948); abridged as *Toreros: Poems of John Gawsworth,* selected by Richard Aldington, edited by Steve Eng (Fontwell, Arundel, West Sussex: Centaur Press, 1990; Nashville, Tenn.: Depot Press, 1990);

Some Poems, edited by Oliver Cox (London: Privately published, 1970);

A Bibliophile's Holiday: Magnetic Fingers (Lewes, East Sussex: Tartarus Press, 1992).

OTHER: Tristram Rainey, *The Doors of Heart: Verses,* foreword by Gawsworth (London: E. Lahr, 1932);

Backwaters: Excursions in the Shades, selected by Gawsworth (London: Denis Archer, 1932);

Known Signatures: New Poems, edited by Gawsworth (London: Rich & Cowan, 1932); revised and enlarged as *Fifty Years of Modern Verse: An Anthology* (London: Secker & Warburg, 1938); abridged as *Fifty Modern Poems by Forty Famous Poets* (Calcutta: Susil Gupta, 1945);

Strange Assembly: New Stories, edited by Gawsworth (London: Unicorn Press, 1932);

Lady Hester Lucy Stanhope, *Remarks Upon Hermodactylus,* translated by Arthur Machen, footnote by Gawsworth (London: Privately printed, 1933);

Richard Middleton, *The Pantomime Man,* edited by Gawsworth (London: Rich & Cowan, 1933);

Wilfrid Ewart, *When Armageddon Came: Studies in Peace and War,* edited by Gawsworth (London: Rich & Cowan, 1933);

Full Score: Twenty-five Stories, edited by Gawsworth as Fytton Armstrong (London: Rich & Cowan, 1933);

The Public School Poets, 3 volumes, edited by Gawsworth (London: Rich & Cowan, 1934)—comprises *The Poets of Merchant Taylors' School, The Poets of Harrow School,* and *The Poets of Eton College;*

Ewart, *Scots Guard,* edited anonymously by Gawsworth (London: Rich & Cowan, 1934);

New Tales of Horror by Eminent Authors, edited anonymously by Gawsworth (London: Hutchinson, 1934);

Thrills, Crimes and Mysteries: A Specially Selected Collection of Sixty-Three Complete Stories by Well-Known Writers, edited by Gawsworth (London: Associated Newspapers, 1935);

E. H. W. Meyerstein, *Selected Poems,* edited by Gawsworth and Maurice Wollman (London: Macmillan, 1935);

M. P. Shiel, *The Invisible Voices,* contributions by Gawsworth (London: Richards, 1935);

Theodore Wratislaw, *Selected Poems,* edited by Gawsworth (London: Richards, 1935);

Edwardian Poetry: Book One, edited anonymously by Gawsworth (London: Richards, 1936);

Thrills: Twenty Specially Selected New Stories of Crime, Mystery and Horror, edited anonymously by Gawsworth (London: Associated Newspapers, 1936);

Crimes, Creeps and Thrills: Forty-Five New Stories of Detection, Horror and Adventure by Eminent Modern Authors, edited anonymously by Gawsworth (London: E. H. Samuel, 1936);

Masterpiece of Thrills, edited anonymously by Gawsworth (London: Daily Express, 1936);

Richards' Shilling Selections from Edwardian Poets, 7 volumes, edited by Gawsworth (London: Richards, 1936–1941);

Wilfred Rowland Childe, *Selected Poems of Wilfred Rowland Childe,* edited by Gawsworth and Wollman (London: Thomas Nelson, 1936);

Neo-Georgian Poetry, 1936–1937, edited anonymously by Gawsworth (London: Richards, 1937);

The Muse of Monarchy: Poems by Kings and Queens of England, edited anonymously by Gawsworth (London: Eric Grant, 1937);

Havelock Ellis, *Poems,* selected by Gawsworth (London: Richards, 1937);

Edgar Jepson, *Memories of an Edwardian and Neo-Georgian,* edited by Gawsworth (London: Richards, 1937);

Ewart, *Aspects of England,* edited by Gawsworth (London: Richards, 1937);

"The Dowson Legend," in *Essays by Divers Hands, Being the Transactions of the Royal Society of Literature of the United Kingdom,* New Series, volume 17, edited by E. H. W. Meyerstein (London: Oxford University Press, 1938), pp. 93–123;

Twenty Tales of Terror: Great New Stories by Modern Masters of the Macabre, edited anonymously by Gawsworth (Calcutta: Susil Gupta, 1945);

Harry Milner, *Until Bengal: Poems in War,* introduction by Gawsworth (Calcutta: Susil Gupta, 1945);

"Letters in French Barbary: A War Despatch, 1943," in *Essays by Divers Hands, Being the Transactions of the Royal Society of Literature of the United Kingdom,* New Series, volume 24, edited by Clifford Bax (London: Oxford University Press, 1948), pp. 135–159;

Shiel, *The Best Short Stories of M. P. Shiel,* selected by Gawsworth (London: Gollancz, 1948);

"Magnetic Fingers: A Bibliophile's Holiday," in *Holidays and Happy Days,* edited by Oswell Blakeston (London: Phoenix House, 1949), pp. 129–146;

Thomas Burke, *The Best Stories of Thomas Burke,* selected by Gawsworth (London: Phoenix House, 1950);

Shiel, *Science, Life, and Literature,* foreword by Gawsworth (London: Williams & Norgate, 1950);

Ellis, *From Marlowe to Shaw: Studies, 1876–1936, in English Literature,* edited by Gawsworth (London: Williams & Norgate, 1950);

Ellis, *Sex and Marriage; Eros in Contemporary Life,* edited by Gawsworth (London: Williams & Norgate, 1951);

Alfred Tennyson, *The Poetical Works of Tennyson,* edited by Gawsworth, Macdonald Illustrated Classics, no. 19 (London: Macdonald, 1951; New York: Coward-McCann, 1951);

John Milton, *The Complete English Poems of Milton,* edited by Gawsworth, Macdonald Illustrated Classics, no. 25 (London: Macdonald, 1953);

"Two Poets 'J. G.,'" in *Frederick Rolfe and Others: A Miscellany of Essays on John Gray, Henry Williamson, Ronald Firbank, Andre Raffalovich and Frederick Baron Corvo,* edited by Cecil Wolfe (Aylesford, U.K.: St. Albert's Press, 1961), pp. 167–172;

"Regent Street 'Royalists,'" in *Parnassus Near Piccadilly: An Anthology—The Café Royal Centenary Book,* edited by Leslie Frewin (London: Leslie Frewin, 1965);

Memoir by Gawsworth, in *Richard Aldington: An Intimate Portrait,* edited by Alister Kershaw and Fréderick-Jacques Temple (Carbondale: Southern Illinois University Press, 1965);

"John Gawsworth . . . On M. P. Shiel: A Selection," compiled by Steve Eng, in *Shiel in Diverse Hands: A Collection of Essays,* edited by A. Reynolds Morse, *The Works of M. P. Shiel,* volume 4 (Cleveland: Reynolds Morse Foundation, 1983).

SELECTED PERIODICAL PUBLICATIONS–
UNCOLLECTED: "Machen and Gwent," as Fytton Armstrong, *Space,* 9 (March 1931): 29–30;

"Priest of the Mysterious," *New English Weekly,* 5 (5 November 1936): 76–77;

"M. P. Shiel Centenary," *Aylesford Review,* 7 (Autumn 1965): 133–134;

"The Poet and the Philosopher: Gawsworth and M. P. Shiel," *Aklo* (Spring 1988): 48–51.

The English lyric poet John Gawsworth enjoyed styling himself as a "man of letters" in the urbane, eclectic, nineteenth-century sense of the term. His prolific career as poet, poetry editor, and editor of short stories and essays (anthologies and individual collections)—as well as that of bibliographer and magazine editor—made a wide if not always deep impression. Gawsworth was an energetic literary leader of the second rank. He was also an eccentric, colorful public personage, claiming to be king of a mythical kingdom linked to the Caribbean island of Redonda, which he had never visited but promoted vividly in the press. Gawsworth yearned to be an immortal English poet but is more remembered today for his Redonda charade and his tireless advocacy of fantasy authors such as Arthur Machen and M. P. Shiel. Gawsworth has rightly been termed the English counterpart of American writer, fantasy editor, and publisher August Derleth.

"John Gawsworth" was the pen name for Terence Ian Fitton Armstrong ("Fitton" became "Fytton" in his own later versions of the name). He was born on 29 June 1912 in the Baron's Court district of London to Frederick Percy and Ethel Jackson Armstrong. His mother was related to the family of Mary Fitton of Gawsworth Hall, in Cheshire, who was purportedly the "Dark Lady" of William Shakespeare's sonnets (a legend since refuted). Armstrong also claimed kinship (on his mother's side) to John Milton's third wife and (on his father's side) to dramatist Ben Jonson and poet Lionel Johnson. Young "Terry" Armstrong graduated from Merchant Taylors' School in London in 1928, where one of his horror-story heroes, Richard Middleton (author of "The Ghost Ship," 1912), had attended. At Merchant Taylors', Armstrong may well have known fellow student Hilary Machen, son of Arthur Machen.

Armstrong claimed his father abused him. His parents divorced when he was young, and in 1928 his mother went to Canada and married her former husband's brother. Armstrong stayed behind, working at Andrew Block's bookstore in Denmark Street, Soho, and living in a shabby, gaslit garret surrounded by his used-book collection. Foyle's bookstore in Charing Cross Road was one of his haunts, and in his essay "Magnetic Fingers: A Bibliophile's Holiday" (1948) he recaptured his halcyon adolescence as a book scout. Lawrence Durrell, in his *Spirit of Place: Letters and Essays on Travel* (1969), remarked that had Armstrong "cared to be a bookseller he would now be the greatest one in England."

Armstrong's fanatical zeal for books and manuscripts introduced him to many living authors from the 1890s and the Edwardian period. Such connections helped him inflate his precocious "man of letters" reputation. Soon he was calling himself "John Gawsworth," evoking Gawsworth Hall and probably inviting confusion with John Galsworthy.

Gawsworth met Arthur Machen in the 1930s, corresponding with him from 1929 until Machen's death in 1947. Machen was a reader for the publisher Ernest Benn, operating from his home in Buckinghamshire, and Gawsworth worked in the sales department. Gawsworth privately printed two booklets of photos of Machen residences, and Machen introduced Gawsworth's short story *Above the River* in its slender book edition (1931). The tale is a Machenesque, dreamy fantasy set in Wales. By 1933 Gawsworth was writing Machen's biography—over his hero's objections, as recorded in Machen's letters. The amateurish book was never published; its three drafts are housed at the library of the University of California at Los Angeles.

Gawsworth's Machen fixation persisted in verse as well. In one of his earliest poetry efforts, *Fifteen Poems, Three Friends* (1931), a five-verse cycle, "Siluria," was dedicated to Machen. It is filled with liquid Welsh place-names such as Abergavenny and Llanthony, and three of the poems made it into *The Collected Poems of John Gawsworth* (1948). The best one, "Roman Headstone," was picked by Richard Aldington for the even more selective *Toreros: Poems of John Gawsworth* (1990). It was written near Caerleon, site of Machen's novel *The Hill of Dreams* (1907) and evokes the thrill of a tourist who fancies he glimpses a girl's ethereal face in the twilight. He imagines she is Julia, wife of a Roman centurion.

Machen had been launched by the "Keynotes" series in the 1890s, published by John Lane's Bodley Head—so had Shiel, a horror, mystery, and science-fiction author and one-time friend of Machen. Shiel became Gawsworth's next hero, and Gawsworth documented Shiel's books in his *Ten Contemporaries: Notes toward Their Definitive Bibliography* (1932). Its 1933 sequel covered fantasy short-story writers Thomas Burke, John Collier, and Oliver Onions.

Shiel, like Machen, was in his latest decline after a similar, brief American revival in the 1920s. Gawsworth began ferreting out lost Shiel stories and publishing them. His first fantasy anthology, *Strange Assembly: New Stories* (1932), featured two stories each by Shiel and Machen. Works by these authors appeared in Gawsworth's next two anthologies, *Full Score: Twenty-five Stories* (1933) and *New Tales of Horror by Eminent Authors* (1934), and were included in all the others that followed. *Full Score* even republished Gawsworth's "Above the River" with Machen's friendly if ambivalent commentary. Typical of Gawsworth's loyalty to Shiel (and to Machen, among other older authors), he also secured the author's Civil List pension for him.

Gawsworth married Barbara Kentish, social editor of *The Daily Mail,* in 1933. Her employer recruited Gawsworth to compile some mystery-horror anthologies, which the newspaper published at Christmas-time as premiums. Such anthologies were used in newspaper wars to lure subscribers, and Gawsworth edited several for different publishers: *Thrills, Crimes and Mysteries: A Specially Selected Collection of Sixty-Three Complete Stories by Well-Known Writers* (1935); *Crimes, Creeps and Thrills: Forty-Five New Stories of Detection, Horror and Adventure by Eminent Modern Authors* (1936);

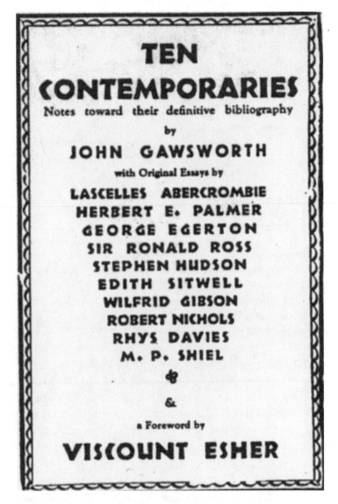

Cover for the first of the two bibliographies Gawsworth published in 1932 and 1933

Thrills: Twenty Specially Selected New Stories of Crime, Mystery and Horror (1936); and *Masterpiece of Thrills* (1936), which included one of the earliest book appearances for Durrell, an author Gawsworth personally discovered. His one-man fantasy/mystery-horror movement was analogous to the eleven *Not at Night* volumes edited by Christine Campbell Thompson (1925–1936) and Charles Birkin's anthologies (1932–1936). British anthologists Hugh Lamb and Peter Haining have dipped into these often bulky books for stories to reprint. In *The Year's Best Horror Stories Series IX* (1981) American horror editor Karl Edward Wagner compared the 1980s horror explosion to "those thousand-page super-dreadnaught-class horror anthologies published in England in the 1930s—particularly those edited by John Gawsworth." Cumulative sales for Gawsworth's volumes were around two hundred thousand.

The anthologies included many "collaborations," with Gawsworth's byline appended to those of other writers. He would sit in a pub, touching up or completing sundry story fragments by writers such as E. H. Visiak or Shiel. (The Shiel-Gawsworth tales were collected as "The Seven Limbs of Satan" but the volume was never published.) Among the best of these collaborations was "The Shifting Growth," written with Edgar Jepson, an old friend of Shiel, Machen, and Middleton; it appeared in *Crimes, Creeps and Thrills*. The story belongs in a subgenre that might be dubbed "weird surgery," with a doctor operating on a girl who has a monster growing in her intestine:

> I made a longer incision than I usually do, nearly the whole length of the growth, for it still seemed to be rippling, and opened up the colon on to a black-and-red spongy mass, dragging at the needle which held it fast. And from the middle of that seething sponge there stared up at me two set, unwinking eyes.
>
> An octopus! . . . Uncompressed, it looked as if it would have filled a drain-pipe, and split the colon of an ox. And the eyes were still staring, stupidly.

"The Shifting Growth" prompted Haining to say in *The Nightmare Reader* (1973) that Gawsworth played "a major role in the propagation of the British horror story . . . He could also write a genuinely macabre tale along with the best of them." Most of his few, memorable tales have been reprinted.

"Scylla and Charybdis," in *New Tales of Horror*, is set in Machen's Usk region of Wales, but the plot is more like Algernon Blackwood's "The Willows" (1907), with its malignant, antique trees and the pagan terror they evoke. "How It Happened," in *Thrills*, is a brief *conte cruel* in the vein of Guy de Maupassant in which a madman confesses how he murdered his sweetheart and his own brother, whom she preferred. The slayer's detachment is chilling as he hangs his lover from a tree branch: "but Margery did not seem to understand. The jerkings gave way to stillness, a lovely stillness."

Gawsworth continued to champion other writers. In 1938 he delivered a lecture to the Royal Society of Literature in London on poet Ernest Dowson, challenging Dowson's reputation as a hopeless drunkard. Gawsworth himself was an alcoholic, and his own compulsive collecting and selling of books was partly inspired by his lust for liquor. In some of his own early poems Gawsworth had emulated Dowson, then had begun striving toward a more modern originality within the tight format of rhyme and meter. Many readers respected his sonnets, and his ballad-style verses—somewhat like those of A. E. Housman—were often rich with grim irony. In addition to his own poetry books, he edited single-author

collections (including Shiel's) and various anthologies.

Gawsworth had become a member of the Royal Society of Literature in 1933 and a Fellow in 1938; in 1939 he won its Benson Silver Medal for his "work in general." (T. E. Lawrence had written to Robert Graves on 11 May 1934: "He is a scribbler, like us.") Also in 1939 he founded *The English Digest,* which he edited until 1941.

The last poem in his *Legacy to Love: Selected Poems, 1931–1941* (1943), "December 12, 1940," stated solemnly that even poets must risk their lives in wartime. As Terence Armstrong, Gawsworth joined the army in 1942 and the Royal Air Force in 1944, turning his military tenure into a literary campaign. In Algiers he chased down poetry and poets and eventually delivered a lecture on North African literature; in Cairo, he was one of the "Salamander" British war poets (with G. S. Fraser, Erik de Mauny, and John Waller); in Italy, he hunted up the philosopher Benedetto Croce; and from Italy and India he published several poetry broadsides, booklets, and books. Poems such as "Moving Back" ("We are going back again / To the mud and the rain / Where the guns complain / and the stones stain") revealed Gawsworth as a World War I–style poet adjusting to World War II.

Gawsworth's career peaked in the late 1940s, when he succeeded Muriel Spark as editor of *The Poetry Review* from 1949 to 1952. Gawsworth was an urbanely balanced editor, printing the work of traditional poets such as Walter de la Mare along with that of modernists such as Durrell and Michael Hamburger. Gawsworth simultaneously edited *Enquiry*–a magazine of philosophy and parapsychology that reprinted Graves's *The White Goddess* (1948)–as well as *The Literary Digest*. With his definitive *Collected Poems* Gawsworth reached his lyrical zenith.

Gawsworth's life had moments as colorful or fantastic as anything he wrote. For example, on 14 April 1949 he intervened when poet Roy Campbell tried to assault Stephen Spender at a poetry reading. Gawsworth was fired from *The Poetry Review* in 1952, though Edith Sitwell and others protested, and the magazine lost much of its prestige. Then there was his connection with the "kingdom" of Redonda. Shiel's father had staked a whimsical claim to the Caribbean island of Redonda and crowned his son "king" in a farcical ceremony when Shiel was fifteen years old. The British annexed the island, but Shiel never forgot his fanciful kingdom. On 5 October 1936 he and Gawsworth had cut their wrists with a penknife, performing a blood-pact ritual that decreed

Gawsworth to be king of Redonda upon Shiel's death.

When Shiel died in 1947, Gawsworth thus became "King Juan I" of Redonda. He issued "State Papers" and bestowed the titles of "Duke" and "Duchess" on various figures ranging from Machen, Derleth, Ellery Queen, and Dylan Thomas to Inspector Robert Fabian of Scotland Yard and movie stars Dirk Bogarde and Diana Dors. This running parody of stuffy aristocracy was the delight of the press. Reporters enjoyed interviewing Gawsworth in pubs, paying for his drinks and earning their own dukedoms in exchange. Various Caribbean travel books have jokingly honored him as King Juan I of Redonda.

Gawsworth had divorced his first wife, Barbara, in 1948. That same year he married Estelle Gilardeau; they also divorced. In 1955 Gawsworth married Doreen Emily Ada (Rowley) Downie, whom he renamed "Anna." By the early 1960s they were living at 35 Sutherland Place in an apartment building owned by Charles Wrey Gardiner, once editor of *The Poetry Quarterly* and founder of Grey Walls Press. One of their neighbors, poet-scholar John Heath-Stubbs, remembers that Gawsworth in a fit of rage hurled his typewriter out the window—smashing it and further curtailing his career. He continued filling notebooks with his hand-scrawled lyrics, however, selling them to the book dealers, and hundreds of unpublished Gawsworth poems have thus survived.

Gawsworth published ephemeral booklets commemorating Machen's centenary in 1963 and persuaded Derleth to accept two Shiel titles at Arkham House, the leading publisher of fantasy books in the United States. Gawsworth also had been a close drinking friend of British horror author John Metcalfe (whose wife, American novelist Evelyn Scott, was one of Gawsworth's *Poetry Review* contributors). After Metcalfe's death in 1965 Gawsworth became his literary executor.

Anna Gawsworth left her husband, and for a time in the 1960s Gawsworth lived with Eleanor Brill, an unofficial "Queen of Redonda." When their apartment building was sold in 1969, he lacked a permanent address, so was ineligible for Social Security. Gawsworth was sleeping where he could—in friends' houses and even on benches in Hyde Park—when the BBC discovered him and gave him a television tribute on 7 July 1970, hosted by Durrell. Gawsworth performed at his tipsy, bohemian best, reading aloud his "Four A.M.– January 3, 1970 (The Princess Beatrice Hospital)," which ends, "Damn you Poetry!"

Gawsworth was a diabetic and in his final days wrote poems from various hospital sickbeds. On the

I MADE A LONGER INCISION THAN I USUALLY DO

Illustration from Gawsworth's 1936 anthology Crimes, Creeps and Thrills, *for Gawsworth and Edgar Jepson's "The Shifting Growth," in which the narrator operates on a girl who has an octopus growing in her colon*

verge of death he bequeathed his literary rights to poet Ian Fletcher and to publisher Jon Wynne-Tyson of the Centaur Press, son of novelist Esmé Wynne-Tyson. He also anointed Wynne-Tyson "King Juan II" of Redonda. Wynne-Tyson is an environmentalist and editor of *The Extended Circle: A Commonplace Book of Animal Rights* (1985), as well as a horror-tale author (*The Twilight Zone* magazine) and novelist whose *So Say Banana Bird* (1984) has a Caribbean setting with a Redonda motif.

Gawsworth died of a pulmonary embolism at Brompton Hospital (Kensington, London) on 23 September 1970. *The New York Times* lamented the passing of a "POET AND 'KING' OF TINY ISLAND" (27 September 1970). Two days after his death, an unexpected family legacy arrived, which could have sustained him for the rest of his life.

REALM of REDONDA

This Volume Is from
the Bookshelves of

M. P. SHIEL, (1865-1947)

[H.M. King Felipe I, 1880-1947]

and

JOHN GAWSWORTH (1912-   )

[H.M. King Juan I, 1947-   ]

Bookplate reflecting Gawsworth's satirical claim to the throne of a Caribbean island (from Steve Eng, ed., "John Gawsworth: Unforgotten: A Tribute Anthology," Romantist, no. 6–7–8 [1986])

Although Gawsworth's contemporaries often dismissed him as a ne'er-do-well dilettante, he deserves credit for his championing of other writers, especially in the fantasy field, and for his better poetry. In *When the Rat-Race Is Over: An Essay in Honour of the Fiftieth Birthday of John Gawsworth* (1962) poet Hugh MacDiarmid wrote, "The race is not to the swift nor the battle to the strong. You will not be denied your niche in the great temple of English Literature."

Interviews:
Eric Philips, "H. M. the King of Redonda," *Writer* (October 1962): 3–5;
Maggie Angeloglou, "The King Who Washed Edith Sitwell's Windows and Took Dylan Thomas Home to Sleep on the Sofa," London *Evening Standard* (3 May 1965): 10.

Bibliographies:
J. H. R. Owen, *John Gawsworth: Some Publications 1931–1944* (Vasto, Italy: Privately printed, 1944);
A. Reynolds Morse, *The Works of M. P. Shiel,* volume 2 (Cleveland: Reynolds Morse Foundation, 1980), pp. 299–304;

Paul de Fortis, "John Gawsworth," in *The Kingdom of Redonda 1865–1990,* edited by de Fortis (Upton, Cheshire: Aylesford Press, 1991), pp. 93–94.

References:
Arthur Caddick, "Marks of Royal Favour," *Cornish Review,* no. 22 (Winter 1972): 4–21;
Robert Coram, "Guano and Literature," in his *Caribbean Time Bomb: The United States' Complicity in the Corruption of Antigua* (New York: Morrow, 1993), pp. 84–95;
Roger Dobson, Godfrey Brangham, and R. A. Gilbert, eds., *Arthur Machen, Selected Letters: The Private Writings of the Master of the Macabre* (London: Aquarian Press, 1988), pp. 168–208;
Lawrence Durrell, "Some Notes on My Friend John Gawsworth 1962," in his *Spirit of Place: Letters and Essays on Travel,* edited by Alan G. Thomas (New York: Dutton, 1969), pp. 17–23;
Steve Eng, "Men About Machen: John Gawsworth 'Machen's Boswell,'" *Avallaunius,* 10 (Spring 1993): 18–23;
Eng, "Profile: John Gawsworth," *Night Cry: The Magazine of Terror,* 2 (Spring 1987): 73–85;
Eng, ed., "John Gawsworth Unforgotten: A Tribute Anthology," *Romantist,* no. 6–7–8 (1982–83–84 [1986]): 85–106;
F. Dubrez Fawcett, "King of All the Seagulls," *Men Only,* 75 (November 1960): 58–60;
Ian Fletcher, "John Gawsworth: The Aesthetics of Failure," *Malahat Review,* 63 (October 1982): 206–219;
Sue Strong Hassler and Donald M. Hassler, eds., *Arthur Machen and Montgomery Evans: Letters of a Literary Friendship, 1923–1947* (Kent, Ohio: Kent State University Press, 1994);
Hugh MacDiarmid, *When the Rat-Race Is Over: An Essay in Honour of the Fiftieth Birthday of John Gawsworth* (London: Twyn Barlwm Press, 1962);
Jon Wynne-Tyson, "Two Kings of Redonda: M. P. Shiel and John Gawsworth," *Books at Iowa,* 36 (April 1982): 15–22.

Papers:
The chief collection of John Gawsworth's books, manuscripts, and correspondence is at the University of Iowa, Iowa City. Another large collection of books, letters, and some manuscripts is at the Harry Ransom Humanities Research Center, University of Texas at Austin. Minor collections exist at the University of New York at Buffalo (University Library: Poetry/Rare Books Collection), and at the library at the University of Reading, England.

William Golding

(19 September 1911 – 19 June 1993)

Joe Sanders

See also the Golding entries in *DLB 15: British Novelists, 1930–1959; DLB 100: Modern British Essayists, Second Series;* and *Yearbook: 1983.*

BOOKS: *Poems* (London: Macmillan, 1934; New York: Macmillan, 1935);

Lord of the Flies (London: Faber & Faber, 1954; New York: Coward-McCann, 1955);

The Inheritors (London: Faber & Faber, 1955; New York: Harcourt, Brace & World, 1962);

Pincher Martin (London: Faber & Faber, 1955; New York: Capricorn, 1956); republished as *The Two Deaths of Christopher Martin* (New York: Harcourt, Brace, 1957);

The Brass Butterfly: A Play in Three Acts (London: Faber & Faber, 1958); republished with introduction by Golding (London: Faber & Faber, 1963);

Free Fall (London: Faber & Faber, 1959; New York: Harcourt, Brace & World, 1960);

The Spire (London: Faber & Faber, 1964; New York: Harcourt, Brace & World, 1964);

The Hot Gates, and Other Occasional Pieces (London: Faber & Faber, 1965; New York: Harcourt, Brace & World, 1966);

The Pyramid (London: Faber & Faber, 1967; New York: Harcourt, Brace & World, 1967);

The Scorpion God: Three Short Novels (London: Faber & Faber, 1971; New York: Harcourt Brace Jovanovich, 1972);

Darkness Visible (London: Faber & Faber, 1979; New York: Farrar, Straus & Giroux, 1979);

Rites of Passage (London: Faber & Faber, 1980; New York: Farrar, Straus & Giroux, 1980);

A Moving Target (London: Faber & Faber, 1982; New York: Farrar, Straus & Giroux, 1982; revised edition, New York: Farrar, Straus & Giroux, 1984);

Nobel Lecture, 7 December 1983 (Leamington Spa, U.K.: Sixth Chamber, 1984);

The Paper Men (London: Faber & Faber, 1984; New York: Farrar, Straus & Giroux, 1984);

William Golding (photograph © Jerry Bauer; from the dust jacket for The Paper Men, *1984)*

An Egyptian Journal (London & Boston: Faber & Faber, 1985);

Close Quarters (London: Faber & Faber, 1987; New York: Farrar, Straus & Giroux, 1987);

Fire Down Below (London: Faber & Faber, 1989; New York: Farrar, Straus & Giroux, 1989);

To the Ends of the Earth (London: Faber & Faber, 1991)—comprises *Rites of Passage, Close Quarters,* and *Fire Down Below;*

The Double Tongue (London: Faber & Faber, 1995; New York: Farrar, Straus & Giroux, 1995).

PLAY PRODUCTIONS: *The Brass Butterfly,* Oxford, New Theatre, 24 February 1958; London, Strand Theatre, April 1958; New York, Lincoln Square Theatre, West Side YMCA, 11 December 1965.

PRODUCED SCRIPTS: "Our Way of Life," radio, *Third Programme,* BBC, 15 December 1956;

"Miss Pulkinhorn," radio, *Third Programme,* BBC, 20 April 1960;

"Break My Heart," radio, *Third Programme,* BBC, 19 March 1961.

OTHER: "Envoy Extraordinary," in *Sometime, Never: Three Tales of Imagination,* by Golding, John Wyndham, and Mervyn Peake (London: Eyre & Spottiswoode, 1956; New York: Ballantine, 1957), pp. 3–60.

SELECTED PERIODICAL PUBLICATIONS–UNCOLLECTED: "The Writer in His Age," *London Magazine,* 4 (May 1957): 45–46;

"Pincher Martin," *Radio Times,* 38 (21 March 1958): 8;

"The Anglo-Saxon," *Queen,* 215 (22 December 1959): 27–30;

"Miss Pulkinhorn," *Encounter,* 15 (August 1960): 27–32;

"Androids All," review of *New Maps of Hell,* by Kingsley Amis, *Spectator,* 206 (24 February 1961): 263–264;

"Before the Beginning," review of *World Prehistory,* by Grahame Clark, *Spectator,* 206 (26 May 1961): 768;

"It's a Long Way to Oxrhynchus," *Spectator,* 207 (7 July 1961): 9;

"The Condition of the Novel," *New Left Review,* (January–February 1965): 34–35;

"Egypt and I," *Holiday,* 34 (April 1966): 32, 46–49;

"Delphi: The Oracle Revealed," *Holiday,* 42 (August 1967): 60–61, 87–88, 90, 150.

William Golding is an unusually controversial writer of the fantastic. First of all, his stature as a writer has been questioned despite–or possibly because of–the popular acceptance of his work. Secondly, critics have had difficulty agreeing exactly which of his works are fantastic. Golding's relation to science fiction was generally uncertain even at the beginning of his career. Kingsley Amis's *New Maps of Hell: A Survey of Science Fiction* (1960) mentions him in passing as one "who comes nearer than anybody so far to being a serious writer working within science fiction," yet faults him for letting his literary ambitions interfere with the "coherence and concision" of his writing. In reply, while reviewing Amis's book in "Androids All" (1961), Golding includes himself among "addicts and writers of S.F.," though he calls such people "strange creatures" because of their concentration on ideas at the expense of characterization, sex, humor, and wit. Nevertheless, according to Brian Aldiss in "William Golding: An Appreciation" (1993), Golding is "the only Nobel Prize Laureate to have regarded himself, at least in one phase of his career, as a science fiction writer."

William Gerald Golding was born on 19 September 1911 in Cornwall, to Alec Golding, a schoolmaster, and Mildred Golding, a suffragette. He attended the Marlborough School. As Golding describes his childhood, he was torn between light and darkness, confidence that the world could be understood and mastered versus certainty that this task was beyond human ability. In his essay "The Ladder and the Tree" (1960) Golding writes that his father "inhabited a world of sanity and logic and fascination," but the boy himself felt a nullifying, almost-sentient force from the graveyard next to their home, growing stronger as night fell, extending into the darkness of their own cellar. Golding also was fascinated, as he wrote in his essay "Egypt in My Inside" (1965), by Egyptian art that reflects awareness of the presence of unknowable powers intervening in human life, as shown by the artists' creation of painted shapes that still "outstare infinity in eternity." At the time, Golding did not attempt such creation himself; in his essay "Billy the Kid" (1960) he describes himself as a schoolyard bully who escaped fear of the darkness beyond human knowledge by trying to subjugate the world to his ego.

Golding earned his bachelor's degree in English literature at Brasenose College, Oxford, in 1935. In 1939, after spending a few years at small-time theater work in London, he married Ann Brookfield, a chemist, and began teaching at Bishop Wordsworth's School in Salisbury. He served in the Royal Navy during World War II, once spending three days adrift on a raft after his ship was sunk. In an essay titled "Fable" (1965) he explains how his wartime experiences changed him:

> Before the second World War I believed in the perfectability of social man; that a correct structure of society would produce goodwill; and that therefore you could remove all social ills by a reorganization of society. . . . After the war I did not because I was unable to. I had discovered what one man could do to another. . . . I am thinking of the vileness beyond all words that went on, year after year, in the totalitarian states. . . . there were things done during that period from which I still have to avert my mind lest I should be physically sick. . . . I must say that anyone who moved through those years without understand-

ing that man produces evil as a bee produces honey, must have been blind or wrong in the head.

Considering Golding's description of his childhood, this understanding must have been less a revelation than a confirmation of the darkness that underlies human consciousness. In his fiction he attempts to show how attractive but dangerous egotistic certainty can be. That includes, of course, certainty that one has established the boundaries of the natural and supernatural.

After the war, Golding returned to teaching. Encouraged by his wife and inspired by his observation of young boys, he began writing fiction. His first published novel, *Lord of the Flies,* appeared in 1954 to encouraging reviews, but Aldiss describes him at the time as a typical writer of borderline science fiction, complaining that the publishers were not promoting his work vigorously enough.

In *Lord of the Flies* a group of schoolboys are marooned on a tropical island during some future war—the reason the book may be considered as borderline science fiction. The boys form a tribal society involving reverence for a deity embodied in a wild pig's head. The novel never suggests, however, that Beelzebub, lord of flies, is actually present; instead the boys' unacknowledged fears and desires take shape in the savage god they worship. In "Fable," however, Golding describes how the writing of what he intended to be a fable, a straightforward story with a moral, got out of hand when he was writing about one of the boys, Simon, first spying on others worshiping the pig's head: "It was at this point of imaginative concentration that I found that the pig's head knew Simon was there. In fact the Pig's head delivered something very like a sermon to the boy; the pig's head spoke. I know because I heard it." This discovery elated Golding. Rather than constructing a "fable," he discovered that he was expressing myth—"something which comes out from the roots of things in the ancient sense of being the key to existence, the whole meaning of life, and experience as a whole," as he said in a 1959 interview with Frank Kermode. Golding never refers to "the pig's head" as more than that (the one capitalization is probably a typo), nor does he deny that the "sermon" could have emerged from his own unconscious. But he is impressed by the power of that visitation, wherever it came from, shattering the most tightly knit literary intentions and mocking any attempt to view it from one conscious perspective.

Consequently, all of Golding's fiction, fantastic or otherwise, displays the attitude that underlies fantasy: the universe is not susceptible to human under-

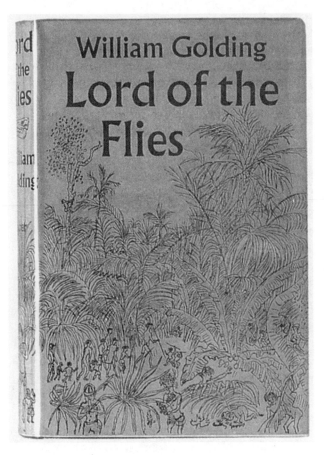

Dust jacket for Golding's first novel, published in 1954, about a group of boys who descend into savagery after they are marooned on a deserted island (from R. A. Gekoski and P. A. Grogan, William Golding: A Bibliography, 1934–1993, *1994)*

standing or control. His writing that can be labeled explicitly fantastic does not feature magical spells or cursed revenants. Humans create their own magic—probably; no one can be sure. Golding focuses on the tensions created by humans' absolute need to achieve the absolutely impossible—and the fantasies that conflict creates.

Golding's second novel, *The Inheritors* (1955), is sometimes included in lists of his fantastic fiction because it is set in prehistoric times. The novel includes few or no elements that are unequivocally supernatural. The main focus is on the consciousness of the wondering, innocent primitive people who are about to be exterminated by the more fearful (and intelligible to readers) variety of humans who are modern man's direct ancestors. The novel might be considered part of the subclass of science fiction written about the distant past, such as H. G. Wells's "A Story of the Stone Age" (1897). But although *The Inheritors* is intensely speculative fiction, that does not make it science fiction. Most science-fiction writers who consider prehistoric people are concerned with

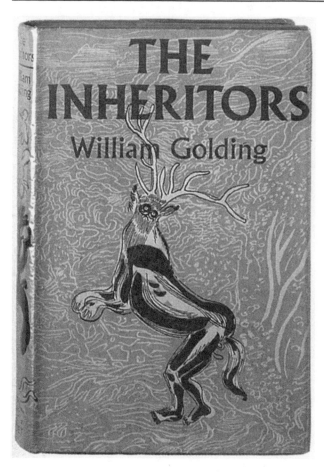

Dust jacket for Golding's second novel, published in 1955, about the extermination of an innocent prehistoric race by the direct ancestors of modern humans (from R. A. Gekoski and P. A. Grogan, William Golding: A Bibliography, 1934–1993, *1994)*

superior characters born ahead of their time, who either lead their tribe upward (as in Wells's story) or, as in Jack London's *Before Adam* (1906), are dragged down by the brutes around them. In plot, Golding's novel somewhat resembles Lester del Rey's "The Day Is Done" (1939), but is undiluted by del Rey's sticky sentimentality. *The Inheritors* never equates change with progress.

With *Pincher Martin* (1955), though, Golding at last wrote a novel that can be classified rather firmly as fantastic. The action of *Pincher Martin* can be quickly told: during World War II, Christopher Hadly Martin's ship is torpedoed, and he is cast away, alone, on a bleak rock in the ocean. After several days of increasing torment, he becomes delirious and sinks into oblivion. His body later drifts to an inhabited coast and is discovered. Such a brief summary, however, misses the point of the novel. The last sentence of the book announces that Martin's body still has its seaboots on. Since in the narration of Martin's struggle to survive it is certain that he

kicked his boots off while thrashing about in the water, the reader must reevaluate the truth of the whole narrative. It becomes clear that Martin's real life ends while he convulses in the water, and that everything following is an illusion.

Moreover, throughout the narrative, many clues (especially flashbacks) suggest that readers must reevaluate their first, sympathetic picture of Martin as a man fighting heroically against overwhelming odds to survive—it is revealed, for instance, that as the torpedo struck his ship, Martin was deliberately giving an order that would cause the death of his best friend. On the rock, he actually denies death because he fears judgment, as he cries out, defiantly but with unintentional irony, "I'm damned if I'll die!"

Looking back over the apparent action, readers recognize that Martin has imagined his stay on the rock out of two central aspects of his existence: pain and isolation. He convinces himself that he is in a real place by imagining rocks poking his body as starvation consumes him. He plans absurdly grandiose projects to summon help. The fact is, however, that Martin has always been a loner, suffering because of it but always exploiting anyone who gets too close to him. Remembering his life, he pictures climbing a wall of living human faces that are so brittle that he must move on, shattering more people as he climbs. He also remembers himself in an agony of loneliness, exclaiming, "Can't anyone understand how I feel?" He craves, in other words, exactly the intimacy that he rejects.

This self-defeating way of life is echoed in Martin's clinging to pain as a survival technique on the rock. It cannot succeed. Rather than safely distracting Martin's intelligence from discrepancies in the surface texture of his environment, pain erodes his control and permits him to perceive more incongruities. When he must give up on sane survival, Martin tries the role of madman, but that also falls apart as the rock begins to disintegrate. Finally, Martin must face God, a figure in black seaboots, who concludes that Martin is incapable of understanding why he has become what he is and so sets about dissolving his last fragments of being "in a compassion that was timeless and without mercy."

Pincher Martin often is compared to Ambrose Bierce's "An Occurrence at Owl Creek Bridge" (1892), another tale in which the ending reveals that the central character has imagined a series of experiences to avoid admitting that he is dead. Bierce's protagonist, however, remains an innocent cipher, and he tries to build his postdeath existence out of appreciation of nature and warm, domestic yearning.

Golding's more complex protagonist has only selfish, unpleasant memories to shape into his fantasy, and Golding was bemused to see how readers missed that aspect of the character, as he said in the Kermode interview: "I went out of my way to damn Pincher as much as I could by making him the most unpleasant, the nastiest type I could think of, and I was interested to see how critics all over the place said, 'Well yes, we are like that.' I was really rather pleased."

It might be objected that Martin's incriminating memories are more obscure, less immediate than the scenes on the rock. Several, such as a fear of the darkness in the basement of his childhood home, seem to echo Golding's descriptions of his own childhood; it is possible that the character has not been developed independently enough for readers to apprehend him. But Golding would reply that there is no other way to present a character such as Pincher Martin directly, since the man himself uses all his skill and energy to avoid seeing himself clearly, because he wants to avoid recognizing the moral implications of his actions.

Even Golding's most clearly nonfantastic novels give a similar effect of vivid detail but authorial detachment. Readers become aware of the world in which characters act only as the characters themselves experience it. Things happen. The characters make sense of events as best they can. At times, this world is a baffling place, full of apparent incongruities. Moreover, the characters sometimes discover that their perceptions and the personal choices based on them are quite mistaken. Only rarely, however, does Golding suggest that there is some absolute Truth—conscious or not, benign or not—somewhere past the boundaries of human perception, a glimpse of which might resolve the muddle.

In *The Paper Men* (1984), for example, a writer who is fleeing from a persistent academic critic believes that he catches glimpses of the man in different cities around the world; he is sure that he is being pursued with uncanny skill by the wretched scholar who wants to make a life's work out of dissecting a creator's soul. Later, the critic complains that he has been catching glimpses of the writer in still other cities; he is sure that the writer is taunting him by staying miraculously just out of reach. Rather than assuming the presence of supernatural traveling doppelgängers, readers may simply suppose that two distraught people are imagining what they want and/or dread to see. The novel is Golding's most fully developed comment on the folly of literary interpretation. Late in his career, he was ironically impressed that more had been written about him than he had written himself, but he was

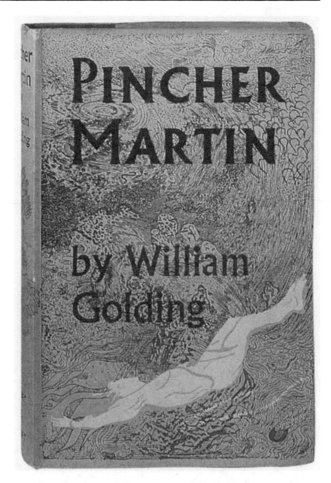

Dust jacket for Golding's 1955 novel about a naval officer whose struggle for survival after his ship is torpedoed turns out to be an after-death fantasy (from R. A. Gekoski and P. A. Grogan, William Golding: A Bibliography, 1934–1993, *1994)*

confident that he had eluded the critics, seeing himself as "A Moving Target"—the title essay in his second collection of nonfiction (1982).

Two additional books deserve attention in considering Golding as a writer of fantasy or science fiction: one because it is sometimes labeled fantastic, the other because its fantastic nature has not received enough comment. *The Scorpion God* (1971) collects three short novels set in exotic times and locales. This fact, along with Golding's detached technique and disillusioned attitude, may be why some commentators have seen fantastic overtones throughout the book. One story, "Envoy Extraordinary" (a prose version of his 1958 play *The Brass Butterfly*), is historical science fiction, as an inventor offers a Roman emperor a steamship, high explosives, and a printing press; the story is, however, chiefly concerned with resistance to new concepts and with how the emperor manages to save the civilized world from powered machinery, long-distance warfare, and

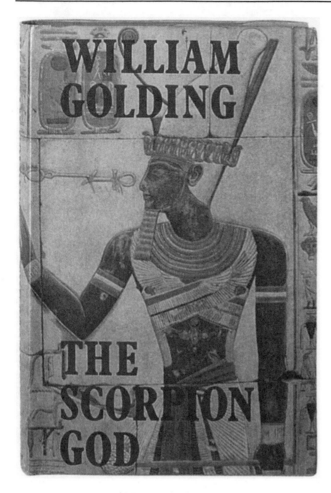

Dust jacket for Golding's 1971 collection of short stories set in the distant past (from R. A. Gekoski and P. A. Grogan, William Golding: A Bibliography, 1934–1993, *1994)*

mass-produced books. In "The Scorpion God," set in ancient Egypt, another court smugly lives by its presuppositions, more amused than disturbed by the travel tales of Liar, the court jester, who reports marvels such as snow, people with pale skins, and non-incestuous sex. Though the story ends with Liar triumphant, his brave new vision of bloody conquest and a dynasty extending all along the river is both realistic and coldhearted; he sounds a lot like Pincher Martin. Finally, "Clonk Clonk" is set in prehistoric Africa, where men make loud noises and take themselves seriously. Meanwhile, the somewhat more realistic women actually get their own way, and Golding implies that this arrangement has persisted. In all, these stories are less involved with the fantastic or the supernatural than with how humans fail to perceive nature correctly.

The same could be said of *Darkness Visible* (1979). Nevertheless, it is Golding's other fantastic novel. During the World War II blitz in London, fire fighters discover a child wandering out of the flames.

No one claims him—not surprising in the wartime chaos—and the left half of his body is hideously burned. He is given the name Matty and treated with the mixture of pity and disgust that society thinks appropriate for a disfigured orphan. His ugliness, for example, affronts Sebastian Pedigree, a schoolteacher on the verge of active child molestation, whose routine Matty disrupts. As a young adult, Matty can be shoved into menial work, in which his "unguessable mode of the mind" will not bother anyone. However, after human communication is denied him, Matty begins reading the Bible with insane intensity and performing bizarre, private rituals.

Up to this point, readers feel about Matty much as the "normal" people around him do: he is pathetic, but his consciousness is too maimed to be accommodated. When he begins keeping a journal to record the visitations of "elders" who reassure him that he is meant for some great purpose, readers see this idea as another symptom of insanity. At the same time, though, readers are introduced to Sophy—beautiful, brilliant, idolized by all around her, and insane in a different, vicious way. She always has felt that all of existence was meant to serve her, and she feels more powerfully herself as she becomes more "weird," dark, and contemptuous of others. Despite what her accomplices in a kidnapping scheme believe, Sophy's real goal is to procure a helpless child to kill. When Matty disrupts that scheme and is burned to death in the process, readers remember that his supernatural visitors had revealed a few days earlier that he was to guard a child by becoming "a burnt offering." As in *Pincher Martin,* the whole frame of reference in the novel appears to be reversed; Matty's insane delusions are validated, while Sophy's manipulations of conventional belief are negated.

The conclusion of the novel also strongly resembles *Pincher Martin.* Sitting alone in a park, Pedigree has or imagines a vision of Matty standing before him. The old man protests that he has never actually hurt a child (in contrast, though he does not realize it, to Sophy's intent) but begs for help before he actually does so. In response, Matty changes: "Sebastian watched in terror as the man before him was consumed, melted, vanished like a guy in a bonfire; and the face was no longer two-tone but gold as the fire and stern and everywhere there was a sense of the peacock eyes of great feathers and the smile round the lips was loving and terrible." This being gives Pedigree the only "cure" possible for him: death.

Again, readers are left with an unfathomable puzzle. Sophy is all too easily believable; one can understand the forces that warped her. But Matty's origin is beyond comprehension. It is difficult to accept the idea that a benign supernatural power would create an individual who must go through life-long suffering and humiliation to achieve a "good" purpose. (If this situation resembles the life of Jesus, Matty is a Christ with no disciples and no surviving gospel.) The elders do tell Matty that the child he is to save will change the world for the better sometime in the future. As the novel ends, however, Sophy is likely to escape punishment, free to continue her amusements. Furthermore, the title of the novel is a quote from John Milton's *Paradise Lost* (1667) describing the light from the flames of Hell. Try as they may, many readers will find it difficult to accept John Calvin Batchelor's enthusiastic conclusion that "In holding out the possibility that one man—ugly, unloved, untouched, reviled—can for a moment beat the devil with faith alone, Golding has written a cheer for human courage."

For fifteen years after World War II, Golding concentrated his reading in the classical Greeks, and his viewpoint seems close to the Greek picture of humans at the mercy of powers erupting out of the darkness around and within individuals. In any event, William Golding, who died in 1993, was a distinctive, powerful writer. Even though his fiction seldom is unequivocally fantastic, he clearly represents the loss of faith in human comprehension that has made fantasy a viable form of fiction for contemporary writers.

Interviews:

"Portrait," *Time* (9 September 1957): 118;

Owen Webster, "Living with Chaos," *Books and Art* (March 1958): 15–16;

Frank Kermode, "The Meaning of It All," *Books and Bookmen,* 5 (October 1959): 9–10;

Owen Webster, "The Cosmic Outlook of an Original Novelist," *John O'London's* (28 February 1960): 7;

John W. Aldridge, "Mr. Golding's Own Story," *New York Times Book Review* (10 December 1961): 56–57;

"The Well-Built House," in *Authors Talking* (London: BBC Broadwater Press, 1961), pp. 18–19;

Maurice Dolbier, "Running J. D. Salinger a Close Second: An Interview with William Golding," *New York Herald Tribune Books* (20 May 1962): 6, 15;

Douglas M. Davis, "Golding, the Optimist, Belies His Somber Pictures and Fiction," *National Observer* (17 September 1962): 4;

Davis, "A Conversation with Golding," *New Republic* (4 May 1963): 28–30;

James Keating, "The Purdue Interview with William Golding," in *Lord of the Flies: Text, Notes, Criticism,*

edited by James R. Baker and Arthur P. Ziegler Jr. (New York: Putnam, 1964), pp. 189–195;

Bernard F. Dick, "The Novelist Is a Displaced Person: An Interview with William Golding," *College English,* 26 (March 1964): 480–482;

Jack Biles, *Talk: Conversations with William Golding* (New York: Harcourt Brace Jovanovich, 1970);

Victoria Glendinning, "Golding: The Old Man and the Sea," *Sunday Times* (19 October 1980): 39;

James Baker, "An Interview with William Golding," *Twentieth Century Literature,* 28 (Summer 1982): 130–170;

John Haffenden, *Novelists in Interview* (London: Methuen, 1985), pp. 97–120;

John Carey, "William Golding Talks to John Carey: 10–11 July 1985," in *William Golding: The Man and His Books: A Tribute on His 75th Birthday,* edited by Carey (London: Faber & Faber, 1986), pp. 171–189.

Bibliographies:

Jack I. Biles, "A William Golding Checklist," *Twentieth Century Literature,* 17 (April 1971): 107–122;

J. Don Vann, "William Golding: A Checklist of Criticism," *Serif,* 8 (June 1971): 21–26;

R. A. Gekoski and P. A. Grogan, *William Golding: A Bibliography, 1933–1994* (London: Deutsch, 1994).

References:

Brian Aldiss, "William Golding: An Appreciation," *Locus,* 31 (August 1993): 58;

Kingsley Amis, *New Maps of Hell: A Survey of Science Fiction* (New York: Harcourt, Brace, 1960; London: Gollancz, 1961);

Henry Avril, "The Pattern of *Pincher Martin,*" *Southern Review,* 9 (March 1976): 3–26;

Howard S. Babb, *The Novels of William Golding* (Columbus: Ohio State University Press, 1970);

James R. Baker, *William Golding: A Critical Study* (New York: St. Martin's Press, 1965);

Baker, ed., *Critical Essays on William Golding* (Boston: G. K. Hall, 1988);

John Calvin Batchelor, "Golding Beats the Devil," *Village Voice,* 5 (November 1979): 43, 47;

Jack I. Biles and Robert O. Evans, eds., *William Golding: Some Critical Considerations* (Lexington: University Press of Kentucky, 1979);

Biles and Carl R. Kropf, "The Cleft Rock of Conversion: *Robinson Crusoe* and *Pincher Martin,*" *Studies in the Literary Imagination,* 2 (October 1969): 17–43;

A. S. Byatt, "William Golding: Darkness Visible," in her *Passions of the Mind: Selected Essays* (London: Chatto & Windus, 1991; New York: Turtle Bay, 1991), pp. 169–173;

Don Crompton, *A View from the Spire: William Golding's Later Novels,* edited and completed by Julia Briggs (New York: Blackwell, 1985);

Cecil Davis, "'The Burning Bird': Golding's *Poems* and the Novels," *Studies in the Literary Imagination,* 13 (Spring 1980): 97–117;

Bernard F. Dick, *William Golding* (New York: Twayne, 1967; revised, 1987);

L. L. Dickson, *The Modern Allegories of William Golding* (Tampa: University of South Florida Press, 1990);

Lawrence S. Friedman, *William Golding* (New York: Ungar, 1993);

James Gindin, "'Gimmick' and Metaphor in the Novels of William Golding," *Modern Fiction Studies,* 6 (Summer 1960): 145–152;

Samuel Hynes, "Grief, Sheer Grief, Grief, Grief," *New Republic,* 13 (September 1982): 36–37;

Arnold Johnston, *Of Earth and Darkness: The Novels of William Golding* (Columbia: University of Missouri, 1980);

Mark Kinkead-Weekes and Ian Gregor, *William Golding: A Critical Study* (London: Faber & Faber, 1967; revised, 1984);

Stephen Medcalf, *William Golding* (Essex, U.K.: Longman, 1975);

Bernard S. Oldsey and Stanley Weintraub, *The Art of William Golding* (New York: Harcourt, Brace & World, 1965);

Norman Page, ed., *William Golding: Novels, 1954–67* (Basingstoke & London: Macmillan, 1985);

John Peter, "The Fables of William Golding," *Kenyon Review,* 19 (Autumn 1957): 577–592;

Michael Quinn, "An Unheroic Hero: William Golding's 'Pincher Martin,'" *Critical Quarterly,* 4 (Autumn 1962): 247–256;

Philip Redpath, *William Golding: A Structural Reading of His Fiction* (Totowa, N.J.: Barnes & Noble, 1986);

Virginia Tiger, *William Golding: The Dark Fields of Discovery* (London: Calder & Boyars, 1974).

Aldous Huxley

(26 July 1894 – 22 November 1963)

Johan Heje
Greve Gymnasium, Denmark

See also the Huxley entries in *DLB 36: British Novelists, 1890–1929: Modernists; DLB 100: Modern British Essayists, Second Series; DLB 162: British Short-Fiction Writers, 1915–1945;* and *DLB 195: British Travel Writers, 1910–1939.*

BOOKS: *The Burning Wheel* (Oxford: Blackwell, 1916);
Jonah (Oxford: Holywell, 1917);
The Defeat of Youth and Other Poems (Oxford: Blackwell, 1918);
Limbo (London: Chatto & Windus, 1920; New York: Doran, 1920);
Leda (London: Chatto & Windus, 1920; New York: Doran, 1920);
Crome Yellow (London: Chatto & Windus, 1921; New York: Doran, 1922);
Mortal Coils (London: Chatto & Windus, 1922; New York: Doran, 1922);
On the Margin: Notes and Essays (London: Chatto & Windus, 1923; New York: Doran, 1923);
Antic Hay (London: Chatto & Windus, 1923; New York: Doran, 1923);
Little Mexican & Other Stories (London: Chatto & Windus, 1924; republished as *Young Archimedes, and Other Stories* (New York: Doran, 1924);
Those Barren Leaves (London: Chatto & Windus, 1925; New York: Doran, 1925);
Along the Road: Notes and Essays of a Tourist (London: Chatto & Windus, 1925; New York: Doran, 1925);
Selected Poems (Oxford: Blackwell, 1925; New York: Appleton, 1925);
Two or Three Graces and Other Stories (London: Chatto & Windus, 1926; New York: Doran, 1926);
Jesting Pilate: The Diary of a Journey (London: Chatto & Windus, 1926; New York: Doran, 1926);
Essays New and Old (London: Chatto & Windus, 1926; New York: Doran, 1927);
Proper Studies (London: Chatto & Windus, 1927; Garden City, N.Y.: Doubleday, Doran, 1928);
Point Counter Point (London: Chatto & Windus, 1928; Garden City, N.Y.: Doubleday, Doran, 1928);

Aldous Huxley

Arabia Infelix, and Other Poems (London: Chatto & Windus/New York: Fountain Press, 1929);
Holy Face and Other Essays (London: Fleuron, 1929);
Do What You Will: Essays (London: Chatto & Windus, 1929; Garden City, N.Y.: Doubleday, Doran, 1929);
Brief Candles: Stories (London: Chatto & Windus, 1930; Garden City, N.Y.: Doubleday, Doran, 1930);
Vulgarity in Literature: Digressions from a Theme (London: Chatto & Windus, 1930);
Appenine (Gaylordsville, Conn.: Slide Mountain Press, 1930);

The World of Light: A Comedy in Three Acts (London: Chatto & Windus, 1931; Garden City, N.Y.: Doubleday, Doran, 1931);

Music at Night and Other Essays (London: Chatto & Windus, 1931; Garden City, N.Y.: Doubleday, Doran, 1931);

The Cicadas and Other Poems (London: Chatto & Windus, 1932; Garden City, N.Y.: Doubleday, Doran, 1932);

Brave New World (London: Chatto & Windus, 1932; Garden City, N.Y.: Doubleday, Doran, 1932);

Texts and Pretexts: An Anthology with Commentaries (London: Chatto & Windus, 1932; New York: Harper, 1933);

Rotunda: A Selection from the Works of Aldous Huxley (London: Chatto & Windus, 1932);

T. H. Huxley as a Man of Letters, Imperial College of Science and Technology, Huxley Memorial Lecture (London: Macmillan, 1932);

Retrospect: An Omnibus of Aldous Huxley's Books (Garden City, N.Y.: Doubleday, Doran, 1933);

Beyond the Mexique Bay (London: Chatto & Windus, 1934; New York: Harper, 1934);

What Are You Going to Do about It? The Case for Constructive Peace (London: Chatto & Windus, 1936; New York: Harper, 1937);

Eyeless in Gaza (London: Chatto & Windus, 1936; New York: Harper, 1936);

1936 . . . Peace? (London: Friends Peace Committee, 1936);

The Olive Tree and Other Essays (London: Chatto & Windus, 1936; New York: Harper, 1937);

Ends and Means: An Enquiry into the Nature of Ideals and into the Methods Employed for Their Realization (London: Chatto & Windus, 1937; New York: Harper, 1937);

Stories, Essays, and Poems (London: Dent, 1937);

The Most Agreeable Vice (Los Angeles: Ward Ritchie, 1938);

The Gioconda Smile (London: Chatto & Windus, 1938);

After Many a Summer (London: Chatto & Windus, 1939); republished as *After Many a Summer Dies the Swan* (New York: Harper, 1939);

Words and Their Meanings (Los Angeles: Ward Ritchie, 1940);

Grey Eminence: A Study in Religion and Politics (London: Chatto & Windus, 1941; New York: Harper, 1941);

The Art of Seeing (New York: Harper, 1942; London: Chatto & Windus, 1941);

Time Must Have a Stop (New York: Harper, 1944; London: Chatto & Windus, 1945);

Twice Seven: Fourteen Selected Stories (London: Reprint Society, 1944);

The Perennial Philosophy (New York: Harper, 1945; London: Chatto & Windus, 1947);

Science, Liberty, and Peace (New York: Harper, 1946; London: Chatto & Windus, 1947);

Verses and a Comedy (London: Chatto & Windus, 1946);

The World of Aldous Huxley: An Omnibus of His Fiction and Non-Fiction over Three Decades, edited by Charles J. Rolo (New York: Harper, 1947);

Ape and Essence (New York: Harper, 1948; London: Chatto & Windus, 1949);

The Gioconda Smile: A Play (London: Chatto & Windus, 1948; New York: Harper, 1948);

Prisons, with the "Carceri" Etchings by G. B. Piranesi (London: Trianon, 1949; Los Angeles: Zeitlin & Ver Brugge, 1949);

Themes and Variations (London: Chatto & Windus, 1950; New York: Harper, 1950);

The Devils of Loudun (London: Chatto & Windus, 1952; New York: Harper, 1952);

Joyce, the Artificer: Two Studies of Joyce's Method, by Huxley and Stuart Gilbert (London: Chiswick Press, 1952);

A Day in Windsor, by Huxley and J. A. Kings (London: Britannicus Liber, 1953);

The French of Paris, text by Huxley, photographs by Sanford H. Roth (Paris: Editions du Chêne, 1953; New York: Harper, 1954);

The Doors of Perception (London: Chatto & Windus, 1954; New York: Harper, 1954);

The Genius and the Goddess (London: Chatto & Windus, 1955; New York: Harper, 1955);

Heaven and Hell (London: Chatto & Windus, 1956; New York: Harper, 1956);

Adonis and the Alphabet, and Other Essays (London: Chatto & Windus, 1956); republished as *Tomorrow and Tomorrow and Tomorrow, and Other Essays* (New York: Harper, 1956);

Collected Short Stories (London: Chatto & Windus, 1957; New York: Harper, 1957);

Brave New World Revisited (London: Chatto & Windus, 1958; New York: Harper, 1958);

Collected Essays (New York: Harper, 1959);

On Art and Artists, edited by Morris Philipson (London: Chatto & Windus, 1960; New York: Harper, 1960);

Selected Essays, edited by Harold Raymond (London: Chatto & Windus, 1961);

Island (London: Chatto & Windus, 1962; New York: Harper, 1962);

Literature and Science (London: Chatto & Windus, 1963; New York: Harper & Row, 1963);

The Crows of Pearblossom (New York: Random House, 1967; London: Chatto & Windus, 1968);

Great Short Works of Aldous Huxley, edited by Bernard Bergonzi (New York: Harper & Row, 1969);

The Collected Poetry of Aldous Huxley, edited by Donald Watt (London: Chatto & Windus, 1971; New York: Harper & Row, 1971);

Moksha: Writings on Psychedelics and the Visionary Experience, 1931–1963, edited by Michael Horowitz and Cynthia Palmer (New York: Stonehill, 1977; London: Chatto & Windus, 1980);

The Human Situation: Lectures at Santa Barbara 1959, edited by Piero Ferrucci (New York: Harper & Row, 1977; London: Chatto & Windus, 1978);

Jacob's Hands, by Huxley and Christopher Isherwood (New York: St. Martin's Press, 1998; London: Bloomsbury, 1998);

Complete Essays, edited by Robert S. Baker and James Sexton (Chicago: I. R. Dee, 2000).

PLAY PRODUCTIONS: *The Discovery,* by Frances Sheridan, adapted by Huxley, London, 1924;

The World of Light, London, Royalty Theatre, 30 March 1931;

The Gioconda Smile, London, New Theatre, 1948; New York, Lyceum Theatre, 1950;

The Genius and the Goddess, by Huxley and Ruth Wendell, New York, Henry Miller Theatre, 1957; Oxford, Oxford Playhouse, 1962.

PRODUCED SCRIPTS: *Pride and Prejudice,* scenario by Huxley and Jane Murfin, motion picture, M-G-M, 1940;

Madame Curie, treatment by Huxley, motion picture, M-G-M, 1943;

Jane Eyre, scenario by Huxley, motion picture, 20th Century-Fox, 1944;

A Woman's Vengeance, adaptation by Huxley from his *The Gioconda Smile,* motion picture, Universal-International, 1948.

OTHER: Frances Sheridan, *The Discovery: A Comedy in Five Acts,* adapted by Huxley (London: Chatto & Windus, 1924; New York: Doran, 1925);

The Letters of D. H. Lawrence, edited by Huxley (London: Heinemann, 1932; New York: Viking, 1932);

An Encyclopedia of Pacifism, edited by Huxley (London: Chatto & Windus, 1937; New York: Harper, 1937).

For four decades Aldous Huxley was a major figure in the literary mainstream, yet he is now chiefly remembered for a novel that is, by any definition, science fiction. In this respect his position is similar to that of H. G. Wells, who wrote much else besides science fiction but whose reputation has endured as the great pattern-setter for

Huxley's first wife, Maria Nys Huxley, in the 1920s

twentieth-century science fiction. Similarly, Huxley's novel *Brave New World* (1932) created a thematic pattern for many subsequent works. Moreover, *Brave New World* was not Huxley's only foray into the futuristic or the fantastic.

Aldous Leonard Huxley, born on 26 July 1894 in Surrey, had a family background that predestined him for a distinguished career in the world of science or the world of letters. His father, Leonard Huxley, a classics master at Charterhouse and later editor of the *Cornhill Magazine,* was the son of T. H. Huxley, the famous biologist and expounder of Darwinism; his mother, Judith Arnold Huxley, was the granddaughter of one of the major educators of the Victorian period, Thomas Arnold of Rugby, and niece of Matthew Arnold. Her sister, Mrs. Humphry Ward, was an admired novelist. Sir Julian Huxley, biologist of world renown and the first director-general of UNESCO, was one of Aldous Huxley's two elder brothers; they also had a younger sister.

Huxley was an avid reader from his earliest years and received an education that befitted his background: Eton and Balliol College, Oxford, from which he graduated in 1916 despite significant damage to his eyesight, caused by keratitis in 1911. While at Oxford he was introduced to Lady Ottoline Morrell, whose country home, Garsington, was a salon for members of England's intellectual elite. Among her house guests Huxley met many people who were, or became, notable scholars or writers. With some of them, most importantly D. H. Lawrence and Bertrand Russell, he formed lasting friendships. At the age of twenty-two he was a published poet, and within a few years he had established a reputation as a promising and provocative essayist, short-story writer, and novelist. He married Belgian-born Maria Nys in 1919, and their son, Matthew, was born in 1920.

Garsington obviously provided inspiration for Huxley's first novel, *Crome Yellow* (1921), written much in the manner of Thomas Love Peacock: a group of people are gathered at a country house, and their characters are exposed through various complications in their relationships but most of all through their conversation. Novelties and fads of the early 1920s are glanced at lightheartedly. This novel set a pattern for his next three novels, climaxing in *Point Counter Point* (1928); certain themes and character types reappeared in new disguises, but the canvas in these novels grew larger, and the satire often more virulent. Always witty and erudite, Huxley came to represent a postwar generation disenchanted with the beliefs and standards of the prewar era, more or less sincerely testing out new mindsets. Though he experimented with increasingly complex forms of narration and tended to view the maladies of his time in psychological rather than sociopolitical terms, he was, and remained, above all concerned with ideas. His novels are, in a sense, enlarged versions of the essays he wrote throughout his life, providing commentaries on an immense variety of topics. Concerned as he was with the future of humanity in a world of apparently uncontrollable change, he was naturally attracted by the utopian and the science-fiction tale, fictional forms that are basically fueled by ideas and speculation on what those ideas may mean if they are transferred into reality.

Brian W. Aldiss posits in his *Trillion Year Spree: The History of Science Fiction* (1986) that "*Brave New World* is arguably the Western world's most famous science fiction novel." With this novel, which has never been out of print since its first publication in February 1932, Huxley reached a larger public than ever before or after. Most of his other novels seem to have faded along with the time they were written in, but his name is inseparable from this book, which has obtained the status of a classic and has, together with George Orwell's *Nineteen Eighty-Four* (1949), provided a whole frame of reference for half a century of debates on what—with a slight rephrasing of a Huxley essay title—may be called the future of the present. In the history of science fiction it stands out as a seminal work, a model for later cautionary tales set in the future.

Originally, *Brave New World* appears to have been conceived by Huxley as a light diversion. He had in mind a parody of Wells's utopias, notably *Men Like Gods* (1923). He had, he said twenty-five years later in a letter to Mrs. Arthur Goldsmith, an American acquaintance,

"been having a little fun pulling the leg of H. G. Wells," but then he "got caught up in the excitement of [his] own ideas." Like others of his generation, he was skeptical about the belief in evolutionary progress that had been prominent in the thinking of the late-nineteenth and the early-twentieth centuries and that had been almost personified by Wells. Though some of Wells's utopias are actually anti-utopias, in his later works he seemed able to fall back on the conviction that science and reason would prevail in the end. This belief in the impartiality and inherent benevolence of science and technology was precisely what raised Huxley's doubts. The allure of technology is that it makes life easier; the danger is that science and technology are also tools in a quest for power. *Brave New World* depicts the ultimate technocracy.

Similar misgivings had been voiced by Russell in *The Scientific Outlook*, which, newly published, may have been on Huxley's table when he set to work on his novel in the summer of 1931. Behind the massive industrialization undertaken in the Soviet Union, Russell saw an ascendant oligarchy of scientific experts in alliance with party bureaucrats. Russell envisaged a "world State," already in the making in the United States as well as in the Soviet Union, where all aspects of human existence would be controlled by "scientific manipulation."

The opening lines of *Brave New World* are a model example of how a science-fiction concept is introduced into a known setting: "A squat grey building of only thirty-four stories. Over the main entrance the words, CENTRAL LONDON HATCHERY AND CONDITIONING CENTRE, and, in a shield, the World State's motto, COMMUNITY, IDENTITY, STABILITY." On the following pages a group of students are being introduced to the marvels of the Centre by its Director. The basis of the unalterable stability of the World State is demonstrated: "Bokanovsky's process," cloned fetuses in bottles, up to ninety-six in number, on a production line, each being exposed to the stimuli, or lack of such, that will fit them for their future stations in a caste hierarchy as members of the Alpha elite, or as Betas, Deltas, Gammas, or "semi-moron" Epsilons. In the second chapter the tour proceeds to the "NEO-PAVLOVIAN CONDITIONING ROOMS," the infant nurseries where further conditioning takes place with the use of hypnopedia, repetitive sleep-teaching. Certain desirable reflexes are firmly implanted in the infants' subconscious minds, desirable for the caste they were "decanted" into, and for a society based on mass production and mass consumption.

In chapter three, with a shift to cinematic crosscuts, the perspective widens. Sex, now completely divorced from procreation, is encouraged as an innocuous pastime (as long as it is strictly promiscuous) along with games involving an elaborate apparatus that increases consumption, and the "feelies" ("virtual reality" would be the cur-

Huxley in 1926 with his son, Matthew

rent term) with "scent-organ accompaniment," which have replaced old-time movies as the medium of mass entertainment. The reader gets the first snapshots of some of the major characters caught in medias res. Most significant at this point is the introduction of Mustapha Mond, "The Resident Controller for Western Europe. . . . One of the Ten World Controllers," who gratifies the students by his unplanned presence. Through his discourse the reader gets a sketchy outline of what has happened to the world in the six centuries that have passed from A.D. 1932 to A.F. 632, the year 632 After Ford.

Though *Brave New World* marks a new departure in Huxley's fiction, it continues the satiric mode of his earlier writings and deals with contemporary issues he had touched on before, both in novels and essays. In science fiction he had found a new, effective mold for his satire. Industrial mass production—as exemplified in Henry Ford's production line, the movie industry, the manipulative slogans of mass advertising, the development of air transport, drugs, even the invention of the zipper, all perfectly visible features of the contemporary scene—could be linked with Pavlovian behaviorism, Sigmund Freud's view of family and the human psyche, and trends toward uni-

formity at the expense of individual choice evident in communism and fascism, and certainly not absent in the capitalistic West. In science fiction Huxley's work is distinctive in encompassing so many contemporary phenomena, not just one or a few of them, and displaying them in what might be their logical extremes.

As early as in *Crome Yellow* Mr. Scogan, an eccentric Wellsian, thrilled his lady listeners with his vision of a scientifically regulated society: "An impersonal generation will take the place of Nature's hideous system. In vast state incubators, rows upon rows of gravid bottles will supply the world with the population it requires. The family system will disappear; society, sapped at its very base, will have to find new foundations; and Eros, beautifully and irresponsibly free, will flit like a gay butterfly from flower to flower through a sunlit world." Eleven years later, in *Brave New World,* the sinister implication of the "new foundations" is seen to be the complete regimentation, beyond recall, of the human mind.

Perhaps the most alarming feature of Huxley's anti-utopia is the perpetuated contentment of its genetically engineered inhabitants. In Mustapha Mond's words, "People are happy; they get what they want, and they never want what they can't get." The interlude between a desire and its gratification has been eliminated, for that interlude may breed discontent and would thus be a threat to "social stability," but of course no desire is admitted that cannot be gratified in the form of material comfort or sensual pleasure. Medical technology has abolished sickness and old age: peace of mind is ensured by free access to soma, the all-purpose happiness drug, and the compulsory monthly shot of VPS, Violent Passion Surrogate. The family, a dirty word out of humanity's "viviparous" past, has been replaced by the communal decree "everybody belongs to everybody else." Religion has become parodic Ford worship, and the cross has been replaced by the T, the Ford sign. History is discarded as "bunk" (as Ford had actually done in an interview in 1919) and is locked away in the World Controller's safe, as is "high art," another potential source of unrest. Poetry exists only as commercial jingles (funny parodies of them), which bear out the sleep-taught maxims of the World State.

For a time the plot focuses on two Alpha malcontents who "shared . . . the knowledge that they were individuals." One is an unfulfilled artist; the other, Bernard Marx, is troubled by his less-than-Alpha size (possibly caused by a slightly incorrect dosage at the bottle stage) and his unorthodox monogamous infatuation with an uncomprehending "Alpha Minus" female, Lenina. He obtains permission to take her on an excursion to Malpais (Spanish for "bad country"), a "Savage Reservation" in New Mexico. The life of the Native Americans on the Reservation presents a squalid contrast to the technical efficiency of the World State. Their community is primitive and agricultural; they die of diseases or old age; and their lives are ruled by strict tribal custom and a mix of religious ritual. During their visit Bernard and Lenina meet John, the Savage, and Bernard conceives a scheme to get back at his boss, the Director of the Hatchery and Conditioning Centre, who had threatened him with exile in Iceland. The Savage is, it appears, the Director's son. His mother had been lost on a trip to the Reservation, and a Native American had become his adoptive father. Bernard arranges for the Savage to be taken to London, where he causes a sensation and the downfall of the Director, who finds himself faced with a young man who addresses him with the unspeakable word "Father."

The Savage is a misfit in both worlds. Never accepted by the Native Americans as one of their kind, his cultural baggage is *Shakespeare's Collected Works,* a cause of laughing incomprehension among World State citizens. He soon discovers that they are not the beautiful people of a "brave new world" who had delighted Miranda in *The Tempest* (1611). He is horrified by their cloned uniformity and isolates himself, trying to fight off his illicit lusting, as he sees it, for Lenina. Guilt-ridden after witnessing his mother dying in a soma haze, he faces Mustapha Mond in

a pivotal confrontation. Impervious to the World Controller's dialectics, he maintains his individuality and persists in claiming "the right to be unhappy." But it is a solitary stance, and solitude is not granted him. When rumors of his masochistic excesses attract sensation-hungry crowds to the remote lighthouse where he has sought refuge, he commits suicide.

The role of the Savage has been a matter of divergent opinions in critical assessments of *Brave New World.* He cannot be said to represent a viable alternative to the World State philosophy set forth with inexorable clarity by the World Controller, and yet he stands, in his neurotic way, for the value of free choice. But for him no choice seems possible. He can neither return as an outsider to Malpais nor embrace the comfortable servitude of the World State. All cards seem stacked in his disfavor. In a foreword to a 1946 edition of the novel Huxley expressed regret for this trap and suggested that the Savage should have been given a third possibility, "in a community of exiles and refugees . . . living within the borders of the reservation." But this option, one might argue, would be less consistent with the premises Huxley had laid out for his World State, the most significant being its finality, its unalterability.

Huxley returned to his most famous book on several other occasions. When George Orwell's *Nineteen Eighty-Four* appeared in 1949 and invited comparisons with *Brave New World,* Huxley wrote Orwell an appreciative letter but found it doubtful that the "boot-on-the-face" tyranny described by Orwell could endure. Future governments would be more likely to employ the "less arduous" means of control he had envisaged in his own novel. In 1958, twenty-six years after the publication of *Brave New World* and thirteen years after World War II, Huxley took stock in *Brave New World Revisited* and could point to much that seemed to bring his vision of the future closer to reality sooner than he had anticipated. In this series of interconnected essays he dealt with topics such as overpopulation, overorganization, the subliminal persuasion developed in advertising and visual media, and other trends that seemed to indicate that, to paraphrase Sir Winston Churchill, "never have so many been manipulated so much by so few." The question remained whether the human race, being "moderately gregarious" by nature but not a race of termites, could be educated to value freedom. Or would humans always, as thought by Fyodor Dostoevsky's Grand Inquisitor in his 1879–1880 novel, *The Brothers Karamazov* (a model for Huxley's World Controller), be ready to lay down freedom and say to their rulers, "Make us slaves, but feed us"?

In two of his later novels Huxley included fantastic elements in otherwise realistic settings. In *After Many a Summer* (1939), written shortly after he had settled in California with his wife and son in 1938, speculations on longevity set the stage for a comic-horror conclusion. An eighteenth-century English nobleman is revealed to have discovered a life-prolonging effect from eating the viscera of carp and turns out to be still alive and over two hundred years old, though degenerated into happy apehood. In *Time Must Have a Stop* (1944), a best-seller in the United States, one of the characters, a pleasure-loving libertine, refuses to accept his own death and clings to a somehow ineffectual afterlife, struggling to keep his separate essence from being absorbed by the luminous center of things. These novels show the influence of Huxley's friend Gerald Heard, the British mystic, whose philosophy drew upon Buddhism as well as psychoanalysis. Like all of the novels Huxley published in the 1930s and 1940s, they sparked critical debate and varying assessments.

No mention of the potential of nuclear physics had been made in *Brave New World*—a "failure of foresight," Huxley called this omission in his 1946 foreword, for nuclear technology had been "a popular topic of conversation for years before the book was written." In 1948, when he wrote his second novel set in the future, *Ape and Essence,* his theme was the consequences of atomic warfare. The short novel opens, symbolically, in Hollywood on the day of Mahatma Gandhi's assassination in 1947, but this opening turns out to be only a frame for the actual story, a rejected motion-picture script found in a dumpster. Three or four generations after the destruction of most of the world in an atomic war, an expedition sets out from New Zealand, which was untouched because of its geographic isolation, to explore California, where humanity is presumed to be extinct. That is not the case, but the descendants of the few survivors have regressed into a primitive, apelike existence, scavenging among the ruins of a past civilization. Sex is limited to the annual rutting period, and then as an orgy of violence. Women are despised and contemptuously referred to as "vessels" because they are seen as carriers of the curse that the majority of infants are born deformed. The most deformed babies are killed, and their mothers are cruelly whipped. Logically, Belial is worshiped, for has it not been proven that he has won, and so must be propitiated? Religious rituals, administered by a hierarchy of castrated priests, are depicted in detail as Christianity reversed.

Ape and Essence was not well received. Huxley was accused of morbidity and of indulging in sadistic horrors for their own sake. In hindsight, it is possible to give the novel credit as an early serious treatment of the postnuclear holocaust theme and for warnings that are still pertinent. In a long sequence the Arch-Vicar, the head priest, explains the philosophy of Belianism to a captive New Zealand scientist:

> From the very beginning of the industrial revolution
> He foresaw that men would be made so overweeningly

Dust jacket for Huxley's classic 1932 dystopian novel about a twenty-fifth-century Britain in which people are totally controlled by technology (from Modern First Editions: Catalogue 297 *[London: Bertram Rota, 2001])*

bumptious by the miracles of their own technology that they would soon lose all sense of reality. And that's precisely what happened. These wretched slaves of wheels and ledgers began to congratulate themselves on being the Conquerors of Nature. Conquerors of Nature, indeed! . . . Just consider what they were up to during the century and a half before the Thing. Fouling the rivers, killing off the wild animals, destroying the forests, washing the topsoil into the sea, burning up an ocean of petroleum, squandering the minerals. . . . An orgy of criminal imbecility. And they called it Progress.

Only Belial, he argues, could have put that concept of progress into human minds. *Ape and Essence* presents an unmitigated dystopia, but in contrast with *Brave New World,* a glimmer of hope is let in when the scientist escapes with his newfound girlfriend to join a community of "Hots," people banished because they are in heat throughout the year.

At one point the Arch-Vicar contemplates the possibility, unpalatable to this Satanic priest, that things could

Dust jacket for Huxley's 1958 essay collection, in which he assesses how far society has moved toward the conditions he predicted in Brave New World

have turned out differently: "Eastern mysticism making sure that Western science should be properly used; the Eastern art of living refining Western energy; Western individualism tempering Eastern totalitarianism . . . it would have been the kingdom of heaven." During the last two decades of his life Huxley's writings were to a great extent influenced by his study of Eastern mystics. In *The Perennial Philosophy* (1945), an anthology of quotations with commentary, he tried to define the common core of transcendental philosophy and mystical experience throughout the ages: the perception of the basic oneness of humanity and God, atman and Brahman, underlying all religion. In two controversial books, *The Doors of Perception* (1954) and *Heaven and Hell* (1956), he discussed his own experiments with hallucinogens (mescaline and LSD). Though he found similarities between the states of mind induced by these drugs and the visions of mystics, he never claimed to have had such visions himself or to have achieved any kind of transcendence, only increased self-

knowledge. This admission, and his awareness of the potential negative effects of the drugs he tested, have often been overlooked by critics of these books. He did, however, remain interested in the possibility of a mind-liberating drug without negative side effects.

In his last novel, *Island,* written and published a year before his death of cancer in 1963, he invents such a drug, called moksha, and in his description of its effects he drew upon his own experiences in *The Doors of Perception.* Moksha is used by the inhabitants of Pala, a fictional island in the Indian Ocean. In the nineteenth century a Scots surgeon had come to Pala to treat the local raja for a tumor, and the two men formed a lifelong friendship. A bond was created between Western science, applied beneficially, and ancient Buddhist religion. A truly utopian community developed, which at the beginning of the novel has existed for about a hundred years. Almost point by point this novel can be viewed as an antithesis to *Brave New World.* The people of Pala live in a network of extended families. Family planning is practiced; genetic improvement is ensured by artificial insemination; sickness and death (going into "the Clear Light") are dealt with communally; aggression is channeled; and children are carefully educated in the spiritual exercises that will make them harmonious, knowledgeable members of the community—all by a discerning application of Western science combined with Eastern spirituality. Humanity is at peace with nature; in one scene a Buddha figure in a living room is encircled by a live cobra. Moksha is used to enhance any experience—from love, to classical music, to the contemplation of the unity of all being. The Western, Manichaean dichotomy of good and evil has been resolved in "the reconciliation of yes and no lived out in total acceptance and the blessed experience of Not-Two."

The utopia is not meant to last, however; Pala is already being infiltrated by multinational oil companies and a mainland dictator wanting to exploit Pala's natural resources. In the end the defenseless Palanese community is simply snuffed out by the brute force of the "Modern World." Only the mynah birds with their parrot-like cry of "Attention"—the first and the last word in the novel—remain as reminders of what has been destroyed.

Island received a tepid reception from reviewers and is rarely ranked among Huxley's best books. The least friendly critics called the islanders brainwashed and found moksha similar to soma. Viewed more objectively, the novel can be regarded as an attempt to popularize ideas that had occupied Huxley for many years but that might easily seem abstruse by clothing them in the garment of fiction. He had been at pains to create a plot and credible characters and to depend on dialogue. *Island,* moreover, harks back to a classical utopian tradition, ranging from Plato, Thomas More, and Francis Bacon to William Morris, Samuel Butler, Edward Bellamy, and Wells, even to the point of letting the protagonist, a spying journalist and later a convert, be shipwrecked on an imaginary island, where the utopian marvels are unfolded–a tradition sometimes deprecated by Huxley. With this novel he, the satirist, had joined the club as a serious-minded member. But despite earnest efforts, he could not escape the didacticism inherent in the genre.

In 1956, after Maria Huxley's death from cancer the year before, Huxley married Laura Archera, a psychotherapist, who shared his commitments to mysticism and experimentation with drugs. These commitments have remained a matter of some controversy without affecting his position as a satirist, a science-fiction writer, a philosopher, a utopian, and a belated polyhistor with roots in nineteenth-century liberal humanism. His wide-ranging intellect and his untiring search for solutions to the dilemmas facing humanity in the twentieth century continued to surprise and challenge his readers to the end.

Letters:

The Letters of Aldous Huxley, edited by Grover Smith (London: Chatto & Windus, 1969; New York: Harper & Row, 1969).

Bibliographies:

Hanson R. Duval, *Aldous Huxley: A Bibliography* (New York: Arrow, 1939);

Claire John Eschelbach and Joyce Lee Shober, *Aldous Huxley: A Bibliography, 1916–1959* (Berkeley & Los Angeles: University of California Press, 1961; London: Cambridge University Press, 1961);

Thomas D. Clareson and Carolyn S. Andrews, "Aldous Huxley: A Bibliography 1960–1964," *Extrapolation,* 6 (December 1964): 2–21;

Dennis D. Davis, "Aldous Huxley: A Bibliography 1965–1973," *Bulletin of Bibliography of Criticism* (New York: Garland, 1981).

Biographies:

Julian Huxley, ed., *Aldous Huxley, 1894–1963: A Memorial Volume* (London: Chatto & Windus, 1965; New York: Harper & Row, 1965);

Laura Archera Huxley, *This Timeless Moment: A Personal View of Aldous Huxley* (New York: Farrar, Straus & Giroux, 1968; London: Chatto & Windus, 1969);

Sybille Bedford, *Aldous Huxley: A Biography* (2 volumes, London: Chatto & Windus, 1973–1974; 1 volume, New York: Knopf, 1974);

David King Dunaway, *Huxley in Hollywood* (New York: Harper & Row, 1989; London: Bloomsbury, 1989);

Dunaway, *Aldous Huxley Recollected: An Oral History* (New York: Carroll & Graf, 1995);

Nicholas Murray, *Aldous Huxley* (London: Little, Brown, 2002).

References:

Brian W. Aldiss with David Wingrove, *Trillion Year Spree: The History of Science Fiction* (London: Gollancz, 1986; New York: Atheneum, 1986);

John Atkins, *Aldous Huxley: A Literary Study* (London: Calder, 1956; revised, London: Calder & Boyars, 1967; New York: Orion Press, 1968);

Robert S. Baker, *Brave New World: History, Science, and Dystopia* (Boston: Twayne, 1990);

Baker, *The Dark Historic Page: Social Satire and Historicism in the Novels of Aldous Huxley 1921–1939* (Madison: University of Wisconsin Press, 1982);

Peter Bowering, *Aldous Huxley: A Study of the Major Novels* (London: Athlone Press, 1969; New York: Oxford University Press, 1969);

David Bradshaw, *The Hidden Huxley* (London: Faber & Faber, 1994);

Laurence Brander, *Aldous Huxley: A Critical Study* (London: Hart-Davis, 1970; Lewisburg, Pa.: Bucknell University Press, 1970);

June Deery, *Aldous Huxley and the Mysticism of Science* (New York: St. Martin's Press, 1996);

Peter E. Firchow, *Aldous Huxley: Satirist and Novelist* (Minneapolis: University of Minnesota Press, 1972);

Firchow, *The End of Utopia: A Study of Aldous Huxley's Brave New World* (Lewisburg, Pa.: Bucknell University Press, 1984);

John Griffin, *Brave New World by Aldous Huxley* (Harlow, U.K.: Longman, 1990);

Keith May, *Aldous Huxley* (New York: Barnes & Noble, 1972);

Jerome Meckier, *Aldous Huxley: Satire and Structure* (London: Chatto & Windus, 1969; New York: Barnes & Noble, 1971);

Meckier, ed., *Critical Essays on Aldous Huxley* (Detroit: Gale, 1995);

Donald Watt, ed., *Aldous Huxley: The Critical Heritage* (London: Routledge & Kegan Paul, 1975);

George Woodcock, *Dawn and the Darkest Hour: A Study of Aldous Huxley* (London: Faber & Faber, 1972; New York: Viking, 1972).

Papers:

The most substantial collection of Aldous Huxley's few remaining papers (following the destruction of most in a fire) is at the library of the University of California at Los Angeles. Some are also at the Stanford University Library.

Anna Kavan
(Helen Woods Ferguson Edmonds)
(10 April 1901 – 5 December 1968)

Darren Harris-Fain
Shawnee State University

BOOKS: *A Charmed Circle,* as Helen Ferguson (London: Cape, 1929); as Anna Kavan (London & Chester Springs, Pa.: Peter Owen, 1994);

The Dark Sisters, as Ferguson (London: Cape, 1930);

Let Me Alone, as Ferguson (London: Cape, 1930); as Kavan (London: Peter Owen, 1974);

A Stranger Still, as Ferguson (London: John Lane, 1935); as Kavan (London & Chester Springs, Pa.: Peter Owen, 1995);

Goose Cross, as Ferguson (London: John Lane, 1936);

Rich Get Rich, as Ferguson (London: John Lane, 1937);

Asylum Piece and Other Stories, as Anna Kavan (London: Cape, 1940; New York: Kesend, 1980);

Change the Name (London: Cape, 1941; London & Chester Springs, Pa.: Peter Owen, 1993);

I Am Lazarus: Short Stories (London: Cape, 1945);

Asylum Piece (Garden City, N.Y.: Doubleday, 1946)—comprises *Asylum Piece and Other Stories* and *I Am Lazarus;*

The House of Sleep (Garden City, N.Y.: Doubleday, 1947); republished as *Sleep Has His House* (London: Cassell, 1948; New York: Kesend, 1980);

The Horse's Tale, by Kavan and K. T. Bluth (London: Gaberbocchus Press, 1949);

A Scarcity of Love (Southport & London: Angus Downie, 1956; New York: Herder & Herder, 1972);

Eagles' Nest (London: Peter Owen, 1957);

A Bright Green Field, and Other Stories (London: Peter Owen, 1958);

Who Are You? (Lowestoft, U.K.: Scorpion, 1963);

Ice (London: Peter Owen, 1967; Garden City, N.Y.: Doubleday, 1970);

Julia and the Bazooka, and Other Stories, edited by Rhys Davies (London: Peter Owen, 1970; New York: Knopf, 1975);

My Soul in China: A Novella and Stories, edited by Davies (London: Peter Owen, 1975);

My Madness: The Selected Writings of Anna Kavan, edited by Brian W. Aldiss (London: Pan, 1990);

Mercury (London & Chester Springs, Pa.: Peter Owen, 1994);

The Parson (London & Chester Springs, Pa.: Peter Owen, 1995).

Helen Woods Ferguson Edmonds, who wrote her best-known work under the pseudonym Anna Kavan, is one of the most enigmatic of modern British writers. Her haunted life is reflected in her work, which is permeated with powerful language and surreal imagery akin to the fantastic fiction of writers such as Franz Kafka and J. G. Ballard. Her fictions are filled with dream-like, if not nightmarish, visions of warped realities and distorted imaginings. Such intensity may be part of the reason why for many years Kavan was not widely read at all, let alone as part of the tradition of British fantastic literature. Yet, as Brian W. Aldiss and other critics have pointed out, much of her work is fantastic in nature, and her novel *Ice* (1967) is one of the most distinctive works of science fiction since World War II. Moreover, her preoccupation with depicting psychological dramas through bizarre imagery foreshadows a similar concern with "inner space" in New Wave science fiction of the 1960s and 1970s. What Aldiss says in his introduction to *Ice* applies to much of her work: "this is no novel of old-fashioned realism; it is a metaphysical adventure, where the scenery is not painted to ape reality but to glide into the wings, revealing something more frightening beyond it."

Kavan was born Helen Emily Woods on 10 April 1901 in Cannes, France; her parents were Claude Charles Edward Woods and Helen Bright Woods. Her well-to-do English parents traveled extensively in her childhood, sometimes leaving her with relatives in England rather than taking her with them. When she was six her parents placed her in a boarding school in Rialto, California. Thus, much of her childhood was unhappy. First, she felt betrayed and abandoned by her parents, and she especially found her mother emotion-

Anna Kavan

ally distant; second, her father committed suicide in 1915, when she was fourteen. Following her father's death, she attended boarding schools in Switzerland and England. She was academically talented enough to be offered the opportunity to attend Oxford, but her mother did not give her enough money to do so. On 10 September 1920 Woods married Donald Ferguson, eleven years her senior. He took her with him to Burma, where he worked as a railway engineer. In 1922 the two had a son, Bryan Ferguson, but the marriage was a failure, and that same year she left her husband and returned to Europe. During this time, biographer D. A. Callard speculates, she began using drugs—first cocaine, then opium, then heroin. She was a heroin addict for the last forty years of her life.

During one of her visits to France, over the winter of 1925–1926, she met her longtime lover, Stuart Edmonds, a wealthy amateur painter. Later in life Kavan destroyed most of her letters and almost all of her diaries; however, she preserved her diary from July 1926 to November 1927, which recounts her passionate affair with Edmonds. They lived together for some time, but it is unclear whether they were ever officially married or if their marriage—she eventually assumed the name Helen Edmonds—was common-law. Early in

their relationship she became pregnant and had an abortion; later she bore Edmonds a daughter, but the child died in infancy.

In the 1920s and 1930s she began to publish novels as Helen Ferguson. In one of her first books, *Let Me Alone* (1930), she writes about a character named Anna Kavan, whose father abandoned her and who ends up marrying a man she does not love. (The character also appears in her 1935 novel, *A Stranger Still*.) Helen Ferguson was obviously the model for Anna Kavan, and later in her career the author adopted her character's name not only as her pen name but as her own.

Most of the Ferguson novels are realistic fiction, but *Goose Cross* (1936) is closer to fantasy. The discovery of a Roman skeleton brings down a curse on an English village. The romantic plot of the novel is at the forefront, but also important to the story is how the curse unexpectedly acts to refine the village inhabitants who survive its effects. Like the other Ferguson novels, *Goose Cross* received mixed reviews and found only a limited readership.

An important transitional period in the writer's life and career occurred following her breakup with Edmonds in the late 1930s. (The end of their relationship is the basis of the 1975 book *Honeysuckle Girl*, the

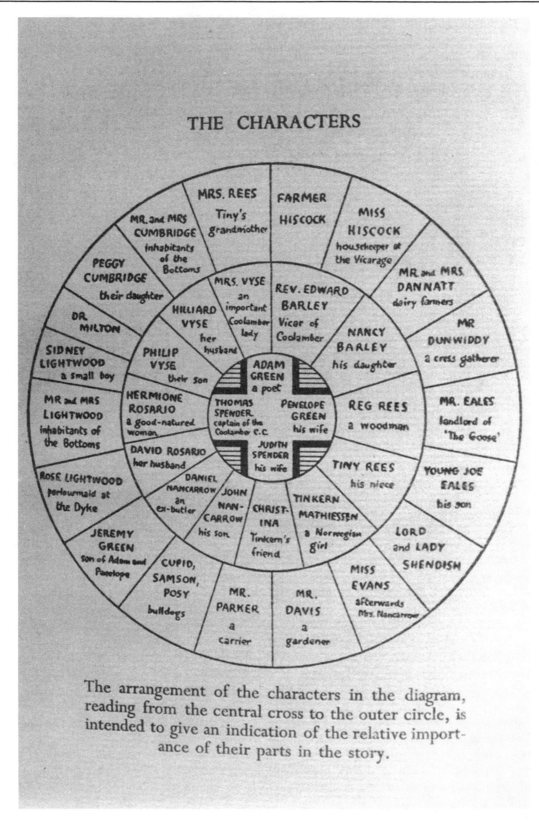

THE CHARACTERS

The arrangement of the characters in the diagram, reading from the central cross to the outer circle, is intended to give an indication of the relative importance of their parts in the story.

Author's diagram of the characters in her 1936 novel, Goose Cross, *which she published under the name Helen Ferguson (from Anna Kavan,* Goose Cross, *1936)*

last novel by her friend Rhys Davies, who first met her in the 1930s.) The two were different in many ways, and he abused alcohol just as she abused heroin; also, among the deleterious effects of heroin use is a substantial weakening of the libido, and Edmonds did not hide his infidelity. Ferguson had previously been treated for depression and drug addiction (during most of her lifetime, drug addiction was treated in England as an illness, and registered addicts such as Ferguson received drugs from the government, which tried various ways to cure the addicted), but the failure of her relationship with Edmonds brought about a massive breakdown and a lengthy hospitalization. She emerged as Anna Kavan, and her writing was even more intense than her earlier efforts as Ferguson.

Her first book as Kavan was *Asylum Piece and Other Stories* (1940). Unlike her previous work, which was for the most part conventionally romantic if rather personal and psychological, this collection includes many stories with fantastic elements. Most of Kavan's fantastic fiction stems from two sources: the stylistic experimentation in which she engaged when she began writing as Kavan, and her attempt to capture heightened or distorted perceptions and emotions. For instance, the stories in *Asylum Piece and Other Stories* are based on her experiences as a psychiatric patient. In the title story the asylum is a cage, and its inmates are birds. As in Ken Kesey's novel *One Flew over the Cuckoo's Nest* (1962), the world described by characters with severe mental illnesses such as schizophrenia strikes readers as fantastic with its depictions of their delusions and hallucinations. The posthumous collection *Julia and the Bazooka, and Other Stories* (1970), like *Asylum Piece and Other Stories,* includes some pieces that are fantastic in nature.

During this period Kavan traveled extensively and ended most of her connections with other people, limiting her relationships to a select few—including her doctor, K. T. Bluth; her publisher; and fellow writer Davies. In 1942 her son, whose relationship with her was not close, was killed while serving in the Royal Air Force. Her fictional characters often found themselves repelled by other people, and this repeated trait likely has its basis in Kavan's tortured and often erratic personality. Kavan published several books in her lifetime, but she did not earn enough from them to support herself entirely, especially not in the comfortable lifestyle she had enjoyed with Edmonds. She added to her income by writing articles for magazines such as *Harper's Bazaar* and *The New Yorker* and by working as an assistant editor on Cyril Connolly's *Horizon,* which also published her work. In addition, she purchased, reno-

Helen Emily Woods circa 1914. She changed her name to Anna Kavan in 1939.

vated, and sold houses on the side, painted as a hobby, and continued to travel the world.

Her novel *Sleep Has His House* (1948), published in the United States a year earlier as *The House of Sleep,* is like much of Kavan's work in its use of surrealistic imagery as a reflection of extreme psychological states. The book, narrated using the stream-of-consciousness technique, concerns an unhappy young girl and how she creates a fantasy world within her mind. Although *Asylum Piece* (1946), the American publication of her first two collections, *Asylum Piece and Other Stories* and *I Am Lazarus* (1945), had been well received, *Sleep Has His House* fared poorly in the United States and Britain alike.

As was often the case, Kavan was consoled by Bluth, her doctor. In addition, she collaborated with Bluth, a man of literary interests, on her next book, *The Horse's Tale* (1949). The book is an animal fable about an extraordinary circus horse named Kathbar who can recite poetry and sing. Fated for the slaughterhouse, Kathbar instead runs away from his owner and becomes a celebrity of sorts as an artist. When his fame declines, he lapses into depression, and after passing out drunk at a party he wakes to find himself in an asylum. There, after some uncertainty about his identity and destiny, Kathbar recovers and decides to return to the circus.

By the 1950s what little literary reputation Kavan enjoyed had evaporated, and she published almost nothing in periodicals and relied on small presses or vanity presses to publish her books—such as *A Scarcity of Love* (1956), based on her love-hate relationship with her mother, who died in 1955. Kavan's career began to turn around, however, when she met publisher Peter Owen, who supported and published almost all of Kavan's work for the remainder of her career and after her death.

Eagles' Nest (1957), like many novels of fantasy, employs the motif of the quest; it also reveals, like much of Kavan's fiction, the influence of Kafka on her work. The protagonist journeys to Eagles' Nest, a fortress that serves as a portal to a hellish, hallucinatory fantasy world. Like many of Kavan's works, this book shows readers her uncanny talent for combining the psychological with the phantasmagoric in a disturbing nightmare landscape:

> I felt I could have put out my hand and touched the volcanic hills, rising like islands from this unstable brilliance, mirages floating in the transparent dazzle. Beyond them, nothing was to be seen but mountains, all of the same stark, forbidding outline, flat-topped, rectilinear, savagely coloured and depthless-looking, as if painted on the cobalt sky; crowding one behind another like a gigantic city of vast skyscrapers, or a monstrous cemetery of colossal coffins stood up on end. There was something frighteningly strange about these angular identical mountains, so different from the grandeur of the snow-capped mountains I knew, and seeming to have no life or soul, as they stretched away to infinity, range beyond range, gruesome in their impressiveness, overpowering, a horror of dead rock.

The language, tone, and imagery of *Eagles' Nest* are similar to Kavan's earlier fiction and anticipate *Ice*—as does a novella titled "New and Splendid" and collected in her next book, *A Bright Green Field* (1958). The novella is not as science-fictional as *Ice,* but it shows Kavan using science-fiction ideas as a means of expression, in this case through her depiction of a futuristic city, modeled on New York, divided by class into the High City and the Lanes.

Kavan settled into a more retired existence in the 1960s, traveling and moving less and devoting herself more to her writing. In *Who Are You?* (1963) she again uses her first marriage as the basis for the story; this time, however, her treatment is more impressionistic and experimental. It evoked positive remarks from Jean Rhys, who praised the novel in a letter to her friend Francis Wyndham, and Anaïs Nin, who wrote about Kavan's fiction in her 1969 study, *The Novel of the Future.* (Despite its title, Nin's book does not concern science fiction.)

Ice is also marked with Kavan's trademark style and concerns. Moreover, it bears a strong similarity to the French *nouveau roman* (New Novel), which Kavan admired, with its abandonment of conventional treatments of fictional elements such as plot and characterization; in addition, the narrative is often disrupted without warning with dream sequences that call into question the division between real and unreal. The apocalyptic novel, which is set in a future ice age that follows a nuclear holocaust and which features a dystopian society, is really more about the search for meaning and identity than it is about the cataclysm that leads to the story. As the narrator of *Ice* says at one point, "My surroundings . . . seemed vaguely familiar, and yet distorted, unreal. My ideas were confused. In a peculiar way, the unreality of the outer world appeared to be an extension of my own disturbed state of mind."

The setting of *Ice* is a nameless northern region filled with ceaseless military action. The male narrator, fearing for a young woman in an unhappy marriage, pursues her as she flees through shifting war zones and the encroaching ice age that threatens them all. Again, there is a strong autobiographical element in the book: the young woman's attempts to survive include flight from an unloving husband and a former lover.

The reputation of *Ice* as a science-fiction novel rests to a large extent on Aldiss, a New Wave science-fiction writer who praised the work both in his introduction to its 1970 publication and in his 1973 *Billion Year Spree: The True History of Science Fiction* (substantially revised and expanded with David Wingrove in 1986 as *Trillion Year Spree: The History of Science Fiction*). In his introduction he calls *Ice* the best science-fiction novel of 1967. Kavan had not written it as a science-fiction work, according to Aldiss, nor was it published as such; in a 1966 letter to her publisher about the manuscript that eventually became *Ice* she describes it as a cross between Kafka and the British television program *The Avengers* (1961–1969). But when her publisher and friend Owen told her that the novel was science fiction, she had no problem with accepting her placement in the category: "That's the way I see the world now," she told him. She read science fiction in the 1960s and especially liked Aldiss's work even before he asked to meet her. Late in life she also became a fan of the popular

Anna Kavan was born in France, and spent her childhood in several European countries and in California. She completed her education in England. She married and for a time lived in Burma. It was during this period that she began writing.

Her marriage failed, and she remarried and spent some time in various parts of Europe. Several books were published, and she continued to write, even during periods of mental illness which she spent in clinics in Switzerland and in England. Her experiences there provided material for her book, *Asylum Piece*.

During part of the war she lived in New York, and later worked as a researcher for a military psychiatric unit. In 1942 she became an assistant editor of *Horizon*, in which some of her own stories were published. She worked with Cyril Connolly, Stephen Spender, Arthur Koestler and other well-known writers.

Anna Kavan's work has been highly praised by critics, although the quality and originality of her writing have only recently become more widely appreciated. Her books have appeared in the USA and this is the third of her books to be published by Peter Owen.

Her chief recreation is painting and her work has been exhibited. She is also interested in architecture and interior decoration.

Rear panel of the dust jacket, inscribed by Kavan, for her 1967 novel Ice
(Special Collections, McFarlin Library, The University of Tulsa)

British science-fiction television show *Doctor Who* (1963–1992).

Kavan's lifelong struggles with depression, suicide attempts, and heroin addiction ended when she died of heart failure in 1968; her body was discovered in her house in London on 5 December, but she may have died a day earlier. Since her death she has approached the status of a literary cult figure among some readers familiar with her books. Likewise, *Ice* is regarded by some readers of science fiction as a classic unlike any other work in the field. Though it is unlikely that her work will ever be widely read because of the darkness of her vision–in a 1949 letter to friend and fellow writer Raymond Marriott she wrote, "As so-called literature becomes more and more commercialised, 'real' writing is bound to take more and more obscure and personal forms until it's finally only intelligible to a small number of sensitive people"–her difficult life and compelling fiction are sure to attract attention from a selective group of readers for years to come.

Biography:

D. A. Callard, *The Case of Anna Kavan* (London: Peter Owen, 1992).

References:

Brian W. Aldiss and David Wingrove, *Trillion Year Spree: The History of Science Fiction* (London: Gollancz, 1986; New York: Atheneum, 1986), pp. 336–337;

Janet Byrne, "Moving toward Entropy: Anna Kavan's Science Fiction Mentality," *Extrapolation,* 23 (Spring 1982): 5–11;

Margaret Crosland, "Experimenting (2)," in her *Beyond the Lighthouse: English Women Novelists in the Twentieth Century* (New York: Taplinger, 1981), pp. 186–192;

Rhys Davies, "Anna Kavan," *Books and Bookmen* (March 1971): 7–10;

Priscilla Dorr, "Anna Kavan: A Critical Introduction," dissertation, University of Tulsa, 1988;

Anaïs Nin, *The Novel of the Future* (London: Peter Owen, 1969), pp. 13, 139, 166, 171.

Papers:

Anna Kavan's papers and correspondence are located at the McFarlin Library, University of Tulsa; at the Harry Ransom Humanities Research Center, University of Texas at Austin; and in the Rhys Davies papers at the National Library of Wales, Aberystwyth.

Gerald Kersh

(26 August 1911 – 5 November 1968)

Robert Carrick

BOOKS: *Jews Without Jehovah* (London: Wishart, 1934);

Men Are So Ardent (London: Wishart, 1935; New York: Morrow, 1936);

Night and the City (London: Joseph, 1938; New York: Simon & Schuster, 1946); republished as *Dishonor* (New York: Avon, 1955);

I Got References (London: Joseph, 1939);

The Private Life of a Private, Being Extracts from the Diary of a Soldier of Britain's New Army, anonymous (London: W. H. Allen, 1941);

They Die with Their Boots Clean (London & Toronto: Heinemann, 1941; New York: Vanguard, 1952);

The Nine Lives of Bill Nelson (London & Toronto: Heinemann, 1942);

The Dead Look On (London & Toronto: Heinemann, 1943; New York: Reynal & Hitchcock, 1943);

Selected Stories (London: Staples & Staples, 1943);

A Brain and Ten Fingers (London & Toronto: Heinemann, 1943);

The Battle of the Singing Men (London: Everybody's Books, 1944);

The Horrible Dummy and Other Stories (London & Toronto: Heinemann, 1944);

Faces in a Dusty Picture (London & Toronto: Heinemann, 1944; New York: McGraw-Hill, 1945);

An Ape, a Dog and a Serpent (London & Toronto: Heinemann, 1945);

Sergeant Nelson of the Guards (Philadelphia: Winston, 1945)—comprises *They Die with Their Boots Clean* and *The Nine Lives of Bill Nelson;*

The Weak and the Strong (London: Heinemann, 1945; New York: Simon & Schuster, 1946);

Neither Man Nor Dog (London & Toronto: Heinemann, 1946);

Clean, Bright and Slightly Oiled (London: Heinemann, 1946);

Sad Road to the Sea (London & Toronto: Heinemann, 1947);

Gerald Kersh (photograph by Carlyle Studios; from the dust jacket for Night and the City, *1946)*

Prelude to a Certain Midnight (London & Toronto: Heinemann, 1947; Garden City, N.Y.: Doubleday, 1947);

The Song of the Flea (London: Heinemann, 1948; Garden City, N.Y.: Doubleday, 1948);

Clock Without Hands (London: Heinemann, 1949);

The Thousand Deaths of Mr. Small (Garden City, N.Y.: Doubleday, 1950; London: Heinemann, 1951);

The Brazen Bull (London: Heinemann, 1952);

The Great Wash (London: Heinemann, 1953); republished as *The Secret Masters* (New York: Ballantine, 1953);

The Brighton Monster and Others (London: Heinemann, 1953);

Guttersnipe: Little Novels (London: Heinemann, 1954);

Men Without Bones, and Other Stories (London: Heinemann, 1955); republished, with different contents, as *Men Without Bones* (New York: Paperback Library, 1962);

Fowler's End (New York: Simon & Schuster, 1957; London: Heinemann, 1958);

On an Odd Note: Science Fiction Stories (New York: Ballantine, 1958);

The Best of Gerald Kersh, edited by Simon Raven (London: Heinemann, 1960);

The Ugly Face of Love and Other Stories (London: Heinemann, 1960; New York: Ace, 1962);

The Implacable Hunter (London: Heinemann, 1961);

The Terribly Wild Flowers: Nine Stories (London: Heinemann, 1962);

More Than Once Upon a Time (London: Heinemann, 1964);

The Hospitality of Miss Tolliver and Other Stories (London: Heinemann, 1965);

A Long Cool Day in Hell (London: Heinemann, 1965);

The Angel and the Cuckoo (New York: New American Library, 1966; London: Heinemann, 1967);

Nightshade & Damnations, edited by Harlan Ellison (Greenwich, Conn.: Fawcett, 1968; London: Hodder Fawcett, 1969);

Brock (London: Heinemann, 1969).

SELECTED PERIODICAL PUBLICATIONS–
UNCOLLECTED: "Jack of Swords," *Saturday Evening Post* (1, 8, 15, 22, 29 October 1949);

"Trip Out on Red Lizzie," *Saturday Evening Post* (27 January 1968): 50–52, 54–55.

Gerald Kersh entered the British world of letters in 1934 with an unusual work. *Jews Without Jehovah* purported to be a novel, but it included observations on some of the idiosyncracies of real members of the Kersh family–to the point that several of the author's uncles and a cousin filed libel suits against him. The book was withdrawn from sale after fewer than a hundred copies had been sold. Kersh persevered, however, and by the end of World War II he had more than a dozen books in print, short-story collections as well as novels. Indeed, in January 1944 *Newsweek* magazine reported that four of Kersh's books were on the London bestseller lists at the end of 1943.

Kersh wrote a total of twenty novels, two autobiographical reminiscences, and ten or more collections of short stories, depending upon how one counts collections including stories that have previously appeared in other collections under the same or different titles. How

many short stories he wrote altogether is, like many aspects of his life and career, a matter of widely varying conjecture. It seems highly unlikely that he wrote the three thousand stories attributed to him by his brother, Cyril Kersh, in a 1990 memoir, but there can be no argument with John Clute's statement in *The Encyclopedia of Science Fiction* (1993) that Kersh was "very prolific in shorter forms," nor with Brian Ash's in *Who's Who in Science Fiction* (1976) that he produced "a prodigious quantity" of stories. In his entry on Kersh, Clute remarks that "many of his numerous short stories are sf or fantasy," and he goes on to give as examples stories that fall into generally recognized categories of speculative fiction, such as "Whatever Happened to Corporal Cuckoo?" (immortality), "Voices in the Dust of Annan" (postholocaust), and "Men Without Bones" (aliens among us). In *The Encyclopedia of Fantasy* (1997) Clute cites examples of fantasy stories written by Kersh: "The Extraordinarily Horrible Dummy" (possession), "In a Room without Walls" (posthumous fantasy), "The Scene of the Crime" (ghost story), "The Brighton Monster" (timeslip/monster), and "The Oxoxoco Bottle" (lost race). He also classes Kersh's 1953 novel *The Great Wash* as science fiction. Stories by Kersh have appeared in such unassailable bastions of their genres as *The Pan Book of Horror* series (for "horror" read "dark fantasy") and Judith Merril's *Year's Best SF* series.

Depending upon which biographical source one reads, Gerald Kersh was born either in London or in Russia–in 1911 according to Clute and others, and in 1909 according to *Newsweek* and yet others. Full agreement on the facts of this man's life seems unlikely, since even Kersh promoted stories about himself of questionable veracity. However, Paul Duncan writes that Kersh's birth certificate reveals he was born on 26 August 1911, in Teddington, a suburb of London. Details of his early education are unknown, but at age thirteen he won a scholarship and attended the Regent Street Polytechnic.

In the newspaper and magazine columns on both sides of the Atlantic and in the biographical notes in his books, Kersh gained a larger-than-life image, undoubtedly enhanced by his good looks, his reportedly prodigious physical strength, and a succession of day jobs. Reviewers of his work attributed to him employment experience in at least twenty types of jobs. All seemed to agree that he had served in the Coldstream Guards during World War II and was a bouncer in a London nightclub before that, and the consensus was that he had wrestled professionally for a while; other than that, accounts varied widely. One biographical source said he had been both a manual laborer and a French teacher, but only *The New York Times,* in Kersh's obituary (8 November 1968), reported that he was a spy for

Britain in World War II, citing the author himself as the source of that information.

Early in his career Kersh worked as a freelance journalist, mostly in London in the 1930s. According to his brother, he contributed many editorial pieces for such Norman Kark publications as *Courier* and *Shelf Appeal.* Duncan says Kersh wrote short stories for *John O'London's Weekly,* and various other references indicate that he wrote for many other periodicals published in London in the 1930s and 1940s. Biographers may never be able to credit him with most of those pieces, however, because many of them were written under pseudonyms; Piers England and Waldo Kellar are just two mentioned by his brother. He wrote a lot of copy for the *Daily Mirror* on whatever subjects were assigned. Unfortunately, the *Mirror* keeps no index, so looking up one freelancer's work is a near-impossible task, especially since Kersh allegedly wrote under many different bylines.

"Comrade Death" was the first of his fantasy stories—actually dark fantasy or horror—to appear between book covers, in Kersh's first collection, *I Got References* (1939). With cardboard characters, B-movie dialogue, and a totally unbelievable plot, "Comrade Death" does not have much going for it. It does, however, reveal a trademark that Kersh used with great effect throughout his career, his talent for describing, in the most graphic terms, things hideous and horrible.

"The Extraordinarily Horrible Dummy," which appeared in *Selected Stories* (1943), deals with the horror of incipient madness and, for some imaginations, the horror of observing possession in the diabolical sense. At a mere 1,500 words, the story is too short to be subtle or to give the characters adequate treatment, but the idea—the transference of evil from a man to a ventriloquist's dummy—is an intriguing one.

"The Gentleman All in Black" appeared in *Today,* the magazine section of *The Philadelphia Enquirer,* in 1946. It is a short deal-with-the-devil story in which Old Nick outsmarts a shrewd businessman, but just barely. The piece is too long to qualify as a vignette and too short to be considered more than a promise of things to come.

Several speculative-fiction pieces appeared in the somewhat unsatisfactory collection *Neither Man Nor Dog,* also published in 1946. There are thirty-seven pieces in this book, most about five pages in length; many of them are no more than character studies, sketches, or vignettes. Some of the stories are reprints from popular London weeklies such as *John O'London's, John Bull, The Bystander,* and *Picture Post,* while others cannot be specifically dated. A few of the pieces are worth noting as part of Kersh's evolution from novice writer to professional. "In a Room without Walls" is a sketch about a *Pal Joey*-

"I have been clean-shaven since 1936, and gray-haired since 1938. The shiny glass reflected my face, strangely young, with a short black mustache."

Illustration by Geoffrey Biggs for Kersh's short story "Note on Danger B" in the 5 April 1947 issue of The Saturday Evening Post

type wiseguy taking advantage of a girl and possibly paying a terrible price. Ten years after its initial publication, it was reprinted by *Esquire,* then one of the highest-paying and increasingly male-oriented American magazines.

The idea of "The Old Burying Place" (reprinted from the *Evening Standard,* 25 May 1938) has become so overused that it seems a bit trite to read about a seemingly ancient tribe digging up an artifact that turns out to be a Piccadilly street sign. It would have been a new twist at the time, however, and probably effective, even though the story was no more than a nine-hundred-word vignette. "The Old Burying Place" was Kersh's first indisputably science-fiction (postholocaust) piece.

"Maria's Christ" (reprinted from *John Bull,* 17 January 1942) could be considered a war story, or a contemporary story of no particular genre, or speculative fiction. The last case can be made on the grounds that the protagonist is convinced a miracle took place—and perhaps it did. It is a modest effort, with flat characterization and a one-trick-pony plot, but the descriptive passages show promise.

"The Conqueror Worm" (reprinted from *The Bystander,* 23 June 1937) is a decidedly far-fetched story of a man whose deed of desperation changes him from a doormat to a petty tyrant. Nevertheless, it deserves credit as an effective horror story despite its manifest weaknesses. Kersh draws a convincing portrait of a coward about to become a killer out of sheer, unsubstantiated fear. That the act of murder would then lead the man to become a domestic and entrepreneurial strongman seems less likely. Kersh makes that point forcefully, however, in the description of the character before and after the murder. "He was one of those pulpy personalities in which it is difficult to find anything definite," Kersh says in the second sentence of the story. But the last line says, "He is acquiring something of the reputation of a man of iron." Such a complete turnaround of character or situation is not uncommon in a Kersh piece.

The ancient theme of the biter getting bitten is virtually guaranteed a good reception if it is competently presented; Kersh does so in "The Ruined Wall," (reprinted from *John O'London's Weekly,* 14 August 1942), depicting an avaricious old French landlady trying to scrub the mess off her walls after a tenant has covered them with his crude paintings. The twist is in her description of the reprehensible tenant: "A little slice of a man with a carroty head and blue eyes, smelling of tobacco and wine. . . . Some kind of Prussian; Von Gugg, Vincent Von Gork. A spy, no doubt. . . .Van Gogh, yes, that's it. Where is the law, where is the justice in the world if men like this can go about the earth wrecking houses with their filthiness and their swinishnesses?"

In "Fantasy of a Hunted Man" (reprinted from *John Bull,* 16 May 1942) a hysterical white woman in the South accuses a black man of rape, and a rabid white crowd pursues the accused with intent to lynch. One could wish that the author had allocated more than the 1,200 or so words to this story and had provided a reasonable explanation for one white pursuer's conviction that he has literally been transfigured into the hunted black man. However, Jack Sullivan in *The*

Penguin Encyclopedia of Horror and the Supernatural (1986) found the "poetic justice" of this story to be "deliciously satisfying." There are other speculative-fiction stories in this collection–"An Undistinguished Boy" (alternate history), "The Earwig" (dream realization, reprinted from *Picture Post,* 22 October 1938), and "Who Wants a Liver-Coloured Cat?" (a haunting, reprinted from *John Bull,* 28 February 1942)—but they are better considered practice exercises than finished and polished stories.

The Saturday Evening Post, at that time one of the most popular magazines in the United States, began a long relationship with Kersh in April 1947 when it published a striking story by him. "Note on Danger B," about the breaking of the sound barrier, appeared six months before Captain Charles E. "Chuck" Yeager accomplished that feat. A mock foreword signed by Kersh states that the sound barrier has been broken, despite the existence of Dangers A and B. "Danger A" is explained as the hostile forces an airplane encounters when it approaches the speed of sound. Those forces were all too real, as the many pilots who failed their attempts in conventional aircraft during the 1940s discovered. When Kersh wrote this story, neither he nor anyone else knew that when the aircraft passed from subsonic to supersonic speeds, nose-heavy changes in trim set up structural vibrations that tore the airplanes apart.

Kersh had the erroneous notion that more power was the answer to driving the aircraft (even if it were a soft, blunt cylinder) through the barrier. For whatever reason, however, in his story the aircraft that accomplished the mission was designed in the ultrastreamlined shape of the spade on playing cards. This notion was the essentially correct one. In October 1947 Yeager broke the sound barrier in a Bell X-1 airplane–not spade-shaped, perhaps, but especially designed to conquer Danger A.

However, the Danger B envisioned by Kersh–age reversal in human beings when the vehicle in which they are traveling exceeds one thousand miles per hour–does not and cannot exist under the currently accepted laws of physics. Twentieth-century lunar astronauts did age more slowly on their trips than those who stayed home, but they could never turn back the clock under the theory of relativity. Still, readers who were not physicists could certainly be excused for wondering about that, having seen the first "impossibility"–the breaking of the sound barrier—resolved so quickly after publication of Kersh's story.

A month after the publication of "Note on Danger B," Kersh's name appeared again in *The Saturday Evening Post* with another story of extreme speculation, though of an entirely different sort. "The Royal Impostor" deals with deceit and with an incredible degree of

The Monster *By GERALD KERSH*

The weird creature that came out of the sea has remained a
mystery for two hundred years. Do we know the truth now?

Illustration by Robert Riggs for Kersh's short story "The Monster" in the 21 February 1948 issue of The Saturday Evening Post. *It was
retitled and republished as the title story in his 1953 collection,* The Brighton Monster and Others.

mechanical dexterity. That aspect is perhaps too incredible, but the story shows what the writer could do with the standard story elements if he gave himself enough room to work. The characters are well developed, and the plot, apart from the substitution of an android for the king, is quite intriguing and, though complex, is feasible. The intricacies of making clocks provide an unusual backdrop for the action. One sees Kersh beginning to develop the elaborate, individualistic style that so often hinted at letting the reader in on amazing or scandalous revelations and that so many readers found to be the captivating difference between Kersh's work and that of his contemporaries. For example, "The Royal Impostor" begins: "Secrets such as Pommel told me burn holes in the pockets of the brain. If I could tell you the real name of the King and his country, your eyebrows would go up and your jaws would go down—

and then, more likely than not, you would damn me for a sensational rogue and a dirty liar."

Also in 1947 Kersh's short morality tale "Seed of Destruction" was published by *Esquire*. It was a model story for what was still at that time basically a family magazine with one of the biggest circulations in the United States. "Seed of Destruction" was exotic but easy to understand, included no naughty words or unchaste thoughts, and provided a twist of irony at the end.

Continuing to capitalize on Kersh's popularity, editor Ben Hibbs published another of his stories in *The Saturday Evening Post* in 1947. "Voices in the Dust" proved to be one of the Kersh pieces most sought out by anthologists, with at least six eventual republications, one of them in German. It begins as a straightforward narrative in the familiar "club story" format, with the explorer-cum-trader relating his quest, a search through tribal lands for the lost ruins of the ancient city of Annan. Early on, however, fairies are mentioned; they appear in the ruins of the city, and the explorer manages to capture one. So, with a little feint in the direction of Faerie, Kersh introduces readers to the aftermath of World War III and its mutants. "Annan," it is eventually revealed, is the corrupted pronunciation of "London." The same basic idea—the aftermath of Armageddon—has been done repeatedly since, but Kersh's tale was one of the early versions.

A profitable year of sales to American magazines was rounded off with the publication of "Ladies or Clothes" in the December 1947 issue of *Esquire*. It is a monologue by the venomous old widow of Potiphar, Pharaoh's chief officer. She tells her grandson that had she been a bit more persuasive in coaxing into her bed a certain slave, one Yosif, who owned a coat of many colors, she would have "solved our Jewish Problem for Pharaoh."

"The Monster" (probably better known under its reprint title, "The Brighton Monster," in the 1953 Kersh collection of the same name) was published in *The Saturday Evening Post* in February 1948. A Japanese man is blasted back in time exactly two hundred years by the atomic bomb dropped on Hiroshima, ending up in the sea off Brighton. There he is picked up by fishermen and treated by them, and the other inhabitants of their village, as if he were a sea monster. In a state of shock and total confusion the doomed man, after three months of captivity in what amounts to a private zoo, "escapes" into the sea and, no doubt, death by drowning. Half a dozen diverse characters are effectively sketched in this relatively short piece. A tour de force, "The Monster" is one of Kersh's better stories of any kind and certainly near the top of his science-fiction output.

In June 1948 another of Kersh's best stories, "The Mysterious Mona Lisa Smile," appeared in the same magazine. There is almost no physical description of the two characters and little of their personal histories. Yet, after only about 3,500 words, mostly dialogue, readers have extensive insight into the two different characters of Leonardo da Vinci and his patron, the Duke. This brilliant story might seem more appropriately classified as historical than as speculative fiction, except when one reflects that probably no single feature in the entire history of portraiture has given rise to more speculation than the Mona Lisa smile. As the Duke remarks, midway in the story, "What is she smiling at? She might be the Mother of God or she might be the Devil's wife." Almost as an afterthought to this double character study, Kersh gives readers a logical answer to that old question, and possibly a little insight

into the lady's character as well. As he frequently did—with characters ranging from Jesus and William Shakespeare to several protagonists of his own invention—Kersh reused da Vinci and the Duke in at least one other story, "The Dancing Doll," but it cannot be considered speculative fiction.

Kersh then moved away from science-fiction, fantasy, and horror story ideas for a few years. He indulged his fascination for old male characters by selling a couple of mainstream stories featuring the elegant Mr. Ypsylanti to *The Saturday Evening Post* and an adventure serial to the same publication, all in 1949. During 1950 and 1951 he appears to have published only one forgettable romantic novelette and the minor mainstream novel *The Thousand Deaths of Mr. Small*. This decline in output may be because he was changing his life rather drastically at the time: moving first to Canada, then to the United States; writing his sole science-fiction novel, *The Great Wash;* and getting seriously ill for the first time. Kersh said the illness was malaria, but his brother suspected it might have been alcohol-related.

In April 1952 Kersh published a mainstream story in *The Saturday Evening Post,* followed by the fantasy story "The Terrible Ride of Colonel Tessier," which might well have been called "The Man Who Lost the Battle of Waterloo" but for giving the plot away. Then the same magazine began publishing the five-part serial that became Kersh's only science-fiction novel. The serial was published under the title *The Mystery of the Third Compartment* from 22 November through 20 December 1952; a slightly altered and expanded book form was published in both the United States and England in 1953. The British edition, titled *The Great Wash,* was published by Heinemann, and the American edition, titled *The Secret Masters,* was published by Ballantine.

The story is more akin to an Ian Fleming thriller, minus the James Bond–type hero, than classic science fiction, but it does present the threat of using a super-bomb to melt the polar ice caps and destroy most of the world's population. As it happens, Fleming must have been writing *Casino Royale,* his first Bond book, at the same time Kersh was writing this one, as they were both published in 1953.

Fortunately for Kersh, his literary reputation does not depend on this novel. Even as light reading it has some flaws that are difficult to forgive, even given the greatest willingness to suspend disbelief. Among these weaknesses are the dependence on absurd coincidence to introduce a major character; the ease with which an undercover agent infiltrates a criminal organization that has spared no expense to remain secret; the assertion that three escaping prisoners, armed with a single pistol, can figure out, in about thirty seconds, how to totally destroy a massive, hugely protected installation; and the fortuitous existence of an easily accessed Achilles' heel that enables the heroes to blow up the whole nasty enterprise.

On the other hand, aspects of the presentation give the piece a certain panache characteristic of much of Kersh's work. The descriptions and the narrative techniques are generally good, with appropriate color. The dialogue is realistic to the time and place. The characterization, while not always in the depth one might desire, is generally adequate for the purposes of the story. An interesting aspect of the book are the frequent asides, not essential to the plot or the action but perhaps titillating to the enlightened reader and, incidentally, revelatory of the breadth of Kersh's knowledge of and interest in certain historical periods and their literature, notably that written by Shakespeare, A. E. Housman, Edgar Allan Poe, Rudyard Kipling, and Wilfred Owen.

The Brighton Monster and Others was published by Heinemann in 1953 and includes examples of Kersh's best speculative fiction. "Frozen Beauty" is too short to permit meaningful characterization and is in fact not much more than the "What if . . ." from which so many speculative stories have derived. In this case, the question is what if some ancient citizens of this planet were frozen as instantaneously as possible—is there any chance at all that the spark of life could be retained? The answer, at least so far, is no, but it is a fascinating speculation, especially with the development of the science of cryogenics.

To consider "The Queen of Pig Island" speculative fiction may be a bit of a stretch, but it certainly required a strong imagination to devise the four bizarre characters who comprise the cast, and one cannot help being reminded by these malformed creatures, as well as by the setting, of H. G. Wells's *The Island of Doctor Moreau* (1896). Also, the lingering death of the limbless Lalouette, unable to fetch food or water for herself, would certainly qualify the story as horror. Of all of Kersh's works, this story probably comes the closest to meeting the criteria Aristotle deemed essential to tragedy.

"Whatever Happened to Corporal Cuckoo?" is the tale of an immortal who seems to be unable to avoid soldiering—and painful, front-line soldiering at that. In a story unusually long for Kersh, a correspondent named Kersh meets American soldier Le Cocu on a troopship returning to the United States at the end of World War II. After translating some of François Villon's medieval slang—something few contemporary Frenchmen could do—Le Cocu tells Kersh that he was born in 1507 and shows the reporter a body hideously

Illustration by Robert Fawcett for Kersh's short story "The Mysterious Mona Lisa Smile" in the 26 June 1948 issue of The Saturday Evening Post

scarred from participation in nearly every war since the Battle of Turin in 1536. He claims that Ambroise Paré (an actual famous surgeon of the European Renaissance) treated his split skull with an improvised battlefield remedy that not only healed what should have been a deadly wound but also resulted in virtual immortality for the soldier. When the doctor took him in and began treating him like royalty, Le Cocu suspected that there was a financial motive. One of the doctor's assistants confirmed that Paré's concoction had worked on Le Cocu but not on everyone else; if the physician could find out why and make the adjustment to universal application, he would become god-like and, not incidentally, the richest man ever to walk the planet. So Le Cocu stole the doctor's notes and ran away. The problem was that although Le Cocu had the ingredients, he could not get the proportions right, or the temperature, or something, because he could not make the formula work on anyone else. When Kersh meets him on the troopship he is anxious to get home and back to his experiments. The reporter fails to find out just where "home" is, however, and is ostensibly writing the story to try to find Le Cocu and discover what happened.

Kersh's intimations that the doctor failed to make an extra copy of his recipe and that the soldier could not learn another trade in more than four hundred years require hefty application of the willing suspension of disbelief on the part of the reader, but even with such flaws in logic the story is a gripping one. First, Kersh forces the reader to accept a highly unlikely personal history by providing the claimant with knowledge he could not have had if he were lying. Next, he enlists pity and sympathy for Le Cocu, not just for the horrendous scars and disfigurements on his body but also for his never-ending punishment in having to face more—and worse—again and again. Finally, he intrigues the reader with one of the fondest hopes of all humanity: that out there, somewhere, is the secret of eternal, youthful, healthy life.

Also in *The Brighton Monster and Others* are two stories of lesser quality: "White Horse with Wings" and "The Copper Dahlia." Once again, Kersh claims to be no more than the medium for another man's story as he relates the tale of the "White Horse with Wings." A World War II Greek Resistance fighter, escaped from German torturers, claims that he was saved from death or recapture by the mythical winged horse, Pegasus. Kersh tells the story without embellishment, pointing out that "in the delirium that came when he was wounded and desperate" the man might have dreamed that the great horse saved him. At the end, however, he adds, "Christos could not possibly have made his way back without assistance." One of the few Kersh stories that is straight science fiction, though not particularly convincing, is "The Copper Dahlia," about aliens who, with the best intentions, are going to kill humankind with kindness.

"Men Without Bones," published in *Esquire* in 1954, is one of three Kersh stories mentioned by Clute in *The Encyclopedia of Science Fiction;* it is one of four cited by Mike Ashley in *Who's Who in Horror and Fantasy* (1977), and Sullivan refers to it simply as "Kersh's masterpiece" in *The Penguin Encyclopedia of Horror and the Supernatural.* Once again, as with "Seed of Destruction," the story could serve as a model for what was popular at the time with the readers of *Esquire,* which by then featured tough stories for men. "Men Without Bones" offers a setting similar to Joseph Conrad's *Heart of Darkness* (1902), with half-mad scientists peering under rocks they should not; it is short enough to be read on the train to work; and it concludes with an italicized tag line guaranteed to get one's attention and start the adrenalin flowing. It was Kersh's only speculative fiction of the year, but it was a set piece likely to maintain his reputation with his growing number of fans while his life again underwent major changes.

In 1938 Kersh had married Alice Thompson Rostron, divorcing her in 1943 to marry his second wife, Clair Alyne. In 1955 he divorced Alyne and married his third wife, an American named Florence Sochis. They moved permanently to the United States, and Kersh filed for U.S. citizenship, which he received in 1959. It is impossible to say how these important changes in Kersh's life affected him as a writer, but his nights as a free-spending London bon vivant were behind him, and days of serious illness were not far ahead. He still had one good novel left in him—many say his best—the mainstream *Fowler's End* (1957), and nearly a dozen speculative shorter pieces worth reading.

The collection *Guttersnipe: Little Novels* appeared in 1954, but it includes only three speculative-fiction pieces, all reprints from American magazines. The 1955 collection *Men Without Bones, and Other Stories* includes some of the author's best work, but with the exception of one story, every piece is a reprint. The exception is "Carnival on the Downs," which, together with "The Scene of the Crime," is one of only two ghost stories by Kersh. It is unusual and nicely written, but strange. Horror editor Mary Danby thought enough of the story to include it in the anthology *65 Great Tales of the Supernatural* (1979), but one wonders what supernatural agency found these rather pedestrian principals sufficiently interesting to resurrect annually.

The speculative-fiction pieces in the Kersh collections that appeared after 1955 were either reprints or were too bizarre to be noticed by any of the major reviewers of Kersh's work. In March 1957 *The Saturday Evening Post* published its first Kersh story in fourteen months, a long gap for them between pieces by one of their favorite contributors. "Murder's Eye" was not a particularly convincing or memorable story. His second story to appear in *The Saturday Evening Post* in 1957, however—"The Secret of the Bottle" (retitled "The Oxoxoco Bottle" when it was reprinted in *Men Without Bones, and Other Stories*)—is one many critics believe to be his best.

Kersh's imagination is on display in this narrative centering on a document alleged to have been written by the misanthropic American writer Ambrose Bierce, who disappeared in Mexico in 1914. In the story, as himself, Kersh says of Bierce, "He was a great writer. . . . One of America's greatest." Given Kersh's obvious interest in things mysterious and his admiration for the American writer, it is not surprising that Bierce, a subject of enduring speculation, should be cast in a Kersh fantasy involving other mysteries that are never resolved.

He seemed not to like the look of his shadow on the path in the moonlight when he caught an unexpected glimpse of it.

Dr. Kurt Brevis, one of the world's greatest atomic scientists, had disappeared. Was he murdered? Was he behind the Iron Curtain? Here's the exciting tale of a man too dangerous to live.

The Mystery of the Third Compartment

A Novel By GERALD KERSH *in five parts*

OH no!" says Superintendent Halfacre, of Scotland Yard. "You're not going to try and write this story, are you now?"

Before I can say, "I am," George Oaks says, "Yes, he is, Halfacre! I know Albert Kemp. He'll write the story all right, mark my words. . . . Eh, Albert?"

"I must put it down, at least," I reply.

We are in my summerhouse, drinking brown ale in the cool of the evening. Only forty-eight hours have passed, yet it seems that a long time has trickled away since last we sat here, and that times have changed for the better, and the world has grown sweeter since then. George Oaks is smiling and content, in spite of three stitches in his forehead.

Halfacre has the air of a man who has nothing to complain of, and even I am happy in my way, although my broken nose, newly set, aches most abominably.

"Your story won't wash," says Superintendent Halfacre to me. "We'll deny it. So will the Federal Bureau of Investigation in America."

George Oaks says, "But who's to stop Albert writing it as pure fiction?"

"Provided nobody can establish identity, for the purpose of suing for libel, slander and defamation," says Superintendent Halfacre, "as far as I know, no one can stop him."

"Well," says George Oaks, very comfortably, "let Albert open his story in the classic style, high, wide and handsome. What?"

19

Opening page, with illustration by James R. Bingham, of the first installment (22 November 1952) of Kersh's science-fiction novel, which was revised and published in book form in 1953 as The Great Wash *in Britain and as* The Secret Masters *in the United States*

This story is beautifully realized, in more ways than one. First, there is the gimmick of the strange, beautifully named Oxoxoco Bottle–Kersh's capitalization of "Bottle" conveys the suggestion that one is dealing with no common tourist artifact. Its unusual shape creates a sense of mystery even before the reader knows that it contains a message from the recondite Bierce. Second, Kersh has duplicated Bierce's writing style almost perfectly; indeed, a reader familiar with the acerbic cynicism of the older writer could easily believe that the account had been written by Bierce. This plausibility strengthens the illusion of reality. Third, it is an interesting story of a Shangri-la in the Western hemisphere and of the enormously wealthy descendants of an ancient race of superior humans capable of amazing powers of healing and rejuvenation. It becomes a horror story when Bierce begins to suspect that when his host speaks of having him for a special family banquet, the man means just that: Bierce is to *be* the banquet. Wisely, Kersh leaves Bierce's fate unknown.

A few months later, in March 1958, Kersh published another story, "River of Riches," in *The Saturday Evening Post*. Although Judith Merril reprinted this story in the fourth volume of the series she edited for Dell, *The Year's Greatest Science Fiction and Fantasy* (1959), it does not come close to the quality of "The Secret of the Bottle." As he often did, the author used a modified "club story" approach; the story is not actually told by one club member to others in the club lounge, but Kersh purports to be relating another person's adventure as it was told to him.

This piece provides a good example of a tendency apparent in some Kersh stories that contributes to their failure to live up to their initial promise: gilding the lily. "River of Riches" shows the potential of being an exciting adventure up to the point where the storyteller begins winning gold and precious stones by the handful from Mato Grosso cannibals in a simple gambling game akin to marbles. He gives the chief his rifle and, in return, is given a double handful of emeralds, which he estimates to be worth $120,000. The suspension of disbelief wavers; then "An uncut diamond of the Brazilian variety, as big as your two fists" is wagered, and disbelief, willing or otherwise, can no longer be suspended. As is usually the case in such soldier-of-fortune stories, the storyteller manages to get away with his life, but with none of the treasure.

Kersh continued to publish stories with speculative-fiction connections. "Prophet Without Honor," published in *On an Odd Note: Science Fiction Stories* (1958), is a contemporary story but includes the science-fiction element of a prophecy of Armageddon in 1995. "The Death Tunnel," which appeared in *The Saturday Evening Post* in January 1959, is unmistakably similar to (though not derivative of) Poe's "The Cask of Amontillado" (1846) but not quite chilling enough to be considered horror.

Kersh had one more story published by *The Saturday Evening Post* in 1959 that can be considered fantasy. The story was "An Imaginary Heir," better known as "The Shady Life of Annibal," the title under which it appeared in *The Ugly Face of Love and Other Stories* (1960). It is a good story (if a bit wacky, involving as it does an imaginary child), though not one of the Kersh classics. Its strongest feature is the figure of protagonist Bella Barlay, unusual because Kersh did not often do a good job of depicting female characters—which is probably why there are so few of them, at least in his speculative fiction. Bella, though no beauty, becomes a famous actress, largely because she has to pretend to interact with the nonexistent brother invented by her parents. Once again the author used the "as told to" gimmick he so liked, ostensibly just recording what he was told.

By this time Kersh was living in a series of remote towns in New York State, suffering from various ailments, in debt, and not making much money. He put a good face on things for his British friends, relaxing only with his brother, as Cyril Kersh recalls in his memoir. In February 1960 Kersh wrote to Cyril: "I was taken to the hospital in Middletown . . . Suspicion of abscesses in the colon . . . I lost about three stones, and Flossie with virus pneumonia. Not one hour of peace in twelve years. Well, I'm home again, neatly stitched and getting back to work, being deep– oh, so deep! in hock." A year later he was back in the hospital in an oxygen tent, recovering from viral pneumonia and undergoing surgery to remove a rib.

In April 1962 *The Saturday Afternoon Post* published Kersh's "wonderful invention" story, "The Unsafe Deposit Box," which was picked up at the end of the year by Merril for inclusion in *The 8th Annual of the Year's Best SF* (1963). Later that year, *Playboy* published "A Lucky Day for the Boar," an elaborate fantasy (although *Playboy* reprinted it in *The Playboy Book of Crime and Suspense* in 1966). Again, the story does not rank with the best of Kersh–the plot, involving the artificial aging of a royal conspirator in order to extract a confession, is far too convoluted to be readily believable–but it is entertaining, if one suspends disbelief, and it is unmistakably Kersh.

In 1962 Heinemann published *The Terribly Wild Flowers: Nine Stories,* the title story from which had appeared in the magazine *Fantasy and Science Fiction* in October 1958. The story is, as the title suggests, about flowers that attack animals and humans. Publication of his stories in the big American magazines was rare by this time, but the one that had used his material most, *The Saturday Evening Post,* printed "A Bargain with Cashel" in April 1963. The story is an interesting variation on the venerable theme of selling one's soul to the devil—selling one's time to him instead.

The story itself does not merit extensive dissection, but there are several curious aspects to it. In his only other deal-with-the-devil story, "The Gentleman All in Black," one of the first periodical pieces of Kersh's to be published in America, the man making the deal gives Satan just one second of his time, and Satan uses that second to have the man kill himself. As though he is closing that ancient loophole, the protagonist of "A Bargain with Cashel" (obviously Kersh) says, "Naturally, I have read about deals with the devil, and so forth; how deadly it can be to sell even a second of one's time, in which one may utter a fateful word or pull a trigger. I stipulate, none of that! The time I sell may not be used to hurt me." Kersh also offers an opinion of the state of the art of storytelling at that time when he says of Cashel, a science-fiction magazine publisher: "Since storytelling is a dying art and conjecture is its last gasp, little Cashel's back is bowed from stooping to scrape the bottom of an oft-rinsed barrel." Merril included this story in *The 9th Annual of the Year's Best SF* in 1964.

The following year, "Somewhere Not Far from Here" was published in *Playboy* and again anthologized by Merril, in *The 11th Annual of the Year's Best SF* (1966). This piece appears to be a straightforward war or adventure story in which a suicide squad of soldiers attacks an enemy stronghold to obtain explosives, which their side must have at all costs. Despite terrible casualties, they accomplish their task, because of individual feats of courage, self-sacrifice, and strength—about what one expects from a story of this kind. Upon reflection and another reading, however, one may find more than that in the story.

For one thing, this war is a nameless, dateless struggle, and the attacking "free men" are battling a faceless enemy. Thoughts of Franz Kafka are inescapable. Perhaps Merril saw it as a parable, a kind of companion piece to the story some critics regard as Kersh's masterpiece, "Whatever Happened to Corporal Cuckoo?" The boy narrator says, "when I saw John gritting his teeth in pain, I knew there was no such thing as home, and peace was an old man's story." Certainly that matches the pessimism of the older story. Or perhaps, along with Ox, the soldier whose individual strength saves the mission, Merril saw the optimistic side. After the team wins against the odds, Ox says, "There's always a way to deal with things. Despair is the enemy. To hope on and manage yourself, that is to be one of the free men."

Dust jacket for the 1953 British book version of Kersh's novel about the foiling of a plot to use a superbomb to melt the polar ice caps (Bruccoli Clark Layman Collection)

In 1965 Kersh was diagnosed as having cancer of the throat, and his larynx was removed. In letters to his brother he seems undismayed. His comedy novel *A Long Cool Day in Hell* was published by Heinemann that year. In 1966 he produced another novel, *The Angel and the Cuckoo*—which at least one critic, Duncan, considers the best of his Soho books. By that time his cancer had spread to the base of his tongue, requiring additional major surgery. When he wrote to his brother about the situation, he said that he was finishing another novel (presumably *Brock,* which was published by Heinemann in 1969 after the author's death). He seemed indefatigable, but his brother, who visited him in 1967, found the house in which he was living in Cragsmoor, New York, to be "little more than a shack":

quite isolated with sparse and not very good furniture, no television, one room piled with old newspapers, while a small mountain of beer cans dominated the back garden. . . . The place was cold and shabby and I had the firm impression that Gerald and Flossie really were on the poverty line, particularly with his small earnings swallowed by horrendous medical costs.

Kersh's last published work appears to have been "Trip Out on Red Lizzie," which was surprisingly good, considering his physical condition at the time. It was published by *The Saturday Evening Post* on 27 January 1968. This imaginative science-fiction story about a likable alien stranded on Earth nine quadrillion miles away from his home planet was the thirty-sixth Kersh story (two of them book-length serials) the magazine had published since 1947.

Kersh uses a couple of clever devices in this story. The first is to make the alien a London screever—that is, an artist who works with chalk on stone sidewalks. What the alien does is thus neatly tied into the story: if he gets the picture of his home planet right, he will instantly be returned there. The second is the use of Red Lizzie, a potent workingman's drink popular in London at the time, as an essential catalyst to getting the alien launched homeward. As Kersh describes Red Lizzie, "It was made by mixing the rinsings of old port casks with wood alcohol and water, and they said of it, in the style of the old gin-mill advertisement, that on this stuff you could get stupefied for sixpence, homicidal for a shilling, and a clean cell for nothing." Kersh makes it clear that the alien's body needs the sugar and his soul needs the soothing. As an extra, Kersh gets the double entendre of "trip out" in the title, meaning not only the trip out to the planet Bvenis, but getting high, in the hippie terminology of the time. *The Saturday Evening Post* honored Kersh by running the story again—a rare occurrence in the big-circulation American magazines—in 1991.

The fame of speculative-fiction writers who are known primarily from their contributions to magazines is often evanescent. Once they stop writing, all but the most talented of them are usually remembered dimly, if at all. Yet, twenty-five years after Gerald Kersh's death on 5 November 1968 from cancer complications, Clute wrote of him: "GK's strengths as an author are everywhere evident: a strong and vivid sense of character, a colourful style and a capacity to infuse his stories with a deep emotional charge (sometimes sentimentalized). He has strong admirers."

References:

"Amazing Career of Gerald Kersh," *Newsweek* (3 January 1944): 62–63;

Paul Duncan, "A Kershian Fable," *Paperback Pulp & Comics Collector,* 31–39;

Duncan, "The Nights and Cities of Gerald Kersh," 10 February 1999 <http://www.harlanellison.com/Kersh/index.htm>;

Cyril Kersh, *A Few Gross Words: The Street of Shame, and My Part in It* (London: Simon & Schuster, 1990);

James Sallis, "Feverish Country, This," *FlashPoint,* Web Issue 4 (Winter 2001); <http://www.flashpoint-mag.com/sallis.htm>.

C. S. Lewis

(29 November 1898 – 22 November 1963)

Bernadette Lynn Bosky

See also the Lewis entries in *DLB 15: British Novelists, 1930–1959; DLB 100: Modern British Essayists, Second Series;* and *DLB 160: British Children's Writers, 1914– 1960.*

BOOKS: *Spirits in Bondage: A Cycle of Lyrics,* as Clive Hamilton (London: Heinemann, 1919); as Lewis (San Diego: Harcourt Brace Jovanovich, 1984);

Dymer, as Hamilton (London: Dent, 1926; New York: Dutton, 1926); as Lewis (London: Dent, 1950; New York: Macmillan, 1950);

The Pilgrim's Regress: An Allegorical Apology for Christianity, Reason and Romanticism (London: Dent, 1933; revised edition, London & New York: Sheed & Ward, 1935; revised again, London: Bles, 1943; New York: Sheed & Ward, 1944);

The Allegory of Love: A Study in Medieval Tradition (Oxford: Clarendon Press, 1936; New York: Oxford University Press, 1958);

Out of the Silent Planet (London: John Lane, 1938; New York: Macmillan, 1943);

Rehabilitations and Other Essays (London & New York: Oxford University Press, 1939);

The Personal Heresy: A Controversy, by Lewis and E. M. W. Tillyard (London & New York: Oxford University Press, 1939);

The Problem of Pain (London: Centenary Press, 1940; New York: Macmillan, 1943);

The Screwtape Letters (London: Bles, 1942; New York: Macmillan, 1943); enlarged as *The Screwtape Letters and Screwtape Proposes a Toast* (London: Bles, 1961; New York: Macmillan, 1962); enlarged again as *The Screwtape Letters; with Screwtape Proposes a Toast* (New York: Macmillan, 1982);

A Preface to Paradise Lost (London & New York: Oxford University Press, 1942);

Broadcast Talks: Reprinted with Some Alterations from Two Series of Broadcast Talks ("Right and Wrong: A Clue to the Meaning of the Universe" and "What Christians Believe") Given in 1941 and 1942 (London: Bles,

C. S. Lewis

1942); republished as *The Case for Christianity* (New York: Macmillan, 1943);

Christian Behaviour: A Further Series of Broadcast Talks (London: Bles, 1943; New York: Macmillan, 1943);

Perelandra (London: John Lane, 1943; New York: Macmillan, 1944); republished as *Voyage to Venus* (London: Pan, 1953);

The Abolition of Man: Reflections on Education with Special Reference to the Teaching of English in the Upper Forms of Schools, Riddell Memorial Lectures, Fifteenth Series (London: Oxford University Press, 1943; New York: Macmillan, 1947);

Beyond Personality: The Christian Idea of God (London: Bles, Centenary Press, 1944; New York: Macmillan, 1945);

That Hideous Strength: A Modern Fairy-Tale for Grown-Ups (London: John Lane, 1945; New York: Macmillan, 1946); abridged by Lewis as *The Tortured Planet* (New York: Avon, 1946); republished as *That Hideous Strength* (London: Pan, 1955);

The Great Divorce: A Dream (London: Bles, Centenary Press, 1945; New York: Macmillan, 1946);

Miracles: A Preliminary Study (London: Bles, Centenary Press, 1947; New York: Macmillan, 1947; abridged edition, with new preface by Lewis, New York: Association Press, 1958; revised complete edition, London: Collins, 1960; New York: Macmillan, 1978);

Vivisection (Boston: New England Anti-Vivisection Society, 1947; London: National Anti-Vivisection Society, 1948);

Arthurian Torso: Containing the Posthumous Fragment of The Figure of Arthur by Charles Williams and A Commentary on the Arthurian Poems of Charles Williams by C. S. Lewis (London & New York: Oxford University Press, 1948); republished as *Taliessin through Logres; The Region of the Summer Stars, by Charles Williams. And Arthurian Torso, by Charles Williams and C. S. Lewis* (Grand Rapids, Mich.: Eerdmans, 1974);

Transposition and Other Addresses (London: Bles, 1949); republished as *The Weight of Glory and Other Addresses* (New York: Macmillan, 1949; revised and enlarged, edited by Walter Hooper, 1980);

The Lion, the Witch, and the Wardrobe (London: Bles, 1950; New York: Macmillan, 1950);

Prince Caspian: The Return to Narnia (London: Bles, 1951; New York: Macmillan, 1951);

Mere Christianity (London: Bles, 1952; New York: Macmillan, 1952)—revised and enlarged edition of *Broadcast Talks, Christian Behaviour,* and *Beyond Personality;*

The Voyage of the Dawn Treader (London: Bles, 1952; New York: Macmillan, 1952);

The Silver Chair (London: Bles, 1953; New York: Macmillan, 1953);

The Horse and His Boy (London: Bles, 1954; New York: Macmillan, 1954);

English Literature in the Sixteenth Century Excluding Drama, Oxford History of English Literature, volume 3 (Oxford: Clarendon Press, 1954; New York: Oxford University Press, 1954); republished as *Poetry and Prose in the Sixteenth Century,* Oxford History of English Literature, volume 4 (Oxford: Clarendon Press, 1990);

The Magician's Nephew (London: Bodley Head, 1955; New York: Macmillan, 1955);

Surprised by Joy: The Shape of My Early Life (London: Bles, 1955; New York: Harcourt, Brace, 1956);

The Last Battle (London: Bodley Head, 1956; New York: Macmillan, 1956);

Till We Have Faces: A Myth Retold (London: Bles, 1956; New York: Harcourt, Brace, 1957);

Reflections on the Psalms (London: Bles, 1958; New York: Harcourt, Brace, 1958);

The Four Loves (London: Bles, 1960; New York: Harcourt, Brace, 1960);

Studies in Words (Cambridge: Cambridge University Press, 1960; enlarged, 1967; New York: Cambridge University Press, 1990);

The World's Last Night and Other Essays (New York: Harcourt, Brace, 1960;

A Grief Observed, as N. W. Clerk (London: Faber & Faber, 1961; Greenwich, Conn.: Seabury Press, 1963); as Lewis (London: Faber & Faber, 1964; Greenwich, Conn.: Seabury Press, 1964);

An Experiment in Criticism (Cambridge: Cambridge University Press, 1961; New York: Cambridge University Press, 1992);

They Asked for a Paper: Papers and Addresses (London: Bles, 1962);

Letters to Malcolm: Chiefly on Prayer (London: Bles, 1964; New York: Harcourt, Brace & World, 1964);

The Discarded Image: An Introduction to Medieval and Renaissance Literature (Cambridge: Cambridge University Press, 1964);

Poems, edited by Hooper (London: Bles, 1964; New York: Harcourt, Brace & World, 1965);

Studies in Medieval and Renaissance Literature, edited by Hooper (Cambridge: Cambridge University Press, 1966; New York: Cambridge University Press, 1979);

Of Other Worlds: Essays and Stories, edited by Hooper (London: Bles, 1966; New York: Harcourt, Brace & World, 1967); enlarged as *Of This and Other Worlds,* edited by Hooper (London: Collins, 1982); republished as *On Stories: And Other Essays on Literature* (New York: Harcourt Brace Jovanovich, 1982);

Christian Reflections, edited by Hooper (London: Bles, 1967; Grand Rapids, Mich.: Eerdmans, 1967);

Spenser's Images of Life, edited by Alastair Fowler (Cambridge: Cambridge University Press, 1967);

Narrative Poems, edited by Hooper (London: Bles, 1969; New York: Harcourt Brace Jovanovich, 1972);

Selected Literary Essays, edited by Hooper (Cambridge & New York: Cambridge University Press, 1969);

God in the Dock: Essays on Theology and Ethics, edited by Hooper (Grand Rapids, Mich.: Eerdmans, 1970); republished as *Undeceptions: Essays on Theology and Ethics* (London: Bles, 1971);

The Dark Tower and Other Stories, edited by Hooper (London: Collins, 1977; New York: Harcourt Brace Jovanovich, 1977);

A Cretaceous Perambulator (the Re-examination Of), by Lewis and Owen Barfield, edited by Hooper (Oxford: Oxford University C. S. Lewis Society, 1983);

Boxen: The Imaginary World of the Young C. S. Lewis, edited by Hooper (London: Collins, 1985; San Diego: Harcourt Brace Jovanovich, 1985);

Present Concerns, edited by Hooper (London: Collins, 1986; San Diego: Harcourt Brace Jovanovich, 1986);

Christian Reunion: And Other Essays, edited by Hooper (London: Collins, 1990);

All My Road before Me: The Diary of C. S. Lewis, 1922–1927, edited by Hooper (London: HarperCollins, 1991; San Diego: Harcourt Brace Jovanovich, 1991);

The Collected Poems of C. S. Lewis, edited by Hooper (London: HarperCollins, 1994).

Collections: *Screwtape Proposes a Toast and Other Pieces* (London: Collins, 1965);

The Complete Chronicles of Narnia, 7 volumes (Harmondsworth: Penguin, 1965; New York: Macmillan, 1970);

A Mind Awake: An Anthology of C. S. Lewis, edited by Clyde S. Kilby (London: Bles, 1968; New York: Harcourt, Brace & World, 1969);

Fern-Seed and Elephants, and Other Essays on Christianity, edited by Hooper (London: Collins, 1975);

The Joyful Christian: 127 Readings from C. S. Lewis, edited by Henry William Griffin (New York: Macmillan, 1977);

The Cosmic Trilogy (London: Bodley Head, 1990).

RECORDING: *The Four Loves,* read by Lewis, Parish of the Air / Episcopal Radio-TV Foundation, 1975.

OTHER: *George MacDonald: An Anthology,* edited by Lewis (London: Bles, 1946; New York: Macmillan, 1947);

Essays Presented to Charles Williams, edited by Lewis (London: Oxford University Press, 1947; Grand Rapids, Mich.: Eerdmans, 1966);

Joy Davidman, *Smoke on the Mountain: The Ten Commandments in Terms of Today,* preface by Lewis (Philadelphia: Westminster Press, 1954; London: Hodder & Stoughton, 1955);

Selections from Layamon's "Brut," edited by G. L. Brook, introduction by Lewis (Oxford: Clarendon Press, 1963).

Although C. S. Lewis published, as Peter J. Kreeft notes in his *C. S. Lewis: A Critical Essay,* "some

Lewis in July 1919, about four months after his first book, Spirits in Bondage: A Cycle of Lyrics, *was published*

sixty first-quality works of literary history, literary criticism, theology, philosophy, autobiography, Biblical studies, sermons, formal and informal essays, a spiritual diary, [and] short stories," as well as poetry, of particular interest to readers of fantasy and science fiction are Lewis's novels, which combine those elements with allegory, myth, romance, and satire. A professor who won awards for his academic work and received five honorary doctorates in England and France, Lewis was a gregarious man, known for his love of tobacco and alcohol. His biographer A. N. Wilson says that "his jolly, red, honest face was that of an intellectual bruiser"; his earlier biographers Roger Lancelyn Green and Walter Hooper write of his appearance at lectures: "There strode in a big man with shabby clothes, looking like nothing so much as a prosperous butcher, who began addressing his audience in a loud, booming voice and with tremendous gusto." Lewis's wit and honesty attracted a wide circle of friends and thousands of admirers but alienated others, including many of his fellow writers. Passionate about his dislikes and loves, Lewis never left a neutral acquaintance, listener, or reader.

Clive Staples Lewis was born on 29 November 1898 in Dundela Villas, Belfast, the second child of

Albert Lewis, a prosecuting attorney, and Florence Augusta Hamilton Lewis, known as Flora; his brother, Warren Hamilton Lewis, had been born on 16 June 1895. According to Wilson, Albert Lewis was a "soulful poet" and a skilled and funny raconteur. In *Surprised by Joy: The Shape of My Early Life* (1955) Lewis describes his father's side of the family as "true Welshmen, sentimental, passionate, and rhetorical, easily moved both to anger and to tenderness; men who laughed and cried a great deal and who had not much of the talent for happiness." His paternal grandfather, Richard Lewis, came from a line of Welsh farmers but was born in Ireland; he was a master boilermaker for the Cork Steamship Company. He was also—though Lewis does not mention the fact in *Surprised by Joy*—a writer who made up science-fiction stories to amuse his children and who read essays to fellow members of the Workman's Reading Room at the steamship company. The essays are largely theological and, Green and Hooper note, "surprisingly eloquent for a man who had so little education."

Lewis describes his mother's family as "a cooler race. Their minds were critical and ironic and they had the talent for happiness in a high degree." They were of a higher social class than Lewis's father's family, with what Green and Hooper call "a strong ecclesiastical tradition" that included an ancestor who was bishop of Ossory. Lewis's maternal grandfather, Thomas Hamilton, was rector of St. Mark's in Dundela, on the outskirts of Belfast. Lewis's mother was highly educated for a woman of her time: she had studied mathematics and logic at Queen's College in Belfast and had written magazine articles.

The family was inclined to nicknames: Warren was usually Warnie but sometimes Badger, Badgie, or Badge, while from age four Clive was Jack, Jacks, Jacko, Kricks, or Klicks. Despite their almost three years' difference in age, the brothers were close companions. They had a vivid imaginative life, telling stories and making up histories that C. S. Lewis began writing down when he was five. Influenced by the "humanized animals" in Beatrix Potter's *The Tale of Peter Rabbit* (1902) and *The Tale of Squirrel Nutkin* (1903) and by stories of knights and chivalry such as Mark Twain's *A Connecticut Yankee in King Arthur's Court* (1889) and Sir Arthur Conan Doyle's *Sir Nigel,* which was serialized in *The Strand* in 1905–1906, he created a medieval Animal-Land with mice in armor. Later, Animal-Land was joined with Warren's imaginary version of India to form a land called Boxen, about which Lewis wrote stories from age twelve to fourteen. Some of the Boxen stories have been published, and critics generally agree that they give little hint of Lewis's later ability: they are

dry, with little sense of wonder or of the numinous, although they do reveal a sense of humor.

Lewis's early childhood included yearly summer trips to a seaside resort and a nurse, Lizzie Endicott, who told him Irish folktales. From his nursery window he could see the Castlereagh Hills, which he mentions in *Surprised by Joy* as the source of his first feelings of *Sehnsucht,* or romantic, bittersweet longing.

Albert Lewis had a house, Little Lea, built farther out from the city center, and the family moved into it in 1905. Soon after the move Warren was sent to Wynyard House, a boarding school near Watford in Hertfordshire, England; Lewis was taught at home by a governess and spent many hours in solitary reading. By 1907 the household included their grandfather Lewis; a housemaid and a cook; and pets such as a dog, a mouse, and a canary. In the diaries he kept from the age of nine, Lewis reports reading John Milton's epic poem *Paradise Lost* (1667) when he was ten, but otherwise his reading seems more normal for a boy of that age: the books of E. Nesbit, Conan Doyle's Sherlock Holmes stories, and H. Rider Haggard's exotic adventure novels, which he continued to enjoy for the rest of his life.

One of the key events that formed Lewis's personality occurred at 6:30 A.M. on 23 August 1908, when his mother died of cancer. Since she had needed round-the-clock nurses, Lewis's grandfather had had to move out in March, and he had died a month later of a stroke. According to Green and Hooper, "The effect of Flora's death on Albert Lewis was to alienate him from his two sons just at the time when mutual comfort was most needed"; Lewis recalls in *Surprised by Joy* that his father "spoke wildly and acted unjustly." Lewis was devastated: without a mother and feeling distant from his father, he felt that all security had gone.

Lewis and Warren became closer than ever—"Two frightened urchins huddled for warmth in a bleak world," as Lewis dramatically puts it in *Surprised by Joy*. Emotional support also came from the family of his mother's cousin, Hope Ewart. The boys had a standing invitation to visit her nearby mansion, Glenmacken (called "Mountbracken" in *Surprised by Joy*), and she provided a motherly and civilizing influence. Still, the scar left by his mother's death shaped Lewis's life.

Lewis's father sent him to a series of boarding schools, mostly in England. In September 1908 he joined Warren at Wynyard House; he found his brother's presence one of the few tolerable things about the school. In *Surprised by Joy* he refers to it as "Belsen," after the Nazi concentration camp. Green and Hooper characterize the school as "at once brutalizing and intellectually stupefying"; the headmaster, the Reverend Robert Capron, may have been insane and was later institutionalized. The high-church

Anglo-Catholic services held twice every Sunday, however, awakened Lewis's religious feelings. Warren went to Malvern College in the fall of 1909; their father kept Lewis at Wynyard, where he was even more miserable, until the end of the 1909–1910 academic year, when the school was closed because of parental complaints. One bright spot for Lewis in 1910 was seeing James M. Barrie's *Peter Pan* performed in London; the play left a vivid impression on him.

For the autumn term of 1910 Lewis was enrolled in Campbell College, two miles from Little Lea; he lived at the school but visited home every Sunday. His memories of his short time there were as pleasant as those of Wynyard were disagreeable. At Campbell College, Lewis began to enjoy learning. His teacher J. A. McNeill introduced him to Matthew Arnold's poem "Sohrab and Rustum" (1853), which became a lifelong favorite. In November 1910 Lewis was sent home because of illness. He rested, reading almost constantly—especially fairy tales—for two months.

From January 1911 to June 1913 Lewis attended Cherbourg, a small preparatory school of seventeen boarding students and some day students near Malvern. There, for the first time, he made friends with boys his own age. His first published works, two essays and a poem, appeared in the *Cherbourg School Magazine*.

Lewis also lost his faith in Christianity at Cherbourg. He was influenced by Germanic mythology, which stirred his emotions and seemed to him to have as much possibility of being true as Christianity. He first encountered the mythology in a supplement to the December 1911 issue of *The Bookman* in which several of Arthur Rackham's color illustrations for Margaret Armour's translation of Richard Wagner's *Siegfried; and The Twilight of the Gods* (1911) were reproduced. Lewis read widely in Norse myth and became enamored of all things "Northern."

In June 1913 Lewis took the entrance examination for Malvern College, despite being in bed with fever at the time, and earned a junior scholarship. Warren, however, had just withdrawn from Malvern, having been asked to leave because he had been caught smoking (both brothers had been smokers for years). At Malvern, Lewis "reacted against the whole public-school ethos," as Joe R. Christopher writes in *C. S. Lewis*. In *Surprised by Joy* Lewis records his dislike of the importance placed on athletics, of the social hierarchy, and of a system in which younger students were imposed on in many ways, including sexually, by older ones. Still, he loved the school library; in later years he also fondly remembered Harry Wakelyn Smith, who taught classics and English. Lewis studied Virgil, Horace, and Euripides as well as the poetry of Milton and William Butler Yeats. Yeats stimulated Lewis's

Dust jacket for Lewis's 1926 narrative poem, published under a pseudonym taken from his mother's birth name, about a young man's rebellion against society (Marion E. Wade Center, Wheaton College, Wheaton, Illinois)

interest in Celtic mythology, although Northern myth was still more vital to him. During the summer term of 1914 he wrote *Loki Bound*, a play combining Norse mythology with Greek tragic form.

Lewis's love of Northern mythology was shared by Arthur Greeves, a neighbor at Little Lea. The two had known each other for years, but in 1914 this common interest cemented a lifelong friendship, conducted mainly through correspondence, that was second only to the affection between Lewis and his brother. Lewis's letters to Greeves were published as *They Stand Together* in 1979.

Albert Lewis had become reacquainted with his old headmaster from Lurgan College, William T. Kirkpatrick, when the teacher needed his help in a minor legal matter. Kirkpatrick had retired and was doing individual tutoring; Warren studied with him to prepare for the entrance examination to the Officer Training College at Sandhurst, and, since Lewis was ill-suited to public-school life, his father sent him to study with Kirkpatrick at the latter's home, Gastons, in Great

Bookham, Surrey. When he arrived on 19 September 1914, Lewis was fifteen and Kirkpatrick, called "the Great Knock" by the Lewis family, was sixty-six. Wilson describes the tutor as "an old-fashioned nineteenth-century rationalist, whose favorite reading consisted of [Sir James George] Frazer's *The Golden Bough* [1890] and [the philosopher Arthur] Schopenhauer." Under Kirkpatrick's influence Lewis became increasingly convinced that Christianity was an attractive myth system but not true. In his correspondence with Greeves, who was a devout Christian, the arguments grew intense; Lewis was as staunch a polemicist for atheism as he later was for Christianity. Finally, the boys agreed not to write about the topic. To please his father, however, Lewis was confirmed at St. Mark's Church on 6 December 1914. The married but misogynist Kirkpatrick reinforced not only Lewis's atheism but also his low impression of marriage and women.

To Lewis, Kirkpatrick—who is reflected in the character MacPhee in Lewis's novel *That Hideous Strength: A Modern Fairy-Tale for Grown-Ups* (1945)—represented all things rational; in *Surprised in Joy* he credits Kirkpatrick with his own ability to argue and even to think well. During his two and a half years at Gastons, Lewis blossomed intellectually. He studied Henrik Ibsen's plays; William Morris's poems and prose; Alfred Tennyson's "Morte d'Arthur" (1842); Edmund Spenser's *The Fairie Queene* (1590, 1596); Homer, Sophocles, and Aeschylus in Greek; and *Beowulf* (circa 1000) and *Sir Gawain and the Green Knight* (circa 1375) in modern English translations. He read the works of Aristotle, Milton, John Keats, John Ruskin, and Virginia Woolf. Even Kirkpatrick thought that Lewis read too much, but he wrote glowingly in letters to Lewis's father about the boy's intellectual acumen.

In 1916 Lewis picked up in a bookstall a copy of *Phantastes* (1858), by the Christian writer George MacDonald. The archetypal myths in the novel stirred him deeply. In the introduction to an anthology of extracts from MacDonald's works that he edited in 1946, Lewis says that what *Phantastes* "did to me was to convert, even to baptise . . . my imagination. It did nothing to my intellect nor (at that time) to my conscience. Their turn came far later and with the help of many other books and men."

Kirkpatrick and Lewis's father decided that Lewis should go to a university and become a fellow or, at least, a schoolmaster. Lewis agreed to the plan, though he really wanted to be a poet and romance writer. Between Easter 1915 and Easter 1917 he wrote fifty-two poems, none of them particularly good. On 4 December 1916 he went to Oxford to take the scholarship examination. Though he was elected to a scholarship in University College, he had to pass another examination before matriculating. It included Lewis's bane—mathematics—so he returned to Bookham to study algebra with Kirkpatrick; he also studied German and Italian.

As an Irishman, Lewis would have been exempt from service in World War I, but he wanted to serve. He returned to Oxford on 20 March 1917; he did not pass the algebra part of the examination, but as a prospective soldier he was allowed to matriculate anyway. On 10 June he was drafted into an Officer's Training Corps cadet battalion housed at Keble College, which was being used as a barracks. There he met Edward Francis Courtenay "Paddy" Moore, a fellow recruit. Lewis became friends with Moore and his family, especially with his mother, Janie.

Lewis was sent to France with the Third Battalion, Somerset Light Infantry, on 17 November 1917. In February 1918 he was hospitalized with trench fever; on 15 April he was wounded by a stray English shell during the Battle of Arras and was sent to a London hospital. In July he moved to a convalescent home near Bristol. In mid October he was assigned to Ludgershall, near Andover, Hampshire. By that time Lewis had learned that Paddy Moore, who had asked Lewis to look after his mother if anything should happen to him, had been killed in action earlier that year. Lewis was demobilized on 29 December 1918 with the rank of second lieutenant; he returned to Oxford in January 1919.

Lewis's first published book, the poetry collection *Spirits in Bondage: A Cycle of Lyrics,* was published in March 1919 under the pseudonym Clive Hamilton. The poems, written during the war, most after 1917, reflect Lewis's atheism, combined with a dualism in which spirit is beauty but the body is evil. Some poems show Lewis's interest in Irish myth, while others reflect his war experiences. The poems are derivative, more interesting for the insights they provide into Lewis's thought than for their quality.

At Oxford, Lewis was finally in his element. His tutors included E. F. Carritt, F. P. Wilson, E. E. Wardale, and Geonger Gordon; he joined the Martlets, a literary and debate society, speaking on William Morris, James Boswell, and Spenser. He also met Yeats, whose poetry he admired. In the summer of 1920 Janie Moore and her daughter, Maureen, moved to Oxford, renting a small house with Lewis's financial help. Lewis hid the extent of his involvement with Moore—especially the financial aspects—from his father, who did not trust her, and from the university, which would not have approved of an undergraduate entering into such an arrangement.

Much has been written about Lewis's relationship with Moore, and the full truth will probably never be known. Lewis lived with her for decades, supporting her financially and placidly interrupting his scholarship to perform trivial errands for her. Moore was a complex, difficult woman, possessive and not particularly intelligent but generous, gregarious, and affectionate. Some writers speculate that the relationship was sexual, but others point out that Lewis's history left him vulnerable to the appeal of a maternal figure and that he took seriously the wartime promise to his dead friend. The negative side of Moore is reflected in Lewis's depiction of the mother in *The Screwtape Letters* (1942), the positive aspects in the Great Lady in Heaven in *The Great Divorce: A Dream* (1945).

Lewis continued to write poetry after returning to Oxford, but he did not submit any of it to the undergraduate periodicals. On 24 May 1921 he won the Chancellor's English Essay Prize for a piece on the topic of optimism. Among the lifelong friends he made as an undergraduate was Owen Barfield; their relationship was marked by friendly disagreements and vigorous intellectual debate. He also met Nevill Coghill, a Christian who became his colleague in English at Oxford and whose friendship helped shape Lewis's thought.

Lewis took firsts in honour moderations (Greek and Latin literature), greats (philosophy and history), and English. He received a B.A. in 1922 and another in 1923. Despite encouragement from his teachers, he did not immediately apply for a fellowship at Oxford; he also turned down other teaching opportunities because they would take him too far from his household with the Moores. He remained at Oxford, supported partly by his father and partly by correcting examinations and coaching students in essay writing.

In the fall of 1924 Lewis received a temporary post as a philosophy tutor at University College. On 20 May 1925 he was elected to a fellowship at Magdalen College as tutor in English language and literature, a field that was more to his liking. Probably inspired by Kirkpatrick's example, Lewis was a brilliant but difficult tutor, bracing to some students and intimidating to others. One of his first students, John Betjeman, who later became poet laureate, provides a scathing picture of Lewis in his autobiographical poem *Summoned by Bells* (1960). Green and Hooper point out, however, that some of Lewis's seemingly malicious remarks actually came from his charitable assumption that his students had read more widely or were more intelligent than was the case. Lewis's lectures were lively and well attended; they abounded in quotations recited verbatim from memory, with those not in English given first in the original language and then in translation. Lewis's reading lists concentrated on primary texts rather than criticism.

As a new fellow, Lewis was assigned to teach a weekly class at Lady Margaret Hall, a women's college in North Oxford. Green and Hooper report that "Con-

Dust jacket for Lewis's 1938 science-fiction novel—the first volume in his Space Trilogy—in which a philologist is kidnapped and taken to Mars (Marion E. Wade Center, Wheaton College, Wheaton, Illinois)

trary to rumor, Lewis neither looked down on women undergraduates nor refused to tutor them: he made no distinctions between them and his male pupils—and made no special allowances."

In 1926 Lewis published a long narrative poem, *Dymer,* again under the Hamilton pseudonym. He had begun the poem as early as 1918, set it aside, and gone back to it in 1922. Christopher characterizes it as "the story of a young man's rebellion against society and his seeking of the Spirit behind *sehnsucht*"—the melancholy longing Lewis often felt. The physical appearance of the magician in the poem may be based on that of Yeats. The poem was positively reviewed in the *Sunday Times,* but not until a year after publication; it was uneven artistically, and sales were poor.

In 1926 Lewis met J. R. R. Tolkien, who had just been elected Rawlinson and Bosworth Professor of Anglo-Saxon at Oxford. Within a year, according to Green and Hooper, they were "meeting in each other's rooms and talking far into the night." They shared an interest in "things Northern," as well as many literary values. Tolkien was a Catholic while Lewis was still an atheist but, stirred by the study of the works of John Donne, George Herbert, and Sir Thomas Browne, was coming to see Christianity as more and more beautiful. In 1927 he began learning Old Icelandic and joined Tolkien in the Oxford Icelandic club, "The Coalbiters"; the name is a metaphor for those who sit around the fire telling stories. Tolkien was Lewis's closest friend until the 1950s, and the two men critiqued each others' work in manuscript.

Lewis considered 1929 the pivotal year of his conversion back to Christianity. The conversion would not have been likely while the rationalist Kirkpatrick was still alive, but he had died in 1921. Literary influences that led Lewis toward Christianity included books by MacDonald, John Bunyan's *Grace Abounding to the Chief of Sinners* (1666), the works of the German mystic Jacob Boehme, Thomas Traherne's *Centuries of Meditations* (1908), and G. K. Chesterton's *The Everlasting Man* (1925). Lewis had begun to see Christianity as the truth behind Frazer's dying-god myth, and, he recalls in *Surprised by Joy,* "In Trinity Term 1929 I gave in, and admitted that God was God, and knelt and prayed: perhaps, that night, the most dejected and reluctant convert in all England." He compares his search for God to the search of a mouse for the cat. The 1929 conversion was to theism, not yet to Christianity; but Lewis did begin to attend church services.

Lewis and his brother had been estranged from their father for some years. After Albert Lewis retired in 1928 he became even more difficult, but Lewis began visiting him and spent Christmas 1928 with him. As his father's health declined, Lewis cared for him as much as his university duties would allow. An operation on 3 September 1929 revealed advanced cancer, and Albert died on 24 September. Lewis and Warren were surprised to find themselves deeply disturbed by their father's death and by the process of sorting through the contents of Little Lea in preparation for selling it. One result was the discovery of diaries, letters, and other papers that Albert had saved. Warren took on the job of organizing and typing up the papers, which totaled 3,563 single-spaced pages bound in eleven volumes; among them were some of Lewis's letters to Greeves that Lewis borrowed back for the project.

Warren retired from the military, and with the proceeds from the sale of Little Lea the brothers bought the Kilns, a house near Oxford, for themselves and Janie and Maureen Moore. In mid October 1930 they moved in, and it was Lewis's home for the rest of his life. The household also included a dog, Mr. Papworth; a maid; and a gardener, Fred Paxton, who became the model for Puddleglum the Marshwiggle in Lewis's *The Silver Chair* (1953). After Warren reenlisted in September 1931, Lewis spent weeknights in his rooms at Magdalen College and weekends and vacations at the Kilns; Maureen, by then a young woman, often picked him up in the family car and brought him to the Kilns for lunch.

In 1930 Lewis began a novel, "The Moving Image"; the manuscript has never been found, but Lewis described it in a 22 June 1930 letter to Greeves as "almost a Platonic dialogue in a fantastic setting with dialogue intermixed." He completed two narrative poems: "The Queen of Drum," about a queen who rejects Christianity for faerie, and "The Nameless Isle," using motifs from Emanuel Schikaneder and Wolfgang Amadeus Mozart's opera *Die Zauberflöte* (The Magic Flute, 1791); both were published in a posthumous volume in 1969. Still considering himself primarily a poet, he began to write religious lyrics.

On 19 September 1931 Lewis invited Tolkien and Hugo Dyson to his rooms for dinner, and they discussed Christianity until four o'clock in the morning. On 28 September, Lewis fully accepted Christianity while riding with his brother–who had himself recently reconverted–to Whipsnade Zoo. A few weeks later, on 11 October 1931, Lewis wrote to Greeves, "Now the story of Christ is simply a true myth: a myth working on us in the same way as the others, but with this tremendous difference that *it really happened.*"

During a two-week vacation in Ireland in August 1932 Lewis found a way to write about his conversion. *The Pilgrim's Regress: An Allegorical Apology for Christianity, Reason and Romanticism* (1933) is an allegorical story clearly influenced by Bunyan's *The Pilgrim's Progress from This World to That Which Is to Come, Delivered under the Similitude of a Dream Wherein Is Discovered, the Manner of His Setting Out, His Dangerous Journey, and Safe Arrival at the Desired Countrey* (1678). Lewis's pilgrim, John, like Bunyan's pilgrim, undertakes a journey past many ideological pitfalls and finally finds faith. The book received some favorable reviews but was not a commercial success. It also occasioned controversy–the first, but far from the last, of Lewis's books to do so. It is an abrasive work that does not forgo easy attacks on or generalizations about churches and social trends; Lewis himself came to view it as too harsh. It was also too complicated for many readers; Lewis wrote an explanatory preface and annotations for the 1943 edition.

In September 1935 Lewis completed *The Allegory of Love: A Study in Medieval Tradition* (1936), a work he had begun in July 1928. In an 18 September 1935 letter to the publisher, Lewis said, "The book as a whole has two themes: 1. The birth of allegory and its growth from what it is in Prudentius to what it is in Spenser. 2. The birth of the romantic conception of love and the long struggle between its earlier form (the romance of adultery) and its later form (the romance of marriage)."

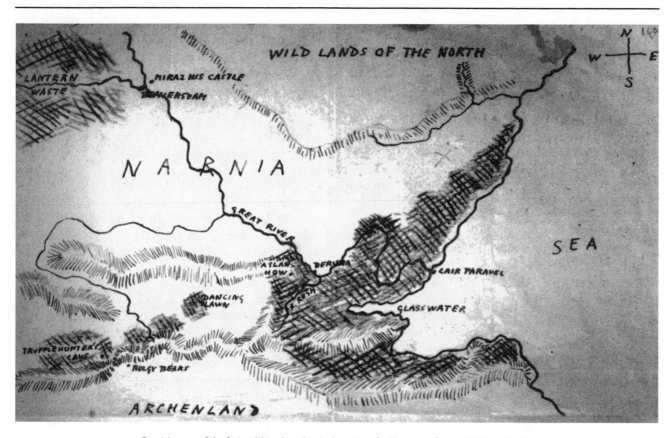

Lewis's map of the fictional kingdom that is the setting for his series of seven children's books
(Bodleian Library, Oxford University)

Dedicated to Barfield, the book made Lewis's academic reputation. Reviews were positive, and scholars praised the work in letters to Lewis—even E. M. W. Tillyard, with whom Lewis was engaged in a fierce academic debate concerning the nature of poetry. The book won the Hawthornden Prize in 1936 and the Israel Gollancz Memorial Prize for literature in 1937.

The Allegory of Love also served to introduce Lewis to Charles Williams. Lewis had read Williams's *The Place of the Lion* (1931), a supernatural novel concerning Platonic Forms breaking into everyday reality, and had sent Williams a letter praising it; coincidentally, Williams, an editor at Oxford University Press in London, had just seen and been impressed by the proofs of Lewis's literary study. A correspondence led to a friendship that lasted until Williams's death in 1945 and a literary influence that was even more enduring.

Lewis met another friend, the physician R. E. "Humphrey" Havard, by catching influenza in 1934 or 1935. Havard was a recent convert to Roman Catholicism; after discussing theology with him, Lewis invited him to join the conversations with Tolkien and others in his rooms at Magdalen.

From these friendships and the precedent of the Coalbiters developed a literary circle, the Inklings. The name is a pun on insight—"having an inkling"—and the predominance of writers, who work in ink, among the members. The Inklings had begun in the early 1930s as a literary dining club organized by an undergraduate in University College. That club, to which Lewis and Tolkien were recruited, ended in 1933, but, according to William White, Tolkien recalled that the name was transferred to an "unelected and undetermined circle of friends who gathered about C.S.L. and met in his rooms at Magdalen." Williams, who moved with Oxford University Press from London to Oxford to escape the German bombing during World War II, joined the Inklings in September 1939. From 1939 through 1945 the group met at least twice a week, generally once in Lewis's rooms and once at the Eagle and Child pub (which the Inklings called the "Bird and Baby"). After 1950 the meetings in Lewis's rooms ended, but they continued at the Eagle and Child and other Oxford pubs; Lewis attended until shortly before his death. At the meetings the members read aloud from their works in progress, including Tolkien's *The Hobbit* (1937), and discussed topics ranging from T. S. Eliot's poetry to whether dogs have souls.

Lewis's first novel, *Out of the Silent Planet*, was published in 1938. It was the first volume of his Space Trilogy (also known as the Cosmic Trilogy or the Ransom Trilogy), one of the two major pillars of Lewis's fame as a writer of fantastic fiction. The story is a scientific romance, like those of H. G. Wells, Jules Verne, and Edgar Rice Burroughs, but the cosmology is Christian and—showing the influence of Lewis's work on *The Allegory of Love*—medieval. Elwin Ransom, a philologist, is kidnapped by the amoral physicist Weston and the greedy industrialist Devine. They take him to Mars, known by its inhabitants as Malacandra, because they believe that a community of one of the three sentient species there desires a human sacrifice. Ransom escapes from Weston and Devine, learns the languages of the Martians, and discovers that his fellow earthlings are the savages, while the races of Mars are intelligent and caring. Earth is known to them as Thulcandra, the "silent planet"; it is ruled by the Bent One, a planetary spirit that revolted, like Satan. Weston and Devine kill a Malacandran and are tried and sent back to Earth; Ransom accompanies them.

Lewis's world building, while enjoyable, is primitive by later standards of science fiction—the novel is definitely a romance rather than a work of scientific extrapolation, as Lewis himself explained in an essay published in *Of Other Worlds: Essays and Stories* (1966). For instance, his Mars has the canals that were part of the popular idea of the planet, although scientists in 1938 did not believe in their existence. Lewis excels in his presentation of nonhuman but sentient races, the *hrossa, sorns,* and *pfifltriggi,* and the novel explores differences in perception as Ransom comes to see the Malacandrans as normal and Thulcandrans as strange.

Lewis develops a vital Christian universe in which space is not cold, empty, and black but sings and shines with the presence of God; his *eldila,* angel-like presences, and *Oyarsa,* the great *eldil* who is the genius or spirit of each planet, have medieval and Renaissance predecessors but are original creations. In a 17 November 1957 letter to a fan, Lewis said that he was influenced by Olaf Stapledon's novel *Last and First Men* (1931), J. B. S. Haldane's scientific work *Possible Worlds* (1927), and Wells's novel *The First Men in the Moon* (1901); he also credited David Lindsay's *A Voyage to Arcturus* (1920) with showing him that an interplanetary story could have a strong spiritual or supernatural dimension. *Out of the Silent Planet* was well received, both in reviews and in later scholarship, although it did not sell outstandingly well.

Warren Lewis was called back to the army when World War II broke out in 1939; in May 1940 he was among troops evacuated from Dunkirk. Afterward he was assigned to patrol the outskirts of Oxford with the Home Guards. C. S. Lewis, who still carried shrapnel from World War I—some of which was surgically removed in 1944—did not fight in World War II but served the war effort as a popular morale-building Christian apologist. On 22 October 1939 he preached before Oxford University in the Church of St. Mary the Virgin on the topic "None Other Gods: Culture in War Time." That same year his friend Ashley Sampson asked him to contribute a book to the Christian Challenge series that Sampson was editing for the publisher Geoffrey Bles. *The Problem of Pain* (1940) was designed to answer the question of how a loving and omnipotent God could allow suffering in humans and in animals.

In July 1940 Lewis conceived of the work that brought him to the attention of the general public. Originally titled "From One Devil to Another," *The Screwtape Letters* was probably finished by Christmas. It records the advice of an experienced devil, Screwtape, to his nephew, Wormwood. The soul Wormwood is assigned to secure—called his "patient"—is an ordinary man who is capable of following influences from "the Enemy," God. He is killed during an air raid and goes to heaven, for which Wormwood will be punished harshly. The book is filled with keen psychological insights and sharp humor. Influences may include *Breve fra Helvede* (1866), which Lewis seems to have read while studying with Kirkpatrick; the work was written in Danish by Valdeman Adolph Thisted and translated into English by Julie Sutter as *Letters from Hell,* with an introduction by MacDonald, in 1884. In a conversation with Hooper, documented in *C. S. Lewis: A Biography,* Lewis acknowledged inspiration from Stephen McKenna's *Confessions of a Well-Meaning Woman* (1922). The diabolical letters were published as a weekly column in the *Manchester Guardian* from 2 May through 28 December 1941 and immediately attracted overwhelming positive attention, offending only a few who missed the satirical point. The book version, published in 1942 and reprinted eight times that year alone, was Lewis's first financial success. He gave much of his new wealth to charity.

Still, Lewis was hardly unknown when *The Screwtape Letters* came out. He had been speaking on the radio since 1941 at the invitation of Dr. James W. Welch, director of religious broadcasting for the British Broadcasting Corporation (BBC), who had been impressed by *The Problem of Pain.* Lewis wrote the scripts and traveled to London for the fifteen-minute broadcasts; mail poured in from listeners, and a show answering the letters only increased the response. The broadcasts were published as *Broadcast Talks: Reprinted with Some Alterations from Two Series of Broadcast Talks ("Right and Wrong: A Clue to the Meaning of the Universe" and "What Christians Believe") Given in 1941 and 1942* (1942; republished as *The Case for Christianity,* 1943);

Christian Behaviour: A Further Series of Broadcast Talks (1943); and *Beyond Personality: The Christian Idea of God* (1944); in 1952 Lewis collected and revised them as *Mere Christianity*. Robert Speaight wrote in *The Tablet* (26 June 1943), "Mr. Lewis is that rare being–a born broadcaster; born to the manner as well as the matter." Also in 1941 Lewis began speaking at Royal Air Force bases in England. On Sunday, 8 June 1941, he delivered his best-known sermon, "The Weight of Glory," at the Church of St. Mary the Virgin, Oxford University. The sermon was published a few months later in the November 1941 issue of *Theology*.

The second volume of Lewis's Space Trilogy, *Perelandra,* was published in 1943. As *The Allegory of Love* sparked Lewis's imagination toward *Out of the Silent Planet, Perelandra* is the outgrowth of Lewis's lectures on Milton's *Paradise Lost,* delivered between 1939 and 1941 and published in 1942 as *A Preface to* Paradise Lost. Perelandra–known to earthlings as Venus–has not yet fallen into sin. Most of the planet is covered by floating islands; the "forbidden fruit" for its only sapient inhabitants, the queen and her husband, is to stay overnight on the only solid land. Weston, cored out and replaced by the evil he channels to become "the Un-man," has come there to tempt the queen, who is known as the Green Lady. He is capable of both sophisticated theological temptations and small, pointless cruelties. Ransom, transported to Perelandra by the planetary intelligences to do battle with Weston, fights with only human strength but finally defeats the Un-man. The book ends with a glorious pageant in which the planetary intelligences celebrate the victory. *Perelandra* was Lewis's personal favorite among his works of fiction.

That Hideous Strength: A Modern Fairy-Tale for Grown-Ups, the third volume of the Space Trilogy, was published in 1945. The nonfiction text behind this novel is *The Abolition of Man: Reflections on Education with Special Reference to the Teaching of English in the Upper Forms of Schools* (1943), delivered as lectures at the University of Durham in 1943. Many critics claim that the setting of *That Hideous Strength* is modeled on the University of Durham, though Lewis denied it; the academic infighting, politics, and one-upmanship of the novel owe more to Lewis's life at Oxford. Unlike its predecessors, *That Hideous Strength* is set in a realistic, almost mundane world of town-and-gown politics and marital adjustments. But fantastic elements are introduced into that setting: the head of a murderer that is being kept alive and used to channel evil spirits; the magician Merlin, awakened from centuries-long sleep; and the planetary spirits from the previous two books. Like *Perelandra,* the novel is the story of a battle between good and evil; but this time the battle takes place on Thulcandra, the silent planet.

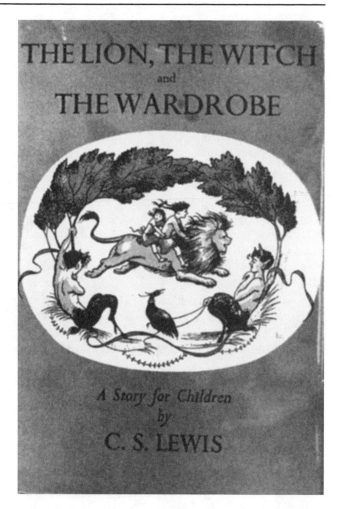

Dust jacket for Lewis's 1950 novel, in which four siblings go through the back of an old wardrobe and find themselves in the land of Narnia (Marion E. Wade Center, Wheaton College, Wheaton, Illinois)

That Hideous Strength has been frequently called "a Charles Williams novel written by C. S. Lewis" partly because, as Lewis's only novel set on Earth, it resembles Williams's seven fantasy novels. Moreover, the group that Mr. Fisher-King–as Ransom is called in this novel–assembles around himself is reminiscent of the Companions of the Co-inherence, the spiritual fellowship in Williams's Arthurian poetry. Ransom himself–who, because he is a philologist, is often said to be inspired by Tolkien–resembles Williams more than Tolkien in this novel. Lewis, however, does connect the story to Tolkien's Middle-earth: Merlin's mention of "Numinor" refers to Tolkien's "Númenór" from *The Silmarillion* (1977); Tolkien had been reading the manuscript for that work to Lewis. Wilson says that the crush of the young wife in the novel, Jane Studdock, on Ransom may be based on the infatuation with Lewis of a teenager, June Flewett, who was living and working as a domestic servant at the Kilns while Lewis was writing the work. Most critics contend that Jules, a Cockney scientist, is a satiric portrait of Wells in his later years. Green and Hooper disagree, pointing out that Lewis never met Wells. Devine from *Out of the Silent Planet* appears in *That Hideous Strength* as Lord Feverstone, an advocate for the National Institute of Coordinated Experiments–a group with the ironic acronym N.I.C.E.–that wants to resurrect Merlin and use his powers for its nefarious purposes.

Sales of *That Hideous Strength* were good, though the reviews, especially by science-fiction aficionados, were largely negative. Esteem for the novel has increased over the decades, although many readers are daunted by the misogyny, or at least sexism, that is shown in the relationships of men and women in the book, and by what certainly appears to be homophobia in the depiction of the repulsive lesbian, "Fairy" Hardcastle.

Immediately after finishing *That Hideous Strength* Lewis began to write *The Great Divorce: A Dream,* which was serialized in the *Manchester Guardian* beginning in November 1944 and published in book form in 1945. Warren recorded in his diary that the idea had come to Lewis in 1932 as "a sort of infernal day-excursion to Paradise." According to Puritan theology, the damned are shown heaven as additional torture; here, a busload of souls from hell are not only allowed to visit the outskirts of heaven but are invited to remain there if they choose to reject the sin that resulted in their damnation. Only one soul chooses not to return to hell, showing that heaven and hell are separated by one's own choices. The title is a takeoff on William Blake's poem *The Marriage of Heaven and Hell* (circa 1793). Lewis also clearly had Dante's *Divine Comedy* (written circa 1310–1314; published, 1472) in mind: George MacDonald is the narrator's guide, as Virgil is Dante's in *The Inferno. The Great Divorce* was not as popular as *The Screwtape Letters,* but many readers consider it a more mature theological work.

Williams died on 14 May 1945. Lewis wrote in a letter to Sister Penelope, a friend, on 28 May 1945, "Death has done nothing to my idea of him, but he has done–oh, I can't say what–to my idea of death. It has made the next world much more real and palpable." Lewis's acts to commemorate his friend included editing and contributing to *Essays Presented to Charles Williams* (1947) and a series of university lectures on Williams's Arthurian poetry that he published, along with an unfinished study by Williams of King Arthur, as *Arthurian Torso* (1948).

By 1947 Janie Moore was bedridden, and her care fell to Lewis. In April 1950 she had to be placed in a nursing home, where Lewis visited her every day until she died on 12 January 1951. By that time Warren, who had retired from the military a second time and returned to the Kilns at Christmas 1932, had become an alcoholic; he was most apt to drink in stressful times when Lewis could most use his support. Another misfortune for Lewis during the late 1940s was that his friendship with Tolkien began to cool.

After the Space Trilogy, the second major pillar of Lewis's fame as a writer of fantastic fiction is what Green and Hooper call "that unexpected creation of his middle age," The Chronicles of Narnia. Lewis believed that good children's books should be enjoyable reading throughout one's life; in a lecture published in *On Stories: and Other Essays on Literature* (1982) he says, "When I was ten, I read fairy tales in secret and would have been ashamed if I had been found doing so. Now that I am fifty I read them openly." The seven Narnia books are fantasies written for children but intended to be appreciated by adults. The books were produced quickly, with Lewis writing later ones while the first was being illustrated by Pauline Baynes and set in proof. Though the volumes were released yearly from 1950 to 1956, Lewis had probably finished writing them by 1953.

The first book in the series, *The Lion, the Witch, and the Wardrobe,* has achieved fame apart from the rest, winning the Lewis Carroll Shelf Award in 1962. The work had its origin when Lewis was sixteen and imagined, as he says in an essay collected in *Of Other Worlds: Essays and Stories,* "a picture of a Faun carrying an umbrella and parcels in a snowy wood." He started writing the book in 1939, when three schoolgirls were evacuated to the Kilns because of World War II. When Lewis took up the story again in 1948, the girls developed into the Pevensie children–Peter, Susan, Edmund, and Lucy– who are "sent away from London during the Air-Raids" in 1940 to "the house of an old Professor who lived in the heart of the country." The children, exploring the huge house, find a forgotten wardrobe, the back of which opens onto the magical land of Narnia.

Narnia has been both praised and blamed for its intermingling of mythologies, including not only classical fauns and Beatrix Potter-like talking animals but also Father Christmas and a Christ-like lion named Aslan (Turkish for "lion"). Lewis was influenced by Nesbit's children's stories; Green and Hooper report he was also highly affected by "The Wood That Time Forgot," a children's novel by Green that he read in manuscript and that was never published. Lewis writes in an essay included in *Of Other Worlds: Essays and Stories* that Aslan "bounded into" the story relatively late in the composition of *The Lion, the Witch, and the Wardrobe,* but "once He was there He pulled the whole story together, and soon He pulled the other six Narnia stories after him." The story concludes with the sacrificial death and resurrection of Aslan, defeating the evil White Witch who has condemned Narnia to perpetual winter and establishing the children on thrones in the Great Hall of Cair Paravel as rulers of the land. After a benevolent reign, they return to England—where no time has passed—through the wardrobe.

Lewis made a false start on the sequel to *The Lion, the Witch, and the Wardrobe*: on their arrival in Narnia the Pevensie children are greeted by a standard English lamppost; Lewis's first impulse was to tell the story of its arrival in the fantasyland. A fragment of this work survives in manuscript. Instead, however, Lewis turned to an adventure story, *Prince Caspian: The Return to Narnia*, in which the children are recalled to Narnia in 1941 to rescue Prince Caspian, a descendant of the old royalty of Narnia and rightful heir to the throne, from his evil uncle, the tyrant Miraz. In Narnia more than a thousand years have passed; Cair Paravel lies almost in ruins and barely recognizable. With the help of the children and Aslan, Caspian prevails in the struggle with his uncle. Lewis's narrative voice is more assured and less precious here than in *The Lion, the Witch, and the Wardrobe;* both the adventure and the characters are more well-rounded and convincing.

The third book, *The Voyage of the Dawn Treader,* is set in 1942. Susan and Peter have become too old to travel to Narnia; with maturity has come preoccupation with the mundane world and a disinclination to believe in Narnia. Lucy and Edmund are accompanied to Narnia—where three years have passed since their previous adventure—by their cousin Eustace Clarence Scrubb. They must join King Caspian X, as Prince Caspian is now known, on a sea journey to find seven friends of his father who were exiled by his wicked uncle. At first, Eustace, raised to be a modern scientific—that is, unimaginative—sort, is a burden to the Pevensies; one theme of the novel is Eustace's psychological and moral growth, which is produced by many trials, including transformation into a dragon. A major accomplishment in the work is Lewis's creation of the valiant soldier Reepicheep, king of the mice. The captain of the *Dawn Treader,* Drinian, steadfast and settled, acts as a foil to the dramatic mouse. At the end of *The Voyage of the Dawn Treader* Aslan tells Lucy and Edmund that they, too, are aging and will not come back to Narnia.

In *The Silver Chair* a few weeks have passed on Earth since the events of *The Voyage of the Dawn Treader.* The novel begins at Experiment House, a scathing satire of the trends in modern education that Lewis criticized in *The Abolition of Man.* Eustace and his schoolmate Jill Pole escape through a door that leads to Narnia, where seventy years have passed since Eustace's previous visit; there they find they are needed to rescue Prince Rilian, Caspian's heir, from the underground lair of the Green Witch. The children repeatedly misjudge those they meet or miss important signs left for them,

Dust jacket for the sixth volume in Lewis's Chronicles of Narnia, published in 1955, in which the origin of the kingdom is recounted (Marion E. Wade Center, Wheaton College, Wheaton, Illinois)

like Parzival failing to ask the right questions in his search for the Holy Grail. After some genuinely scary scenes, Aslan helps the children and their companion, the pessimistic frog-like "Marsh-wiggle" Puddleglum, rescue Rilian. Back in England, Eustace and Jill confront the bullies of Experiment House and win.

The fifth and seventh books, *The Horse and His Boy* and *The Last Battle,* begin in Narnia instead of in England. They are also the most controversial of the books. Both feature the Calormenes, whose culture is tyrannical and inimical to Narnia; it is also highly reminiscent of Muslim or Arab cultures, and Lewis's depiction of it is often criticized as condescending or even racist. Yet, in *The Last Battle* a Calormene soldier is elected into eternity because he lived a moral life and honored Aslan in his heart, even though he thought he worshiped another—false—god: this development is, perhaps, condescending but certainly not racist. Similarly, the treatment of Susan in *The Last Battle* is often seen as sexist; but *The Horse and His Boy* includes some of Lewis's best female characters, including Aravis, a

Calormene princess who is a valiant rider on her talking horse, Hwin.

The Horse and His Boy returns to the time of the reign of the four Pevensies in Narnia. The male protagonist, Shasta, is riding to the North on his talking horse, Bree, as he flees the Calormene empire; he is actually the king of Archenland, who was rescued from the sea as a baby by Aslan and raised as the son and virtual slave of a Calormene fisherman. Besides action and some strong characters, *The Horse and His Boy* offers several good comic scenes. The book won the Carnegie Medal Commendation of the British Library Association in 1955.

Lewis finally explains the lamppost in Narnia—and depicts the creation of that entire world—in the sixth book, *The Magician's Nephew*. Set in 1900, the time of Lewis's own childhood, the novel concerns Digory Kirke, who grows up to be the "old Professor" of *The Lion, the Witch, and the Wardrobe*, and Polly Plummer, his friend and neighbor. Magical rings owned by Digory's Uncle Andrew transport the children to a "Wood Between the Worlds," from which they find themselves in the dismal, literally deadly Land of Charn. There they awaken Queen Jadis, who becomes the White Witch of *The Lion, the Witch, and the Wardrobe*. Narnia has not yet been created, and the children witness Aslan singing it into existence.

If *The Lion, the Witch, and the Wardrobe* is Narnia's story of Resurrection from the Gospels, and *The Magician's Nephew* is Narnia's Book of Genesis, then *The Last Battle* is its Book of Revelation. It features a false prophet: Shift, an ape who disguises a donkey in a lion skin and presents him as Aslan. After the final battle between the Narnians and the Calormenes, Aslan escorts his chosen ones through a stable door, which is actually a door into eternity. The novel concludes, "All their life in this world and their adventures in Narnia had only been the cover and the title page: now at last they were beginning Chapter One of the Great Story, which no one on Earth has ever read: which goes on for ever: in which every chapter is better than the one before." *The Last Battle* won the Carnegie Medal for best children's book in 1956.

"The critical reception of the seven books," Green and Hooper note, "was varied and usually guarded." The books have gained popularity over the decades, and a set published in paperback by Puffin between 1977 and 1979 was a best-seller. Lewis always stressed that the Narnia books were not Christian allegories, though many critics disagree; certainly, they are not allegories in the sense of *The Pilgrim's Regress* but constitute a unique myth, although based in Christianity.

In a chronological bibliography of Lewis's books the Narnia novels are interrupted by only three titles: *Mere Christianity* in 1952; *English Literature in the Sixteenth Century Excluding Drama,* a major scholarly project that was published as volume three in the Oxford History of English Literature series, in 1954; and *Surprised by Joy,* his first autobiography, in 1955. During this time two major changes occurred in Lewis's life.

In June 1954, after having spent his entire career up to that time at Oxford, Lewis accepted the chair of Medieval and Renaissance English at Cambridge. At Oxford he had been passed over for the Merton Professorship of English Language in 1947 and the poetry chair in 1951. According to Wilson, "Even colleagues who were Christian found Lewis's career as a popularizer embarrassing." Thus, Lewis moved from Magdalen College, Oxford, to Magdalene College, Cambridge. Oxford tried to entice Lewis back in 1957 and always listed him as an honorary fellow, but Lewis was much happier at Cambridge. He could travel to the Kilns for vacations and most weekends; more important, he had no tutorial duties. Lewis's Cambridge lectures formed the basis of his *Studies in Words* (1960), *The Discarded Image: An Introduction to Medieval and Renaissance Literature* (1964), and the posthumous *Spenser's Images of Life,* assembled by Alastair Fowler from Lewis's notes and published in 1967.

The other major change in Lewis's life in the 1950s was his relationship with an American poet, Joy Davidman. It began in 1950 when she wrote to him from her home in Westchester County, New York, where she was unhappily married to William Gresham. Davidman, then in her thirties, had converted to Christianity in 1946, partly because of the influence of Lewis's books. They met when Davidman visited England in September 1952; while she was there, Davidman discovered that her husband had been unfaithful and that he wanted a divorce. She immediately returned to the United States to get the divorce, and came back to England in 1954 with her sons, David and Douglas. That year her *Smoke on the Mountain: The Ten Commandments in Terms of Today* was published with a preface by Lewis. She moved from London to Oxford the following year.

Lewis began his final completed work of fantastic fiction, "Bareface," in 1955 and finished it in February 1956; the publisher insisted that he change the title, and *Till We Have Faces: A Myth Retold* appeared in 1956. The novel retells the story of Cupid and Psyche, a classical tale first recorded by Apuleius. Lewis's twist, which had come to him as early as 1923—he tried the theme twice in poetry as an undergraduate—is that Psyche's homely older half sister, Orual, the queen of the realm of Glome, is not jealous but genuinely cannot see the palmore than a few moments. How could it, when its whole effort was to achieve a contradiction?—to awake merely personal, selfish, prudential hopes and fears for things that can only be realised in proportion as the merely personal, selfish, and prudential have been (at least for the time being) sloughed off?

One thing that blunts grief in childhood is the mass of other miseries which surround it. I was taken into the bedroom where my Mother lay dead, to see the body. There was nothing that a grown-up would call disfigurement—except for that total disfigurement which is death itself. Grief was overwhelmed in terror; nor have I ever been able to this day to conceive how any corpse can be thought beautiful. The ugliest man alive is an angel of beauty (for me) compared with the loveliest of the dead. I have seen plenty of dead people since, and my impression has always been the same; namely, that death reveals man as an animal. That first view of death in my Mother's sick-room, that and all the horrible subsequent paraphernalia of coffin, flowers, hearse and black clothes, added richly to the furniture of my nightmares. The dreams about insects did not disappear, but the spectres multiplied.

The years spent in the new house before my Mother's illness had been very happy; they had also been very solitary, since my Mother was away for the greater part of the year. I loved solitude (except after dark). I once overheard my Father say of me to my grandfather: "He is the most easily amused child I ever saw. Give him pencil and paper and he'll be quiet for hours." And so I was, quiet at a little card-table in the corner of a room we called the "study" though in fact it was the room in which everyone usually sat. But I think I soon preferred to be elsewhere. I had found out an attic for myself which I had, in a childish way, fitted up as a study of my own. Works of art, of my own composition, or cut from the highly-coloured Christmas numbers of magazines, were pinned on the walls. My pen and ink-pot and pad and paint-box were also there: for by now I could write as well as draw. Here my earliest stories were written and illustrated with enormous delight. They were an attempt to combine my two favourite literary pleasures—"dressed animals" and "knights in armour"; for Beatrix Potter's little books were now reaching me and Conan Doyle's Sir Nigel was appearing monthly in The Strand. As a natural result I wrote about medieval mice or rabbits who rode out in plate armour and killed, not giants but cats. Already the mood of the systematiser was strong in me—the mood which made Trollope build up from novel to novel his

Manuscript page for Lewis's first autobiography, Surprised by Joy, *published in 1955 (Bodleian Library, Oxford University, Dep. d.241 f.22)*

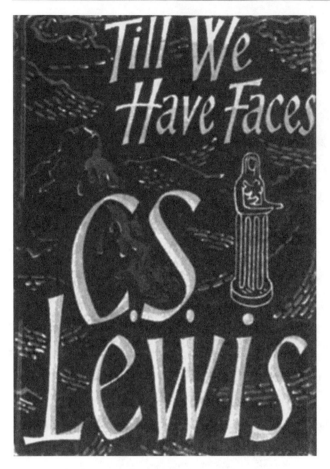

*Dust jacket for Lewis's final completed work of fantastic fiction, a
retelling of the myth of Cupid and Psyche published in 1956
(Marion E. Wade Center, Wheaton College, Wheaton, Illinois)*

ace built for Psyche by Cupid; she fears that Psyche has gone insane or married a monster. Orual's stark and powerful narrative voice is off-putting to some readers. At first a worshiper of the barbarian stone goddess Ungit, Orual advances in spiritual development when she is taught Platonism by the Fox, an educated Greek slave. With maturity and acceptance she can finally surrender to God: "How can the gods meet us face to face," Orual asks, "until we have faces?" In contrast to the sweetness of the Narnia books, *Till We Have Faces* is a knotty, difficult work; the immediate reaction to it in England disappointed Lewis, though it was received more favorably in the United States.

On 23 April 1956 Lewis married Davidman in a civil ceremony, ostensibly—and perhaps actually—just so she could remain in England. In early 1957, however, Davidman was diagnosed with bone cancer, and Lewis married her again on 21 March 1957—this time in a religious ceremony officiated by the Reverend Peter Bide in her room at Churchill Hospital in Oxford. Some biographers think that even then Lewis was not in love with her but married her so that it would not be

improper for him to take her to the Kilns to nurse her until she died. When, instead, she experienced a remission in late 1957, Davidman became Lewis's wife in the full sense. In 1958 Lewis told Coghill, "I never expected to have, in my sixties, the happiness that passed me by in my twenties." In August 1958 the couple traveled to Ireland. Davidman helped Lewis with *Reflections on the Psalms* (1958), a topic Lewis had thought about since the 1940s.

In 1958, in response to a request for tapes to be broadcast on the radio in the United States, Lewis wrote ten scripts concerning *storge* (affection), *philia* (friendship), *eros* (sexual love), and *agape* (gift-love or charity). The talks were not as widely broadcast as anticipated, because some thought that the discussion of *eros* was too brash for American audiences. Lewis adapted the talks into *The Four Loves*, which was published in March 1960. Cassettes of the talks were made commercially available in 1970.

Davidman's cancer returned in October 1959. Nonetheless, the couple vacationed in Greece in 1960; the trip, Lewis's only excursion outside the British Isles since World War I, was Davidman's idea. Soon after Davidman's death on 13 July 1960 Lewis wrote his second autobiography, *A Grief Observed,* an account of their last years together; it was published under the pseudonym N. W. Clerk in 1961. In the book Lewis says of Davidman, "Her mind was lithe and quick and muscular as a leopard."

After Davidman's death Lewis worked on, but did not finish, a story about Helen of Troy ten years after the Trojan War. The idea had occurred to Lewis around 1956, and he had returned to the project after his and Davidman's trip to Greece. The fragment was published posthumously as "After Ten Years" in the collections *Of Other Worlds: Essays and Stories* and *The Dark Tower and Other Stories* (1977).

Lewis created two final masterworks, one of literary criticism and one of religious writing. *An Experiment in Criticism* (1961) began as a paper presented to the Martlets on 14 November 1940, which Lewis developed into his essay "On Stories," first published in *Essays Presented to Charles Williams* (1947). The essay and the book are of particular interest to readers of popular fiction, including fantastic fiction. Lewis examines various ways of approaching a book and shows how some strategies of appreciation fit better with some kinds of fiction than with others. *Letters to Malcolm: Chiefly on Prayer,* the last book Lewis wrote, was published posthumously in 1964; some scholars have tried to identify the person to whom the letters are written, though most contend that "Malcolm" is fictitious and that the "correspondence" is a device Lewis uses to elaborate his views on prayer and acceptance.

From 1959 to 1962 Lewis collaborated on a revision of the Psalms for the Book of Common Prayer; it is impossible to know how much of the finished product is Lewis's work. By late 1961, however, he was suffering from kidney, heart, and prostate problems. His health fluctuated, including an unexpected revival from a coma following a heart attack on 15 July 1963. After that recovery, Lewis finally retired from Cambridge. Warren cared for him throughout this period, until his death on 22 November 1963.

Lewis had a rich, though controversial, posthumous career, thanks largely to his tireless editor and literary executor, Walter Hooper. Hooper unquestionably did invaluable work by republishing Lewis's uncollected pieces in accessible volumes, but some critics contend that Lewis had good reasons for leaving some fragments and even whole pieces unpublished, and that some of the material Hooper resurrected may be of interest for the light it sheds on Lewis's other work but is not a credit to the author in itself. A more serious charge was raised by Kathryn Lindskoog in *The C. S. Lewis Hoax* (1988). She accused Hooper of using his position as Lewis's literary executor to perpetrate his own versions of Lewis's works. The most significant charge for readers of Lewis's fantastic fiction concerns *The Dark Tower and Other Stories*. The volume includes two short stories that were published in *The Magazine of Fantasy and Science Fiction* during Lewis's lifetime: "The Shoddy Lands" (February 1956) and "Ministering Angels" (January 1958). "The Shoddy Lands," in which an elderly don literally walks inside the mind of a boring and pretty woman, can be seen as highly sexist; it is best viewed as a comment on any imprecise mind, not as an overall comment on women. "Ministering Angels" is a lighthearted tale of space-station concubines set on a Mars that is definitely not Malacandra. "The Forms of Things Unknown," not published during Lewis's lifetime, is a clever story in which the Gorgons live on the moon and turn all the astronauts sent there to stone. Many readers, however, do not realize that the mysterious figure at the end is a Gorgon. Lewis's recognition of this defect may account for his failure to publish it.

"The Dark Tower" is the piece Lindskoog attacks. Hooper presents it as the truncated beginning of another novel in the Space Trilogy, probably written immediately after *Out of the Silent Planet* but abandoned in 1939; MacPhee and Ransom are characters in it. It is not about space travel but about traveling in time, first through a viewing machine and then by switching bodies. One major image is surreal and disquieting, reminiscent of those in Lindsay's *A Voyage to Arcturus:* a horrible figure stabs the unicorn-like horn in his forehead into the spines of human beings, who submit to its

Lewis's wife, Joy Davidman Lewis, in 1960, the year of her death

poison and become automata. According to Lindskoog, the piece is a forgery. Other critics contend that Lewis knew that the fragment went nowhere and wisely shelved it.

C. S. Lewis accomplished enough for many lifetimes: he was a poet, a literary scholar and critic, a Christian apologist and theologian, an autobiographer, and a novelist. Yet, all of his work is of a piece, expressing his love of God's creation and his dedication to that "something more" at which he believed all earthly joys hinted. Using the vehicle of fantastic fiction, Lewis left many views of the real world, as well as of that "something more," all of them striking to the imagination and satisfying to the heart.

Letters:

Letters of C. S. Lewis, edited, with a memoir, by W. H. Lewis (London: Bles, 1966; New York: Harcourt Brace Jovanovich, 1975; revised and enlarged edition, edited by Walter Hooper, London: Collins/ Fount, 1988; San Diego: Harcourt Brace, 1993);

Letters to an American Lady, edited by Clyde S. Kilby (Grand Rapids, Mich.: Eerdmans, 1967; London: Hodder & Stoughton, 1969);

Sheldon Vanauken, *A Severe Mercy: C. S. Lewis and a Pagan Love Invaded by Christ, Told by One of the Lovers* (New York: Harper & Row, 1977);

They Stand Together: The Letters of C. S. Lewis to Arthur Greeves, 1914–1963, edited by Hooper (New York: Macmillan, 1979; London: Collins, 1979);

Letters: C. S. Lewis–Don Giovanni Calabria. A Study in Friendship, translated and edited by Martin Moynihan (London: Collins, 1989);

Letters to Children, edited by Lyle W. Dorsett and Marjorie Lamp Mead (New York: Simon & Schuster, 1995).

Bibliographies:

Joe R. Christopher and Joan K. Ostling, *C. S. Lewis: An Annotated Checklist of Writings about Him and His Work* (Kent, Ohio: Kent State University Press, 1974);

Walter Hooper, "A Bibliography of the Writings of C. S. Lewis," in *Light on C. S. Lewis,* edited by Jocelyn Gibb (New York: Harcourt Brace Jovanovich, 1976), pp. 117–160;

Hooper, *C. S. Lewis: A Companion and Guide* (San Francisco: HarperSanFrancisco, 1996), pp. 799–883;

Janine Goffar, *The C. S. Lewis Index: A Comprehensive Guide to Lewis's Writings* (Westchester, Ill.: Crossway, 1998).

Biographies:

Roger Lancelyn Green and Walter Hooper, *C. S. Lewis: A Biography* (London: Collins, 1974; New York: Harcourt Brace Jovanovich, 1974);

Humphrey Carpenter, *The Inklings: C. S. Lewis, J. R. R. Tolkien, Charles Williams, and Their Friends* (London: Allen & Unwin, 1978);

James T. Como, ed., *C. S. Lewis at the Breakfast Table, and Other Reminiscences* (New York: Macmillan, 1979);

Margaret Patterson Hannay, *C. S. Lewis* (New York: Ungar, 1981);

Brian Sibley, *Shadowlands: The Story of C. S. Lewis and Joy Davidman* (London: Hodder & Stoughton, 1985);

William Griffin, *Clive Staples Lewis: A Dramatic Life* (San Francisco: Harper & Row, 1986);

George Sayer, *Jack: C. S. Lewis and His Times* (London: Macmillan, 1988); republished as *Jack: A Life of C. S. Lewis* (Westchester, Ill.: Crossway, 1994);

Douglas H. Gresham, *Lenten Lands* (New York: Macmillan, 1988; London: Collins, 1989);

A. N. Wilson, *C. S. Lewis: A Biography* (New York: Norton, 1990);

Michael Coren, *The Man Who Created Narnia: The Story of C. S. Lewis* (Grand Rapids, Mich.: Eerdmans, 1996).

References:

Lionel Adey, *C. S. Lewis's "Great War" with Owen Barfield* (Victoria, B.C.: ELS Monographs, 1978);

Michael Aeschliman, *The Restitution of Man: C. S. Lewis and the Case against Scientism* (Grand Rapids, Mich.: Eerdmans, 1983);

Anne Arnott, *The Secret Country of C. S. Lewis* (London: Hodder & Stoughton, 1974);

Owen Barfield, *Owen Barfield on C. S. Lewis,* edited by G. B. Tennyson (Middletown, Conn.: Wesleyan University Press, 1989);

David Barratt, *C. S. Lewis and His World* (Grand Rapids, Mich.: Eerdmans, 1988);

Sally A. Bartlett, "Humanistic Psychology in C. S. Lewis's *Till We Have Faces:* A Feminist Critique," *Studies in the Literary Imagination,* 22 (Fall 1989): 185–198;

John Beversluis, *C. S. Lewis and the Search for Rational Religion* (Exeter: Paternoster Press, 1985);

Ann Bonsor, "'One Huge and Complex Episode': The Diary of C. S. Lewis," *Contemporary Review,* 260 (March 1992): 145–149;

Perry C. Bramlett, *C. S. Lewis and Life at the Center: Prayer, Devotion, and Friendship* (London: Peake, 1996);

Patrick J. Callahan, "The Two Gardens in C. S. Lewis's *That Hideous Strength,*" in *SF: The Other Side of Realism—Essays on Modern Fantasy and Science Fiction,* edited by Thomas D. Clareson (Bowling Green, Ohio: Bowling Green University Popular Press, 1971), pp. 147–156;

David C. Campbell and Dale E. Hess, "Olympian Detachment: A Critical Look at the World of C. S. Lewis's Characters," *Studies in the Literary Imagination,* 22 (Fall 1989): 199–215;

Corbin Scott Carnell, *Bright Shadow of Reality: C. S. Lewis and the Feeling Intellect* (Grand Rapids, Mich.: Eerdmans, 1974);

Humphrey Carpenter and Christopher Tolkien, eds., *The Letters of J. R. R. Tolkien* (London: Allen & Unwin, 1981);

Michael J. Christensen, *C. S. Lewis on Scripture: His Thoughts on the Nature of Biblical Inspiration, the Role of Revelation and the Question of Inerrancy* (Waco, Tex.: Word, 1979; London: Hodder & Stoughton, 1979);

Joe R. Christopher, *C. S. Lewis* (Boston: Twayne, 1987);

Christopher, "C. S. Lewis, Love Poet," *Studies in the Literary Imagination,* 22 (Fall 1989): 161–173;

Richard B. Cunningham, *C. S. Lewis: Defender of the Faith* (Philadelphia: Westminster Press, 1967);

Christopher Derrick, *C. S. Lewis and the Church of Rome* (San Francisco: Ignatius, 1982);

"Don v. Devil," *Time,* 50 (8 September 1947): 65–74;

David C. Downing, *Planets in Peril: A Critical Study of C. S. Lewis's Ransom Trilogy* (Amherst: University of Massachusetts Press, 1992);

Colin Duriez, *The C. S. Lewis Encyclopedia: A Complete Guide to His Life, Thought, and Writings* (Westchester, Ill.: Crossway, 2000);

Duriez, *The C. S. Lewis Handbook* (Grand Rapids, Mich.: Baker, 1990);

Bruce I. Edwards, ed., *The Taste of the Pineapple: Essays on C. S. Lewis as Reader, Critic, and Imaginative Writer* (Bowling Green, Ohio: Bowling Green State University Popular Press, 1988);

Paul F. Ford, *Companion to Narnia* (New York: Harper & Row, 1980);

Edmund Fuller, "The Christian Spaceman: C. S. Lewis," in *Books with Men behind Them* (New York: Random House, 1962), pp. 143–168;

Jocelyn Gibb, ed., *Light on C. S. Lewis* (New York: Harcourt Brace Jovanovich, 1976);

Evan K. Gibson, *C. S. Lewis, Spinner of Tales: A Guide to His Fiction* (Grand Rapids, Mich.: Christian University Press, 1980);

Douglas Gilbert and Clyde S. Kilby, *C. S. Lewis: Images of His World* (Grand Rapids, Mich.: Eerdmans, 1973);

Terry W. Glaspey, *Not a Tame Lion: The Spiritual Legacy of C. S. Lewis* (Nashville, Tenn.: Cumberland House, 1996);

Donald E. Glover, *C. S. Lewis: The Art of Enchantment* (Athens: Ohio University Press, 1981);

Beatrice Gormley, *C. S. Lewis: Christian and Storyteller* (Grand Rapids, Mich.: Eerdmans, 1997);

Mark R. Hillegas, ed., *Shadows of Imagination: The Fantasies of C. S. Lewis, J. R. R. Tolkien, and Charles Williams* (Carbondale: Southern Illinois University Press, 1969);

David Holbrook, *The Skeleton in the Wardrobe: C. S. Lewis's Fantasies—A Phenomenological Study* (Lewistown, Pa.: Bucknell University Press, 1991);

Paul L. Holmer, *C. S. Lewis: The Shape of His Faith and Thought* (New York: Harper & Row, 1976);

Walter Hooper, *C. S. Lewis: A Companion and Guide* (San Francisco: HarperCollins, 1996);

Hooper, *Imagination and the Spirit: Essays in Literature and the Christian Faith,* edited by Charles A. Huttar (Grand Rapids, Mich.: Eerdmans, 1971);

Hooper, *Past Watchful Dragons: The Narnian Chronicles of C. S. Lewis* (New York: Macmillan, 1974);

Thomas Howard, *C. S. Lewis, Man of Letters: A Reading of His Fiction* (Worthing, Sussex: Churchman, 1987);

William G. Johnson and Marcia K. Houtman, "Platonic Shadows in C. S. Lewis' Narnia *Chronicles,*" *Modern Fiction Studies,* 32 (Spring 1986): 75–87;

Paul A. Karkainen, *Narnia Explored* (Grand Rapids, Mich.: Fleming H. Revell, 1979);

Carolyn Keefe, ed., *C. S. Lewis: Speaker and Teacher* (Grand Rapids, Mich.: Zondervan, 1971);

Clyde S. Kilby, *The Christian World of C. S. Lewis* (Grand Rapids, Mich.: Eerdmans, 1964);

Kilby, "Holiness in the Life of C. S. Lewis," *Discipleship Journal,* 22 (1984): 14–16;

Kilby, *Images of Salvation in the Fiction of C. S. Lewis* (Wheaton, Ill.: Harold Shaw, 1978);

Don W. King, "The Distant Voice in C. S. Lewis's *Poems,*" *Studies in the Literary Imagination,* 22 (Fall 1989): 175–184;

Gareth Knight, *The Magical World of the Inklings: J. R. R. Tolkien, C. S. Lewis, Charles Williams, Owen Barfield* (Longmead, Shaftesbury, Dorset: Element, 1990);

Peter J. Kreeft, *C. S. Lewis: A Critical Essay* (Grand Rapids, Mich.: Eerdmans, 1969);

Kreeft, "C. S. Lewis and the Case for Christianity," in *The Intellectuals Speak Out about God,* edited by Roy Abraham Varghese (Chicago: Regnery, 1984);

Kreeft, *C. S. Lewis for the Third Millennium: Six Essays on the Abolition of Man* (San Francisco: Ignatius, 1994);

Kreeft, *The Shadow-Lands of C. S. Lewis: The Man behind the Movie* (San Francisco: Ignatius, 1994);

John Lawlor, *Patterns of Love and Courtesy: Essays in Memory of C. S. Lewis* (Chicago: Northwestern University Press, 1966);

Kathryn Lindskoog, *The C. S. Lewis Hoax* (Portland, Ore.: Multnomah, 1988);

Lindskoog, *C. S. Lewis, Mere Christian,* 4th edition (Chicago: Cornerstone Press, 1997);

Lindskoog, *Journey into Narnia* (Pasadena, Cal.: Hope, 1997);

Lindskoog, *The Lion of Judah in Never-Never Land* (Grand Rapids, Mich.: Eerdmans, 1973);

Lindskoog and Gracia Fay Ellwood, "C. S. Lewis: Natural Law, the Law in Our Hearts," *Christian Century,* 101 (14 November 1984): 1059–1061;

Lindskoog and David Mortimer, *Finding the Landlord: A Guidebook to C. S. Lewis's* The Pilgrim's Regress (Chicago: Cornerstone Press, 1995);

Lindskoog and Patrick Wynne, *Light in the Shadow Lands: Protecting the Real C. S. Lewis* (Portland, Ore.: Multnomah, 1994);

Terry Lindvall, *Surprised by Laughter: The Comic World of C. S. Lewis* (Nashville, Tenn.: Star Song, 1995);

Marion Lochhead, *The Renaissance of Wonder in Children's Literature* (Edinburgh: Canongate, 1977);

Michael H. Macdonald and Andrew A. Tadie, eds., *The Riddle of Joy: G. K. Chesterton and C. S. Lewis* (Grand Rapids, Mich.: Eerdmans, 1989);

C. N. Manlove, *C. S. Lewis: His Literary Achievement* (New York: Macmillan, 1987);

Gilbert Meilaender, *The Taste for the Other: The Social and Ethical Thought of C. S. Lewis* (Grand Rapids, Mich.: Eerdmans, 1978);

Angus Menuge, ed., *C. S. Lewis, Light-Bearer in the Shadowlands: The Evangelistic Vision of C. S. Lewis* (Westchester, Ill.: Crossway, 1997);

David Mills, ed., *The Pilgrim's Guide: C. S. Lewis and the Art of Witness* (Grand Rapids, Mich.: Eerdmans, 1998);

Peter Milward, *A Challenge to C. S. Lewis* (London: Associated University Presses, 1995);

John W. Montgomery, *Myth, Allegory and Gospel* (Minneapolis: Bethany Fellowship, 1974);

Brian Murphy, *C. S. Lewis* (Mercer Island, Wash.: Starmont House, 1983);

George Musacchio, *C. S. Lewis, Man and Writer: Essays and Reviews* (Belton, Tex.: University of Mary Hardin-Baylor, 1994);

Doris T. Myers, *C. S. Lewis in Context* (Kent, Ohio: Kent State University Press, 1994);

A. K. Nardo, "Decorum in the Fields of Arbol: Interplanetary Genres in C. S. Lewis's Space Trilogy," *Extrapolation*, 20 (Summer 1979): 118–128;

J. I. Packer, "Still Surprised by Lewis," *Christianity Today*, 42 (7 September 1998): 54, 56–60;

Leanne Payne, *Real Presence: The Holy Spirit in the Works of C. S. Lewis* (Westchester, Ill.: Cornerstone Books, 1979);

John Peters, *C. S. Lewis–The Man and His Achievement* (Exeter: Paternoster Press, 1985);

Thomas C. Peters, *Simply C. S. Lewis: A Beginner's Guide to the Life and Works of C. S. Lewis* (Westchester, Ill.: Crossway, 1997);

Richard Purtill, *C. S. Lewis's Case for the Christian Faith* (New York: Harper & Row, 1981);

Purtill, *Lord of the Elves and Eldils: Fantasy and Philosophy in C. S. Lewis and J. R. R. Tolkien* (Grand Rapids, Mich.: Zondervan, 1974);

Robert J. Reilly, *Romantic Religion: A Study of Barfield, Lewis, Williams, and Tolkien* (Athens: University of Georgia Press, 1971);

Katherine A. Rogers, "Augustinian Evil in C. S. Lewis's *Perelandra*," in *The Transcendent Adventure: Studies of Religion in Science Fiction/Fantasy*, edited by Robert Reilly (Westport, Conn.: Greenwood Press, 1985), pp. 84–91;

Lee D. Rossi, *The Politics of Fantasy: C. S. Lewis and J. R. R. Tolkien* (New York: R. R. Bowker, 1984);

Martha C. Sammons, *A Guide through Narnia* (Wheaton, Ill.: Shaw, 1979);

Peter J. Schakel, *Reading with the Heart: The Way into Narnia* (Grand Rapids, Mich.: Eerdmans, 1979);

Schakel, *Reason and Imagination in C. S. Lewis: A Study of Till We Have Faces* (Exeter: Paternoster Press, 1982);

Schakel, ed., *The Longing for a Form: Essays on the Fiction of C. S. Lewis* (Kent, Ohio: Kent State University Press, 1977);

Schakel and Charles A. Huttar, eds., *Word and Story in C. S. Lewis* (Columbia: University of Missouri Press, 1992);

Stephen Schofield, *In Search of C. S. Lewis* (South Plainfield, N.J.: Bridge, 1983);

Jeffrey D. Schultz and John G. West, eds., *The C. S. Lewis Readers' Encyclopedia* (Grand Rapids, Mich.: Zondervan, 1998);

Brian Sibley, *C. S. Lewis through the Shadowlands* (Grand Rapids, Mich.: Fleming H. Revell, 1994);

Sibley, *The Land of Narnia: Brian Sibley Explores the World of C. S. Lewis* (New York: HarperCollins, 1990);

John Sims, *Missionaries to the Skeptics: Christian Apologists for the Twentieth Century–C. S. Lewis, Edward John Carnell, and Reinhold Neibuhr* (Macon, Ga.: Mercer University Press, 1995);

Robert Houston Smith, *Patches of Godlight: The Patterns of Thought of C. S. Lewis* (Athens: University of Georgia Press, 1981);

Gunnar Urang, *Shadows of Heaven* (London: SCM Press, 1970);

Philip Vander Elst, *C. S. Lewis* (London: Claridge, 1996);

John Wain, "Pleasure, Controversy, Scholarship," *Spectator*, 193 (1 October 1954): 403–405;

Andrew Walker and James Patrick, eds., *A Christian for All Christians: Essays in Honor of C. S. Lewis* (London: Hodder & Stoughton, 1990);

Chad Walsh, *C. S. Lewis: Apostle to the Skeptics* (New York: Macmillan, 1949);

Walsh, *The Literary Legacy of C. S. Lewis* (New York: Harcourt Brace Jovanovich, 1979);

John G. West Jr., "Politics from the Shadowlands: C. S. Lewis on Earthly Government," *Policy Review*, no. 68 (Spring 1994): 68–70;

William Luther White, *The Image of Man in C. S. Lewis* (Nashville, Tenn.: Abingdon Press, 1969).

Papers:

C. S. Lewis's papers are in the Bodleian Library at Oxford University and in the Marion Wade Collection at Wheaton College, Wheaton, Illinois.

David Lindsay

(2 March 1878 – 16 July 1945)

Edgar L. Chapman
Bradley University

BOOKS: *A Voyage to Arcturus* (London: Methuen, 1920; New York: Macmillan, 1963);

The Haunted Woman (London: Methuen, 1922; Hollywood, Cal.: Newcastle, 1975);

Sphinx (London: John Long, 1923; New York: Carroll & Graf, 1988);

Adventures of Monsieur de Mailly (London & New York: Melrose, 1926); republished as *A Blade for Sale* (New York: McBride, 1927);

Devil's Tor (London: Putnam, 1932; New York: Arno, 1978);

The Violet Apple and The Witch, edited by J. B. Pick, with an introduction by Colin Wilson (Chicago: Chicago Review Press, 1976);

The Violet Apple (London: Sidgwick & Jackson, 1978).

David Lindsay was an Anglo-Scottish fantasy writer whose work has been far more widely read and discussed after his death than it ever was during his lifetime, when his lack of understanding of the literary marketplace, his imperfect knowledge of literary technique, and his obsession with a personal and private vision gained him only a few discerning readers. C. S. Lewis's belated praise for Lindsay's seminal work, *A Voyage to Arcturus* (1920), and a resurgence of interest in sophisticated fantasy, beginning in the 1960s with the paperback sales of J. R. R. Tolkien's *The Lord of the Rings* (1954–1955), have helped to arouse considerable interest in Lindsay's writing for scholars of fantastic romances. Though Lindsay's novels have never gained an audience comparable to that of Tolkien, Lewis, or Ursula K. Le Guin, he has still reached a sizable number of readers a generation after his death.

Judgments about the value of *A Voyage to Arcturus* continue to vary. Some critics such as Gary K. Wolfe regard Lindsay's work as "among the most remarkable works of philosophical fiction of the twentieth century," and C. N. Manlove, though with reservations, has acknowledged the imaginative force of Lindsay's Tormance as a concretely created

David Lindsay

world. By contrast, other acute critics, such as Kathryn Hume and Brian Aldiss, have been distinctly cool toward both the novel and Lindsay's vision. Few would deny, however, that Lindsay's novel was an influential work in its impact on Lewis and later Loren Eiseley, Colin Wilson, and no doubt many other intelligent readers as well. In an age when British fantastic fiction tended to imitate H. G. Wells and such pulp-magazine entertainers as Edgar Rice Burroughs, or when solitary fantasy writers such as E. R. Eddison were retreating into private worlds of their own creation, Lindsay attempted to use the conventions of popular fiction to express a philosophic and transcendentalist vision.

David Lindsay was born into a middle-class family in the London suburb of Blackheath on 2 March 1878, but not much is known about his early life. His father, Alexander Lindsay, had been born in Scotland but had left it at an early age to go to London, where he found work for a finance company in the City, heart of the London financial district. In Alexander Lindsay's family background there were some important figures, including the sixteenth-century poet Sir David Lindsay. Bessy Bellamy, Lindsay's mother, came from a respectable farming family in Warwickshire. David, the future novelist, was the youngest of three children, following a brother, Alexander, and a sister, Margaret. Their father's desertion of the family when Lindsay was thirteen led to difficult times and financial stringency; however, Lindsay's mother was able to move the family into the household of her sister.

Although Lindsay won a university scholarship, his father's defection seems to have blighted Lindsay's hopes for a university education. Nevertheless, he continued to nurse literary ambitions, which had apparently originated during his attendance at Lewisham Grammar School. As a youth, Lindsay evidently had been an avid reader of the better romantic fiction of the later nineteenth century: the fantasies of George MacDonald, the adventure novels of Robert Louis Stevenson, the exotic "lost race" romances of H. Rider Haggard, and probably the science fiction of Wells. However, unable to attend a university or to indulge his literary ambitions, Lindsay was forced to take a job with Price Forbes, a firm of insurance brokers in the City. The necessity of earning a living obliged him to work for this firm from 1894 to 1914. During these years Lindsay lived a relatively tranquil life, winning the respect of his colleagues and supervisors despite his retiring nature. He still desired to become a writer, and he enlarged his intellectual and aesthetic interests through reading German philosophy, especially the work of Arthur Schopenhauer and Friedrich Nietzsche. He also became an avid devotee of classical music.

When World War I broke out, Lindsay's calm existence was overturned. Despite his age (he was thirty-six), Lindsay was inducted into military service with the British army, and he served in various capacities throughout the duration of the war, though he was not obliged to leave Great Britain and enter combat at the front.

In 1916 other momentous changes occurred in Lindsay's life. Not long after breaking off an engagement that had languished for sixteen years, he married Jacqueline Silver, a lively young woman of literary enthusiasms who was more than twenty years younger than he. At that time he also decided to use his savings to break away from his business career and devote himself to writing. His bride is said to have been of a rather romantic temperament, and she believed fervently in Lindsay's potential as an author of imaginative fiction.

Before Lindsay undertook this new career, however, he was obliged to serve two more years in the British army; but then the couple made a complete break with London (and a literary circle in which Lindsay had established some contacts) by moving to a cliffside house in St. Columb Minor, a small town in Cornwall. There Lindsay began to write industriously, though it took some time to define a direction for his energy; indeed, some critics have asserted that his entire literary career was a series of failed attempts to attain that end. His first published novel, *A Voyage to Arcturus,* was produced in a frenzied burst of activity in 1919 and 1920 and published late in 1920. But Lindsay's plot involving a visit to a distant planet made the novel seem remote from the mainstream of contemporary British fiction, and its curious collection of characters who are clearly allegorical or symbolic probably discouraged sales.

A Voyage to Arcturus remains Lindsay's most provocative, if also at times his most puzzling, work. On the surface, this allegorical novel is cast in the formula of pre–World War II science fiction, when voyages to other planets were generally imagined as eccentric experiments by daring inventors of spaceships. The tale also shows kinship with novels dealing with Gothic and occult motifs. But the real source of *A Voyage to Arcturus* is the nineteenth-century tradition of quest romance developed by British Romantic poets in such narrative poems as William Wordsworth's *The Prelude* (1850), Percy Bysshe Shelley's *Alastor* (1816), and John Keats's *Endymion* (1818). This tradition had been continued by such late Romantic poets as William Morris and William Butler Yeats (in *The Wanderings of Oisin* [1889] and *The Shadowy Waters* [1900]) and in such Romantic novels as Edgar Allan Poe's *The Narrative of Arthur Gordon Pym, of Nantucket* (1838) and George MacDonald's *Lilith* (1895).

As *A Voyage to Arcturus* begins, the reader may initially expect a thriller full of Gothic atmosphere unfolding in a shadowland of occultism. In the first chapter Lindsay's protagonist, Maskull, accompanied by an odd companion named Nightspore, attends a seance in London, in an ambience replete with trappings of neo-Romantic mysticism. Maskull and Nightspore witness a bizarre materialization—the apparition of a strange man from another plane of existence. Although the seance is attended by the usual group of prosperous eccentrics and described in considerable detail, the only attending character of importance besides Maskull and Nightspore is an unexpected intruder named Krag. A short but muscular and beardless man, Krag confronts the materialized figure and drives it away, or perhaps exorcises it. Krag also makes references to mysterious entities called Surtur and Crystalman.

Krag informs Maskull that he can learn more about the apparition only if he makes the journey to "Crystalman's country," the planet Tormance, an inhabited world in the Arcturus system. Though Maskull responds with disbelief and questions Krag's sanity, nevertheless his curiosity is aroused, and he gradually accepts Krag's credibility because of their mutual acquaintance with Nightspore. Further dialogue establishes that Maskull is ideally equipped to take on a spiritual quest, since he has no job, no family, and in short no earthly ties or responsibilities. Krag instructs Maskull to go to the remote observatory at Starkness on the northeastern coast of Scotland. When Maskull and Nightspore arrive, however, they find the observatory abandoned and in disrepair. But when Krag arrives, they are beamed off to Tormance, located near the double star Arcturus. They travel in an odd cigar-shaped crystal torpedo, which was the most popular of the imagined shapes of the spaceship in this early era of science fiction.

At this point in the narrative Lindsay's originality begins to emerge. On Tormance, Maskull is separated from his companions but begins an unavoidable pilgrimage to find the meaning of existence through encounters with the beings who reside on the alien planet. The source of life is described as "Surtur," also known as Muspel, the life force; but Surtur, though sometimes treated as a creator figure, is also an elusive concept, rather than a divinity with a personality. In opposition to Surtur is "Crystalman," who is identified with death and thus associated with nonbeing.

Some critics have tended to speak of Crystalman as Lindsay's version of the concept of the devil or the power of the demonic principle, but this interpretation is imprecise. The symbolic figure of the devil posited by Christianity tends to serve destructive ends, or death and nonbeing, but the devil is not himself the essence of nonbeing. For a time, Maskull

and the reader believe that Krag is serving Crystalman; as a result, Krag seems to be a demonic agent or force. But ultimately Maskull learns that this view of Krag is mistaken.

As Maskull journeys through the landscape of Arcturus in an attempt to gain a better understanding of Surtur and Crystalman, he meets various beings who offer help (or sometimes hindrance) and advice (some of it misleading). Each encounter tends to carry symbolic implications, though Lindsay's intended meaning is not always clear, and sympathetic readers may offer a variety of plausible interpretations for many incidents.

Lindsay had the ability to give an entire milieu an ambience or aura implying the nature of the place. Each region Maskull travels through tends to represent an intellectual or psychological state. The region ruled by Joiwind and Panawe, for instance, is a world of naive emotionalism and innocence, a state of mind that, while charming and enjoyable, cannot remain Maskull's permanent residence. Joiwind seems to embody an innocent state of the psyche when feelings of romantic love awaken, without concern for the complexities and frustrations caused by sexuality. Similarly, her consort, Panawe (whose name suggests a sense of awe for all being), seems to represent a phase of unshaped religious feeling usually awakened in adolescence—a psychic state when one may be submerged in what William James called the experience of oceanic feeling.

Maskull's main purpose is to discover the nature of Surtur, the source of divine fire (or spirit), and the identity of Krag, whom he considers to be an enemy. Yet, the novel demonstrates that there is a major difference between appearance and reality. As Maskull encounters one state of being or mental outlook after another, he learns that no philosophical position can provide lasting happiness or offer the ultimate explanation of existence.

Maskull kills some of the characters he encounters; others lose their lives because of his actions. Their deaths, however, do not have the same emotional resonance as the deaths of humans would have, because readers recognize that the characters represent ideas or psychological states. In the middle sections of the novel Maskull meets and explores various states of being such as commitment to self-sacrificial service (the philosophy of Spadevil); the attraction of life as a "natural man," living in an unspoiled nature (Polecrab's world); the appeal of philosophic idealism (the realm of Corpang); and the surrender to sexuality (Sullenbode). After meeting these beings and deciding to move beyond their outlooks to a more challenging or fulfilling realm,

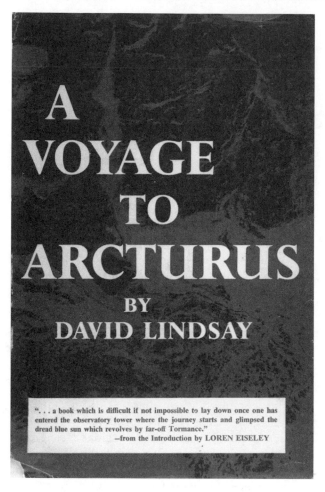

Dust jacket for the 1963 American edition of Lindsay's first book and best-known work, his philosophical and allegorical 1920 novel about a journey to the planet Tormance

Maskull has traveled through much of the landscape of Tormance. At last, after an arduous three-day journey, Maskull comes to a decisive moment when he must accept his own death.

But Maskull's death does not bring his extinction or the end of the novel: rather, this event is a metamorphosis or transformation that results in the submerging of Maskull's consciousness in the world of Nightspore. This being, who early in the book was presented as Maskull's companion, is now revealed to be simply another aspect of Maskull's mind (his subconscious, or his imagination, or visionary powers, depending on one's choice of interpretations). As Nightspore, Maskull ascends to a tower that provides a final vision of the whole pattern of existence, a revelation of the nature of ultimate reality.

What he sees becomes one of the two final surprises of the novel. Throughout the book, Surtur has been treated as though it is a numinous, god-like power, engaged in a war with Crystalman, the force

of nonbeing, in a conflict that the reader expects Surtur will ultimately win. But when Maskull-Nightspore ascends the tower, he discovers that Surtur does not exist except in himself: "*There was nothing.* He was standing on the top of a tower measuring not above fifteen feet each way. Darkness was all around him." Through this epiphany, Maskull-Nightspore learns that only the few courageous individuals who carry the force or vision of Surtur are able to sustain the unending battle with nonbeing.

This revelation is both shocking and tonic. Instead of finding a powerful divine force to help him, Lindsay's prototypical hero comes to realize that the burden of continuing the conflict with spiritual emptiness and nonbeing rests only on the courageous few like himself. This conclusion reflects the influence of the philosophy of Schopenhauer, as some of Lindsay's interpreters, such as Wolfe, have noted. But Wolfe also suggests that the works of mystics who reject the phenomenal world, such as the medieval author of *The Cloud of Unknowing,* also strongly influenced the ending of Lindsay's fantasy. Nevertheless, even Maskull-Nightspore's stunning discovery is followed by a final surprise: on descending the tower, Lindsay's hero meets Krag, whom Maskull has considered an antagonist throughout the book. Now, however, Krag appears to Maskull as an ally against Crystalman. Moreover, in a moment readers remember vividly, Krag reveals that his true name is pain, which is the cost of striving against stagnation, or of surrender to the forces of pleasure, or nonbeing.

The epiphanies of Lindsay's ending underscore the theme that experiences of leisure can only be temporary respites from the struggle of life to actualize itself, and the hard-earned corollary that philosophic or religious outlooks that stress serenity or consolation rather than struggle may actually abet complacency and nonbeing. Of course, the revelation of Krag's identity, with its implication that pain is necessary for spiritual growth, may strike some readers as bringing Lindsay close to a masochistic philosophy; others have been reminded of Nietzsche's philosophy, as Wolfe notes, though Nietzsche was apparently less potent than Schopenhauer as an influence on the novel.

Lindsay's essential vision was established, however imperfectly, in *A Voyage to Arcturus.* The reading public in Great Britain was scarcely ready for such an allegory, however, and the disappointing sales of the novel impelled Lindsay to attempt to present his ideas and symbols in more familiar and popular forms. In some respects, Lindsay resembles other British fantasy writers of his generation in his search for a form that not only would enable him to describe his vision but also would prove attractive to readers.

Lindsay's second published novel, *The Haunted Woman* (1922), adopts the Gothic mode to present a tragic fantasy. Though some critics regard this novel as Lindsay's most readable and carefully crafted work, it did not sell much better than its predecessor. *The Haunted Woman* deals with the search for meaning by Isbel Loment, a woman who tries to live a normal life despite a deep, repressed visionary talent. Though she is engaged to a man of ordinary middle-class aspirations, her residence in an aging mansion leads to a belated recognition of a kindred soul in Mr. Henry Judge, the youthful owner. Isbel's most dramatic moment of discovery occurs when she wanders into a haunted room of the mansion that releases her slumbering occult powers. The use of an ancient house is a common stage prop in Gothic fiction, symbolizing the power of the past or of dark subconscious or supernatural forces, but in this case, only one room of the house exerts a psychic influence.

Isbel's quest for a better rapport with the mysterious Mr. Judge, which follows her self-discovery, is doomed. Her involvement with Judge results in his death, and though Isbel gains some illumination from the experience, the resolution of the novel does not totally clarify its meaning. A sense of psychological frustration hangs over the ending of *The Haunted Woman*.

Although Lindsay turned to the Gothic tradition, following the precedent set by earlier Romantics who chose the Gothic novel when they sought a more popular form than the quest romance, readers expecting conventional Gothic thrills will be disappointed. Though well constructed, the novel maintains a somber and muted tone that fails to create the melodramatic excitement aficionados of Gothic fiction enjoy, as J. B. Pick, one of the most ardent and sympathetic critics of the novel, notes in an introduction to a 1987 paperback edition. Moreover, Lindsay's ambiguous treatment of the supernatural no doubt disappoints the usual lover of Gothic tales. The tightness and compression of *The Haunted Woman* suggest that Lindsay's sense of novelistic form had greatly improved in the composition of this novel. Most readers, however, are likely to prefer the stimulating atmosphere of Tormance and the imaginative vision of *A Voyage to Arcturus*.

After the commercial failure of *The Haunted Woman*, Lindsay produced *Sphinx* (1923), another exercise in Gothic fiction. In this novel the hero, Nicholas Cabot, an amateur psychologist, has developed a machine for exposing the dreams of the other characters. Like *The Haunted Woman,* the novel is set in contemporary England, and again it ends on a note of tragedy as Lore Jensen, one of the most sympathetic characters, commits suicide after she comes to realize that she has wasted her musical talents and settled for a life of mediocrity. But the tragedy is offset by an ending that apparently unites her with the hero in some realm beyond death. The title of the novel alludes to a modern recasting of the riddle of the sphinx, which apparently may be solved by the study of one's dreams. While *Sphinx* offers some insight into Lindsay's desire to rise above mediocrity and achieve some form of recognition, it remains an awkward attempt to show how the supernatural or the realm of spirit that Lindsay envisioned impinged on everyday reality.

In his fiction of this period Lindsay was attempting to use a novel-of-manners technique to describe a world of mundane surface reality that intersects with a hidden world of myth or transcendent reality. In a surprising way, Lindsay's approach is comparable to the fiction of the Australian master Patrick White in such novels as *Voss* (1957). But the comparison immediately reveals Lindsay's weaknesses. To begin with, White's command of realistic technique allowed him to avoid working in a specialized genre, such as Gothic fiction. Moreover, while White felt a contempt for the banal surfaces of social intercourse resembling Lindsay's dislike of them, White's depictions of contemporary manners are masterful and convincing, whereas Lindsay's novels are seldom able to sustain the credibility of their social surfaces. Even more significantly, if Lindsay's representations of contemporary manners are weaker than White's, his works also seem flawed by less control of the mythology or symbolism they introduce. Nevertheless, Lindsay's novels are seldom without some interest for the student of symbolic fantasy.

After publishing three novels that did not sell widely, Lindsay desperately tried to find an audience by writing a light adventure novel, *Adventures of Monsieur de Mailly,* an attempt at a swashbuckler modeled on the works of Alexandre Dumas *père* and Rafael Sabatini. This book was brought out in 1926 in Great Britain and the following year in the United States as *A Blade for Sale*. This effort to compromise with commercial values and popular taste, however, failed to improve Lindsay's status as a novelist who received good reviews but whose works failed to make money. In addition, Lindsay's attempt to become a popular entertainer no doubt created some psychological strain. In more than one novel Lindsay shows contempt for the writer who compromises his art by seeking to please a superficial reading public rather than expressing his inner self.

Lindsay's final published novel, *Devil's Tor* (1932), was a more ambitious effort in the mode of fantasy. A rewriting of a novel he had initially drafted in 1923 titled "The Ancient Tragedy," *Devil's Tor* is one of Lindsay's most ambitious works, because it sets out to fuse the picturesque and rugged landscape of Cornwall with the world of Norse and Celtic mythology that Lindsay found fascinating. In *Devil's Tor* Lindsay makes direct use of striking fantasy icons: a magic stone from India, which an adventurer, Hugh Drapier, takes to England; and a hill near Drapier's family home called Devil's Tor, which conceals an ancient barrow, or tomb. After Drapier and his cousin Ingrid discover the tomb, Drapier is killed accidentally. But Saltfleet, an explorer on a quest and the actual hero of the novel, arrives and, besides wooing and winning Ingrid, deciphers the mystery of Devil's Tor by learning that it is haunted by the spirit of a mother goddess figure.

Though this novel is quite long, it makes a vigorous attempt to describe Lindsay's sense of a numinous and transcendental reality found in ancient European myths. Moreover, in its use of English natural landscapes, it seems a more congenial expression of Lindsay's talent than the Gothic narratives he had been devising.

Despite its stimulating use of Norse and Celtic mythology and some favorable reviews, *Devil's Tor* was not successful, and its failure, the last of a series of commercial failures, seemed to sound the death knell for Lindsay's career. Perhaps Lindsay's ideas were too complex to find embodiment in this novel, and perhaps it employed too many plot complications. Yet, it is hard to deny that *Devil's Tor* is a more effective expression of Lindsay's talent than any work he had written after *A Voyage to Arcturus*.

Devil's Tor has been reprinted only once, and copies of the novel are exceedingly hard to locate. Because of its failure, and no doubt also because of tight publishing budgets during the Great Depression, Lindsay was unable to get another novel published in his lifetime, nor were publishers enthusiastic about reprinting *A Voyage to Arcturus*, despite continued interest in that book. Nevertheless, Lindsay continued to labor at his writing, though his frustration mounted.

Lack of sales produced straitened circumstances for Lindsay and his family. In the early years of their marriage, Lindsay's wife had given birth to two daughters, Diana (born in 1919) and Helen (born in 1921). Though Lindsay evidently enjoyed fatherhood and domestic tranquility, the repeated failure of his novels to earn money forced the family to find a less expensive mode of living. They were obliged to move from Cornwall to Ferring, near Worthing and Brighton, in Sussex in 1928, and then to the resort town of Brighton in 1938, where they earned some income as the enterprising Jacqueline Lindsay began to take in boarders. By this point, it was her industry as a landlady rather than his novels that provided the main support for the family. Moreover, in the later decades of his life, Lindsay's preference for a reclusive and austere lifestyle, as well as bitterness over the failure of his novels, produced great tension in his marriage and family life.

One of his most sympathetic interpreters, Bernard Sellin, has suggested that Lindsay's fiction might have been more successful if the author had been more energetic at pursuing literary contacts. However, positive reviews did not help the sales of Lindsay's fiction, perhaps because the author's insights into the tastes of the mass reading audience did not encourage him to respect that audience greatly. His sales might not have improved even if he had enjoyed more frequent contact with other writers. Indeed, Lindsay's obsession with philosophical themes and a passionate commitment to defining a private vision would have made it hard for him to become a widely read novelist under the most congenial circumstances.

Despite Lindsay's perseverance and diligence in revising unpublished work, his later years were clearly rather lonely and embittered. Some consolation was provided by the pleasures of domesticity and by Lindsay's lifelong love of music, especially Richard Wagner, and his love of picturesque scenery, of which there was much to enjoy both in Cornwall and in Sussex. Moreover, a friendship with L. H. Myers, a minor novelist who shared Lindsay's pessimism and his belief in a transcendentalist vision, provided some intellectual companionship from 1926 until Myers's suicide in 1944.

In the final months of Lindsay's life, *A Voyage to Arcturus* received an unexpected boost when C. S. Lewis, by then a well-known lay theologian and respected literary scholar at Oxford, commented favorably in a 1944 lecture at a Merton College literary society about the influence of its romanticism on his mind in his youth. But such eleventh-hour praise, however gratifying—and there is no evidence that Lindsay even learned of it—came too late to inject life into his moribund literary career. The disenchanted Lindsay died on 16 July 1945, partly as a result of the trauma from a German bomb striking his house, but mainly from complications resulting from an abscess in his jaw. At this point his work appeared to be virtually unknown.

In the years after his death, however, Lindsay's reputation refused to die, and his fame even began to grow slowly. *A Voyage to Arcturus* was republished in 1946, perhaps as a result of publicity ensuing from Lindsay's death the preceding year, and again in 1963, when interest in literary fantasy was beginning to grow. An American edition was also published that year by Macmillan, with an enthusiastic but somewhat confusing introduction by Eiseley, who had gained an impressive reputation as an anthropologist for his meditative classic *The Immense Journey* (1957). An American paperback edition of *A Voyage to Arcturus* published in 1968 by Ballantine did much to enlarge Lindsay's reading audience. In the excitement of a new generation's discovery of Lindsay, even an experimental motion picture based on *A Voyage to Arcturus* was made by a student moviemaker.

In the 1970s scholars began investigating Lindsay's life and career, and some of his other novels were republished. His life and work were the subjects of a 1970 monograph by Colin Wilson, J. B. Pick, and E. H. Visiak. Pick also edited a 1976 edition of two previously unpublished novels: *The Violet Apple,* which was probably written in the 1920s, and the unfinished fragment *The Witch,* which was Lindsay's final work of fiction, on which he labored obsessively in the waning years of his life. Lindsay's reflections in his journal were also made available for scholars in a typescript titled "Philosophical Notes," housed at the National Library of Scotland in Edinburgh. Neither of the two new novels led to a major reestimation of Lindsay's importance, but they do add to understanding of his work.

The Violet Apple had been rejected by several publishers and then received some minor revisions from Lindsay before being put into storage. However, the novel is readable and frequently lively. It describes the development of an unexpected and slowly ripening romantic relationship between a successful playwright, Anthony Kerr, and Haidee Croyland, the fiancée of a friend. To add a mythic dimension to the story, Lindsay presents a radical revision of the Judeo-Christian myth of the fall from innocence in Eden. In Lindsay's version, the eating of the apple releases his characters from bondage to the world of superficiality and mediocrity. The "innocence" in which Anthony and Haidee live is an unthinking acceptance of societal notions of success and happiness.

Anthony, a well-known author of light comedy, is a portrait of the writer as social success. He represents a condition that Lindsay both envied and feared; on the one hand, he has achieved freedom from monetary worries and a measure of fame, which Lindsay, like most sane writers, ardently desired. On the other hand, Anthony has rejected the deeper and more urgent demands of his imagination; his life of comfortable mediocrity is a form of imaginative death, and he is about to inter his spirit further in an agreeable but passionless marriage to a pleasant woman named Grace.

His counterpart, Haidee, though more attuned to her imaginative and passionate inner self, is about to make a similar mistake by marrying Jim, a man for whom her feelings are tenuous. She feels drawn to Anthony, and he reciprocates her interest. Although Anthony is depicted as an honorable man who hates deception, and Haidee at first has no intention of deceiving her fiancé, the two begin to meet, at first casually and apparently by accident, but later by intention in order to resolve their confusion. The decisive moment comes when each decides to eat one of the small apples that have come into their possession, the fruit of a tree grown from a mysterious seed Anthony inherits—a seed believed to have come from the mythic tree of knowledge in the garden of Eden. The consumption of these apples opens their eyes to the commonplace mediocrity of the social world they live in comfortably and makes them aware of the possibilities of the world of the spirit.

Although the novel presents a long opening section in which the nature of the apples is discussed, and some of the characters question the credibility of the Eden myth and speculate on comparative mythology, Lindsay clearly implies that the apples possess some magic power to liberate the faculty of imaginative vision. Although Lindsay insists that the power of the apples does not symbolize sexuality, Anthony and Haidee feel a strong mutual physical attraction. But this desire is energized by their realizations, after their decisive acts, of how closely attuned their spiritual aspirations are. Since their fiancés have become uneasy because of the obvious attraction between Anthony and Haidee, both are able to break their engagements rather easily and confront the future together as kindred souls.

Unlike the three novels that preceded its composition, *The Violet Apple* concludes on a note of happiness and reconciliation. Moreover, Lindsay's handling of the social setting and manners of the story is credible, and his employment of an intrigue plot is at times adroit. As the story moves from light courtship intrigue to Haidee and Anthony's discovery of their passion, the novel tends to gather strength and momentum.

Cover for the 1975 American edition of Lindsay's 1922 Gothic novel, about a woman with psychic powers

Indeed, the failure of *The Violet Apple* to find a publisher in the 1920s seems surprising to readers of later generations. Although the novel does not reveal a significant enlargement of Lindsay's vision, it was probably his only novel after *A Voyage to Arcturus* that had a chance to become a major commercial success during Lindsay's lifetime. Moreover, Haidee, from whose point of view much of the action is seen, is undeniably Lindsay's most attractive female character and perhaps his most sympathetic protagonist.

Lindsay's imaginative revision of the Eden myth in *The Violet Apple* reveals a softening of his attitude toward Christian mythic archetypes in his later work. This increased sympathy for Christianity, which in his youth and early writing he had rejected and caricatured, also appears in the final unfinished novel, *The Witch*. But the Christian archetypes are blended with many other images and archetypes from Teutonic, Norse, and Celtic myth. The work

seems to attempt a final ambitious synthesis of Lindsay's ideas: he apparently labored at *The Witch* in the years following the commercial failure of *Devil's Tor*, and though he was unable to complete it, the story remains a substantial fragment of around fifty thousand words.

The main theme of the novel is the spiritual quest of Ragnar Pole for the illumination that can be provided by Urda Noett, the witch of the title. However, as the novel explains, Urda's witchcraft is not to be considered a vulgar kind of magic, but the ritualistic command of ancient powers that can lead a person beyond the superficiality of ordinary existence into an understanding of the mythic forces that represent the ultimate reality of the universe.

As in *A Voyage to Arcturus,* Lindsay's hero must undergo various initiations in his search for spiritual enlightenment. However, his education takes place in the environment of the Sussex Downs instead of on a distant planet. So, although Ragnar enjoys love with an attractive woman, Faustine Gaspary, he must pass through the experience of romantic love to other spiritual states. According to Colin Wilson in his introduction to *The Witch,* Ragnar progresses through three distinct stages on his spiritual journey, symbolized by the metaphor of "three musics." Urda's "music" represents the third stage of the soul, apparently the world of vision or philosophic contemplation. The ultimate destination for Ragnar remains undescribed, but it is clear that Urda represents an "earth mother" archetype familiar to students of Jungian psychology of the sort already introduced in *Devil's Tor.*

Although *The Witch* offers much of interest for students of Lindsay's work, it often proves to be tedious reading. Lindsay appears to be more concerned with expressing his philosophic themes through dry exposition or seemingly endless discussion than with dramatizing them in narrative. Perhaps the frustration of many rejections had sapped his enthusiasm for fiction, or perhaps Lindsay was trying to define his themes clearly in one last effort. At any rate, despite its length and intellectual seriousness, *The Witch* must be judged a rather unsatisfactory fragment.

A biographical study of Lindsay by Sellin, a French scholar, was published in 1981, and Wolfe's monograph appeared in 1982. But after this flurry of scholarly activity, Lindsay's literary stock leveled off. In the late 1980s and the 1990s, traditional romantic quest fantasy of the *Voyage to Arcturus* type seemed less provocative and attractive to many readers. Rather than rereading the fantasy classics of the past, many admirers and scholars of the genre appeared to be devoting their attention to the work that their contemporaries, such as Gene Wolfe, Stephen R. Donaldson, Judith Tarr, and Jane Yolen, are producing.

Primarily because of *A Voyage to Arcturus,* David Lindsay has a secure place in the history of twentieth-century fantasy. As Wolfe has noted, Lindsay in his later works was unable to repeat the "clarity of vision" expressed in *A Voyage to Arcturus.* To a lesser extent, his other novels, notably *The Haunted Woman, Devil's Tor,* and the posthumous *The Violet Apple,* add something to his stature and remain interesting works that express a highly personal and stimulating vision—a curious late Romantic transcendentalism that tends to reject the phenomenal world in a manner resembling ancient gnosticism. But Lindsay's primary contribution to the tradition of British fantasy lies in the powerful imagery and drama of Maskull's extraordinary pilgrimage to Tormance.

Letters:

Adam International Review, 15, nos. 346–348 (1971).

Biography:

Bernard Sellin, *The Life and Works of David Lindsay,* translated by Kenneth Gunnell (Cambridge: Cambridge University Press, 1981).

References:

Brian Aldiss and David Wingrove, *Trillion Year Spree: The History of Science Fiction* (London: Gollancz, 1986; New York: Atheneum, 1986);

John Clute and John Grant, eds., *The Encyclopedia of Fantasy* (New York: St. Martin's Press, 1997);

Kathryn Hume, *Fantasy and Mimesis* (New York: Methuen, 1984);

C. S. Lewis, "On Stories," in his *Of Other Worlds: Essays and Stories,* edited by Walter Hooper (New York: Harcourt, Brace & World, 1966), pp. 3–21;

C. N. Manlove, "David Lindsay, *A Voyage to Arcturus* (1920)," in his *Scottish Fantasy Literature: A Critical Survey* (Edinburgh: Canongate, 1994), pp. 153–169;

J. B. Pick, introduction to Lindsay's *The Haunted Woman* (Edinburgh: Canongate, 1987);

Eric S. Rabkin, "Conflation of Genres and Myths in David Lindsay's *A Voyage to Arcturus," Journal of Narrative Technique,* 7 (1977): 149–155;

Colin Wilson, E. H. Visiak, and Pick, *The Strange Genius of David Lindsay* (London: John Baker, 1970);

Gary K. Wolfe, *David Lindsay* (Mercer Island, Wash.: Starmont House, 1982);

Wolfe, "David Lindsay and George MacDonald," *Studies in Scottish Literature,* 13 (October 1974): 131–145.

Naomi Mitchison

(1 November 1897 – 11 January 1999)

Salvatore Proietti
Università di Roma "La Sapienza"

See also the Mitchison entries in *DLB 160: British Children's Writers, 1914–1960* and *DLB 191: British Novelists Between the Wars.*

BOOKS: *The Conquered* (London: Cape, 1923; New York: Harcourt, Brace, 1923);

When the Bough Breaks, and Other Stories (London: Cape, 1924; New York: Harcourt, Brace, 1924);

Cloud Cuckoo Land (London: Cape, 1925; New York: Harcourt, Brace, 1926);

The Laburnum Branch: Poems (London: Cape, 1926; New York: Harcourt, Brace, 1926);

Black Sparta: Greek Stories (London: Cape, 1928; New York: Harcourt, Brace, 1928);

Anna Comnena (London: Gerald Howe, 1928);

Nix-Nought-Nothing: Four Plays for Children (London: Cape, 1928; New York: Harcourt, Brace, 1929);

Barbarian Stories (London: Cape, 1929; New York: Harcourt, Brace, 1929);

The Hostages, and Other Stories for Boys and Girls (London & Toronto: Cape, 1930; New York: Harcourt, Brace, 1931);

Comments on Birth Control (London: Faber & Faber, 1931);

Kate Crackernuts: A Fairy Play (Oxford: Alden, 1931);

Boys and Girls and Gods (London: Watts, 1931);

The Corn King and the Spring Queen (London: Cape, 1931; New York: Harcourt, Brace, 1931); republished as *The Barbarian* (New York: Cameron, 1961);

The Price of Freedom: A Play in Three Acts, by Mitchison and Lewis E. Gielgud (London: Cape, 1931);

The Powers of Light (London: Pharos, 1932);

The Delicate Fire: Short Stories and Poems (London & Toronto: Cape, 1933; New York: Harcourt, Brace, 1933);

The Home and a Changing Civilisation (London: John Lane, 1934);

Naomi Mitchison's Vienna Diary (London: Gollancz, 1934; New York: Smith & Haas, 1934);

Beyond This Limit (London: Cape, 1935);

Naomi Mitchison in 1987 (photograph by Broderick Haldane)

We Have Been Warned: A Novel (London: Constable, 1935; New York: Vanguard, 1936);

The Fourth Pig: Stories and Verses (London: Constable, 1936);

An End and a Beginning, and Other Plays (London: Constable, 1937);

Socrates, by Mitchison and Richard H. S. Crossman (London: Hogarth Press, 1937; Harrisburg, Pa.: Stackpole, 1938);

The Moral Basis of Politics (London: Constable, 1938; Port Washington, N.Y.: Kennikat Press, 1971);

The Alban Goes Out (Harrow, Middlesex: Raven, 1939);

As It Was in the Beginning: A Play in Three Acts, by Mitchison and Gielgud (London: Cape, 1939);

The Kingdom of Heaven (London & Toronto: Heinemann, 1939);

Historical Plays for Schools, 2 volumes (London: Constable, 1939);

The Blood of the Martyrs (London: Constable, 1939; New York: McGraw-Hill, 1948);

The Bull Calves (London: Cape, 1947);

Men and Herring: A Documentary, by Mitchison and Denis Macintosh (Edinburgh: Serif, 1949 [i.e., 1950]);

The Big House (London: Faber & Faber, 1950);

Spindrift: A Play in Three Acts (London: S. French, 1951);

Lobsters on the Agenda (London: Gollancz, 1952);

Travel Light (London: Faber & Faber, 1952; New York: Penguin–Virago, 1987);

Graeme and the Dragon (London: Faber & Faber, 1954);

The Swan's Road (London: Naldrett, 1954);

The Land the Ravens Found (London: Collins, 1955);

To the Chapel Perilous (London: Allen & Unwin, 1955);

Little Boxes (London: Faber & Faber, 1956);

Behold Your King: A Novel (London: Muller, 1957);

The Far Harbour: A Novel for Boys and Girls (London: Collins, 1957);

Five Men and a Swan (London: Allen & Unwin, 1957);

Other People's Worlds (London: Secker & Warburg, 1958);

Judy and Lakshmi (London: Collins, 1959);

A Fishing Village on the Clyde, by Mitchison and George William Lennox Patterson (London: Oxford University Press, 1960);

The Rib of the Green Umbrella (London: Collins, 1960);

The Young Alexander the Great (London: Parrish, 1960; New York: Roy, 1961);

Karensgaard: The Story of a Danish Farm (London: Collins, 1961);

Presenting Other People's Children (London: Hamlyn, 1961);

The Young Alfred the Great (London: Parrish, 1962; New York: Roy, 1963);

Memoirs of a Spacewoman (London: Gollancz, 1962; New York: Berkley, 1973);

The Fairy Who Couldn't Tell a Lie (London: Collins, 1963);

Alexander the Great (London: Longmans, 1964);

Henny and Crispies (Wellington: New Zealand School Department of Education, School Publications Branch, 1964);

Ketse and the Chief (London: Nelson, 1965; Camden, N.J.: Nelson, 1967);

When We Become Men (London: Collins, 1965);

A Mochudi Family (Wellington: New Zealand School Department of Education, School Publications Branch, 1965);

Friends and Enemies (London: Collins, 1966; New York: John Day, 1968);

Return to the Fairy Hill (London: Heinemann, 1966; New York: John Day, 1966);

The Big Surprise (London: Kaye & Ward, 1967);

Highland Holiday (Wellington: New Zealand School Department of Education, School Publications Branch, 1967);

African Heroes (London & Sydney: Bodley Head, 1968; New York: Farrar, Straus & Giroux, 1969);

Don't Look Back (London: Kaye & Ward, 1969);

The Family at Ditlabeng (London: Collins, 1969; New York: Farrar, Straus & Giroux, 1970);

The Africans (London: Blond, 1970);

Sun and Moon (London: Bodley Head, 1970; Nashville: Nelson, 1973);

Cleopatra's People (London: Heinemann, 1972);

Small Talk . . . : Memories of an Edwardian Childhood (London: Bodley Head, 1973);

A Life for Africa: The Story of Bram Fischer (London: Merlin, 1973; Boston: Carrier Pigeon, 1973);

Sunrise Tomorrow: A Story of Botswana (London: Collins, 1973; New York: Farrar, Straus & Giroux, 1973);

The Danish Teapot (London: Kaye & Ward, 1973);

Oil for the Highlands? (London: Fabian Society, 1974);

All Change Here: Girlhood and Marriage (London: Bodley Head, 1975);

Sittlichkeit (London: Birkbeck College Press, 1975);

Solution Three (London: Dobson, 1975; New York: Warner, 1975);

Snake! (London: Collins, 1976);

The Brave Nurse and Other Stories (Cape Town & New York: Oxford University Press, 1977);

The Two Magicians, by Mitchison and Dick Mitchison (London: Dobson, 1978);

The Cleansing of the Knife and Other Poems (Edinburgh: Canongate, 1979);

You May Well Ask: A Memoir, 1920–1940 (London: Gollancz, 1979);

The Vegetable War (London: Hamilton, 1980);

Images of Africa (Edinburgh: Canongate, 1980);

Mucking Around: Five Continents over Fifty Years (London: Gollancz, 1981);

Margaret Cole, 1893–1980, by Mitchison, John Parker, and John Saville, edited by Betty Vernon (London: Fabian Society, 1982);

What Do You Think Yourself? Scottish Short Stories (Edinburgh: Harris, 1982);

Not by Bread Alone (London & New York: Boyars, 1983);

Among You, Taking Notes: The Wartime Diary of Naomi Mitchison 1939–1945, edited by Dorothy Sheridan (London: Gollancz, 1985);

Beyond This Limit: Selected Shorter Fiction of Naomi Mitchison, edited by Isobel Murray (Edinburgh: Scottish Academic Press in conjunction with the Association of Scottish Literary Studies, 1986);

Naomi Mitchison (Edinburgh: Saltire Society, 1986);

Early in Orcadia (Glasgow: Drew, 1987);

As It Was (Glasgow: Drew, 1988)–comprises *Small Talk* and *All Change Here;*

A Girl Must Live: Stories and Poems (Glasgow: Drew, 1990);

The Oath-Takers (Nairn, Scotland: Balnain, 1991);
Sea-green Ribbons (Nairn, Scotland: Balnain, 1991).

OTHER: *An Outline for Boys and Girls and Their Parents,*
edited by Mitchison (London: Gollancz, 1932);

*Re-Educating Scotland: Being a Statement of What Is Wrong
with Scottish Education and What It Might Yet Become,
with a Number of Practical Proposals for Its Betterment,
Put Forward by the Education Committee of Scottish Convention,* edited by Mitchison, Robert Britton, and
George Kilgour (Glasgow: Published by Scoop
Books for Scottish Convention, 1944);

Frederic Bartlett and others, *What the Human Race Is Up
To,* edited by Mitchison (London: Gollancz,
1962);

"The Little Sister," in *Pulenyane's Secret,* by Ian Kirby
(Cape Town: Oxford University Press, 1976);

"The Wild Dogs," in *The Animal that Hides in the Trees,*
by Megan Biesele (Cape Town: Oxford University Press, 1977);

"Words," in *Dispatches from the Frontiers of the Female Mind,*
edited by Jan Green and Sarah Lefanu (London:
Women's Press, 1985), pp. 164–174.

SELECTED PERIODICAL PUBLICATION–
UNCOLLECTED: "The Profession of Science Fiction:
Wonderful Deathless Ditties," *Foundation,* 21 (Feb-
ruary 1981): 27–34; republished as "Wonderful
Deathless Ditties" in *The Profession of Science Fiction:
SF Writers on Their Craft and Ideas,* edited by
Maxim Jakubowski and Edward James (New
York: St. Martin's Press, 1992), pp. 34–43.

Naomi Mitchison's literary career covers more
than seventy years, with an output of almost one hundred titles, including plays, poetry, prose fiction, and
political tracts. Her novels and short stories belong to a
diversified array of genres, from fairy tales to historical
fiction and from science fiction to fantasy, with settings
ranging from faraway planets to southern Africa and
from the Roman Empire to the Arthurian world. Her
science-fiction production is relatively small, amounting
to three novels and a handful of short stories (mostly
reprinted in the 1990 collection *A Girl Must Live: Stories
and Poems,* which also includes a few original tales); nevertheless, modern critics are more forcefully acknowl-
edging her prominence in the landscape of contemporary
British science fiction. With her first and most important
science-fiction novel, *Memoirs of a Spacewoman* (1962),
Mitchison "almost single-handedly invented feminist
SF," as Patrick Parrinder wrote in 1990.

Mitchison was born Naomi Mary Margaret
Haldane in Edinburgh on 1 November 1897. Her
father, John Scott Haldane, was an Oxford physiology

professor from a family that included other distinguished academics and statesmen; her mother, Louisa
Kathleen Trotter, was a descendant of the Tory elite
and had a strong personality. Around her family, and
in particular around her brother, geneticist and polemicist J. B. S. Haldane, a veritable clan flourished, starting
in the late 1920s, that in biographer Gary Werskey's
words "embodied the liberal virtues of the intellectual
aristocracy" as opposed to the conservative views of
landed or financial patricians. Contrary to the more
monolithically humanistic tendencies of the other leading intellectual "clan" of the period, the canonical
Bloomsbury group, Haldane and the others were, first
and foremost, philosophers, ideologists, and populariz-
ers of science; they saw science–and in particular biology–as a way of unifying speculative inquiry and
practical social reform. Haldane wrote in *Daedalus*
(1924) that the biologist, as a bold revolutionary of bodies and minds, was about to become "the Romantic figure" of the twentieth century. This view, and the whole
debate on science during the 1920s and 1930s, deeply
influenced Mitchison's science fiction.

Among these radical scientists, both Haldane and
J. D. Bernal wrote some science fiction, while Haldane's
wife, Charlotte Haldane, was the author of *Man's World*
(1926), a dystopia of women's oppression that cast
many doubts toward her husband's faith in genetics. In
other words, in those years science fiction was a legitimate tool in British mainstream intellectual debate, and
Mitchison was in the middle of that mainstream.
Among her friends and acquaintances were writers
such as H. G. Wells, Olaf Stapledon, Gerald Heard,
and Aldous and Julian Huxley, as well as W. H.
Auden, D. H. Lawrence, and Wyndham Lewis (who
illustrated her 1935 short novel *Beyond This Limit*), and
in later years scientists such as James D. Watson (to
whom she dedicated *Solution Three* [1975] and who dedicated *The Double Helix: A Personal Account of the Discovery of
the Structure of DNA* [1968] to her) and Niels Bohr.

Educated at Oxford, Mitchison began her lifelong commitments to professional writing and to political activism in the mid 1920s. In all fields she maintained a less triumphalist, more skeptical attitude than
that of her male cohorts, without their flirtings with
Stalinism and eugenics. Indeed, her first attempt at science fiction, the 1929 story "Cardiff A.D. 1935" (from
Barbarian Stories), is an (unsuccessful) anti-Stalinist apo-
logue. As further evidence of an early and deep interest in science fiction, her 1935 political novel *We Have
Been Warned* includes a final dystopian vision of a fascist Britain.

Her public activism, which informs much of her
journalism as well as her many autobiographical books,
brought her to participate in the family planning move-

34

ghosts & fairies. He has never seen any fairies, but he says he saw 3 ghosts. They were not at all transparent, but he saw a bumble bee fly through a lady ~~road~~ walking down a path. None of them were ghosts of dead people, but in two cases the people were in london, & in the other he saw the ~~ghost~~ of a little girl go into a room, ~~crying~~ dressed in blue, & going after it immediatly he saw the <u>real</u> little girl sitting there dressed in white! My Father & Boy fled precipitately as soon as they heard his motor but my mother & I got on with him quite well, we found him silly, but amusing.

Page from Naomi Haldane's diary for 1909 (from Naomi Mitchison, Small Talk . . . : Memories of an Edwardian Childhood, *1973)*

ment in the late 1920s and in later feminist, pacifist, and Scottish nationalist movements. She also ran for Parliament as a Labour candidate in 1935 and served as a representative in local councils of the Highlands for some thirty years. Her husband, G. Richard Mitchison, whom she married in 1916 and who died in 1970, was an important Labour figure, elected to the House of Commons in 1945 and appointed as cabinet minister and made a life peer in 1964. The Mitchisons had two daughters and three sons; all three of the latter have become distinguished academic figures in the fields of medicine and zoology.

From 1937 Mitchison lived in Carradale, Kyntire, Scotland. She also traveled widely in the pursuit of her journalistic and political interests; among other things, she actively supported the post-Depression recovery efforts in the southern United States and the anticolonialist struggles of Botswana and Zambia. In fact, from the early 1960s onward, Botswana became her second home, and the Bakgatla tribe adopted her as an honorary "mother" and adviser. In her foreword to *Images of Africa* (1980) Mitchison described her role as "attempting to build bridges which will allow communication where none existed before or where it had gone wrong." This emphasis on communication in the attempt "to build bridges of understanding" can be taken as paradigmatic of her whole opus, and in her science fiction it tempers her confidence in the promises of scientific inquiry.

Themes of understanding and communication are also central in her historical fiction, starting with her debut novel, *The Conquered* (1923). This cluster, which includes many Scottish novels such as the acclaimed *The Bull Calves* (1947), is the largest in her popular opus. In this genre, most remarkable is *The Blood of the Martyrs* (1939), a retelling of the persecution of Christians under the Roman Empire during Nero's times, which forcefully allegorizes the contemporary Nazi persecution of the Jews. Mitchison is a pioneer in the modern popular revamping of this genre. But these works, unlike nineteenth-century nationalist-imperialist romances and unlike modern soap-opera-like potboilers, manage to conjoin adventure plots with a peculiar vein of allegorical didacticism. Thus, Mitchison's historical tales are usually set in periods of harsh, even fratricidal, conflicts, from prehistoric times to classical antiquity, the Middle Ages, and World War II, and explore the viewpoint and the daily life of oppressed, colonized, and vanquished groups.

Within historical fiction, Mitchison often tests the limits of realist conventions. Among these borderline works is the "prehistoric fiction" of *The Powers of Light* (1932) and *Early in Orcadia* (1987). The turning point was *The Corn King and the Spring Queen* (1931), a mix of

historical novel, romance, fable, and fantasy. Set in Greece and Eastern Europe, along the Black Sea, and building on James G. Frazer's studies on ancient rites and mythologies, the novel begins with the forced marriage of the young witch Erif Der ("red fire") to Tarrik the Corn King, and with her attempts at rebellion. The arrival of a shipwrecked philosopher is substantial in bringing about their release from the grip of black magic. Both Erif Der (now the Spring Queen) and Tarrik then undergo a quest that will allow them to reach a new awareness of the world they live in, and will give them a chance to choose for themselves an everlasting bond (a magic of a different kind), no longer based on brutality and undisputed tradition. With a distinctive, if light-toned, feminist viewpoint, the novel–like many of Mitchison's innovative fantasies–addresses issues of power and authority, and is thus a possible precursor to Samuel R. Delany's *Nevèrÿon* series (1979–1994) as well as to Mary Renault's many popular novels.

Mitchison had a remarkable production of fantasies and fairy tales, often published as children's literature. Early examples are in the collection *Barbarian Stories* (1929). *The Fourth Pig: Stories and Verses* (1936) is the only one that assumes an overt tone of political (socialist) allegory. *The Big House* (1950) is dominated by the Scottish setting, emphasized by a pervasive use of Gaelic language, and is again a parable about growth as the discovery of common areas in the encounter with the new and unknown; during a Halloween celebration a fisherman's son and a rich girl from the "big house" meet and receive a visit from a fairy prince, who brings them on a magical trip in time. *Travel Light* (1952) is a fantasy with feminist elements, set in a world resembling that of *The Corn King and the Spring Queen,* at a later time, and with the presence of diverse mythological elements drawn from Anglo-Saxon, Greek, and Asian traditions. The fabulous story of a king's daughter, cast out by the evil queen and raised among bears, dragons, and unicorns, is told in a lighthearted style against the background of the rise of the more modern and "secular" world of Christianity. Young Halla's quest toward Micklegard (that is, Constantinople) becomes a personal quest for growth and self-determination. The meeting with the mysterious Wanderer will change her life and bring her back to the world of humans. Her own wandering leads her through adventures–experiences of both communication and violence–that teach her the necessity both of breaking free of fixed, established habits and of keeping roots in (and memories of) the various modes of civilization she encounters. By "traveling light" she learns to remain always ready for new occasions and neverending opportunities. *To the Chapel Perilous* (1955) is an ironic rewriting of the Grail legends, which introduces in the middle of the chronicle a group of journalists giving their reports about the Arthurian knights and their lives.

Later examples include an endearing fable for young children, *The Fairy Who Couldn't Tell a Lie* (1963), and the title story in *Five Men and a Swan* (1957), which can only be called an example of magic realism with a Scottish working-class setting. "Nagli's First Princess" and "Death of a Peculiar Boar," included in *A Girl Must Live,* use the weapons of parody and irony, aimed at traditional and sword-and-sorcery hero figures (respectively, a dragon and an Arthurian knight). In the same collection, "Miss Omega Raven" (1972) and "Like It Was" are feminist allegories of maturation and self-discovery, with a use of irony that borders on a sense of the grotesque similar to that of Angela Carter. Finally, fantasy and supernatural elements can be found in the Botswana stories of *Images of Africa*–arguably the masterpiece of her latest years–as a way to explore the confrontation between technological modernity and traditional African life, whether as salvific resources ("The Half-Person and the Scarlet Bird") or as tools of archaic and inhumane oppression ("The Finger," included by Gardner Dozois in his anthology *Best Science Fiction Stories of the Year 1980* [1981]).

The most sustained articulation of these themes can be found in Mitchison's first science-fiction novel, *Memoirs of a Spacewoman,* which parallels in scope and complexity some of the problematics pioneered by Stapledon and addressed, in the same years, in other European masterpieces by Ivan Yefremov and Stanisław Lem. The novel revolves around a joyous, panoramic description of a dozen encounters with alien species, including sentient echinoderms, centipedes, dolphinoids, giant butterflies, hermaphroditic Martians, and symbiotic invertebrates. These meetings are recounted in the first-person retrospective narrative of Mary, a communication expert in many missions of space exploration. In this future world Earth has reached global unification and gender equality, overcoming national and (apparently) class distinctions, and, with the friendly help of the Martians, is undertaking the exploration of the galaxy. The hopeful attitude of the early 1960s, with the women's and Third World liberation movements, finds an expression in this depiction of the new ethical issues and relationships of an emancipated humanity. *Memoirs of a Spacewoman* is what Wells would have called a kinetic utopia, open-ended in its programmatic willingness to question continually its own roots and beliefs and to learn from its mistakes: a world that, as Mary says of one of her colleagues in one of the most self-conscious moments in the novel, "one may explore . . . endlessly, always learning something new."

Naomi Haldane with her brother, the future geneticist J. B. S. Haldane, at Eton College in 1910

At the same time, this novel is a bildungsroman that presents character growth as a never-ending process of formation, without the pursuit of any prescribed end state of integration. Indeed, the fact itself of the contact and dialogue with alien worlds is what renders this openness an inevitable goal if one chooses–as Mitchison and this future Earth do–to avoid the risk of imperialistic anthropocentrism; even at the personal level, any notion of a "stable personality" is questioned and invalidated by these contacts, as the narrator herself states: the acceptance of continual change is part of any "explorer's" daily experience. The scientific-cognitive horizons of this novel are those of post-Einsteinian and post-Heisenbergian physics, wherein the very presence of the traveling observers may and does affect the visited culture, and the goal of noninterference (in an endless tension with the search for fruitful exchanges) is both a legal directive and an ingrained trait.

Furthermore, the "scientific" core is not technocratic engineering or astronautics, as in much pulp science fiction, but biology and anthropology, with an

Mitchison with Avrion and Lois, two of her five children

larly, Mary volunteers to serve as the host for the grafting onto her body of an alien symbiotic creature, both a rewarding and emotionally painful experience that will eventually lead to the alien's successful grafting on of a Martian creature, and thus to the start of a possible new species. This incident best of all epitomizes an ideal of understanding that does away with power hierarchies between researcher and object of study without giving up the goal of scientific curiosity.

Mary is a representative of Earth culture vis-à-vis the galaxy, but also one for whom the grafting is another experience of mothering, on a par with those of her three children, and her backward look embraces both domestic and professional events. In other words, Mary is a protagonist who literally fuses individual bodily experience with the body politic, private pleasure with public responsibility, in a feminist and humanist ideal of harmony that rejects any segregation of science from other branches of cognition. Liberation through empathetic and corporeal "alienation" often entails major personal and ethical hardships; her grief at the loss of the graft is devastating and sincere. Also, Mary is often on the verge of interfering: both in the case of the centipedes, who sadistically slaughter the harmless "Roundies," and in the case of the butterflies, who have transformed their own caterpillar offspring into a virtual subrace in the search for a sort of eugenic purity.

During these episodes, the ethical assumptions of Mary's culture are evoked, historicized, and debated. The need for suspended animation ("time-blackout") during interstellar travel has, for example, resulted in a redefinition of concepts of family, conjugal bonds, and friendship. Mothering now means spending a few years on Earth for the child's early socialization, and partnership commitments can no longer be lifetime issues, to be interrupted traumatically. Thus, Mary has three children by three different lovers (one African, one Martian, one Scandinavian), remains a close friend with all of them, and tries to meet them and the children as often as possible. Also, Mary keeps moving between worlds and returning to an ever-changing one: for her, inevitably, the locales she visits are important as distorting mirrors reflecting her memories of the past and her experience of the present. This plot—with its effect of estrangement or, literally, of alienation—builds the novel as a parable on the state of affairs not only in Mary's world but also the reader's. Haldane's and the scientists' faith in human perfectibility is re-elaborated by Mitchison through the filter of fallibility; she could be called a critical optimist.

emphasis on alien reproduction and sexuality. Contrary to the post-Darwinian (male) tradition of British science fiction from Wells onward (including J. B. S. Haldane), humanity's striving toward better conditions does not entail a gradual forfeiting of the body's role. Instead, communication and understanding are both intellectual and physical processes; bodily knowledge is foregrounded throughout *Memoirs of a Spacewoman*. Readers find this element first of all in the playful, detailed analyses of the various alien biologies, cultures, and sexual mores, which are the main charm of the book. If there is such a thing as "the sense of wonder" in science fiction, this novel is one of its best examples. One illustration is the "five-choiced world" of the starfish-like "radiates," whose culture in all fields, from aesthetics to mathematics, is arranged along a much more complex system of alternatives than earthly dichotomies. Other crucial episodes include Mary's parthenogenetic conception of her haploid daughter, Viola, accidentally "activated" by Mary's Martian friend and confidant Vly, who "talks" through tactile communication. Simi-

In 1976 the New English Library "SF Master Series," edited by Harry Harrison (who, as an anthologist, had published several Mitchison stories) and Brian

W. Aldiss, granted *Memoirs of a Spacewoman* a paperback reprint that brought Mitchison to the attention of a wider science-fiction readership; in 1985 the novel was also included in the prestigious Women's Press series of feminist science fiction. These editions have bestowed on it the status of a science-fiction classic and a place in the history of British feminist writing.

Mitchison herself paid homage to her masterpiece by returning to the same universe in three more stories. "Conversation with an Improbable Future" (1990) recapitulates, again in the personal narrative form, some of the major themes of *Memoirs of a Spacewoman:* the ethical implications of time-blackouts (new notions of family and child-rearing), and the pains and rewards, both personal and professional, resulting from the commitment to exploring. Ultimately this commitment is to a never-ending process of individual and collective self-realization: "All the same, once there are problems aching, so to speak, to be worked on, solved, we can't stop, can we? In my own field there have been disappointments and misunderstandings. But we go on."

"What Kind of Lesson?" (1989) chronicles the contact, from establishment to breakup, with a humanoid species living in symbiosis with a kind of algae. It records, in a way that echoes Lem's *Solaris* (1961), the dilemmas of failure in a nonteleological universe:

> And in the end, always, always, we are left with the unpleasantness, the anxiety, of a lesson put before us by what or whom or why is not known. Nor is it helpful to question or discuss. It must, we suppose, be a lesson intended to lead us further, to teach something of the utmost importance. But this lesson is in an unknown and unknowable script or speech, and so, whatever our willingness, we cannot learn from it.

In "I Couldn't Tell the Papers" (1990) two women biologists have a cheerful discussion about a newly discovered species of egg-laying humanoids and about how this reproductive system has affected their culture and gender roles (females do the chasing, while males accept their courtship by artfully cooking and eating one of their own unfertilized eggs). The story is a playful, lighthearted celebration of cultural diversity and plurality.

Mitchison wrote several other stories involving women and science. "Mary and Joe" (1970) is a tongue-in-cheek, secular, feminist rewriting of the founding myth of Christianity set in the age of genetically engineered reproduction, from immaculate conception (biologist Mary's inexplicable pregnancy) to passion (her daughter, antiestablishment activist Jaycie, is almost burned to death in an "accident" involving the police) and resurrection (Mary saves her daughter with a graft of her own compatible skin tissue). "After the

Accident" (1970) is a skeptical feminist allegory on self-determination: after a nuclear war, a biologist gives birth to the first genetically engineered baby, connected to the prospect of future colonization of high-gravity planets; maternal and professional pride get fused again in humanity's last hope. "Far from Millicentral Station" (1990) is a comic tale that exposes the limits of traditional splits between reason and emotion. Only the uncollected 1985 story "Words" proposes a pessimistic view of scientific curiosity, portraying the hubris of a scientist who dies while experimenting with brain stimulation. It is a cautionary tale of the will to knowledge turning into self-consuming addiction.

In other stories as well, the warning tone comes to the foreground. In "The Valley of the Bushes" (1976) murdering the explorers who get too close is presented as the inevitable option for a pastoral, egalitarian, matriarchal "lost race" that has managed to balance some advanced technology with unexplained powers derived from the botany and geochemistry of its homeland. More directly, some plots revolve around ecological disasters, with images of impotence ("Take-over," 1990) and self-delusion ("The Factory," 1973). Even more bluntly, Mitchison's reflections on war are stories of total annihilation, opposing all justificatory or minimizing ideologies with the sarcasm of hopelessness. In "Out of the Deeps" (1974) the story of a global nuclear war is told from the viewpoint of the dolphins. Humans fail to acknowledge them as sentient beings and try to use them as weapons, but the dolphins eventually retreat back to the oceans while humans wipe out all life from the surface of the planet. In "Rat-World" rats are Earth's new dominant species after the extinction of humanity during the "Great Darkness." The masterpiece "Remember Me," from *What Do You Think Yourself? Scottish Short Stories* (1982) and reprinted in *Beyond This Limit: Selected Shorter Fiction of Naomi Mitchison* (1986), is the mournful personal narrative of an aged grandmother trying to survive in a Scottish Highlands community after an officially minor "theater missile" nuclear exchange has resulted in holocaust; as she writes, supplies are running out, and so are the psychological resources of domesticity and a good neighborhood. A slightly hopeful opening is present only in "Somewhere Else," in which readers follow the vicissitudes of a group of children living in a world where mutagenic chemicals have spawned animals such as the "pincers" (giant crustaceans) that threaten their lives on a daily basis and where it is forbidden to inquire about the past. But knowledge cannot be kept hidden forever, and if science has been a force of destruction, it can also be recuperated and reused as a tool of resistance.

This trust in people's ability to improve their lot seems to vanish from Mitchison's other two science-

Dust jacket for Mitchison's 1975 novel, in which scientists rule the world after a global catastrophe

fiction novels: *Solution Three* and *Not by Bread Alone* (1983). In both, humanity is incapable of self-determination and can save itself only under the firm guidance of an enlightened caste, the scientific elite. This pessimism is transparently a result of the crisis of 1960s hopes in the age of transnational capitalism and environmental havoc. Furthermore, unlike her debut novel and her stories, these books do not endow their characters with any significant dramatic force. Mitchison's humanist ideal was first and foremost a dynamic harmony between individual and collective bodies; in these books free agency is no longer an option, and the ensuing clash of equally depersonalizing tendencies makes for two much duller works.

In *Solution Three* the issue is population policy; after a global catastrophe, the "Professorials" have taken over and imposed their "solutions" to the problems of war, hunger, and population growth. In this partly utopian, peaceful society facing the condition of scarcity, most new births, as well as wheat crops, are obtained through cloning, while heterosexual relationships have been ruled out as unclean and repellent. The Professorials have kept for themselves both heterosexuality and technocratic leadership. The expert has become a self-appointed hero and a benevolent dictator. When things, both human and agricultural, start going wrong, the Professorials launch a new solution: heterosexuality shall be enforced as an antidote against impoverished gene pools. A minimum of hope resides in this society's ability to reverse its actions and in its commitment to the erasure of race and gender hierarchies; the foreshadowing of Solution Four, with the acceptance of heterosexual along with gay and lesbian relationships, of physical maternity along with cloning, represents an opening toward a future of diversity and plurality. Still, this world needs to go through a stage of nearly complete control of most aspects of life.

The epigraph to *Solution Three* presents this condition as a "horrid idea"; in *Not by Bread Alone* the ruling elite of scientists becomes instead the only available way out of the undesirable present. In this bleakest of Mitchison's novels Earth is ruled, without any democratic control, by a multinational cartel called PAX, which holds the global monopoly of the food market. Through genetic engineering, food is available and free for all, and the world is a sort of consumerist nightmare. But benevolent capitalism eventually collapses, and in the ensuing famine, the only apparent hope for recovery lies in the pseudo-utopia started by a group of PAX scientists in Australia, with the help of an aboriginal community. For Mitchison, the only antidote to the dark pessimism of tales such as this one and "Remember Me" is the separated society of the happy few, back to the patrician ideal of Haldane and Bernal.

Naomi Mitchison's writing career continued into her nineties; she died on 11 January 1999 at the age of 101. The trajectory of her work, from hope to closure, has tragic proportions emblematic of larger trends. In literary terms, her science fiction includes one fundamental book and a few significant short stories. Mitchison's fantasy works are being rediscovered, and new reprints have been appearing in the 1990s. Her novels, and in particular *The Corn King and the Spring Queen, Travel Light,* and *To the Chapel Perilous,* are recognized as original, sophisticated works and as anticipations of contemporary women's writing in the genre, as a result of Mitchison's clearly feminist approach to "traditional" mythology and folklore, from classic Greek and Roman to Arthurian legends. Critical reconsiderations of *Memoir of a Spacewoman* are becoming more appreciative. Mitchison acknowledged science fiction as an important part of her cultural background, from William Morris (the ideal of harmony between work and creativity has its roots there) to modern figures such as Arthur C. Clarke and Doris Lessing, including the American pulp tradition. Younger writers such as Josephine Saxton mention Mitchison as an important influence, and many feminist writers have tackled her favorite themes.

Given that biology and genetics have become a central preoccupation of science fiction, her reputation is bound to increase even more.

Biographies:

Gary Werskey, *The Visible College: A Collective Biography of British Scientists and Socialists of the 1920s* (London: John Lane, 1978);

Jill Benton, *Naomi Mitchison: A Century of Experiment in Life and Letters* (London: Pandora, 1990); republished as *Naomi Mitchison: A Biography* (London: Pandora, 1990; New York: New York University Press, 1992);

Jenni Calder, *The Nine Lives of Naomi Mitchison* (London: Virago, 1997).

References:

Jenni Calder, "More Than Merely Ourselves: Naomi Mitchison," in *A History of Scottish Women's Writing*, edited by Douglas Gifford and Dorothy McMillan (Edinburgh: Edinburgh University Press, 1997), pp. 444–455;

Phyllis Lassner, "From Fascism in Britain to World War: Dystopic Warnings," in her *British Women Writers of World War II: Battlegrounds of Their Own* (New York: St. Martin's Press, 1998), pp. 58–103;

Sarah Lefanu, "Difference and Sexual Politics in Naomi Mitchison's *Solution Three*," in *Utopian and Science Fiction by Women: Worlds of Difference*, edited by Jane L. Donawerth and Carol A. Kolmerten (Syracuse, N.Y.: Syracuse University Press, 1994; Liverpool: Liverpool University Press, 1994), pp. 153–165;

Lefanu, *In the Chinks of the World Machine: Feminism and Science Fiction* (London: Women's Press, 1988; Bloomington: Indiana University Press, 1988);

Elizabeth Longford, "Introduction," in *Travel Light* by Mitchison (London: Virago, 1985);

Patrick Parrinder, "Scientists in Science Fiction: Enlightenment and After," in *Science Fiction Roots and Branches*, edited by Rhys Garnett and R. J. Ellis (London: Macmillan, 1990), pp. 57–78;

Parrinder, "Siblings in Space: The Science Fiction of J. B. S. Haldane and Naomi Mitchison," *Foundation*, 22 (June 1981): 49–56;

Susan M. Squier, "Naomi Mitchison: The Feminist Art of Making Things Difficult," in *Solution Three* by Mitchison (New York: Feminist Press, 1995), pp. 161–183.

Papers:

Collections of Naomi Mitchison's papers are at the National Library of Scotland, Edinburgh, and at the Harry Ransom Humanities Research Center, University of Texas at Austin.

George Orwell
(Eric Arthur Blair)
(25 June 1903 – 21 January 1950)

Johan Heje
Greve Gymnasium, Denmark

See also the Orwell entries in *DLB 15: British Novelists, 1930–1959; DLB 98: Modern British Essayists, First Series;* and *DLB 195: British Travel Writers, 1910–1939.*

BOOKS: *Down and Out in Paris and London* (London: Gollancz, 1933; New York: Harper, 1933);

Burmese Days (New York: Harper, 1934; London: Gollancz, 1935);

A Clergyman's Daughter (London: Gollancz, 1935; New York: Harper, 1936);

Keep the Aspidistra Flying (London: Gollancz, 1936; New York: Harcourt, Brace, 1956);

The Road to Wigan Pier (London: Gollancz, 1937; New York: Harcourt, Brace, 1958);

Homage to Catalonia (London: Secker & Warburg, 1938; New York: Harcourt, Brace, 1952);

Coming Up for Air (London: Gollancz, 1939; New York: Harcourt, Brace, 1950);

Inside the Whale, and Other Essays (London: Gollancz, 1940);

The Lion and the Unicorn: Socialism and the English Genius (London: Secker & Warburg, 1941);

Animal Farm: A Fairy Story (London: Secker & Warburg, 1945; New York: Harcourt, Brace, 1946);

Critical Essays (London: Secker & Warburg, 1946); republished as *Dickens, Dali and Others* (New York: Reynal & Hitchcock, 1946);

James Burnham and the Managerial Revolution (London: Socialist Book Centre, 1946);

The English People (London: Collins, 1947);

Nineteen Eighty-Four (London: Secker & Warburg, 1949; New York: Harcourt, Brace, 1949);

Shooting an Elephant, and Other Essays (London: Secker & Warburg, 1950; New York: Harcourt, Brace, 1950);

England Your England and Other Essays (London: Secker & Warburg, 1953); republished as *Such, Such Were the Joys* (New York: Harcourt, Brace, 1953);

George Orwell (Eric Arthur Blair) in 1946
(photograph by Vernon Richards)

The Orwell Reader: Fiction, Essays, and Reportage, edited by Richard H. Rovere (New York: Harcourt, Brace, 1956);

George Orwell: Selected Writings, edited by George Bott (London: Heinemann, 1958);

The Collected Essays, Journalism, and Letters of George Orwell, 4 volumes, edited by Sonia Orwell and Ian Angus

(London: Secker & Warburg, 1968; New York: Harcourt, Brace & World, 1968);

Orwell: The War Broadcasts, edited by W. J. West (London: Duckworth/BBC, 1985); republished as *Orwell: The Lost Writings* (New York: Arbor House, 1985);

Orwell: The War Commentaries, edited by West (London: Duckworth/BBC, 1985; New York: Pantheon, 1986);

The Complete Works, edited by Peter Davison, 20 volumes (London: Secker & Warburg, 1986–1998; revised and updated volumes, 1998–2001).

Editions and Collections: *A Collection of Essays* (Garden City, N.Y.: Doubleday, 1954);

Collected Essays (London: Secker & Warburg, 1961);

Orwell's Nineteen Eighty-Four: Text, Sources, Criticism, edited by Irving Howe (New York: Harcourt, Brace & World, 1963);

Decline of the English Murder, and Other Essays (Harmondsworth, U.K.: Penguin, 1965);

Nineteen Eighty-Four, edited by Bernard Crick (Oxford: Clarendon Press, 1984);

Nineteen Eighty-Four: The Facsimile of the Extant Manuscript, edited by Peter Davison (New York: Harcourt Brace Jovanovich / Weston, Mass.: M & S Press, 1984).

PRODUCED SCRIPTS: *The Voyage of the Beagle,* adapted by Orwell from work by Charles Darwin, radio, BBC, 1946;

Animal Farm, radio, BBC, 1947.

George Orwell gained an enduring international reputation with his two last works of fiction, the political fable *Animal Farm: A Fairy Story* (1945) and his near-future dystopia, *Nineteen Eighty-Four* (1949). Although he was never primarily a writer of fantastic fiction, these works have been extremely influential in the fields of fantasy and science fiction. In these works, as in the journalism, reportage, essays, and realistic fiction that filled the rest of his career, he gauged the contemporary European scene of the troubled 1930s and 1940s with critical insight drawn from personal experience and a deep moral commitment. His two landmark contributions to twentieth-century fantastic fiction were thus not so much a departure from his previous work as a more effective medium for voicing his moral and political concerns.

The responses that *Animal Farm* and *Nineteen Eighty-Four* received naturally brought these books to the attention of readers and writers of fantasy and science fiction, and even though in publishing terms they were mainstream books by a mainstream author, those in the field of fantastic fiction quickly

adopted the novels as their own, including them in their respective canons and reflecting their influence. In particular, *Animal Farm* demonstrated how fantasy could comment on specific political issues, and *Nineteen Eighty-Four* provided a host of themes and images for futuristic depictions of nightmarish societies, from Ray Bradbury's science-fiction novel *Fahrenheit 451* (1953) to Anthony Burgess's *A Clockwork Orange* (1962) to Terry Gilliam's motion picture *Brazil* (1985), written by Gilliam, Charles McKeown, and Tom Stoppard.

Orwell was born Eric Arthur Blair on 25 June 1903 in Motihari in Bengal, India. (George Orwell was the pen name he adopted for his first book and used for all his subsequent publications, though he never legally changed his name.) His father, Richard Walmesley Blair, served as a minor official in the government department that administered the British opium trade monopoly. Eric spent most of the first nine years of his life with his mother, Ida Mabel Blair, and two—later three—sisters in a small market town, Henley-on-Thames, in southeast England. He later ironically described himself as a person born into "the lower-upper-middle class," with pretensions but not the money to belong to the upper middle class. The almost obsessive preoccupation with class distinctions characteristic of much of what he wrote originated from childhood experiences, especially as a scholarship recipient in a private boarding school, St. Cyprian's near Eastbourne, and later at the most prestigious of British public schools, Eton, from which he graduated in 1921. In a retrospective essay, "Such, Such Were the Joys," first published posthumously in the September–October 1952 issue of *Partisan Review,* he described his life at St. Cyprian's as one lived in constant fear of arbitrary authority and punishments, and with constant reminders of his inferior position as a scholarship student among the sons of wealthier people. Some critics have even suggested that St. Cyprian's partially inspired the nightmare world of *Nineteen Eighty-Four.* In the presentation he gives of himself in *The Road to Wigan Pier* (1937), Orwell writes about his struggle to overcome his "snobbishness," which he saw as the most ineradicable result of his schooling.

His distrust of authority and hatred of repression were further strengthened by the five years he spent in Burma as an officer in the Indian Imperial Police between 1922 and 1927. In *The Road to Wigan Pier* and elsewhere he describes his feeling of guilt and isolation at serving a system he found unjust and oppressive without having anybody to whom he dared confide his secret thoughts. After his return to England his determination to become a writer was

Orwell as a young man, with pet rabbit

by two remarkable documentaries: *The Road to Wigan Pier,* an exploration of the living conditions of the unemployed in the depressed industrial north of England, and *Homage to Catalonia* (1938), about the seven months he spent in Spain during the Spanish Civil War. He went there as a journalist in December 1936 but soon joined active combat on the Republican side for four months as a corporal in the militia of the Workers' Party of Marxist Unification (Partido Obrero de Unificación Marxista, or POUM), and was then stuck for more than a month in Barcelona, where he witnessed the beginning of the destruction of the POUM and anarchist militias by the Communists. On his return to the front he was wounded, but even as a discharged member of the now-outlawed POUM militia he was in danger, and he and his wife only narrowly escaped the country in June 1937.

To Orwell the internecine fighting between parties that were supposed to be united in their war against fascism was a shock, and *Homage to Catalonia* marks a turning point in his political outlook. He saw himself as a socialist and continued to do so for the rest of his life, but he was never a member of a political party, and for him socialism was first of all a matter of "justice and common decency." Even before Spain, Orwell had expressed impatience with the Marxist theorizing of left-wing intellectuals, and in Spain the Communists, Orwell realized, were employing methods for acquiring power similar to those employed by the Fascists. The common man was the sufferer. In "Looking Back on the Spanish War," written in 1942 and included as a postscript in the 1952 American edition of *Homage to Catalonia,* he summed up his experience of, among other things, wartime propaganda:

> I saw great battles reported where there had been no fighting, and complete silence where hundreds of men had been killed. I saw troops who had fought bravely denounced as cowards and traitors, and others who had never seen a shot fired hailed as the heroes of imaginary victories; and I saw newspapers in London retailing these lies and eager intellectuals building emotional superstructures over events that had never happened.

These lines came to represent a major theme in *Animal Farm* and *Nineteen Eighty-Four,* both of which he was already planning.

During World War II Orwell worked for more than two years as a program producer for the Eastern Service of the British Broadcasting Company (BBC). Its main purpose was to help boost the morale of Indian soldiers fighting in British service.

beginning to mature at the same time as he wanted to expiate his "weight of guilt": "I felt that I had got to escape not merely from imperialism but from every form of man's dominion over man. I wanted to submerge myself, to get right down among the oppressed, to be one of them and on their side against the tyrants." He worked briefly as a dishwasher in Paris in 1929 and as a teacher at private schools in Middlesex and Uxbridge between 1932 and 1933, meanwhile trying to write. The eventual result was *Down and Out in Paris and London* (1933), Orwell's first published book (after several rejections of this work and others), a description of two periods during which he had shared the life of casual workers, tramps, and outcasts. It was well reviewed and cleared his way into professional writing, even though he had to hold another job, as a clerk in a used-book store in London, from 1934 to 1936. In June 1936 he married Eileen O'Shaughnessy.

Down and Out in Paris and London was followed by four novels, which all include autobiographical elements, most obvious in *Burmese Days* (1934), and

Orwell's involvement in what was basically a propaganda operation was both a frustrating and a learning experience for him and may be counted among the sources of inspiration for his two subsequent masterpieces. He also continued to contribute reviews and articles on wartime issues (and, more specifically, on issues that British society would face after the war) to newspapers and magazines. When he left the BBC in November 1943 he was ready to write *Animal Farm,* which he did in three months. It was not published, however, until August 1945, when the war was over, purportedly because of paper rationing but mostly because of the unmistakable fact that it parodied the history of an important war ally, the Soviet Union. When published, it immediately hit the best-seller lists in both Great Britain and the United States, was soon translated into many languages, and was banned throughout the Soviet-controlled part of the world. As a result of its success, for the first time in his life Orwell was freed of financial anxieties.

He had chosen the time-honored form of the animal fable, in which animals are given human characteristics while keeping something of their animal natures, for his story about a revolution that goes bad when its power-hungry leaders establish themselves as a new ruling class and gradually adopt the vices of the ousted tyrant. In the expository first chapter the decay of Manor Farm is suggested by the brutish drunkenness of its owner, Mr. Jones, which gives the farm animals an opportunity for a secret gathering in the barn, where they listen to a speech given by the aging boar Old Major. The gallery of animal characters is introduced, and each is given his or her predominant trait. Old Major's speech is a denunciation of dictatorial man and the evil tyranny he exercises over animals, as well as an admonition to them never to adopt his corrupt ways. The speech concludes with the revolutionary slogan "All animals are equal," which has already been undercut by the awkward question: "Are rats comrades?" A song, "Beasts of England," conjures a picture of a utopian animal paradise, "the golden future time."

In the second chapter the focus is transferred to the pigs, who turn out to be more intelligent than the other animals and who are now busy preparing for the revolution by elaborating Old Major's ideas into a "system of thought, to which they gave the name of Animalism." They do not meet with much understanding from the other animals until Mr. Jones's mismanagement of the farm reaches the point where he forgets to feed the animals. Then, literally overnight, he and his wife are driven out, and the animals are left in charge. The principles of Animalism are set down in "Seven Commandments," the chief of which again is "All animals are equal." But at the end of this chapter about their glorious revolution, it appears that the pigs have appropriated the day's provision of milk for their own benefit.

The Seven Commandments become a gauge of how far the pigs' betrayal of the revolution has advanced with each chapter. One by one they are modified to suit the pigs' comfort at any given moment. The animals' memories are too short, too uncertain to call the bluff. Similarly, the history of the revolution and the following battles against attacks from hostile human neighbors are gradually falsified and finally fade into myth. The victory won in the first of these battles was a result of the ingenious strategy of one of the two leading pigs, Snowball; but when he is brought down in a coup by his competitor, Napoleon, who has a pack of fierce dogs at his command, the history of the battle is revised: the victory was Napoleon's work. The now-absent Snowball becomes the scapegoat for the misfortunes that befall the animals, including those caused by Napoleon's mistakes. The Sunday meetings that were supposed to be the forum for decisions are abolished when Napoleon has established his dictatorship. Feeble attempts at revolt are cruelly suppressed. "Traitors" make public confessions and have their throats torn out by Napoleon's dogs. In the end the animals are no better off than at the beginning: every distinction between the pigs and the former human oppressors seems to have vanished, and the Commandments are reduced to hilarious absurdity: "All animals are equal but some animals are more equal than others."

Like many classical animal fables, *Animal Farm* is an allegory. Point by point the story is constructed so as to bring out parallels with the actual history of the Russian revolution and the rise of the Soviet Union: Manor Farm is Russia; Mr. Jones is the tsar; Old Major's speech is a parody of Karl Marx and Friedrich Engels's *Communist Manifesto* of 1848; the pigs are the Bolsheviks, who established themselves as a privileged bureaucratic power elite; Snowball is Leon Trotsky, who organized the Red Army but lost in the power struggle with Stalin (Napoleon) and became the almost archetypal traitor in Stalinist mythology; and Napoleon's dogs are Stalin's secret police, the GPU, a predecessor to the KGB. The list could be continued with Stalin's five-year plans for the industrialization of Russia, the crushing of the peasants' rebellion against collectivization, the notorious purges of the late 1930s, the German-Soviet treaty of 1939, the war against Germany, and many minor details. A notable deviation is Squealer, the

Eileen O'Shaughnessy, whom Orwell married in 1936

pig who could "turn black into white," the master manipulator who seems to some extent modeled on Adolf Hitler's minister of propaganda, Joseph Goebbels, thus indicating what Orwell saw as the essential sameness of totalitarian systems.

Among the common animals, Boxer, the strong but somewhat dull-witted carthorse, stands out as the ever-loyal and trusting representative of the working class without whom, it is implied, no power structure can exist. He patiently puts up with whatever trial the animals are exposed to and is rewarded by being sold to the knacker when his strength fails him. In a sense he is the hero of Orwell's fable, ineffectual in his inability to connect the facts he actually observes but retaining his basic decency. Other more or less minor figures fit equally well into the allegory. A special position is reserved for Benjamin, the intelligent donkey who, in words sometimes echoing Thomas Hobbes, refuses to believe that anything will ever change.

Though the ingenuity of Orwell's allegory will probably be lost on most future readers, to whom the Stalinist era will be increasingly remote history, *Animal Farm* is likely to continue to be read as a classic. It

has a sheer entertainment value not too characteristic of Orwell's other works, a combination of humor and pathos, and great consistency in balancing the two aspects of the characters: their animal identities and their function as recognizable human types. Though certain literary antecedents may be named, *Animal Farm* is a deeply original work and may be said to belie the view of some critics that Orwell did not possess much creative originality as a fiction writer. It can be read, as was Orwell's intention, as a cautionary tale, not just about the Russian revolution but about revolutions in general, indeed about the very concept of revolution. By showing what may go wrong in a revolution, the novel becomes a call for more awareness of the mechanics of power and a better analysis of history—and of human nature—than the one offered by Marxism. It was not meant to endorse the belief of a Benjamin—or of Hobbes or Swift—that change is not possible.

As a work of fantasy, *Animal Farm* is conventional but still noteworthy. In the Western world the tradition of the animal fable dates back at least as far as the fables of Aesop, and in English literature one of the more significant practitioners of the form was Geoffrey Chaucer. While Orwell was consistent with the tradition in using animals to satirize human foibles, his contribution was to employ the animal fable for specifically political ends. He was not the first writer to do so, but with *Animal Farm* he became the best known, influencing later writers such as Art Spiegelman, whose *Maus* graphic novels (1986, 1991) relate the stories of Holocaust victims and survivors with the Nazis as cats and the Jews as mice.

The 1940s was not a time that encouraged optimism: World War II was followed by the Cold War and the specter of atomic warfare. One type of totalitarianism seemed to have been defeated, while another, the Stalinist variety, had gained power. Orwell's outlook is generally regarded as pessimistic, mainly on the basis of the nightmarish picture of a totalitarian world order given in his last novel. It should be kept in mind, however, that *Nineteen Eighty-Four* is not meant as a prediction of a future Orwell imagined would actually happen, as has often been assumed, but as another cautionary tale about trends discernible in the contemporary world. It is about 1948, the year in which he finished writing it, as much as it is about 1984 (the last two digits reversed). In particular, it is about the prospect that had been part of his Catalonian experience and that worried him most of all: the possibility, apparently aggravated by modern means of mass communication, of distorting and even falsifying real facts to suit the purposes of those in power. If history, which must be the basis of a political consciousness, can be distorted, even obliterated, then individual memory, the basis of human identity, can be obfuscated to the point of obliteration. Orwell believed in the existence of objective reality where, in words he used several times, two plus two make four.

He had been planning the novel since 1940, and completing it was an immense effort for him, hampered as he was by serious outbreaks of the tuberculosis that he had suffered from since his excursion into the world of the submerged poor in Paris and London. It took him more than two years to write the book, and when it finally appeared in print in June 1949, it was greeted with almost unanimous critical acclaim and soon became another bestseller. By that time, however, he was dying. "My new book is a Utopia in the form of a novel. I ballsed up rather, partly owing to being so ill while I was writing it," he wrote to fellow author Julian Symons on 4 February 1949. He had also had private sorrows. In the spring of 1945 his wife, with whom he had adopted a son, died unexpectedly during an operation. A few months before his death he married Sonia Brownell, a friend for some years, who became the assiduous guardian of his literary reputation.

It has often been pointed out that in creating *Nineteen Eighty-Four* Orwell gleaned from earlier anti-utopian novels. *Nineteen Eighty-Four* bears some similarity to H. G. Wells's *When the Sleeper Wakes* (1899), in which the protagonist is transported into a world of technological tyranny two hundred years into the future. Wells had been Orwell's favorite author when he was young. He shared not only Wells's fascination with utopian thinking but also his critical attitude toward the British class system. However, Wells's later belief in science and rationality as the ultimate problem solvers had, in Orwell's opinion, been outdated since World War I. After all, both Hitler and Stalin had been able to harness science in the service of their dictatorships. Some scholars have also pointed to *Swastika Night* (1937) by Katharine Burdekin (writing as Murray Constantine) as a likely model. A more significant influence on Orwell's novel was probably *We* (1924), by Russian novelist Evgeny Zamyatin. In Zamyatin's dystopia individuality has been all but obliterated; personal names have been replaced by numbers; people's lives are regulated down to the minutest details; and those who do not conform are tortured into submission, subjected to corrective brain treatment with X rays, or publicly executed by a chemical process that might be described as vaporization, the word used in *Nineteen Eighty-Four* about the sudden disappearance of unwanted persons. Orwell reviewed Zamyatin's novel in 1946 and found that it

was a better novel than Aldous Huxley's *Brave New World* (1932) insofar as it provided a more credible motive for the power elite to stay on top than Huxley had done. In Orwell's view no totalitarian system could exist without a ruling class motivated by power hunger, the wish to exercise power over others and keep it at any cost.

The most direct inspiration for *Nineteen Eighty-Four* came, however, from a work of nonfiction: *The Managerial Revolution* (1941) by James Burnham, an American economist whose ideas Orwell argued against in a 1946 pamphlet. Burnham was a neo-Machiavellian thinker who did not believe that democracy would ever exist except as democratic trappings of no real significance. There would always be a ruling oligarchy possessed of power and economic privilege and intent on keeping its advantages. In the future the "managers," businessmen, technicians, and soldiers would become the real controllers of the means of production. Burnham predicted the disappearance of national states and the emergence of three superpowers, based in Europe (Germany), Asia (Japan), and America. They might be at war with each other, but none of them would be strong enough to win predominance over the others. This situation is paradoxically reflected in the pattern of the world of *Nineteen Eighty-Four*.

Throughout the novel the narrative viewpoint is that of Winston Smith, an employee in the Ministry of Truth, where his work consists of adapting or falsifying information. The setting is London, "chief city of Airstrip One," a province of Oceania, one of the three superstates (the other two are Eurasia and Eastasia). The setting was easily recognizable to many contemporary readers, because it is that of wartime and postwar London with its bomb sites, buildings in disrepair, faulty supply of electricity, shortages, rationing, and identity cards—only worsened by decades of uninterrupted war. The city is in general decay except for the towering concrete structures of the four ministries that make up the power apparatus: the Ministry of Truth, the Ministry of Peace, the Ministry of Plenty, and the ominous Ministry of Love, each concerned with the opposite of what its name indicates. The reversal of values and the corruption of language are evident in the three slogans of the ruling Party, repeated everywhere: WAR IS PEACE, FREEDOM IS SLAVERY, and IGNORANCE IS STRENGTH. Also everywhere are huge posters portraying Big Brother, the mythical Party leader, whose searching eyes "looked deep into Winston's own."

A significant feature of Orwell's future world is that the only kind of technology that seems to have

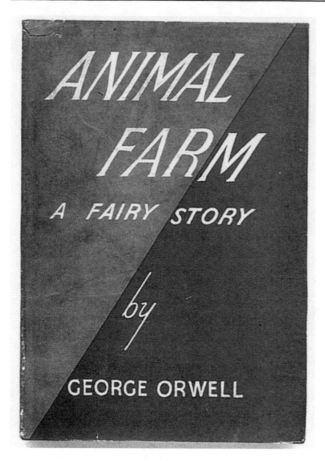

Dust jacket for Orwell's 1945 allegory, in which a barnyard represents the Soviet Union

advanced is that of surveillance. Winston's apartment, like the apartments of other Party employees, is equipped with a telescreen through which he can at any time be watched by the feared Thought Police. An atomic war in the 1950s is mentioned, but the war between the superstates that has been going on since then seems to be conducted with World War II technology. The continuous state of war and war hysteria is simply a prerequisite for upholding the rule of the Party. Since historical records are constantly altered or destroyed, it is difficult to determine the actual course of the war, which is in any case obscured by propaganda announcements of spurious victories. The enemy may be Eurasia or it may be Eastasia; the main thing is that there always is an enemy, who can be an object of hatred. Another such object is the archtraitor, Goldstein, reminiscent of Trotsky and as mythical as Big Brother. That the enemy may change from one day to the next, without questions being asked, is an aspect of the indoctrination with "doublethink," defined as "the power of holding two contradictory beliefs in one's mind simultaneously, and accepting both of them." Private

emotions are channeled into the daily session of "Two Minutes Hate," reinforced by public hangings of "traitors." An atmosphere of paranoia prevails; children are encouraged to inform on their parents; and sex is reduced to the duty of propagation.

Winston belongs to the middle stratum of society, the Outer Party, which serves the Inner Party elite. Below him are "the proles," who are not submitted to the rigorous thought control of Party members, but instead are kept in place and fed with vacuous, machine-made entertainment ("prolefeed"). Like the middle-class protagonists of Orwell's realistic novels, Winston dreams of a different life, in his case well aware that such dreams are branded as "thoughtcrime." About forty, he is old enough to have vague memories of the time before the 1950s war, in which his parents perished. He collects little mementos of that time, including a yellowed diary, to which he confides his secret subversive thoughts. Writing is his way of "staying sane," of keeping a record of whatever scraps of objective reality he is capable of assembling.

In part two of the novel Winston's loneliness is temporarily broken by his clandestine affair with Julia, another Ministry of Truth employee. She is much younger than Winston and has no recollection of the time before Big Brother's regime. His notions of revolt she regards as foolish. She has learned to go through the motions of obedience to the Party, including taking the pledge of chastity of the "Junior Anti-Sex League," to which she belongs. Her defiance of the Party consists in cheating it whenever possible and snatching whatever opportunity for private gratification comes her way. Not insignificantly, sexuality is the one aspect of a private life least accessible to control. In their different ways Winston and Julia represent the only conscious opposition to the system that appears in the novel, its only evidence that opposition can exist, if only on a private plane. For a short time they enjoy a furtive domestic idyll in a room above a junk shop in a prole quarter, which eventually turns out to be a trap set by the Thought Police.

The affair with Julia strengthens Winston's hope of finding fellow conspirators, who can confirm the existence of an oppositional "Brotherhood." Naively, he stakes his hope on O'Brien, a high-ranking Inner Party member, who lends him "The Book," supposedly written by Goldstein. This favor turns out to be another ruse. Winston's arrest takes place when he is reading "The Book." The part he manages to read reveals the Party's means of attaining control, though not its ends. The explication of these is reserved for part three, in which Winston is imprisoned in the Kafkaesque Ministry of Love and

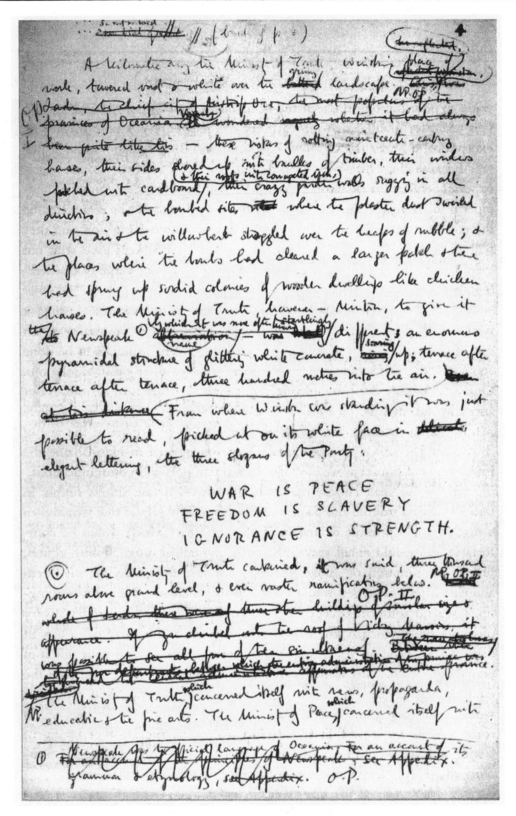

WAR IS PEACE
FREEDOM IS SLAVERY
IGNORANCE IS STRENGTH.

Page from a draft for Orwell's 1949 novel, Nineteen Eighty-Four, *about life in Britain under a totalitarian government thirty-five years in the future (University College London)*

subjected to torture by the demoniac O'Brien. "They can make you say anything–anything–but they can't make you believe it. They can't get inside you," Julia had said; but the purpose of O'Brien's torture is not to extract confessions but to eradicate Winston as an individual, to destroy his precarious hold on a subjective identity. After the horrors of Room 101, where Winston's last defense falls and he betrays his loyalty to Julia, the last vestige of a private emotion, he is ready to accept whatever truth the Party finds expedient, even if it says that two plus two make five. The Party has obtained its end, which is power for its own sake, power to create its own solipsistic reality. At the close of the novel Winston, Orwell's typified "Last Man in Europe" (his original title for the novel), has been reduced, so to speak, to a product of his torturer's mind.

In an appendix Orwell explains "The Principles of Newspeak," which in the novel is being introduced as the coming official language of Oceania. He had earlier, in his essay "Politics and the English Language" (1946), tried to expose the staleness and clichés of political jargon and demonstrate the connection between clear thinking and good writing. The purpose of Newspeak is to prevent both through a reduced vocabulary devoid of nuances. The theory is that thoughts deprived of words become virtually unthinkable. Conceptual distinctions are blurred by creations such as "doublethink," and value judgments are simplified when "bad" is replaced by "ungood." Newspeak will, of course, make the expression of private emotions, as in Winston's diary, unthinkable too.

The horrors of *Nineteen Eighty-Four* have been criticized for being excessive or unbelievable. Orwell emphasized that the novel was meant as a satire, displaying certain totalitarian ideas in their extreme consequence. In a review of Orwell's posthumously published *Shooting an Elephant, and Other Essays* (1950) E. M. Forster wrote of *Nineteen Eighty-Four* that "There is not a monster in that hateful apocalypse which does not exist in embryo today." It is difficult to point to any major inconsistency that may detract from the overall impact of Orwell's vision, and its detailed realism makes it all the more distressing.

The influence of *Nineteen Eighty-Four* on later fiction, both mainstream and science fiction, has been considerable. Orwell influenced science fiction by presenting a vision of a future world that, rather than possessing advanced technology as in Huxley's dystopian *Brave New World,* is at a technological standstill, if not actually in worse shape than the present. Wells in his works of the 1930s and 1940s presented a glorious future made possible in part by science;

Huxley parodied such a vision with his world of great scientific advances employed for dubious ends. Orwell's contribution was to show that neither scientific nor political progress was inevitable. In so doing, he offered a possible route for generations of science-fiction writers. However, his main concern was with the political dangers he saw as present, despite the futuristic setting of the novel. By making the warning "Big Brother Is Watching You" proverbial, Orwell may have made it less likely that Big Brother will ever come into existence.

Since his death from tuberculosis on 21 January 1950 Orwell has come to be identified primarily with his two fantastic novels, *Animal Farm* and *Nineteen Eighty-Four.* Widely read and admired by people who would not consider themselves readers of fantasy or science fiction, both novels have also been accepted in those genres by readers, writers, and critics. While the relevance of these novels may diminish as the historical factors that motivated them become increasingly distant, they stand as significant contributions to British fantasy and science fiction of the mid twentieth century.

Bibliography:

Gillian Fenwick, *George Orwell: A Bibliography* (Winchester, U.K.: St. Paul's Bibliographies, 1998; New Castle, Del.: Oak Knoll Press, 1998).

Biographies:

Peter Stansky and William Abrahams, *The Unknown Orwell* (London: Constable, 1972; New York: Knopf, 1972);

Stansky and Abrahams, *Orwell: The Transformation* (London: Constable, 1979; New York: Knopf, 1980);

Bernard Crick, *George Orwell: A Life* (Boston: Little, Brown, 1980);

Michael Shelden, *Orwell: The Authorized Biography* (New York: HarperCollins, 1991).

References:

W. F. Bolton, *The Language of 1984: Orwell's Language and Ours* (Oxford: Blackwell, 1984);

Jenni Calder, *Animal Farm and Nineteen Eighty-Four* (Buckingham, U.K.: Open University Press, 1987);

Peter Davison, *George Orwell: A Literary Life* (Basingstone, U.K.: Palgrave, 1996; New York: St. Martin's Press, 1996);

Averil Gardner, *George Orwell* (Boston: Twayne, 1987);

J. R. Hammond, *A George Orwell Companion* (London: Macmillan, 1982);

Graham Holderness, Brian Loughery, and Nahem Yousaf, eds. *George Orwell: Contemporary Critical*

Essays (Basingstoke, U.K.: Palgrave, 1998; New York: St. Martin's Press, 1998);

Christopher Hollis, *A Study of George Orwell: The Man and His Works* (London: Hollis & Carter, 1956);

Irving Howe, *1984 Revisited: Totalitarianism in Our Century* (New York: Harper & Row, 1983);

Howe, ed., *Orwell's Nineteen Eighty-Four: Text, Sources, Criticism* (New York: Harcourt, Brace & World, 1963);

Stephen Ingle, *George Orwell: A Political Life* (Manchester & New York: Manchester University Press, 1994);

Daniel Lea, ed., *George Orwell: Animal Farm / Nineteen Eighty-Four* (Cambridge: Icon Books, 2001);

Geoffrey Meyers, *Orwell: Wintry Conscience of a Generation* (London & New York: Norton, 2000);

Meyers, *A Reader's Guide to George Orwell* (London: Thames & Hudson, 1975; Totowa, N.J.: Littlefield, 1977);

Meyers, ed., *George Orwell: The Critical Heritage* (London: Routledge & Kegan Paul, 1975);

Valerie Meyers, *George Orwell* (London: Macmillan, 1991);

John Newsinger, *Orwell's Politics* (Basingstoke, U.K. & New York: Palgrave, 1999);

Daphne Patai, *The Orwell Mystique: A Study in Male Ideology* (Amherst: University of Massachusetts Press, 1984), pp. 253–263;

Richard Rees, *George Orwell: Fugitive from the Camp of Victory* (London: Secker & Warburg, 1961);

Patrick Reilly, *Nineteen Eighty-Four: Past, Present, and Future* (Boston: Twayne, 1989);

Alan Sandison, *The Last Man In Europe: An Essay on George Orwell* (London: Macmillan, 1974); republished as *George Orwell After 1984* (London: Macmillan, 1986);

Peter Stansky, ed. *On Nineteen Eighty-Four* (New York: W. H. Freeman, 1983);

William Steinhoff, *George Orwell and the Origins of 1984* (Ann Arbor: University of Michigan Press, 1976);

Raymond Williams, *George Orwell* (London: Fontana, 1971; New York: Viking, 1971);

Williams, ed. *George Orwell: A Collection of Critical Essays* (Englewood Cliffs, N.J.: Prentice-Hall, 1974);

Tom Winnifrith and William V. Whitehead, *1984 and All's Well?* (London: Macmillan, 1984).

Papers:

The main body of George Orwell's manuscripts, personal papers, and correspondence is in the George Orwell Archive, University College, London.

Mervyn Peake

(9 July 1911 – 17 November 1968)

Tanya Gardiner-Scott
Mount Ida College

See also the Peake entries in *DLB 15: British Novelists, 1930–1959* and *DLB 160: British Children's Writers, 1914–1960.*

BOOKS: *Captain Slaughterboard Drops Anchor* (London: Country Life, 1939; New York: Macmillan, 1967);

Shapes and Sounds (London: Chatto & Windus, 1941; New York: Transatlantic, 1941);

Rhymes Without Reason (London: Eyre & Spottiswoode, 1944);

Titus Groan (London: Eyre & Spottiswoode, 1946; New York: Reynal & Hitchcock, 1946); corrected version, edited by G. Peter Winnington (Harmondsworth, U.K.: Penguin, 1981);

The Craft of the Lead Pencil (London: Wingate, 1946);

Letters from a Lost Uncle (from Polar Regions) (London: Eyre & Spottiswoode, 1948);

Drawings by Mervyn Peake (London: Grey Walls, 1949 [i.e., 1950]);

The Glassblowers (London: Eyre & Spottiswoode, 1950);

Gormenghast (London: Eyre & Spottiswoode, 1950; New York: Weybright & Talley, 1967); corrected version, edited by Winnington (Harmondsworth, U.K.: Penguin, 1982);

Mr. Pye (London: Heinemann, 1953);

Figures of Speech (London: Gollancz, 1954);

Titus Alone (London: Eyre & Spottiswoode, 1959; New York: Weybright & Talley, 1967); revised and enlarged version, edited by Langdon Jones (London: Eyre & Spottiswoode, 1970); corrected version, edited by Winnington (Harmondsworth, U.K.: Penguin, 1981);

The Rhyme of the Flying Bomb (London: Dent, 1962);

Poems and Drawings (London: Keepsake, 1965);

A Reverie of Bone: And Other Poems (London: Rota, 1967);

Selected Poems (London: Faber & Faber, 1972);

A Book of Nonsense (London: Peter Owen, 1972);

The Drawings of Mervyn Peake (London: Davis-Poynter, 1974);

Mervyn Peake in 1946 (photograph © Hulton Getty)

Mervyn Peake: Writings and Drawings, edited by Maeve Gilmore and Shelagh Johnson (London: Academy Editions / New York: St. Martin's Press, 1974);

Twelve Poems, 1939–1960 (Hayes, Middlesex: Bran's Head, 1975);

Boy in Darkness (Exeter: Wheaton, 1976; revised edition, London: Hodder Children's Books, 1996);

Peake's Progress, edited by Gilmore (London: Allen Lane, 1979; Woodstock, N.Y.: Overlook, 1981); corrected version, edited by Winnington (Harmondsworth, U.K.: Penguin, 1981);

Mervyn Peake: Ten Poems, edited by Brian Sibley (London: Mervyn Peake Society, 1993).

PLAY PRODUCTION: *The Wit to Woo,* London, Arts Theatre, 12 March 1957.

PRODUCED SCRIPT: *Titus Groan,* radio, Third Programme, British Broadcasting Corporation, 1 February 1956.

OTHER: *Ride a Cock-Horse and Other Nursery Rhymes,* illustrated by Peake (London: Chatto & Windus, 1940; New York: Transatlantic, 1944);

Lewis Carroll, *The Hunting of the Snark: An Agony in Eight Fits,* illustrated by Peake (London: Chatto & Windus, 1941);

C. E. M. Joad, *The Adventures of the Young Soldier in Search of the Better World,* illustrated by Peake (London: Faber & Faber, 1943; New York: Arco, 1944);

Samuel Taylor Coleridge, *The Rime of the Ancient Mariner,* illustrated by Peake (London: Chatto & Windus, 1943);

Christina Hole, *Witchcraft in England,* illustrated by Peake (London: Batsford, 1945; New York: Scribners, 1947);

Carroll, *Alice's Adventures in Wonderland and Through the Looking Glass,* illustrated by Peake (Stockholm: Zephyr Books, 1946; London: Wingate, 1954; New York: Schocken, 1979);

Maurice Collis, *Quest for Sita,* illustrated by Peake (London: Faber & Faber, 1946; New York: Day, 1947);

The Brothers Grimm, *Household Tales,* illustrated by Peake (London: Eyre & Spottiswoode, 1946; New York: Schocken, 1979);

Robert Louis Stevenson, *Dr. Jekyll and Mr. Hyde,* illustrated by Peake (London: Folio Society, 1948; New York: Duchesne, 1948);

Stevenson, *Treasure Island,* illustrated by Peake (London: Eyre & Spottiswoode, 1949; New York: Schocken, 1979);

"How a Romantic Novel Was Evolved," in *A New Romantic Anthology,* edited by Stefan Schimanski and Henry Treece (London: Grey Walls, 1949), pp. 80–89;

Johann Wyss, *The Swiss Family Robinson,* illustrated by Peake (London: Heirloom Library, 1949; New York: Chanticleer, 1950);

"Boy in Darkness," in *Sometime, Never: Three Tales of Imagination,* by Peake, William Golding, and John

Wyndham (London: Eyre & Spottiswoode, 1956; New York: Ballantine, 1957), pp. 129–185;

Sketches from Bleak House, edited by Leon Garfield and Edward Blishen (London: Methuen, 1983).

To label Mervyn Peake as a fantasy writer is to focus on his Titus novels—*Titus Groan* (1946), *Gormenghast* (1950), and *Titus Alone* (1959; second edition, 1970), arguably his most well-known prose—as well as his novel *Mr. Pye* (1953) and his short stories. He was also a poet, a painter, one of the best illustrators of his time, and a playwright, working in a variety of media until his health declined from Parkinson's disease during the 1950s and 1960s.

Regarded as a maverick or "major minor" writer, Peake is not easily labeled. He wrote in the tradition of Charles Dickens and Laurence Sterne, yet he can also be linked with the bildungsroman (the novel of growth and development); Gothic fantasy, which W. P. Day in *In the Circles of Fear and Desire* (1985) defines as a parody of romance and realism; and the postmodern novel. Although he is one of many writers, including J. R. R. Tolkien and C. S. Lewis, who used self-contained alternate worlds linked to reality as a way of exploring the issues of his time, his vision is much less comforting. Peake uses literary tradition in an ironic way, omnisciently narrating his stories, using exaggeration and metonymy to convey the qualities he wants the reader to consider (much as he does in his paintings), and delighting in Gothic trappings and semifeudal settings. The result is a particular kind of fantasy rooted firmly in the known world.

Mervyn Laurence Peake was born on 9 July 1911 in Kuling, in central southern China, to Dr. Ernest Cromwell Peake, an Edinburgh-trained missionary doctor, and Amanda Elizabeth Powell Peake, his missionary nurse wife. Kuling was their summer home, where they and their elder son, Ernest Leslie (called Lonnie), and later Mervyn spent the hot seasons. His father worked in a hospital at Hengchow (Henyang) in the Hunan area, but Mervyn spent his first seven months in Kuling because of a rebellion against the Manchu dynasty that caused unrest in other parts of the country. The following year the Peakes moved to Tientsin, where Dr. Peake ran the London Missionary Society hospital from 1913 to 1923.

From the time he was able to hold a pencil, Peake was gifted as an artist and encouraged by his family to draw whenever possible. He held his pencil the Chinese way, thumb on one side and first, second, and third fingers on the other to balance it, and he retained a Chinese sense of word and image as aspects of the same whole throughout his life. He went first to Tientsin Grammar School, traveling by donkey from the mis-

Peake and Maeve Gilmore at their wedding in December 1937

sionary compound to the school. In 1922 his "A Letter from China" was published in the London Missionary Society magazine for children, *News from Afar*. In 1924, three years after he had written it, "Ways of Travelling" appeared in the same magazine; both pieces were profusely illustrated, a habit he carried into much of what he wrote.

In 1923 the family left China, and Peake went to Eltham College, a school for the sons of missionaries that Lonnie had attended since 1914. Peake's father and uncles had also been enrolled there. Peake's reputation was more that of an athlete (cricket, rugby, and the high jump) than of a scholar—he failed spelling—but he was heavily influenced in his reading tastes by the Drake brothers, English teachers at the school. He drew and wrote copiously, and he enjoyed his time there; Eltham College is the basis for the young Titus Groan's comically cast school days in *Gormenghast*. It was also where Peake met his lifelong friend Gordon Smith, with whom he collaborated on two projects and shared his fertile creative imagination.

In 1929 Peake left Eltham College and went to the Croyden School of Art, where he received some training in painting. In December of that year he went on to the Royal Academy School for a planned five-year period of study. At this time painters were forming groups and putting on shared exhibitions; Peake belonged to several groups simultaneously and took part in a variety of art shows. He also gained recognition as a costume designer for his intricate designs for a production of Karel and Josef Čapek's *Ze života hmyzu* (1921; translated as *The Life of Insects,* 1923). Though his still life *Cactus* had been accepted by the Royal Academy and he had won the Arthur Hacker prize for a different painting, he objected to the rigidity of the teaching styles and left the academy in 1933 when his place as a student was not renewed.

Peake then moved to an artists' colony, founded by one of the Drake brothers, on the Channel island of Sark. He was one of the founding artist members and during this time became known for his portraits, consistently rated highly and commissioned throughout his career. He also became known locally for his soccer-playing on the Sark team, and Eric Drake is quoted by biographer John Watney as describing Peake in retrospect as an example of "joyous immediacy completely free—repeat completely—of the inhibitions of . . . any . . . form of intellectualism." This capacity for intense spontaneity heavily influences the form of the Titus novels. His knowledge of Sark also influences his depiction of the rooftops of Gormenghast Castle.

After several exhibitions by the Sark Group and one at the Royal Society of British Artists in 1935, Peake was invited to teach at the Westminster School of Art; this engagement lasted until 1941, when the school was evacuated during World War II. While at the Westminster School he met Maeve Gilmore, a sculptor and painter, and they married in December 1937. That same year he had a one-man exhibition. He and Gilmore had three children: two boys, Sebastian and Fabian, and a girl, Clare.

In 1939 *Captain Slaughterboard Drops Anchor* was published; inspired by Peake's love for pirates (and, Smith suggests, for Gilmore) and copiously illustrated, it recounts the adventures of Captain Slaughterboard, his crew, and his special companion, the Yellow Creature. Most of the copies of the first edition were destroyed in a warehouse fire caused by the London Blitz, and it was not republished until 1945, when, after the war, reviewers were not so worried about its fantastic-grotesque illustrations and their effects on children. It has been in print continuously since 1967.

Throughout this time Peake was doing costume designing, writing poetry (both nonsense and serious), and continuing to exhibit paintings in a variety of

London venues. He has been linked with the New Romantic school of poetry, as his poems often address moments of creativity and disillusionment and integrate the world of emotions and personal experience with myth.

He and Gilmore both had exhibitions in 1939, his in the Leicester and hers in the Wertheim Galleries. When World War II began, he was put to work fitting other civilians with gas masks, and she was pregnant. Sebastian was born on 7 January 1940, and shortly thereafter Peake branched into another major area in this most creative decade of his life and began to write the first of the Titus books.

Unsuccessful in his application to be a war artist, Peake was drafted in 1940 into the artillery. He could no longer paint, because of the lack of space for his materials, so he took notebooks (publishers' dummies) with him. He used them for illustrations (commissioned by Chatto and Windus as a result of his first book) and went on writing *Titus Groan,* which he published in 1946. He would sketch the characters as he wrote them into life, thereby complementing the verbal with the visual, although with the direct effect of the war on his art career, he had to focus more specifically on writing than at any previous time. For a while he was part of an anti-aircraft-gun battery on the Isle of Sheppey in the Thames estuary, and then he was posted to Blackpool, where he had plenty of time to write. In December of that year Chatto and Windus published *Ride a Cock-Horse and Other Nursery Rhymes,* with Peake's illustrations. These also had mixed reviews because of their "horrible beauty" and were, it was suggested, more appropriate for adults, given his trademark techniques of chiaroscuro, exaggeration, and elongation.

In June 1941 Peake was posted back to London, where he continued his friendships with figures such as Graham Greene and Dylan Thomas. He never belonged to any literary group, but he knew most of the writers, actors, and artists in London at the time. One of the foremost book illustrators of his time, he was a personal friend of Walter de la Mare and knew and sketched Laurence Olivier, Vivien Leigh, and many other theater people. He was also able to rent a studio so he could paint again when not on duty. He was then posted to the Lake District, where again the problem of space caused him to work on illustrations and the novel. He was commissioned to illustrate an edition of Lewis Carroll's 1876 work *The Hunting of the Snark: An Agony in Eight Fits* (1941); he published a book of poetry, *Shapes and Sounds* (1941); and he had another exhibition of drawings at the Leicester Galleries.

While in the Lake District he worked on *A Reverie of Bone: And Other Poems* (1967), a melancholic meditation on death and on skeletal beauty, animal and human, with grotesque details transformed into objets d'art. He also produced illustrations for Christina Hole's *Witchcraft in England* (1945), and he continued to write *Titus Groan,* sketching the characters as he wrote to intensify his sense of them.

Army life was becoming less bearable. A letter to Smith dated 7 March 1942 reads, "Oh God, I'm sick, sick, sick of it–the perpetual littleness of the life," a reflection of the ever-rebellious Titus. In April 1942 he forged a pass, having been denied permission for compassionate leave, and went home to see his wife, who gave birth to their second son, Fabian. Soon after he went back she was informed that he had suffered a nervous breakdown and had been sent to the Neurosis Centre in Southport. During this time he wrote chapters 56 and 57 of *Titus Groan*–"The Dark Breakfast" and "The Reveries," the latter his only chapter in Joycean internal monologue–and managed to persuade the matron to type his book for him to that point. He was put on indefinite sick leave, returning home in September 1942. He was still working on the novel and, newly commissioned by Chatto and Windus, on illustrations for a 1943 edition of Samuel Taylor Coleridge's 1798 poem *The Rime of the Ancient Mariner.* These are particularly noteworthy for their use of chiaroscuro; their eerie drawings of "Life in Death," predictive of the skeletal survivors of the concentration camps he later saw; and their sensitivity to Coleridge's text. Peake's army discharge finally came through on 30 April 1943, and he finished *Titus Groan* shortly thereafter. It was published in 1946.

Titus Groan introduces the world of Gormenghast, ancestral seat of the Groan dynasty, a castle filled with eccentric retainers, ever-confusing spatial arrangements, and punctiliously observed traditional rituals that consume the time and energy of all involved. The Groan family consists of Sepulchrave, the current lord; his wife, Gertrude; his daughter, Fuchsia; the young Titus, born at the beginning of the novel and even as a baby fighting his dynastic destiny; and the epileptic, monomaniacal aunts, Cora and Clarice.

The story takes the reader through the growth and development of the rebellious young earl in this quasi-Gothic environment, an alternate world situated in another time and place and completely isolated from the known world. There are various subplots, the most important of which are those dominated by Titus's increasingly demonic double, the ingenious, malevolent upstart former-kitchen-boy Steerpike, whose goal is total control of the castle. At first Steerpike engages the reader's sympathy as a rebel against an oppressive, traditional social order, but he soon manipulates all with whom he comes into contact. He explores hidden parts of the castle, plays the clown for Fuchsia, and encour-

Peake with his sons, Fabian and Sebastian

ages the aunts in their ambitions to the throne of Gormenghast. Targeting Sepulchrave as the reason for their relegation to inferior parts of the castle, Steerpike suggests that they burn Sepulchrave's beloved library at the time the family is gathered there to celebrate young Titus's christening and make arrangements for a breakfast in his honor, both which are interrupted by the fire. He also positions himself to be a rescuer-figure, thus ensuring admiration. In the fire Sourdust, the incumbent Master of Ritual, who controls the heart of the castle and the everyday doings of its inhabitants, is killed. A Hitleresque figure in the way he usurps power, Steerpike eventually worms his way into the position of private secretary to the new Master of Ritual, Barquentine, son of Sourdust.

There are two other important subplots, also involving retainers and notable violence. The obese cook Swelter and the earl's emaciated retainer Flay have a bitter, fatal rivalry that results in Swelter's dramatic death at the culmination of a moonlit duel; and Keda, Titus's wet-nurse, has two sculptor-lovers who fight to the death over her.

Another crucial character is Dr. Alfred Prunesquallor, the somewhat androgynous castle doctor, who

like Flay is fiercely loyal to the Groan dynasty. He is renowned for his creative flights of verbal fancy and his sharp brain. He becomes the detective figure of Gormenghast Castle, the one who learns most of Steerpike's brilliant machinations and who appreciates the caliber of the young man's calculating mind as no other can. His sister Irma, who initially makes a career out of being a virgin and is as prosaically literal as he is imaginatively verbose, is one of the more comic castle characters, particularly as Steerpike easily turns her head with his flattery.

The other consequence of the fire in the library is that the earl, his cultural refuge gone, goes mad and thinks he is one of the castle owls. Steerpike mocks the earl in front of Flay, who reacts by throwing one of Gertrude's cats at him, thus causing Flay's banishment by a furious Gertrude, who usually responds only when her birds and animals are threatened.

At the end of the novel, although Titus is little more than a year old, the community gathers for him to assume his father's title after Sepulchrave has allowed himself to be eaten by the owls. Steerpike, having been ultimately responsible for the earl's madness and demise, is gaining in power and influence, unbeknownst to most, and is poising himself for a takeover. Titus's earling celebration is marked in part by his refusing to comply with the ritual and dropping the sacred objects into Gormenghast Lake. As he does so, he cries out, and the Thing, Keda's bastard daughter, cries out in enthusiastic response. She is in the tradition of mischievous nature spirits, so much so that nobody is sure exactly how to deal with her when she disrupts castle rituals, and Peake develops her in *Gormenghast* as the symbol of the total freedom for which Titus longs.

The last few pages of the novel show Rottcodd, the Curator of the Bright Carvings made by the best of the commoners, looking down on the returning procession from his high window and musing on the changes, anathema to the community, that he can sense in the year and more since he was first visited with the news of the birth of the seventy-seventh earl. There is obviously more to come.

Fantastic though the setting and rituals may be—perhaps in part a reflection of Peake's memories of China transmuted into another setting—his grip on human drives and eccentricities is sure, and his rhythmically written visual prose, evocative vocabulary (often a feature of wartime writing), and imaginative perspective all carefully guide the reader into the fantastic, the quasi-Gothic, and the otherworldly. Peake plays with the reader's sense of time, looping it back and forth so that it works on both a linear and a cyclic ritualistic level. The seasons are part of his intensification of mood, and, as yet another marker of time passing, they help to focus the dual pull of stasis and change that is such a major part of the castle. Overall, change is something the inhabitants of Gormenghast try to avoid, which is what makes Steerpike, an agent of extreme change who is attempting to destroy the old order, so threatening. The reader experiences time stretched out in moments of individual tension for the characters, condensed, static, speeding up, and even at times completely negated when individual characters pass out, as when Fuchsia faints at one point. As Colin Manlove remarks in his *Modern Fantasy: Five Studies* (1973), "Time seems to be going both backwards and forwards, and the net effect is that the temporal sequence appears frozen."

Another way Peake plays with the mimetic is in his use of narrative structure, as he intersperses different narrative strands with an intrusive third-person narrator. Episodes in the days before Steerpike's burning of Sepulchrave's library are stretched into separate chunks.

Not only does Peake play with the reader's sense of time and space, he also switches between animate and inanimate at a speed that piles image on image. One example of the way identity shifts and changes is a description of Flay, the earl's valet:

> His black suit, patched on the elbows and near the collar with a greasy sepia-coloured cloth, fitted him badly but belonged to him as inevitably as the head of a tortoise emerging from its shell or the vulture's from a rubble of feathers belong to that reptile or that bird. His head, parchment-coloured and bony, was indigenous to that greasy fabric. It stuck out from the top window of its high black buildings as though it has known no other residence.

This example also demonstrates just how convoluted Peake's sentences can be.

In Dickensian fashion Peake uses verbal and visual signals to identify characters, as well as odd names, so that the reader is constantly interpreting on a variety of levels. For example, Barquentine, the Master of Ritual, has a peg leg and a distinctive style of swearing; he stands out not only visually but also aurally. The narrator directs the readers' gaze so that they see characters through the eyes of others and are led to focus on the metonymic in sometimes all-absorbing detail.

Another device Peake uses to great effect is chiaroscuro, light and dark. One example comes from the preliminaries to the duel between Flay and Swelter, as the radiance of the "humpbacked moon"

> poured through the open wall at the far end of the Hall of Spiders. Beyond the opening it danced and glittered

on the hissing water that had formed great walled-in lakes among the roofs. The rain slanted its silver threads and raised spurts of quicksilver on striking water. The Hall itself had the effect of a drawing in black, dove-grey and silver ink.

Word and image interpenetrate to great effect.

Discharged from the army, Peake continued to work on illustrations, placing *Titus Groan* with a publisher and doing artistic work for the Ministry of Information. In 1945, just at the end of the war, he was finally appointed as a war artist and went, under the auspices of London's *Leader Magazine,* to Europe with Tom Pocock, whose writing he was to illustrate. The two went through Paris to Germany and back, and Peake took a side trip to see the Bergen-Belsen concentration camp a month after its liberation. He sketched the dying in the hospital set up by the British and wandered around what was left. Years later he transmuted what he had seen into parts of his dystopian third novel, *Titus Alone.*

He spent the rest of the year preparing *Titus Groan* for publication and continued to illustrate various classics—*The Rime of the Ancient Mariner* in 1943, *Alice's Adventures in Wonderland* (1865) and *Through the Looking-Glass* (1871) in 1946, and Robert Louis Stevenson's *Treasure Island* (1883) in 1949—though he was hampered by postwar conditions in Britain. In 1946 he, his wife, and his two sons went back to the island of Sark, where they could live more spaciously, and Peake worked on his sequel, *Gormenghast,* also set in the world of Gormenghast Castle. Peake memorialized the contours of the Sark coastline in his mapping of the castle roofscapes during the flooding toward the end of the novel. Yet, despite the family's happiness on Sark and his ability to make frequent trips back to London to stay in touch with his editors and publishers, Peake decided in 1949 that he needed to return to the mainland permanently.

Gormenghast was published in 1950, as was a collection of poetry, *The Glassblowers,* and Peake won the 1951 Heinemann Prize for Literature. The novel focuses on the same themes as *Titus Groan*—loyalty, love, evil, menace, and freedom—but its concern with the themes of evil and freedom is particularly sharp.

When the novel opens, Titus is seven. Peake brings the reader up to date on the living and the dead and then ushers the reader into the "present" of the story. Titus is immersed in his schooling. Peake provides a gallery of eccentric schoolmasters and boys' games as context in yet another expansion of his castle setting. Part of the fantastic element in Gormenghast Castle is the sense that there is always room for more.

*Manuscript page, with Peake's drawing of the character Swelter, for his projected operatic version
of his 1946 novel,* Titus Groan *(Collection of Mrs. Maeve Peake)*

As Titus matures over the next ten years, he explores his environment and learns about power and responsibility. He increasingly wants to be seen as his own person, not simply a cardboard earl, and much of the novel is taken up with his struggles. Frustrated at his dynastic duties, he takes every possible opportunity to escape from the castle, exploring its hinterlands and catching glimpses of the Thing, his wild, free foster sister, to whom he becomes increasingly attracted as a person as well as a symbol and whom he almost rapes toward the end of the novel. Peake makes it clear that her death by lightning marks a maturation point for his young protagonist, but he belabors the point through his omniscient narrator, and Titus's maturation is perhaps not as well conveyed as it might be, seen differently.

Titus sees Steerpike as the epitome of the ritual he has come to resent. Although their final battle is viewed by the castle community as the earl defending his heritage, for the seventeen-year-old Titus it becomes a personal contest, a first blooding that, despite himself, elevates him to mythic stature.

Peake develops Steerpike as an increasingly demonic character who ultimately becomes completely megalomaniac. He imprisons and starves the aunts to death after playing sadistically with them from time to time; he gets rid of Nanny Slagg, the children's old nurse; he plots Titus's demise in ever-increasing ritual obligations; and he woos Fuchsia, all the while intending that he then be the instrument of her punishment for being involved with a commoner. After he has been tracked down and the full extent of his crimes known, he sees himself in mythic terms: "He was watching himself, but only so that he should miss nothing. He was the vehicle through which the gods were working. The dim primordial gods of power and blood." By the time he dies, his rational capacities have completely vanished, and he has come terrifyingly close to achieving his objective, despite the community's stand against him led by Gertrude and Dr. Prunesquallor and the flooding of the castle itself in a spontaneous abortion of him.

In the eyes of the community, including Steerpike (in his way a traditional satanic rebel), for Titus to kill Steerpike is to exorcise the castle of its evil. In Titus's own view, "I want to be myself, and become what I make myself, a person, a real live person and not a symbol any more. That is my reason! He must be caught and slain. He killed Flay. He hurt my sister. He stole my boat. Isn't that enough? To hell with Gormenghast." Shortly afterward, Fuchsia's drowning, which may be suicide or an accidental death, is discovered, serving as another intensification of Titus's personal reasons for playing his mythically scripted role and killing his demonic double.

Gormenghast is multifaceted. Its pace is faster than that of *Titus Groan*, as it works on the level of plot more than setting. The novel crosses genre lines with its detective plot of the unmasking and eventual defeat of the murderous outlaw Steerpike; its bildungsroman theme, with the earl as a young man and savior of his world finally turning his back on everything to which he has been bred; and its comic romance elements, predominantly in the lovingly humorous depiction of the marital adventures of schoolmaster Bellgrove and Irma, Prunesquallor's sister. The subplots tie in closely: Steerpike's courting of Fuchsia with a view to seducing and disgracing her, as well as his murder of his superior, Barquentine, the Master of Ritual, in a fiery holocaust that leaves Steerpike burned too; the androgynous Prunesquallor's attempts to advise Irma on her marital games and her final conquest of Bellgrove; and the Thing, symbol of freedom.

Again the fantastic is present through setting, vocabulary, and perspectives. As Peake says in *Gormenghast,* "The walls of Gormenghast were like the walls of paradise or the walls of an inferno. The colours were devilish or angelical according to the colour of the mind that watched them," thus firmly placing the burden of interpretive responsibility on the individual reader.

In both *Titus Groan* and *Gormenghast* are reflections of what Anthony Burgess, in his introduction to a 1968 edition of the former, called "an era of horrors." In the first is a fake haunt, with a human skull gilded and used as an object of terror, and in the second is Steerpike's sadism and eventual madness. The old reasons for doing things no longer hold in this new world. Titus is an existential hero who does what he wants and nearly fulfills the Gothic pattern of destroying his identity, as Steerpike does.

Gormenghast is thus a depiction of self-deluded romantics, with their fulfilling of multiple roles—Steerpike as eventual Master of Ritual and thus upholder of tradition as well as villain, Titus as earl and private person—and a detective plot to root out the evil. After this purge is accomplished, Titus leaves the castle, becoming an actor divorced from his setting, an absurd, unimpressive hero, even an antihero. Thus Gormenghast, the emblem of stasis, empire, and self-perpetuation, loses its young hope, though his mother thinks his trip will be cyclic: "There is nowhere else. You will only tread a circle, Titus Groan. There's not a road, not a track, but it will lead you home. For everything comes to Gormenghast."

In both Britain and the United States the first two novels have had respectable, though not overwhelming, sales, in part because of their visual quality, their delib-

3 Trafalgar Studios
Manresa Rd. Chelsea. SW3.

Dear Goatie.

Herewith a most curious request. When I went to Eyre & Spottswood ("migraine" to you) I was appalled at being asked whether I would condense into about 200 words the "oomph" of Gormenghast.. I cant think of another word. Something which will give readers an idea of what they are letting themselves in for. The "blurb" in other words. I said, "Look here", (or some such opening gambit) " I cant write my own "blurb" for the dust cover — its *indecent*. "True", said they (in effect) but authors have so scolded us in the past when they have read the blurbs we've given them that we are asking writers to try to say what they've been driving at — Keeping out superlative adjectives *if they can*!

First page of a 1947 letter from Peake to his lifelong friend and sometime collaborator Gordon Smith
(from Gordon Smith, Mervyn Peake: A Personal Memoir, *1984)*

erately evocative vocabulary, their metonymic focus, and their seminal images, rooted in the Gothic fantastic, of the castle, the mother-figure that attempts to contain all. Also significant are the bildungsroman theme and, as Margaret Ochocki points out in her 1982 article "*Gormenghast:* Fairytale Gone Wrong?," the fairy-tale and mythic patterns. Their moderate sales may be a result of mixed reader reactions to them, from enthusiasm to dismissal, with seemingly little in between; they are also a result of the fact that Peake does not make *Titus Groan* or *Gormenghast* easy allegories.

His blend of the fantastic, the bizarre, and the everyday, coupled with his highly literary, visual prose, make Peake a challenging writer to read, and with his "major minor" status as a writer he is something of a cult figure among readers of fantasy. *Titus Groan* and Peake's two other books about Titus have always had a readership, though they are an acquired taste, despite the fact that Peake was a contemporary of Tolkien and Lewis, whose fantasies have inspired huge markets of devoted readers.

With their suggestive echoes of Adolf Hitler's rise to power and their depictions of violence, ambition, and megalomania, all three Titus novels provide an emotional index of the time of their creation. Peake grapples with an ongoing artistic dilemma: when reality seems extreme, fantastic, or horrific, how does a writer convey these things in a way that will not seem desensitizing to saturated readers? In this sense postmodernism is parallel to the Gothic; each is in reaction to an earth-shattering event that changed the face of the known world.

For Gothic writers such as Matthew G. Lewis, that event was the French Revolution and its bloody aftermath; for writers such as Graham Greene, Elizabeth Bowen, Malcolm Lowry, Evelyn Waugh, George Orwell, and Peake, that event was World War II, with its images of human savagery and cruelty on a scope never envisioned, and the dawn of the atomic age. Peake shares certain preoccupations with his contemporaries, though he uses the alternate universe of Gormenghast to explore them—the overturning of social hierarchies; the guilt and burden of the past and its expectations of the new generation; social stagnancy and enervation (part of the legacy of imperialism as represented by Gormenghast Castle and conveyed in the ritualistic repetitions within its society); and the difficulty of love. Peake acts as a sensor of his times, tapping into the currents of thought and mood around him.

But above all Peake explores the themes of identity and the relativity of perception. In his depiction of the self-perceptions of various characters as opposed to their public personae he lays out for his readers the gaps and imaginative leaps between appearance and reality.

When they moved back to England in 1949, the Peakes settled in Chelsea for a time, and Peake taught portraiture at the Central School of Art in Holborn, one of the few times he had a steady income. He also was increasingly in demand as an illustrator and became more interested in working in the theater as a writer.

The Chelsea apartment was too cramped, however, and the family decided to buy a house in Smarden, Kent. This expensive purchase meant that money, never plentiful, became an urgent need. Peake decided to write a novel he hoped would sell well, *Mr. Pye* (1953). In this novel he pays homage to Sark and its islanders by creating Mr. Pye, an evangelist who goes on a mission to the island, has all kinds of encounters with the Sarkese, and, in a burst of magic realism, grows horns when he does evil and wings when he does good. While the setting and characters are vivid, the whimsical, quasi-allegorical fantasy of the novel was off-putting to readers used to the grandeurs of Gormenghast, and the novel did not do as well as hoped.

Meanwhile, the Peakes had put the Smarden house on the market, moved back to London, and finally gained possession of the house his father had left to him in Wallington. The Smarden house was sold, and Peake turned his attention to making *Titus Groan* an opera. But nothing came of this project, and he decided to develop an idea for a play, *The Wit to Woo,* produced in 1957 but not published until *Peake's Progress* (1979) appeared. He kept his studio in London, and the family moved to Wallingford, where he and Gilmore painted and he wrote. Throughout this time he was continuing to illustrate others' books, but he was not getting as many offers as he once had, and his main hope was that the play would lift them out of their financial bind. The signs of what was diagnosed as Parkinson's disease, including tremors in his hands, were beginning at this time.

Peake had begun *Titus Alone* in 1954 and had been working throughout this time on short fiction. "The Weird Journey" had been commissioned and published in *Harvest* in 1948. This story clearly illustrates what John Batchelor dubs Peake's technique of "concentrating on the word" and allowing "the word to release the image and the image to release meaning." A dream vision, "The Weird Journey" is filled with fantastic alliterations such as "daylight darkness, a summer of sepia and . . . the brilliance of light." It is structured around four waking nightmares. The dreamer is on a journey already fated, stepping in his own footsteps in artificial snow, going back to his origins in order to examine the influence of the past on the present, a nightmare vision of the suburban future,

Dust jacket for the second volume (1950) in Peake's Titus trilogy, in which seventeen-year-old Titus kills his demonic rival, Steerpike

the dehumanized conformity that smothers creativity. He fears change, sees the future as frightening, and ultimately desires annihilation even as he deplores it. Peake uses color, or the lack of it, as a powerful metaphor, as well as water images, which are also common in his novels. This story, like his others that are horror-gothic fantastic in conception and execution, is both familiar and strange.

"The Connoisseurs," inspired by a social encounter Peake had, came out in *Lilliput* in 1950; Batchelor mentions that the Peakes produced a dramatic (and still unpublished) version of the story at Smarden in 1952. The story spoofs the pretensions of those who dabble in art. His other realistic story, based on a piece of family history, is "I Bought a Palm Tree," unpublished until its appearance in *Peake's Progress*. In 1955 he went on a trip to Yugoslavia as a writer for the British Broadcasting Corporation, but the writing and the sketches he did were never used. Peake's play in blank verse, *The Wit to Woo,* is the story of a young man who fakes his own death and pretends to be someone else to get the girl he loves.

Though Olivier and Leigh were enthusiastic about it when they saw the script, the play was not staged until 1957, when it closed after a few days.

In 1956 the Peakes went to Spain for a restorative holiday, and he returned less strained and more able to work on *Titus Alone*. That same year Peake was commissioned to write a story for a volume called *Sometime, Never: Three Tales of Imagination,* along with William Golding and John Wyndham. His contribution was "Boy in Darkness," a semi-allegorized, fantastic Titus story (though the boy is never named) about one of his escapes from the castle. The boy meets a hyena-man and a man-goat, both of whom are controlled by the evil, vampiric Lamb, who loves to feed on his victims' terror and has a history of turning humans into beasts. Titus manages to turn the two grotesque beast-men, all that remains of the Lamb's original entourage, against their master, and in the last possible moment of freedom, the boy kills the human-hating Lamb, thus releasing the men within the other two. They then lead him to freedom. Reminiscent of other fantastic metamorphoses, from Circe's beast-men in Homer's *Odyssey* through H. G. Wells's *The Island of Dr. Moreau* (1896), Peake's tale has peculiar weight because of his complete inversion of traditional Christian imagery in the figure of the Lamb and his dystopian vision of a world destroyed. The wreckage, the dust, and the squalor, coupled with the increasing fear of dissolution throughout the story, make "Boy in Darkness" horrific and powerful, and it uses the theme of the boy's stubborn resistance in a way similar to parts of *Titus Alone*.

Titus Alone was published in 1959, at a time when Peake's illness was becoming worse. He had been under considerable financial pressure for many years, and the lack of success of *The Wit to Woo* had taken its toll. With the help of Gilmore, who wrote what he dictated when he could not write, he had finished the novel, but he was unable to edit it for publication. Thus, the first edition came out under the direction of Maurice Temple Smith of Eyre and Spottiswoode, the Peakes making the cuts he had proposed. In 1970 Langdon Jones reedited the novel, restoring many of the cuts Temple Smith had suggested and made with Gilmore's approval, but what Peake intended can never be fully known. The message of dystopian urgency in the novel is clear, as is its panoramic social scope. It tackles the age-old problem of conformity to and transgression of social norms. Titus's problem is that he has changed societies, and his points of reference are only in his mind in this "brave new world."

The novel traces Titus's journey once he has left the familiar terrain of Gormenghast, crossed a desert, and arrived in a dystopian universe where he is a displaced person with no papers, carrying the memory of the reality of Gormenghast in his heart and mind. Tracked by the police, with their spy globes and identical robotic hunters, he finds himself in a universe of fast cars, sophisticates, and sleek city buildings, the likes of which he has never seen. He encounters Muzzlehatch, a deliberately anachronistic father figure who maintains his own zoo, drives an ancient car, and has his own sense of history. Muzzlehatch dislikes the way the world is changing and welcomes Titus's Gormenghast-haunted vision. After their first, somewhat abrasive encounter, he and his former lover Juno save Titus from the police when the boy falls through a glass roof into the middle of a cocktail party (an episode based on Peake's own boyhood experience of falling through the roof of his father's operating room). Juno, fulfilling a traditional female role as Peake portrays her, vouches in court to take care of Titus, extending a quasi-maternal, quasi-sexual protection to him, while seeing him as a younger version of Muzzlehatch. When Titus tires of Juno and breaks off their relationship, he leaves, disables a spy device that is trailing him, and finds Muzzlehatch again. The latter saves him from the police at the cost of his own zoo, and sends him with a special symbol to the Under-River—a community of criminals, former Nazi capos, and displaced persons into whose ranks Titus can vanish.

In these episodes Peake may be drawing on his memories of the London underground during the Blitz as well as the Europe he saw when he traveled for the *Leader*. His descriptions of the environs of this counterculture are reminiscent of Henry Moore's drawings. Peake also depicts the sadistic capo Veil and his abused victim and former camp inmate, the Black Rose, focusing on the latter's desire for "clean linen," a fantasy recorded by many survivors. In manuscript he describes Veil as having the same bicolored face that Steerpike has after he is burned, suggesting that Titus's encounter with Veil is a battle between good and evil on the epic scale of that other, earlier one—at least as it was seen at the time by the obviously biased castle community. Peake also writes about a scientist and his "death ray," something that Temple Smith objected to as too science-fictional and in that sense dated.

Muzzlehatch, his animals dead, arrives in time to rescue the Black Rose and kill Veil, taking the former to Juno's house. Titus, having expressed his sense of being overwhelmed by the suffering of his survivor-companions, goes partway with them and then wanders on. The Black Rose dies as she has dreamed, on clean sheets. Muzzlehatch then leaves Juno to track the scientist who has destroyed his zoo, symbol of a better world. He gains entry (in a section restored in the second edition) to the factory where clones are created and learns the dimensions of this scientifically controlled project (think "death factory"). With the Black Rose dead, Juno becomes the target of an investigation, acquires a new lover, Anchor, and goes with him to try to find Titus.

Titus encounters Cheeta, the dwarfish daughter of the scientist for whom Muzzlehatch is searching. She is the quintessential predatory modern woman, "bizarre, utterly feminine, and delicious . . . frozen at the very taproot . . . without heartache. . . . So clear, so crisp, so empty. In short, so civilized." He wants her body; she wants his mind. When she cannot have it, she decides to destroy it by creating a fake Gormenghast based on his reminiscences in delirium when they first met and convincing Titus that he is insane. Peake depicts Cheeta and Juno as polar opposites, suggesting that the only possible interest in either of them is a carnal one; at the same time, he embodies aspects of Titus's head/heart dichotomy in each, thus ensuring his defection from both.

Cheeta, having involved even her scientist father in her evil plans to derange Titus, is overwhelmed when Muzzlehatch, Juno, Anchor, the robotic police tracers, and some Under-River characters show up. Muzzlehatch confronts Cheeta's father to tell him that his factory is to be destroyed; Muzzlehatch is then killed when the police stab him. Titus, his sanity saved, defeats Cheeta's plans. Again harking back to fairy tale and myth, the beautiful dwarf with the icy heart is reduced to running away screaming, her plans thwarted.

Titus, Juno, and Anchor, shaken and grieving, take advantage of the panic and leave, and Titus asks to be parachuted from their craft. He lands in the woods, falling through the air as though he is being reborn, and shortly thereafter finds himself at the edges of Gormenghast Castle. Reassured of its reality, he turns away and leaves in another direction, having become his own person.

Titus Alone did not do as well as the other Titus novels. Its prose style is spare and lean, a far cry from the baroque intensities and setting of the first two novels. It is also in multiple sections of varying length and has science-fiction elements; its vision is dystopian, though its theme, of the young man finding himself, is familiar. Peake refers not only to the capo-inmate relationship but also to the smell of the death camps, as expressed through Titus's first impression of the "death factory," and later his description of the effect of Muzzlehatch's bomb in the factory hints at the atomic bomb. Muzzlehatch conveys a haunting comment on the changes in the world he has known—"Once there were islands all a-sprout with palms: and coral reefs and sands as white as milk. What is there now but a vast shambles of the heart? Filth, squalor, and a world of little men." Yet, having voiced the pain of change and the disillusionment of his time through Muzzlehatch, Peake at the end of the novel reaffirms his faith in human resilience and the chance of a fresh start.

Peake had plans to write many more Titus novels, as shown in the few pages of "Titus Awakes" that he left, which consist of a "preadventure" set in Gormenghast Castle, two pages that start with the last sentence of *Titus Alone,* and a potential cast of characters and list of encounters Titus might have. But Peake's illness had progressed to the point where his writing was impossible to read, and his concentration for all but drawing was greatly impaired. Gilmore valiantly crusaded on his behalf, promoting him, sorting through his great store of unpublished pieces (written and drawn in a variety of genres) for works to bring out, and getting him to illustrate *The Rhyme of the Flying Bomb* (1962), a poem he had written in 1949. The illustrations are roughly blocked in, as compared to his earlier fine draftsmanship, but they are eerily effective considering the atmosphere of the Blitz conveyed in the poem. His poems continued to appear, and Gilmore had two of his fantastic stories, "Same Time, Same Place" and "Danse Macabre," published in 1963 in consecutive issues of *Science Fantasy,* championed by Michael Moorcock. A major influence in bringing Peake to wider critical notice, Moorcock also recruited Jones to reedit the manuscripts of *Titus Alone.*

"Same Time, Same Place" is not dated; "Danse Macabre" was written in 1954. The former has a protagonist who needs to break free of his seedy household. He chooses love as his vehicle, engaging in a clandestine, passionate romance with a girl curiously immobile on her chair, a dehumanizing technique Peake uses repeatedly. The young man agrees to marry the girl, but then he discovers that she is a dwarf and her friends are figures from a carnival. He runs back to the home he has so recently rejected, returning to childish dependence in what amounts to psychic suicide. In this story Peake criticizes the failure of marriage and the family and the deadening rut of relationships. The fantastic is present in the zoomorphic figures he injects into the story.

"Danse Macabre" was originally told around a fireside on Boxing Day (26 December), a traditional time for telling ghost stories in Britain. It also has failed adult relationships as its theme, involving a couple who hurt each other, and their clothes, which want to stay together. Batchelor compares Peake's use of everyday details with that of M. R. James and the narrator's mental state with those of Edgar Allan Poe's narrators. Upset at the separation from his wife and unsettled by what is happening to his possessed clothes, which he finds entangled with hers, the narrator becomes increas-

ingly hollow, as does his wife; the clothes embody all of the passion that the people no longer feel. The image of the clothes and their fierce desire to kill the humans who stand in their way is visually disturbing, particularly as they represent a force stronger than the individual, and the ending of the story is suitably eerie: "We were both dead."

Peake's reputation toward the end of his life was growing, even as critics placed him outside the mainstream. He went through shock treatments and frequent hospitalizations, including brain surgery in 1960, to help correct the ever-increasing tremors that were affecting his physical ability to work. His ability to draw remained the longest, but the depredations of his illness robbed him of memory and language except in rare moments. He spent the last four years of his life in private hospitals; his wife writes of his final years in her moving biography, *A World Away* (1970).

Peake died on 17 November 1968, when new markets for fantasy were opening up; he was becoming something of a cult figure; and the acknowledgment of his creative achievements as a writer was increasing. The Titus books were republished in both Britain and the United States in hardback in 1967 and paperback in 1968, along with some of the sketches from the manuscripts, now at University College, London. Reprints came out steadily through the 1970s, and there were translations of the novels into various foreign languages. In 1979 his wife published *Peake's Progress,* collecting plays, poems, early prose, drawings, and short stories into one volume. The books Peake had illustrated also were reprinted in the 1970s, and in 1983 his hitherto unpublished *Sketches for Bleak House* appeared. In 1988 the Overlook Press brought out new American editions of the Titus books, marking the first time that the second edition of *Titus Alone* or "Titus Awakes," attached to the *Titus Alone* volume with an introduction by John Watney, had come out independently in the United States. Also included in the volume is a section titled "Critical Assessments," for which G. Peter Winnington wrote a critical introduction on the reception of the novels and collected twelve previously published papers on the novels. He also edited *Peake Studies,* a journal he published every six months. The Mervyn Peake Society in Britain published a volume of critical essays, *Peake Papers* (1994), further enhancing scholarship on this increasingly important though controversial author. (In 1977 forty-three critics had listed him in both categories of "most underrated" and "most overrated authors since 1902.")

While categorizing Peake's novels remains problematic, and readers either love them or cannot get through them, he has finally gained recognition as a significant writer and illustrator of his time. In a 24 October 1943 letter he sent to his lifelong friend Smith, Peake wrote, "I want to create between two covers a world, the movements of which—in action, atmosphere and speech—enthrall and excite the imagination." In this endeavor, he was successful.

Bibliography:

Dee Berkeley and G. Peter Winnington, "Peake in Print: A Bibliographical Checklist," *Mervyn Peake Review,* 13 (Autumn 1981): 8–35; 14 (Spring 1982): 15–35.

Biographies:

Maeve Gilmore, *A World Away: A Memoir of Mervyn Peake* (London: Gollancz, 1970);

John Watney, *Mervyn Peake* (London: Joseph, 1976);

Gordon Smith, *Mervyn Peake: A Personal Memoir* (London: Gollancz, 1984);

Sebastian Peake, *A Child of Bliss: Growing Up with Mervyn Peake* (Oxford: Lennard, 1989);

Malcolm Yorke, *Mervyn Peake: My Eyes Mint Gold, a Life* (London: Murray, 2000);

G. Peter Winnington, *Vast Alchemies: The Life and Work of Mervyn Peake* (London: Peter Owen, 2000).

References:

John Batchelor, *Mervyn Peake: A Biographical and Critical Exploration* (London: Duckworth, 1974);

Ronald Binns, "Mervyn Peake: Situating Gormenghast," *Critical Quarterly,* no. 21 (Spring 1979): 21–33;

Hugh Brogan, "The Gutters of Gormenghast," *Cambridge Review,* 95 (23 November 1973): 38–42; reprinted in *Mervyn Peake Review,* no. 18 (Spring 1984): 8–17;

Tanya Gardiner-Scott, *Mervyn Peake: The Evolution of a Dark Romantic* (New York: Peter Lang, 1989);

Gardiner-Scott, "'These Varying Voices': The Shorter Fiction of Mervyn Peake," in *Peake Papers 1994* (London: Mervyn Peake Society, 1994), pp. 17–33;

Colin Greenland, "From Beowulf to Kafka: Mervyn Peake's *Titus Alone,*" *Foundation,* no. 21 (1981);

Rob Hindle, "'Something of a Holocaust': The Titus Novels and the Second World War," in *Peake Papers 1994* (London: Mervyn Peake Society, 1994), pp. 127–141;

Bruce Hunt, "Psychology of the Bildungsroman," *Mervyn Peake Review,* no. 6 (Spring 1978): 10–17;

Rosemary Jackson, *Fantasy: The Literature of Subversion* (London: Methuen, 1981);

Sally Jacquelin, "Gormenghast: The Construction of a Body of Maternal Images," in *Peake Papers 1994* (London: Mervyn Peake Society, 1994), pp. 97–110;

Pierre-Yves Le Cam, "Gormenghast, A Gothic World?" in *Peake Papers 1994* (London: Mervyn Peake Society, 1994), pp. 111–125;

Edmund Little, *The Fantasts: Studies in J. R. R. Tolkien, Lewis Carroll, Mervyn Peake, Nicolay Gogol and Kenneth Grahame* (Amersham: Avebury, 1984), pp. 54–73;

Colin Manlove, *The Impulse of Fantasy Literature* (Kent, Ohio: Kent State University Press, 1983), pp. 115–126;

Manlove, *Modern Fantasy: Five Studies* (Cambridge: Cambridge University Press, 1973), pp. 207–257;

Mark McGuiness, "Gormenghast and Beyond: The Centre of Imaginative Gravity in Mervyn Peake's Titus Books," in *Peake Papers 1994* (London: Mervyn Peake Society, 1994), pp. 83–95;

Margaret Ochocki, "*Gormenghast:* Fairytale Gone Wrong?" *Mervyn Peake Review,* no. 15 (Autumn 1982): 11–17;

David Punter, *The Literature of Terror: A History of Gothic Fictions from 1765 to the Present Day* (London: Longman, 1980), pp. 373–380;

Cristiano Rafanelli, "Titus and the Thing in *Gormenghast,*" *Mervyn Peake Review,* no. 3 (Autumn 1976): 15–20;

Joseph Sanders, "The Passions in the Clay: Mervyn Peake's Titus Stories," in *Voices for the Future,* edited by Thomas D. Clareson (Bowling Green, Ohio: Bowling Green State University Popular Press, 1984), pp. 75–105;

Ann Yeoman, "'Arabesque in Motion': The Dreamscape of Gormenghast," *Peake Studies,* 4, no. 1 (Winter 1994): 7–24;

Yeoman, "The Cry of a Fighting Cock: Notes on Steerpike and Ritual in *Gormenghast,*" in Peake's *Titus Alone,* edited by G. Peter Winnington (London: Penguin, 1981), pp. 322–331.

Papers:

The D. M. S. Watson Library of University College, London, has the manuscripts of Mervyn Peake's Titus novels. Microfilms are also available. The Imperial War Museum in London, the Bodleian Library at Oxford, and the Berg Collection at the New York Public Library have additional Peake letters and manuscripts.

John Cowper Powys

(8 October 1872 – 17 June 1963)

Maureen F. Moran
Brunel University, London

See also the Powys entry in *DLB 15: British Novelists, 1930–1959.*

BOOKS: *Odes and Other Poems* (London: Rider, 1896);

Poems (London: Rider, 1899);

The War and Culture: A Reply to Professor Münsterberg (New York: G. Arnold Shaw, 1914); republished as *The Menace of German Culture: A Reply to Professor Münsterberg* (London: Rider, 1915); republished under original title (London: Village Press, 1975);

Visions and Revisions: A Book of Literary Devotions (New York: G. Arnold Shaw, 1915; London: Rider, 1915); republished with a new introduction by Powys (London: Macdonald, 1955);

Wood and Stone: A Romance (New York: G. Arnold Shaw, 1915; London: Heinemann, 1917);

Confessions of Two Brothers, by Powys and Llewelyn Powys (Rochester, N.Y.: Manas Press, 1916; London: Sinclair Browne, 1982);

Wolf's-Bane: Rhymes (New York: G. Arnold Shaw, 1916; London: Rider, 1916);

One Hundred Best Books, with Commentary and an Essay on Books and Reading (New York: G. Arnold Shaw, 1916; London: Village Press, 1975);

Rodmoor: A Romance (New York: G. Arnold Shaw, 1916; London: Macdonald, 1973);

Suspended Judgments: Essays on Books and Sensations (New York: G. Arnold Shaw, 1916); republished as *Suspended Judgements: Essays on Books and Sensations* (London: Village Press, 1975);

Mandragora: Poems (New York: G. Arnold Shaw, 1917; London: Village Press, 1975);

The Complex Vision (New York: Dodd, Mead, 1920; London: Village Press, 1975);

Samphire: Poems (New York: Seltzer, 1922; London: Village Press, 1975);

The Art of Happiness, Little Blue Books, no. 414 (Girard, Kans.: Haldeman-Julius, 1923; London: Village Press, 1974);

John Cowper Powys, circa 1920

Psychoanalysis and Morality (San Francisco: Jessica Colbert, 1923; London: Village Press, 1975);

Ducdame (Garden City, N.Y.: Doubleday, Page, 1925; London: Richards, 1925);

The Religion of a Sceptic (New York: Dodd, Mead, 1925; London: Village Press, 1974);

The Secret of Self-Development, Little Blue Books, no. 112 (Girard, Kans.: Haldeman-Julius, 1926; London: Village Press, 1974);

The Art of Forgetting the Unpleasant, Little Blue Books, no. 1264 (Girard, Kans.: Haldeman-Julius, 1928; London: Village Press, 1974);

Wolf Solent, 2 volumes (New York: Simon & Schuster, 1929; London: Cape, 1929);

The Meaning of Culture (New York: Norton, 1929; London: Cape, 1930; enlarged edition, New York: Norton, 1939; London: Cape, 1939);

Debate! Is Modern Marriage a Failure? by Powys and Bertrand Russell (New York: Discussion Guild, 1930; North Walsham, Norfolk: Warren House Press, 1983);

The Owl, the Duck, and–Miss Rowe! Miss Rowe! (Chicago: Black Archer Press for William Targ, 1930; London: Village Press, 1975);

In Defence of Sensuality (New York: Simon & Schuster, 1930; London: Gollancz, 1930);

Dorothy M. Richardson (London: Joiner & Steele, 1931);

A Glastonbury Romance (New York: Simon & Schuster, 1932; London: John Lane, 1933);

A Philosophy of Solitude (New York: Simon & Schuster, 1933; London: Cape, 1933);

Weymouth Sands (New York: Simon & Schuster, 1934; revised as *Jobber Skald* (London: John Lane, 1935); original version republished (London: Macdonald, 1963);

Autobiography (New York: Simon & Schuster, 1934; London: John Lane, 1934);

The Art of Happiness (New York: Simon & Schuster, 1935; London: John Lane, 1935);

Maiden Castle (New York: Simon & Schuster, 1936; London: Cassell, 1937); unabridged edition, edited by Ian Hughes (Cardiff: University of Wales Press, 1990);

Morwyn; or, The Vengeance of God (London: Cassell, 1937);

The Enjoyment of Literature (New York: Simon & Schuster, 1938); revised as *The Pleasures of Literature* (London: Cassell, 1938);

Owen Glendower: A Historical Novel (2 volumes, New York: Simon & Schuster, 1940; 1 volume, London: John Lane, 1942);

Mortal Strife (London: Cape, 1942);

The Art of Growing Old (London: Cape, 1944);

Dostoievsky (London: John Lane, 1947);

Obstinate Cymric: Essays 1935–1947 (Carmarthen: Druid Press, 1947);

Rabelais: His Life, The Story Told by Him, Selections Therefrom Here Newly Translated, and an Interpretation of His Genius and His Religion (London: John Lane, 1948; New York: Philosophical Library, 1951);

Porius: A Romance of the Dark Ages (London: Macdonald, 1951; New York: Philosophical Library, 1952); unabridged edition, edited by Wilbur T. Albrecht (Hamilton, N.Y.: Colgate University Press, 1995);

The Inmates (London: Macdonald, 1952; New York: Philosophical Library, 1952);

In Spite of: A Philosophy for Everyman (London: Macdonald, 1953; New York: Philosophical Library, 1953);

Atlantis (London: Macdonald, 1954);

Lucifer: A Poem (London: Macdonald, 1956);

The Brazen Head (London: Macdonald, 1956);

Up and Out (London: Macdonald, 1957);

Homer and the Aether (London: Macdonald, 1959);

All or Nothing (London: Macdonald, 1960);

John Cowper Powys: A Selection from His Poems, edited by Kenneth Hopkins (London: Macdonald, 1964; Hamilton, N.Y.: Colgate University Press, 1964);

Real Wraiths (London: Village Press, 1974);

Romer Mowl and Other Stories, edited by Bernard Jones (St. Peter Port, Guernsey: Toucan Press, 1974);

Two and Two (London: Village Press, 1974);

You and Me (London: Village Press, 1975);

After My Fashion (London: Pan, 1980);

Paddock Calls: A Play, introduction by Charles Lock (London: Greymitre, 1984);

Three Fantasies, afterword by Glen Cavaliero (Manchester: Carcanet Press, 1985);

Horned Poppies: New Poems (North Walsham: Warren House Press, 1986);

The Diary of John Cowper Powys, 1930, edited by Frederick Davies (London: Greymitre, 1987);

Singular Figures: Six Lectures, edited by Paul Roberts (Colchester: Footprint Press, 1989);

The Diary of John Cowper Powys, 1931 (London: Jeffrey Kwintner, 1990);

Elusive America, volume 1 of *The Uncollected Essays of John Cowper Powys,* edited by Roberts (London: Cecil Woolf, 1994);

Petrushka and the Dance: The Diaries of John Cowper Powys, 1929–1939, edited by Morine Krissdóttir (Manchester: Carcanet Press, 1995);

The Dorset Year: The Diary of John Cowper Powys, June 1934–July 1935, edited by Krissdóttir and Roger Peers (Bath: Powys Press, 1998).

PLAY PRODUCTION: *The Idiot,* adapted by Powys and Reginald Pole from the novel by Fyodor Dostoevsky, New York, Republic Theater, 7 April 1922.

SELECTED PERIODICAL PUBLICATION–UNCOLLECTED: "Shillyshally," *Between Worlds: An International Magazine of Creativity,* 1 (Spring–Summer 1961): 205–213.

In keeping with the value he placed on the private imagination and a sense of individuality, John Cowper

Phyllis Playter in 1929. A writer, she was Powys's companion from 1921 until his death.

Powys holds a unique place in British fantasy and science-fiction literature. His published output spans novels, fantasy fables and stories, autobiography, literary criticism, popularizations of his philosophy, poetry, diaries, letters, book reviews, and appreciations. His early literary reputation was based on his philosophical and critical essays, which were attractive to the "common man" and capitalized on his prominence as an inspirational public lecturer in the United States. But Powys is remembered today primarily for his fiction, much of it ostensibly in the realist mode, in which he embeds macabre and fantastic elements such as apparitions, magician seers, mythic archetypes, giants, fairies, and miraculous events. His vision of the universe is a dynamic, pluralistic one in which the inanimate, the sensual, and the spiritual or supernatural are fluidly integrated. The individual's creative energy—be it sexual or intellectual—and imaginative powers half create and half perceive this undifferentiated reality. To possess such a visionary imagination, one must reject a dualistic view of reality that separates body and soul, male and female, and good and evil. Set side by side

with the everyday, which he depicts in all its mundane, cruel, and even disgusting detail, the fantastic becomes just another dimension of the real. Receptiveness to it is often the key factor that impels Powys's central characters to acknowledge their subconscious inclinations, accept their weaknesses and strengths, and begin their journey to fulfillment and peace.

Critics tend to group Powys's fiction into three phases: the early romances and "Wessex quartet"; the historical epics combining myth, legend, and fantasy; and the final extravagant fables. All display a concern with the individual's divided consciousness, advocate a holistic vision of the spiritual and physical dimensions of life, and oppose cruelty and champion the downtrodden and the weak. But some thematic strands emerge only gradually: opposition to dogmatism; a concern with the exercise of power; an ability to accept the destructive and evil, as well as the creative, forces in human life; identification with the inanimate and elemental; and a spiritualized reveling in bodily sensation. Powys's later fiction develops the fantastic elements more overtly than do the early works, and his final fantasies eschew realism altogether in favor of child-like fables in which causality and plausibility give way to the episodic and irrational. These tales, however, continue to attack authoritarian absolutes, to delight in sensation and the physical cosmos, and to embrace the creative and the destructive, the sensual and the spiritual, and the subhuman and the supernatural as equally valid aspects of experience.

Powys was born in Shirley, Derbyshire, on 8 October 1872, the first of eleven children of the Reverend Charles Francis Powys and Mary Cowper Powys. Powys rejected his father's orthodox evangelical Christianity and Victorian patriarchal conservatism, but he says in his *Autobiography* (1934) that he was strongly influenced by his father's child-like simplicity, feeling of kinship with even the most humble aspects of the natural world, and ability to appreciate a quality "beyond normal reality" in all places and people. His mother, descended from the poets John Donne and William Cowper, passed on to her children a delight in literature, a morbid sensitivity, and a hatred of cruelty. Each child's individuality was nurtured, and two of them, in addition to John Cowper, became well-known writers: Theodore Francis, born in 1875, whose novels *Black Bryony* (1923) and *Mr. Weston's Good Wine* (1927) provide sharp allegories drawing on English village life; and Llewelyn, born in 1884, who is remembered for autobiographical works such as *Dorset Essays* (1935) and *Earth Memories* (1938).

In 1879 Powys's father became curate in Dorchester, Dorset; in 1885 he was appointed vicar in Montacute, Somerset. In his *Autobiography* Powys says that he first identified his "imaginative sensuality" and ambition to be a magician as a child in the Wessex countryside: "My head was always full of some fantastical transaction that broke up the normal world." For Powys, the essence of magical power is the capacity of each individual to create a private worldview. At the same time, he says, no one is ever truly alone: the imaginative energy of consciousness can project itself into an understanding of other entities, both human and nonhuman. To recognize this creative power of consciousness, he says in his *Autobiography*, "is synonymous with your being alive."

Powys was educated at Sherborne School in Somerset and at Corpus Christi College of Cambridge University, where he studied history. After graduating from the latter with a second-class B.A. in 1894, he taught English literature at girls' schools in Brighton and Eastbourne. In 1896 he published a small collection of largely undistinguished poems. That same year he married Margaret Alice Lyon, the sister of a Cambridge friend. Margaret Powys appears to have been an unassuming woman of largely conventional domestic interests, in striking contrast to Powys's flamboyant, self-dramatizing, and enthusiastic personality.

In 1898 Powys gave a sample lecture on Arthurian legend for the Oxford University Extension Committee, then offered a series of probationary lectures on Alfred Tennyson. In 1899 he was appointed an extension lecturer for the university and published a second volume of poetry. During the next ten years he also provided extension lectures for Cambridge University and the University of London on authors ranging from William Shakespeare to nineteenth-century English writers. His eloquence drew large audiences and resulted in invitations to set up lecture series in Dresden and Leipzig and to give lectures in Hamburg. In 1905 he made a successful lecture tour of the United States sponsored by the Society for the Extension of University Teaching in Philadelphia.

Powys and his wife had a son, Littleton Alfred Powys, in 1902 but separated a few years later. Powys says little about the relationship in his autobiography, but he provided financial support for his wife until her death in 1947 and spent time with his son each summer.

Throughout his life Powys suffered from gastric ulcers, and in 1909 he resigned his position as Oxford lecturer for reasons of health. That same year, however, he began a new career as a professional lecturer in the United States. No transcripts or recordings of his lectures exist, but recollections by Maurice Browne in his autobiography, *Too Late to Lament* (1955), and by Henry Miller in his *The Books in My Life* (1952) emphasize Powys's mesmeric power and common touch.

Speaking largely without notes, often to audiences of more than two thousand people for up to two hours, Powys endeavored to incorporate himself into the consciousness of the authors whose works he explicated. This imaginative sympathetic identification with other people, places, and things is the essential methodology of his fiction and accounts for its fantastic features.

The firm of his stage manager, G. Arnold Shaw, published many of Powys's early books, including the collection of critical essays *Visions and Revisions: A Book of Literary Devotions* (1915), the novels *Wood and Stone* (1915) and *Rodmoor* (1916), and poetry collections in 1916 and 1917. In these early novels competing worldviews are tested through characters or groups set in opposition to each other. Tensions are not well dramatized, the plots are static, and the characters are largely two-dimensional. Nonetheless, Powys makes clear his view that the critical life struggle for any individual is the need to resolve the opposition between the mystical and the materialistic interpretations of existence and between good and evil. Most of his early protagonists fail or are, at best, only partially successful in this quest. In *Wood and Stone* the opposition is figured in the struggle between the sadistic quarry-owning capitalists Mortimer Romer and his daughter, Gladys, and their powerless victims, particularly the sensitive stonemason James Anderson, whose inability to cope with the contending forces of love and power lead to his breakdown and suicide. In *Rodmoor* the writer Adrian Sorio moves from New York to the East Anglian village of the title, where he fails to reconcile the dualities typified by his two loves: the down-to-earth Nance Herrick and the perverse, dangerous Philippa Renshaw, who is both his intellectual soul mate and his temptress. Only the destruction of the self provides release from his divided consciousness, and he dies insane. In *After My Fashion*, written in 1919 but not published until 1980, Richard Storm, another New York writer, torn between two women in the United States and England, struggles to find a middle way between opposing modes of perception: the analytical and rational, associated with science, materialism, and masculinity, and the creative and synthesizing, associated with artistic vision, mystical ecstasy, and femininity.

In *The Complex Vision* (1920) Powys gives a systematic exposition of his philosophy. He emphasizes the need for introspection, which facilitates both an imaginative projection into the consciousness of others and a better understanding of the self. He advocates a Wordsworthian model of the imagination that creates the object it contemplates; it is the key faculty for eroding false oppositions and uniting the self with the not-self and for reaching beyond the material order to an invisible mystical reality. Paradoxically, though, Powys

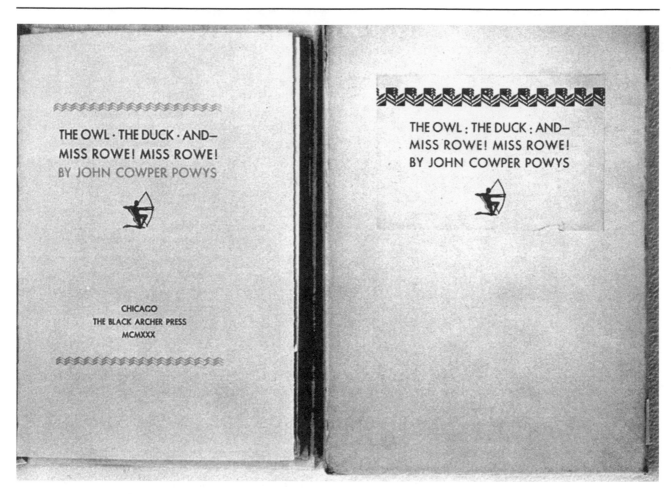

Title page and box for the limited edition of Powys's early fantasy story (from Dante Thomas,
A Bibliography of the Writings of John Cowper Powys: 1872–1963, *1975)*

asserts that an impenetrable mystery lies at the heart of every person, place, and object. True morality, he says, consists in maintaining this individuality in the face of all forms of oppression, whether scientific, emotional, political, or social.

Powys was romantically, if chastely, linked with several intelligent women during his years in the United States; among them was Frances Gregg, a friend of Ezra Pound's. On a lecture tour in 1921 he met Phyllis Playter, an aspiring writer from Kansas who was twenty-one years his junior. Immediately attracted to each other, they lived together until his death; Playter read and commented on drafts of his novels and suggested characters and plot developments. From 1923 to 1930 they resided in an apartment building at 4 Patchin Place in New York City in which E. E. Cummings also lived. But Powys's professional routine as a peripatetic lecturer made him a largely solitary figure. He was not part of any established literary circle; this isolation may explain the old-fashioned oratorical style and structure of his fiction, which owe more to medieval romances and panoramic nineteenth-century novels than to the spare experimental fiction of the early twentieth century. Nonetheless, his friends included Dreiser, whom he admired as a fellow "Magician" concerned with moral rather than aesthetic issues. Their relationship was an intense one; it was not homosexual—Powys always denied that he was homosexual—but was based, Powys wrote in his *Autobiography,* on a deep "magnetic attraction . . . due to the diffusion of some mysterious occult force through the material envelopes of our physical frames." Dreiser claimed that he once saw Powys's astral projection in New York City; Powys always refused to discuss the incident.

Powys's earliest novels include little that might be termed fantastic, but the unjustly neglected *Ducdame* (1925) is more confident and complex in its suggestions of dimensions beyond the here-and-now. It also establishes Powys's view that access to "the eternal vision" cannot be gained solely through the intellect. The dark mysterious forces of sensation and primordial nature must be accommodated; this is the realm of the Great Earth Mother, a symbol of the lost golden age when all dimensions of reality, including the invisible, were interrelated and immediately and intuitively accessible. Powys's protagonist, the Dorset squire Rook Ashover, lives in fear of the feminine principle and of the natural order with its imperatives of birth, death, and rebirth, which are in conflict with his masculine sense of order and duty. His preference is for the escapist "Cimmery Land" described by the elderly gypsy Betsy Cooper as a "dreamland where folks do live like unborn babies." He is unwisely drawn to the impersonality of this imaginary idealized country; for him, "real" nature is a disturbing force peopled by grotesques such as the idiot Binnory and Betsy's monstrous twin grandchildren. Rook, however, has a mystical meeting with his as yet unconceived son and, as a result, becomes reconciled to accepting a place in the natural order. Although he cannot sustain a relationship with a woman, he decides to produce an heir to carry on the family name. Powys's reservations about the adoption of such a stoic resignation to duty instead of a joyous commitment to a multilayered universe—or "multiverse," as Powys called it—can be seen in Rook's destruction: he dies as his son is born.

Powys's view of the physical universe as a living thing and his claim that one can escape a stifling social order by dwelling on the moments of intense creative insight when the soul glimpses "the eternal vision" was an appealing theory of liberation in the aftermath of World War I. It conveyed power and value on the individual, since, as Powys wrote in *The Meaning of Culture* (1929), "Not the wretchedest human being but has his share in the creative energy that builds the world." Powys's work was well received by reviewers in both the United States and Britain, and by the end of the 1920s his reputation as a stimulating popularizer was established. *The Meaning of Culture* was on the best-seller list for months.

Powys's next four novels have been termed the Wessex cycle. Set in the English West Country, they show a writer whose narrative and structural control have noticeably matured. Although only *A Glastonbury Romance* (1932) has significant elements of fantasy, all of the novels deal with the struggle of individuals to resolve internal tensions and to form relationships with other psyches who construct "reality" in different ways. A celebration of difference rather than an attempt to blend and erode contrasts emerges as a key theme. Oppositions abound between men and women, illusion and truth, nature and civilization, the animate and inanimate, the human and the nonhuman, and the disgusting and the sublime. Powys's chief concern in the Wessex cycle is to find a narrative

method that will enable him to accommodate these opposites and to evoke an imaginative response based on tolerance and acceptance.

In *Wolf Solent* (1929) the main struggle of the eponymous protagonist, a London history teacher who suddenly resigns and moves to the Wessex countryside, is to achieve a whole self, to accept that he is both body and soul, and to love the ugly and repugnant as well as the beautiful. Powys gives the reader access to the character's psyche at all levels, including his dreams, fantasies, and illusions, in order to depict his gradual fusion of self and increasing tolerance of other personalities. In the end Wolf reaches a calm, stoic understanding of himself and his connection to a wider natural order. As is increasingly typical of Powys's fiction, fantastically grotesque characters and subplots expose a dark side of human experience and indicate the diversity of human beings, all of whom are entitled to acceptance unless they are bent on sadistic cruelty. The physically disgusting, even the excremental, are legitimate parts of the universe. The four American and three English printings of *Wolf Solent* in its year of publication, as well as its 1930 and 1931 reprints, attest to its popularity.

In 1930 Powys ventured into fantasy by publishing a limited edition of a short story, *The Owl, the Duck, and—Miss Rowe! Miss Rowe!* Set in a location based loosely on his Patchin Place apartment, the piece displays his talent for depicting the interpenetration of spiritual and physical orders by combining realistic characters with a ghost, the fictional characters of a writer who formerly lived in the building, two divine beings, and some sentient inanimate objects.

With the royalties from *Wolf Solent* Powys was able to retire from lecturing; by then he had spoken in all but two states and had become a popular cult figure. He and Playter moved to Phudd Bottom, a farmhouse near Hillsdale in upstate New York, where he wrote the critical study *Dorothy M. Richardson* (1931), *A Glastonbury Romance, A Philosophy of Solitude* (1933), and his *Autobiography*.

A Glastonbury Romance presented a challenge to readers who had admired *Wolf Solent*. The novel is a vast panorama with many characters, representing various attitudes to the supernatural, some of whom make psychic contact with the spiritual energies underpinning the Arthurian myth. Symbols such as the Holy Grail suggest that links with a timeless collective psyche are possible. According to Powys's 1955 preface to the third printing of the novel, "Its message is that no one Receptacle of Life and no one Fountain of Life poured in that Receptacle can contain or explain what the world offers us." Set in the 1930s, the novel focuses on John "Bloody Johnny" Geard, the mystical mayor of

Glastonbury, who plans a revival of the religious spirit, "a new outburst of magic and miracle." Geard is in contact with the spirit of Merlin and is able to heal the sick and even bring the dead back to life. "Bloody Johnny's" power is that of simplicity of heart, compassion, and generosity. He is open to the victim, the outcast, and the repugnant. Those on his side, such as Sam Dekker, the vicar's son who leaves his mistress to serve the poor, show the same capacity to embrace the grotesque and the disgusting; for Sam this capacity is symbolized by his vision of the Grail, with its painful feeling of being pierced in the bowels from below by a spear. Opposed to Geard is Philip Crow, an industrialist from Norfolk who refuses to acknowledge the supernatural. Character types from the earlier novels are reworked, such as the repressed sadist, bookseller, and Merlin expert Owen Evans, akin to Brand Renshaw (*Rodmoor*) and Squire Urquhart (*Wolf Solvent*), and the androgynous Persephone Spear, a female Rook Ashover who is seeking escape from the dimension of fleshly sensation; these characters are linked by their self-destructive yearning for oblivion. The novel also includes types who recur in Powys's more mythological and fantastic later fiction: the elderly spinster here is one of the mad or rejected women who retain powerful ties to the primitive energy of the cosmos. Surprisingly, however, the selfless tolerance and compassion of the magus do not succeed unconditionally: while the mystical characters capture the reader's sympathy and seem to win the battle against the scientific-mechanistic spirit of the modern age, Geard dies in the flood that destroys Crow's industrial empire.

The many subplots, the absence of a convincing analysis of social and political realities, and the at times overwritten and mystical prose are barriers for many readers, but Powys's minute attention to physical detail, sympathy for every aspect of the cosmos, understanding of the individual psyche, and authoritative presentation of the manifestation in legend and mythic symbol of an archetypal cultural consciousness make the novel a major achievement. Fantasy and material reality are combined so that the everyday incorporates the supernatural, dramatizing the theme of "the presence of a *double world,* every motion and gesture in the first being a symbol of something that was taking place in the second."

Having worked on the novel for more than a year, Powys counted on royalties from it to sustain him financially; but the book was a commercial failure. According to Richard Heron Ward's *The Powys Brothers* (1935), some reviewers, such as J. D. Beresford, hailed the novel as a landmark in twentieth-century fiction, but others condemned its "erotic bunkum" and dismissed it as "pretentious and almost unbearably dull."

Only four thousand copies had been sold by August 1932; Powys's expected royalties of $3,000 totaled no more than $780. Moreover, threatened with litigation by a Glastonbury resident who believed that he had been libeled in the novel, Powys's publishers agreed to a settlement that gave the man all forthcoming royalties in lieu of damages.

In 1934 Powys returned to Britain with Playter. They settled briefly in Dorset and moved in 1935 to Corwen in Wales, the country of Powys's paternal ancestors. As a result of the legal problems he had encountered with *A Glastonbury Romance* Powys published *Weymouth Sands* (1934) in England as *Jobber Skald* (1935), the name of the main character, disguising the setting with fictitious place-names. Neither this novel nor the final one in the Wessex cycle, *Maiden Castle* (1936), can be termed fantasies, although both portray a mystical dimension that is perceived as a living reality by the imagination or the subconscious.

Weymouth Sands concerns several lonely characters who fail in their personal relationships. Their inability to project themselves imaginatively and sympathetically into the minds and feelings of others is the source of cruelty, disillusionment, and oppression. Powys continues to assert the existence of a spiritual order "dimly visible" past "our existing world of forms and impressions." Places of marginality, such as the sand linking the sea with the dry land, are important symbols of this double dimension. In *Maiden Castle* the story of the repressed and overly spiritualized Dud No-Man, as he named himself on learning of his illegitimacy, has two main strands: his unconsummated love for and abandonment by the circus girl Wizzie Ravelston, whom he "buys" from her brutal employer, and his discovery of the father he never knew: the Welsh eccentric and magus figure named Uryen Quirm, who seeks to make contact with the ancient supernatural powers that were once worshiped at the earthwork Maiden Castle near Dorchester. The full text of the novel was published for the first time in 1990, restoring Powys's thematic elaborations, additional authorial reflections, and passages of philosophical debate that provide a coherent argument for the multidimensional nature of the cosmos.

From this point Powys moved to fiction that establishes a self-contained fantasy world. *Morwyn; or, The Vengeance of God* (1937), an attack on vivisection, draws on Dante's *Inferno* and other myths of the underworld to describe a journey to hell. The narrator, his dog, a Welsh girl named Morwyn, and her vivisectionist father are cast into the earth by a meteorite and descend through its various levels. Morwyn's father, who is killed in the initial fall, continues to accompany the group in the form of a spirit. He finds himself in suitable company, for Powys's hell is reserved for the

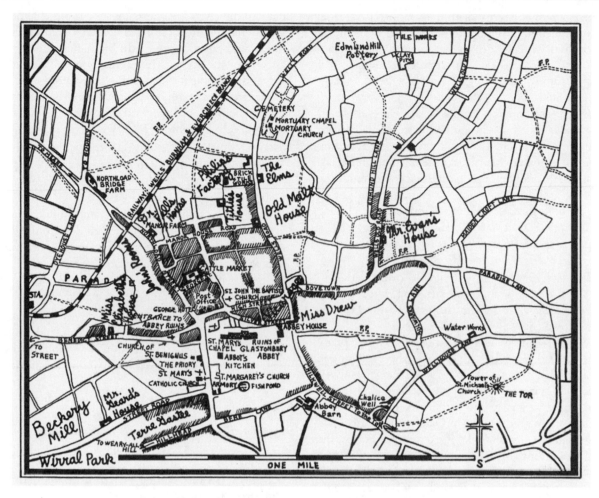

Map, with notations by Powys, of the setting for his 1932 novel, A Glastonbury Romance *(from Dante Thomas,*
A Bibliography of the Writings of John Cowper Powys: 1872–1963, *1975)*

cruel and oppressive. Famous sadists, such as Nero, the Marquis de Sade, and Tomás de Torquemada, inhabit the first level. The next level is a primeval stench-ridden abyss where two sea monsters do perpetual destructive battle. They represent science and religion, evil institutions united in their reliance on torture (in the case of science, torture of animals in experiments) to secure and assert "the truth." Below this level is a realm where the ancient god Cronos, or Saturn, sleeps with the Great Earth Mother, awaiting the advent of a new golden age. For Powys the eternal vision lies below the dark abyss of evil, which must not be avoided but must be crossed through the exercise of selflessness and compassion, whatever the cost. Suffering becomes a positive path to the fourth dimension of reality; the victim is the true inheritor of Saturn's new kingdom. As the group escapes, led to the surface by Socrates, the narrator has a vision of François Rabelais, who explains that God is an immanent as well as a transcendent force but is found only "wherever a man refuses to do evil that

good may come, wherever a man is merciful and pitiful *even unto his hurt.*" Finally, Morwyn goes to the United States to preach antivivisectionism; she is accompanied by Black Peter, the dog. The narrator returns to Wales.

The romantic battle of the human consciousness to reach such mystical understanding is the theme of the historical novel *Owen Glendower* (1940). The title character is the real-life fifteenth-century Welsh rebel who attempted to overthrow the English rulers of his country. In the novel Glendower has psychic gifts that he uses to release his soul from the material world whenever he wishes, but he never becomes a magus who can surrender the self and obliterate duality and difference. He chooses to preserve his independent identity, with tragic results: his desire to prove his control over his soul makes him hold back from pressing his advantage over the English, and he and his followers are destroyed by the unimaginative men of action. Though he is defeated, he becomes a legend and an inspiration to his people, and at his death his spirit becomes a living energy within the very landscape. Powys's depiction of the minute particulars of medieval life combines with the archetypal imagery and mythological texture of the novel to reinforce the sense of another reality transcending the everyday world of sensation and linking past to present.

In Wales, Powys was almost a recluse, addicted to long walks and raw eggs, olive oil, and milk, which he drank for his ulcer. Though frequently in agonizing pain, he was always cheerful, courteous, and enthusiastic about the minutiae of daily existence and about the lives of his visitors. In addition to fiction, he produced books of philosophy and literary criticism, including *Dostoievsky* (1947) and *Rabelais: His Life, The Story Told by Him, Selections Therefrom Here Newly Translated, and an Interpretation of His Genius and His Religion* (1948).

Powys's new departure into historical fiction in *Owen Glendower* was followed in 1951 by *Porius: A Romance of the Dark Ages*. At the time it was Powys's favorite novel, but it was given a mixed reception by critics. In part, this reaction stemmed from the many cuts Powys had to make to find a publisher, resulting in a narrative that is disjointed and lacks direction. Even in this abbreviated form the novel is verbose: the printed version runs to more than six hundred pages but deals only with the week in October 499 when Saxons invaded the British Vale of Edeyrnion. Porius, the heir of the ruling British family in the Vale, is part Roman, part Celt, and related to the aboriginal giant people; he rejects imposed orthodox Christian dogma and admires the heretic Pelagius. Another alternative perspective is provided by the primitive "forest people," a matriarchal society that worships the Earth Mother. The elderly "Three Aunties," the last in the royal line of the forest people, foster a tragic alliance with the Saxons. A more effective medium for the mystical powers of the feminine principle is Myrrdin Wyllt, or Merlin, the most fully developed magus in Powys's fiction and quite different from the legendary figure–as are most other members of the Arthurian court in the novel. Ugly, disheveled, and smelling of fungus, he is a channel to the earth in its animate and vegetative manifestations and a medium with connections to the primitive past and the supernatural. He has magical powers, but his real strength lies in his ability to find these powers in the weak and discarded, in selfless love, and in the earthly animalism of human beings: "What the world wants is more common-sense, more kindness, more indulgence, more leaving people alone," he says. Porius's release of Myrrdin Wyllt from his imprisonment by Nineue in the rocks of Snowdon promises hope for "innumerable weak and terrified and unbeautiful and unconsidered and unprotected creatures" through the banishment of imperial power, "a world of blind authority." This heroic rescue is possible because Porius has learned to share Merlin's commitment to humanity's roots in the earth: by mating with a female Giant, he has renewed his connections with the primeval and the pagan. Touching the numinous that is immanent in the physical gives him the strength to accept solitude; to forget sorrow, tragedy, and cruelty; to endure, to be content, and even to enjoy.

The unabridged version of the novel, published in 1995, does not significantly alter the plot or the range of characters. But it does reinforce Powys's vision of a material reality interpenetrated by the marvelous. The characters are more fully drawn, and motivations and action, including fantastic sequences that troubled early reviewers, are more clearly explained. *Porius* in its entirety makes an even more persuasive case for Powys's view of a world in which natural and supernatural elements coexist and are of equal significance.

The fiction of Powys's final years increasingly takes the form of fairy tale and fable. The plots, such as they are, draw less and less on recognizable places and social situations and increasingly on mythic stories and science-fiction scenarios and conventions. The language becomes simple and often humorous; the action is episodic and often implausible; and the characters are broadly sketched, with little representation of their reflective processes. The complex, fantastic plots and the oblique and rambling style of these late works were out of joint with the then-current taste for naturalistic and strongly focused fiction, and they were not well received by the reading public.

In *The Inmates* (1952) John Hush, a sexual fetishist confined to a mental hospital, plans to use a helicopter to free his fellow inmates; the novel illustrates Powys's view that those who wield power are less sane than those they categorize as "mad." *Atlantis* (1954), which replaced *Porius* as Powys's favorite among his books, had a mixed critical reception like the earlier work, and for similar reasons. Some critics found it fey and arch, while others read its blend of myth, philosophy, and fantastic invention as an eloquent homage to the multiverse. The elderly Odysseus, bored at home, visits the lost continent of Atlantis; overthrows its hideous ruler, who represents the false scientific spirit that would dissect and destroy purely out of curiosity; then goes on to America. The amusing anthropomorphizing of animals and inanimate objects dramatizes Powys's belief in the interrelationship of all entities in a living, dynamic cosmos. The novel also offers advice on obtaining personal fulfillment in the form of the gradual illumination that comes to Zeuks, the irreverent farmer and reputed son of Pan, who sees that resignation to life's tragedies and surrender to life's delightfulness are equally important.

Powys's son, who had become an Anglican, then a Catholic, priest, died in a motorcycle accident in 1954. In 1955 Powys and Playter moved to another Welsh town, Blaenau Ffestiniog. Powys's next novel, *The Brazen Head* (1956), returns to the Middle Ages to make many of the same thematic points as *Atlantis* and *The Inmates*. Roger Bacon, portrayed here as a scientist, magician, and heretic, has been exiled to an isolated monastery, where he fashions a brass head to produce oracular prophecies. St. Bonaventura and Peter Peregrinus, an evil soldier of fortune and alchemist, set out to defeat him and gain power for themselves. Sexual energy plays an important role in the work: the genitalia of the virgin Ghosta enliven the prophetic powers of the head, while Peter Peregrinus's destructive magical lodestone must be in contact with his genitals to function. While the plot is fantastic, the novel is pointedly satiric in its caricatures of righteous dogmatic clerics and sets up a valid contrast between wholesome scientific endeavor, on the one hand, and sinister curiosity and rigid orthodoxy, on the other. *The Brazen Head* also once again emphasizes the invisible psychic reality that embodies and links "all that exists, whether super-human, human, or sub-human, whether organic or inorganic."

Powys's final fantasies are far more surrealistic and extravagant in their implausibilities, arbitrary situations, and capricious non sequiturs and were not generally understood. They rest on the assumption that human beings, gods, devils, fairy-tale archetypes, and even abstract concepts all exist on an equal footing. In some of the works the characters engage in space travel in which they penetrate the very limits of the cosmos.

Up and Out (1957) is made up of two lengthy short stories. In the title work two couples, survivors of the world's destruction by nuclear holocaust, wander in space, have philosophical discussions, and encounter Time (a slug), Eternity (a nasty fog), God, and the devil. The work is uncharacteristically nihilistic for Powys: at the end the four earthlings, God, and the devil leap into the abyss of space and destroy themselves. "The Mountains of the Moon: A Lunar Love Story" is a more coherent tale in which the moon is peopled by intuitive creatures with intense inner lives. The plot concerns the search of Lod Zed's children, Rorlt and Lorlt, for suitable mates. Such a partnership represents a complete self, with both sexual and cerebral faculties accommodated and accepted.

Powys received an award from the Freie Akademie der Künste (Free Academy of the Arts) in Hamburg in July 1958. In 1959 he published *Homer and the Aether,* a loose translation of and commentary on *The Iliad*. The text, which gives much greater insight into Powys's thinking than into Homer's epic, is noteworthy

Powys's two-volume 1940 novel, about a fifteenth-century Welsh rebel leader with psychic powers, in its original box (from Dante Thomas, A Bibliography of the Writings of John Cowper Powys: 1872–1963, *1975)*

for its reaffirmation of the power of the imagination to project consciousness even into the inanimate and to comprehend the life energy in all other beings.

Elements of crude farce and stilted, childish dialogue render *All or Nothing* (1960) unpalatable to many readers. Once again, a quartet wanders in space: this time it consists of the twins John o'Dreams and Jill Tewky and the giant Urk's children, Ring and Ting. The young people visit the sun, and John kills Urk to keep him from devouring it; journey to Vindex, a star in the Milky Way, where they find the sexually potent Cerne Giant; and create a new star dedicated to the ancient British queen Boadicea, who represents matriarchy and the wisdom of feminine principles. Just as consciousness incorporates both creative and destructive urges, Powys shows, all of existence holds the same opposites in a productive tension—as is symbolized in the novel by the Fountain of Bubble and Squeak, with its ephemeral empty bubble, representing nothingness, and its squeaking skull, which urges life out of death.

The All of creation includes the Nothing out of which it comes and to which it finally tends.

In 1962 Powys received an honorary Litt.D. from the University of Wales and ninetieth-birthday tributes on the British Broadcasting Company Welsh Home Service and in magazines and newspapers. He died on 17 June 1963 in the Blaenau hospital. While some prominent writers and critics, such as George Steiner and Angus Wilson, asserted his importance, and translations of his works appeared in France, Germany, and India, at his death most of his work was out of print, and his reputation among academics and general readers was mixed. To some he had the status of a cult artist-actor-priest; to others he was a muddled thinker with ill-controlled verbosity. His obituary notices suggest the range of opinion about him: *The Times* (London) called him "rich and versatile," and *The Scotsman* praised him as an "author, philosopher and poet," but the *Daily Herald* summarized his philosophy as "laziness—his key to happiness." Perhaps the most objective analysis was provided by *The Sunday Telegraph*, which assessed him as a "great individualist."

More late fantasies were published after Powys's death; for the most part they are slighter than those that appeared during his lifetime but retain his colloquial and slangy style, childish humor, dislike of brutality, and use of space travel as an allegory for the imaginative journey to wisdom. *Real Wraiths* (1974) puts four ghosts in the company of a group of unlikely "underworld" disputants, such as Pluto and the devil; *Two and Two* (1974) follows the magician Wat Kums on his journey through space in search of knowledge; and *You and Me* (1975) explores the nature of love using a childish, nursery tale format. *Three Fantasies* (1985) comprises three short stories. "Topsy-Turvy" animates the furnishings of Powys's Blaenau Ffestiniog room and sends the spirits of two of them—Topsy, a drawing, and Turvy, the door handle—to a spiritual dimension to converse with the irascible, somewhat silly ghosts of writers such as Walt Whitman and legendary figures such as Dido and Aeneas. The first part of "Abertackle" is a mocking fantasy of village life peopled by ridiculous characters, such as Squire Neverbang, Lady Wow, and Ooly-Fooly, who take free love, incest, and tea parties equally seriously; in the second part, one character explores outer space, identifies the devil with Hate, and discovers that he is a mere invention and can thus be eliminated. "Cataclysm" begins by attacking vivisectionists but quickly mimics "Up and Out" with an apocalyptic space journey undertaken by the heroic free spirit Auntie Zoo-Zoo and her friend Ve Zed into various universes; at the end they are eaten by the giant Gyges.

Powys's concept of the multiverse, with its intermingled dimensions of the physical and the spiritual, challenges traditional dualistic modes of thought. Moreover, the value he places on the psyche as the source of creative dreams and fantasies is a counterbalance to the Freudian view of the unconscious as threatening and of fantasy as expressing unhealthy repressed impulses. For Powys, the excremental and the sacramental are equally valid; convention and orthodoxy teach otherwise, and the imposition of such externally derived values is to be resisted. Tragedy and cruelty stem from abuse of power, whether social, physical, sexual, or intellectual. Powys's message is that one should oppose this domination of the individual, the seat of reality: defy the absolute, forget the painful past, accept one's own nature, and enjoy the affirmation of life.

Letters:

Letters of John Cowper Powys to Louis Wilkinson: 1935–1956, edited by Louis Wilkinson (London: Macdonald, 1958);

Letters to Glyn Hughes, edited by Bernard Jones (Stevenage: Ore, 1971);

Letters to Nicholas Ross, selected by Nicholas and Adelaide Ross, edited by Arthur Uphill (London: Rota, 1971);

Letters 1937–54, edited by Iorwerth Peate (Cardiff: University of Wales Press, 1974);

Letters from John Cowper Powys to C. Benson Roberts, edited by C. Benson Roberts (London: Village Press, 1975);

Letters of John Cowper Powys to His Brother Llewelyn, volume 1, edited by Malcolm Elwin (London: Village Press, 1975);

Letters to Clifford Tolchard from John Cowper Powys, edited by Clifford Tolchard (London: Village Press, 1975);

The Letters of John Cowper Powys to G. R. Wilson Knight, edited by Robert Blackmore (London: Cecil Woolf, 1983);

Letters of John Cowper Powys to Sven-Erik Täckmark, edited by Cedric Hentschel (London: Cecil Woolf, 1983);

Powys to a Japanese Friend: The Letters of John Cowper Powys to Ichiro Hara, edited by Anthony Head (London: Cecil Woolf, 1989);

The Letters of John Cowper Powys to Hal W. and Violet Trovillion, edited by Paul Roberts (London: Cecil Woolf, 1990);

The Letters of John Cowper Powys to Frances Gregg, volume 1, edited by Oliver Marlow Wilkinson and Christopher Wilkinson (London: Cecil Woolf, 1994);

The Letters of John Cowper Powys to Glyn Hughes, edited by Frank Warren (London: Cecil Woolf, 1994).

Bibliographies:

Lloyd E. Siberell, *A Bibliography of the First Editions of John Cowper Powys* (Cincinnati: Ailanthus Press, 1934);

Derek Langridge, *John Cowper Powys: A Record of Achievement* (London: Library Association, 1966);

Dante Thomas, *A Bibliography of the Writings of John Cowper Powys: 1872–1963* (Mamaroneck, N.Y.: P. P. Appel, 1975).

Biographies:

Louis Wilkinson, *Welsh Ambassadors* (London: Chapman & Hall, 1936);

Wilkinson, *The Brothers Powys* (Cincinnati: Auburncrest Library, 1947);

Wilkinson, *Seven Friends* (London: Richards, 1953);

Kenneth Hopkins, *The Powys Brothers: A Biographical Appreciation* (London: Phoenix House, 1967);

Belinda Humfrey, ed., *Recollections of the Powys Brothers: Llewelyn, Theodore and John Cowper Powys* (London: Peter Owen, 1980);

Alan Howc, *John Cowper Powys, Theodore Francis Powys, Llewelyn Powys: A Reader's Guide and Checklist of the Principal Writings of the Powys Family* (Bath: Powys Society, 1991).

References:

Joe Boulter, *Postmodern Powys: Essays on John Cowper Powys* (Kidderminster: Crescent Moon, 2000);

Richard Breckon, *John Cowper Powys–the Solitary Giant* (London: Village Press, 1973);

Maurice Brown, *Too Late to Lament* (London: Gollancz, 1955);

Glen Cavaliero, *John Cowper Powys: Novelist* (Oxford: Oxford University Press, 1973);

C. A. Coates, *John Cowper Powys in Search of a Landscape* (London: Macmillan, 1982);

H. P. Collins, *John Cowper Powys: Old Earth Man* (London: Barrie & Rockliff, 1966);

H. W. Fawkner, *Amorous Life: John Cowper Powys and the Manifestation of Affectivity* (Kidderminster: Crescent Moon, 1998);

Fawkner, *The Ecstatic World of John Cowper Powys* (Rutherford, N.J.: Fairleigh Dickinson University Press / London: Associated University Presses, 1986);

Jeremy Hooker, *John Cowper Powys* (Cardiff: University of Wales Press, 1973);

Hooker, *John Cowper Powys and David Jones: A Comparative Study* (London: Enitharmon Press, 1979);

Hooker, *Writers in a Landscape* (Cardiff: University of Wales Press, 1996);

Belinda Humfrey, ed., *Essays on John Cowper Powys* (Cardiff: University of Wales Press, 1972);

Humfrey, ed., *John Cowper Powys's 'Wolf Solent': Critical Studies* (Cardiff: University of Wales Press, 1990);

G. Wilson Knight, *Neglected Powers: Essays on Nineteenth and Twentieth Century Literature* (London: Routledge & Kegan Paul, 1971);

Knight, *The Saturnian Quest: A Chart of the Prose Works of John Cowper Powys* (London: Methuen, 1964);

Morine Krissdóttir, *John Cowper Powys and the Magical Quest* (London: Macdonald, 1980);

Dennis Lane, ed., *In the Spirit of Powys: New Essays* (Lewisburg, Pa.: Bucknell University Press / London: Associated University Presses, 1990);

Roland Mathias, *The Hollowed-out Elder Stalk: John Cowper Powys as Poet* (London: Enitharmon Press, 1979);

Henry Miller, *The Books in My Life* (Norfolk, Conn.: Laughlin, 1952);

Janina Nordius, *"I am myself alone": Solitude and Transcendence in John Cowper Powys* (Goteberg, Sweden: Acta Universitatis Gothoburgensis, 1997);

Powys Journal, 1– (1991–   );

Powys Notes, 1– (1985–   );

Powys Review, 1– (1977–   );

Review of English Literature, special Powys issue, 4 (January 1963);

Jeremy Robinson, ed., *Rethinking Powys: Critical Essays on John Cowper Powys* (Kidderminster: Crescent Moon, 1999);

Robinson, *Sensualism and Mythology: The Wessex Novels of John Cowper Powys* (Kidderminster: Crescent Moon, 1990);

A. P. Seabright, *Powys: The Ecstasies of Crazy Jack: John Cowper Powys* (Kidderminster: Joe's Press, 1993);

Richard Heron Ward, *The Powys Brothers: A Study* (London: John Lane, 1935).

Papers:

The major collection of John Cowper Powys's manuscripts, previously in the private collection of E. E. Bissell, has been donated to the Powys Society; it is housed at the Dorset County Museum, Powys Centre, Dorchester. Diaries, unpublished letters and poems, and corrected typescripts are also in the National Library of Wales. Other collections of Powys family papers are in the Harry Ransom Humanities Research Center at the University of Texas, Austin; at Colgate University, Hamilton, New York; at Syracuse University; and at Churchill College, Cambridge.

Eric Frank Russell

(6 January 1905 – 28 February 1978)

Amelia A. Rutledge
George Mason University

BOOKS: *Sinister Barrier* (Kingswood, Surrey: World's Work, 1943; Reading, Pa.: Fantasy Press, 1948);

Dreadful Sanctuary (Reading, Pa.: Fantasy Press, 1951; London: Science Fiction Club, 1953; revised edition, New York: Lancer, 1963; London: New English Library, 1967);

Sentinels from Space (New York: Bouregy & Curl, 1953); republished as *The Star Watchers* (London: Science Fiction Club, 1954);

Deep Space (Reading, Pa.: Fantasy Press, 1954; London: Eyre & Spottiswoode, 1956);

Men, Martians, and Machines (London: Dobson, 1955; New York: Roy, 1956);

Three to Conquer (New York: Avalon, 1956; London: Dobson, 1957);

Wasp (New York: Avalon, 1957; expanded edition, London: Dobson, 1958; unabridged edition, New York: Ballantine, 1986);

Great World Mysteries (London: Dobson, 1957; New York: Roy, 1957; Toronto: McClelland, 1957);

The Space Willies; Six Worlds Yonder (New York: Ace, 1958); *The Space Willies* enlarged as *Next of Kin* (London: Dobson, 1959; New York: Ballantine, 1986);

Far Stars (London: Dobson, 1961);

The Great Explosion (London: Dobson, 1962; New York: Dodd, Mead, 1962);

Dark Tides (London: Dobson, 1962);

The Rabble Rousers (Evanston, Ill.: Regency, 1963);

With a Strange Device (London: Dobson, 1964); republished as *The Mindwarpers* (New York: Lancer, 1965);

Somewhere a Voice (London: Dobson, 1965; New York: Ace, 1965);

Ghosts (London: Batsford, 1970);

Astrology and Prediction (London: Batsford, 1972; New York: Drake, 1973);

Like Nothing on Earth (London: Dobson, 1975);

The Best of Eric Frank Russell, edited by Alan Dean Foster (New York: Ballantine, 1978);

Eric Frank Russell

Design for Great-Day, by Russell and Foster (New York: Tor, 1995).

Eric Frank Russell was one of the most prolific producers of science fiction in England during the 1950s. Although his first novel, *Sinister Barrier* (1943), is often cited in histories of science fiction for its connections with the magazine *Unknown,* he was best known to readers of science fiction for his short stories, more than half of which appeared in John W. Campbell's *Astounding Stories* (later *Astounding Science-Fiction*). The salient characteristics of his short fiction are an ironic, often humorous questioning of hierarchies and a casual approach to the "science" content in a period when "hard" science fiction was still dominant. His novels are less varied in content than the short stories, tending to focus on the subjection of the human race to external manipulation, which is rarely benevolent.

Russell was born on 6 January 1905 in Camberley, Surrey; his father was an instructor at the Military College, Sandhurst, and Russell spent part of his childhood in Egypt and the Sudan. Almost nothing else is known, since Russell was notoriously resistant to revealing even minimal biographical information. Writing to the editor of *Other Worlds* in January 1953, he began by stating, "I have an almost pathological dislike of biographical sketches." Educated in several branches of engineering, including crystallography, metallurgy, and quantity surveying, he also served twice in the military, in the King's Regiment from 1922 to 1926 and in the Royal Air Force from 1941 to 1945. He and his wife, Ellen, were married in 1930, and their only child, Erica, was born in 1934. He worked as a technical consultant for a Liverpool engineering firm, but his avocation was writing. By the mid 1950s Russell was a full-time professional writer. Although his interest in strange phenomena led him to write books such as *Great World Mysteries* (1957), *Ghosts* (1970), and *Astrology and Prediction* (1972), the bulk of his writing was science fiction.

Russell was a founding member of the British Interplanetary Society (1933), although he is officially listed as a member beginning in 1935. He began writing and submitting stories in the late 1930s; his first short story, "The Saga of Pelican West," was published in *Astounding Stories* in 1937. Campbell was impressed by Russell's aptitude and writing style, and his fiction appeared in *Astounding Stories* and other American magazines throughout his career. Russell adopted American idioms in his writing—only rarely does a "Britishism" creep in—possibly because most of the science fiction he read had been published in American magazines. He may also have realized that he was thus more appealing to the expanding American audience for science fiction. Russell learned his craft initially through imitation, first of Stanley G. Weinbaum and then of H. G. Wells, as Russell's "The Seeker of Tomorrow" (*Astounding Stories,* 1937) demonstrates. This rather awkward story, written in collaboration with Leslie J. Johnson, a minor science-fiction writer, shows Wells's influence in every paragraph. Russell quickly discovered his own expressive mode—fast-paced action, characters sketched rather than developed, and well-crafted prose. During the period between 1937 and 1949 he entered his mature phase.

Russell was a talented raconteur, though his range was limited, and in the first years of his career as a science-fiction writer he developed most of his characteristic themes and devices. He wrote a few gad-get-oriented stories that were published in *Astounding Science-Fiction,* including "The Seeker of Tomorrow" (1939), with its time machine. Another is "Seat of Oblivion" (1941) in which a scientist perfects a personality-transfer device that is appropriated by a criminal, whom he succeeds in trapping in the body of another criminal in time to assure his capture. Much more accomplished was one of his last such stories, "The Mechanical Mice" (*Astounding Science-Fiction,* 1941), inspired by and published under the name of Maurice Hugi, originator of the plot that was substantially reworked by Russell with Hugi's permission. In this story an inventor designs a self-propagating machine that uses mechanical "mice" to steal the necessary parts. The working of the machine itself is the focus in a way that Russell quickly abandoned.

In this period Russell also wrote three of the four stories that constitute his only series fiction: the Jay Score stories, ultimately collected in *Men, Martians, and Machines* (1955), his most popular collection of tales. These stories were praised by Anthony Boucher in *Modern Fantasy and Science Fiction* as "a rousing inventive space adventure" and by P. Schuyler Miller in *Astounding Science-Fiction* as "an old and familiar formula applied." Variations on these comments became the typical reviewers' responses to Russell's short stories and novels; similar comments are made when the works are republished. There is a full panoply of gadgets, from Jay Score (J-20) himself, a robot (although this fact is revealed only gradually in "Jay Score"), to the "pocket A-bomb" that shifts the balance in the more perilous situations the oddly assorted crew encounters. The other stories in the series, "Mechanistria" (1942), "Symbiotica" (1943), and "Mesmerica" (1956), are tales of initial contacts on planets that are more memorable than the events that occur. Mechanistria is inhabited by sentient machinery; Mesmerica's inhabitants are telepathic illusionists. "Symbiotica," the most complex of the tales, presents a human/tree symbiosis along with an array of inventively menacing plants. Russell does not explore the biological or psychological implications of these life-forms; they are simply there. He uses a story pattern familiar to viewers of television science-fiction series: the crew encounters a new race and manages, with Jay Score's help, a difficult escape.

The Jay Score stories also introduce Russell's inclusiveness, sometimes cited as a rare early example of racial tolerance: the ship's doctor is black, and part of the crew is Martian. This inclusiveness must be qualified, however, since Russell employs an implicit stereotyping by class and occupation, as seen in "Jay Score":

On the outward runs toward Mars, the Asteroids or beyond, they have white Terrestrials to tend the

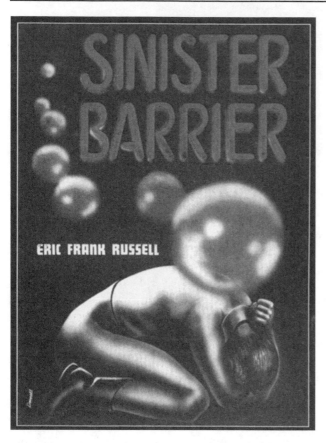

Dust jacket for the 1948 U.S. edition of Russell's first novel, published in Britain in 1943, in which aliens foment quarrels among earthlings so as to produce the emotional energy on which they subsist

yet another successful experiment in creation. A surprise ending and an ironic point of view were becoming the most enduring hallmarks of a Russell story.

The most important themes in the future settings of Russell's fiction were those of the power of passive resistance and the inherent absurdity of authoritarian structures, whether military hierarchies or galactic empires. In "Late Night Final" (*Astounding Science-Fiction,* 1948) a group of Earth humans suborns a whole crew of alien invaders by making them welcome, thus exploiting their homesickness. The martinet commander is the last to give in, but his surrender is inevitable. The galactic empire of "Metamorphosite" (1946), also published in *Astounding Science-Fiction,* has been infiltrated by several races bent on undermining its structures of oppression. Its most aggressive move is blocked by a race that turns out to be its own ancestors, Terrans evolved beyond all recognition; even the human race, Russell suggests, can outgrow its negative tendencies.

Species chauvinism was another target for Russell's satire, and in "Homo Saps" (published in 1941 under the pseudonym "Webster Craig") and "Muten" (1948), both published in *Astounding Science-Fiction,* pretension is deflated by the recognition of sentience in Earth animals. Martians in the former tale discover that camels are the truly intelligent Terran species, and the talking horse of "Muten" has the last laugh. In "The Undecided" (*Astounding Science-Fiction,* 1949) Russell presents the first of his "arrogant alien" stories, the would-be attackers or conquerors who cannot prevail against human ingenuity. This theme is a commonplace of early science fiction, but Russell excelled in making the aliens look absurd and their downfall the logical result of their overconfidence.

In 1943 Russell published his first novel, *Sinister Barrier,* an expanded version of a 1937 story published in *Unknown.* As critics have pointed out, Russell was strongly influenced by the writings of Charles Fort, a collector of unexplained phenomena and promulgator of the theory that humans were "property" of some more powerful race. The alien Vitons of Russell's novel have isolated Earth as a source of the emotional energy on which they live; in order to maintain their supply, they have fomented dissension throughout history. The hero, Bill Graham, a government agent plenipotentiary, assembles a group of scientists to create the necessary weapon to expel the Vitons. Russell gives more attention to the device in this novel than in any of his other works except the early short fiction, but there is little consistency of detail, and the drug by which humans become able to see the Vitons—a mixture of mescaline and methylene blue, assisted by a topical application of iodine—is too improbable for

engines because they're the one who perfected modern propulsion units, know most about them and can nurse them like nobody else. All ships' surgeons are black Terrestrials because for some reason none can explain no Negro gets gravity-bends or space nausea. Every outside repair gang is composed of Martians who use very little air, are tiptop metal workers and fairly immune to cosmic-ray burn.

Russell moved toward fantasy in "With a Blunt Instrument" (*Unknown,* 1941), a mixed-genre piece, part detective fiction and part fantasy, in which an Australian aborigine's power of suggestion really works; but it is a minor piece. He later wrote a few gothic horror tales, but this subgenre was not one that he explored frequently.

In this period he also wrote two stories focused on cosmogony: "Mana" (1937) and "Hobbyist"(1947), both published in *Astounding Science-Fiction.* In the former story, the last man on Earth, Omega, endows a race of ants with intelligence, "mana," as his final gesture. In the latter, a self-assured explorer leaves a new planet, unaware that the "hobbyist" has just checked him off as

anything but a spoof of the elaborate pseudoscience of science fiction in its early years.

Russell's well-paced plot succeeds despite a proliferation of repetitious disasters. Writers such as E. E. Smith had long ago posited manipulative galactic beings operating in vast sweeps of outer space, but Russell was almost the first to give this idea a "local" setting, making it a popular one for writers and readers alike. The protagonist of *Sinister Barrier* is also typical of Russell's principal characters: mature and competent, but not exceptional except in determination. Russell did not favor the youthful, all-around genius that populated a great deal of science fiction at that time. Critics at the time questioned the originality of the basic plot, but at least one later commentator, Sam Moskowitz, dates the popularity in science fiction of the Fortean premise "we are property" from *Sinister Barrier*.

Russell continued his variations on the Fortean theme in his next two novels, *Dreadful Sanctuary* (1951) and *Sentinels from Space* (1953). The former novel offers a purely Earth-based version of manipulation, with a secret society convinced that Earth is a penal colony for Mercury, Venus, and Mars and that they represent the only humans who have evolved beyond the status of incarcerated prisoner. They are intent on sabotaging Earth's space program because it is seen as a threat to the "necessary" quarantine of Earth, and they recruit new members by means of a mind-altering machine. Although some critics have found an element of interest in the question posed to all candidates for the controlling group, "How do you know that you are sane?," much of the novel is a chase-and-adventure sequence focused on exposing the group and making one successful moon shot.

In *Sentinels from Space* Russell uses benevolent aliens as his outside manipulators; their task is to maintain peace and unity among Terrans and their space colonies long enough for all humans to evolve into their next stage, "homo in excelsis." Russell adds interest to the plot by creating several mutant talents, the result of exposure to radiation on the colony planets; these groups, such as the pyrotics—telepathic fire-starters—need to be maneuvered into not using their talents for partisan gain. *Sentinels from Space* also differs from other Russell stories in its development of a female character who is more than simply an incidental figure, although all Russell females conform to the science-fiction stereotypes of the 1940s and 1950s. Russell's female characters are dependable supporters of the heroes' efforts; in addition, they tend to be conservative and cautious in contrast to the more adventurous males.

While Russell's novels of the early 1950s show slight variations and little progress in developing themes, he was producing much of his most memorable short fiction, including "Allamagoosa" (*Astounding Science-fiction,* 1955), which won a Hugo Award. "Allamagoosa" represents a new story type for Russell, the "snafu" story, a plot that allowed him to display his satirical skills. A spaceship crew, confronted with a preinspection inventory, find one item listed that they cannot identify; so they try subterfuge, reporting that the object disintegrated during flight. When the list misprint is translated, they are left to account for what never happened. Russell is at his best in this story, combining ridicule, a successful mystery, and a joke.

Aliens figure more prominently than before in the short fiction of this period, usually arrogant invaders such as the mimics in "Exposure" (*Astounding Science-Fiction,* 1950), whose downfall is assured by their rigid adherence to rules that forbid them to change their disguise once it is adopted; the outcome seems obvious to the reader until one final revelation indicates the extent of the aliens' blindness. Russell also wrote about benevolent aliens, the best known of which is the protagonist of "Dear Devil" (*Other World Stories,* 1950), a Martian poet who is allowed to settle on Earth and who befriends the human remnants of a world-destroying war.

The aliens of "The Waitabits" (*Astounding Science-Fiction,* 1955) force human colonizers to reflect on their own self-confidence; if aliens as slow as the "Waitabits" exist, what would happen if one met a race whose time perceptions were proportionately faster than those of humans? Russell's story "Diabologic" (*Astounding Science-Fiction,* 1955), which introduced a new term into the science-fiction vocabulary, shows one version of the cautious approach to exploration. The explorer's defense against his captors is specious reasoning that leaves them trapped in logical circles mostly of their own making. As a device, "diabologic" figured in some of Russell's later stories, most notably in *The Space Willies* (1958).

One of Russell's best passive-resistance stories, "I Am Nothing" (*Astounding Science-Fiction,* 1952), is sometimes cited as his most effective antiwar story as well. David Korman, machine-like in his pursuit of conquest, is reformed by an encounter with a severely troubled child from one of the planets he is attacking. Persuaded to communicate the trauma that has left her nearly speechless, she writes, "I am nothing and nobody. My house went bang. My cat was stuck to a wall. I wanted to pull it off. They wouldn't let me. They threw it away." Korman's conversion verges on the sentimental—it occurs too quickly—but his epiphany is one of Russell's best moments.

Russell's tendency to satirize the foibles of empire-builders did not necessarily free him from a tacit acceptance of the concept of empire, and at least once

Dust jacket for Russell's 1951 novel, about a secret society that tries to sabotage Earth's space program to protect the planet from aliens

this understanding manifested itself in explicit xenophobia. "The Timeless Ones" (*Science Fiction Quarterly,* 1952) is a "yellow peril" story in which Russell ironically converts his favored motif of "passive resistance" into a tool used by enemies, who are perceived only by a clearsighted, antibureaucratic protagonist. An anthropologist encounters a race that never resists conquests but will do any servile task if only allowed to breed. As in *Sinister Barrier* or *Dreadful Sanctuary,* the protagonist insists on active resistance to the threat; but his attempt to issue a warning is blocked by obtuse authorities who see "shape prejudice," the most abhorrent form of bigotry in this civilization of races with widely varying body configurations, in his report. Russell's simultaneous use of two of his "trademarks" increases the bitterness of the piece, which ends with the protagonist staring at a sign that reads, "Ah-Fong, Laundry."

Russell did not write horror fiction often (much of it can be found in the 1962 collection *Dark Tides*), but two of his strongest gothic stories were written during

this time: "The Rhythm of the Rats" (*Weird Tales,* 1950) and "I Hear You Calling" (*Science Fantasy,* 1954). "The Rhythm of the Rats" is a version of the Pied Piper story, narrated in retrospect as the experience of a nine-year-old, and "I Hear You Calling" uses a drunken sailor in search of a one-night stand as the focus for a well-wrought piece of black humor and true horror.

Russell wrote three novels in the second half of the 1950s: *Three to Conquer* (1956), *Wasp* (1957), and *The Space Willies.* Russell tended to expand previously published short stories into novels; the results tend to be disappointing, and only *Wasp,* which was conceived as a novel from the beginning, has real narrative coherence. *Three to Conquer* first appeared as a three-part serial in *Astounding Science-Fiction* as "Call Him Dead" (1955) and is the story of a telepath who is able to track down invaders who take over human minds; the novella does not gain from increased detail. Further, the true narrative interest lies in the ingenuity with which the telepath eludes detection, not in an exploration of the aliens themselves.

Wasp, on the other hand, is one of Russell's most coherent and satisfying narratives. It is a story of the successful political sabotage efforts of a young Terran agent, disguised as a native of the Sirian empire, against the Sirians. Science fiction provides the exotic setting of an alien planet and some of the hardware, but most of the agent's work is done with inflammatory messages, letter bombs, and selective gunplay. The agent, a Terran raised on a Sirian planet, bears a strong resemblance to Rudyard Kipling's Kim, and indeed, Russell's plot seems to owe as much to John Buchan or Kipling as it does to the conventions of science fiction.

Russell expanded the short story "Plus X" (*Astounding Science-Fiction,* 1956) into *The Space Willies.* The story falls into the "arrogant alien" class of Russell's science fiction; this time the Terran outwits his alien captors by means of an imaginary double, "Eustace," on whom he blames any chance mishaps that occur. He manages to convince the aliens that they, too, have doubles called "Willies," hence the title of the novel. Although the idea is promising, this novella is a less-successful exemplar of Russell's alien-contact stories.

One of Russell's last two novels, *The Great Explosion* (1962), is also an expanded short story. The original short story, "And Then There Were None" (*Astounding Science-Fiction,* 1951), is an encounter between Terran explorers and colonists who had adopted Mahatma Gandhi's principles as their mode of organization. In classic Russell fashion, some of the explorers, converted by what they see, leave their restrictive former lives to join the colonists. The material added for the novel, involving a colony of health-conscious nudists, fails to add much to the narrative, but the basic story, although somewhat romantic in its positing of a cultural ethos based on passive resistance, retains its effectiveness.

With a Strange Device (1964), published in the United States in 1965 as *The Mindwarpers,* resembles *Dreadful Sanctuary* in its use of a mind-altering machine to sabotage research efforts by convincing scientists such as the protagonist, Harper, that they are guilty of brutal murders and must abandon everything to evade pursuers. It is the weakest of Russell's novels; the device that qualifies the story as science fiction is concealed until near the end of the story, and the extended description of Harper's flight is unfocused, giving the expression of exhausted creativity.

After the early 1960s Russell wrote almost no fiction. In a 19 October 1972 letter, written to Alan Dean Foster and quoted in Foster's introduction to *The Best of Eric Frank Russell* (1978), Russell said that he had nothing new to say and that most science-fiction plots were praised by young readers only by reason of the latter's inexperience. Still, despite the weaknesses of his later novels, his short stories of the late 1950s show no diminution of Russell's inventiveness. There were "snafu" stories such as "A Study in Still Life" (*Astounding Science-Fiction,* 1959), which is even more effective than the award-winning "Allamagoosa," and "Into Your Tent I'll Creep" (*Astounding Science-Fiction,* 1957), which explains why dogs seem to rule humanity and which is his most fully realized human/animal story. "Sole Solution" (*Fantastic Universe,* 1956) is likewise the best-crafted of his cosmogony stories, with its poetic compactness and its description of a Creator motivated by loneliness. Quite possibly, however, Russell's recognition of the limitations imposed by the small number of story types he usually employed led to his retirement from writing. He died on 28 February 1978.

The reasons for Russell's silence in the last years of his life are a matter of speculation. But the eight novels and nearly eighty short stories he produced are, within the limitations of the time period and culture in which they appeared, well-written if not far-reaching science-fiction narratives, possessing a humorous touch for which the era, and the genre, had great need. Russell was posthumously inducted into the Science Fiction and Fantasy Hall of Fame in 2000.

Bibliographies:

Francis Valéry, *Eric Frank Russell: A Bibliography* (Chicago: Weinberg, 1990);

Phil Stephensen-Payne and Sean Wallace, *Eric Frank Russell, Our Sentinel in Space: A Working Bibliography,* third edition (Leeds: Galactic Central, 1999).

References:

Malcolm Edwards, "Eric Frank Russell, 1905–1978," in *Science Fiction Writers: Critical Studies of the Major Authors from the Early Nineteenth Century to the Present Day,* edited by Everett F. Bleiler (New York: Scribners, 1982), pp. 197–202;

Heinz-Wenzel Fabry and P. Wenzel, "Mythisch-religiöse Themen in der Very Short Story: Eric Frank Russells 'Sole Solution' und Fredric Browns 'Answer'," *Anglistik and Englischunterricht,* 23 (1984): 129–140;

Sam Moskowitz, "Eric Frank Russell," in his *Seekers of Tomorrow: Masters of Science Fiction* (Cleveland: World, 1966), pp. 133–150.

Papers:

Eric Frank Russell's science-fiction-related papers, manuscripts, and correspondence with science-fiction readers and writers, including John W. Campbell, are located in the Sydney Jones Library, University of Liverpool.

Sarban
(John W. Wall)
(6 November 1910 – 11 April 1989)

Edgar L. Chapman
Bradley University

BOOKS: *Ringstones and Other Curious Tales* (London: Davies, 1951; New York: Coward-McCann, 1951);

The Sound of His Horn (London: Davies, 1952; New York: Ballantine, 1960);

The Doll Maker and Other Tales of the Uncanny (London: Davies, 1953); title work republished as *The Doll Maker* (New York: Ballantine, 1960; London: World, 1962);

The Sound of His Horn and The King of the Lake (East Sussex: Tartarus Press, 1999).

Edition: *Ringstones* (New York: Ballantine, 1961).

Publishing under the pseudonym "Sarban," John W. Wall earned a reputation as an author of stylish neo-Gothic fantasy, primarily from his three short novels or novellas, *Ringstones* (1951), *The Sound of His Horn* (1952), and *The Doll Maker* (1953), which is perhaps his masterpiece. Two of these novellas originally appeared in volumes accompanied by a few short stories. He also enjoyed a brief period of commercial success in the early 1960s through paperback reprints of these novellas. This rather limited canon was enough to create a following for Sarban, with the appeal perhaps increased by the mystery surrounding Wall's identity and his use of the intriguing pseudonym; but his failure to capitalize on his initial success and his lack of sustained publication allowed his reputation to fade.

Until the 1980s Sarban's identity was not widely known except to insiders in publishing and book reviewing. He was born John William Wall in Mexborough, South Yorkshire, on 6 November 1910. His parents were George William Wall, a passenger guard on the Great Central Railway, and Maria Ellen Moffatt Wall; he had four older siblings. Wall earned scholarships to the Mexborough School in 1922 and to Jesus College, Cambridge, in 1930, from which he graduated three years later. Interested in the Middle East and in Asian languages, he joined the Consular Service in Sep-

tember 1933 and began a career as a diplomat, working in such places as Beirut, Tabriz, Casablanca, and Cairo. In 1946 he met Eleanor Alexander (née Riesle), whom he married on 20 January 1950; the couple later had a daughter, Jocelyn. Wall's wife was instrumental in encouraging him to publish the stories he had begun writing at the end of 1947.

The restrictions of his profession regarding publication while in active service obliged Wall to adopt a pseudonym. Although his horror fantasy had little to do with the diplomatic work in which he was engaged, publication under his own name might have created an image that would have seemed politically injudicious or even frivolous. Finally, the use of a pseudonym may have accorded with the author's desire for privacy: throughout his life, Wall maintained a polite reserve about his personal life. Wall's choice of the name "Sarban" suggests affinities with H. H. Munro, a British author of satires and satiric horror tales who published under the pen name of "Saki."

Sarban's three long works of fiction all deal with an innocent protagonist who becomes enmeshed in an enslaving situation and gradually discovers that not only is he or she enacting the role of a ritual victim but also he or she actually feels a longing to surrender to this role as a passive participant in the reenactment of a mythic pattern. Such an initiation into a hidden world of pagan and ancient British ritual provides the main theme of *Ringstones,* Sarban's first long novella, written in 1947. This work describes the experiences of Daphne Hazel, an athletic young student at Towerton College, in her first employment as a governess at a lonely Northumbrian manor house during a school vacation.

The story is presented mainly through a first-person account by Daphne to her boyfriend, Piers DeBourg, though her story is preceded and followed by a frame narrative involving a discussion between Piers and an unnamed narrator, a fellow student at Piers's university (probably Cambridge). The narrator of the frame sec-

Sarban (John W. Wall; by permission of the Estate of John Wall)

tions describes himself as a bemused visitor to Piers's family home in the bleak northern city of Newcastle. Sarban's use of such a framing narrative is a recurring device in much of his fiction. This traditional technique reveals the influence of Victorian and Edwardian models of fiction, such as Emily Brontë, H. G. Wells, Robert Louis Stevenson, Joseph Conrad, and Henry James, for instance, and perhaps Arthur Machen. Moreover, Daphne's situation as a governess, overseeing three children at an isolated manor called Ringstones, provides an irresistible reminder of James's masterpiece of horror fiction, *The Turn of the Screw* (1898). As in James's novella, Sarban's heroine undergoes a somewhat puzzling interview in London, is hired, and journeys to a remote manor house where she meets an uncommunicative housekeeper and children who seem, despite apparently normal surface behavior, to conceal some scandalous secret and to act strangely at times.

Despite the obvious parallels with James's story, which are so strong as to suggest that *The Turn of the Screw* was a conscious model, Sarban's melodrama also presents some contrasts to James's masterpiece. For instance, Daphne's mysterious employer, Dr. Ravelin, is not a parent or relative of the children residing at Ringstones, but merely a temporary guardian concerned with their welfare. There are three children, a

boy and two girls, and they are supposedly not native speakers of English, for Daphne is hired primarily to improve their speech. Whereas James's boy has been sent home from a respectable private school for mysterious reasons involving discipline, and whereas James's repressed children seem to have some unwelcome knowledge of the alleged misconduct of their uncle's valet and the previous governess, the children in Sarban's story possess merely impressive energy and threatening innocence. Most significantly, *Ringstones* moves suspensefully to a different resolution, an ending that restores order but creates disquieting overtones.

There is also a sharp contrast between Daphne and the Jamesian governess of *The Turn of the Screw*. Although both are drawn into the undercurrents of the world they enter innocently, the Jamesian protagonist is a repressed clergyman's daughter whose fascinated attempts to probe into the nature of the valet's mysterious and allegedly immoral conduct reveal a subconscious obsession with sexuality. Her narrative focuses compulsively on the appearance of the ghosts of the valet and the former governess, specters that some readers consider hallucinations created by the narrator's own overheated imagination.

By contrast, the central section of Sarban's novella is narrated by a young woman who is less reflective and more active than the governess in *The Turn of the Screw*. On the surface, at least, Daphne is more at ease with herself and less repressed than the Jamesian protagonist; but Sarban portrays her as having unacknowledged desires, especially a subconscious willingness to submerge herself in archaic fertility rituals. The name of Sarban's heroine carries mythic overtones: in classical myth, as retold by Ovid, Daphne was a nubile young woman who aroused the lust of the god Apollo and was obliged to flee by running until she was transformed into a laurel tree by the goddess Artemis or Diana. The surname of Sarban's heroine, Hazel, emphasizes her natural and "pagan" qualities. Like the mythic Daphne, Sarban's heroine is nearly captured and reduced to sexual bondage by a nemesis who is actually a divinity; but also like the Greek Daphne, Sarban's Daphne receives a last-minute reprieve.

Before the action intensifies, much of Daphne's narrative is devoted to establishing an eerie atmosphere. Daphne's employer, Dr. Ravelin, is drawn after the character type of the eccentric scholar or mad scientist of many Gothic stories; the housekeeper and her husband, Mr. and Mrs. Sarkissian, are also eccentric and grotesque figures; and Ringstones is located near an ancient Celtic or druidic circle of stones.

But the central plot of Sarban's novella revolves around Daphne's gradual seduction by the children she is supposed to tutor. Her major problem is Nuaman, the fifteen-year-old lad, whom Daphne at first considers merely a mischievous rebel. The two girls, Marvan and Ianthe, are natural followers, but they appear to be devoted to mindless physical diversions and impervious to conventional notions of right and wrong. If Nuaman at first seems an archetype of Pan, his female companions may suggest prepubescent nymphs. But the northern English setting raises suggestions of ancient Celtic or Norse gods or fertility spirits. At any rate, as Nuaman gradually reveals his powers and his tendency to exert dominance, Daphne finds herself both attracted to and repelled by him.

At last, in a dream sequence, Daphne envisions herself being led by Sarkissian to the stone circle, where she and the semiliterate Polish servant woman, Katia, are initiated into servitude as vassals under Nuaman's power. Both young women are stripped nude and harnessed to Nuaman's chariot, which they are expected to pull willingly. To her surprise, Daphne discovers that she welcomes such a submission. The scene is sketched vividly and peopled by a throng of what appear to be pagan warriors and athletes—both male and female and all dressed scantily—engaged in exercise or practice with weapons. Not only are Nuaman and his sisters involved in this establishment of archaic sexual bond-

age, but Daphne perceives that the others readily accept his dominance.

However, at the final moment, on the point of surrendering entirely to Nuaman, Daphne feels the need to resist. She utters a cry and flees to the protection of Dr. Ravelin, the authority figure who fortuitously returns from town. Like the protagonists in Sarban's other major stories, Daphne feels both a masochistic temptation to yield to her oppressor and a stronger opposing urge to resist.

After Daphne has recounted her intense dream in her long narrative for Piers, her story comes to an abrupt end. It is supposed to be an experiment in fiction, she claims; but Daphne is not known to be particularly imaginative. In a long closing sequence, Piers and the narrator of the frame sections decide, after reading Daphne's story, to hurry to Ringstones to investigate. When they arrive, they find that Daphne is safe and apparently working for a modern middle-class physician, Dr. Hancock, and his family, rather than the mysterious Dr. Ravelin of her narrative. Since her charges are only two small girls of Egyptian origin and no tragedies have occurred, her tale involving Nuaman perhaps was indeed a work of fiction inspired by a visit to the ruins of the abandoned house of Ringstones.

Perfectly natural explanations can be offered for every puzzling event in Daphne's narrative: there was once a Dr. Ravelin who owned and tried to maintain Ringstones, but the upkeep was too expensive, and he abandoned the house. Daphne's surrender to Nuaman's enchantments is explained as a dream in which Daphne wandered off into an earlier time. Yet, there are hints that all is not what it seems, and the surface of Daphne's world conceals disturbing emotions and a real experience of sexual bondage, for which a cut on her left wrist may be a memento. Such ambiguous hints suggest that Daphne may have stepped through some mysterious gate into a primitive world ruled by Nuaman and nearly fallen under his dominance, only to be saved by Dr. Ravelin's timely return. As Daphne's surface composure collapses in front of her visitors, and she seems on the point of yielding to frightening memories, Piers grabs her hands and reassures her, "The doctor did arrive in time, you know. He did arrive."

Thus Sarban's novel, while not tragic in the mode of *The Turn of the Screw,* concludes on a note of horror and ambiguity somewhat similar to James's classic novella. Whatever interpretation is given to *Ringstones,* the novella remains a haunting story, though its homage both to James and to Gothic tradition should not encourage an overrated estimate of it. Despite its powerful scenes, the closing sequence tends to be too long, and some elements of the plot seem superfluous. Nevertheless, Sarban's writing in *Ringstones* is vivid and often poetic, and his style is notable in this work, as else-where, for lucidity and control. American reviewers were moderately enthusiastic about *Ringstones. The New Yorker* reviewer described Sarban's imagination as "without bounds in an old-fashioned, *Castle of Otronto* way." *The San Francisco Chronicle* critic called him "a writer of the very highest order." *The Saturday Review of Literature,* however, was less favorable.

Sarban's short stories displayed many of the same themes and concerns as his novellas. For example, in "Capra" (1951, published in *Ringstones and Other Curious Tales*), the theme of revival of archaic myth is devel-oped once again when a glamorous woman named Diana keeps a rendezvous with a creature who appears to be an ancient Grecian satyr. The fascination with relationships of dominance and submission recurs in "The Khan," another story appearing in *Ringstones and Other Curious Tales,* in which an Englishwoman in the Near East falls under the dominance of a mysterious masculine figure.

Sarban's second major novella, *The Sound of His Horn,* shows a clear indebtedness to Conrad's novella *Heart of Darkness* (1899). Sarban's narrator in this work is a masculine protagonist, and Sarban introduces him to an imagined world that can be considered a science-fiction setting. *The Sound of His Horn* is mainly composed of a narrative told by a former British officer, Alan Querdilion, to a group of friends after a dinner party. Querdilion's tale describes his horrifying experience during World War II as a German prisoner. But the reader gradually learns with surprise that the intern-ment occurs in an alternate history, in which the Ger-mans won the war. Sarban's novella is one of the earliest alternate-history novels in which the Nazi Reich triumphed, although many others have appeared since its publication, in part because of its Ballantine paper-back reprint in 1960 and the success of Philip K. Dick's novel *The Man in the High Castle* two years later.

The Sound of His Horn is vividly imagined. Aside from Querdilion, the novella employs only sketchy characterizations, but its controlled and deliberate pace creates a cumulative effect of growing horror as Quer-dilion recounts the story of his captivity and describes his dawning realization that he has somehow entered an alternate reality. At length, Querdilion finally dis-covers not only that the Nazi Reich somehow tri-umphed in the war but also that he is living in the unpleasant year 102 of the "First Millennium as fixed by Our First Fuehrer and Immortal Spirit of German-ism."

Gradually, Querdilion learns that Count von Hackelberg (in whose castle Querdilion is a prisoner) rules a vast forested area set aside as a hunting preserve where, the Englishman discovers to his horror, the

Cover for the 1960 paperback edition—the first U.S. publication— of Sarban's 1952 novella, in which a British army officer in World War II suddenly finds himself more than one hundred years in the future in an alternate reality in which Germany has won the war

Count hunts human prey, usually scantily dressed or nude young women. Other aspects of the Nazi world order are not described but implied through casual hints. The cities of the triumphant Reich remain off-stage, and little direct comment is made about the Holo-caust, although the tale emphasizes the importance of the Nazi concept of a superior Teutonic race. The use of human beings as game for the Count's hunts is justi-fied by the usual Nazi ideological argument that the Germans are the "superior" race. Obviously, the ritual-ized hunt of human prey, which invokes the mythic trappings of ancient Teutonic warlords galloping through a primitive forest in pursuit of deer or wolves, is a metaphor expressing the victorious German state's attitude toward the peoples it has conquered.

Once Querdilion learns that far from being a prisoner of war, he has wandered into an alternate historical world where Teutonic overlords enact barbaric rituals, *The Sound of His Horn* comes to a suspenseful climactic sequence. Accompanied by a young woman captive, Querdilion is forced to become one of the humans who must play the role of game pursued by Hackelberg. Although being turned loose in the forest enables Querdilion to elude the hunters, escape over the fence surrounding the estate, and return to his own twentieth century, the hunting scenes linger disturbingly in his memory.

At times Querdilion surprises both himself and the reader by feeling a sense of pleasurable terror in the pursuit, somewhat like the welcome feeling of surrender and fetishism described in Daphne's dream of submission to Nuaman at the climax of *Ringstones*. Querdilion and the other intended victim of the Count's hunt seem to feel a surge of perverse enjoyment in the threat of being pursued, captured, and destroyed by the lord of the castle. The sadism of the dominating master evokes a temptation to yield and become a victim of this archaic ritual. Though this bizarre reaction may be rationalized as a result of Querdilion's captivity, it also seems to be a displacement of conventional sexual desire. Nevertheless, despite his inner ambivalence, Querdilion's desire for freedom and self-preservation triumphs over latent masochism.

Querdilion's emotional conflict provides one of the most disturbing elements of the story. Novelist and critic Kingsley Amis, who wrote an introduction for the 1960 Ballantine edition of the novel, found the barbaric sadism of the Count's hunt for young women somewhat disquieting, though he apparently did not perceive Querdilion's ambivalent response. In fact, he argued that "much of the novel is taken up with Querdilion himself being hunted, and I can find no indication that he or Sarban are secretly getting some discreditable thrill out of that." But if Amis may have glossed over Querdilion's own response, he does comment that a momentary enjoyment of the Count's sadism does not exclude the possibility of a moral condemnation of it.

Perhaps it should be observed that Querdilion's emotional ambivalence enriches his characterization. However, one of the most thorough analysts of Sarban's work, Peter Nicholls, tends to regard nearly all of Sarban's protagonists as masochists tempted by heartless sadists and obliged not only to fight against their would-be oppressors but also to resist their own inner inclinations. On this view, moreover, the sadists, though apparently demonic, represent "something that

has been lost to modern civilized society—or at least suppressed by it." Whether the reader agrees with such an interpretation or not, it is obvious that the dominating sadists of Sarban's fiction exercise a fascinating power over the imagination, especially in Sarban's fantasy vision of Nazi triumph.

Despite its narrative vigor and suspense, however, *The Sound of His Horn* is disappointing in its failure to offer a memorable or revealing portrait of Hackelberg as a personality or to draw other Nazi types effectively. Aside from the Count, the chief representative of Nazism is predictably sketched as a sadistic doctor who explains the rules of this world to Querdilion while treating his injuries in captivity. (It is possible that the doctor's ministrations include an injection that tends to decrease Querdilion's resistance to the Count's rule and make him more passive.) But Hackelberg, the supreme embodiment of the Nazi concept of the dominating master race, is seen primarily as a mysterious and distant presence, a symbolic icon of barbarism and sadism. Rather than being introduced as a personality, the Count is depicted primarily through the attitudes of his servants and through the terrifying experience of the hunt.

Although Hackelberg is presented as a mythic presence rather than a realistic character, the nature of his mythic identity has provoked some interesting speculation. Nicholls has suggested that Hackelberg is an avatar of a numinous figure in German myth, the "Wild Huntsman," a preternatural character who corresponds to the numinous figure in British myth of Herne the Hunter. While this interpretation is plausible, these traditional figures were, though frightening, somewhat ambiguous. Yet, there can be little doubt that as an avatar of the programmatic Nazi myth of robust Teutonic paganism, the Count plays the role of a destructive and demonic figure in *The Sound of His Horn*.

Not much notice of *The Sound of His Horn* was given by American reviewers at its belated publication in 1960, although it did receive a favorable review in *The New York Times*. Whatever one's final judgment of this novella, it is an impressive exercise in narrative suspense. At the end of his story, Querdilion has become inwardly disturbed by his memory of the terror he has described. Like Conrad's Marlow, who narrates *Heart of Darkness*, Querdilion has gained an experience of human bestiality and depravity. Whereas Marlow learned a pragmatic wisdom based on stoicism and self-discipline from his experience, Querdilion has not acquired a comparable gain. His narrative allows his listeners (and Sarban's readers) to reexperience his terrifying ordeal; but his comments on it do not reveal any growth in moral insight. In short, Sarban's novella fails to attain the mature moral vision found in Conrad's.

Sarban's third major work, *The Doll Maker,* shows advances in discipline, technique, and artistry over his earlier novellas. In plot and theme, this short novel returns to the concerns of *Ringstones.* Once again the setting is a remote rural estate, and the protagonist is a naive young woman who, despite herself, falls under the temporary domination of a sinister but attractive male. Sarban develops a highly controlled third-person narrative voice for *The Doll Maker,* and instead of relying on primitive myth to create terror, he turns to the more familiar Gothic theme of possession by a demonic or alien force.

The plot of *The Doll Maker* is relatively simple. Clare Lydgate, an eighteen-year-old student at a drab English boarding school, discovers adventure and romance at the remote country estate nearby. But her adventure comes at the price of nearly falling under the power of Niall Sterne, the young master of Brackenbine. Clare's need for a tutor in Latin provides her with the opportunity to visit Brackenbine, since Niall's mother is a Latinist; but Clare also learns the art of sneaking out of a window at her school to roam the estate, with its legends of a dark past, and soon she begins a romance with its mysterious master. Though a former tutor contracted an unusual illness and died after visits to Brackenbine, and other young women associated with Brackenbine have disappeared or died under questionable circumstances, Clare disregards these ominous precedents and falls in love with the sophisticated Niall, who lives by a credo of ambitious aestheticism.

Attractive but amoral, Niall is an obsessive minor artist who devotes himself to carving wooden dolls and, by some form of magic, animating them for what seems to be a fairy pageant in the woods outside his sprawling manor house. In his quest to create the perfect doll, which would be a means to make human beauty eternal, Niall somehow manages to imprison the spirits of young women in his wooden images. The means whereby Niall animates his dolls and captures the spirits of his admirers in them is unclear, although it is supposedly linked to chemicals stored in his studio. It is finally revealed that Niall gives his victims injections and persuades them to perform a ritual in which they swear unquestioning obedience to him. But the source of Niall's power is never satisfactorily explained. However, its symbolism is rather clear: Niall's art of woodcarving is an artificial and carefully nurtured fetish, which stands in opposition to the natural world of woods and flowers on the estate outside the house.

Although Clare apparently does not lose her virginity to Niall, she falls in love with him not only because of her fascination with his charismatic charm but also because of his promise of a secret world where

Cover for the first U.S. edition (1960) of Sarban's 1953 Gothic novella, in which an artist imprisons the souls of his lovers in the dolls he creates

she may be immortal. Her doubts of his sincerity do not surface until she discovers that he also has begun to seduce Jennifer Gray, another girl from the school. Shocked and disillusioned, Clare secretly investigates his studio and learns the real aim of his art is to imprison his victims rather than liberate them. Thereupon, like other Sarban protagonists, Clare struggles to escape the domination of her oppressor and at length manages to liberate herself when she burns Brackenbine.

Despite its Gothic aura, this novel ends on a positive note, with another symbolic element. While Clare convalesces from injuries received in the fire, her favorite teacher comforts her with gentle remarks about nature's powers of renewal, which will soon regenerate the burned-over land of Brackenbine. Clare stares at some coltsfoot in her sickroom and hears her mentor remark, "I'm glad you're going to be nineteen, next summer, Clare." Throughout the novel, coltsfoot has been a metaphor of natural beauty and renewal, in contrast to the perverse "life-in-death" of Niall's carving of wooden dolls. At the resolution of the novel, the presence of coltsfoot and the emphasis on Clare's approaching maturity suggest a hopeful conclusion. Thus, beneath its Gothic atmosphere and plot, *The Doll Maker* is in reality the story of Clare's rite of passage from adolescence to adulthood.

The symbolic meaning of Niall's art is less easy to describe. In a broad sense, the novel juxtaposes natural life and growth, with its inevitable ills (including aging and death), to an artificial and specious immortality gained through art and the liquid chemicals in the tubes, evidently some kind of drugs whose allegorical significance remains obscure. Yet, the evil involved in Niall's work does not seem to be inherent in the creation of art itself but in the artist's indifference to the human cost of his artistry. Although Sarban obviously intends to offer a fictional statement about the dangers of art, the full implications of his symbolism remain ambiguous.

The Doll Maker, though more mature in narrative technique than Sarban's earlier novellas, is not without flaws. The author demonstrates a greater control over his narrative tone and characters in this tale, but there is a concomitant decrease of narrative force and emotional power. Nor is his conscious effort to employ symbolism entirely satisfactory, as it usually is in Gothic fiction by more assured masters, such as Nathaniel Hawthorne and Edgar Allan Poe. One *New York Herald-Tribune* reviewer placed *The Doll Maker* in the tradition of both Henry and M. R. James; beyond that, however, the rather late publication in paperback of this novel in North America, coming seven years after the first British edition, seems to have generated little interest among reviewers. These three books, nevertheless, were enough to create a reputation for Sarban "as a

subtle, literate teller of tales conscious of the darker and less acceptable implications that underlie much popular literature, according to John Clute and Chris Bell in *The Encyclopedia of Fantasy* (1997).

Although Sarban did not publish any new books after 1953, several unpublished manuscripts indicate that he continued his writing activities at least into the 1970s. In 1966 he retired from the Consular Service, though he continued working for the Foreign Office in a teaching capacity in London and Cheltenham. He and his wife separated in 1971. He retired to Monmouthshire in 1977 and died in 1989. Ten years later the previously unpublished fantasy story *The King of the Lake* was published by Tartarus Press in an edition with *The Sound of His Horn.*

On the whole, Sarban's contribution to the traditions of British fantasy rests on his three novellas. Despite the brevity of his literary career and the limited canon of fantasy stories he published, Sarban's fiction is notable for some memorable qualities. His work is characterized by a mature style, which may be vivid and sensuous or disciplined and austere. His fiction also is impressive in its creation of narrative suspense and in its ability to re-create the seductive power of numinous archaic figures from ancient myth. Although Wall in his role as Sarban was only a minor writer, his small body of fiction is probably an enduring contribution to the British fantasy tradition.

References:

Peter Nicholls, "Sarban," in *Supernatural Fiction Writers,* volume 2, edited by E. F. Bleiler (New York: Scribners, 1985), pp. 667–673;

R. B. Russell, "Sarban," *Lost Club Journal,* <http://freepages.pavilion.net/users/tartarus/wall.html>.

Papers:

Sarban's papers, including his unpublished manuscripts, are in the possession of his family.

Nevil Shute
(Nevil Shute Norway)
(17 January 1899 – 12 January 1960)

Corbin S. Carnell
University of Florida

BOOKS: *Marazan* (London: Cassell, 1926);

So Disdained (London: Cassell, 1928); republished as *The Mysterious Aviator* (Boston: Houghton Mifflin, 1928);

Lonely Road (London: Cassell, 1932; New York: Morrow, 1932);

Ruined City (London: Cassell, 1938); republished as *Kindling* (New York: Morrow, 1938);

What Happened to the Corbetts (London: Heinemann, 1939); published as *Ordeal* (New York: Morrow, 1939);

An Old Captivity (London: Heinemann, 1940; New York: Morrow, 1940);

Landfall: A Channel Story (London: Heinemann, 1940; New York: Morrow, 1940);

Pied Piper (London: Heinemann, 1942; New York: Morrow, 1942);

Pastoral (London: Heinemann, 1944; New York: Morrow, 1944);

Most Secret (London: Heinemann, 1945; New York: Morrow, 1945);

Vinland the Good (London: Heinemann, 1946; New York: Morrow, 1946);

The Chequer Board (London: Heinemann, 1947; New York: Morrow, 1947);

No Highway (London: Heinemann, 1948; New York: Morrow, 1948);

A Town Like Alice (London: Heinemann, 1950); republished as *The Legacy* (New York: Morrow, 1950); republished as *A Town Like Alice* (New York: Ballantine, 1981);

Round the Bend (London: Heinemann, 1951; New York: Morrow, 1951);

The Far Country (London: Heinemann, 1952; New York: Morrow, 1952);

In the Wet (London: Heinemann, 1953; New York: Morrow, 1953);

Slide Rule: The Autobiography of an Engineer (London: Heinemann, 1954; New York: Morrow, 1954);

Nevil Shute

Requiem for a Wren (London: Heinemann, 1955); published as *The Breaking Wave* (New York: Morrow, 1955);

Beyond the Black Stump (London: Heinemann, 1956; New York: Morrow, 1956);

On the Beach (London: Heinemann, 1957; New York: Morrow, 1957);

The Rainbow and the Rose (London: Heinemann, 1958; New York: Morrow, 1958);

Trustee from the Toolroom (London: Heinemann, 1960; New York: Morrow, 1960);

Stephen Morris (London: Heinemann, 1961; New York: Morrow, 1961).

Nevil Shute Norway, who wrote under the name Nevil Shute, is not much studied in literature courses, nor are there many articles and books about him; but his annual income from royalties was extensive, and most of his twenty-four books are still in print. He was a novelist whose work as an engineer informed his narratives, and some of his books include science-fiction elements—including his best-known novel, the nuclear holocaust tale *On the Beach* (1957).

If Shute's novels are considered escapist, one must note that none of his characters escape responsibility. In fact, responsibility is a major theme in Shute, one of the things that appeals to readers.

Nevil Shute Norway was born on 17 January 1899 to Arthur Hamilton Norway and Mary Louisa (Gadsden) Norway in Ealing, west of London. He reported in *Slide Rule: The Autobiography of an Engineer* (1954) that what he wanted most as a boy was to "mess around" with machines. He had a bad stammer, a problem he never completely overcame. His background was upper middle class; his father was a civil servant who was made head of the postal service in Ireland, and in 1912 the family moved to Dublin, where he spent happy summers. During the academic year he attended Shrewsbury School in England. His older brother, Fred, was killed in France in World War I, and young Nevil served in the medical corps during the Easter Rebellion, when his father's post office was burned. He wanted to be in the Flying Corps but was rejected because of his stammer. He enlisted in the infantry just before the war ended.

In 1918 Shute entered Oxford, where he did not distinguish himself, getting third-class honors in engineering. During his college years he wrote poetry. After graduating in 1922, he became a junior stress and performance calculator at the de Havilland Aircraft Company, where he learned to fly. He also bought a typewriter, perhaps encouraged by the writing activities of his family: his grandmother had been a writer of children's books; his father had published travel books; and his mother edited a volume of correspondence about the family's experiences in the Sinn Fein rebellion. Still, he did not initially intend to become a full-time professional writer, and in *Slide Rule* he explains why he published as Nevil Shute, not Nevil Norway: he

was concerned that his bosses "would probably take a poor view of an employee who wrote novels on the side," and he feared other engineers would consider him "to be not a serious person." But he enjoyed writing and kept at it.

In June 1923 Shute sent his first novel, "Stephen Morris," to a publisher. Despite three rejections, he wrote a second novel, "Pilotage," in fourteen weeks in early 1924; but it, too, was repeatedly turned down. He later spoke of this early work as not being particularly good, but these two novels about a young engineer were published after his death as *Stephen Morris* (1961), with some excision of philosophizing and lengthy introductory sections.

Two years after joining de Havilland, Shute left to join the Airship Guarantee Company as chief calculator for the *R.100,* a giant rigid airship, a job he held for the next six years. In 1930 an airship developed by the air ministry, the *R.101,* came apart during trials, killing forty-four men. This event preoccupies Shute in *Slide Rule,* and he observes that his project, having to be cost efficient as a private venture, produced a better airship than the government-subsidized *R.101.* Shute was apparently a good engineer and did important work on retractable landing gear and in-flight refueling.

As an engineer Shute found writing a relaxing activity and usually took only about six months to produce a novel. His first published novel, *Marazan* (1926), is about Philip Stenning, a man involved with British civil aviation after World War I, who gets caught up in avenging the death of a friend. He goes to Italy in search of Mattani, the murderer, and succeeds in killing him in self-defense. Julian Smith, author of the 1976 Twayne volume on Shute, calls *Marazan* a "rattling good yarn" reminiscent of John Buchan.

Between 1924 and 1930 Shute worked on the airship and for relaxation flew a small plane and wrote more novels about flying. His next novel, *So Disdained* (1928), reflected his love of England and of aviation as well as his concern for pilots who, after serving in the war, were now poorly paid. The American edition was called *The Mysterious Aviator.*

After the *R.101* crashed, the *R.100* was sold for scrap, in spite of the fact that it had flown successfully to Canada and back. In 1931 Shute founded a new company to build planes, Airspeed Limited, which employed a thousand workers. Later that year he married Frances Mary Heaton, a doctor at York Hospital. Though he mentions his wife and family only briefly in his autobiography, it seems to have been a happy marriage. It is likely that his wife provided the medical information he needed to describe various accidents and illnesses in his fiction.

Some critics believe that Shute's good literary work really started with his next novel, *Lonely Road* (1932), though some hold that it was not until *What Happened to the Corbetts* (1939) that Shute showed his mature abilities. Certainly the more he wrote, the more artistically shaped his novels were. *Lonely Road* is the complex story of a man named Malcolm Stevenson, who runs a shipping line and gets involved in intrigue; it is much like an early Graham Greene novel. Though Shute was a Tory in background and inclination, he ends the story with the protagonist confessing a broad faith in the democratic process.

Working hard to make Airspeed a success, Shute published no novels between 1932 and 1938. *Lonely Road* was made into a movie in 1936, and Shute started writing again. In 1938 he resigned from Airspeed and published *Ruined City,* selling the movie rights almost immediately. These first two movie sales, and several later ones, added substantially to his income.

Shute's next novel, *What Happened to the Corbetts,* is set in the near future, as he anticipated the coming of World War II. When the war began, Shute was highly critical of American isolationism. He sent his wife and their two young daughters to Canada for their safety. He joined the British navy and worked on weapons development. The rather prescient *What Happened to the Corbetts* is the story of a young lawyer named Peter Corbett; his wife, Joan; and their three small children, who are sleeping in the garage because of wartime bombing. They begin living on their small yacht to escape bombing and disease, and later they retreat to France, hoping to get passage to Canada. Though the novel employs little futuristic extrapolation, it is part of two long-standing traditions in science fiction, tales of the near future and narratives about future wars.

The characters are ordinary people muddling through with courage and integrity, a theme Shute incorporated in his other four war novels: *Landfall: A Channel Story* (1940); *Pied Piper* (1942); *Most Secret* (1945), which was written in 1942 but withheld from publication for a time by Admiralty censors for security reasons; and *Pastoral* (1944). Another novel, *An Old Captivity* (1940), about an aerial expedition to trace early Norse settlers in Greenland and Scottish explorers in North America, was written for relaxation and was meant to be escapist in the midst of the war.

Landfall is rather light reading also, but George Orwell found that it brought out "the essential peculiarity of war, the mixture of heroism and meanness." *Pied Piper,* about an elderly British lawyer named John Howard who rescues seven refugee chil-

Dust jacket for Shute's 1957 novel, set in 1962, in which the last people left alive on Earth after a nuclear holocaust await death in Australia

dren of various backgrounds from France just before the German invasion, brought Shute fame in England and in the United States. He had deliberately aimed his book at American readers, hoping that the United States would end its isolation.

His first postwar book was *Vinland the Good* (1946), a screenplay and his least successful work. It was an adaptation of the Viking segments in *An Old Captivity.* Screenwriting was not Shute's forte; as Smith states, "The novel was his form."

After the war Shute went to Burma to work for the Ministry of Information, but he did not stay long, returning to England and his full-time writing career in 1945. *The Chequer Board* (1947) grew out of his time in Burma. Its main character, Jackie Turner, is a "little man" who is nevertheless called on to make a difference, even though he is dying—inoperable shrapnel fragments are destroying his brain. His life becomes intertwined with three other lives as Shute tells this story of the struggle against racial prejudice and stereotyping.

In 1947 Shute traveled by car around the United States, seeking a firsthand glimpse into the real America. The following year he published *No Highway,* which returns to a favorite subject, civil aviation. *No Highway* is the story of Theodore Honey, a homely, eccentric research scientist who predicts the structural failure of a transatlantic airliner at 1,440 hours of flying time. When people will not listen to him, he secretly sabotages the plane while it is still on the ground so that it is unable to fly. In 1951 the story was made into a motion picture (titled *No Highway in the Sky* in the United States) starring James Stewart.

Shute wrote his next novel, *A Town Like Alice* (1950), in three and a half months; Smith suggests it was "a kind of income insurance policy . . . he wrote what he himself called a 'potboiler' to recoup the funds he had spent during his six months of travel" in 1948–1949, when he flew his own plane to Australia and back. The materials all come from his Australian experiences. *A Town Like Alice* has a simple plot: a man bequeaths a fortune to a niece, Jean Paget, with the stipulation that she not touch the principal until she is thirty-five, eight years hence. She learns that an Australian soldier whom she thought the Japanese had killed is alive and looking for her. They marry, and she uses the money to further the economic and social life of an Australian town, partly by attracting young women to it and thereby getting men to live there. Shute followed this novel with *Round the Bend* (1951), the story of a mystical aviator.

In 1950 Shute moved permanently to Australia, partly to avoid the higher taxes in England. For eight months he did no writing. Then he began *The Far Country* (1952), set in Australia and centering on another resourceful young woman, Jennifer Morton, who comes to Australia from England. Jennifer repeatedly compares life in England with life Down Under. She rejects the Labour government but values English ways, as do most Australians.

Shute enjoyed living in Australia, and he was well liked by the people there, who responded to his enthusiasm for their country. He bought a hundred acres of farmland south of Melbourne, expanding his holdings over the years. In 1951 he suffered a minor heart attack that forced him to give up flying his own plane.

During this period, in spite of his stammer, Shute began to lecture on professional writing. Among the topics he discussed were the elements he believed fiction readers want: information, romance, heroism, and a happy ending—even if it involves death. As Smith points out, Shute's next novel, *In the Wet* (1953), supplied those four things, and it added a

fifth element—topicality, in its depiction of the activities of Queen Elizabeth II, inspired by events surrounding her coronation. Like *Round the Bend,* this novel synthesized Christian and Buddhist beliefs and allusions as part of the story. Moreover, *In the Wet* includes a vision of the 1980s, in which Australia is the center of a thriving British empire free of socialism and with a prosperous royalty. In this respect the novel participates in the science-fiction tradition of envisioning a radically different future based on contemporary observations and trends.

Shute next turned to writing *Slide Rule,* which traces his life up to 1938. Smith posits that "the book is a disappointment because it stops short of the most potentially interesting years of his life—World War II and his growing success as a novelist." Shute then reworked a novel titled "Blind Understanding," which he had abandoned five years earlier, and the result was *Requiem for a Wren* (1955). It is the story of a World War II veteran and lawyer's attempt to discover the truth behind the family parlormaid's suicide.

In his best-known work, *On the Beach,* Shute takes up his most ambitious subject yet: the destruction of the world in a nuclear holocaust. Because he intended that one of the main characters should be American, Shute traveled to the United States again in 1954 to see what Americans were like, spending time in Oregon and in the Rockies. Smith observes that *On the Beach* "has more mood than plot"; the title is taken from T. S. Eliot's poem "The Hollow Men" (1925). The novel tells how in 1962 a nuclear war begins with the bombing of Tel Aviv and ends thirty-seven days later, presumably in total devastation. Southern Australia is the last part of the world to be affected by the spreading deadly radioactivity, which will reach there within a year. The novel depicts the things people focus on in their final weeks and days—alcohol, auto racing, church attendance, vegetable gardens, and suicide drugs. Yet, in many respects life goes on as before: American nuclear submarine captain Dwight Towers continues to buy gifts for his wife and children in Connecticut even though they are already dead. But he helps to bring closure to the novel; when he sees his men stricken with radiation sickness, he loads them on his submarine and sinks it one last time, himself aboard, in the depths of the sea. Other characters end their lives with cyanide pills.

Science-fiction writers had predicted the development of nuclear weapons well before the first atomic bombs were dropped on Hiroshima and Nagasaki in 1945, and authors were quick to foresee the possibility of worldwide destruction through such weapons years before nuclear stockpiles had risen to such a level. Thus, *On the Beach* is hardly unique in its topic. Shute's treatment of the subject, however, is noteworthy, both for the vividness of his depiction of the war's effects, especially on his characters, and in the remarkable popularity of the book.

Smith observes that Shute "probably did more than any other writer or thinker of the 1950s to make a large audience understand that men must suffer equally the results of what they do at home or allow to happen far away." Shute was surprised that *On the Beach* should be his most popular novel. It confirmed his belief that readers respond to sincerity more than they seek escape.

In 1958 a crew arrived in Melbourne to film the 1959 movie version of *On the Beach,* starring Gregory Peck, Ava Gardner, Fred Astaire, and Anthony Perkins. (Changes were made in the story to explain why so many Americans are in Australia.) Shute was quite unhappy with the movie, particularly with the decision to involve the character of Dwight Towers in a sexual affair, because he had tried to show that Towers still thought of his wife as being alive.

Shute finished only two novels in his last four years: *The Rainbow and the Rose* (1958), about a pilot reviewing the life of his mentor, and *Trustee from the Toolroom* (1960), which opens in West Ealing, where Shute lived as child, and is about an accomplished engineer. His work on the latter was impaired somewhat by a stroke he suffered in December 1958. Nevertheless, Shute gave some thought to continuing his autobiography in a volume to be titled "Set Square," and he began a new novel that was to metaphorically depict the Second Coming of Christ in the southern Australian wilderness. He was working on it when he died on 12 January 1960.

Though there is not much critical interest in Nevil Shute today, his books continue to be in print and are read throughout the English-speaking world and in a few translations. He remains admirable for his workman-like fiction, his desire to please his readers, and his compassion and deep humanity. He also earned a small but important role in British science fiction, particularly for *On the Beach,* one of the most striking depictions of nuclear holocaust in the literature.

References:

David Martin, "The Mind That Conceived 'On the Beach,'" *Meanjin,* 19 (June 1960): 193–200;
Julian Smith, *Nevil Shute* (Boston: Twayne, 1976).

Papers:

Nevil Shute's manuscripts are housed at the National Library of Australia, with microfilm copies in the Arents Library at Syracuse University.

Olaf Stapledon

(10 May 1886 – 6 September 1950)

William F. Touponce
Indiana University–Purdue University at Indianapolis

See also the Stapledon entry in *DLB 15: British Novelists, 1930–1959.*

BOOKS: *Latter-Day Psalms* (Liverpool: Young, 1914);

A Modern Theory of Ethics: A Study of the Relations of Ethics and Psychology (London: Methuen, 1929; New York: Dutton, 1929);

Last and First Men: A Story of the Near and Far Future (London: Methuen, 1930; New York: Cape & Smith, 1931);

Last Men in London (London: Methuen, 1932; Boston: Gregg Press, 1976);

Waking World (London: Methuen, 1934);

Odd John: A Story Between Jest and Earnest (London: Methuen, 1935; New York: Dutton, 1936);

Star Maker (London: Methuen, 1937; New York: Berkley, 1961);

Saints and Revolutionaries (London: Heinemann, 1939);

New Hope for Britain (London: Methuen, 1939);

Philosophy and Living, 2 volumes (Harmondsworth, U.K.: Penguin, 1939);

Darkness and the Light (London: Methuen, 1942; Westport, Conn.: Hyperion, 1974);

Beyond the "Isms" (London: Secker & Warburg, 1942);

Seven Pillars of Peace (London: Common Wealth, 1944);

Old Man in New World (London: Allen & Unwin, 1944);

Sirius: A Fantasy of Love and Discord (London: Secker & Warburg, 1944);

Death into Life (London: Methuen, 1946);

Youth and Tomorrow (London: St. Botolph, 1946);

The Flames: A Fantasy (London: Secker & Warburg, 1947);

Worlds of Wonder: Three Tales of Fantasy (Los Angeles: Fantasy, 1949);

A Man Divided (London: Methuen, 1950);

To the End of Time: The Best of Olaf Stapledon, edited by Basil Davenport (New York: Funk & Wagnalls, 1953);

The Opening of the Eyes, edited by Agnes Z. Stapledon (London: Methuen, 1954);

Olaf Stapledon

4 Encounters (Hayes, Middlesex: Bran's Head Books, 1976);

"Nebula Maker" (Hayes, Middlesex: Bran's Head Books, 1976);

Far Future Calling: A Radio Play, edited by Harvey Satty (New York: Olaf Stapledon Society, 1978);

Far Future Calling: Uncollected Science Fiction and Fantasies of Olaf Stapledon, edited by Sam Moskowitz (Philadelphia: Train, 1979).

Collection: *An Olaf Stapledon Reader,* edited by Robert Crossley (Syracuse, N.Y.: Syracuse University Press, 1997).

OTHER: "Experiences in the Friends' Ambulance Unit," in *We Did Not Fight 1914–18: Experiences of War Resisters,* edited by Julian Bell (London: Cobden- Sanderson, 1935), pp. 359–374;

"Literature and the Unity of Man," in *Writers in Freedom: A Symposium,* edited by Herman Ould (London: Hutchinson, 1942), pp. 113–119;

"Letters to the Future," edited by Robert Crossley, in *The Legacy of Olaf Stapledon: Critical Essays and an Unpublished Manuscript,* edited by Patrick A. McCarthy, Charles Elkins, and Martin Henry Greenberg (New York: Greenwood Press, 1989), pp. 99–120.

SELECTED PERIODICAL PUBLICATIONS– UNCOLLECTED: "Theory of the Unconscious," *Monist* [Chicago], 37 (July 1927): 422–444;

"The Location of Physical Objects," *Journal of Philosophical Studies,* 4 (January 1929): 64–75;

"The Remaking of Man," *Listener,* 5 (8 April 1931): 575–576;

"The Dialectic of Science," *London Mercury,* 39 (January 1939): 454–455;

"Escapism in Literature," *Scrutiny* [Cambridge, England], 8 (December 1939): 298–308;

"Morality, Scepticism and Theism," *Proceedings of the Aristotelian Society,* 44 (1943–1944): 15–42;

"Education for Personality-in-Community," *New Era in Home and School,* 27 (March 1946): 63–67;

"Data for a World View: 1. The Human Situation and Natural Science," *Enquiry* (April 1948): 13–18;

"Data for a World View: 2. Paranormal Experiences," *Enquiry,* 1 (May 1948): 13–18;

"Interplanetary Man?" *Journal of the British Interplanetary Society,* 7 (November 1948): 213–233;

"Personality and Living," *Philosophy,* 24 (April 1949): 144–156;

"Man's Future," *Prediction,* 14 (April 1949): 4–6;

"Science Finds a New Universe," *Prediction,* 15 (August 1949): 14–16;

"The Ways of Peace," *One World,* 3 (October–November 1950): 178–185.

Olaf Stapledon was one of the most distinguished writers of science fiction in English in the period between World War I and World War II. He was often proclaimed the successor of H. G. Wells, and he and Wells corresponded for almost a decade. Stapledon openly acknowledged his debt to Wells, but he lacked Wells's intellectual certainties even when he criticized him. Like many writers of the 1930s, such as W. H. Auden and George Orwell, Stapledon expressed in his work a crisis of conscience, a loss of faith in capitalism and parliamentary democracy, and a sense of contempt for organized religion. Unlike Orwell, who was a participant greatly affected by the Spanish Civil War, Stapledon remained a socialist, and a pacifist, all of his life.

As a science-fiction writer, he was concerned with the fate of humanity in the universe, which he believed was not just matter but also spirit. For Stapledon, the purpose of humanity in the universe was to understand the nature of this spirit, insofar as was humanly (or in some of his novels, superhumanly) possible. He considered the most distinctive thing about humanity to be its power of standing outside itself, in ecstasis, its capacity for disinterested objectivity even in the face of its own ultimate destruction. The experience of the spirit in Stapledon's fiction is often austere and its fate tragic, tied up with transcending the tortured and isolated individual self by means of a telepathic consciousness capable of spanning the vast totality of an indifferent universe. By participating in the final fate of this evolving spirit, which becomes a larger cosmic consciousness or "personality-in-community," Stapledon's narrators often discover a strange source of almost mystical exaltation.

All of Stapledon's works demand of their reader a move toward a more cosmic perspective. Stapledon never used the term "science fiction," preferring to call his texts "essays in myth creation" or "romances of the future." His literary concepts and fictional techniques– what he called fantastic fiction of a semiphilosophical kind–defy traditional literary classification. They have been called "philosophical epics," "cosmic macrohistories," or "mythic panoramas" and are often not about the fate of specific individuals but rather that of many life-forms evolving and mutating during eons of time throughout the entire cosmos.

Although his literary reputation declined in England during the 1940s, and he had little affection for American culture and the pulp-magazine science fiction of the 1930s and the 1940s that came to dominate the genre, Stapledon remains one of the most influential figures in science fiction in any language. His influence on Stanisław Lem, for instance, is well known. For British writers of the generation that succeeded him, such as Arthur C. Clarke and Brian W. Aldiss, Stapledon's imagination showed the way to their own visions. To these writers he was not just a figure of the past. In his foreword to the fiftieth-anniversary edition of Stapledon's *Star Maker* (1937) Aldiss remarked that "whatever it may be–novel, myth, prose poem, vision–*Star Maker*

Stapledon as an ambulance driver during World War I

remains light years ahead, something towards which the rest of us are still traveling."

William Olaf Stapledon was born into comfortable bourgeoise circumstances, to William Clibbett and Emmeline Miller Stapledon, on 10 May 1886 in Wallasey, near Liverpool, England. For most of his life Stapledon lived on the Wirral peninsula adjacent to Liverpool, in a series of houses constructed with his family's financial resources. His family was in commercial shipping in Liverpool and Port Said, Egypt. The first six years of Stapledon's childhood were spent in that international crossroads, an environment that may have played some part in his later intellectual rejection of nationalism and "tribalism."

According to Sam Moskowitz, Stapledon was an only child and rather lonely; his closest friend was Rip, a rough-haired terrier who was a likely source of inspiration for *Sirius: A Fantasy of Love and Discord* (1944), the story of a superintelligent dog. Stapledon's parents were relatively old when he was born, and they seem to have sheltered him. He got along extremely well with his father, who taught him about the natural sciences, but somewhat less so with his mother, who was possessive and fearful for his welfare, even after Stapledon married. Nonetheless, his mother certainly mediated to him

some of his socialist ideas, for her idol was John Ruskin, with whom she corresponded extensively. Stapledon's agnosticism seems also to be derived from his parents; his father subscribed to no religious sect at all, and his mother was Unitarian.

His formal schooling was late. His elementary education was conducted at Abbotsholme, a progressive boarding school that he attended for six years. In 1905 he entered Balliol College, Oxford, graduating with a B.A. in modern history in 1909 and an M.A. in 1913. Moskowitz reports that during this period Stapledon attained his full physical growth of five feet, eight inches and 140 pounds, which seldom varied for the rest of his life. He was muscular and rowed in the college eight, the competitive rowing team. At Oxford he produced his first known writings, which prefigure some of the concerns expressed in his cosmic histories. His earliest known publication, "The Splendid Race," which discusses the use of eugenics to fashion an improved humanity, appeared in *The Old Abbotsholmian* of 1908. Also in 1908 he gave a lecture to the Historical Society of Balliol on the voices of Joan of Arc, which may be a prefiguring of his interest in the theme of telepathic mind invasion.

After his graduation from Oxford, Stapledon spent a year as an assistant master at Manchester Grammar School, teaching history. Judging from the semi-autobiographical *Last Men in London* (1932), it was a frustrating experience. His unorthodox teaching methods apparently irritated other teachers. In 1910 he entered the family business in Liverpool while also working in a shipping agency in Port Said, running a motorboat to reach and board ships to see if they needed coal before or after their canal passage. He enjoyed the boating but was again frustrated by the paperwork that accompanied such a business. According to Moskowitz, Stapledon's family–particularly his mother–did not want him away from home anyway and discouraged his Port Said efforts. They were also happy when a hoped-for position at the University of Wales fell through.

In an effort to establish some kind of independent intellectual life for himself, Stapledon then joined the Workers' Educational Association (WEA), lecturing extramurally from Liverpool University to workingmen on literature and industrial history. These lectures frequently stressed left-wing political views, for he was immersed in socialist philosophy at the time. Moskowitz posits that Stapledon's political views kept him from obtaining a permanent academic position. At any rate, by the outbreak of World War I he was committed to pacifist ideas. Not wanting just to stand aside while others were involved in the fighting, however, Stapledon joined the Friends Ambulance Unit in

December 1915, serving mainly the wounded of a French division in Champagne, the Argonne, and Lorraine. He served as an ambulance driver in France until January 1919 and was awarded the Croix de Guerre. He wrote about his wartime activities in an essay for *We Did Not Fight 1914–18: Experiences of War Resisters* (1935) and fictionalized them through his character Paul in *Last Men in London*.

His first book, however, was *Latter-Day Psalms* (1914), a collection of poems published with the financial assistance of his father. Though his cadences are vaguely Whitmanesque, his diction is traditionally "poetic," and his subjects are conventional for a leftist intellectual of his time (they include atheism, social revolution, the plight of the workingman, and sympathy for the devil). Writing poetry interested Stapledon all of his life, and there is more of it in *Last Men in London*. But on the whole this volume was rather undistinguished, never garnering him any critical praise. No one seriously argues that these poems are important to the history of modernist poetry; however, critics concerned with the internal development of Stapledon's notion of spirit see him wrestling forty years later with the same dilemmas enunciated in these pieces. For instance, Patrick A. McCarthy argues that the poems taken in sequence "trace a spiritual journey from the simple rejection of the world as he finds it [which operates without the presence of a just God] to a more complex and ambiguous affirmation of transcendent spiritual verities."

Stapledon married Agnes Zena Miller, a first cousin from Australia, on 16 July 1919. Stapledon and his new wife, whose family was also in shipping, had met frequently during their childhoods. They corresponded regularly during the war and became engaged by letter. Their daughter, Mary Sidney, was born in 1920; their son, John David, in 1923. But Stapledon remained financially dependent on his father, who bought the newly married couple a house in West Kirby, where they lived until 1940. Stapledon was ambivalent about his father's money throughout his life, feeling protected by the capitalist system he had intellectually rejected.

Stapledon continued his employment with the WEA. However, feeling that he wanted to explore his true intellectual interests, he went to Liverpool University for a Ph.D. in philosophy. His thesis—called "Meaning"—was completed in 1925. It was never published, but Stapledon went on to publish a series of articles in respected professional philosophical journals on various topics. In 1927, for instance, he published an article in *The Monist* on Sigmund Freud's theory of the unconscious. Officially, Stapledon took a skeptical view of Freud's theories, though this hesitation did not stop his

narrators from making Freudian observations about their subjects. For instance, the fictional biographer of *Sirius* frequently offers Freudian interpretations of the relationship between his wife, Plaxy, and the dog, Sirius, suggesting that Plaxy's ambivalence toward Sirius stems from the fact that in her unconscious the dog represents her father.

From 1925 onward Stapledon's lecturing for the WEA was in philosophy and psychology. He continued to write poetry, realizing however that it was not his strong point. He also published his first book of philosophy, *A Modern Theory of Ethics: A Study of the Relations of Ethics and Psychology* (1929). No one knows why Stapledon turned to writing science fiction to express his ideas. His decision to write fiction might have come from a vacation experience on the Welsh seacoast, probably in the mid 1920s, when he and his wife heard the human-like crying of the seals splashed by the cold rising tide. From this experience Stapledon had a vision of human nature remade to fit alien environments. In 1930, probably after several years of work, Stapledon published his vast future history of mankind, *Last and First Men: A Story of the Near and Far Future*. It sold better in England than in the United States (going into four printings), but according to Moskowitz, the reviews by some of the most important critics in the United States were nothing short of superlative. These reviews—and the generally positive reception of the book—determined the future direction of Stapledon's life. He became a full-time writer and a part-time lecturer, though he still depended on his family's money for a livelihood.

Since it covers billions of years in human evolution on three planets and through eighteen species of man, *Last and First Men* obviously defies easy summary. Furthermore, it is as rich in extrapolative details as it is abstract and ironic in style. One example of extrapolative detail producing cognitive estrangement is the physical appearance of Stapledon's Last Men, who inhabit Neptune. They have been genetically altered to live in the tremendous pressure of that planet, evolving new sense organs in the process. They possess a pair of occipital eyes to afford 360-degree vision, as well as an upward-looking "astronomical eye" on the crowns of their heads with which they study the cosmos. Besides the familiar eye colors, there are orbs of topaz, emerald, amethyst, and ruby. It seems that the human and the animal interpenetrate in these creatures, so that there have developed "innumerable physiognomic types." Stapledon's narrator, who is one of the Last Men, says that the First Men—that is, twentieth-century earthlings—would probably miss the humanity of the Last Men, seeing them as "old Egyptian deities with animal heads." But they are much more, in every feature. Sta-

Agnes Zena Miller, whom Stapledon married in 1919

pledon's narrator makes it clear that they preserve useful features from all stages of humanity's development. In addition, they possess a facial expression and bodily gestures peculiar to their own species, "luminous," yet pungent with "ironical significance."

Their irony no doubt stems from the fact that they have telepathically observed all periods of human evolution in the past from the standpoint of a more developed consciousness. Internally they possess a special organ within the brain that allows telepathic communication within the "multi-sexual" group and, in certain moments of supreme experience, with the entire race. They have seen the huge fluctuations of joy and woe that make up Stapledon's myth of "racial adventure." But also, because they have achieved spiritual maturity and a philosophical mind, they possess something more than irony: an ecstatic acceptance of fate, or as Stapledon puts it, "the dispassionate ecstasy which salutes the Real as it is and would not change one jot of it." Still living within human history, however fantastically remote, they are themselves caught up in a time of crisis. Because an unprecedented deluge of radiation from a nearby star threatens to destroy the sun, they have embarked on two mighty projects: first, to explore the entire extent of the human past in order to contem-

plate the totality of the "whole great saga of man" as a completed work of tragic art, thereby transfiguring grief into ecstasy; and second, to disseminate among the stars the seeds of a new humanity.

This latter task is the more difficult one for them, and not just for technical reasons. It turns out that because they have learned the "supreme art of ecstatic fatalism" so well, they find it almost intolerably repugnant to continue the "arid labour" of designing and producing in vast quantities an artificial human seed small enough to be blown along on the solar winds (which are coming from the very star that will destroy them). Thus, they also need the past in order to learn over again "that other supreme achievement of the spirit," loyalty to life embattled against death.

As interesting as the other human species are, the essence of the book lies in the Last Men and their projects. Because they are embodiments of Stapledon's myth of the future, they are the ones who enunciate his major themes: the relentless acceptance of fate and the search for the "cosmic ideal" of an awakened universe, a cosmic spirit, which someday may be embraced (continued on a much larger scale in *Star Maker*). Moreover, their projects provide the motivation for the book, since with their journeys into past time they hope to influence earlier epochs—the reader's time—with their own philosophy. Stapledon makes clear, however, that modern humans' puny brains are not capable of holding such grandeur in contemplation. Stapledon's Neptunian narrator ironically points out in the introduction that the "actual writer" (Stapledon himself), though he seeks to tell a plausible story, "neither believes it himself nor expects others to believe it. Yet the story is true." Near the end he also expresses the view that the book, so admirable in conception, has issued from Stapledon's brain "in such disorder as to be mostly rubbish." In this manner another major theme of Stapledon's is enunciated: the failed vision of cosmic totality created by all-too-human limitations.

The Last Men also provide the major metaphor that is the key to understanding the thematic structure of Stapledon's imaginative universe: "Man himself is music." Stapledon conceived of the whole cosmic adventure of mankind as a symphony in progress, which may or may not achieve its just conclusion. Again, the totality of this pattern of intertwining themes that evolve and die cannot be grasped by a normal human mind, according to Stapledon's Neptunian narrator. Indeed, only in the state of the racially awakened mind can the Last Men themselves hear this music of the spheres. Nonetheless, something of this polyphonic pattern of cosmic events, the perfection of the whole, is what the Neptunian narrator manages to construct in his narrative.

Stapledon is aware that formally he is not writing a polyphonic novel on a vast scale (such as that of Frank Herbert's *Dune* series, beginning in 1965, or Stephen Baxter's Xeelee series, beginning in 1987); yet, the musical metaphor still expresses something that is essential to modern novelistic consciousness: its open-ended, unfinished qualities. Consequently, Stapledon's myths are not closed structures limiting humanity's horizons; rather, they live on in their unfinished state. In this sense they do not have the function of traditional myths but instead act more like fictional constructs known to be fictions and accepted as such, as "a fiction needed for the rationalizing of our experience," which is how Stapledon's Neptunian narrator expresses it. Without some such myth the meaning of life, and human loyalty to it, would collapse. Furthermore, his human narrators frequently express their own unreliability, which is hardly a prime characteristic of the narrators of traditional myth, who frequently claim to be telling god-inspired truth.

What ultimately happens to the two projects of the Last Men is revealed in Stapledon's next book, *Last Men in London,* published in 1932, the year his father died. It is a kind of sequel to *Last and First Men.* Readers learn in the epilogue of the earlier novel that the dissemination has probably failed, but it is by no means certain that it has. By remaining so ambiguous about the fate of the dissemination, Stapledon has left himself another open-ended thread with which to weave another story. But since radiation has increased the degeneration of mankind, the racial mode of contemplation used by the Last Men is no longer possible. The data that were still being collected would never be incorporated in the single racial consciousness, in the aesthetic apprehension of the Cosmos by the fully awaked Spirit of Man, leaving them only with "the blind recollection of past light."

Formally, *Last Men in London* is more of a novel than its predecessor, providing a closer look at the home life of one of the Last Men, as well as a human protagonist controlled by a "Neptunian parasite." Indeed, the book documents the struggles of the young man, Paul, with the society of World War I Britain and with his controller, so much so that readers are tempted to agree with the narrator that it is not the record of one isolated consciousness (which Paul in the early part mostly thinks himself to be) but a "strange hybrid sprung from the intercourse of a purely Terrestrial mind and a Neptunian mind, earth-infected." Certainly, it is a good psychological novel of paranoia, as Paul comes to the horrifying realization that he is inhabited by another, an alien being bent on shaping his ego. The Neptunian narrator, in fact, tortures Paul into accepting that he must not fear death but must make his own con-

tribution to the spirit, to "the intolerable, the inhuman, beauty" of the music of the spheres; the narrator thus fills Paul's mind with images of cosmic pain and grief, including the leitmotiv of a dead mare, already decaying. From its hindquarters projects the "hideously comical" face of its unborn foal, symbolizing a world powerless to be born.

Printings of *Last Men in London* were small, and it never attained the popularity of *Last and First Men.* Moskowitz opines that perhaps because more than half of it was devoted to the agonies of World War I, the book was doomed to have only a narrow appeal to science-fiction readers who were expecting more cosmic vistas. Nevertheless, Stapledon received letters of praise from noted scientists such as J. B. S. Haldane (whose own brief synopsis of the next forty million years, called "The Last Judgement," published in 1927, certainly influenced Stapledon). He began a correspondence with Wells and received more invitations to lecture than he could possibly accept. Apparently he made a conscious decision not to move to London, feeling that he would be absorbed there and that he had a more important role to play as a provincial intellectual. He continued to hold his WEA job, began calling himself a socialist, and became a member of the Fabians.

During this period he was sympathetic to Marxism but critical of it. Stapledon spoke frequently at peace rallies, trying at one time to circulate a peace petition to be signed by millions of British citizens. He contributed articles, reviews, and letters to such journals as *The London Mercury, New Statesman, Leader,* and *The Listener.* Despite his active public life in the 1930s, Stapledon managed to devote several hours of each day to his garden. He was also fond of hiking, swimming, and participating in folk-dancing societies with his family. Stapledon also enjoyed making elaborate toy boats for his children. To his neighbors he seemed a friendly fellow, rather eccentric (he swam in the lake at all times of the year) but otherwise unexceptional.

Despite all of this activity, both public and private, during the second half of the 1930s Stapledon wrote two of his greatest books, *Odd John: A Story Between Jest and Earnest* (1935) and *Star Maker.* For *Odd John* (and the later *Sirius,* which also purports to be a biography) he adopted a narrative strategy that made the book much more accessible. Both of his earlier books were narrated by a superior being and aimed at the First Men, who cannot comprehend fully the meaning of the books but who can be given glimpses of the future in order that they may become more alert to their real status in the universe and catch a glimpse of the self-detached ecstasy of the truly human. In *Odd John* there is more of a sharing of superhuman vision with ordinary people, so much so that it can be consid-

Cartoon drawn by Stapledon on the back of a photograph and sent to Miller in 1916 (from Talking Across the World: The Love Letters of Olaf Stapledon and Agnes Miller, 1913–1919, *edited by Robert Crossley, 1987)*

ered Stapledon's first real novel, for the narrator is simply a journalist fascinated by John Wainwright's story, examining documents and reporting on conversations and interviews. In general, readers' moral reactions to John and their points of view are conditioned by the narrator's, though they may part company with his judgment on some occasions. Readers do not have any such guide for their response to attributes of the Last Men such as their ritual cannibalism, which the narrator of *Last and First Men* simply reports.

The events of *Odd John* include murder and incest, which may indeed shock readers, but Stapledon manages to evoke a sympathetic fascination for John, who possesses a superhuman intellect and is searching for others of his kind. At first he picks up a general buzz of telepathic "noise" put out by the normal species of humans, but soon he is able to focus on outstanding themes. Not coincidentally, the first trace of other superhuman mentality is revealed by music, played on a recorder by a man who is an inmate in an insane asylum. Through his playing (which the other patients take to be noise) the young John is shown for the first time "just precisely the true, appropriate attitude of the adult human spirit to its world," curiously pious yet aloof, which is the starting point of maturity in Stapledon's philosophy. Appropriately enough, the only ordinary music invented by *Homo sapiens* that is of interest to this "mad" person is the contrapuntal and complexly layered music of Johann Sebastian Bach.

John eventually assembles a colony of superhuman beings on an island in the Pacific, where he embarks on the two "supreme tasks" of the awakened spiritual community: to help in the practical task of world building (John makes it clear that his community is communist and that to a limited extent he admires the model of Soviet Russia) and to employ itself to the best of its capacity in intelligent worship of the universe. Since the normal human species is irrevocably infected with nationalism, militarism, chauvinism, and other subhuman elements that prevent its awakening into a higher awareness, John and his group would gladly destroy humanity if they could: "*Homo sapiens* has little more to contribute to the music of this planet, nothing in fact but vain repetition. It is time for finer instruments to take up the theme," he says to his biographer, who feels that John must be right, partly because he realizes with John that humanity would certainly destroy the superhumans.

The activities of the superhuman community on the island provide some good science-fiction elements, even by modern standards of extrapolation. Because the inhabitants are telepaths, they no longer need to use human language, or do so only elliptically. They have discovered a way of manipulating matter on the atomic level with their psychic abilities, so that they have a potentially unlimited source of power. Furthermore, these "juvenile freaks" (for so they are regarded by the outside world) are experimenting on the embryos of captured humans in order to produce more superhumans. They exhibit mental dominance and can administer "hypnotic inoculation" to any hostile figures invading the settlement, making them see fearful things. They can also administer "oblivifaction" of memory to any friendly visitors leaving the island. Eventually, however, and before they can come to full power as a community, their island is discovered and (self)destroyed. Yet, John Wainwright does achieve his final attitude of ecstasy in the face of oblivion through the awakened community of supernormal peers.

In 1937 Methuen published *Star Maker,* which returns to the cosmic themes of *Last and First Men,* only on a much larger scale. Treating the two-billion-year history of the human race in just a few paragraphs, Stapledon goes on to tell the history of the entire universe (other universes are considered, as well). *Star Maker* has been compared to a dream quest or vision, as the human narrator journeys through the universe in search of its creator, the Star Maker. The narrator's native powers of thought and imagination are aided by beings of superhuman development. Again Stapledon uses the device of the unreliable narrator, whose record of the journey turns out to be after all "no more reliable than the rigamarole of any mind unhinged by the impact of experience beyond its comprehension." But as the narrator journeys through the universe, readers see myriad creatures—nautiloids, symbiotic ichthyoid-arachnoids, bird composites, plantmen, living stars and nebulae—who reenact the same human spiritual crises seen on Earth: their "chrysalis" worlds are all capable of achieving true community on a worldwide scale and of finally conceiving the appropriate spiritual attitude toward the universe, but may destroy themselves through selfishness.

As the narrator achieves greater telepathic sympathy with alien life-forms, he experiences the birth of his "third mind"—not as a fusion with the other in higher synthesis, but as an always-present "contrapuntal harmony of each in relation to the other," one that does not subsume or abolish differences. In the early stages of the journey the narrator believes that human history is shaped by a progressive improvement in the species and a gradual awakening of the human spirit. Later, however, he sees cosmic proof against such a theory, as entire cultures revert to barbarism, followed by protracted periods of subhuman savagery. He laments the horror that "all struggle should be finally, absolutely vain," and in this horror it seems to him that the Star Maker must be Hate itself.

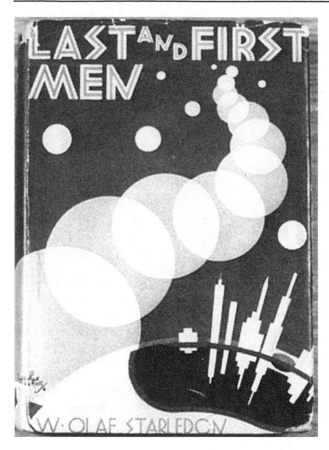

Dust jacket for the 1931 U.S. edition of Stapledon's 1930 novel, in which human beings undergo evolutionary adaptations that allow them to live on other planets (courtesy of The Lilly Library, Indiana University)

When the narrator finally meets the Star Maker it appears as a bright, blinding star that evolves to greater and greater insight into itself by learning from its previous creations. Struck down by the blinding light of this ruthless maker, the narrator now realizes that the creator's primary motivating spirit is contemplative, not loving or benign. Eventually, he learns to accept its creative acts as good and affirms that he must praise them. At the end he discusses the cycle of previous universes. Several are literally made up of music and resemble the tonal world depicted in his short fantasy story "A World of Sound," collected in *Far Future Calling: Uncollected Science Fiction and Fantasies of Olaf Stapledon* (1979).

Star Maker elicited an outpouring of appreciative reviews, including one from Bertrand Russell, published in the *London Mercury* (1937); in his review, Russell praised Stapledon's "fine intellectual courage," saying that his writing had "a quality of austere beauty." Also during this period Stapledon made initial contact with the world of science-fiction magazines and writers through Eric Frank Russell, a member of the British Interplanetary Society and a budding British

science-fiction writer himself. Stapledon's reaction to American pulp science fiction (and to America as well) was that it was pretty adolescent material, especially in the area of love interest, and of uneven quality, though he was surprised by the amount of it.

When World War II broke out, Stapledon lectured on social and psychological subjects at army and Royal Air Force bases, under an educational program organized by the War Office. Closer to home, he became a local air-raid warden. In 1940 the family moved into a new house at Simon's Field, near Caldy. During the war years Stapledon continued his writing career with such philosophical and political books as *Philosophy and Living* (1939), *Saints and Revolutionaries* (1939), and *New Hope for Britain* (1939). As a social prophet, Stapledon was by all accounts sadly mistaken about Adolf Hitler, the ferocity of fascism, and the extermination of the European Jews during World War II. However, in March of 1939 the Stapledons took in an Austrian refugee student of Jewish ancestry, Wolfgang Brueck, who came to be regarded as a family member. Another way that Stapledon was affected by the war was the sinking of his son's ship, the HMS *Aldenham,* by a mine in the Adriatic Sea in 1944. David Stapledon was one of the few survivors.

Although during this period Stapledon published a series of articles in *Scrutiny* on literary and critical topics such as the nature of escapism in literature, his fictional output was limited to one book, *Darkness and the Light* (1942). The book is a kind of allegory of the forces besetting the modern soul, organized contrapuntally by two themes, those of darkness and "the triumphing light." It offers two futures for the world: one in which humanity degenerates into barbarism and is finally exterminated by a species of mutated rat, and the other a utopian one in which humanity is awakened into a true spiritual community by Tibetan monks. Although he did not predict the rise of fascism, Stapledon in this book foresees along the dark path, in a kind of alternate reality, the domination of Europe by a Fourth Reich. As part of their propaganda war against the Tibetans, the fascists create a "synthetic religion" to motivate the masses against them and generally manipulate the population in a manner that anticipates Orwell's *Nineteen Eighty-Four* (1949). Along the path toward light a modified Marxist-socialist world state ensues, at once supermodern and yet in a way medieval, for most people live in small, self-sufficient villages.

Stapledon never took utopian thought to be the last word about humanity, however. Soon the "forwards" or visionary philosophers of this society of light detect a widespread and perhaps more fundamental principle of darkness (conceived in the mythical form of dark titans brawling in the snowy light of the universe, it owes much to Norse mythology) that threatens to extinguish the light. Rather than give way to nihilism and despair, they propose that the human race dedicate itself to the spiritual struggle for racial awakening that will constitute a "heroic venture of sacrificing everything in the attempt to destroy the 'titans' with the lucidity of the human spirit." The experiment fails when a plague nearly destroys the human race, but in the distant future the narrator sees again the rise of a new species of humanity loyal to the light.

Darkness and the Light simply restates many of Stapledon's themes. Because much of its fictional content was so rapidly overtaken by real events at the end of the war (such as the atomic bomb), it became one of the author's rarest books until it was reprinted in the United States by Hyperion Press in 1974. It remains fascinating to read, however, if only because of the oddity of Tibetan biological warfare. Instead of bombarding the world with their own ideology, they inject into their native soil toxins that produce amnesia, undermining the grip of the "synthetic religion" among the invading armies. This book also marks a significant departure in Stapledon's conception of the nature of ultimate reality. Whereas previously he had conceived of the Star Maker as blinding light, he now sees ultimate reality in terms of darkness, as wholly Other than man, and his deepening agnosticism is apparent.

Old Man in New World (1944) is basically a socialist allegory about the reactions of an austere old revolutionary to a pageant celebrating the founding of the New World State and put on by the much more relaxed children of the revolution. The old man is concerned with maintaining the order that he fought to create; the young man—a twenty-three-year-old "product of the Revolution"—who brings him as an honored guest to the ceremonies is concerned with preventing that order from stagnating. Although the old man finds himself emotionally moved by the ceremony, he cannot tolerate the carnival spirit that erupts. Clowns, comedians, and jesters burlesque the seriousness of the pageant, suggesting the willingness of the younger generation to accept criticism. In the climax to the ceremony a "court fool" even sits on the speakers' platform and mimics the political leaders who address the crowd. This brief but well-executed novelette, with its pageant displaying the otherness created by repressive revolutionary socialism, represents Stapledon's inversion of his own serious themes. Caught between two worlds, the old man responds emotionally to the message of the fool, but cannot fit it into the system of thought that carried him through the revolution.

Among Stapledon's later books, none has been so popular as *Sirius,* which many literary critics feel is his best novelistic achievement as well. Almost unique among Stapledon's works, which seldom have a well-rounded character acting as central consciousness, *Sirius* tells with verisimilitude (borrowing some of its convincing details from John Herries McCulloch's *Sheep Dogs and Their Masters,* 1938) the story of a super-intelligent dog's tragic attempt to live in the human world. Because it dramatizes with sympathy the conflicts that distress Sirius throughout his life, particularly the conflict between his "wolf-nature" and his compassionate civilized mentality, it makes Stapledon's theme of the necessity of leading the awakened spiritual life accessible in a way that his other, more austere books do not. Stapledon chose a dog to embody what in his view makes people most human: the ability to hear and compose the music of the spirit.

The book, subtitled *A Fantasy of Love and Discord,* has two main characters: the dog, Sirius, and Plaxy, his human "sister" and lover. The music of their lives is structured as a duet of variations upon three themes, as Sirius himself points out. First there is the difference in their biological natures, which tends to separate them. Then there is the love between them, which unites them and actually feeds on these differences. Lastly there is sex, which alternates between tearing them apart because of their biological remoteness and welding them together because of their love. (Because its subject matter includes sexual relations between a young woman and a superintelligent dog, *Sirius* was rejected by Methuen and was published by Secker and Warburg. Stapledon was somewhat ahead of his time in his willingness to discuss interspecies sexual relationships, which were hardly talked about at all in American science fiction until the 1950s.)

Sirius suggests to Plaxy that there is a fourth theme to their music, which is perhaps the unity of the other three: the journey along the way of the spirit, together and yet worlds apart. For her part Plaxy believes that they have a treasure in common, "a bright gem of community," and that she herself is a partner in a higher entity, the human part of Sirius-Plaxy.

When Sirius is finally hunted down and killed by the "human" forces of prejudice, Plaxy sings one of his strange songs, a mixture of the hounds' baying blended with human voices, as his requiem. Facing the dawn, she feels that the power of his music—which he has also sung in human churches—epitomizes something common to all awakening spirits on Earth and in the farthest galaxies. For although Sirius has never experienced the pleasures of human eyesight, "the music's darkness was lit up by a brilliance," a color that he himself has never seen, but that is "glimpsed by the quickened mind everywhere." From the internal evidence of musical themes, then, one could argue that Stapledon intends readers to understand *Sirius* to be a

LAST MEN IN LONDON

BY

W. OLAF STAPLEDON
Author of "LAST AND FIRST MEN"

METHUEN & CO. LTD. LONDON

Dust jacket for Stapledon's 1932 novel, in which a man living in England during World War I finds his consciousness invaded by that of a Neptunian descendant of the human race who lives far in the future

polyphonic novel of ideas, with the songs of Sirius giving voice to otherness in a dialogical "view of humanity from outside of humanity," which is how the parson of the church where Sirius sings interprets them. Formally, *Sirius* represents the closest Stapledon ever came to writing a modern science fiction novel while still working within the narrative conventions of popular Victorian fiction.

Stapledon was increasingly interested in extrasensory perception (ESP) and other psychic powers, as evinced by articles that he wrote for *Prediction* magazine and *Enquiry* after World War II. He argued that growing evidence of paranormal experience might soon revolutionize the worldview of physics. Two of his later novels, *Death into Life* (1946) and *The Flames* (1947), speculate on paranormal experiences.

Death into Life takes up the theme of the Other in a more mystical manner. Called by Stapledon "an imaginative treatment of the problem of survival after death," it tells the story of a rear gunner in a British bomber who is

"annihilated" along with all his companions. The gunner awakes, however, to find himself first a part of a spirit bomber crew, then the spirit of all those killed in battle, then the spirit of Man, then the spirit of the cosmos, then the universal Spirit, yearning toward a "dark Other," who is utterly inaccessible and indifferent to humanity's fate. True to his habit of contrapuntal structuring, Stapledon contrasts this lofty theme with brief passages enunciating the simple theme of personal love back on Earth. Although Stapledon conceives of the solar system as a "commonwealth of minded worlds" with humans genetically transformed to inhabit them, he does not objectify these worlds in the manner of *Last and First Men* or *Star Maker*. The book suffers, therefore, from a highly internalized and philosophical narrative structure, as well as a lack of a clearly defined point of view.

The Flames, by contrast, takes up the theme of the dark Other with a controlled and sustained irony that makes it one of Stapledon's best literary efforts. An epistolary novel, it takes the form of a communication from a psychologist writing from an insane asylum to report to a scientific friend that he has conversed with a living and intelligent flame—a "salamander," one of a species of gaseous organisms that has been hibernating since the first of the planets whirled into space. This flame tells the initially paranoid psychologist, Cass, about the struggles of the cosmic mind to consummate its union with "the hyper-cosmical Lover," God. What the cosmic mind learns instead is that ultimate reality is the Wholly Other, completely unintelligible and entirely indifferent to the most sacred values of the awakened minds of the cosmos. The flames themselves, in a crisis that is typically human and Stapledonian, are divided about what to do. Some insist on abandoning the struggle of the spirit in favor of a "purely epicurean" way of life; others continue to hope for union with God. A third party emerges in the sun, combining the spiritual commitment of the first with the agnosticism of the second. Cass pledges loyalty to this new party, but the terrestrial flames do not (they align themselves with the theistic party). They persecute Cass in an attempt to convert him to their viewpoint, finally becoming the malignant force Cass once thought they were.

Stapledon remained politically active through the 1940s. When the crisis over Western access to Berlin was at its height, he went against Cold War attitudes by attending two peace conferences that were controversial and seen in America as communist fronts—the Wroclaw Congress in Poland (August 1948) and the New York Cultural and Scientific Conference for World Peace (March 1949). At the latter conference he was the only delegate from western Europe given a visa by the U.S. State Department.

Stapledon wrote articles about both congresses, expressing a degree of optimism because at least Russian intellectuals had been willing to talk to their Western counterparts for the first time since World War II. In New York he had his first and only personal contact with American science-fiction writers (including Fletcher Pratt and Frederik Pohl) at an evening meeting of the Hydra Club, an organization formed by such writers during the late 1940s and early 1950s. But in New York he was also frightened by the anticommunist hysteria and war fever reflected in a *Life* magazine report of the event. He returned to Britain exhausted, expressing the fear that war might break out at any moment.

During 1948 Arthur C. Clarke arranged for Stapledon to speak before the British Interplanetary Society. Stapledon's address, on adaptations of human beings to colonize the planets and on the possibility of a "commonwealth of worlds" throughout the galaxy, received widespread publicity. Although Clarke's conception of the Overmind in his own novel *Childhood's End* (1953) is probably an adaptation of the "cosmic mind" of *Star Maker,* during the discussion that followed Stapledon's address Clarke stated that he did not think that humanity could ever take part in a galactic culture, even assuming that the technical difficulties involved could be overcome. The human mind would be strained to the utmost to deal with a solar civilization of even a dozen worlds. Clarke felt that a galactic civilization implied an impossible increase in complexity.

Clarke's remarks express the first doubts about the type of cosmic science fiction Stapledon established. Only in the last decades of the twentieth century did these doubts find full aesthetic expression in the works of cyberpunk authors such as Bruce Sterling, whose Shaper/Mechanist novel *Schismatrix* (1985) finds "posthumanity" shattered into thousands of factions, each vying with the others in the absence of any unifying vision of what is human. Stapledon himself seems to have believed that, given his definition of spiritual symbiosis, such a vision of cosmic totality was possible, however fantastically it might be accomplished in his fiction by telepathy and other paranormal devices.

In his later years Stapledon was a science-fiction writer who was more remembered than read. He began to develop an interest in art, trying his hand at paintings, most notably a portrait of his character Odd John. In 1950 Stapledon visited Yugoslavia and attended an international summer school in France organized by the Women's League for Peace and Freedom. He returned only a few weeks before his death, which was sudden and unexpected: on 6 September 1950 he suffered a massive heart attack after chopping wood at his home. Stapledon was cremated, and his ashes were spread near Simon's Field. His last work, *A Man Divided* (1950), is a story that Stapledon called "a symbolical expression of psychological conflicts that are widespread today."

Dust jacket for Stapledon's 1937 novel, in which the narrator travels through the universe in search of its creator

Stapledon's posthumous *The Opening of the Eyes* (1954) was edited by Agnes Stapledon. Parts of this book—which critics agree is a failure both as philosophical statement and literary art—are important only because of their relation to other works or to the interpretation of Stapledon's later political views and his agnostic mysticism. Another posthumous work, *4 Encounters* (1976), composed sometime after World War II but not published until a quarter century after its author's death, is even less finished than *The Opening of the Eyes* but in other respects is a less perplexing piece of work. Not trying to communicate or express the ineffable, the narrative describes four apparently unrelated encounters with different sorts of people—a Christian, a scientist, a mystic, and a revolutionary—who expound their philosophies in dialogues with the narrator. "Nebula Maker" (1976) is the greatest of Stapledon's posthumous books. Probably written in the mid 1930s, it was part of an early attempt to write *Star Maker*. Its theology is considerably different from *Star Maker*—it speaks of a God literally behind the universe—and the nebulae are anthropomorphized to a much greater extent.

In the years since his death, a considerable body of literary criticism about Stapledon has emerged. There are book-length studies, several articles, and a special issue of *Science Fiction Studies* devoted to his work. One of the most interesting debates centers around the question of Stapledon's relationship to dialectical thought. Curtis C. Smith has surveyed Stapledon's novels and examined especially the dialectical pattern of history in *Last and First Men* and *Star Maker*. Writing from a largely Freudian perspective, Leslie A. Fiedler found Stapledon to be a man permanently divided against himself—like his work as a whole destined never to achieve closure. In 1989 Robert Shelton published an essay in *The Legacy of Olaf Stapledon: Critical Essays and an Unpublished Manuscript* on the moral philosophy of Stapledon that directly challenged Fiedler's antidialectical reading.

Much of this criticism gives ample testimony to the assessment that as a writer and a thinker in the field of science fiction, Stapledon was ahead of his time. Certainly, whatever may be the fate of these academic debates and opinions, Stapledon remains a vital science-fiction writer whose works offer the reader more than the obvious pleasures provided by best-sellers and cult favorites of the genre. Using and transforming a rich tradition of philosophical thought in seeking answers to the problems of the spirit in modern technological culture, his writings have clearly contributed much to what Aldiss has called the "speculative wealth" of science fiction.

Letters:

Robert Crossley, ed., *Talking Across the World: The Love Letters of Olaf Stapledon and Agnes Miller, 1913–1919* (Hanover, N.J.: University Press of New England, 1987).

Bibliography:

Harvey J. Satty and Curtis C. Smith, *Olaf Stapledon: A Bibliography* (Westport, Conn.: Greenwood Press, 1984).

Biography:

Robert Crossley, *Olaf Stapledon: Speaking for the Future* (Syracuse, N.Y.: Syracuse University Press, 1994).

References:

K. V. Bailey, "A Prized Harmony: Myth, Symbol and Dialectic in the Novels of Olaf Stapledon," *Foundation,* 15 (January 1979): 53–66;

J. B. Coates, "Olaf Stapledon," in his *Ten Modern Prophets* (London: Muller, 1944), pp. 151–166;

Robert Crossley, "Famous Mythical Beasts: Olaf Stapledon and H. G. Wells," *Georgia Review,* 36 (Fall 1982): 619–635;

Crossley, "Olaf Stapledon and the Idea of Science Fiction," *Modern Fiction Studies,* 32 (Spring 1986): 21–42;

Crossley, ed., "The Letters of Olaf Stapledon and H. G. Wells, 1931–1942," in *Science Fiction Dialogues,* edited by Gary Wolfe (Chicago: Academy Chicago, 1982), pp. 27–57;

Charles Elkins, "The Worlds of Olaf Stapledon: Myth or Fiction?" *Mosaic,* 13 (Spring/Summer 1980): 145–152;

Leslie A. Fiedler, *Olaf Stapledon: A Man Divided* (New York: Oxford University Press, 1983);

Walter H. Gillings, "The Philosopher of Fantasy: How Dr. Olaf Stapledon Discovered Science Fiction Magazines," *Scientifiction: The British Fantasy Review,* 1 (June 1937): 8–10;

John Huntington, "Olaf Stapledon and the Novel about the Future," *Contemporary Literature,* 22 (1981): 349–365;

John Kinnaird, *Olaf Stapledon* (Mercer Island, Wash.: Starmont House, 1986);

E. W. Martin, "Between the Devil and the Deep Sea: The Philosophy of Olaf Stapledon," in *The Pleasure Ground: A Miscellany of English Writing,* edited by Malcolm Elwin (London: Macdonald, 1947), pp. 204–216;

Patrick A. McCarthy, *Olaf Stapledon* (Boston: Twayne, 1982);

Sam Moskowitz, "Olaf Stapledon: Cosmic Philosopher," in his *Explorers of the Infinite: Shapers of Science Fiction* (Cleveland: World, 1963), pp. 261–277;

Science Fiction Studies, special Stapledon issue, edited by McCarthy, 9 (November 1982);

Curtis C. Smith, "Olaf Stapledon's Dispassionate Objectivity," in *Voices of the Future: Essays on Major Science Fiction Writers,* edited by Thomas D. Clareson (Bowling Green, Ohio: Bowling Green University Popular Press, 1976), pp. 44–63.

Papers:

The major archive of Olaf Stapledon's papers, including manuscripts, is at the Sydney Jones Library at the University of Liverpool. Another collection of correspondence is located at the Harry Ransom Humanities Research Center, University of Texas at Austin. The H. G. Wells Collection at the University of Illinois at Urbana-Champaign also has twenty-six letters from Stapledon to Wells.

William F. Temple

(9 March 1914 – 15 July 1989)

Darren Harris-Fain
Shawnee State University

BOOKS: *Four-Sided Triangle: A Romance* (London: Long, 1949; New York: Frederick Fell, 1951);

The Dangerous Edge (London: Long, 1951);

The True Book about Space-Travel (London: Muller, 1954); republished as *The Prentice-Hall Book about Space Travel* (New York: Prentice-Hall, 1954);

Martin Magnus, Planet Rover (London: Muller, 1955);

Martin Magnus on Venus (London: Muller, 1955);

Martin Magnus on Mars (London: Muller, 1956);

The Automated Goliath, published with *The Three Suns of Amara* (New York: Ace, 1962);

Battle on Venus, published with *The Silent Invaders* by Robert Silverberg (New York: Ace, 1963);

Shoot at the Moon (New York: Simon & Schuster, 1966; London: Whiting & Wheaton, 1966);

The Fleshpots of Sansato (London: Macdonald, 1968).

Edition: *The Three Suns of Amara,* published with *Battle on Venus* (New York: Ace, 1973).

OTHER: "The Kosso," in *Thrills,* edited anonymously by Charles Birkin (London: Philip Allan, 1935), pp. 37–48;

"Is Space Travel Possible?" by Temple (anonymous) and Arthur C. Clarke, in *Dan Dare's Space Book,* edited by Temple (anonymous), Marcus Morris, and Frank Hampson (London: Hulton, 1952), pp. 10–16;

"Discoverer of Radium–The Story of Marie Curie," by Temple (anonymous) and Clarke, in *The Girl Book of Modern Adventurers* (London: Hulton, 1952), pp. 97–110;

"Explorers of Mars" and "How to Say Hello to a Martian," in *The Authentic Book of Space,* edited by H. J. Campbell (London: Hamilton, 1954), pp. 7–14, 64–65;

"Ice Patrol" and "Treasure of the Gorge," in *The World-Wide Book for Boys* (London: Beaver, 1957), pp. 7–24, 40–52;

"Vera in the Stone Age," in *Gay Stories for Girls* (London: Beaver, 1957), pp. 33–43, 66;

William F. Temple

"Coco-Talk," in *New Writings in SF 7,* edited by John Carnell (London: Dodson, 1966), pp. 129–147;

Contributor, *The DoubleBill Symposium: Being 94 Replies to "A Questionnaire for Professional Science Fiction Writers and Editors,"* edited by Bill Bowers and Bill Mallardi (Akron, Ohio: D:B Press, 1969), pp. 131–136;

"The Unpicker," in *Androids, Time Machines, and Blue Giraffes: A Panorama of Science Fiction,* edited by Roger Elwood and Vic Ghidalia (Chicago: Follett, 1973); restored and revised as "Scrutiny," in *Space Stories,* edited by Mike Ashley (London: Robinson Children's Books, 1996), pp. 165–174.

SELECTED PERIODICAL PUBLICATIONS–
UNCOLLECTED: "Mr. Craddock's Life-Line," as
Temple Williams, *Amateur Science Stories*, 1 (October 1937): 1–8; republished as "Mr. Craddock's
Amazing Experience," *Amazing Stories*, 13 (February 1939): 42–51;

"Lunar Lilliput," *Tales of Wonder*, 2 (Spring 1938): 100–122;

"The Smile of the Sphinx," *Tales of Wonder*, 4 (Autumn 1938): 42–60; expanded version, *Worlds Beyond*, 1 (December 1950): 68–99;

"No Chance," *New Worlds*, 4 (August 1939): 4–9, 30;

"Experiment in Genius," *Tales of Wonder*, 11 (Summer 1940): 33–45; expanded version, *Future/Science Fiction Stories*, 2 (November 1951): 8–31;

"The Monster on the Border," *Super Science Stories*, 2 (November 1940): 60–76;

"The Three Pylons," *New Worlds*, 1 (June 1946): 43–58;

"Way of Escape," *Thrilling Wonder Stories*, 32 (June 1948): 46–54;

"Miracle Town," *Thrilling Wonder Stories*, 33 (October 1948): 86–100;

"The Brain Beast," *Super Science Stories*, 5 (July 1949): 8–51; restored as "Mind Within Mind," *Authentic Science Fiction Monthly*, 33 (15 May 1953): 54–137;

"A Date to Remember," *Thrilling Wonder Stories*, 34 (August 1949): 121–128;

"Wisher Takes All," *Reveille* (14 October 1949): 13;

"For Each Man Kills," *Amazing Stories*, 24 (March 1950): 92–110;

"The Triangle of Terror," *Weird Tales*, 42 (May 1950): 50–62;

"Martian's Fancy," *New Worlds*, 7 (Summer 1950): 38–53;

"Forget-Me-Not," *Other Worlds Science Stories*, 2 (September 1950): 18–38;

"The Bone of Contention," *Thrilling Wonder Stories*, 37 (October 1950): 122–132;

"Conditioned Reflex," *Other Worlds Science Stories*, 3 (January 1951): 102–120;

"The Two Shadows," *Startling Stories*, 23 (March 1951): 106–121;

"You Can't See Me!" *Fantastic Adventures*, 13 (June 1951): 64–77;

"Double Trouble," *Science Fantasy*, 3 (Winter 1951–1952): 37–47;

"Counter-Transference," *Thrilling Wonder Stories*, 40 (April 1952): 98–111;

"Limbo," *Nebula Science Fiction*, 3 (Summer 1953): 3–35;

"Destiny Is My Enemy," *Nebula Science Fiction*, 5 (September 1953): 3–37;

"The Whispering Gallery," *Fantastic Universe*, 1 (October–November 1953): 128–142;

"Moon Wreck," *Boy's Own Paper*, 76 (November 1953): 22–23, 55–58;

"Pawn in Revolt," *Nebula Science Fiction*, 4 (Autumn 1953): 30–50;

"Pilot's Hands," *Nebula Science Fiction*, 7 (February 1954): 74–120;

"Space Saboteur," *Boy's Own Paper*, 76 (March 1954): 42–43, 70–73;

"Errand of Mercy," *Authentic Science Fiction Monthly*, 43 (March 1954): 69–91;

"Standard Style," *Science Fantasy*, 11 (December 1954): 2–5;

"Eternity," *Science Fantasy*, 12 (February 1955): 84–111;

"Man in a Maze," *Authentic Science Fiction Monthly*, 54 (February 1955): 43–64;

"The Lonely," *Imagination*, 6 (July 1955): 102–112;

"Better Than We Know," *Science Fiction Quarterly*, 3 (August 1955): 60–67;

"Mansion of a Love," *Nebula Science Fiction*, 13 (September 1955): 43–49;

"Uncle Buno," *Science Fantasy*, 16 (November 1955): 89–110;

"Earth Satellite Charlie-One," *Boy's Own Paper*, 78 (January 1956): 18, 54–56;

"The Girl from Mars," *Heiress* (September 1956): 32–33;

"Outside Position," *Nebula Science Fiction*, 18 (November 1956): 3–19;

"The Green Car," *Science Fantasy*, 23 (June 1957): 105–128;

"The Different Complexion," *New Worlds*, 76 (October 1958): 44–64;

"The Undiscovered Country," *Nebula Science Fiction*, 35 (October 1958): 53–63;

"Magic Ingredient," *Science Fantasy*, 38 (December 1959): 33–60;

"'L' Is for Lash," *Amazing Science Fiction Stories*, 34 (July 1960): 24–60;

"Sitting Duck," *New Worlds Science Fiction*, 100 (November 1960): 4–23;

"The Unknown," *Amazing Stories*, 35 (March 1961): 44–64;

"That Impossible She," *New Worlds Science Fiction*, 115 (February 1962): 2–3, 112–114;

"A Niche in Time," *Analog*, 73 (May 1964): 67–72;

"Beyond the Line," *Fantastic Stories of the Imagination*, 13 (September 1964): 36–46;

"The Legend of Ernie Deacon," *Analog*, 75 (March 1965): 74–80;

"Talking about John Wyndham: Plagiarism in SF," *Binary*, 8 (March 1965): 11–14;

"The Man Who Wasn't There," *Tit-Bits* (16 December 1967): 4; expanded version, *Amazing Science Fiction*, 52 (November 1978): 76–81;

"Echo," *Famous Science Fiction,* 5 (Winter 1967–1968): 66–75;

"The Year Dot," *Worlds of If,* 19 (January 1969): 43–61;

"When in Doubt—Destroy!" *Vision of Tomorrow,* 1 (August 1969): 17–25;

"The Life of the Party," *Vision of Tomorrow,* 1 (February 1970): 40–58;

"Unhappy Ending," *Story and Stanza,* no. 10 (1980): 24–25;

"Testimony," *Interzone,* 65 (November 1992): 26–31.

Great Britain has a long tradition of fantasy and science fiction, but for most of British literary history these have been (and continue to be) categories in which authors work who are not necessarily defined (by themselves or others) as fantasy or science-fiction writers. Science fiction in particular began to be seen as a separate type of writing in the United States after the appearance of pulp magazines devoted to the form in the late 1920s, when the term "science fiction" came into use, and the early 1930s. The break has always been less distinct in Britain, but some writers—often directing their work toward the American magazines—nonetheless took on the label of "science-fiction writer." William F. Temple is one example.

William Frederick Temple, born in Woolwich, Kent, on 9 March 1914, was the oldest child of William and Doris Temple. When he was two, his family moved to Eltham, a village not far from London. His early memories included air raids during World War I and an acquaintance with fantasy writer and fellow Eltham resident E. Nesbit. Later in his childhood his mother's poor health made him a caretaker of sorts for his younger siblings, Jack and Vera; his mother died of tuberculosis while Temple was a student at Woolwich Polytechnic. He attended the school at the urging of his engineer father, but rather than following in his father's footsteps, Temple was attracted to more artistic pursuits. Later in life he said that seeing the movie *The Lost World* (1925), based on Arthur Conan Doyle's 1912 novel of the same title, and reading the scientific romances of H. G. Wells in his youth were important influences in shaping his future direction.

At first, however, Temple made his living from a job with the London Stock Exchange. He was not particularly drawn to finance, but he saw it as an opportunity to earn money while figuring out how he could do what he really wanted: write. Like many aspiring science-fiction writers in the twentieth century, Temple entered the field not as a writer but as a fan. He was active in science-fiction fandom, which is distinctive for its organization and its dedication to a particular type of writing; he was also a member of the British Interplanetary Society, which combined an interest in rocketry with an interest in science fiction. One of Temple's fellow members in the society was Arthur C. Clarke, another science-fiction fan and aspiring writer, and the two were housemates in the 1930s.

Temple lived with his father when he began working; but his father remarried, and Temple's new stepmother, unhappy with his steadily growing library of books and magazines, disposed of some of his papers, so he set out on his own. In his first apartment he met his landlady's granddaughter, Joan Streeton. Though he only stayed at the flat briefly, his relationship with Streeton developed into a lifelong partnership, and the two eventually married on 16 September 1939. In the meantime, Temple briefly returned home following his father's breakup with his second wife, then rented a flat with Clarke and Maurice Hanson that soon became an informal center of British science-fiction fandom.

The intellectual and literary stimulation Temple received from Clarke and other fans and aspiring writers was productive. In the mid 1930s Temple began submitting stories to British and American genre magazines. One of his first efforts was a horror story called "The Kosso." It was published in 1935 in *Thrills,* part of a popular series of horror anthologies edited by Charles Birkin. However, like most genre writers of the 1930s and 1940s, Temple published his work predominantly in the many science-fiction and fantasy magazines that proliferated between the world wars, such as *Tales of Wonder* and *Super Science Stories.* Many of these stories remain uncollected.

Mike Ashley, who has done more than any other critic to promote Temple's posthumous reputation, praises him as a writer of ideas. For instance, "The Smile of the Sphinx" (1938) takes as its premise the possibility that cats, rather than being domesticated animals, are instead alien creatures. In "A Date to Remember" (1949) Martians promote human progress by inhabiting the minds of geniuses, while the Martians in "You Can't See Me!" (1951) provide imaginary friends for every person on Earth.

Temple's efforts to establish a career as a professional writer were disrupted by his service in World War II, which also led him and his fiancée to move up their wedding date from November 1939 to September, when war broke out. Temple enlisted in the military but was not mobilized at first. In August 1940 he and his wife had a daughter, Anne. Shortly thereafter Temple entered active service as a signaler with the Royal Artillery in Italy and northern Africa. He tried to write while home on leave and even during the war, at one point misplacing a draft that expanded his 1939 magazine story "Four-Sided Triangle" into a novel. In May 1943 his son, Peter, was born; the infant died seven months later of an infection.

After the war Temple picked up where he had left off, returning to the Stock Exchange as head clerk and placing stories with magazines such as *Thrilling Wonder Stories* as well as American periodicals such as *Amazing Stories* and *Weird Tales*. In 1947 a second son, Cliff, was born. Temple also contributed to various anthologies and published a crime novel, *The Dangerous Edge,* in 1951.

Temple became active in British science-fiction circles again after the war. He was associated with the group of writers and enthusiasts (including Clarke and John Wyndham) who met regularly in the White Horse pub, celebrated in Clarke's collection *Tales from the White Hart* (1957). Those who gathered at the White Horse were instrumental in reviving British science-fiction fandom after the war, and Temple was once more involved with fan activities and conventions. In addition, Temple was one of the first contributors to one of the most important science-fiction magazines in Britain, *New Worlds*.

Capitalizing on his popularity with readers of magazine science fiction and on the new trend of publishing magazine work in book form, Temple finally finished his first book, *Four-Sided Triangle: A Romance* (1949), an expansion of a previously published work serialized in *Amazing Stories* in 1939. The plot of the novel is a good representation of the type of concept- driven story that appeared with great regularity in the science-fiction pulp magazines. The basis of the story is a love triangle in which two men are in love with the same woman, who loves one of the men. With all the resourcefulness of a stereotypical science-fiction character from the pulp era, the man whom she does not love decides to clone the woman, hoping that he can have his ideal woman too. However, the cloned woman, like the original, loves the other man—hence the four-sided triangle of the title. There is more to the novel than its imaginative premise, however, as Temple realistically describes how people might behave in such circumstances. A low-budget movie version of the novel was released in 1953.

The history of the novel also illustrates the relationship between imagined and real science in modern science fiction. When Temple was at work revising and expanding the story into a novel in the early 1940s, he planned to make his characters the first people on earth to use atomic power. After the United States ended the war with Japan by dropping atomic weapons on Hiroshima and Nagasaki, however, Temple was forced to change this part of his story.

Like most popular fiction of the period, *Four-Sided Triangle* was largely ignored in the mainstream press, although it was avidly discussed among science-fiction fans. In the field the story has become a minor classic—especially in its expanded novel form, which most critics agree is superior to the original magazine story. In addition, the story gained a larger audience when it was adapted for the screen.

The success of *Four-Sided Triangle* and the sale of *The Dangerous Edge* encouraged Temple to try something he had long wanted to do: retire from the Stock Exchange, which he did in 1950, and attempt to make his living from writing. However, at first he encountered difficulty in placing his stories—partly because his American agent, the well-known science-fiction collector Forrest J. Ackerman, was asking too much for his work. He met with better success with Scott Meredith as his agent, but he was forced to find work as a printer to support his family. He later tried again to work full time as a writer, but he sometimes found himself seeking other work to supplement his unsteady income from his various publications.

Another example of a science-fiction concept story can be found in Temple's tale "Conditioned Reflex" (1951). A Martian robot that escapes to Earth tries to convince the humans it meets that human beings are also robots, the products of Martian exploration of Earth thousands of years ago. The people do not believe it, but when the Martian robot leaves behind a device that works in controlling other humans, the truth of the robot's claims is realized. Yet another example is "The Lonely," published in the July 1955 issue of *Imagination*. The entire thrust of this story rests on its idea—namely, following a major catastrophe the last woman in London finds the last man in London, only to discover that he is homosexual.

A particularly striking story that reveals Temple's imagination is "The Green Car" (1957). After a hit-and-run accident, the car thought responsible is revealed to have been lost in the ocean in an accident in 1940. What might seem like the setup for a ghost story instead is used for a science-fiction concept. When the car is found, it contains water and a humanoid creature. Although the creature dies, the speculation that its undersea people had duplicated the 1940 car as a vehicle to explore the world of air-breathing people is accepted by the characters.

Though Temple never used his fiction as a platform for his political and social ideas, some indication of his concerns can be found in stories such as "Uncle Buno" (1955), "The Undiscovered Country"

(1958), and "The Different Complexion" (1958). "Uncle Buno" concerns the relationship between a young human boy and an elderly Martian who teaches the boy more about life than his human family does. In "The Undiscovered Country" a captured alien from Pluto turns her mental powers against her captors only because of her treatment. Finally, in "The Different Complexion" the initial view of Martians as ugly by human standards is reversed in the course of a romance between the two races. In all of these stories, Temple sympathizes with the alien or the outsider and critiques the tendency to judge others by one's own limited cultural standards.

Despite such noteworthy stories and the modest attention *Four-Sided Triangle* received, Temple was unable to parlay its success into the type of career enjoyed in the 1950s and 1960s by science-fiction writers such as Clarke or Wyndham. Instead, Temple continued to write extensively for the magazines, with occasional book publications such as his science-fiction juveniles featuring astronaut Martin Magnus; his work on a science-fiction comic called *Rocket;* and other occasional works. His novels *The Automated Goliath* (1962), *The Three Suns of Amara* (1962), and *Battle on Venus* (1963), all expansions of earlier magazine publications, are standard science-fiction adventure stories with little literary merit, lacking the imagination of *Four-Sided Triangle*. All three were published in the United States as Ace doubles (two books bound together); and while such books are widely collected and often include noteworthy works, Ace would publish even the most conventional of space operas. (A space opera is basically a horse opera—that is, a Western—in space, usually involving two-dimensional characters, trite concepts, amazing spaceships and weaponry, and plenty of action and adventure, usually dealing with galactic battles.)

Less conventional was Temple's novel *Shoot at the Moon* (1966), which, in fact, parodies many of the existing conventions in science fiction, putting to effective use the satirical wit that made Temple popular with magazine readers and within fandom. The story, about a trip to the moon, includes enough extrapolation to qualify as science fiction, since a moon landing was not accomplished until three years after the publication of the novel and since an exploration involving many characters has still not happened. The various comic characters caught up in the lunar murder mystery at the heart of *Shoot at the Moon* provide much of the interest of the book. Nonetheless, the book failed to make much of an impact.

At first glance Temple's last novel, *The Fleshpots of Sansato* (1968), seems to be a return to conventional science fiction, and in fact the story includes

Dust jacket for Temple's 1966 novel, a lunar murder mystery that parodies science-fiction conventions

many of the elements of space opera. The protagonist is an agent sent from Earth to a decadent city in a far-off galaxy to investigate reports of a faster-than-light drive for starships. There is more to the book than its standard plot, however. In particular, Temple's depiction of Sansato and its prostitution, while not salacious, is extremely effective and creative, managing to suggest without being explicit.

Temple's production had been diminishing gradually since the late 1950s, and *The Fleshpots of Sansato* was his last novel in large part because of his frustration with publishers. Temple had suffered in his relationships with publishers throughout his career—a later story, "A Niche in Time" (1964), deals with a time traveler who attempts to encourage despairing artists—but the heavy editing of the British paperback of *The Fleshpots of Sansato*, which Temple believed ruined the book in terms of style and content, effectively led him to retire from writing. In 1970 he took a job with a bookseller in Folkestone in

Kent, where he and his wife had moved in the mid 1960s. He published his last story in 1973, and he retired in 1975.

For the remainder of Temple's life he battled his deteriorating health, occasionally attempted to write again, attended a few science-fiction conventions, and indulged in his love of movies. He also saw some of his old stories anthologized in the many collections that appeared in the 1970s and early 1980s. He died at age seventy-five, on 15 July 1989.

The work and career of William F. Temple are representative of many science-fiction writers who attempt to earn their livings as professional writers: competent if not brilliant, imaginative if not always innovative, with a firmer grounding in scientific fact than literary fiction. Like many such writers, he never gained much of a reputation beyond the science-fiction community; this limited exposure may also be a result of Temple's distaste for self-promotion. Also, like several magazine writers in science fiction of the 1940s and 1950s, Temple did not change with the times, and in the 1960s and beyond, readers came to view his work as dated. Nor is it likely that he will ever be read by many uninterested in science fiction. However, one cannot fully understand the development of modern science fiction without understanding writers such as Temple, and a good part of his legacy lies in the role he played in the subgenre at an important stage of its development.

Bibliography:

Mike Ashley, *The Work of William F. Temple: An Annotated Bibliography and Guide* (San Bernardino, Cal.: Borgo, 1994).

References:

Mike Ashley, "Tell Them I Meant Well: A Tribute to William F. Temple," *Foundation,* 55 (Summer 1992): 5–24;

Larry Nowinski, "The Female Characters of William F. Temple: A Limited Study," *Lan's Lantern,* 29 (January 1989): 30–32;

Timothy Nowinski, "Old Ideas with a Twist," *Lan's Lantern,* 29 (January 1989): 53–55.

Papers:

William F. Temple's papers are held by his estate.

J. R. R. Tolkien

(3 January 1892 – 2 September 1973)

Michael W. George
Ohio Northern University

See also the Tolkien entries in *DLB 15: British Novelists, 1930–1959* and *DLB 160: British Children's Writers, 1914–1960.*

BOOKS: *A Middle English Vocabulary* (Oxford: Clarendon Press, 1922);

The Hobbit; or, There and Back Again (London: Allen & Unwin, 1937; Boston: Houghton Mifflin, 1938); revised edition (London: Allen & Unwin, 1951; Boston: Houghton Mifflin, 1952);

Farmer Giles of Ham (London: Allen & Unwin, 1949; Boston: Houghton Mifflin, 1950);

The Fellowship of the Ring: Being the First Part of The Lord of the Rings (London: Allen & Unwin, 1954; Boston: Houghton Mifflin, 1954); revised edition (London: Allen & Unwin, 1966; Boston: Houghton Mifflin, 1967);

The Two Towers: Being the Second Part of The Lord of the Rings (London: Allen & Unwin, 1954; Boston: Houghton Mifflin, 1955); revised edition (London: Allen & Unwin, 1966; Boston: Houghton Mifflin, 1967);

The Return of the King: Being the Third Part of The Lord of the Rings (London: Allen & Unwin, 1955; Boston: Houghton Mifflin, 1956); revised edition (London: Allen & Unwin, 1966; Boston: Houghton Mifflin, 1967);

The Adventures of Tom Bombadil and Other Verses from The Red Book (London: Allen & Unwin, 1962; Boston: Houghton Mifflin, 1962);

Tree and Leaf (London: Allen & Unwin, 1964; Boston: Houghton Mifflin, 1965);

The Tolkien Reader (New York: Ballantine, 1966);

Smith of Wootton Major (London: Allen & Unwin, 1967; Boston: Houghton Mifflin, 1967);

The Road Goes Ever On: A Song Cycle, poems by Tolkien, music by Donald Swann (Boston: Houghton Mifflin, 1967; London: Allen & Unwin, 1968);

Smith of Wootton Major and Farmer Giles of Ham (New York: Ballantine, 1969);

The Father Christmas Letters, edited by Baillie Tolkien (London: Allen & Unwin, 1976; Boston: Houghton Mifflin, 1976);

The Silmarillion, edited by Christopher Tolkien (London: Allen & Unwin, 1977; Boston: Houghton Mifflin, 1977);

Poems and Stories (London: Allen & Unwin, 1980; Boston: Houghton Mifflin, 1980);

Unfinished Tales of Númenor and Middle-earth, edited by Christopher Tolkien (London: Allen & Unwin, 1980; Boston: Houghton Mifflin, 1980);

Finn and Hengest: The Fragment and the Episode, edited by Alan Bliss (London: Allen & Unwin, 1982; Boston: Houghton Mifflin, 1983);

Mr. Bliss (London: Allen & Unwin, 1982; Boston: Houghton Mifflin, 1983);

The Monsters and the Critics and Other Essays, edited by Christopher Tolkien (London: Allen & Unwin, 1983; Boston: Houghton Mifflin, 1984);

The Book of Lost Tales, 2 volumes, edited by Christopher Tolkien, volumes 1 and 2 of *The History of Middle-earth* (London: Allen & Unwin, 1983–1984; Boston: Houghton Mifflin, 1983–1984);

The Lays of Beleriand, edited by Christopher Tolkien, volume 3 of *The History of Middle-earth* (London: Allen & Unwin, 1985; Boston: Houghton Mifflin, 1985);

The Shaping of Middle-earth: The Quenta, the Ambarkanta, and Annals, Together with the Earliest 'Silmarillion' and the First Map, edited by Christopher Tolkien, volume 4 of *The History of Middle-earth* (London: Allen & Unwin, 1986; Boston: Houghton Mifflin, 1986);

The Lost Road and Other Writings: Language and Legend before The Lord of the Rings, edited by Christopher Tolkien, volume 5 of *The History of Middle-earth* (London: Allen & Unwin, 1987; Boston: Houghton Mifflin, 1987);

The Return of the Shadow: The History of the Lord of the Rings, Part I, edited by Christopher Tolkien, volume 6 of *The History of Middle-earth* (London:

J. R. R. Tolkien in 1972 (photograph by Billett Potter)

Unwin Hyman, 1988; Boston: Houghton Mifflin, 1988);

The Treason of Isengard: The History of the Lord of the Rings, Part II, edited by Christopher Tolkien, volume 7 of *The History of Middle-earth* (London: Unwin Hyman, 1989; Boston: Houghton Mifflin, 1989);

The War of the Ring: The History of the Lord of the Rings, Part III, edited by Christopher Tolkien, volume 8 of *The History of Middle-earth* (London: Unwin Hyman, 1990; Boston: Houghton Mifflin, 1990);

Sauron Defeated: The End of the Third Age (The History of the Lord of the Rings, Part IV), edited by Christopher Tolkien, volume 9 of *The History of Middle-earth* (London: HarperCollins, 1992; Boston: Houghton Mifflin, 1992);

Morgoth's Ring: The Later Silmarillion, Part One, The Legends of Aman, edited by Christopher Tolkien, volume 10 of *The History of Middle-earth* (London: HarperCollins, 1993; Boston: Houghton Mifflin, 1993);

The War of the Jewels: The Later Silmarillion, Part Two, The Legends of Beleriand, edited by Christopher Tolkien, volume 11 of *The History of Middle-earth* (London: HarperCollins, 1994; Boston: Houghton Mifflin, 1994);

The Peoples of Middle-earth, edited by Christopher Tolkien, volume 12 of *The History of Middle-earth* (London: HarperCollins, 1996; Boston: Houghton Mifflin, 1996).

OTHER: "Goblin Feet," in *Oxford Poetry,* edited by G. D. H. Cole and T. W. Earp (Oxford: Blackwell, 1915), pp. 64–65;

Geoffrey Bache Smith, *A Spring Harvest,* introductory note by Tolkien (London: Erskine Macdonald, 1918);

"Tha Eadigan Saelidan (The Happy Mariners)," "Why the Man in the Moon Came Down Too Soon," and "Enigmata Saxonica Nuper Inventa Duo," *A Northern Venture: Verses by Members of the Leeds University English School Association* (Leeds: Swan Press, 1923), pp. 15–20;

"Philology, General Works," in *The Year's Work in English Studies,* volume 4 (London: Oxford University Press, 1924), pp. 20–37;

Sir Gawain and the Green Knight, edited by Tolkien and E. V. Gordon (Oxford: Clarendon Press, 1925); revised by Norman Davis (Oxford: Clarendon Press, 1967);

"Philology, General Works," in *The Year's Work in English Studies,* volume 5 (London: Oxford University Press, 1926), pp. 26–65;

"The Nameless Land," in *Realities: An Anthology of Verse,* edited by G. S. Tancred (Leeds: Swan Press / London: Gay & Hancock, 1927), p. 24;

Walter E. Haigh, *A New Glossary of the Dialect of the Huddersfield District,* foreword by Tolkien (London: Oxford University Press, 1928);

"Ancrene Wisse and Hali Meiðhad," in *Essays and Studies by Members of the English Association,* volume 14 (Oxford: Clarendon Press, 1929), 104–126;

"Appendix I: The Name 'Nodens,'" in *Report on the Excavation of the Prehistoric, Roman, and Post-Roman Sites in Lydney Park, Gloucestershire,* Reports of the Research Committee of the Society of Antiquaries of London, no. 9, by Sir R. E. M. Wheeler and T. V. Wheeler (London: Oxford University Press, 1932), pp. 132–137;

"Chaucer as a Philologist: The Reeve's Tale," in *Transactions of the Philological Society* (London: David Nutt, 1934), pp. 1–70;

Songs for the Philologists, by Tolkien, Gordon, and others (London: Privately printed for the Department of English at University College, London, 1936);

"Beowulf: The Monsters and the Critics," *Proceedings of the British Academy,* volume 22 (London: Oxford University Press, 1937), pp. 245–295;

John R. Clark Hall, *Beowulf and the Finnesburg Fragment: A Translation into Modern English Prose,* preface by Tolkien (London: Allen & Unwin, 1940);

"On Fairy-Stories," in *Essays Presented to Charles Williams,* edited by C. S. Lewis (London: Oxford University Press, 1947), pp. 38–89;

"A Fourteenth-Century Romance," *Radio Times,* London, 4 December 1953;

"The Homecoming of Beorhtnoth Beorhthelm's Son," in *Essays and Studies by Members of the English Association,* New Series, volume 6 (London: Murray, 1953), pp. 1–18;

M. B. Salu, *The Ancrene Riwle,* preface by Tolkien (London: Burns & Oates, 1955);

Peter Goolden, ed., *The Old English Apollonius of Tyre,* prefatory note by Tolkien (London: Oxford University Press, 1958);

Ancrene Wisse: The English Text of the Ancrene Riwle, edited by Tolkien, Early English Text Society no. 249 (London: Oxford University Press, 1962);

"English and Welsh," in *Angles and Britons: O'Donnell Lectures* (Cardiff: University of Wales Press, 1963;

Mystic, Conn.: Verry, Lawrence, 1963), pp. 1–41;

"Once upon a Time" and "The Dragon's Visit," in *Winter's Tales for Children: 1,* edited by Caroline Hillier (London: Macmillan, 1965; New York: St. Martin's Press, 1965), pp. 44–45, 84–87;

The Jerusalem Bible, edited by Tolkien and others (London: Darton, Longman & Todd, 1966);

"The Hoard," in *The Hamish Hamilton Book of Dragons,* edited by Roger Lancelyn Green (London: Hamilton, 1970), pp. 246–248;

"Bilbo's Last Song (at the Grey Havens)," broadside (London: Allen & Unwin, 1974; Boston: Houghton Mifflin, 1974);

Sir Gawain and the Green Knight, Pearl, and Sir Orfeo, translated by Tolkien, edited by Christopher Tolkien (London: Allen & Unwin, 1975);

Drawings by Tolkien (Oxford: The Ashmolean Museum, 1976);

Pictures by J. R. R. Tolkien, edited by Christopher Tolkien (London: Allen & Unwin, 1979; Boston: Houghton Mifflin, 1979).

SELECTED PERIODICAL PUBLICATIONS–UNCOLLECTED: "The Battle of the Eastern Fields," *King Edward's School Chronicle,* 26 (March 1911): 22–27;

"From the Many-Willow'd Margin of the Immemorial Thames," anonymous, *Stapeldon Magazine,* 4 (December 1913): 11;

"The Happy Mariners," *Stapeldon Magazine,* 5 (June 1920): 69–70;

"Iumonna Gold Galdre Bewunden," *Gryphon,* New Series, 4 (January 1923): 130;

"The City of the Gods," *Microcosm,* 8 (Spring 1923): 8;

"Henry Bradley, 3 December 1845 – 23 May 1923," *Bulletin of the Modern Humanities Research Association,* 20 (October 1923): 4–5;

"The Cat and the Fiddle: A Nursery Rhyme Undone and Its Scandalous Secret Unlocked," *Yorkshire Poetry,* 2 (October–November 1923): 1–3;

"Some Contributions to Middle-English Lexicography," *Review of English Studies,* 1 (April 1925): 210–215;

"Light as Leaf on Lindentree," *Gryphon,* New Series, 6 (June 1925): 217;

"The Devil's Coach-Horses," *Review of English Studies,* 1 (July 1925): 331–336;

"Sigelwara Land," *Medium Aevum,* 1 (December 1932): 183–196;

"The Adventures of Tom Bombadil," *Oxford Magazine,* 52 (15 February 1934); 464–465;

"Sigelwara Land: Part II," *Medium Aevum,* 3 (June 1934): 95–111;

"The Dragon's Visit," *Oxford Magazine,* 55 (4 February 1937): 342;

"Knocking at the Door: Lines Induced by Sensations When Waiting for an Answer at the Door of an Exalted Academic Person," as Oxymore, *Oxford Magazine,* 55 (18 February 1937): 403;

"Leaf by Niggle," *Dublin Review,* 432 (January 1945): 46–61;

"The Lay of Aotrou and Itroun," *Welsh Review,* 4 (December 1945): 254–266;

"'Ipplen' in Sawles Warde," by Tolkien and S. R. T. O. d'Ardenne, *English Studies,* 28 (December 1947): 168–170;

"MS. Bodley 34: A Re-collection of a Collation," by Tolkien and d'Ardenne, *Studia Neophilolgia,* 20 (1947–1948); 65–72;

"Middle English 'Losenger,': Sketch of an Etymological and Semantic Enquiry," *Essais de Philologie Moderne* (Bibliothèque de la Faculté de Philosophie et lettres de l'Université de Liège, fasc. 129 Paris: Les Belles Lettres, 1953), pp. 63–76;

"Imram," *Time and Tide,* 36 (3 December 1955): 1561;

"Tolkien on Tolkien," *Diplomat,* 18 (October 1966): 39;

"For W. H. A.," *Shenandoah: The Washington and Lee University Review,* 18 (Winter 1967): 96–97;

"Beautiful Place Because Trees are Loved," *Daily Telegraph* (4 July 1972): 16.

The place in fantasy literature earned by J. R. R. Tolkien is indisputable. Tolkien is directly responsible for the rising popularity of fantasy literature in the late twentieth century. While authors such as Anne McCaffrey may dominate the scene of modern fantasy, Tolkien is father to this genre. And while Robert E. Howard may be credited with creating the idea of a European medieval barbarian hero fighting his way through life, Tolkien may be credited with taking this generic concept and giving it public attention. Tolkien created a twentieth-century genre from archaic terminology and legends, but his fame comes more from his ability to create characters and events unforgettable to those who have encountered them. His works have spawned a vast industry that includes calendars and recordings and that capitalizes on his characters.

The characters whom readers encounter in Tolkien's fiction seem real; they display traits readers see in themselves and in those around them. Their situations, problems, and lives reflect parts of the reader's own. The relationship between the simple, microcosmic hobbit and the macrocosmic War of the Rings reminds readers of their relationship to their own universe. The hobbit, like the majority of readers, is the most uncharacteristic type of hero, and his rise to heroic stature is that exceptional event that made early literature popular. Tolkien achieved such realism in characters by basing them partly on personal

experience; and his ability to present the completely foreign world of Middle-earth with such believability is a result of his almost obsessive desire for detail.

John Ronald Reuel Tolkien was born on 3 January 1892 to Arthur and Mabel (Suffield) Tolkien in Bloemfontein, South Africa, where his father was in banking. He had one younger brother, Hilary Arthur Reuel Tolkien. After Arthur Tolkien's death on 15 February 1896, the rest of the family relocated to live a modest life in Birmingham, England. The Tolkien children were first educated by their mother at home; Ronald (as he was called) entered King Edward's School in Birmingham in 1900. Mabel Tolkien's Catholicism was a family scandal that apparently left her on her own with the boys. As a result of her conversion to Catholicism and the state of her finances, the boys were enrolled in the Grammar School of St. Philip, attached to the Birmingham Oratory, a church where Father Francis Xavier Morgan was priest. Mabel Tolkien learned that she had diabetes early in 1904, and she died in November of that year. Father Francis, fearing that the boys would be torn from the Catholic faith, arranged for them to live for a time with an aunt in Birmingham and then moved them into a nearby boarding house. There Tolkien met Edith Bratt, with whom he struck up a close friendship. Tolkien and Bratt began courting, until Father Francis forbade any further contact with her until Tolkien was twenty-one, claiming that it would interfere with his studies. During these early years, Tolkien became fascinated with languages, creating two relatively simple languages with his cousin. This interest began with seeing Welsh names on the sides of railroad cars, and it eventually fueled both Tolkien's academic and imaginative careers.

Tolkien attempted unsuccessfully to win a scholarship to Oxford in December 1910, finally winning an exhibition, another form of financial aid, at Exeter College, Oxford, in December of that year. Between 1915 and 1918, just after receiving First Class Honors in his final examination, Tolkien served with the 11th Lancashire Fusiliers, seeing action in World War I. He married Bratt on 22 March 1916, and his oldest son, John, was born in November 1917. Tolkien served on the staff of the *New English Dictionary* in 1918, then worked as a freelance tutor in 1919.

Tolkien's first printed works were poems. He published four poems and an introduction to a poetry collection before he had even produced a scholarly article or book. In his career Tolkien published a total of twenty-six poems (outside of those appearing in his fiction) and one full volume of poetry that includes many of these, and he left many others unfinished or in revision, several of which his son Christopher has since edited and published.

Tolkien's poetry is well informed by his professional interests–Anglo-Saxon and Middle English poetry. As

Christopher Tolkien has illustrated in his notes to *The Lays of Beleriand* (1985), which includes verse versions of two Middle-earth tales, Tolkien borrowed heavily from the alliterative long lines he studied. Christopher Tolkien in the same work cites an anonymous, though extensive, criticism of one of these poems, *The Lay of Leithian,* pointing out that the poem includes many archaisms that need annotation. This tendency is evident in another of the poems, *The Lay of the Children of Húrin,* with such words as *meed, bale,* and *weened.* To the student and scholar of the English Middle Ages, these terms are relatively accessible; but to the average twentieth-century reader, they are not. Each has a specific meaning that has been lost in the centuries between its popular use and Tolkien's poetry. The poet's use of such words as an aid for the alliterative nature of the poem is an early indication of the influence of Tolkien's profession on his creative endeavors.

The Lay of the Children of Húrin is a remarkable poem. Biographer Humphrey Carpenter situates the composition of *The Lay of the Children of Húrin* with Tolkien's stay in a hospital in Hull in 1917, although Christopher Tolkien describes a twenty-eight-page manuscript of his father's titled "Sketch of the Mythology with especial reference to 'The Children of Húrin,'" with a note on the envelope containing it saying that it was "begun c. 1918."

The story of *The Lay of the Children of Húrin* includes a wide variety of themes, influences, and structures common to Tolkien's later work, and its alliterative style illustrates the powerful influence of early English literature on Tolkien's fiction and poetry. The Anglo-Saxon influence on the poem is obvious. Whenever possible, Tolkien adheres to the scheme of the alliterative long line: a/a/a/x. At times, the more limited Modern English vocabulary forces him to adopt a scheme of a/x/a/x, x/a/x/a, a/a/b/b. Though Tolkien always corresponds to the concept of the alliterative half lines, he is forced to abandon the most popular medieval alliterative meter at times. Still, the poem indicates Tolkien's admiration for and willingness to work within the ancient English epic form.

Tolkien's debt to his scholarly work is evident not only in the ancient meter but also the thematic elements he uses in this poem. Carpenter points out that the fight with the dragon is reflective of *Beowulf,* a poem with which Tolkien was quite familiar, and that the hero's incest and subsequent suicide are reminiscent of Iullervo in the *Kalevala.* But there, according to Carpenter, the literary influences end: "'The Children of Húrin' is a powerful fusion of Icelandic and Finnish traditions, but it passes beyond this to achieve a degree of dramatic complexity and a subtlety of characterisation not often found in ancient legends." Carpenter's assertion is misleading, however, for it almost ignores the influence of Tolkien's first love, language and literature, on his creative work. Other elements besides the alliterative style reveal that Tolkien

Edith Bratt Tolkien in 1916, the year she and Tolkien were married

was heavily influenced by Anglo-Saxon and Middle English poetry. The genre that Tolkien helped to create is now referred to by periodical publishers as "European Fantasy" because of its anachronistic representation of a history of Europe. Tolkien's basic creations are modeled on this European history. His weapons are fantastic aberrations of medieval weapons; his creatures are powerful versions of European folk creations. European mythological traditions permeate Tolkien's poetry and fiction, and the basis of these traditions is the literature Tolkien studied as a scholar.

Perhaps most important for the development of Tolkien's fiction are the elements of a fictional language first seen in these poems and constantly used in *The Hobbit; or, There and Back Again* (1937), *The Lord of the Rings* (1954–1955), and *The Silmarillion* (1977). Moving onward from his early experiments, the young Tolkien, using as a model first Spanish and then Gothic, began to create a more systematized language. Tolkien dabbled with this work his entire life, creating two complete languages to enhance and inform his mythology. Additionally, he created an alphabet that, as Carpenter says, "looked like a mixture of

Hebrew, Greek, and Pitman's shorthand." He used this alphabet to write in a diary for a time. As critics such as Judy Winn Bell have noted, his invented languages, begun when he was quite young, and this new alphabet, which eventually became part of the cover design of *The Lord of the Rings* volumes, converge to inform and heighten the experience of Tolkien's Middle-earth.

Tolkien's first novel profoundly changed his career and his life. *The Hobbit* is an introduction to Tolkien's mythology, but the incidental composition of this work begins first with his poetic works of the 1910s and 1920s (printed in various journals and *The Lays of Beleriand*) and second with ideas on mythology. Carpenter provides an illustrative anecdote: C. S. Lewis (whom Tolkien had first met on 11 May 1926), though believing in God, had a problem with the function of Christ in Christianity. Lewis stated that "myths are lies, even though lies breathed through silver." Tolkien asserted, "No, they are not." He then proceeded to offer a lesson in semiotics: names themselves mean nothing until the items they name are given that name. Names are individual perceptions. Thus, myths are an "invention about truth." Carpenter concludes, "In expounding this belief in the inherent *truth* of mythology, Tolkien had laid bare the centre of his philosophy as a writer."

Tolkien had settled into his private and professional life by the time *The Hobbit* was begun. In 1920 he was appointed as Reader in English Language at Leeds University, where he met E. V. Gordon, a fellow scholar of medieval literature and, in 1925, collaborator on the most authoritative edition of *Sir Gawain and the Green Knight*. Tolkien's second son, Michael, was born in 1920. In 1924 Tolkien became Professor of English Language at Leeds. In the same year, his third son, Christopher, was born. In autumn 1925 Tolkien was elected Rawlinson and Bosworth Professor of Anglo-Saxon at Oxford, and the following year he and Lewis formed "The Coalbiters" (or "Kolbítar" in Icelandic), an informal literary club. Other members included George Gordon and Nevill Coghill, and the group met several times per term to read and discuss Icelandic literature. Tolkien's daughter, Priscilla, was born in 1929. Already steeped in his academic investigation, teaching, and parenting, Tolkien had written a short story titled "Roverandom" for his children. He had been working on his mythology for quite some time, composing stories that eventually formed *The Book of Lost Tales* (1983–1984) and *The Silmarillion*. He had discovered that the imaginative complexities that formed *The Silmarillion* could be used for simpler stories. "Roverandom" was rejected by publishers, but apparently, according to Carpenter, "The children's enthusiasm for 'Roverandom' encouraged him to write more stories to amuse them." This response seems to be the impetus behind *The Hobbit*, which Tolkien completed and published in 1937.

The story of *The Hobbit* introduces readers to the wizard Gandalf and the corrupted figure Gollum, not to mention The One Ring. It introduces Smaug, the dragon, which Tolkien himself asserts was inspired by the dragon of *Beowulf*. And, of course, it introduces the title character, Bilbo Baggins, who lives at Bag End—a name that, according to Carpenter, was inspired by Tolkien's Aunt Jane's farm in Worcestershire, which lay at the end of a lane. Additionally, readers are shown Tolkien's love of nature and the natural world. The novel also introduces the public to the previously private, complex mythological world of Middle-earth, a term found often in medieval English literature.

Bilbo Baggins is a creature with internal urges for adventure that prompt him to agree to be a burglar on a mission with thirteen dwarves to The Lonely Mountain, where the dwarven leader, Thorin, seeks buried ancestral treasure. But the treasure is guarded by the fierce Smaug. In a scene quite similar to the theft of the cup in *Beowulf*, Bilbo performs his thieving skill, stealing a cup, and Smaug becomes infuriated and attacks the countryside.

Bilbo is the unexpected hero. At first hesitant, Bilbo by the end of the novel has accepted his place among the dwarves, and he has become something not quite like any other hobbit. His internal journey from reluctant participant to seasoned adventurer comprises a main theme of this novel.

Though ostensibly a children's book, *The Hobbit* addresses themes that are far from childish. Tolkien tackles, in part, the nature of evil. In *The Hobbit* evil is not easily defeated, and the protagonists are not the ones who physically defeat the evil challenge that fuels the tale. Additionally, the idea that rewards can be a mixed blessing, though fully realized in *The Lord of the Rings*, appears in this book. Possibly the most powerful theme in the novel, though, is the idea that people change. Gandalf's prophetic speech in the beginning—"'Great Elephants!' said Gandalf, 'you are not at all yourself this morning'"—foreshadows what happens to Bilbo. He becomes a different person, as Gandalf indicates: "'My dear Bilbo,' he said. 'Something is the matter with you! You are not the hobbit that you were.'" This emphasis on Bilbo's change is arguably what the book is really about: the idea that hobbits can rise above their status to perform acts of heroism.

In this aspect Tolkien diverges from his professional studies. Medieval literature is about the extraordinary. *Beowulf* is of interest because the hero has the strength of thirty men and seemingly the will to match. Roland is Charlemagne's nephew and a knight. Arthur and his knights are legendary. Bilbo, on the other hand, is a short, relatively humanoid creature with an abundance of hair on his toes, a mild, polite manner, and—at least initially—little drive for adventure. He likes to eat, as do all hobbits, and he is fond of remaining at home in the Shire. Somewhat like Walter Mitty, Bilbo is one of the most unlikely heroes literature had produced until 1937. Not an Edgar Rice Burroughs figure rippling with muscle, nor an Arthur Conan Doyle intellectual, Bilbo is a new brand of hero. He is what each reader could be.

This aspect, both in *The Hobbit* and *The Lord of the Rings,* has prompted much critical attention. Critics such as Dainis Bisenieks and Don Adrian Davidson have called the works powerful because of the development of the hobbits, and W. H. Auden, in a 1954 review of *The Fellowship of the Ring* (1954), agreed that Tolkien gives his "types" great depth. Others have viewed the characterization and plotting of the books as simplistic. G. R. Brown sees types of clear-cut good and bad in *The Lord of the Rings,* and Lin Carter sees the characterization as stereotyped and the philosophy as lacking depth.

Many of these studies proclaiming brilliance on one hand and boredom on the other tend to focus on one major aspect to fuel their arguments: morality. The morality of both works is quite clear: Gracia Fay Ellwood claims that good and evil are absolutely obvious. In all but one instance readers have clear-cut instances of good and evil; the one exception is Gollum, the pitiable creature who has been corrupted by the Ring. Many critics also see Tolkien's two major works as decidedly Christian. William S. J. Dowie sees the morality of *The Lord of the Rings* as having religious contributions. Cheryl Forbes asserts that *The Silmarillion* relies quite heavily on Genesis, and Willis B. Glover claims that Middle-earth is monotheistic in the Christian tradition. Many of these studies attest to Tolkien's own sense of religion as a foundation for the Christianity of the works.

Such a wide variety of critical attention, prompted by both *The Hobbit* and *The Lord of the Rings,* tends to place an extraordinary amount of emphasis on these two works and the Middle-earth works that followed (or preceded them, as the case may be). Tolkien's imaginative writing was not limited to Middle-earth, however, and between *The Hobbit* and *The Lord of the Rings* were stories totally unrelated to that world. In 1945 Tolkien published in *The Dublin Review* a short story titled "Leaf by Niggle," first written between 1938 and 1939. The story, which has virtually no similarities with Tolkien's predominant mythology from *The Lays of Beleriand* or *The Hobbit,* illustrates that Tolkien was able to create alternate worlds that both oppose the reader's and are vastly different from Middle-earth.

Niggle, the protagonist, is much like Bilbo Baggins. Niggle is unusual for his society, which is a rather oppressive sociopolitical system where charity is law and usefulness to society is of prime importance. As a creative painter, Niggle serves no functional purpose in this environment. Yet, this lovable character reminds readers of Tolkien himself. Tolkien cared about his mythology, just as

Tolkien around 1935 (photograph by Lafayette)

Niggle cares so much about his painting that he does not even take the time to pack for his journey. Though his painting, his only occupation, is important, Niggle is interrupted constantly; when help is needed, Niggle is ready and willing, though not always happy, to offer that help.

Farmer Giles of Ham (1949), composed sometime in the early 1930s and published in the absence of a sequel to *The Hobbit,* is another story that abandons the mythology of Middle-earth. Tolkien even read this mirthful tale in place of an unfinished paper on the subject of fairy stories at Worcester College in 1938, and to his surprise it was received with appreciation. *Farmer Giles of Ham* is similar to *The Hobbit* in several ways. Like Bilbo, Giles is reluctant to perform brave tasks. He is a simple farmer, though a bit cantankerous to trespassers. He enjoys being plain, at least at the beginning. As with Bilbo, Giles becomes accustomed to his unusual reputation by the end of the story. Additionally, Chrysophylax, the dragon in *Farmer Giles of Ham,* is quite similar to Smaug in *The Hobbit.* Tolkien emphasizes the evil cunning of both dragons through persuasive, misleading speech when each dragon addresses the respective protagonists. Tolkien's characterization of Chrysophylax tends to hinge not on what the dragon says but on what he does when he speaks. When Chrysophylax speaks with deceptive thoughts beneath his duplicitous words, he licks his lips, "a sign of amusement," according to Tolkien. Smaug receives the same type of characterization.

In 1937 Tolkien began to write a sequel to *The Hobbit*, at the request of Allen and Unwin, his publisher. Not appearing until seventeen years later, this monumental work became Tolkien's signature. *The Lord of the Rings* was published in three parts: *The Fellowship of the Ring* and *The Two Towers* were both published in 1954, and the final episode, *The Return of the King*, was published the following year. There is good reason for the lengthy composition of this sequel. First, Tolkien was involved in his scholarly and teaching tasks. He was elected Merton Professor of English Language and Literature at Oxford in 1945. According to Carpenter, the position required Tolkien to give a minimum of thirty-six lectures per year, "but he did not consider this to be sufficient to cover the subject, and in the second year after being elected Professor he gave one hundred and thirty-six lectures and classes." The amount of time for preparation must have detracted from both Tolkien's academic research and his work on Middle-earth. Equally important is the nature of this sequel: *The Lord of the Rings* compresses Tolkien's vast mythological creation into a coherent whole.

Since *The Lord of the Rings* was published in three volumes, it is often erroneously referred to as a trilogy. Carpenter writes:

> Although the book was one continuous story and not a trilogy—a point that Tolkien was always concerned to emphasise—it was felt that it would be best if it appeared volume by volume under different titles, thus earning three sets of reviews rather than one, and perhaps disguising the sheer size of the book. Tolkien was never entirely happy about the division, and he insisted on retaining *The Lord of the Rings* as the overall title.

The publication of this work was plagued by problems, at least for Tolkien. His spellings were revised according to dictionary spellings (for example, *dwarves* to *dwarfs*, *elvish* to *elfish*, and *elven* to *elfin*). Tolkien also wanted a detailed map of the Shire, a project he eventually allocated to his son Christopher, who compiled Tolkien's several sketches of the Shire. Additionally, Tolkien's original plan for certain color prints and halftones was deemed too expensive by the publisher. As the publication date approached, Tolkien felt uneasy, because he considered *The Lord of the Rings* his most personal work. In a letter dated 2 December 1953, to Father Robert Murray, grandson of Sir James Murray (founder of *The Oxford English Dictionary*) and a close friend, Tolkien wrote, "I am dreading the publication . . . for it will be impossible not to mind what is said. I have exposed my heart to be shot at."

The first volume, *The Fellowship of the Ring*, begins with a piece of Tolkien's poetry, describing rings for the "Elven-kings," the "Dwarf-lords," the "Mortal men," and the "Dark Lord," concluding with: "One Ring to rule them all, One Ring to find them, / One Ring to bring them all and in the darkness bind them / In the Land of Mordor where the Shadows lie." The novel then picks up roughly where *The Hobbit* left off, with Bilbo's life after his adventure. The first chapter is titled "A Long Expected Party," obviously a reference to the title of the first chapter in *The Hobbit*, "An Unexpected Party." During a birthday celebration, Bilbo gives his nephew Frodo the Ring of Invisibility he had acquired on his quest; Gandalf recognizes this ring as the One Ring of power, created by the evil lord Sauron, and he tells Frodo that it must be destroyed. If Sauron regains it, Middle-earth could perish.

In this first part of the sequel readers are introduced to the main characters: Frodo, the protagonist; Sauron, the main antagonist; the Ringwraiths; Sam, Merry, and Pippin, hobbits who accompany Frodo; the mysterious Strider, a man of high stature and leadership abilities; Tom Bombadil, a master of the Old Forest; and Glorfindel, an elf leader. In a place called Rivendell readers meet Elrond, a ring bearer and elven lord, as well as some of Frodo's other companions: Boromir, a human warrior and leader; Gimli, a heroic dwarf; and Legolas, an elf. From Rivendell the company travels to Lothlórien, where they are the guests of Lady Galadriel, a wise and noble elf. But these are just the few characters that can be called major players, for Tolkien has loaded his work with characters. Most play an important part in certain episodes, like the Trolls in *The Hobbit*, but these specific characters have a lasting role in the sequel as a whole.

In addition to setting up the characters, Tolkien continues the commentary on nature that he displayed in *The Hobbit*. Tom Bombadil is a creature of nature, living in the woods, and the landscape actually comes to life in the Ents, animated trees inhabited by spirits and protectors of nature. Tolkien illustrates the differences between the Shire and Mordor by natural surroundings. The Shire is green and lush, while Mordor is seemingly devoid of life. The harsh contrast can be seen as an extension of Tolkien's own opinions about humanity's destruction of its natural surroundings.

This part of the sequel is concerned with educating Frodo about what lies ahead, but it also educates the reader. In *The Hobbit* readers learned little about the mythology of Tolkien's world or its history. Moreover, the earlier book did not include much of the legend behind the Ring and the commotion it causes. *The Fellowship of the Ring* fulfills this purpose, giving readers much of the history of the story.

This didacticism is couched in the foundation of epic: the journey motif. Frodo and his friends—the Fel-

Binding, designed by Tolkien, for the 1937 novel in which he introduces the diminutive, hairy-footed race of human-like creatures called hobbits (from Wayne G. Hammond, J. R. R. Tolkien: A Descriptive Bibliography, *1993)*

lowship—embark on a hazardous journey, fleeing their enemies, and encountering new (and old) foes, barely escaping at times, as they travel to Mount Doom, in the center of Sauron's realm, to destroy the Ring. But the journey is not merely physical. Frodo is the designated ring bearer, but he is also becoming increasingly corrupted by the power of the Ring, so that he must use the Ring carefully and battle himself at every turn.

If the reader doubts that *The Lord of the Rings* is a trilogy, this misconception is dispelled at the end of *The Fellowship of the Ring,* which stops without a resolution. In fact, it ends with an introduction to another episode. The last sentence reads, "Then shouldering their burdens, they set off, seeking a path that would bring them over the gray hills of the Emyn muil, and down into the Land of Shadow."

The Two Towers, the second volume of *The Lord of the Rings,* narrates the experiences of each character after the separation of the Fellowship in the first part and leads to the War of the Ring. The reader meets Treebeard, guardian of the forest and oldest surviving Ent, a character who, in Carpenter's opinion, personifies Tolkien's love of trees. Théoden, king of the men of Rohan, joins the party, as does Éomer, his nephew and successor, and readers are introduced to Faramir, Boromir's brother and a human leader. The welcome defeat of the traitorous wizard Saruman occurs in this volume, as does the reappearance of perhaps Tolkien's only tragic figure—Gollum. Additionally, Tolkien expands his depictions of orcs and goblins. In the characters of Uglúk (a large, black orc) and Grishnákh (a goblin) readers get a glimpse at the inner workings of evil minds. The conversations and actions of these characters shed light on exactly what the hobbits face in an army of orcs and goblins. The book takes several interesting turns, and by the end of this volume, an unexpected hero emerges.

The hobbits of the Fellowship are split up in the middle volume: Frodo's unfortunate encounter with the monster spider Shelob separates him from Sam, while Merry swears allegiance to the leader of Gondor, and Pippin allies himself with the Riders of Rohan. Pulled away from what defines their characters, they become what hobbits are normally not—heroic and adventurous. This theme, first presented in *The Hobbit,* runs throughout *The Lord of the Rings.*

The final volume of *The Lord of the Rings* is titled *The Return of the King,* and it deals with the War of the Ring and the return of the king of Gondor. In this volume Tolkien presents an incredibly intense battle scene, yet the battle is not the focus of the narrative. The focus, if taken allegorically (which Tolkien would never suggest), is on the stubborn will of the English people, or in the case of the novel, of the forces of good. In a sense, this will is the focus of the entire work, for one consistently sees the protagonists overcoming nearly impossible odds to defeat evil.

Tolkien took great pains to tie up loose ends, which is why *The Return of the King* was not published until more than a year after the first two volumes. Additionally, Tolkien wanted to include a series of appendices—the rulers of Gondor; the Tengwar (an alphabet) of Fëanor, leader of an ancient race of elves; the Shire Calendar; and an exhaustive index of names, to assist translators of the work. As of 1952 these appendices existed as only rough drafts and notes, and Tolkien knew that they would take much work to be ready for publication. By 1955 Tolkien had abandoned the name index, which allowed him to work on the other appendices as well as the maps that were added to later printings. During this time Tolkien was also working diligently at lectures for his students, which he still did at about double the required number.

In spite of his having originally abandoned the index of names, he continued to work on it. The index appears in more of a dictionary form as a chapter of Jared Lobdell's *A Tolkien Compass* (1975) titled "Guide to the Names in *The Lord of the Rings.*" More importantly, a full index of names appears as the last item in the Ballantine twenty-fifth anniversary edition of *The Return of the King.* In addition to this index, the Ballantine edition also includes an index to the titles and subjects of poems and songs as well as an index to the first lines, an index of places, and a supplemental list of names and places only appearing in poems and songs. The appendices, as they exist in this edition, cover kings and rulers, chronology, family trees, calendars, writing and spelling, and languages and people, indicating the exhaustive work put into every detail of Middle-earth.

Though receiving mixed reviews, *The Lord of the Rings* became not only popular but also a best-seller once it was forced—by substantiated rumors of an unauthorized American paperback edition published by Ace Books in 1965—into an authorized paperback edition published by Houghton Mifflin in conjunction with Ballantine in the same year. It made Tolkien a rich man, though his lifestyle never reflected his wealth. He remained, for the most part, the same Tolkien, though a bit more hindered by callers, visitors, and fan mail. More importantly, the success of *The Lord of the Rings* allowed Tolkien, after his retirement in 1959, to plunge into his mythology all the more. He would spend hours working on etymologies of his languages, correcting inconsistencies noticed by readers and himself, and revising. The result of this constant work on what readers deem to be fiction but what he deemed, for lack of a better term, to be fictional history, is arguably the most complete look into a fictional world in literature. Through Tolkien's imagination readers experience not only a story but also the culture of the peoples around which the story centers. Tolkien presents differing ideological stances in his work, and his appendices compile a vast amount of information that makes the world real to all reading it. One reads this literature and feels that Tolkien's world existed somewhere before the continent of Europe shifted and broke apart.

But Tolkien did not halt with *The Lord of the Rings.* Around 1958 he began writing *Smith of Wootton Major* (1967), possibly his most extensive non–Middle-earth story. The tale was originally an anecdote for a preface to a poetry volume by George MacDonald, but soon grew into its own volume. Tolkien's experience of retiring from his professorship is expressed in *Smith of Wootton Major,* according to Carpenter's biography:

> *Smith* was unusual in two ways: it was composed on the typewriter—something Tolkien did not normally do—and it was related closely and even consciously to himself. He called it "an old man's story, filled with the presage of bereavement," and elsewhere he said that it was "written with deep emotion, partly drawn from the experience of the bereavement of 'retirement' and of advancing age". . . . It was indeed the last story that he ever wrote.

Its status as Tolkien's last composition gives it a certain emphasis. *Smith of Wootton Major* encompasses within it everything Tolkien believed about mythology. In a way, this story reemphasizes in fiction what Tolkien had so many years earlier told Lewis: mythology is inherently related to reality. Smith, who has received a special passport to Faery—the land where the magic of fairies exists, according to Tolkien's essay "Tree and Leaf" (1965)—is the only character in the story who actually believes in Faery, except for Alf (an elven king living in Smith's village in disguise) and Smith's family. In fact, Tolkien's characterization of Nokes, the antagonist of the tale (if one exists in this story) is quite similar to the doubting Lewis. In the beginning of the tale, when Nokes first sees the silver star that later allows Smith to travel to the land of elves, he replies to Alf's assertion that it is from Faery with complete disbelief and disrespect: "'All right, all right.' he said. 'It means much the same; but call it that if you like. You'll grow up some day. Now you can get on with stoning the raisins. If you notice any funny fairy ones, tell me.'" Nokes does not change his opinion by the end, either. He treats Alf with the same impudence as he had previously, and even after he learns the truth, he feels that his experi-

14   XVI

"What does the writing say?" asked Frodo, who was trying
to decipher the inscription on the arch. "I thought I knew the elf-letters. but I
cannot read these."

"The words are in the elf-tongue of the West of
Middle-earth in the Elder Days," said Gandalf. "But they do not
say anything of importance to us. They say only: The Doors of
Durin Lord of Moria : Speak, friend, and enter. And underneath
small and faint is : Narvi made them. Celebrimbor of Hollin
drew these signs."

This is an archaic use of the elvish character; spelling :—
ENNYN ÐURIN ARAN·VÓRIA: PEDO MELLON A MINNO:
   im Narvi hain echant. Celebrimbor o Eregion teithant i·ndew thin.
        (·K)

Page from a draft for Tolkien's The Lord of the Rings *(1954–1955), with a drawing
of the gate to the Mines of Moria (Marquette University, Milwaukee)*

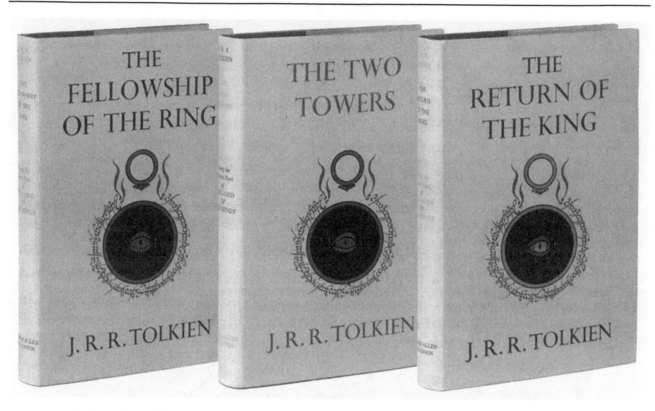

The three volumes of Tolkien's The Lord of the Rings, *which he insisted was a single continuous story and not a trilogy*
(Between the Covers *auction catalogue*)

ence was a dream; he cannot reconcile that Faery actually exists.

The Silmarillion was the last major work of Tolkien's to be published, and Christopher Tolkien was responsible for its completion and publication after the author's death. Yet, as with much of Tolkien's work, this tome was begun long before. In fact, it was submitted to Stanley Unwin as a possible sequel to *The Hobbit* in 1937, but it was deemed unacceptable as a sequel, though praised for its prose style. Tolkien had begun work on this story before any of his other Middle-earth tales, but it had grown over the years. Later work on *The Silmarillion* was hampered by various problems. Tolkien moved late in his life, causing him to reorganize his books and papers. Additionally, on 29 November 1971 his wife, Edith, died after a serious illness. Tolkien moved again from Bournemouth to 21 Merton Street, taking up a position as an honorary resident fellow at Merton College. Thus, work was stalled once again.

Tolkien received great honors toward the end of his life. In 1972 he was made a Commander in the Order of the British Empire, and Oxford conferred an honorary doctorate of letters upon him. But on 2 September 1973 Tolkien was taken ill and died in Bournemouth at age eighty-one. He is buried in Wolvercote Cemetery at Oxford.

Tolkien, possibly prompted by his wife's death, had made arrangements for his son Christopher to complete *The Silmarillion* in the event of his own death. Christopher Tolkien, intimately familiar with the story, not only saw that *The Silmarillion* was published but also edited and made available other works of his father's. An assistant on the *Silmarillion* project was Guy Gavriel Kay, a Canadian who went on to become an acclaimed fantasy writer himself.

Sometime between 1916 and 1917 Tolkien had begun "The Book of Lost Tales," but then abandoned it for several years, only to reconstruct it in a sketch of the mythological history of Middle-earth. What evolved out of this work was *The Silmarillion,* yet the lost tales still remained. They are, as Christopher Tolkien has stated in the foreword to his two-volume edition of *The Book of Lost Tales* (1983–1984), "the first substantial work of imaginative literature by J. R. R. Tolkien, and the first emergence in narrative of the Valar, of the Children of Ilúvatar, Elves and men, of the Dwarves and the Orcs, and of the lands in which their history is set, Valinor beyond the western ocean, and Middle-earth, the 'Great Lands' between the seas of east and west."

Tolkien's development as an artist is difficult to trace, because his work was never complete. He continued to revise *The Hobbit* and *The Lord of the Rings* until near his death. Most of the posthumous publications edited by Christopher Tolkien are incomplete works begun long ago, many before he even created *The Hobbit.* But some development is evident. Tolkien moved from shorter poems on occasional subjects to longer poems and narratives. These expanded narratives hinged around his created mythology, which in itself was born from the languages Tolkien was constantly revising and creating.

One can also see the development of Tolkien's interest in people and nature. Most of Tolkien's protagonists are unlikely heroes, but heroes nevertheless. Bilbo, Frodo, Samwise, Niggle, and Farmer Giles all are rather plain folk, traditionally unworthy of fame yet receiving it anyway. Likewise, Tolkien's concern with nature is reflected in his work. The landscapes of *The Hobbit* and *The Lord of the Rings,* the subject of Niggle's painting, and such characters as Treebeard all indicate the author's concern for the natural world. Tolkien presents various recurrent themes and motifs in his work, and though these are a bit repetitive perhaps, they are also presented in such a way as to be attractive to readers and scholars alike.

More than sixty years after publication of *The Hobbit* Tolkien's works are still in print, selling, and influencing readers the world over. In the late 1960s and early 1970s Led Zeppelin recorded several songs based on Tolkien's work—"Ramble On" (1969) and "Misty Mountain Hop" (1971) are two. Animated versions of *The Hobbit* and *The Lord of the Rings* were released in 1978 and 1980 and are available on videocassette. A live-action movie version of *The Lord of the Rings,* directed by Peter Jackson, is being released in three parts as the books were; the first movie premiered in December 2001. Calendars depicting different artistic renderings of scenes from Tolkien's works are available every year. Moreover, "new" items appear frequently, such as encyclopedias based on Middle-earth and even Middle-earth roleplaying and card games. With the rising interest in and applicability of the World Wide Web, electronic resources featuring Tolkien began to emerge. Dozens, perhaps even hundreds of World Wide Web homepages dedicated to Tolkien, his work, artistic creations relating to Tolkien's work, and Tolkien societies are active. The electronic Tolkien encyclopedia, an evolving resource including analyses of Tolkien's work, subject guides for critical analysis of his works, and an encyclopedia of names, places, and events, is available online. J. R. R. Tolkien's place is indeed firm in fantasy literary circles, and with contemporary resources about Tolkien growing, his place in British literature is secure.

Elijah Wood as the hobbit Frodo Baggins in a promotional still for the 2001 movie The Lord of the Rings: The Fellowship of the Ring *(New Line Cinema)*

Letters:

The Letters of J. R. R. Tolkien: A Selection, edited by Humphrey Carpenter with the assistance of Christopher Tolkien (London: Allen & Unwin, 1981; Boston: Houghton Mifflin, 1981).

Bibliographies:

Richard C. West, *Tolkien Criticism: An Annotated Checklist,* revised edition (Kent, Ohio: Kent State University Press, 1981);

Judith Anne Johnson, *J. R. R. Tolkien: Six Decades of Criticism* (Westport, Conn.: Greenwood Press, 1986);

Wayne G. Hammond, *J. R. R. Tolkien: A Descriptive Bibliography* (Winchester, U.K.: St. Paul's Bibliographies / New Castle, Del.: Oak Knoll Books, 1993).

Biographies:

Daniel Grotta-Kurska, *J. R. R. Tolkien: Architect of Middle Earth* (New York: Warner, 1976);

Humphrey Carpenter, *J. R. R. Tolkien: A Biography* (London: Allen & Unwin, 1977; Boston: Houghton Mifflin, 1977);

Carpenter, *The Inklings: C. S. Lewis, J. R. R. Tolkien, Charles Williams, and Their Friends* (London: Allen & Unwin, 1978; Boston: Houghton Mifflin, 1979).

References:

Judy Winn Bell, "The Language of J. R. R. Tolkien in *The Lord of the Rings,*" in *Mythcon I Proceedings (4–7 September 1970),* edited by Glen GoodKnight (Los Angeles: Mythopoeic Society, 1971): 35–40;

Dainis Bisenieks, "The Hobbit Habit in the Critic's Eye," *Tolkien Journal,* 15 (Summer 1972): 14–15;

Richard E. Blackwelder, *A Tolkien Thesaurus* (New York: Garland, 1990);

Harold Bloom, ed., *J. R. R. Tolkien* (Philadelphia: Chelsea House, 2000);

J. C. Bradfield, *A Dictionary of Quenya and ProtopEldarin and AntepQuenya, with an Index* (Canterbury: J. Bradfield, 1983);

Lin Carter, "The Inklings Produce a Classic: The Achievement of Tolkien and His Influence," in his *Imaginary Worlds: The Art of Fantasy* (New York: Ballantine, 1973), pp. 109–130;

Jane Chance, *The Lord of the Rings: The Mythology of Power* (New York: Twayne, 1992);

Bonniejean Christensen, "Adventures in Manipulation," *English Journal,* 60 (March 1971): 359–360;

Don Adrian Davidson, "Sword and Sorcery Fiction: An Annotated Book List," *English Journal,* 61 (January 1972): 43–51;

David Day, *Tolkien: The Illustrated Encyclopedia* (New York: Collier, 1992);

William S. J. Dowie, "The Gospel of Middle Earth According to J. R. R. Tolkien," *Heythrop Journal,* 15 (January 1974): 37–52;

Colin Duriez, *The J. R. R. Tolkien Handbook: A Comprehensive Guide to His Life, Writings, and World of Middle-earth* (Grand Rapids, Mich.: Baker Book House, 1992);

Gracia Fay Ellwood, "The Good Guys and the Bad Guys," *Tolkien Journal,* 3 (November 1969): 9–11;

E. L. Epstein, "The Novels of J. R. R. Tolkien and the Ethnology of Medieval Christendom," *Philological Quarterly,* 48 (1969): 517–525;

Robley Evans, *J. R. R. Tolkien* (New York: Warner, 1972);

Karen Wynn Fonstad, *The Atlas of Middle-earth* (Boston: Houghton Mifflin, 1991);

Cheryl Forbes, "Answers about Middle-earth," *Christianity Today,* 22 (7 October 1977): 30–31;

Robert Foster, *The Complete Guide to Middle-Earth* (New York: Ballantine, 1978);

Willis B. Glover, "The Christian Character of Tolkien's Invented World," *Criticism,* 13 (1971): 39–53;

Randel Helms, *Tolkien's World* (Boston: Houghton Mifflin, 1974);

Neil D. Isaacs and Rose A. Zimbardo, eds., *Tolkien and the Critics: Essays on J. R. R. Tolkien's The Lord of the Rings* (Notre Dame: University of Notre Dame Press, 1968);

Paul H. Kocher, *Master of Middle-earth: The Fiction of J. R. R. Tolkien* (Boston: Houghton Mifflin, 1972);

Jared Lobdell, ed., *A Tolkien Compass* (La Salle, Ill.: Open Court, 1975);

Jane C. Nitzsche, *Tolkien's Art: A Mythology for England* (London: Macmillan, 1979);

Ruth S. Noel, *The Mythology of Middle-earth: A Study of Tolkien's Mythology and Its Relationship to the Myths of the Ancient World* (London: Thames & Hudson, 1977);

William Ready, *Understanding Tolkien and The Lord of the Rings* (New York: Warner Paperbacks, 1969);

Deborah Webster Rogers and Ivor A. Rogers, *J. R. R. Tolkien* (Boston: Twayne, 1980);

Mary Salu and Robert T. Farrell, eds., *J. R. R. Tolkien, Scholar and Storyteller: Essays in Memoriam* (Ithaca, N.Y.: Cornell University Press, 1979);

T. A. Shippey, *J. R. R. Tolkien: Author of the Century* (London: HarperCollins, 2000; Boston: Houghton Mifflin, 2001);

David Stevens and Carol D. Stevens, *J. R. R. Tolkien—The Art of the Myth-Maker,* revised edition (San Bernardino, Cal.: R. Reginald, 1993);

Catharine Stimpson, *J. R. R. Tolkien,* Columbia Essays of Modern Writers, no. 41 (New York & London: Columbia University Press, 1969);

John Tolkien and Priscilla Tolkien, *The Tolkien Family Album* (London: HarperCollins, 1992).

Papers:
Most of the manuscript materials associated with J. R. R. Tolkien are still in the Tolkien family archives; however, Marquette University at Milwaukee houses several manuscripts of Tolkien's fiction. Items of interest are also at the Department of Western Manuscripts at the Bodleian Library, Oxford.

E. Charles Vivian
(Charles Henry Cannell, Charles Henry Vivian, Jack Mann, Barry Lynd)
(19 October 1882 – 21 May 1947)

Walter Albert

BOOKS: *The Shadow of Christine* (London: Gay & Bird, 1907; New York: Fenno, 1910);

The Woman Tempted Me (London: Melrose, 1909);

The Wandering of Desire (London: Melrose, 1910);

Following Feet (London: Melrose, 1910);

Passion-Fruit (London: Heinemann, 1912);

Divided Ways (London: Holden & Hardingham, 1914);

Peru: Physical Features, Natural Resources, Means of Communication, Manufactures and Industrial Development (London & New York: Pitman, 1914; New York: Appleton, 1914);

With the Royal Army Medical Corps (R.A.M.C.) at the Front (London & New York: Hodder & Stoughton, 1914);

With the Scottish Regiments at the Front (London & New York: Hodder & Stoughton, 1914);

The British Army from Within (London: Hodder & Stoughton, 1914; New York: Doran, 1914);

The Way of the Red Cross, by Vivian and J. E. Hodder Williams (London & New York: Published for *The Times* by Hodder & Stoughton, 1915);

The Young Man Absalom (London: Chapman & Hall, 1915; New York: Dutton, 1915);

The Yellow Streak (Toronto: Warwick & Rutter, 1921);

A History of Aeronautics, by E. Charles Vivian, with a Section on Progress in Aeroplane Design by Lieut.-Col. W. Lockwood Marsh, O.B.E. (London: Collins, 1921; New York: Harcourt, Brace, 1921);

City of Wonder (London: Hutchinson, 1922; New York: Moffat, Yard, 1923);

Broken Couplings, as Charles Henry Cannell (London: Hutchinson, 1923);

The Guarded Woman, as Cannell (London: Hutchinson, 1923);

A Scout of the '45 (London: Religious Tract Society, 1923);

E. Charles Vivian circa 1940

Fields of Sleep (London: Hutchinson, 1923; West Kingston, R.I.: Grant, 1979 [edition suppressed by publisher]; republished, 1980);

People of the Darkness (London: Hutchinson, 1924);

Barker's Drift, as Cannell (London: Hutchinson, 1924);

Ash, as Cannell (London: Hutchinson, 1925);

The Guardian of the Cup, as Cannell (London: Hodder & Stoughton, 1925);

The Passionless Quest, as Cannell (London: Hodder & Stoughton, 1925);

Star Dust (London: Hutchinson, 1925);

The Lady of the Terraces (London: Hodder & Stoughton, 1925);

A King There Was– (London: Hodder & Stoughton, 1926; New York: Arno, 1978);

The Forbidden Door (London & Melbourne: Ward, Lock, 1927);

Robin Hood and His Merry Men (London & Melbourne: Ward, Lock, 1927);

A Tale of Fleur (London & Melbourne: Ward, Lock, 1927);

Man Alone (London & Melbourne: Ward, Lock, 1928);

The Moon and Chelsea, as Cannell (London & Melbourne: Ward, Lock, 1928);

Nine Days (London & Melbourne: Ward, Lock, 1928);

Woman Dominant (London & Melbourne: Ward, Lock, 1929);

Delicate Fiend (London & Melbourne: Ward, Lock, 1930);

One Tropic Night (London & Melbourne: Ward, Lock, 1930);

Double or Quit (London & Melbourne: Ward, Lock, 1930);

And the Devil, as Cannell (London: Bodley Head, 1931);

Innocent Guilt (London & Melbourne: Ward, Lock, 1931);

Unwashed Gods (London & Melbourne: Ward, Lock, 1931);

False Truth (London & Melbourne: Ward, Lock, 1932);

Infamous Fame (London & Melbourne: Ward, Lock, 1932);

Lone Isle (London & Melbourne: Ward, Lock, 1932);

Coulson Goes South, as Jack Mann (London: Wright & Brown, 1933);

Reckless Coulson, as Mann (London: Wright & Brown, 1933);

Girl in the Dark (London & Melbourne: Ward, Lock, 1933);

The Keys of the Flat (London & Melbourne: Ward, Lock, 1933);

Ladies in the Case (London & Melbourne: Ward, Lock, 1933);

Accessory After (London & Melbourne: Ward, Lock, 1934);

Egyptian Nights, as Mann (London: Wright & Brown, 1934);

House for Sale (London: Amalgamated Press, 1934); enlarged as *With Intent to Kill* (London & Melbourne: Ward, Lock, 1936);

Jewels Go Back (London & Melbourne: Ward, Lock, 1934);

Shadow on the House (London & Melbourne: Ward, Lock, 1934);

The Dead Man's Chest, as Mann (London: Wright & Brown, 1934);

The Capsule Mystery (London & Melbourne: Ward, Lock, 1935);

Cigar for Inspector Head (London & Melbourne: Ward, Lock, 1935);

Detective Coulson, as Mann (London: Wright & Brown, 1935);

Seventeen Cards (London & Melbourne: Ward, Lock, 1935);

Barker's Drift (London, 1936);

The Black Prince (London & Melbourne: Ward, Lock, 1936);

Coulson Alone, as Mann (London: Wright & Brown, 1936);

Gees' First Case, as Mann (London: Wright & Brown, 1936);

Who Killed Gatton? (London & Melbourne: Ward, Lock, 1936);

With Intent to Kill (London & Melbourne: Ward, Lock, 1936);

Tramp's Evidence (London & Melbourne: Ward, Lock, 1937); republished as *The Barking Dog Murder Case* (New York: Hillman-Curl, 1937);

.38 Automatic (London & Melbourne: Ward, Lock, 1937);

Grey Shapes, as Mann (London: Wright & Brown, 1937; New York: Bookfinger, 1970);

Nightmare Farm, as Mann (London: Wright & Brown, 1937; New York: Bookfinger, 1975);

The Kleinert Case, as Mann (London: Wright & Brown, 1938);

Maker of Shadows, as Mann (London: Wright & Brown, 1938; New York: Arno, 1976);

Dude Ranch, as Barry Lynd (London & Melbourne: Ward, Lock, 1938);

Evidence in Blue (London & Melbourne: Ward, Lock, 1938); republished as *The Man in Gray* (New York: Hillman-Curl, 1938);

The Rainbow Puzzle (London & Melbourne: Ward, Lock, 1938);

Trailed Down, as Lynd (London & Melbourne: Ward, Lock, 1938);

Ghost Canyon, as Lynd (London & Melbourne: Ward, Lock, 1939);

Problem by Rail (London & Melbourne: Ward, Lock, 1939);

Riders to Bald Butte, as Lynd (London & Melbourne: Ward, Lock, 1939);

Touch and Go (London & Melbourne: Ward, Lock, 1939);

The Ninth Life, as Mann (London: Wright & Brown, 1939; New York: Bookfinger, 1970);

Her Ways Are Death, as Mann (London: Wright & Brown, 1939; New York: Bookfinger, 1981);

The Glass Too Many, as Mann (London: Wright & Brown, 1940; New York: Bookfinger, 1981);

The Impossible Crime (London & Melbourne: Ward, Lock, 1940);

Man with a Scar (London & Melbourne: Ward, Lock, 1940);

And Then There Was One (London & Melbourne: Ward, Lock, 1941);

The Ten-Buck Trail, as Lynd (London & Melbourne: Ward, Lock, 1941);

Curses Come Home (London: Hale, 1942);

George on the Trail, as Lynd (London & Melbourne: Ward, Lock, 1942);

Dangerous Guide (London: Hale, 1943);

Samson (London: Hale, 1944);

Other Gods (London: Hale, 1945);

She Who Will Not (London: Hale, 1945);

Arrested (London: Hale, 1949);

Vain Escape (London: Hale, 1952);

Breath of Paradise (New York, n.d.).

Editions and Collections: *Aia* (New York: Arno, 1978)—comprises *Fields of Sleep* and *People of the Darkness;*

Robin Hood: A Classic Illustrated Edition, compiled by Cooper Edens (San Francisco: Chronicle Books, 2002).

OTHER: *Heard This One? A Book of Funny Stories,* edited by Vivian (London: Pearson, 1922);

Shooting Stars, adapted by Vivian from the motion-picture screenplay by Anthony Asquith and Joe Orton (London: Hurst & Blackett, 1928).

The British novelist and historian Peter Berresford Ellis, who, with Jack Adrian, is preparing a biography and bibliography of E. Charles Vivian, has so far identified ninety-six books published by Vivian under that name and several pseudonyms during his career of four decades as a novelist, journalist, and magazine editor. Fantasy works constitute only about one-fifth of his book-length fiction, including two novels, *Star Dust* (1925) and *The Kleinert Case* (1938), that may be classified as marginal science fiction. And even in these relatively few titles the fantasy element is often slight, appearing in his adventure novels *Woman Dominant* (1929), *Coulson Goes South* (1933), and *The Dead Man's Chest* (1934) as secondary lost-race motifs. Yet, psychic phenomena and Atlantean and Lemurian motifs are prevalent, so that even the marginal works seem colored by an imaginative, poetic vision.

The son of a gentleman farmer, Vivian was born Charles Henry Cannell in Lodden, Norfolk, on 19 October 1882. Little is known about his childhood. When he was around sixteen, he left home after a family quarrel. Apparently breaking off contact with his parents and two sisters, he changed his name to Evelyn Charles Vivian and made his way to South Africa, where he served in the British cavalry during the Boer War of 1899 to 1902.

On his return to England, Vivian embarked on a career in journalism. He worked under Hilaire Belloc, who was editing *Land and Water,* and served as assistant editor of *The English Review* under both its founding editor, Ford Madox Hueffer (better known under the name he adopted after World War I, Ford Madox Ford), and Hueffer's successor, Austin Harrison. During this period he published his first novel, *The Shadow of Christine* (1907), which is characterized by W. O. G. Lofts as having a "genuine eerie atmosphere." Ellis, however, describes the novel—which, like much of Vivian's fiction, is exceedingly difficult to find—in an unpublished letter as "a young man's tale of passion set in the Australian outback."

A more valid precursor of the direction Vivian's fiction later took is *Passion-Fruit* (1912), a novel that includes two obvious prefigurations of Vivian's later work. First, Wilfrid Stevens, a gifted scientist like Leonard Ferrers in *Star Dust,* invents a steel vastly superior in durability to all existing formulas. Like Ferrers's machine that creates gold out of the "ether," Stevens's invention is a threat to national and international interests—although the crisis is averted without the massive destruction of property and loss of life that occur in *Star Dust.* Second, Vivian introduces a character with psychic gifts, who can bestow the power of second sight through hypnosis. The authenticity of the experience is ambiguous, but the "eerie" quality that Vivian imparts to this episode is not.

Vivian married Marion Christmas Harvie in Sussex in 1913. Their only child, Katherine, was born on 25 October 1917.

When World War I broke out in 1914, Vivian was a journalist with the *Daily Telegraph* (London); from 1916 to 1919 he was the editor of *Flying* magazine, which emphasized military aviation. During the war years he published several books of nonfiction but only two novels; according to Ellis, both of the latter had been written before the war.

City of Wonder, Vivian's first lost-race novel, was published in 1922, initiating the period of some eighteen years during which all of his fantasy and adventure fiction was published. Philip Watkins leads his companions Jack Faulkner, who narrates the story, and Cecil Bent into the "wilds that still exist in certain lands of the Pacific" in search of the legendary city of Kir-Asa. The way leads across a great abyss traversed by a "trembling" stone bridge and through the country of the "ghosts who chase

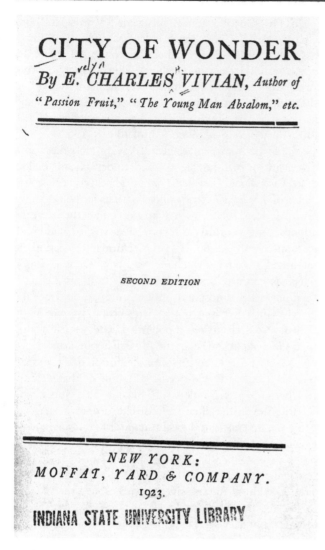

CITY OF WONDER
By E. CHARLES VIVIAN, Author of
"Passion Fruit," "The Young Man Absalom," etc.

SECOND EDITION

NEW YORK:
MOFFAT, YARD & COMPANY.
1923.
INDIANA STATE UNIVERSITY LIBRARY

Title page for the U.S. edition of Vivian's 1922 novel, about three
explorers who find the lost city of Kir-Asa

Even if many of the elements are familiar from the countless lost-race novels written in the wake of H. Rider Haggard's *King Solomon's Mines* (1885), Vivian's novel is distinguished by superior plotting and the shedding of much of the Victorian stylistic baggage—in particular, the stagy dialogue—that can hobble the prose of the most talented writer. Vivian is not a creator of memorable protagonists—Haggard's Zulu warrior Umslopogaas has no counterpart in Vivian's works—but the ones he creates are intelligent and resourceful, with a dogged, sometimes even pedestrian streak that makes his most fantastic adventures, *City of Wonder,* the Aia Saga (1923, 1924), and *The Lady of the Terraces* (1925), seem real. They are also firmly planted in a terrain that Vivian appears to know intimately. Although Vivian's service during the Boer War would have given him some knowledge of Africa, he avoided following in Haggard's footsteps and, instead, set many of his adventures on remote Pacific islands. Ellis reports that Vivian's daughter recalls a cruise her father made to the Near East to gather material for some of the works he wrote under the pseudonym Jack Mann (*Coulson Goes South* particularly benefited from this sojourn), but he never traveled to the Far East or to the South Pacific. Vivian must be seen as one of those gifted armchair travelers who can conjure with apparent accuracy a place they have never visited.

In many of his fantasy and adventure stories Vivian demonstrates a keen interest in the possible survival of descendants of ancient Atlantis and Lemuria in out-of-the-way places. He also proposes the coming to earth of "astral" beings or spirits, some of them so evil that they never blended with matter and survived as shadowy essences, like the murderous "ghosts" in *City of Wonder*. This is the true "eerie" strain in Vivian, and it finds its most significant and convincing expression in the Gees novels that he began writing in 1936.

City of Wonder was followed by two more lost-race novels, *Fields of Sleep* (1923) and *People of the Darkness* (1924), which constitute the Aia Saga. In *Fields of Sleep* Victor Marshall discovers a people, descendants of ancient Babylonian miners, living in a village called Mah-Eng in the interior of a remote island, many of whom are addicted to a narcotic flower that atrophies the vocal cords and renders its victims incapable of living without its perfume. Marshall falls in love with Aia, the daughter of Tara-Hi, hereditary chief of the "silent men," but after a flood destroys the valley he leaves her and returns to England because of obligations he must fulfill. In *People of the Darkness* Victor returns to the island in search of Aia. An eyeless race that dwells underground leads Victor to Aia and her father in the village of Pas-Eng, also inhabited by descendants of Babylonian miners. When a storm and earthquake destroy the village and the remaining silent men, Tari-Hi and Aia are freed from their responsibilities,

women." The entrance to Kir-Asa is guarded by a woman, Nantia, and her army of monkeys; the men pass through this barrier after Bent shoots Nantia. Reaching the outskirts of the lost city, they are greeted by descendants of an ancestor of Watkins's who had made his way to Kir-Asa. The three are taken to be judged by the council of five that will rule until the mad king dies and is succeeded by his eldest son. The intruders participate in a revolution, during which Bent is killed. Watkins's cousin is installed as king, and Watkins declares his intention to remain in Kir-Asa. Faulkner, who has married the new king's daughter but lost her to the "ghosts that chase women," falls into the river and is swept away. He survives long enough to record his adventures and send the manuscript, along with a map, to Watkins's bank. The report reaches its destination; but the map is lost, and Watkins's relatives are unable to retrace the party's steps.

and Aia leaves with Victor for the unknown but tantalizing promises of civilization.

When Victor questions Tara-Hi in *Fields of Sleep* about the origins of his people, he responds: "The people Baal Caesar ruled, the nation that made the world tremble at its conquests and built cities to challenge the ages with their glory. Kings bowed to the dust before the kings of my people, and the plain of Dura shook with the trampling of the hosts when the enemies went out to war." Victor has dim recollections of "scripture lessons" about the great lord Belshazzar; but his city is long since dust, and the present descendants of his people live simply, either bound to the valley by their addiction, or, like Tari-Hi and Aia, by their obligation to protect the silent men and keep the world beyond out of the valley. In *People of the Darkness* Vivian sounds one of his favorite themes by making the underground people remnants of an intellectual caste of Atlanteans, condemned to life underground before the great continent sank beneath the waves.

Vivian's descriptions of the dangerous and difficult expeditions to Mah-Eng and Pas-Eng, the disabling addiction of the silent men, the frightening appearance of the degenerate underground Atlanteans, and, especially, the great earthquake that destroys Pas-Eng are among his finest pages. The rather pedestrian Victor is eclipsed by the secondary character of Erasmus Whauple, whom Victor finds a prisoner of Aia's people in *Fields of Sleep* and who returns with him in search of Aia in *People of the Darkness*. Aia is the first of Vivian's Haggardian heroines; she is reminiscent of Ayesha, the protagonist of *She: A History of Adventure* (1886) and a series of later novels, in her name and in her ability to pass through flames untouched. She is also somewhat too prone to express herself with statements such as "I, being woman, can never be altogether wise . . . proud of my separateness, Victor, yet glad in my beauty that forced your eyes toward me." She is in the lineage of the patient Jessie in *Passion-Fruit*, with neither the savage barbarity of Haggard's Ayesha nor the magnetic beauty of Belle Ashburnham in *Passion-Fruit*. Like many writers, Vivian seems to have been galvanized by his "bad" women and too prone to idealize his heroines out of any resemblance to flesh-and-blood creations.

From 1918 to 1922 Vivian was on the staff of the publisher C. A. Pearson, where he edited *The Novel Magazine;* he then joined Hutchinson's magazine operation, becoming the first editor of *Adventure* in 1922 and of *Mystery Story* in 1923. Both magazines, which featured leading writers of popular fiction, were published for at least two decades, but Vivian gave up the editorship in 1925 to devote himself full-time to his writing career.

In 1925 Vivian published the marginal science-fiction novel *Star Dust,* the account of a brilliant but quirky scientist, Leonard Ferrers, who has built a machine that seems to resemble a giant vacuum cleaner and that can reduce matter to its "primordial elements." It can also—and this is Ferrers's great achievement—create matter out of the "astral" elements from which all material things have evolved. Unlike Wilfrid Stevens in *Passion-Fruit,* who is also a brilliant scientist but is a recluse, Ferrers wants to change the world for the "better" by destroying the materialistic basis of society and, after the resulting chaos has passed, give "people time to live, time to develop, and force them to realize that greed is useless by rendering the objects of their greed valueless." After devoting himself selflessly to his experiments, he falls in love with Anne Osterley, who understands what he wants to do but also sees the threat to Ferrers and to the world posed by his desire to improve the lot of humanity. When Ferrers destroys the monetary system by creating gold, he and Anne are murdered; the murderer is, in turn, killed in the cataclysm that Ferrers unleashes with his machine as he dies. Although the work is somewhat repetitious—Ferrers's intentions are clarified too often by one or another of the characters—Ferrers is a larger-than-life figure somewhat in the vein of the deranged scientists of the *Frankenstein* movies, indifferent to the havoc he will wreak in his single-minded desire to put his plans into effect.

Vivian published two other novels with lost-race elements: *The Lady of the Terraces* in 1925 and *The Forbidden Door* in 1927. *The Forbidden Door* is the more conventional—even pulpish—of the two. It is an adventure story in which Alan Coulson—a precursor of the Rex Coulson character created by Vivian under the Jack Mann pseudonym several years later—and his hard-drinking companion Josiah Drinkwater are engaged by a shady lawyer to help him find Maraquita Terry, the heiress to an unclaimed estate. When she goes "into the hills" to join her cousin, Fleur Delage, the ruthless head of the island's crime syndicate, Coulson and Josiah pursue her in an expedition that mimics the pattern of the lost-race quest novel but has little of its poetic fantasy.

On the other hand, *The Lady of the Terraces* is the first of two splendid South American fantasy/adventure novels. A legendary people, perhaps descendants of the ancient Incas, living in the interior of Peru attract the attention of Colvin Barr, a British colonial employee, "salaried and slave to custom." On a hunt for gold with a companion, Barr turns away from the material quest to look for something different, "something waiting always just over the next horizon, some fullness of experience—one moment, perhaps, that might make a memory to fill years." The most idealistic of Vivian's adventurer-heroes, Barr dies on the eve of realizing his dream. The various sections of the novel are given musical terms as subtitles: the opening section is "moderato e ben marcato," while the final one, in which Barr dies and his companion returns to civilization, is "adagio con brio." These seemingly incompatible terms are expressive of two basic ele-

STAR DUST

By E. Charles Vivian . Author of

"Fields of Sleep," "People of the Darkness," etc.   ::   ::

" Electronic energy. . . is so great and so terrible that it has been seriously put forward that scientific research in this direction should be stopped until it is felt that the human race is sufficiently elevated to be entrusted with the keys of such fearsome storehouses of power."—*Lord Headley in his Presidential Address to the Society of Engineers, Februray 1st, 1921.*

LONDON: HUTCHINSON AND CO.
PATERNOSTER ROW, E.C.

1925

Title page for Vivian's 1925 novel about a scientist who wants to eliminate materialism by rendering people's possessions valueless (Indiana State University Library)

ments in Vivian's fiction, the fire that drives his explorer/wanderer/adventurers always beyond the next horizon and the loss that so often follows the discovery of a city of wonder or a land of the terraces.

The other South American novel, *A King There Was–* (1926), is a work of historical fiction in which the fantasy element is slight. It takes place in the Andean Heights at a time before "Atlantis sank and the Andes were thrust up." The tale, "sung" by "Felipe the Torero," is presumably refined from earlier narratives. It tells of love found and abandoned and of a kingdom threatened by internal dissension within and by the "little hairy men" of the outlands, who eventually overrun the land, sweeping everything before them. The battle sequences, with their almost photographic realism, are one of Vivian's great achievements, but one is reminded of the "adagio" of *The Lady of the Terraces* by the underlying philosophy, to

which one of the characters gives expression: "We live our days in travail, and then are but as shadows that have passed, leaving nor mark nor memory beyond a little time. . . . Children of a day, playing in bitterness, and then to play no more."

The decade in which almost all of Vivian's fantasy fiction was published ended in 1929 with the appearance of *Woman Dominant*. A review in the *Sunday Referee* described it as "good fun and very readable" and commended the author's "fine sense of character" and ability to "create atmosphere swiftly and effectively."

This review, which reads like the checking off of the salient selling points of any genre novel, masks one of the most original of Vivian's adventure works, which presents a sympathetic and probing study of a matriarchal society. It is a fine example of Vivian's fictional treatment of women, which can bog down in Victorian stereotypes but can also portray them as strong and independent. A trip up the Smoky River toward "distant hills" by Josiah Drinkwater of *The Forbidden Door* and his two companions ends in a village in which the male inhabitants are kept docile and passive by being drugged with a powder. The "mother of the powder," the old woman who rules the village, is "much more than a savage, though she is a savage like the rest. The sort of woman who would have been really great, if she had been educated." The arrival of the three "full" men shows some of the younger women, who do not remember the repressive patriarchal regime under which their mothers lived, what a man can be, and the resulting clash leaves the old woman dead and the village in ruins. Vivian escapes the usual pattern of the lost-race novel, in which the main female character is an idealized goddess, and provides major roles for three women: the "mother of the powder"; an Englishwoman known as the "great doctor," who is revered and protected by the natives; and her daughter, who provides the love interest but is no pagan goddess.

Under the Jack Mann pseudonym, which he assumed in the 1930s, Vivian wrote two series: the Coulson adventure novels and the Gees psychic detective cycle. The Coulson novels are enormously entertaining, but only two of them, *Coulson Goes South* and *The Dead Man's Chest,* include fantasy elements. In *Coulson Goes South* a party treks to the legendary "hill of Yarab," where the Arab inhabitants' blood may be mixed with something "far older," such as the race of Atlantis. In *The Dead Man's Chest* a reclusive South Pacific island tribe is ruled by an enlightened leader. The natives are clearly morally superior to one of the English characters, who shoots them in the back and asks what the "lives of four of these stinking animals, or forty of them amount to in comparison with the life of one white man." Coulson replies that "half of the trouble in the Pacific has been caused" by men like that character. The imperialist cast of earlier lost-race fiction is not continued in the Coulson series, which appeared at a time when such a rejection of white superiority was hardly to be expected in genre—or even in mainstream—fiction.

From 1936 to 1940 Vivian published eight mystery novels featuring Gregory George Gordon Green, who is known by his nickname "Gees." The work that opens the series, *Gees' First Case,* is a straightforward mystery story, while the fourth, *The Kleinert Case,* features a haunting and the "super science" interest of *Passion-Fruit* and *Star Dust.* The other six are psychic detective stories and are the most widely collected of all of Vivian's work.

Gees, a "tall, pleasantly ugly, youngish sort of man," advertises himself as equipped to handle matters from "mumps to murder" but most often takes cases in which a supernatural element is present. His office is staffed by Miss Eve Madeleine Brandon, a discreet secretary of intelligence and breeding who only once—in *Her Ways Are Death* (1939)—questions the supernatural dimensions of a case. But then, in the presence of a striking apparition that is apparently unexplainable by the natural laws in which she places such trust, she stammers, "No, not illusion. I was wrong."

After thwarting the Bolsheviks who are planning to create chaos and install a revolutionary government in England in *Gees' First Case,* Gees travels in *Grey Shapes* (1937) to Cumberland, where people still believe that "solid, material things are not all of life," to look into the savage killing of sheep. Only when a shepherd tells him that "no dog as we know dogs is responsible for the outrage" does the case really begin to interest Gees, who senses something "sub-human" and abnormal in it. The nearest neighbor of Gees's employer, Tyrell, is McCoul, who lives in a restored castle with his daughter, Gyda. Gees is particularly struck by Gyda's "perfectly even, shining white teeth" and by both McCouls' repulsive fondness for "red flesh," which Gees describes as "red, dripping stuff." The "beasts" responsible for killing the sheep—and, eventually, the shepherd—are finally identified as the shape-changing McCouls, who are shot and burned at dawn, before they can complete their change back into human form.

Grey Shapes, in spite of the sheep killing and shape-changing, is no conventional novel of lycanthropy. Along with evocative descriptions of the landscape of the region and the customs and habits of its people, Vivian provides extensive antiquarian discussions of local and family history that reaches back to pre-Druidic times. The entire series is marked by this refusal to adhere to stereotypes.

Nightmare Farm (1937) and *Maker of Shadows* (1938) are perhaps the most original works in the Coulson series. In both novels the psychic phenomena are shadows that feed on the human soul. In *Nightmare Farm* the shadows

that drive women mad are the "ghosts that chase women" that the protagonists of *City of Wonder* encountered on their journey to Kir-Asa; they were brought to England by a depraved ancestor of a local family in the seventeenth century. Several details establish the connection with the events of *City of Wonder,* a book with which Gees shows himself to be familiar. He recalls the explanation in the earlier novel of the "ghosts" as elemental spirits so evil that they drive mad the women whose bodies they invade. In an exorcism arranged by Gees, a young woman, Helen Aylener, is freed of the spirit that has taken possession of her; then, in what becomes a recurrent pattern in the series, Gees falls in love with Helen, who is subsequently murdered by another woman who has been invaded by one of the destructive spirits. The same fate befell the young wife of the narrator of *City of Wonder,* and Gees will regularly fall in love with a woman only to lose her to the dark forces he is battling.

Gamel MacMorn, the "maker of shadows," is the first antagonist worthy of Gees. He is an Azilian, a descendant of the race of Atlantis, who captures the souls of humans to extend his own life. The MacMorns go back "to the dawn of things" and "have preserved the old wisdom," which MacMorn continues to practice. Gees destroys MacMorn, but he cannot save Helen, the young woman caught in MacMorn's web; and he is deceived and seduced by Bathsheba Grallach, who has been charged by MacMorn to neutralize Gees, whose knowledge he fears. The discussions of Norse mythology and the descriptions of the "dour" people and of the region, which is haunted by heavy mists that MacMorn uses for his illusions, make this narrative uncommonly satisfying.

History and legend are the strong suits of *The Ninth Life* (1939), in which the last surviving priestess of Sekhmet seeks a final victim to fulfill her covenant with the goddess, and of *Her Ways Are Death,* in which Gees is attracted to Ira Warenn, a woman who possesses knowledge that helped to destroy Atlantis. In the latter novel, even as Gees warns Wrenn of the consequences of venturing into a subject where she is "a thief and an interloper," he allows her to take him with her into the "fourth dimension," where she is ultimately caught and imprisoned. Like Ferrers in *Star Dust,* she has achieved a power that is too dangerous for mortals.

In the last of the Gees series, *The Glass Too Many* (1940), the fantasy elements are subordinated to Gees's investigation into who is trying to murder Sydnor Reed with the administration of "lakiti," a slow-acting Dayak poison. The work is primarily a traditional British country-house mystery; but the murderer is also a "maker of shadows," and in a secret room under the manor some member of the household is practicing ancient rites on a "horned altar." Once again, Gees's fiancée is killed, and at the end of the novel Eve Madeleine Brandon promises to

Advertisement included in Star Dust *for a magazine put out by the same publisher (Indiana State University Library)*

let him know after the Easter holidays whether she will remain with the firm or help him find a suitable "decorative" successor. She had thought at the end of *The Kleinert Case* that Gees might be "awakening" to some recognition of her as a woman; but several novels and several women later, he has still not reached that point.

Vivian's daughter was married in 1939 but continued to live with her parents in London while her husband, Anthony Ashton, served in the army. In 1942 an incendiary bomb destroyed the family's apartment in Longridge Road, Earl's Court, along with Vivian's manuscripts and other papers, but none of the family was injured. They moved to Braham Gardens, where Vivian lived until his death. He published only one novel a year from 1942 to 1945 and nothing in 1946. He died at the Princess Beatrice Hospital, Earl's Court, on 21 May 1947. His wife died in 1964.

Although some of Vivian's books were republished in the United States in the 1970s and early 1980s, no record has been found of any reprints of Vivian's work in England since his death. The lost-race novel has seen its day, and novels of psychic detection have their detractors; but Vivian's work in both of these fields was of uncommonly high quality.

References:

E. F. Bleiler, *The Guide to Supernatural Fiction* (Kent, Ohio: Kent State University Press, 1983), pp. 340–341;

Bleiler, *Science-Fiction: The Early Years* (Kent, Ohio: Kent State University Press, 1990), pp. 776–779;

Peter Berresford Ellis, "Master of Mystery," *Million: The Magazine about Popular Fiction,* no. 6 (November/December 1991): 24–27;

W. O. G. Lofts, "On the Trail of the Mysterious 'Jack Mann,'" *Mystery Reader's Newsletter,* 6 (Autumn 1973): 19–22;

Brian Stableford, "The Gees Series," in *Survey of Modern Fantasy Literature,* volume 2, edited by Frank N. Magill (Englewood Cliffs, N.J.: Salem Press, 1983), pp. 596–600.

Dennis Wheatley

(8 January 1897 – 11 November 1977)

Darren Harris-Fain
Shawnee State University

See also the Wheatley entry in *DLB 77: British Mystery Writers, 1920–1939*.

BOOKS: *The Forbidden Territory* (London: Hutchinson, 1933; New York: Dutton, 1933);

Such Power Is Dangerous (London: Hutchinson, 1933);

"Old Rowley": A Private Life of Charles II (London: Hutchinson, 1933; New York: Dutton, 1934); republished as *A Private Life of Charles II* (London: Hutchinson, 1938);

Black August (London: Hutchinson, 1934; New York: Dutton, 1934);

The Fabulous Valley (London: Hutchinson, 1934);

The Devil Rides Out (London: Hutchinson, 1935; New York: Bantam, 1967);

The Eunuch of Stamboul (London: Hutchinson, 1935; Boston: Little, Brown, 1935);

They Found Atlantis (London: Hutchinson, 1936; Philadelphia: Lippincott, 1936);

Murder Off Miami, by Wheatley and J. G. Links (London: Hutchinson, 1936); republished as *File on Bolitho Blane* (New York: Morrow, 1936);

Contraband (London: Hutchinson, 1936);

The Secret War (London: Hutchinson, 1937);

Who Killed Robert Prentice? by Wheatley and Links (London: Hutchinson, 1937); republished as *File on Robert Prentice* (New York: Greenberg, 1937);

Red Eagle: The Story of the Russian Revolution and of Klementy Efremovitch Voroshilov, Marshal and Commissar for Defence of the Union of Socialist Soviet Republics (London: Hutchinson, 1937); republished as *Red Eagle: A Story of the Russian Revolution and of Klementy Efremovitch Voroshilov* (London: Arrow, 1964);

Uncharted Seas (London: Hutchinson, 1938);

The Malinsay Massacre, by Wheatley and Links (London: Hutchinson, 1938; New York: Rutledge, 1981);

The Golden Spaniard (London: Hutchinson, 1938);

The Quest of Julian Day (London: Hutchinson, 1939);

Herewith the Clues! by Wheatley and Links (London: Hutchinson, 1939; New York: Mayflower, 1982);

Sixty Days to Live (London: Hutchinson, 1939);

Dennis Wheatley as a second lieutenant in the Royal Field Artillery, September 1914

Three Inquisitive People (London: Hutchinson, 1940);

The Scarlet Impostor (London: Hutchinson, 1940; New York: Macmillan, 1942);

Faked Passports (London: Hutchinson, 1940; New York: Macmillan, 1943);

The Black Baroness (London: Hutchinson, 1940; New York: Macmillan, 1942);

Strange Conflict (London: Hutchinson, 1941; New York: Ballantine, 1972);

The Sword of Fate (London: Hutchinson, 1941; New York: Macmillan, 1944);

Total War: A Paper (London: Hutchinson, 1941);

V for Vengeance (London: Hutchinson, 1942; New York: Macmillan, 1942);

Mediterranean Nights (London: Hutchinson, 1942; revised and enlarged edition, London: Arrow, 1962);

Gunmen, Gallants, and Ghosts (London: Hutchinson, 1943; revised edition, London: Arrow, 1963);

The Man Who Missed the War (London: Hutchinson, 1945);

Codeword—Golden Fleece (London: Hutchinson, 1946);

Come Into My Parlor (London: Hutchinson, 1946);

The Launching of Roger Brook (London: Hutchinson, 1947);

The Shadow of Tyburn Tree (London: Hutchinson, 1948; New York: Ballantine, 1973);

The Haunting of Toby Jugg (London: Hutchinson, 1948);

The Rising Storm (London: Hutchinson, 1949);

The Seven Ages of Justerini's: 1749–1949 (London: Riddle, 1949); revised and expanded as *1749–1965: The Eight Ages of Justerini's* (Aylesbury, Buckinghamshire: Dolphin, 1965);

The Second Seal (London: Hutchinson, 1950);

The Man Who Killed the King (London: Hutchinson, 1951; New York: Putnam, 1965);

Star of Ill-Omen (London: Hutchinson, 1952);

To the Devil—a Daughter (London: Hutchinson, 1953; New York: Bantam, 1968);

Curtain of Fear (London: Hutchinson, 1953);

The Island Where Time Stands Still (London: Hutchinson, 1954);

The Dark Secret of Josephine (London: Hutchinson, 1955);

The Ka of Gifford Hillary (London: Hutchinson, 1956; New York: Bantam, 1969);

The Prisoner in the Mask (London: Hutchinson, 1957);

Traitor's Gate (London: Hutchinson, 1958);

Stranger Than Fiction (London: Hutchinson, 1959);

The Rape of Venice (London: Hutchinson, 1959);

The Satanist (London: Hutchinson, 1960; New York: Bantam, 1967);

Saturdays with Bricks, and Other Days under Shell-Fire (London: Hutchinson, 1961);

Vendetta in Spain (London: Hutchinson, 1961);

Mayhem in Greece (London: Hutchinson, 1962);

The Sultan's Daughter (London: Hutchinson, 1963);

Bill for the Use of a Body (London: Hutchinson, 1964);

They Used Dark Forces (London: Hutchinson, 1964);

Dangerous Inheritance (London: Hutchinson, 1965);

The Wanton Princess (London: Hutchinson, 1966);

Unholy Crusade (London: Hutchinson, 1967);

The White Witch of the South Seas (London: Hutchinson, 1968);

Evil in a Mask (London: Hutchinson, 1969);

Gateway to Hell (London: Hutchinson, 1970; New York: Ballantine, 1973);

The Devil and All His Works (London: Hutchinson, 1971; New York: American Heritage Press, 1971);

The Ravishing of Lady Mary Ware (London: Hutchinson, 1971);

The Strange Story of Linda Lee (London: Hutchinson, 1972);

The Irish Witch (London: Hutchinson, 1973);

Desperate Measures (London: Hutchinson, 1974);

The Time Has Come: The Memoirs of Dennis Wheatley, 3 volumes (London: Hutchinson, 1977–1979)—comprises volume 1, *The Young Man Said, 1897–1914;* volume 2, *Officer and Temporary Gentleman, 1914–1919;* and volume 3, *Drink and Ink, 1919–1977,* edited by Anthony Lejeune;

The Deception Planners: My Secret War, edited by Lejeune (London: Hutchinson, 1980).

Editions and Collections: *Those Modern Musketeers* (London: Hutchinson, 1939)—comprises *Three Inquisitive People, The Forbidden Territory, The Devil Rides Out,* and *The Golden Spaniard;*

Early Adventures of Roger Brook (London: Hutchinson, 1951)—comprises *The Launching of Roger Brook* and *The Shadow of Tyburn Tree;*

Worlds Far from Here (London: Hutchinson, 1952)—comprises *Uncharted Seas, The Man Who Missed the War,* and *They Found Atlantis;*

Secret Missions of Gregory Sallust (London: Hutchinson, 1955)—comprises *The Scarlet Impostor, Faked Passports,* and *The Black Baroness;*

Black Magic Omnibus (London: Hutchinson, 1956)—comprises *The Devil Rides Out, Strange Conflict,* and *To the Devil—a Daughter;*

Roger Brook in the French Revolution (London: Hutchinson, 1957)—comprises *The Rising Storm* and *The Man Who Killed the King;*

Death in the Sunshine (London: Hutchinson, 1958)—comprises *The Fabulous Valley, The Secret War,* and *The Eunuch of Stamboul;*

Plot and Counterplot: Three Adventures of Gregory Sallust (London: Hutchinson, 1959)—comprises *Black August, Contraband,* and *The Island Where Time Stands Still;*

Into the Unknown (London: Hutchinson, 1960)—comprises *Sixty Days to Live, Star of Ill-Omen,* and *Curtain of Fear;*

Selected Works, Lymington edition, 6 volumes (London: Hutchinson, 1961).

OTHER: *A Century of Horror Stories,* edited by Wheatley (London: Hutchinson, 1935; Freeport, N.Y.: Books for Libraries Press, 1971);

A Century of Spy Stories, edited by Wheatley (London: Hutchinson, 1938);

Shafts of Fear, edited by Wheatley (London: Arrow, 1965); republished as *Dennis Wheatley's First Book of Horror Stories: Tales of Strange Doings* (London: Hutchinson, 1968);

Quiver of Horror, edited by Wheatley (London: Arrow, 1965); republished as *Dennis Wheatley's Second Book of Horror Stories: Tales of Strange Happenings* (London: Hutchinson, 1968);

Uncanny Tales, 3 volumes, selected by Wheatley (London: Sphere, 1974–1975);

Satanism and Witches: Essays and Stories, selected by Wheatley (London: Sphere, 1974).

Prolific and imaginative if also occasionally repetitive and predictable, Dennis Wheatley is noteworthy in the history of dark fantasy for his treatments of sorcery and black magic and for his distinctive combinations of literary types, resulting in supernatural spy stories and thrillers and in historical horror novels. He is also important for his painstaking work as an anthologist; many readers of horror and weird fiction in Britain and the United States were introduced to these genres through Wheatley's massive collections, such as *A Century of Horror Stories* (1935). So strong was his influence that Keith Neilson, in a chapter on modern horror fiction in Neil Barron's *Horror Literature: A Reader's Guide* (1990), calls Wheatley the most important British horror writer in the period between the world wars, despite the fact that such work comprises only a fraction of his considerable output.

Over the course of a career that spanned more than forty years after he began publishing in his thirties, Wheatley established a reputation as a popular writer of mysteries and thrillers that demanded little from their readers except for a willing suspension of disbelief and a desire to be entertained with exciting and unusual stories. Though his popularity has faded since his death, his books were best-sellers in their time and continue to attract the attention of readers of mystery or horror fiction.

Dennis Yates Wheatley was born in London on 8 January 1897 to Albert David Wheatley and Florence Baker Wheatley (Lady Newton). He was the oldest of three children. In 1908 he began his formal education at Dulwich College, which expelled him for breaking the rules. Feeling that young Wheatley could benefit from a disciplined education, his father then placed him as a cadet aboard the H.M.S. *Worcester,* a training ship moored on the Thames River, where he remained until

Cover for a 1950 British paperback reprint of Wheatley's 1935 novel, about the struggle of the two protagonists to rescue their friend from a sorcerer

1913. He then studied privately for nine months in Germany.

In 1914, with the outbreak of World War I, Wheatley joined the British army and served in the Royal Field Artillery in the City of London Brigade until 1917. He then joined the 36th Ulster Division. He served at several posts throughout Great Britain and saw action in Flanders and France. His active military service came to an end when he developed bronchitis as a result of exposure to chlorine gas and was sent back to England to recover. He remained in the military until 1919, a year after the war ended, leaving with the rank of second lieutenant.

After leaving military service, he began working for the family firm, Wheatley and Son, as a wine merchant. His father's father had founded the business, located in Mayfair. Wheatley started his own family in 1923 when he married Nancy Madelaine Leslie Robinson, with whom he had a son, Anthony Marius Wheatley. Their lavish lifestyle took them into debt, from which his father had to extricate them. Wheatley continued to exercise poor financial judgment early in the marriage, which quickly turned sour as he added to his expenses by keeping a mistress. Again he was rescued, this time by inheriting the family business upon his father's death in 1927.

The choice of writing as a career thus did not come as early in Wheatley's life as it does for many authors. After his father's death he became sole proprietor of the firm, which he renamed Dennis Wheatley, Ltd. Until the Great Depression forced him to liquidate the business in 1931, Wheatley had assumed that his life would be dedicated to selling wine rather than writing popular literature. But after 1931 he focused his energies on writing, which he had considered for some time but had not yet seriously pursued. Also in 1931, Wheatley and his first wife divorced, and that same year he married Joan Gwendoline Johnstone, who supported his writing efforts.

His first published book was the spy novel *The Forbidden Territory* (1933), in which he introduced a trio of heroes who also appear in *The Devil Rides Out,* published two years later. Critics attacked *The Forbidden Territory* for its style but admitted that Wheatley was a skilled storyteller—an assessment that was repeated often throughout his lengthy career. A rapid writer, he soon followed this book with *Such Power Is Dangerous* (1933) and *The Fabulous Valley* (1934), the first published of his many crime novels.

Early in his career Wheatley created the heroes who populate most of his thrillers, among them the Duke de Richleau, a connoisseur of art; secret agent Gregory Sallust; explorer Julian Day; adventurer and spy Roger Brook; and mystery writer Molly Fountain. These adventurous thrillers reveal the influence of Alexandre Dumas *père,* to whose well-known works several of Wheatley's could be compared if not in fact paralleled, as well as Baroness Emma Orczy, author of *The Scarlet Pimpernel* (1905). Wheatley's tendency to focus the bulk of his work around a handful of recurring characters mirrors his willingness to return to familiar formulas in his fiction, a tendency reinforced by the fact that audiences seemed to want such recurrence.

Perhaps Wheatley's best-known work is *The Devil Rides Out.* Combining elements of the spy thriller with those of the weird tale, this 1935 novel involves the efforts of two heroes, the Duke de Richleau and his friend Rex Van Ryn, to extricate their companion, Simon Aron, from the grasp of a sorcerer. The plot is complicated by one of the rescuers falling in love with one of the sorcerer's female subjects. All of these plot elements are used purely in the service of an exciting, entertaining story rather than for any thematic signifi-

cance; the plot itself does not hold up under scrutiny, its effectiveness lessened (as is so often the case in Wheatley's work) by a reliance on a highly implausible deus ex machina ending to resolve the convoluted twists and turns of the story.

Just as interesting as the narrative is one of the stories behind Wheatley's work on *The Devil Rides Out.* The sorcerer in the novel is clearly modeled on the self-proclaimed necromancer Aleister Crowley, who for ten years belonged to the occultist Order of the Golden Dawn before leaving it in 1908, frustrated in his attempts to take control of the Order. He then founded his own occult group, which he called the Argenteum Astrum. Crowley, who eventually dubbed himself the Great Beast, was a controversial figure in Europe not only for his occult practices but also for their acknowledged sensuality. This notoriety, however, did not prevent him from attempting to spread his doctrines through his many writings. W. Somerset Maugham had already used Crowley as an inspiration for his novel *The Magician* (1908), but Wheatley went even further and invited the infamous sorcerer to dinner as part of his research for *The Devil Rides Out.*

Such research was characteristic of Wheatley's creative process. He drew heavily on imagination in his fictional creations, but he relied just as heavily on meticulous investigations of occult beliefs and practices. As Neilson says, Wheatley's "'black magic' books are a veritable catalogue of supernatural lore—Satanism, Black Masses, demonic possession, magical incantations, the conjuring of demons, necromancy, hypnotism, clairvoyance, numerology, palmistry, astrology, ghostly apparitions, enchanted pentacles, astral travel, curses, crystal ball gazing, sex orgies, child sacrifice and time manipulation, to mention a few." And in setting such phenomena in the context of recognizable worlds, whether historical or contemporary, Wheatley also drew on more mundane types of research.

The title of *They Found Atlantis* (1936) gives a good indication of the plot of the novel, which combines legends of the sunken continent with elements of the lost-race novel, a popular subcategory of fantastic fiction in the late 1800s and early 1900s. Unlike most of Wheatley's fantastic fiction, this book comes closer to science fiction than to fantasy or horror.

As in *The Devil Rides Out,* credibility is stretched in other novels featuring the same central characters—the Duke de Richleau, Rex Van Ryn, Simon Aron, and Richard Eaton—whom readers are supposed to find capable and heroic even as they continue to involve themselves in preventable perils. The most noteworthy of these books, in terms of its existence as a cultural artifact if not its aesthetic quality, is *Strange Conflict* (1941). In this novel the heroes again find themselves battling a master of black magic whose evil is intensified by the fact that he is not just an ordinary magician but a Nazi sorcerer.

Wheatley's military background and his strong political beliefs led him to participate in World War II in addition to writing about it in his fiction. In 1940 and 1941 he was a member of the National Service Recruiting Panel, and in 1941 he joined the Joint Planning Staff of the War Council. He remained active in government service for the remainder of the war.

One of the most popular if not widely used subtypes of weird fiction or horror is stories featuring what is generally known as a psychic detective—an investigator of occult phenomena who, though he pries into the supernatural, does so using the methods and tools of the modern detective. Earlier examples include Joseph Sheridan Le Fanu's Dr. Hesselius, Algernon Blackwood's John Silence, and William Hope Hodgson's Carnacki the Ghost-Finder. Wheatley's own psychic detective, Niels Orsen, is featured in four of the stories collected in *Gunmen, Gallants, and Ghosts* (1943). Most scholars of weird fiction agree that Wheatley's efforts in this vein do not quite measure up to those of his predecessors. However, another story in this volume, "The Snake," is one of his best known. The occult is again central: in this case, the story focuses on magic in an African setting.

Wheatley's 1948 novel *The Haunting of Toby Jugg* also combines the supernatural with techniques of the thriller and contemporary concerns. In this case World War II, as in *Strange Conflict,* provides the background to the story, as the protagonist is yet another heroic figure who was injured in the war. However, the war experience and its effects are not the true focus of the plot, which instead revolves around how the hero confronts the various outré horrors that his enemies, set on wrenching his inherited fortune from his grasp, direct his way. Like Wheatley's earlier novels of the supernatural, *The Haunting of Toby Jugg* employs an exciting if incredible narrative, with the ending once more weakened by a resolution that seems to come from nothing the reader has been given up to that point.

Despite critical reservations about works such as *Strange Conflict* and *The Haunting of Toby Jugg,* Wheatley's fiction continued to sell well, and he kept writing novels in which supernatural elements and contemporary ones, especially history and politics, were intertwined. One example is *To the Devil—a Daughter* (1953). In this work the fantasy and horror trope of the amoral necromancer and the science-fiction trope of the mad scientist merge to produce a story of a black magician, Canon Copley-Syle, who plans to take over if not destroy the world by creating thousands of homunculi, human-like creatures whose origins can be traced back through

Christopher Lee as the Satanist defrocked priest Father Michael Rayner and Nastassja Kinski as Catherine in the 1976 movie
To the Devil—a Daughter, *based on Wheatley's 1953 novel of the same title (Hammer Films)*

alchemical lore. His machinations are tied in with communism, which many readers consider the weakest aspect of the novel. Wheatley hated communistic ideas passionately, and at times in this novel and in many of his works he substitutes diatribe for dialogue and screed for scenes. Copley-Syle intends to animate his first artificial creature with the soul of a young woman, Christina, whose Satanist father dedicated her to his dark master when she was born—hence the title of the book. In typical Wheatley fashion, however, the heroine endures trials and terrors until she can be rescued by a brave band of friends. Despite its unlikely mix of contemporary politics and standard supernatural thriller characteristics, as well as its dependence on a traditional Gothic storyline, the novel is often praised as one of Wheatley's most entertaining.

Somewhat similar in its fusion of contemporary political concerns and the weird tale is *The Ka of Gifford Hillary* (1956), which features scheming Russians whose plot against Britain is discovered by a hero who just happens to be dead. Slain by a death ray—Wheatley's supernatural spy thrillers occasionally include science-fiction technology similar to that found in Ian Fleming's James Bond books—Gifford Hillary goes not to the afterlife or oblivion but rather to an astral plane that lies between the natural and supernatural worlds. The "Ka" of the title refers to his astral form, which enables him to learn of the nefarious plans of the Soviets. After doing so, he then faces the challenge of communicating with the natural world, and his return to this world is complicated not only by the problems involved in physical reanimation but also by the fact that his murderer has been killed and Hillary could be suspected of achieving vengeance while in the astral plane. As silly as it all sounds in summary, the novel, like *To the Devil– a Daughter,* also ranks as one of Wheatley's most enjoyable books.

Wheatley returned to familiar territory with his 1960 novel *The Satanist.* Again readers become acquainted with a sorcerer who has evil ambitions; again the detailed descriptions of occult activities are juxtaposed with grandiose political intrigues. While Wheatley never managed to combine the two into a seamless whole as effectively as did the American writer James Blish in his diptych *Black Easter* (1968) and *The Day after Judgment* (1971), efforts such as *The Satanist* are nonetheless exciting to read if not terribly reflective. Furthermore, *The Satanist* is also noteworthy among Wheatley's works for his continuing development of an independent heroine: in *To the Devil–a Daughter,* Christina finally had to be saved by her friends, but in this book the heroine, Mary Morden, fares somewhat better on her own.

Among the best of Wheatley's novels dealing with history and politics is his series of books featuring Gregory Sallust. All of the books in the series are set during World War II, but only *They Used Dark Forces* (1964) and *The White Witch of the South Seas* (1968) include any suggestion of the supernatural. In *They Used Dark Forces* the patriotic Sallust teams up with a sorcerer, Ibrahim Malacou, who, unlike his counterpart in *Strange Conflict,* is opposed to the Nazis rather than working for them. Malacou enables Sallust, of course a master spy, to become an adviser to Adolf Hitler, aided by Hitler's own interest in the occult. The novel even suggests that Sallust may have "assisted" Hitler in his suicide. Though the novel actually employs little of the supernatural compared with related efforts in this mode, it is one of the more effective of Wheatley's works for its intriguing blend of real history and imagination.

Toward the end of his career Wheatley returned to his familiar heroes from *The Devil Rides Out* and other novels in one of his last works dealing with black magic. In *Gateway to Hell* (1970) one of the heroes once more falls into the clutches of a powerful occult enemy, in this case a satanic cult hidden away in Argentina. The plot is predictable: after many adventures, the heroes succeed in rescuing their friend and fighting against the forces of evil.

Somewhat more original is *The Irish Witch* (1973), though it too features a character Wheatley had created earlier–in this case Roger Brook, who had been the hero of several of Wheatley's historical adventure novels. Unlike those earlier works, this Roger Brook adventure involves him with the supernatural, as he fights to free his daughter from the hold of the Irish Witch during the Napoleonic era.

Wheatley's popularity remained high throughout his career up until his death on 11 November 1977, three years after Stephen King published his first novel, *Carrie,* and began a renaissance in horror fiction that led to its recognition as a separate publishing category. In four decades Wheatley produced more than sixty books that sold more than twenty-three million copies. Not only was he the most-read author of horror fiction in Britain during his career, but also his work was translated into twenty-seven languages during his lifetime and sold well in Europe, the United States, and elsewhere. Although this popularity declined after his death, Wheatley remains a significant figure in modern genre fiction both for his own creations and for his influence on the fostering of horror literature at a time when horror existed on the margins of fantasy.

Bibliography:

Iwan Hedman and Jan Alexandersson, *Fyra Decennier med Dennis Wheatley: En Biografi och Bibliografi* (Strangnas, Sweden: Dast, 1973).

T. H. White

(29 May 1906 – 17 January 1964)

Marie Nelson
University of Florida

See also the White entry in *DLB 160: British Children's Writers, 1914–1960.*

BOOKS: *Loved Helen and Other Poems* (London: Chatto & Windus, 1929; New York: Viking, 1929);

The Green Bay Tree; or, The Wicked Man Touches Wood, Songs for Six-Pence, no. 3 (Cambridge: Heffer, 1929);

Dead Mr. Nixon, by White and Roland McNair Scott (London: Cassell, 1931);

Darkness at Pemberley, with illustrations by White (London: Gollancz, 1932; New York & London: Century, 1933);

They Winter Abroad, as James Aston (London: Chatto & Windus, 1932; New York: Viking, 1932);

First Lesson, as Aston (London: Chatto & Windus, 1932; New York: Knopf, 1933);

Farewell Victoria (London: Collins, 1933; New York: Smith & Haas, 1934);

Earth Stopped; or, Mr. Marx's Sporting Tour (London: Collins, 1934);

Gone to Ground; or, The Sporting Decameron (London: Collins, 1935; New York: Putnam, 1935);

England Have My Bones, with illustrations by White (London: Collins, 1936; New York: Macmillan, 1936);

Burke's Steerage; or, The Amateur Gentleman's Introduction to Noble Sports and Pastimes (London: Collins, 1938; New York: Putnam, 1939);

The Sword in the Stone, with illustrations by White (London: Collins, 1938; New York: Putnam, 1939);

The Witch in the Wood, with illustrations by White (New York: Putnam, 1939; London: Collins, 1940);

The Ill-Made Knight, with illustrations by White (New York: Putnam, 1940; London: Collins, 1941);

Mistress Masham's Repose (New York: Putnam, 1946; London: Cape, 1947);

The Elephant and the Kangaroo, with illustrations by White (New York: Putnam, 1947; London: Cape, 1948);

T. H. White

The Age of Scandal: An Excursion through a Minor Period (London: Cape, 1950; London & New York: Oxford University Press, 1986);

The Goshawk, with illustrations by White (London: Cape, 1951; New York: Putnam, 1952);

The Scandalmonger (London: Cape, 1952; New York: Putnam, 1952);

The Master: An Adventure Story (London: Cape, 1957; New York: Putnam, 1957);

The Once and Future King (London: Collins, 1958; New York: Putnam, 1958)—comprises an enlarged version of *The Sword in the Stone; The Witch in the Wood,* revised as *The Queen of Air and Darkness; The Ill-Made Knight;* and *The Candle in the Wind;*

The Godstone and the Blackymor (New York: Putnam, 1959; London: Cape, 1959);

Verses (London: Privately printed by Shenval Press, 1962);

America at Last: The American Journal of T. H. White, edited by David Garnett (New York: Putnam, 1965);

Madame Min's Work Song, music by Ezra Sims (New York: American Composers Alliance, 1975);

The Book of Merlyn: The Unpublished Conclusion to The Once and Future King, prologue by Sylvia Townsend Warner (Austin & London: University of Texas Press, 1977);

A Joy Proposed: Poems, edited by Kurth Sprague (London: Rota, 1980; Athens: University of Georgia Press, 1983);

The Maharajah and Other Stories, edited by Sprague (London: Macdonald, 1981; New York: Putnam, 1981).

OTHER: *The Book of Beasts: Being a Translation from a Latin Bestiary of the Twelfth Century Made and Edited by T. H. White* (London: Cape, 1954; New York: Putnam, 1954);

"The Sale of Midsummer," in *Ghostly, Grim and Gruesome: An Anthology,* edited by Helen Hoke (Nashville: Thomas Nelson, 1976);

"The Tomb of the God," in *Kingdoms of Sorcery,* edited by Lin Carter (Garden City, N.Y.: Doubleday, 1976).

T. H. White is best known for his transformations of stories of the past. His four-volume masterpiece, *The Once and Future King* (1958), gives new life to the works of Sir Thomas Malory, and White also retells, or provides sequels for, stories told by such writers as Jonathan Swift, William Shakespeare, and the anonymous author of the biblical story of the Flood. In addition, his diaries and journals, such as *England Have My Bones* (1936), which he wrote during the years when he first determined to earn his living as a writer, not only have considerable narrative interest in themselves but also can be read as sources for his contributions to English fiction.

Terence Hansbury White was born on 29 May 1906 in Bombay, India, to Garrick Hansbury White, a district superintendent of police, and Constance Edith Southcote Aston White, the daughter of a judge. In 1911, suffering from a stomach infection, he was taken to St. Leonards, East Sussex, where his maternal grandparents lived. He remained with them when his parents returned to India—his father in 1914, followed by his mother in 1915.

White began his formal education in 1920 at Cheltenham College, a public school with a longstanding Anglo-Indian connection and a strong military program. In the summer of 1923 he received a certificate with credits in English, history, geography, French, and mathematics. In January of that year Constance White had been granted a separation from her alcoholic husband on grounds of cruelty; she returned to England and began, with the help of a cousin and her recently graduated son, to attempt to make a living as a pig and poultry farmer. She later wrote that she found herself unable, because she lacked the penny to pay for a stamp, to respond to a letter from her son's former headmaster saying that she must by "hook or crook . . . manage to send my boy to a University."

"The Man," an autobiographical short story collected in *The Maharajah and Other Stories* (1981), is based on this period in White's life. White's sense of injustice at being forced to postpone his university education becomes apparent when his alter ego, Nicky, says that though he "hated the muscular man [his mother's cousin], and hated the arid chicken farm, and hated work, and hated his school, where he ought to be a prefect but was not, he hid these feelings and was ashamed of them and did not recognize them." Nicky's impulse—and White's, too, one can imagine—is to "read himself away, into a less real world."

White spent a year tutoring and was able to enter Queens' College, Cambridge, in 1925. By the end of the year he had earned a scholarship. He made his way back from a trip to Lapland to find he had succeeded brilliantly in his spring examinations. Diagnosed with tuberculosis in 1927, he spent four months in a sanatorium and was then enabled by the generosity of a group of dons to go to Italy for his health. He was advised to "degrade"—that is, to postpone his examinations for a year—but he insisted on taking them and did not perform particularly well. Nevertheless, he wrote what his director of studies considered to be a wild and funny essay on Malory.

In Italy, White began *They Winter Abroad* (1932), wrote several *Saturday Review* articles, and contracted with Chatto and Windus for a book of poems. In 1929 he graduated with distinction from Cambridge; Chatto and Windus published *Loved Helen and Other Poems;* and his thirty-three-line *The Green Bay Tree; or, The Wicked Man Touches Wood* appeared in a Cambridge poets series. The first poems of *Loved Helen and Other Poems* show

White practicing falconry at Stowe School in 1937

White's debt to poets of the English Renaissance, while *The Green Bay Tree* is deliberately imitative of the style of Gerard Manley Hopkins. White continued to write poems for the rest of his life; he sent them in letters to friends, included them in his journals, and incorporated them into his fiction.

In 1930, though he did not consider it worthy of a man who had just graduated from Cambridge with distinction, White took a position as a Latin teacher at St. David's preparatory school in Reigate Hunting, in the south of England. During his two years there he wrote two detective novels (he called them "blood stories") to make money: *Dead Mr. Nixon* (1931), co-authored with Roland McNair Scott, and *Darkness at Pemberley* (1932), both of which include academic characters. In addition, he completed *They Winter Abroad* and worked on *First Lesson* (1932), which were published under the pseudonym James Aston. Both of the Aston novels are set in Italy. The first is a comedy about a group of unlikely candidates for love who are spending the winter there; the second focuses on Belfry, a forty-seven-year-old don who loses his virginity during a sabbatical year in Italy.

In 1932 White lost his teaching position but found a new one at Stowe, a public school that occupied the grounds of a famous country house in Buckinghamshire. At Stowe, in pursuit of gentility, he learned to ride, hunt, and fish; and, partly to overcome his fear,

he learned to fly an airplane. At this time White laid aside "Rather Rum," a never-to-be-completed Aston novel, and wrote *Farewell Victoria* (1933), in which he shows his growing understanding of nature and respect for simple country people. *Farewell Victoria,* which focuses on Mundy, a humble horse groom, encompasses a period from 1858 to 1933.

Earth Stopped; or, Mr. Marx's Sporting Tour (1934), a second novel written during this period, deals with people like Mundy in just one brief chapter that tells how country people teach a young Marxist (who has named himself Marx) to "stop earth," or fill in the tunnels into which hunted animals could escape. It is primarily concerned with the antics of the house guests of the tenth Earl of Scamperdale and ends with a bombing, from an unidentified source, of such proportions that the earth itself seems to have stopped. Its sequel, *Gone to Ground; or, The Sporting Decameron* (1935), is a collection of stories told by survivors of this bombing at the end of a social order.

England Have My Bones, published in 1936, is an engaging series of observations by a highly educated man—who acknowledges the impediments imposed by this status—engaged in the upper-class pursuits of hunting, fishing, and shooting. The chronological series of entries goes far beyond the tedious, repetitive quality of the how-to-hunt, how-to-shoot, how-to-fish sequences of

Burke's Steerage; or, The Amateur Gentleman's Introduction to Noble Sports and Pastimes (1938), a lifeless book apparently written solely because White had an obligation to his publisher. *England Have My Bones* includes references to White's love of flying and his schoolboy fear of ridicule and ends with an account of the March 1935 accident that wrecked his Bentley and left him temporarily half blind. White earned enough from sales of the book to resign his position at Stowe School, move into a gamekeeper's cottage on the grounds, and pursue writing full time.

White unabashedly presents poverty as his reason for writing *The Goshawk* (1951) during the time he was composing the diary entries that became *England Have My Bones*. When he left his second teaching position, his resources, White tells his readers as he introduces the story of his attempt to train the bird he calls Gos, consisted of one hundred pounds, and rent for the cottage in Stowe Ridings in which he was living was five shillings a week. *The Goshawk* was a considerable success but did not solve White's immediate financial problems, since it was not published until 1951. Wren Howard, a representative of the firm of Jonathan Cape who was visiting White in connection with another manuscript, discovered the bulky record of "failure."

The Sword in the Stone (1938) began to earn White the literary fame on which his reputation now rests. Here, as John K. Crane points out in his critical study *T. H. White* (1974), White was able to represent himself in both Merlyn, "the man who thought more about daily existence and its ultimate meaning than most of his contemporaries," and Arthur, "the boy who could never learn enough to place the entire human experience, in its multitudinous forms, in a unified perspective." The first sentences of the book detail the study schedule followed by "the Wart," as Arthur is known in his boyhood, and Kay, the son of Wart's guardian, Sir Ector: "On Mondays, Wednesdays and Fridays it was Court Hand and Summulae Logicales, while the rest of the week it was the Organon, Repetition, and Astrology. In the afternoons the programme was: Mondays and Fridays, tilting and horsemanship; Tuesdays, hawking; Wednesdays, fencing; Thursdays, archery; Saturdays, the theory of chivalry, with the proper measures to be blown on all occasions, terminology of the chase and etiquette." Sir Ector keeps a sparrow hawk named Cully, who can think and who speaks a demented Shakespearean English, for the village priest. Kay and the Wart take the hawk out of the mews and lose it; pursuing it into the Forest Sauvage, Wart meets the comical King Pellinore, who is in perpetual pursuit of the Questing Beast, and comes upon the cottage of the magician Merlyn, who knows the future because he lives backward in time. Merlyn becomes the boys'

tutor. Guided by Merlyn, Wart learns about life by being transformed into a fish, an ant, a hawk, a wild goose, a snake, and a badger. Merlyn also sends Kay and the Wart on an adventure, during which they meet Robin Hood (here called "Robin Wood"), Maid Marian, and Little John.

Word comes that the king, Uther Pendragon, has died without an heir. Shortly thereafter, Sir Ector; Kay, who is preparing to become a knight; and Wart, who is serving as his squire, go to London, where Kay is to participate in a joust. Realizing that he has left his sword at the Castle Sauvage, Kay sends Wart back for it, but Wart finds that Kay's room is locked. Returning to London, he comes upon a sword stuck through an anvil on a stone in a churchyard. Using the wisdom he gained from Merlin, he pulls it out and takes it to Kay. Kay recognizes that it is the sword from the stone that bears the inscription *"Whoso Pulleth Out the Sword of the Stone and Anvil, is Rightwise King Born of All England."* After first claiming that it was he who pulled out the sword, Kay confesses the truth, and Wart becomes King Arthur.

In 1939 White, who had been trying to decide whether to maintain his pacifist beliefs or join the army to fight the Nazis, deferred the decision and moved to Ireland. There he boarded with Paddy and Lena McDonagh in Doolistown.

White's biographer Sylvia Townsend Warner says that writing *The Sword in the Stone* enabled White to have "a dauntless, motherless boyhood" as Wart and an "ideal old age" as Merlyn. *The Witch in the Wood* (1939), on the other hand, seems to have grown from the boyhood White actually had.

White's hatred of his mother's suffocating attentions, of which he wrote in letters to friends such as his former Cambridge tutor, L. J. Potts, remains evident in the opening chapters—even though, on the advice of Potts and the orders of his publisher, he made substantial changes from the manuscript he originally submitted. In the first chapter Gawaine, Gaheris, Gareth, and Agravain, four brothers who will play major roles in the destruction of the Round Table, are introduced as children huddled together in a cold bedroom that has no bed, telling the story of King Uther Pendragon and their grandmother Igraine, as their mother, Queen Morgause of Lothian and Orkney, stirs her boiling kettle of revenge (literally and figuratively) in the room below. White comments on the boys' oath of undying loyalty to their mother: "Perhaps we all give the best of our hearts uncritically—to those who hardly think about us in return." When the brothers kill and dismember a unicorn in their effort to please Morgause, she does not even deign to look at the bleeding head they bring home for her. The young King Arthur is more fortunate: Merlyn continues to act as his adviser as he prepares for the wars that will establish his authority as ruler of an extended kingdom. Merlyn is often presented as a comic figure, but his political awareness is astute. He clenches his fists and shakes all over when Kay advocates imposing what is good for people on them by force. Merlyn, who "lives backward in time," knows about Adolf Hitler, "the Austrian . . . who tried to impose his reformation by the sword, and plunged the civilized world into misery and chaos," and he teaches his student that victories gained through the deaths of men who do not belong to the knightly class are not cause for unqualified rejoicing. *The Witch in the Wood* ends with a genealogical chart showing that the triumphant young King Arthur, son of Igraine and Uther Pendragon, lay with Morgause, the daughter of Igraine and her husband, the earl of Cornwall, resulting in the birth of Mordred.

The Ill-Made Knight (1940) is the story of Lancelot, who thus labels himself because of his ugly face. He and his tutor, Uncle Dap, go to Camelot, and the story of Lancelot and Arthur and Guenever begins to unfold. If one reads Lancelot's behavior in the context of what White says about his own sadistic impulses, it is possible to see that this novel, like the one that preceded it, is semi-autobiographical: Lancelot, like White, "liked to hurt people," knew that it was wrong, and never "committed a cruel action which he could have prevented." The Ill-Made Knight falls in love with Queen Guenever when he sees that his rudeness about her ineptness with a falcon has hurt her; then he determines to leave Camelot to avoid hurting Arthur, whom he loved first and continues to love. Since he is destined to become "the best knight in the world," Lancelot's attempt to escape from love leads to a series of triumphs over lesser knights that provide White the opportunity for digressions about medieval armor, jousts, and tournaments. In the process the old ethics of "might makes right" is transformed into a new ethics of might *for* right. But because of the human weakness of "the Orkney faction," of which Gawaine, Gaheris, Agravaine, and Gareth are the key members, the noble ideals that led to the formation of the Round Table remain far from realization. Lancelot, like Arthur before him, is tricked into fathering a child; but Galahad, Lancelot's son by Elaine, who pretends to be Guenever, will live to see the Holy Grail.

Basic elements of the plot of *The Ill-Made Knight* can be found in Malory's *Le Morte d'Arthur* (1485). What cannot be found in Malory are the rounded characterizations provided by White. In a long digression Guenever is shown to have a seventh sense, which, White explains, follows the acquisition of a sixth sense, the sense of balance. The seventh sense is the means by

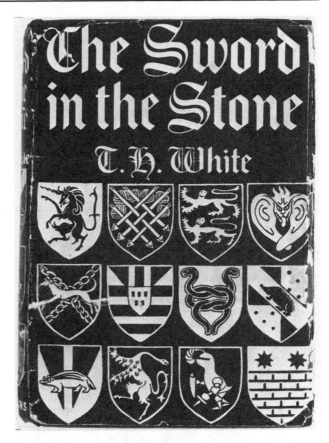

Dust jacket, with coats of arms designed by White, for his 1938 novel, about the early years of King Arthur (from François Gallix, T. H. White: An Annotated Bibliography, *1986);*

which "both men and women contrive to ride the waves of a world in which there is war, adultery, compromise, stultification and hypocrisy." Lancelot has not reached this degree of maturity; but he can reveal to Guenever, and to no one else, his boyhood ambition to become a great healer or to find something of tremendous value, such as the Holy Grail. Arthur's education is shown to be inadequate to the challenges he will face; indeed, it will be a handicap in an imperfect world. And yet, he is a more believable human being than the Arthur in Malory: a man who clings tenaciously to his belief that one can live according to a code of virtue in a less than perfect world.

White does not slavishly follow his source. He selects; he explains; he heightens the drama; and he makes skillful use of Geoffrey Chaucer's device of *occupatio,* which permits a narrator to insert detail even as he claims to be avoiding digression, as when he says, "If you want to read about the beginning of the Quest for the Grail, about the wonders of Galahad's arrival . . . and of the last supper at court, when the thunder came and the sunbeam and the covered vessel and the sweet smell through the Great Hall—if you want to read about these, you must seek them in Malory." He undercuts Galahad's virtue with reports that he played with dolls as a child and said "it is perfectly all right killing people who had not been christened." As for the transformation of Lancelot, White deepens readers' perception of the ill-made knight's sense of his failure to serve his God and his king and to protect his queen with a wistful look back to a past when adults loved faithfully to the end of their lives and with a final vision of Lancelot's tears that uses Malory's words: "And ever . . . Sir Lancelot wept, as he had been a child that had been beaten."

The fourth part of White's Arthurian tetralogy, *The Candle in the Wind,* first appeared in 1958, when all four parts were published in one volume as *The Once and Future King* (here *The Witch in the Wood* is retitled *The Queen of Air and Darkness*). This part begins with Morgause's fifth son, Mordred, whose anger is directed toward Arthur, his father, leading Agravaine, whose anger is directed at Guenever, toward revenge for wrongs suffered before they were born. Gawaine attempts to reason with Mordred, who cannot be dissuaded. The scene shifts to Sir Lancelot and Guenever as aging lovers; Guenever, the wiser of the two, doubts that Arthur can continue to conceal his awareness of their relationship. Arthur enters this scene of domestic tranquillity to tell the two people he loves most about his fatherhood of Mordred, confess his guilt for attempting to kill Mordred by ordering the drowning of all the babies born at the same time as his son, and warn them of the threat posed by Mordred. Gawaine refuses to join his brothers in rebellion against his king and takes Gareth and Gaheris with him as he leaves the court. Mordred confronts Arthur with the adultery of Lancelot and Guenever, and Agravaine forces the king to agree that if Lancelot is found in Guenever's room while Arthur is away on a hunting trip, the knights have permission to take the two prisoner. Lancelot kills Agravaine when the plotters burst into the room but spares Mordred. Gawaine, his loyalties deeply divided, cannot take either side. Gareth and Gaheris stand by their king, but, also loyal to Lancelot, do so unarmed. Lancelot rescues Guenever but, to his regret, kills the unarmed brothers. Guenever and Lancelot escape.

As the old story plays itself out, a fascinating additional story emerges as a result of White's decision to keep much of a text he first intended to produce as a play. Gawaine confronts King Arthur with a summary of what has happened: "the pure and fearless Knight of the Lake, whom you have allowed to cuckold you and carry off your wife, amused himself before he left by murdering my two brothers—both unarmed, and both his loving friends." Guenever, addressing Lancelot, proposes a way to move past the present impasse

toward peace: whatever personal pain their submission may entail, the combatants can appeal to the Pope and abide by his judgment, administered by the bishop of Rochester. She then turns to her lover "with a face of composure and relief—the efficient and undramatic face which women achieve when they have nursing to do or some other employment of efficiency." White's narrative voice then breaks in to express a wisdom that can be gained only by living long enough in an imperfect world: this is the way the world is; the honorable course of action is to recognize and accept it and do the best one can.

Lancelot is banished by order of the bishop of Rochester. Mordred, mad, decides that the proper revenge for his incestuous birth is to seize his father's wife for himself. Gawaine is killed in battle, and Arthur is left to try to reason things out for himself. Merlyn is not available to help the king; he remains in the cave in which Nimue imprisoned him. The old king thinks about Morgause, his half sister; his early wars; his—and White's—persistent questions about why men fight; possessiveness and greed. The fourth book of the tetralogy ends with a conversation between Arthur and a boy named Tom Malory. Arthur knights him Sir Thomas Malory and entrusts him with the task of telling the story of "regis quondam regisque futuri," the once and future king.

White wrote a fifth book to conclude the tragedy of King Arthur and present an antidote to war, but wartime paper shortages precluded its publication; the manuscript was found among his papers after his death, and *The Book of Merlyn: The Unpublished Conclusion to* The Once and Future King was finally published in 1977. When he reappears in the book that bears his name, Merlyn cites a list of sources, beginning with Nennius and Geoffrey of Monmouth and ending with Henry Purcell, Aubrey Beardsley, and White himself (he could have included Alan Jay Lerner and Frederick Loewe if he had truly been gifted with the power of prophecy), to assure the king that they will not be forgotten. Then a new descent into Arthur's past begins. Arthur and Merlyn find themselves in a burrow inhabited by the badger who initiated Wart into the wisdom of the animals; the wise owl, Archimedes; Balin, the merlin; a goat (a creature who did not appear in the transformation series of *The Sword and the Stone*); the king's dog, Cavall; and a humble hedgehog who had begged Wart to spare him when they first met. The animals engage in a rambling discussion of the faults of capitalism, the inadequacies of communism, and the arrogance of the human species. Arthur also revisits the ants, with whom he explores the ideas that can be thought or communicated in a language limited to a minimal number of binary oppositions. With additions that draw attention to the present age of the king (who is not, in the judgment of his animal friends, so old that he is no longer teachable), White retells the story of Wart's transformation into a goose. This retelling, embellished with didactic detail, is clearly intended to serve as preparation for the king's next lesson, but Arthur is not yet ready to learn it. At this point he needs not more political philosophizing but the encouragement of the hedgehog, who has had to sit apart from the other animals because of his fleas. As they respond to the freshness of the English countryside, the hedgehog leads Arthur back to a recognition of his own responsibility, to a sense of what it means—or should mean—to be a king. He tries to make peace with Mordred; but one of Arthur's soldiers lifts his sword to defend himself against a grass snake, Mordred's army interprets the action as an attack on them, and Arthur is killed in the ensuing battle. Guenever, still wiser than Lancelot, persuades her lover that what will be best for him now is total commitment to the service of God and then retires to a convent, where she will rule "efficiently, royally, with a sort of grand contempt . . . her linen clean and fine and scented against the rules of her order." White closes *The Book of Merlyn* with a scholarly citation of the many sources that assert that Arthur will come again.

In 1945 White returned to England and took up residence at Duke Mary's, a cottage in Yorkshire owned by his friend David Garnett. There he wrote *Mistress Masham's Repose* (1946), a sequel to Jonathan Swift's *Gulliver's Travels* (1726). After Lemuel Gulliver's departure from Lilliput in the eighteenth century his associate, Captain Biddel, captures some of the "little people" and takes them back to England, where he puts them on exhibit. The Lilliputians escape when Captain Biddel gets drunk during a visit to Malplaquet, a grand country house, and are carried by a jackdaw that they have raised to an island called Mistress Masham's Repose in the middle of a lake on the grounds of the house. There they establish an ideal society in exile. Notably, their society has no revealed religion (the Big Endian controversy of *Gulliver's Travels* is ended). There are no longer any wars since they have no enemies to fight; families are governed by the mothers; and they all believe that "the most important thing in the world [is] to find out what one like[s] to do, and then do it" (considering White's interests as he expressed them in earlier publications, it is not surprising that two of those things are hunting and fishing). The Lilliputians' ideal educational system helps children learn "Natural History . . . their own History . . . Oeconomy and anything else which dealt with being alive."

In the twentieth century Malplaquet has fallen into a state of decay (the setting bears a strong resemblance to the landscape and architecture of Stowe

Dust jacket for White's 1947 novel, about a second biblical flood that begins in Ireland (from François Gallix, T. H. White: An Annotated Bibliography, *1986);*

school). It is now occupied by Maria, a ten-year-old orphan; her guardian, the vicar Mr. Hater; and Miss Brown, a governess who is "cruel in a complicated way." Maria has two friends: a good-hearted cook with the gift of common sense and a professor who can write only in a twelfth-century style. Maria discovers the descendants of the original Lilliputians and wants to "help" them; she decides, for example, that a fisherman must become an aviator. Her desire to control their lives causes her to race toward ruin "with the speed of a Rake's Progress." The professor becomes aware that he has a teaching responsibility. Calling on Gulliver's experience in Brobdingnag, the land of the giants, he makes her aware of what it is like to be defenseless and made captive. Aided by the cook and the Lilliputians, he rescues Maria from imprisonment by the vicar and Miss Brown, who are trying to steal her inheritance. Finally, stepping out of the world of his fiction at the end of the novel, White speaks directly to David and Ray Garnett's daughter, Amaryllis, telling her that it is still possible to visit the place where the people of the story once lived.

*White in 1954 on the Channel Island of Alderney,
his home from 1947 until his death*

In 1946 White moved to Jersey in the Channel Islands; the following year he moved to another of the islands, Alderney, where he lived for the rest of his life. "Mr. White," the narrator of his next novel, *The Elephant and the Kangaroo* (1947), describes himself "standing in his workshop, or playroom, with his spectacles on the end of his nose and a small oilcan in his hand . . . a tall, middle-aged man, with gray hair and a straggling beard." The description corresponds to White's actual appearance when he lived in Doolistown with the McDonaghs, who recognized themselves as the O'Callaghans of the novel, a not-very-bright Irish Catholic couple. White explains, "Since this is the story of an Ark, it might be fair to say that Mr. White was the elephant, Mrs. O'Callaghan the kangaroo," presumably because of their irreconcilable viewpoints.

The archangel Gabriel comes down the O'Callaghans' chimney and announces that the world is to be destroyed again in a second great flood—a contradiction of the Old Testament promise that there would never be another flood like the one that covered the earth in Noah's time. Mr. White challenges his employee Pat Geraghty's ability to believe in the possibility of a sec-

ond flood, thus making it certain that Geraghty, who always behaves contrary to expectations, will believe that it could happen. He then challenges Geraghty's ability to build an ark, and Geraghty responds by asserting both his belief in the archangel's prophecy and his confidence that he can construct the vessel. Mrs. O'Callaghan expresses her concern about how they will live after the flood is over, but if it means living on grass for a while, as Mr. White assures her that representatives of her species have done before, then she can do it. After all, she has consumed "nittles" (nettles) as a natural remedy. She does not, however, understand how she and her husband, who have been childless up to now, can be expected to be fruitful and multiply. As it turns out, there is no time to build a proper ark; the O'Callaghans' barn will have to do. And there is just time enough to load books that describe the nonlocal animals, but not to collect the animals themselves, before the barn gets up, like an elephant standing on its hind legs, turns upside down, and sails down the River Liffey to Dublin, with the O'Callaghans, Mr. White, his dog Brownie, and a few local species on board. The ark, however, turns out not to be seaworthy; when it crashes against a bridge, the occupants continue floating to Dublin on barrels used as life preservers. White recalls his primary source—Genesis, chapters 6 through 9—with an effective concluding sentence: "It was a perfect rainbow."

Two nonfiction products of White's research into the eighteenth century, *The Age of Scandal: An Excursion through a Minor Period* and *The Scandalmonger,* appeared in 1950 and 1952, respectively. In the introduction to the first book White laments his discovery, on his last visit to Cambridge, that the masters now had to help with the washing up after lunch and speaks of his vicarious enjoyment of "the grand old days of Horace Walpole" and his intention to "give one last, loving and living picture of an aristocratic civilization which we shall never see again."

The Book of Beasts: Being a Translation from a Latin Bestiary of the Twelfth Century Made and Edited by T. H. White followed his two eighteenth-century studies in 1954. The notes for White's bestiary are as copious as the text, and White wrote in a letter to Potts that they were drawn from thirty years of reading. He also told Potts that he considered the task of "translating the twelfth-century Bestiary out of illegible, abbreviated dog-latin into English" a task of "real scholarship," though he did not expect Cambridge to agree that his three scholarly books ought to earn him "a D. Litt. or Ph.D. or whatever it is." His judgment of *The Book of Beasts* would seem to be justified. It has a ten-page bibliography that includes manuscripts in the possession of learned societies that have never been published. His notes include everybody from Aristotle to "the American magazine called *Life*." His more than 125 illustrations are drawn from medieval manuscripts, and his twenty-page appendix, with its "Family Tree" and a diagram that shows the influence of the bestiary tradition on literary works, gives extended attention to the tradition to which he was making a major contribution.

With *The Master: An Adventure Story* (1957), a young-adult novel, White again demonstrates his skill as a master of the twice-told tale. The work to which he gives new life in *The Master* is Shakespeare's *The Tempest* (1611). The island that provides a setting for the action of White's *The Master,* however, could hardly be more different from the island, teeming with life, to which Shakespeare brings his shipwrecked characters. Rockall, the setting for *The Master,* cannot sustain life on its own. The aptly named island—it is "all rock"—houses a helicopter hangar on its top level and a reception room, men's quarters, offices, engines, and water tank on lower levels. Life here is totally dependent on twentieth-century technology. Other reversals of Shakespeare's plot follow. In *The Tempest* Prospero intentionally delivers his erstwhile enemies to his magic island; but Nicky and Judy, the twelve-year-old twin protagonists of *The Master,* are accidentally left on Rockall. Miranda, Prospero's daughter, is an obedient child; but Judy, though she lacks the power to resist the will of the Master—who, like Prospero, completely controls the life of his island—asserts her defiance when she is denied the education her brother receives. Judy is, she says, "not a Plaything To Be Cast Aside, but a Person to Be Reckoned With, who has Made Discoveries, so there." Frinton, the counterpart in the novel to Prospero's spirit servant, Ariel, is the helicopter pilot who brings what the Master needs to extend his 157-year life; but he later takes on a subversive role. And the storm that comes at the beginning of *The Tempest* occurs at the end of *The Master.*

Perhaps White found a point of departure in Alonso's comment in *The Tempest* (act 3, scene 3, lines 47–50) about shapes, gestures, and sounds "expressing, / Although they want the use of tongue, a kind / Of excellent dumb discourse" for the character Pinkie, a black cook who is incapable of communication by any means other than gesture. Another character, Mr. Blenkinsop, a Chinaman, explains that the Master had Pinkie's tongue cut out because Pinkie's ability to think for himself was a threat to the Master's control. The Chinaman's language, which lacks nouns and verbs, has helped the Master to move from English, governed by rules, to a simpler language with which he could directly control his subjects, without words.

Another character, Dr. Totty McTurk, has the responsibility of keeping the Master sane. McTurk's guiding principle is that the mind affects the body and the body affects the mind. For the strong-minded Master, however, it is difficult to maintain the balance, leading to a further reversal of the norms of *The Tempest:* Shakespeare's Stephano and Trinculo, when drunk, lose a degree of control over language. The Master, on the other hand, has progressed so far in studying language that he must be a bit intoxicated to communicate his wishes to those who have not attained his level of linguistic expertise.

The Master wants to take over the world in order to prevent a nuclear war: U.S. president Dwight D. Eisenhower, British prime minister Anthony Eden, and Soviet premier Nikita Khrushchev have atomic bombs, while, as Frinton tells the children, "most politicians can barely sign their names or read a comic strip." As a hurricane begins, Nicky raises a revolver to shoot the Master; but his resistance to the power of the Master's mind is overcome, and he drops the weapon. The Master steps backward, accidentally treading on the children's dog, Jokey. After she bites him, the Master falls and breaks his hip. As he begins a farewell speech in the high style of Shakespeare's Prospero—"Now my charms are all o'erthrown . . ."—his would-be boy assassin asks, "Are you hurt? Can I help?" The book ends as Nicky and Judy are reunited with their parents.

The Godstone and the Blackymor (1959) is a rambling account of White's travels in western Ireland. Responding to a question from "Bunny" (David Garnett) about his bird-training experience, White recalls a friend's kestrel, the hawks of *The Goshawk,* two merlins, and the birds at Fraoch, a shooting lodge on the west coast of Ireland. Mention of the Inniskea Disaster of 1927, in which ten lives were lost at sea, leads into White's account of his own solitary sojourn on one of the Inniskea Islands. There a stone idol, the Godstone, stood before the time of St. Patrick. White includes a poem about the Godstone; he admits that it has some inaccuracies, but he insists that the words cannot be changed because the rhymes are right. He then relates the responses to a questionnaire on the stone, which was administered by children, who, he assumed, were more likely to get answers from their elders than he was. This more scientific approach yields such "facts" as that the stone could render barren ground capable of producing potatoes but not other crops and that it was the pillow of an early Christian hermit. White moves from the etymology of Gaelic names for the cranes of Inniskea to consideration of their migration routes and then to the Latin bestiarists, who, he says, are as bad as the country people when one wants to find answers to serious scholarly questions. The birds of *The Godstone and the Blackymor,* like the birds of White's Arthurian fiction, are visualized in human terms: the barnacle geese of

Dust jacket, with a reproduction of a painting by White of the island on which the work is set, for his 1957 novel, about a mad scientist who wants to take over the world to prevent a nuclear war (from François Gallix, T. H. White: An Annotated Bibliography, 1986)

Inneskea have "the same black shiny gloves, the jet beads, the dress of black and dove gray garnished with white" that he associates with the spinster aunts of his childhood. There is thus no sharp distinction between bird and human, and other oppositions collapse as well. A superior-inferior distinction crumbles when the courtesy of a Nigerian masseur and patent-medicine salesman, James Montgomery-Majoribanks, the "Blackymor" of the title, is graciously expressed in a note of thanks for "overpayment" for his having restored a temporary flexibility to the rheumatic joints of two elderly Irishmen. The superior knowledge of a sixty-year-old dog handler, a man without formal education, also becomes apparent. Mrs. O'Callaghan of *The Elephant and the Kangaroo* briefly reappears in the penultimate chapter, "fervent, loving, tall, thin, humble, and frequently exclaiming that everything was 'loverlay,'" as White acknowledges that English assumptions of superiority to the Irish are baseless. *The Godstone and the Blackymor* does not apologize to the McDonaghs of Doolistown, who did not forgive White for the ungrateful ridicule of

The Elephant and the Kangaroo, but it does acknowledge the dignity of people with whom White spent six years of his life.

White traveled in Italy from November 1962 to February 1963, and from September through December 1963 he lectured at colleges and universities across the United States. The resounding success of his American tour was undoubtedly based to some degree on the fame that the stage and screen adaptations of his Arthuriad—the Lerner and Loewe musical *Camelot* (1960) and the animated Walt Disney version of *The Sword in the Stone* (1963)—brought him, but it must also be attributed to the pleasure he took in lecturing.

The last entry in *America at Last: The American Journal of T. H. White* (1965) is dated 16 December 1963. White was found dead of a heart attack in his cabin aboard the S.S. *Exeter* in Piraeus, the port of Athens, Greece, on 17 January 1964. He is buried in Athens near Hadrian's Arch under a stone that reads "T. H. White, 1906–1964, Author Who from a Troubled Heart Delighted Others Loving and Praising This Life."

Letters:

The Best of Friends: Further Letters to Sydney Carlyle Cockerell, edited by Viola Meyness (London: Hart-Davis, 1956);

The White/Garnett Letters, edited by David Garnett (London: Cape, 1968; New York: Viking, 1968);

Letters to a Friend: The Correspondence between T. H. White and L. J. Potts, edited by François Gallix (New York: Putnam, 1982).

Bibliography:

François Gallix, *T. H. White: An Annotated Bibliography* (New York & London: Garland, 1986).

Biographies:

Sylvia Townsend Warner, *T. H. White: A Biography* (New York: Viking, 1967);

John K. Crane, *T. H. White* (New York: Garland, 1974).

References:

J. R. Cameron, "T. H. White in Camelot: The Matter of Britain Revitalized," *Humanities Association Bulletin,* 16 (Spring 1965): 45–48;

Ed Chapman, "Images of the Numinous in T. H. White and C. S. Lewis," *Mythlore,* 4, no. 4 (1977): 3–10;

John Clute, "T. H. White," in *Supernatural Fiction Writers: Fantasy and Horror, 2: A. E. Coppard to Roger Zelazny,* edited by E. F. Bleiler (New York: Scribners, 1985);

Rodd Cockshutt, "In Search of Theodore White," *Journal of Popular Culture,* 15 (Fall 1981): 86–96;

John K. Crane, *T. H. White* (New York: Twayne, 1974);

Crane, "T. H. White: The Fantasy of the Here and Now," *Mosaic,* 10, no. 2 (1977): 33–46;

Barbara Floyd, "A Critique of T. H. White's *The Once and Future King,*" *Riverside Quarterly,* 1 (1965): 175–180; 2 (1966): 54–57, 127–133, 210–213;

Maureen Fries, "The Rationalization of the Arthurian 'Matter' in T. H. White and Mary Stewart," *Philological Quarterly,* 56 (Spring 1977): 258–265;

François Gallix, "T. H. White et la légende di Roi Arthur," *Mosaic,* 10, no. 2 (1977): 47–63;

Gallix, "T. H. White et la légende di Roi Arthur: De la fantaisie animale au moralisme politique," *Etudes Anglaises,* 34 (April–June 1981): 192–203;

Harold J. Herman, "Teaching White, Stewart, and Berger," in *Approaches to Teaching the Arthurian Tradition,* edited by Maureen Fries and Jeannie Watson (New York: Modern Language Association of America, 1992), pp. 113–117;

Colin N. Manlove, "Flight to Aleppo: T. H. White's *The Once and Future King,*" *Mosaic,* 10, no. 2 (1977): 65–83;

Judith N. Mitchell, "The Boy Who Would Be King," *Journal of Popular Culture,* 17 (Spring 1984): 134–137;

Sven E. Molin, "Appraisals: T. H. White, 1906–1964," *Journal of Irish Literature,* 2, nos. 2–3 (1973): 142–150;

Marilyn K. Nellis, "Anachronistic Humor in Two Arthurian Romances of Education: *To the Chapel Perilous* and *The Sword in the Stone,*" *Studies in Medievalism,* 2 (Fall 1983): 57–77;

Marie Nelson, "King Arthur and the Massacre of the May Day Babies," *Journal of the Fantastic in the Arts,* 11, no. 3 (2001): 266–281;

Nelson, "T. H. White: Master of Transformation," *Neophilologus,* 85 (2001): 309–321;

Nelson, "T. H. White: The Poet behind the Fiction," *Neophilologus,* 83 (1999): 653–659.

Dieter Petzold, "Zwischen Weltkatastrophe und Eukatastrophe: Politik in Fantasy-Romanen," *Inklings,* 4 (1986): 63–86;

Ina Schabert, "Das utopisch Mittelalter der historischen Erzählliteratur," in *Alternative Welten,* edited by Manfred Pfister (Munich: Fink, 1982), pp. 179–186;

Evelyn Schroth, "Camelot: Contemporary Interpretation of Arthur in 'Sens' and 'Matière,'" *Journal of Popular Culture,* 17 (Fall 1983): 31–43;

Nathan Comfort Starr, *King Arthur Today: The Arthurian Legend in English and American Literature 1901–1953* (Gainesville: University of Florida Press, 1954);

Donald R. Swanson, "The Uses of Tradition: King Arthur in the Modern World," *CEA Critic,* 36 (March 1974): 19–21;

Richard C. West, "Contemporary Medieval Authors," *Orcrist,* 3 (Spring-Summer 1969): 9–10, 15;

West, "Malory and T. H. White," *Orcrist,* 7 (Spring–Summer 1973): 13–15;

West, "The Sign of the Unicorn: The Unicorn Motif in Selected Works of Modern Fantasy," in *Selected Proceedings of the 1978 Science Fiction Research Association National Conference,* edited by Thomas J. Remington (Cedar Falls: University of Northern Iowa, 1979), pp. 45–54.

Papers:

The Harry Ransom Humanities Research Center at the University of Texas at Austin has an extensive collection of T. H. White's manuscripts.

Charles Williams

(20 September 1886 – 15 May 1945)

Bernadette Lynn Bosky

See also the Williams entries in *DLB 100: Modern British Essayists, Second Series* and *DLB 153: Late-Victorian and Edwardian British Novelists, First Series.*

BOOKS: *The Silver Stair* (London: Herbert & Daniel, 1912);

Poems of Conformity (London: Oxford University Press, 1917);

Divorce (London: Oxford University Press, 1920);

Windows of Night (London: Oxford University Press, 1925);

An Urbanity (London: Privately printed, 1926);

The Masque of the Manuscript (London: Privately printed, 1927);

A Myth of Shakespeare (London: Oxford University Press, 1928);

The Masque of Perusal (London: Privately printed, 1929);

Poetry at Present (Oxford: Clarendon Press, 1930);

War in Heaven (London: Gollancz, 1930; New York: Norton, 1932);

Heroes and Kings (London: Sylvan, 1930);

Many Dimensions (London: Gollancz, 1931; New York: Pellegrini & Cudahy, 1949);

Three Plays (London: Oxford University Press, 1931);

The Place of the Lion (London: Gollancz, 1931; New York: Norton, 1932);

The Greater Trumps (London: Gollancz, 1932; New York: Pellegrini & Cudahy, 1950);

The English Poetic Mind (Oxford: Clarendon Press, 1932);

Shadows of Ecstasy (London: Gollancz, 1933; New York: Pellegrini & Cudahy, 1950);

Bacon (London: Barker, 1933; New York: Harper, 1934);

Reason and Beauty in the Poetic Mind (Oxford: Clarendon Press, 1933);

James I (London: Barker, 1934; New York: Harper, 1934);

Rochester (London: Barker, 1935);

Cranmer of Canterbury: Acting Edition (Canterbury: H. J. Goulden, 1936);

Charles Williams (photograph by John Spalding)

Thomas Cranmer of Canterbury (London: Oxford University Press, 1936);

Queen Elizabeth (London: Duckworth, 1936);

Descent into Hell (London: Faber & Faber, 1937; New York: Pellegrini & Cudahy, 1949);

Stories of Great Names (London: Oxford University Press, 1937);

Henry VII (London: Barker, 1937);

He Came Down from Heaven (London: Heinemann, 1938; Grand Rapids, Mich.: Eerdmans, 1984);

Taliessin through Logres (London: Oxford University Press, 1938);

The Descent of the Dove: A Short History of the Holy Spirit in the Church (London: Longmans, Green, 1939; New York: Oxford University Press, 1939);

Judgement at Chelmsford (London: Oxford University Press, 1939);

Witchcraft (London: Faber & Faber, 1941; Cleveland: World, 1959);

Religion and Love in Dante: The Theology of Romantic Love (Westminster: Dacre, 1941; Folcroft, Pa.: Folcroft Library Editions, 1974);

The Way of Exchange (London: Clarke, 1941);

The Forgiveness of Sins (London: Bles, 1942; Grand Rapids, Mich.: Eerdmans, 1984);

The Figure of Beatrice (London: Faber & Faber, 1943; New York: Noonday, 1961);

The Region of the Summer Stars (London: Editions Poetry London, 1944);

All Hallows' Eve (London: Faber & Faber, 1945; New York: Pellegrini & Cudahy, 1948);

The House of the Octopus (London: Edinburgh House Press, 1945);

Flecker of Dean Close (London: Canterbury Press, 1946);

Seed of Adam and Other Plays (London: Oxford University Press, 1948);

Arthurian Torso: Containing the Posthumous Fragment of the Figure of Arthur by Charles Williams and a Commentary on the Arthurian Poems of Charles Williams by C. S. Lewis (London & New York: Oxford University Press, 1948);

The Image of the City and Other Essays, selected by Anne Ridler (London: Oxford University Press, 1958);

Selected Writings, selected by Ridler (London: Oxford University Press, 1961);

Collected Plays (London: Oxford University Press, 1963);

Outlines of Romantic Theology, edited by Alice Mary Hadfield (Grand Rapids, Mich.: Eerdmans, 1990);

Charles Williams, edited by David Llewellyn Dodds (Woodbridge, Suffolk & Rochester, N.Y.: Boydell & Brewer, 1991);

The Masques of Amen House (Altadena, Cal.: Mythopoeic Press, 2000).

Edition: *All Hallows' Eve,* introduction by T. S. Eliot (New York: Noonday, 1971).

OTHER: "Stabat Mater Dolorosa," translated by Williams (London: Oxford University Press Music Department, 1926);

A Book of Victorian Narrative Verse, edited by Williams (Oxford: Clarendon Press, 1927);

"Notes on Possible Endings to *Edwin Drood,*" in *The Mystery of Edwin Drood* by Charles Dickens (London: Oxford University Press, 1927), pp. 366–376;

Gerard Manley Hopkins, *Poems,* second edition, edited by Robert Bridges, introduction by Williams (London: Oxford University Press, 1931);

"T. S. Eliot," in *Selected Modern English Essays, Second Series* (London: Oxford University Press, 1932);

A Short Life of Shakespeare with the Sources, abridged by Williams from Sir Edmund Chambers's *William Shakespeare: A Study of Facts and Problems* (London: Oxford University Press, 1933);

Robert Browning, *The Ring and the Book,* retold by Williams (London: Oxford University Press, 1934);

The New Book of English Verse, edited by Williams (London: Gollancz, 1935; New York: Macmillan, 1936);

"Hamlet," "Henry V," and "Troilus and Cressida," in *Shakespeare Criticism, 1919–35,* edited by Anne Bradby (London: Oxford University Press, 1936);

The Story of the Aeneid, retold by Williams (London: Oxford University Press, 1936);

"Queen Victoria," in *More Short Biographies,* edited by R. C. Goffin (London: Oxford University Press, 1938);

The Passion of Christ: Being the Gospel and Narrative of the Passion with Short Passages Taken from the Saints and Doctors of the Church, edited by Williams (London & New York: Oxford University Press, 1939);

Søren Kierkegaard, *The Present Age; and, Two Minor Ethico-religious Treatises,* introduction by Williams (London & New York: Oxford University Press, 1940);

The English Poems of John Milton, introduction by Williams (London: Oxford University Press, 1940);

The New Christian Year, edited by Williams (London & New York: Oxford University Press, 1941);

The Letters of Evelyn Underhill, edited by Williams (London & New York: Longmans, Green, 1943);

"On the Poetry of *The Duchess of Malfi,*" in *The Duchess of Malfi* by John Webster (London: Sylvan, 1945).

SELECTED PERIODICAL PUBLICATIONS–
UNCOLLECTED:

POETRY

"Divites Dimisit," *Theology* (December 1939): 421–424;

"To Michal: After Marriage," *Grasshopper Broadsheets,* third series 10 (1944);

"Ballade of a Street Door," *Mythlore,* 2 (Winter 1971): 18.

DRAMA

"Scenes from a Mystery," *New Witness* (12 December 1919): 70–73.

FICTION

"Et in Sempiternum Pereant," *London Mercury,* 33 (December 1935): 151–158;

"The Noises that Weren't There: Chapter I," *Mythlore,* 2 (Autumn 1970): 17–21;

"The Voice of the Rat: Chapter II," *Mythlore,* 2 (Winter 1971): 17–23;

"Chapter III," *Mythlore,* 2 (Winter 1972): 21–25.

NONFICTION

"The Hero in English Verse," *Contemporary Review* (December 1920): 831–838;

"Autocriticism," *Week-End Review* (18 November 1933): 525;

"Notes on Religious Drama," *Chelmsford Diocesan Chronicle* (May 1937): 75–76;

"The New Milton," *St. Martin's Review* (July 1937): 255–261;

"The Recovery of Spiritual Initiative," *Christendom* (December 1940): 238–249;

"Notes on the Way," *Time and Tide* (28 February 1941): 170–171;

"Paracelsus," *Time and Tide* (27 September 1941): 820–821;

"A Myth of Francis Bacon," *Charles Williams Society Newsletter,* 11 (Autumn 1978); 12 (Winter 1978); 14 (Summer 1979).

Charles Williams is in many ways a paradox: a working-class man who lectured on John Milton at Oxford University; a devoted Christian whose novels explore blasphemies and black magic; an eloquent philosopher of human and divine love whose own romantic life was often deeply troubled. Like those of his friend C. S. Lewis, Williams's talents were evident in several genres: not only poetry and fiction but also plays and various nonfiction, including biography, poetic theory, theology, literary essays, and book reviews. He also left his mark as an editor for Oxford University Press and as a member of the Inklings, a writers' group that included Lewis and J. R. R. Tolkien.

Perhaps most readers know Williams through his seven novels. Critics have praised Williams's novels for their ability to portray spiritual truths, condemned them for their sensationalism, analyzed the precision and delicacy with which Williams writes, and complained of his obscurity. However, most critics agree that Williams's strength as a fiction writer grew throughout his career, and at least the last two novels, *Descent into Hell* (1937) and *All Hallows' Eve* (1945), succeed both aesthetically and philosophically.

Yet, Williams considered himself primarily a poet, and some critics, such as W. H. Auden, find Williams's novels disappointing compared to his poetry. By "Williams's poetry," critics and scholars usually mean his Arthurian poetry, collected in *Taliessin through Logres* (1938) and *The Region of the Summer Stars* (1944). This Arthurian–or, more accurately, Grail–poetry is, as

Roma A. King Jr. writes, "the poetical creation of a coherent mythical vision of man and his place in the larger creation of which he is a part." Some find these poems almost willfully obscure, both in language and in their dependence on a complex set of associations among character, animals, places, and the symbolic associations of each.

Charles Walter Stansby Williams was born on 20 September 1886 in Holloway, North London, England, and baptized at the Anglican church of St. Anne's, Finsbury Park, on 7 November. His only sister, Edith, was born in 1889; she and Charles were close throughout his life. Williams recalled fond memories of London from early on; he could read easily at five years of age, and his parents, Walter and Mary (née Wall) Williams, managed to send him to a private school, St. Mary Magdalene.

His parents provided love, attention, a sense of security, and a sound Christian upbringing. Both highly intelligent, his parents also instilled in Williams a love for literature. Walter Williams occasionally wrote poems, short stories, and plays, some of which were published under his uncle's name, Stansby. Mary Williams's whole family was likewise interested in history and literature, and her brother, Charles Wall, self-published several books on abbeys, castles, and antiquities.

The family finances, however, remained in constant uncertainty and occasional peril. Walter Williams worked for a firm of importers as a foreign correspondence clerk in French and German, but the importing business slumped; then his eyesight began to fail. In 1894 the firm closed, and an eye specialist ordered Williams's father to move from smoke-choked London to the country. In March 1894 the family relocated to St. Albans, where they opened a shop selling stationery and artists' supplies. They had their own house (though they rented two unfurnished rooms for added income) with a garden. The success of the store was uneven, and money was often a concern, but home life included books, long walks, meaningful discussions, and affection.

Williams won yearly prizes for schoolwork and read widely: Jules Verne, Nathaniel Hawthorne, Max Pemberton, and Charles Dickens. His friend George Robinson read Sir Walter Scott, but Williams objected to Scott's loading down a story with forced historical lectures. Williams, his father, and his sister put on amateur plays; a drama written by young Williams, which survives in manuscript, shows his interest in kingship, romance, and battle. He was confirmed on 27 March 1901, in St. Albans.

Williams won an intermediate scholarship to University College in Gower Street, London, and commuted from St. Albans, studying Latin, French, and

English history. However, his parents' overwork and frustration caused tensions at home; after two years at college, the money ran out, and Williams's parents withdrew him. After failing a civil service clerical exam, Williams found his first job (outside the family business) in the New Connexion Methodist Book-room in London. He also took classes at the Working Men's College on Crowndale Road; there he met Fred Page, who became a lifelong friend. Page introduced Williams to Oxford University Press to work as an assistant proofreader for a seventeen-volume edition of William Makepeace Thackeray's works.

Williams joined the Oxford University Press on 9 June 1908. At twenty-two, he began working in the paper, printing, and proofreading department. Unlike his father's jobs, the press offered great career security; more important, it offered Williams opportunities for stimulating conversations and an introduction to the world of letters that might otherwise have been denied him.

Also in 1908 Williams met Florence Conway when both helped at a parish children's Christmas party in St. Albans. Biographer Alice Mary Hadfield describes Conway, the youngest of five daughters of an ironmonger, as "dark and handsome, full of life, dramatic in feelings and in act, and naturally outstanding in amateur theatricals and pageants."

Inspired by love, Williams's writing prospered—in quality and amount, if not in economic reward. He wrote a sequence of eighty-four poems for Conway, *The Silver Stair,* probably more as a gesture of courtship than for publication. However, they were published in 1912, with the encouragement of Page and the vital assistance of Alice Meynell, a well-known Roman Catholic poet. At the beginning of World War I, Williams was declared unfit for military service because of a nervous condition that caused his hands to tremble.

His second book of poetry, *Poems of Conformity,* was published in 1917 by Oxford University Press, again with Page's help. Attention in reviews was small, and sales were smaller, but Williams was encouraged by supporters both inside and outside the press. For a reader of Williams's supernatural novels and mythic poetry, these collections are valuable for insights they provide concerning Williams the man, and because they foreshadow theological ideas in his later works.

After some delays—because of the war, Williams's financial worries, and his fear of responsibility despite deep love—Conway and Williams were married in St. Albans on 12 April 1917. They then moved to a flat she had found at 18 Parkhill Road, London. Their marriage was contentious, yet affectionate; he called her Michal, after King Saul's daughter who laughed at David when he danced before the ark of God.

Williams's wife, Florence Conway Williams—whom he called "Michal"—in costume for a pageant

Williams continued to develop intellectually and spiritually as a result of his experiences in marriage and love, his continued devotion to and quest for critical understanding of Christianity, and his membership in a Rosicrucian order headed by A. E. Waite. Williams's theology was always Christian but both romantic and esoteric. Membership in Waite's order, into which Williams was initiated in late 1917, encouraged Williams's love of symbol and ritual. He always memorized the words to the ceremonies so he could fully participate, and he complained to Anne Ridler that others simply read from cards. Waite's group was highly mystical and comparatively Christian; guided by his Christianity,

*Phyllis Jones, Williams's colleague at the Oxford University Press,
with whom he had a romance from 1924 to 1927*

Williams seems to have taken from it what seemed right and useful, leaving the rest.

By 1920, Hadfield writes, "Charles was a responsible editor for the Press and beginning to hold his own in the London literary world." A third poetry collection, *Divorce,* was published by the Oxford University Press in 1920. The publisher was more enthusiastic than with Williams's first book, but sales were still small. Many of the poems are derivative, influenced by models ranging from Robert Herrick and other seventeenth-century poets to the pre-Raphaelites and William Butler Yeats. Despite the title, *Divorce* includes some of Williams's most human and touching love poems to Michal. A fourth book of domestic poetry, *Windows of Night,* was published by the same press in 1925.

The Williamses' marital conflicts were exacerbated when their only son, Michael Stansby Williams, was born in 1922, as a letter from Williams to John Pellow shows, however joking its tone: "a child is a guest of a somewhat insistent temperament, rather difficult to get rid of, almost pushing. . . . His little voice pulls at my ears; my heartstrings are unplucked." Yet, when Williams later became a champion of romantic love as a religious and self-actualizing path, clearly his relationship with his wife was the source of his belief.

During this period Williams began a third career, as a teacher, despite his lack of a university education. In 1924 he began evening lectures at the Holloway Literary Institute for the London County Council, which

he continued until the outbreak of the war in 1939. The closest analogy in the United States would be continuing-education classes through four-year or community colleges. The students ranged from teenagers who had just left school to retirees, with a concentration of white- and blue-collar workers; they paid a small fee and received no credit, but Williams was an electrifying speaker, and attendance was always good. Like his work at the press, his lectures brought him many friends and a much-needed outlet for his literary and philosophical passions and ideas.

Also at this time Williams met Phyllis Jones, who joined the Oxford University Press staff as the librarian in 1924, when she was twenty-three years old; Williams was in his late thirties. Their relationship was complex and unusual; it provided Williams with artistic inspiration, aesthetic and religious transport, joy and then bitterness, and infidelity to Michal without actual sexual intercourse. Like many office romances, it was an open secret to those at the press, and eventually to Michal, who tolerated it.

Williams's first prose work, *Outlines of Romantic Theology,* coalesced from his lectures, conversations, and experiences. The book was turned down by Oxford University Press in 1924, Nonesuch Press in 1925, and Faber and Gwyer in 1926; many of the ideas show up in other books by Williams, such as *The Figure of Beatrice* (1943), and the original manuscript was finally published by Eerdmans in 1990. In it Williams explores the potentials and pitfalls of human marital love as a way of knowing, even emulating, the love and unity of God. The work is highly influenced by Williams's growing interest in Dante and the stories of the Grail, seminal influences on his thought that increased in power as the years passed.

Williams was also writing novels and failing to sell them. The first was an odd blend of H. Rider Haggard–style adventure and the kind of exploration of love, power, and theology that characterizes Williams's later novels; finally published as *Shadows of Ecstasy* by Gollancz in 1933, it was originally called "The Black Bastard." Critics, including Gunnar Urang and Edmund Fuller, have shown how Williams's novels concern themselves with the use and misuse of supernatural power; this statement certainly applies to Williams's first-written novel, but the emotional tone differs from that of his other novels—subtly prurient about the misuse of power it condemns. Nigel Considine is an African explorer who has learned to transcend earthly limitations by a kind of magical asceticism, extending his life indefinitely. Planning to take over the world, Considine is clearly malign, using others as his tools. Yet, while his path is condemned, its grandeur is also shown, and the more lawful alternatives that offer transcendence–poetry, Christianity, and romantic love–are less fully developed than in Williams's later novels. This tone, along with stereotypes of darkest Africa and its primitive magic, makes *Shadows of Ecstasy* Williams's most problematic novel for most readers.

In a smaller arena Williams found personal satisfaction, social acclaim, and some artistic success writing a series of poems and masques based on his experiences at the Oxford University Press and those of his co-workers. The poem *An Urbanity,* "The Carol of Amen House" (words by Williams and music by Hubert J. Foss), and *The Masque of the Manuscript* were self-published in 1927; *The Masque of Perusal* followed in 1929. These works, related poems, a third masque (written in 1930 but never performed or printed), and explanatory material are collected in *The Masques of Amen House* (2000) from Mythopoeic Press. This material is more allegorical or mythic than supernatural; as with Williams's early poetry, the main attraction for a reader of Williams's fantastic fiction and poetry is a glimpse into the author's life and ideas.

The masques and poetry reflect Williams's increasing responsibility and presence at the Oxford University Press. Though he spent much of his office time on his creative work–of which his superiors at the press were tolerant–he also accomplished much as an editor and writer for the press. In 1927 he edited and wrote the preface for *A Book of Victorian Narrative Verse* and contributed an essay concerning possible endings to the Oxford edition of Charles Dickens's unfinished novel, *The Mystery of Edwin Drood.* By this time his passion for Jones had ended, although they remained friends.

While Williams's fiction and poetry were promising, they were not remunerative enough for a young professional supporting his wife and son. Thus Williams also began popular literary projects for the Oxford University Press. With his energy, his enthusiasm for literature, and his ability to share this enthusiasm with others, he was a natural. For *A Myth of Shakespeare,* published in 1928, Williams provided a mock-Elizabethan-verse framework for excerpts from William Shakespeare's plays; quickly going into a second printing, the volume was his first commercial success.

The end of Williams's apprentice period came in 1930, with works that were finally noticed by the public and that included some of his first mature writing. *Poetry at Present*–studies of other poets with Williams's own verse interspersed–benefited his reputation as both a poet and a critic. Williams wrote many reviews and essays, only a small fraction of which have been reprinted; in January 1930 he began regularly reviewing for the literary page of the *News-Chronicle,* thanks to the suggestion of a friend from the Oxford University

Press who was leaving the job. Lawrence R. Dawson Jr. reports that "Williams wrote eighty-five reviews of 319 books which were . . . variously termed 'detective fiction,' 'mysteries,' 'thrillers,' and 'murder stories.'"

A small edition of poems, *Heroes and Kings,* was published in 1930; it includes some Arthurian poetry, as well as "Flint Castle," inspired by Shakespeare's *Richard II* (1595), and poems to Michal, Michael, and Jones. That year Williams collected some of his verse plays and other Arthurian poetry into the volume *Three Plays* (1931). Making good on the promises of the masques and *A Myth of Shakespeare,* Williams also became a well-known–if always considered idiosyncratic–dramatist. His specialty was religious plays, by which he meant, as he clarified in one essay, not drama about religion but drama "concerned with the relations of man with God"; in such plays, the religion is not a didactic design "imposed from without," but the enactment of necessary conflict within the situation.

These two volumes include pieces from Williams's cycle of poems concerning the Grail, which he considered his most important work. Williams was interested in the Holy Grail as early as 1908, an interest clear in the masques and in his *Outlines of Romantic Theology.* It was also his best poetic inspiration.

In 1930 Williams also debuted as a published novelist. *War in Heaven,* originally titled "The Corpse," succeeds where *Shadows of Ecstasy* is uneven. It also blends Williams's supernatural ideas with a popular genre, in this case the mystery; however, while the story begins with intrigue over a murder, its heart is the discovery of the Holy Grail in a small parish in England. As in many of Williams's novels, the characters define themselves by their relation to the supernatural item; those who agree to serve it and God prosper, while those who seek personal dominion hurt themselves even more than they do their opponents. *War in Heaven* is also acknowledged as Williams's most accessible novel, pleasing even to those readers who may be confused by the theology or the action of some of the other novels. T. S. Eliot compared the novel to G. K. Chesterton's *The Man Who Was Thursday* (1908), though he stated Chesterton "suffers by the comparison."

By the time *War in Heaven* appeared, Williams had established one hallmark of his fiction: realistic depictions of common people encountering supernatural forces in and through everyday English life. In one set of critical terms, this type of fantasy is "low fantasy," supernatural but taking place in this world, as opposed to the other-world "high fantasy" of Tolkien's *The Hobbit* (1937) or *The Lord of the Rings* (1954–1955). In this way Williams is an ancestor to, though rarely a direct influence on, the supernatural-horror genre of the later twentieth century, established as best-seller material by

Ira Levin's *Rosemary's Baby* (1967) and William Peter Blatty's *The Exorcist* (1971) and developed in novels by such authors as Stephen King and Peter Straub.

For Oxford University Press, Williams edited and wrote the new introduction to a second edition of the poetry of Gerard Manley Hopkins, published in 1931. His Arthurian poems began to appear in anthologies and journals: "Percevale's Song" and "Taliessin's Song of Lancelot's Mass" were both published in 1931 in poetry collections edited by Lascelles Abercrombie. Williams strongly identified with the bard Taliessin, the viewpoint character of many of his Grail poems.

Williams's middle novels—*Many Dimensions, The Place of the Lion,* and *The Greater Trumps*—were published by Gollancz in early 1931, late 1931, and 1932, respectively. Lacking the philosophical and psychological depth of his final novels, they nevertheless show progress toward that depth from *War in Heaven,* which itself showed focus and single direction lacking in *Shadows of Ecstasy.* Like *War in Heaven,* each of these middle novels is centered around a spiritual force or item, which intrudes into the natural world: respectively, the stone of Solomon, which can alter time and space at the wishes of its wearer and can infinitely replicate itself; Platonic forms, such as a Lion that embodies strength or a Butterfly that figures forth beauty; and tarot cards, in fact the original deck and an accompanying set of mystically dancing gold figures. Characters must navigate the interpenetration of the natural and the supernatural, frightening in itself but also capable of reflecting and even encouraging their own best or worst natures.

Williams's middle novels show both his strengths and weaknesses as an artist. He writes what George Parker Winship Jr. calls "a weird prose"—not "slovenly," but "the prose of a novelist whose readers do not insist upon being met half-way, who are willing to venture into a murky limbo of rhetoric" in which Williams presents decisive, almost startling insights into psychological and spiritual perception. In key passages, readers feel informed and uplifted, although the exact meaning or even nature of the events may seem elusive. This simultaneous depth and murkiness is apparent in many key scenes, such as when Chloe Burnett submits her will to that of the stone in *Many Dimensions,* or when Nancy Coningsby in *The Greater Trumps* experiences a traffic policeman as an embodiment of the tarot card The Emperor. These examples show another aspect of Williams's middle novels: despite sensational events such as attempted murder by magic (*The Greater Trumps*), attack by a carrion-breathed dragon (*The Place of the Lion*), or time travel and teleportation (*Many Dimensions*), the plot turns on more subtle moments, decisions made by or even perceptions experienced by the characters.

Williams's characters, especially in these first five novels, are often compelling but rarely successful as complete individuals. Especially, critics have argued about Sybil Coningsby in *The Greater Trumps,* whose assured spiritual insight and equanimity can either charm or annoy. Williams's most believable characters in his middle novels are those in transition—those who are for the first time facing supernatural forces that confront them with choices and the consequences of their own natures: Chloe Burnett in *Many Dimensions,* for example, or Damaris Tighe in *The Place of the Lion.*

Though *The Greater Trumps* is the weakest of the three middle novels in plot and character, it includes some of Williams's more captivating metaphysical imagery. In it he develops the idea of the "great dance" of creation, shown in a table of golden figures who represent the Major Arcana (greater trumps) of the tarot deck. All of the figures dance, perpetually and inexplicably; the Fool alone may stand still—or may have the most subtle dance of all. These figures were perhaps modeled on a kind of tarot-based chess, called Rosicrucian Chess or Enochian Chess, that Williams learned from his Rosicrucian mentor, Waite.

Many Dimensions, with its time-travel elements, is noteworthy as the most science-fictional of Williams's novels. In a September 1949 review in *The Atlantic* Edward Weeks called it "a metaphysical novel, perhaps, or better still a mathematical one of the Einsteinian variety." Critics of science fiction note that Williams handles the paradoxes of time travel in a rigorously philosophical way.

By the 1930s Williams had reached maturity as an artist and as an economic provider. *Poetry at Present* was followed in 1932 by *The English Poetic Mind,* based on lectures Williams delivered as a special course for the City Literary Institute at the London Day Training College in 1931, a thematic appreciation of poets including Shakespeare, Milton, and William Wordsworth. The book received mixed reviews, generally praising Williams's insights and decrying the obscurity of some of his prose. Williams also began a series of popular biographies for various London publishers; the first was *Bacon,* about Francis Bacon, in 1933. A third book of general poetry criticism, *Reason and Beauty in the Poetic Mind,* was also published in 1933; in it, Williams traces that theme through the works of such writers as Shakespeare, Milton, Wordsworth, and John Keats.

The only short story Williams ever published, "Et in Sempiternum Pereant," appeared in 1935. It features Lord Arglay, one of the protagonists of *Many Dimensions,* who discovers an entrance to Hell and must confront his hatred of Giles Tumulty, a villain in *Many Dimensions* and *War in Heaven.*

Williams achieved both increased artistic success and greater acknowledgment with his later plays, such as *Cranmer of Canterbury,* commissioned by the Friends of the Canterbury Cathedral and performed at the Canterbury Festival in June 1936, the year after Eliot's contribution, *Murder in the Cathedral.* Published by the Oxford University Press in 1936, Williams's play tells the story of Cranmer, a gentle and peaceful man in times of religious ferment, who served as archbishop of Canterbury under Henry VIII and was burned at the stake by Queen Mary. Told in what Agnes Sibley calls a "stylized, poetic" way, the play includes no overt supernatural events but receives some attention for an enigmatic, sarcastic, mythic figure called "The Skeleton."

Most of Williams's writing energy around this time went into the popular biographies: *James I* (1934); *Rochester* (1935); *Queen Elizabeth* (1936); *Thomas Cranmer of Canterbury* (1936); and *Henry VII* (1937). Comparisons between Williams's play about Cranmer and the biography show his versatility—and his unwillingness to let research go to waste. Reviews of the biographies were mixed.

Still, as Williams quickly produced workman-like nonfiction to bring in money, he was composing two of his major works, one in prose and one in poetry. Generally seen by critics as one of Williams's two or three best novels, *Descent into Hell* was published in 1937.

In this novel Williams explores his doctrines of co-inherence and substitution. As it says in the Bible, Williams states, all Christians are literally one in Christ—not merely in a way of speaking, but as "a fact of experience," as he puts it in *Descent into Hell.* Thus, Williams reasons, people can substitute for each other—literally carry the burden of another's pain or worry—as Christ substituted himself on the cross for everyone's sins. This sacrifice is not just a willed magical act, directed by the individual, but also a constant condition of life, too often unrecognized. Williams explored perversions of the way of exchange and its holy image in all forms of his writing.

Critics regard *Descent into Hell* as Williams's most structurally satisfying novel, mapping the crossed ascent and descent of two characters. The ascending character is Pauline Anstruther, a young woman terrified by appearances of her doppelgänger—an eerie exact double. She is taught the truths of co-inherence and substitution by Peter Stanhope, a playwright whose mentoring relationship to her is much like that of Williams to Lois Lang-Sims (as seen in *Letters to Lalage: The Letters of Charles Williams to Lois Lang-Sims,* 1989). Since co-inherence is limited by neither space nor time, Pauline is finally able to substitute herself for a martyred ancestor during his burning, thus ending her own haunting. Conversely, the title refers to the path of

CHARLES WILLIAMS

THE PLACE OF THE LION

A NEW NOVEL

PRICE 3s NETT

Mundanus Ltd
VICTOR GOLLANCZ PUBLISHER
1931

Wrapper for the second of Williams's three "middle novels," which features an attack by a carrion-breathed dragon (courtesy of The Lilly Library, Indiana University)

Lawrence Wentworth, a man of small vices and smaller virtues, who falls willing victim to a succubus because true love—or even true companionship—is too irritatingly demanding for him. Williams makes clear that the little things count most, in the most literal sense. As he states in an essay in *The Image of the City and Other Essays* (1958), the choice is always between good and evil, community and selfishness: "The choice exists everywhere, at every minute, as a fundamental."

With *Descent into Hell,* as Charles Moorman points out, Williams shifted away from "adventure" and increasingly "toward an attempt to picture salvation and damnation as they exist among the people of Williams' own time." Certainly there is sensational supernaturalism, although this novel is missing the murders and political machinations, the chases and plots of the first five novels. Wentworth's damnation is as much from a small lie he tells—violating the only sense of integrity he has, that of an historian—as it is because of the more dramatic succubus, whose lure tempts him to tell that lie in order to return to her more quickly.

The setting of the novel is Battle Hill, a common housing development near London, but also a place where barriers are thinner than usual between life and death, past and present. The supernatural forces make each character more of what he or she has chosen to be, from Pauline's serene, dying aunt, Margaret, to petty and self-centered Myrtle Fox. Lily Sammile is a completely supernatural creature, a combination of Lilith (Adam's rebellious first wife) and the devil Sammael.

Williams's first book of Grail poetry, *Taliessin through Logres,* was published in 1938. Writing his poems about Taliessin and the Grail paid little, but Williams considered it his lifework—more of a vocation. He may have been drawn to the tragedy of Arthur, Guinevere, and Lancelot; but more central was the story of the Grail and the quest to establish God's kingdom, orderly and just, in England. The poems are difficult, with diagrammatic associations—characters with animals, cities and their roles in the story with parts of the human body and their functions—sometimes influenced by the cabalism of Waite. Many criticize the poems as too dry; yet, the persistent and careful reader will find deep passion in the story and its various quests.

The Grail poems, like Williams's two final novels, explore the doctrines of co-inherence, substitution, and exchange. Love is a way of exchange; so is money, honest work exchanged for honest pay. R. J. Reilly points out that the Taliessin poems also, like *Descent into Hell,* show that "the practices of substitution and interchange can and do operate in the past as well as the present and the future." For instance, Taliessin imagines all Christian poets indebted to Virgil substituting for him at his death.

Williams entered the last stage of his life in 1938, when the Oxford University Press offices moved from London to Southfield House, Hilltop Road, Oxford, to avoid the German bombs of World War II. Michal remained in London—fearlessly, as Williams often remarked—with their son, while Williams, along with coworker Gerry Hopkins, was taken into the household of a professor, H. N. Spalding, at 9 South Parks Road. Visits from Michal went pleasantly, even rejuvenating their marriage. Williams's office at the press, a converted bathroom, was actually quite a wartime luxury, but Williams missed London and the old press offices. He wrote that he felt like "a snail without a shell." His manner of dress never fit with the Oxford style, and his lack of education and wealth made him feel more like an outsider than ever.

Yet, Oxford offered one overwhelming compensation: the friendship of Lewis, a professor there at the time, and others in the Inklings, a group that gathered for discussions that ranged across politics, art, religion, and life; literary critique; and above all, fellowship. Lewis and Williams had first exchanged letters in 1936; Williams admired Lewis's study of medieval literature, *The Allegory of Love* (1936), and Lewis praised Williams's novel *The Place of the Lion*. In Lewis, Williams found an intellectual equal who showed the same keen interest in many of Williams's major passions—if not exactly the same views.

The other key member of the Inklings was Tolkien, famous for his fantasy novels *The Hobbit* and later *The Lord of the Rings*. Less famous but also vital Inklings included Warnie Lewis (C. S. Lewis's brother), Owen Barfield, and Hugo Dyson; Dorothy L. Sayers was a famous associate of the group, but a peripheral one. Humphrey Carpenter's *The Inklings: C. S. Lewis, J. R. R. Tolkien, Charles Williams and Their Friends* (1978) chronicles this period in Williams's life and the nature of the Inklings as a group. The Inklings read works in progress to each other and were encouraging, though not uncritical: Carpenter records Lewis's reference to Williams's "obscurity" and Dyson's phrase "clotted glory from Charles."

Lewis also helped move Williams's teaching, already popular, to a new level. In January 1938 Williams's lecturing prompted his only visit to the Continent, when he delivered "On Byron and Byronism" at the Sorbonne. Then, because of Lewis's encouragement and influence, Williams began to lecture at Oxford, beginning in 1940 with lessons on Milton. As Hadfield writes, "We can only dimly imagine what the Milton lectures meant to Williams. . . . Within five months of his arrival, here he was, a self-made literary man with no university degree, lecturing . . . to educated undergraduates of a great university, under the sponsorship of men of academic reputation." Williams began to lecture regularly at the university and to tutor at St. Hilda's College.

In this period some of Williams's most profound nonfiction books were published, beginning with *He Came Down from Heaven,* published in 1938, the fifth in a series from Longmans called "I Believe: A Series of Personal Statements." Dedicated "To Michal by whom I began to study the doctrine of glory," the book is divided into two parts. The first four chapters examine God's relationship with humanity, while the last three examine three kinds of human relationships: romantic love, behavior toward others, and building a community.

That book was followed by *The Descent of the Dove: A Short History of the Holy Spirit in the Church,* published in 1939 and chosen for the Religious Book Club. In this volume of lay theology Williams explains the concepts, essential to his work, of the Way of Affirmation and the Way of Rejection, both paths to reach understanding of

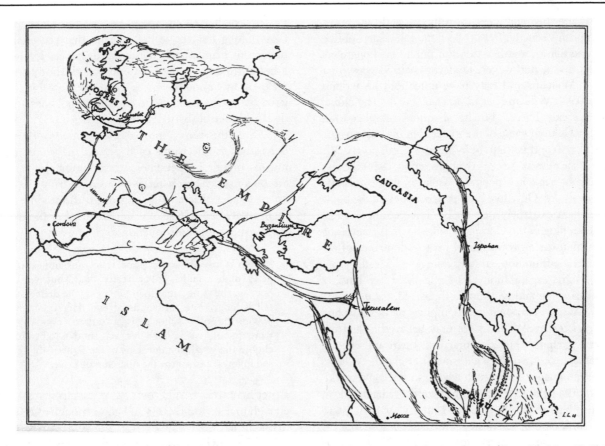

Endpaper, with map by Lynton Lamb, for Williams's 1938 book of Arthurian poems, Taliessin through Logres (*from Alice Mary Hadfield,*
Charles Williams: An Exploration of His Life and Work, *1983*)

God: "The one Way was to affirm all things orderly until the universe throbbed with vitality; the other to reject all things until there was nothing anywhere but He." The latter is the choice of the ascetic and many other mystics, while the former is the choice of lovers and artists. Followers of the Way of Affirmation permeate his novels, from Roger and Isabel Ingram in *Shadows of Ecstasy* to Roger Furnival in *All Hallows' Eve*. In *Taliessin through Logres* Taliessin follows the Way of Affirmation, while Dindrane, also known as Blanchefleur, chooses the Way of Rejection.

The poet who best embodied the Way of Affirmation for Williams was Dante; and so in the early 1940s Williams produced studies of Dante that combine theology and literary analysis. Dacre Press released a small edition of *Religion and Love in Dante: The Theology of Romantic Love* in 1941, and Faber and Faber produced a more mainstream publication, *The Figure of Beatrice,* in 1943. The latter is both a study of Dante and the most complete explication of Williams's own ideas concerning romantic love and its relationship to religious experience. Williams insisted that, as John Heath-Stubbs writes, "For the lover, at the moment of his first falling in love, the beloved was actually an image of the divine perfection." Williams demonstrates this perception in his novels, in Philip Travers's love for Rosamond Murchison in *Shadows of Ecstasy,* in Nancy Coningsby's love for Henry Lee in *The Greater Trumps,* and in the maturing love of Lester Furnival for her husband in *All Hallows' Eve*.

While mining Dante's theology, Williams explored the other side of the supernatural in *Witchcraft,* a nonfiction study published in 1941. Intended for a popular audience, yet almost willfully difficult in many places, it is best read by those already familiar with the topic; but it does provide insight into Williams's view of magic. The book concerns itself "more with the lower level that with any nobler dream," Williams writes; he allows for a kind of high magic, practiced by Renaissance and early-modern figures such as John Dee and Henry Vaughan, but primarily "the nobler idea of virtue mingled with power" that developed into modern science was kept secret by esoteric societies, "or it did in fact degenerate into base and disgusting evils." This predominant, debased strain of magic, called "goetia," informs Williams's final novel, *All Hallows' Eve*.

On 18 February 1943, at fifty-six years of age, Williams finally got his university degree, when Oxford bestowed on him an honorary master of arts. There was some talk of Williams joining the Oxford English faculty, perhaps after his retirement from the press. In the meantime Williams edited a 1943 collection of the letters of Evelyn Underhill for another London publisher, Longmans. A noted mystic and writer, Underhill held views sympathetic to Williams and may have influenced his writing. Also in 1943 Williams began a novel, titled "The Noises That Weren't There," but he abandoned it after three chapters. He used some of the material in his final novel.

The second volume of Williams's Grail poetry, *The Region of the Summer Stars,* was published in 1944; the title comes from a line in a poem by Taliessin in the medieval *Mabinogion* tales. Only five newspapers reviewed the book, two of them extremely negatively. The volume includes "The Founding of the Company," in which Williams outlines a plan for a group based on the doctrines of co-inherence, substitution, and exchange—as Heath-Stubbs writes, "some organization of an essentially 'lay' kind, of Christians living and working in the world, yet under the law of Grace." As shown in biographies of Williams and in *Letters to Lalage,* Williams not only believed in substitution and exchange but also practiced them and encouraged others to do so. In Taliessin's household, Williams presents an image of how such a community could work.

In 1944 the war was ending, and Williams began making plans to move back to London or perhaps to accept some appointment at Oxford. He also wrote his final, and perhaps greatest, novel, *All Hallows' Eve.* This novel, like *Descent into Hell,* shows Williams's deepest understanding of eternity—not the common concept of it as a person's daily life extended infinitely, but life of the bodiless spirit, in which all times are one. Moreover, in both cases, Williams uses the novels to depict co-inherence and exchange (and their perverse alternatives of self-isolation and forced, self-willed magic) more concretely and accessibly than in his other work.

All Hallows' Eve begins at the end of the war, in London—but also in the City, the supernatural reality always present within and through London, in which two young women find themselves wandering, at first unaware that they have been killed by a crashing plane. Evelyn Mercer and Lester Furnival, like Wentworth and Pauline in *Descent into Hell,* choose downward and upward paths, respectively. Yet, *All Hallows' Eve* concentrates on Lester's ascent, an ordeal of self-awareness and forgiveness (of self and others) more realistic and compelling than Pauline's.

As *Descent into Hell* has its succubus and Lily Sammile, *All Hallows' Eve* has a goetic sorcerer, Simon the Clerk. In one vivid supernatural scene, Simon recites the Tetragrammaton (the holy name of God) in reverse to kill his servant, Betty Wallingford, who is also his illegitimate daughter, so that she can be his tool in supernatural realms. Lester, who had not treated Betty well during life, offers to substitute for her as the object of the malign spell. Not only are Simon's intentions frustrated, but

Lester feels herself supported in turn by the shape of a cross, lifting her above the miasma that represents the dangerous magic. Later, Lester accompanies Evelyn into a homunculus, a malformed and parodic body supplied for them by Simon the Clerk, but uses the vehicle to say good-bye to the flesh and to exchange apologies and pardons with her husband, Richard.

Still, the most important events are not the spells, but rather the decisions each person makes, determining his or her proper fate. At one point, besieged by Simon's magic, Lester receives strength from the homiest of images: Richard getting up in the middle of the night to get her a glass of water, saving her the trouble. Eliot writes in his introduction to the novel:

> Evelyn is a woman who appears too insignificant, too petty in her faults, to be really 'bad,' but yet, just because she is no more than pettiness, she delivers herself willingly into the hands of evil. Her friend, who makes the other choice, is a rather commonplace woman; but, having lived just well enough to be able to choose the good, she develops in the light of that good she follows, and learns the meaning of Love.

Lester may well be Williams's strongest character, human enough to need forgiveness and good enough to be willing to ask for it.

The novel is also noteworthy for two patterns of imagery, as evocative as the gold mist and figures in *The Greater Trumps* but more coherent. The first is water—not only Lester's glass of water from Richard but also the waters of baptism, and of rain, which is cleansing but dissolving. The second is the glory into which Lester disperses at the end of the novel: the rain becomes a red wash of fire and blood and roses.

Later in 1945 *The House of the Octopus* was published, a play written at the request of the United Council of Missionary Education. On an island in the "outer seas," the pagan empire of P'o-lu attempts to conquer by undermining the Christian church there. The plot is led by Assantu, the son of a sorcerer; a Christian island girl is martyred and returns as a ghost. The play also features a character called the Flame, which plays an ambiguous role much like that of the Skeleton in *Cranmer of Canterbury.*

Williams's final book was a biography, *Flecker of Dean Close,* published posthumously in 1946. Williams also continued to work on a study of King Arthur; at his death, he had finished five chapters, which were published in 1948, along with commentary by Lewis on Williams's Grail poetry, in *Arthurian Torso.*

By March 1945, Williams looked tired and ill. On the day after the war ended, in May 1945, Williams "was seized with pain," as Hadfield writes; "His wife came from London, he was taken to Radcliffe Hospital, and operated on" for intestinal problems on 14 May. He never recovered and died the following day. Williams was buried in St. Cross Churchyard, Holywell, Oxford, where his tombstone reads simply "Poet," and then, referring to one of his many terms for God, "Under the Mercy."

In honor of his dead friend, Lewis edited *Essays Presented to Charles Williams,* published in 1947. Only the preface concerns Williams directly, but all the essays cover literature dear to Williams, from Haggard's spectacular adventures to the *Divine Comedy.* In addition to *Arthurian Torso,* a collection of Williams's plays was published in 1948.

Though Williams has never become as famous as Lewis or Tolkien, attention to his life and works has continued to grow in a kind of punctuated evolution. Williams has been written about both by those who knew him—including Ridler, correspondent Lang-Sims, coworker and biographer Hadfield, and more famous friends such as Lewis, Eliot, and Auden—and by those attracted to his fiction, poetry, plays, theology, literary studies, historical writings, life, and personality.

Critics and scholars have primarily written about Williams's fiction and poetry, both as works of art and as vehicles of Williams's theology. After a slow, steady growth of studies in the 1950s and early 1960s, critical attention blossomed in the late 1960s and early 1970s. Williams benefited from the increased popularity of *The Lord of the Rings* and from the cultural strains that promoted Tolkien to stardom: a counterculture fascination with forms of consciousness and utopian alternatives, as well as growing literary interest in fantasy and science fiction. Another, smaller spike in activity occurred in the 1980s, surrounding and occasioned by the centenary of Williams's birth. Much of this critical work has been encouraged by academic and semiacademic associations such as the Mythopoeic Society, the Charles Williams Society of England, and the International Association for the Fantastic in the Arts.

Charles Williams remains an unusual author whose work leaves few readers neutral. Though some find his writing occasionally obscure, his novels appeal to many readers of fantasy and science fiction, offering a combination of myth with adventure, deep psychological and spiritual insights with everyday life. Supernatural and mythic elements may attract such readers to Williams's poetry and plays as well. Finally, the unity of Williams's thought may draw readers to the nonfiction, from reviews to theological studies and biographies, in which one can fully experience the integrity of Williams's art and ideas.

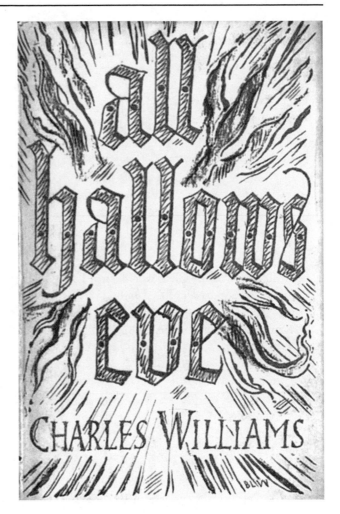

Dust jacket for Williams's final novel, published in 1945, in which two women take divergent paths in the afterlife (courtesy of The Lilly Library, Indiana University)

Letters:

Letters to Lalage: The Letters of Charles Williams to Lois Lang-Sims, introduction and notes by Glen Cavaliero (Kent, Ohio: Kent State University Press, 1989).

Bibliography:

Lois Glenn, *Charles W. S. Williams: A Checklist* (Kent, Ohio: Kent State University Press, 1975).

Biographies:

Humphrey Carpenter, *The Inklings: C. S. Lewis, J. R. R. Tolkien, Charles Williams and Their Friends* (London: Allen & Unwin, 1978; Boston: Houghton Mifflin, 1979);

Alice Mary Hadfield, *Charles Williams: An Exploration of His Life and Work* (London: Oxford University Press, 1983);

John Rateliff, "'And Something Yet Remains to Be Said': Tolkien and Williams," *Mythlore* (Spring 1986): 48–54.

References:

W. H. Auden, "Charles Williams: A Review Article," *Christian Century* (January–June 1956): 552–554;

Bernadette Lynn Bosky, "Charles Williams and the Golden Dawn," *Mythlore* (Winter 1986): 25–35;

Bosky, "Charles Williams: Occult Fantasies, Occult Fact," *Modes of the Fantastic: Selected Essays from the Twelfth International Conference on the Fantastic in the Arts,* edited by Robert A. Latham and Robert A. Collins (Westport, Conn.: Greenwood Press, 1995), pp. 176–185;

Robert McAfee Brown, "Charles Williams: Lay Theologian," *Theology Today* (July 1953): 212–229;

Glen Cavaliero, *Charles Williams: Poet of Theology* (Grand Rapids, Mich.: Eerdmans, 1983);

Lawrence R. Dawson Jr., "Reflections of Charles Williams on Fiction," *Ball State Teacher's College Forum* (Winter 1964): 23–29;

David Llewellyn Dodds, "An Introduction to the Unpublished Williams," *Charles Williams Newsletter* (Spring 1993): 7–22;

Dodds, "Magic in the Myths of J. R. R. Tolkien and Charles Williams," *Inklings Jahrbuch für Literatur und Ästhetik* (1992): 37–55;

T. S. Eliot, "The Significance of Charles Williams," *Listener* (19 December 1946): 894–895;

Edmund Fuller, *Charles Williams's* All Hallows' Eve (New York: Seabury Press, 1967);

Alice Mary Hadfield, *An Introduction to Charles Williams* (London: Hale, 1959);

John Heath-Stubbs, *Charles Williams* (London: Longmans, Green, 1955);

Mark R. Hillegas, ed., *Shadows of Imagination: The Fantasies of C. S. Lewis, J. R. R. Tolkien, and Charles Williams* (Carbondale: Southern Illinois University Press, 1969);

Thomas Howard, *The Novels of Charles Williams* (New York: Oxford University Press, 1983);

Charles A. Huttar and Peter Schakel, eds., *The Rhetoric of Vision: Essays on Charles Williams* (Lewisburg, Pa.: Bucknell University Press, 1996);

Roma A. King Jr., *The Pattern in the Web: The Mythical Poetry of Charles Williams* (Kent, Ohio: Kent State University Press, 1990);

Gareth Knight, *The Magical World of the Inklings: J. R. R. Tolkien, C. S. Lewis, Charles Williams, Owen Barfield* (Longmead, Shaftesbury, Dorset: Element, 1990);

Gisbert Kranz, ed., "Proceedings of the International Charles Williams Symposium," *Inklings Jahrbuch für Literatur and Ästhetik* (1987): 59–296;

C. S. Lewis, "The Novels of Charles Williams," in his *On Stories,* edited by Walter Hooper (New York: Harcourt Brace Jovanovich, 1982);

Lewis, ed., *Essays Presented to Charles Williams* (London & New York: Oxford University Press, 1947);

C. N. Manlove, "Fantasy as Praise: Charles Williams," in his *The Impulse of Fantasy Literature* (Kent, Ohio: Kent State University Press, 1983), pp. 15–30;

Charles Moorman, *Arthurian Triptych: Mythic Materials in Charles Williams, C. S. Lewis, and T. S. Eliot* (Berkeley: University of California Press, 1960);

Geoffrey Parsons, "The Spirit of Charles Williams," *Atlantic Monthly* (July–December 1949): 77–79;

R. J. Reilly, *Romantic Religion: A Study of Barfield, Lewis, Williams, and Tolkien* (Athens: University of Georgia Press, 1971);

George Reynolds, "Dante and Williams: Pilgrims in Purgatory," *Mythlore* (Autumn 1986): 3–7;

Mary McDermott Shideler, *The Theology of Romantic Love: A Study in the Writings of Charles Williams* (New York: Harper, 1962);

Agnes Sibley, *Charles Williams* (Boston: Twayne, 1982);

Patricia Meyer Spacks, "Charles Williams: A Novelist's Pilgrimage," *Religion in Life* (Spring 1960): 277–288;

Peter Sutcliffe, *The Oxford University Press: An Informal History* (Oxford: Clarendon Press, 1978);

Gunnar Urang, *Shadows of Heaven: Religion and Fantasy in the Writing of C. S. Lewis, Charles Williams, and J. R. R. Tolkien* (Philadelphia: Pilgrim, 1971);

Chad Walsh, "Charles Williams' Novels and Contemporary Mutation of Consciousness," in *Myth, Allegory, and Gospel: An Interpretation of J. R. R. Tolkien, C. S. Lewis, G. K. Chesterton, Charles Williams,* edited by Edmund Fuller and others (Minneapolis: Bethany Fellowship, 1974);

George Parker Winship Jr., "This Rough Magic: The Novels of Charles Williams," *Yale Review* (December 1950): 285–296.

Papers:

A large collection of Charles Williams's papers is in the Marion E. Wade Center, Wheaton College, Wheaton, Illinois. In England the largest collection is in the Bodleian Library, Oxford. The archives of the Oxford University Press in Oxford and the Victor Gollancz publishing house also hold some documents. Additional papers are at the Harry Ransom Humanities Research Center, University of Texas at Austin; the Houghton Library, Harvard University; and the archives of the Charles Williams Society in Kings College Library, University of London.

S. Fowler Wright

(6 January 1874 – 25 February 1965)

Darren Harris-Fain
Shawnee State University

BOOKS: *Scenes from the Morte d'Arthur,* as Alan Seymour (London: Erskine MacDonald, 1919);

Some Songs of Bilitis (Birmingham: Poetry, 1921);

The Amphibians: A Romance of 500,000 Years Hence (London: Merton, 1925; New York: World, 1949);

The Song of Songs and Other Poems (London: Merton, 1925; New York: Cosmopolitan, 1929);

The Ballad of Elaine (London: Merton, 1926);

Deluge: A Romance (London: Fowler Wright, 1927; New York: Cosmopolitan, 1928);

The Island of Captain Sparrow (London: Gollancz, 1928; New York: Cosmopolitan, 1928);

Dawn (New York: Cosmopolitan, 1929; London: Harrap, 1930);

Police and Public: A Political Pamphlet (London: Fowler Wright, 1929);

The Riding of Lancelot: A Narrative Poem (London: Fowler Wright, 1929);

The World Below–includes *The Amphibians* (London: Collins, 1929; New York: Longmans, Green, 1930); published separately as *The Dwellers* (London: Panther, 1954);

Elfwin (London: Harrap, 1930; New York: Longmans, Green, 1930);

The King Against Anne Bickerton, as Sydney Fowler (London: Harrap, 1930); republished as *The Case of Anne Bickerton* (New York: Boni, 1930); republished as *Rex v. Anne Bickerton* (Harmondsworth, U.K.: Penguin, 1947);

The Bell Street Murders, as Fowler (London: Harrap, 1931; New York: Macaulay, 1931);

By Saturday, as Fowler (London: John Lane, 1931);

Crime and Co., as Fowler (New York: Macaulay, 1931); republished as *The Hand-Print Mystery* (London: Jarrolds, 1932);

Dream; or, The Simian Maid (London: Harrap, 1931; Westport, Conn.: Greenwood Press, 1985);

The Hanging of Constance Hillier, as Fowler (London: Jarrolds, 1931; New York: Macaulay, 1932);

S. Fowler Wright

Red Ike, by Wright and J. M. Denwood (London: Hutchinson, 1931); republished as *Under the Brutchstone* (New York: Coward-McCann, 1931);

Seven Thousand in Israel (London: Jarrolds, 1931);

Beyond the Rim (London: Jarrolds, 1932);

The Life of Sir Walter Scott: A Biography (London: Poetry League, 1932; New York: Haskell House, 1971);

The New Gods Lead (London: Jarrolds, 1932);

Arresting Delia, as Fowler (London: Jarrolds, 1933; New York: Macaulay, 1933);

Lord's Right in Languedoc (London: Jarrolds, 1933);

Power (London: Jarrolds, 1933);

The Secret of the Screen, as Fowler (London: Jarrolds, 1933);

David (London: Butterworth, 1934);

Who Else But She? as Fowler (London: Jarrolds, 1934);

Prelude in Prague: A Story of the War of 1938 (London: Newnes, 1935); republished as *The War of 1938* (New York: Putnam, 1936);

Three Witnesses, as Fowler (London: Butterworth, 1935);

Vengeance of Gwa, as Anthony Wingrave (London: Butterworth, 1935); as S. Fowler Wright (London: Books of Today, 1945);

The Attic Murder, as Fowler (London: Butterworth, 1936);

Four Days War (London: Hale, 1936);

Post-Mortem Evidence, as Fowler (London: Butterworth, 1936);

Was Murder Done? as Fowler (London: Butterworth, 1936);

Four Callers in Razor Street, as Fowler (London: Jenkins, 1937);

Megiddo's Ridge (London: Hale, 1937);

The Screaming Lake (London: Hale, 1937);

The Adventure of Wyndham Smith (London: Jenkins, 1938);

The Hidden Tribe (London: Hale, 1938);

The Jordans Murder, as Fowler (London: Jenkins, 1938; New York: Hillman-Curl, 1939);

The Murder in Bethnal Square, as Fowler (London: Jenkins, 1938);

Ordeal of Barata (London: Jenkins, 1939);

Should We Surrender Colonies? (London: Readers Library, 1939);

The Wills of Jane Kanwhistle, as Fowler (London: Jenkins, 1939);

A Bout with the Mildew Gang, as Fowler (London: Eyre & Spottiswoode, 1941);

The Rissole Mystery, as Fowler (London: Rich & Cowan, 1941);

Second Bout with the Mildew Gang, as Fowler (London: Eyre & Spottiswoode, 1942);

The Siege of Malta: Founded on an Unfinished Romance by Sir Walter Scott (London: Muller, 1942);

Dinner in New York, as Fowler (London: Eyre & Spottiswoode, 1943);

The End of the Mildew Gang, as Fowler (London: Eyre & Spottiswoode, 1944);

The Adventure of the Blue Room, as Fowler (London: Rich & Cowan, 1945);

Justice, and The Rat: Two Famous Stories (London: Books of Today, 1945);

Too Much for Mr. Jellipot, as Fowler (London: Eyre & Spottiswoode, 1945);

The Witchfinder (London: Books of Today, 1946);

Who Murdered Reynard? as Fowler (London: Rich & Cowan, 1947);

The Throne of Saturn (Sauk City, Wis.: Arkham House, 1949; London: Heinemann, 1951);

Spiders' War (New York: Abelard, 1954);

With Cause Enough? as Fowler (London: Harvill, 1954);

Cortéz: For God and Spain (Ludlow: FWB, 1996);

Inquisitive Angel (Ludlow: FWB, 1996);

Song of Arthur (Ludlow: FWB, 1996);

S. Fowler Wright's Short Stories (Ludlow: FWB, 1996).

Editions: *Deluge: A Romance; and Dawn* (New York: Arno, 1975);

Electronic-text versions of many of Wright's essays, stories, novels, and nonfiction books are available online at *The Works of Sydney Fowler Wright* <http://www.sfw.org.uk>.

OTHER: *Voices on the Wind: An Anthology of Contemporary Verse,* 3 volumes, edited by Wright (London: Merton, 1922–1924);

Poets of Merseyside: An Anthology of Present-Day Liverpool Poetry, edited by Wright (London: Merton, 1923);

Poems: Chosen by Boys and Girls, 4 volumes, edited by Wright and R. Crompton Rhodes (Oxford: Blackwell, 1923–1924);

Birmingham Poetry 1923–24, edited by Wright (London: Merton, 1924);

From Overseas: An Anthology of Contemporary Dominion and Colonial Verse, edited by Wright (London: Merton, 1924);

Some Yorkshire Poets, edited by Wright (London: Merton, 1924);

A Somerset Anthology of Modern Verse, 1924, edited by Wright (London: Merton, 1925);

The County Series of Contemporary Poetry, 15 volumes, edited by Wright (London: Merton, 1925–1926; London: Fowler Wright, 1926–1928; London: Empire Poetry League, 1926–1927; London: Fowler Wright, 1928–1930);

Edward Bulwer-Lytton, *The Last Days of Pompeii: A Redaction,* edited by Wright (London: Vision, 1948);

"Obviously Suicide," in *Beyond the End of Time,* edited by Frederik Pohl (Garden City, N.Y.: Permabooks, 1952), pp. 321–324;

"The Better Choice," in *Science-Fiction Adventures in Mutation,* edited by Groff Conklin (New York: Vanguard, 1955), pp. 310–311.

TRANSLATIONS: Dante, *The Inferno* (London: Fowler Wright, 1928; New York: Cosmopolitan, 1928);

Alexandre Dumas *père, Marguerite de Valois* (London: Temple, 1947);

Dante, *The Purgatorio* (Edinburgh: Oliver & Boyd, 1954);

Dante, *The Paradiso* (Ludlow: FWB, 1996).

Although S. Fowler Wright did not specialize in science fiction or fantasy—he wrote detective fiction and historical novels, as well—perhaps the most important part of his voluminous output is the fraction of it devoted to the fantastic. Within this field he is noteworthy for his particular worldview: in contrast with the more optimistic assessments of human nature and progress offered by near contemporaries such as H. G. Wells and by later science-fiction writers, Wright's voice was one of caution, if not alarm, about what human beings would do with technological changes and better-organized social structures. For the most part, he attempted to convey such ideas through fiction that most resembled some of the popular styles of writing in early-twentieth-century Britain.

Sydney Fowler Wright was born on 6 January 1874 in Birmingham, England. His family were devoted Protestants—his father was a Baptist lay minister, and one of his sisters was a missionary—but Wright eventually rejected organized religion in favor of a broader personal theism. Wright also developed certain principles for conduct: he ate no meat other than fish; he did not smoke; and he drank little. Such idiosyncrasy was typical of Wright, who also thought birth control and automobiles were evil and who did not believe that children (including his own) should read the Bible. He was educated in Birmingham at King Edward's School, and although he left the school as a teenager in order to educate himself (he later taught himself French and Italian), he remained in Birmingham to begin his career as an accountant in 1895, the same year he married Nellie Ashbarry.

By this time Wright had developed the worldview that decades later manifested itself in his fiction. Something of a Romantic in his beliefs about the importance of personal freedom and in his admiration for nature, and an admirer of Jean-Jacques Rousseau on matters of human nature and social institutions, Wright was distrustful, if not disdainful, of many modern social and technological developments. The scientific worldview so central to modern science fiction comes under attack in much of Wright's fiction. Wright often presents readers with earlier historical periods or almost pastoral environments in contrast to the modern industrialized world.

Wright's literary career began slowly. While he worked as an accountant, he wrote poetry on the side. In 1917 he helped to found the Empire Poetry League in Birmingham, which stimulated him to devote more time to writing. Such time was hard to come by, since he had a regular job and a large family to support: in his and Nellie's twenty-three years of marriage before her death in 1918 they had three sons and three daughters. In 1919, at age forty-five, Wright published his first book, a pseudonymous retelling of scenes from Sir Thomas Malory's *Le Morte d'Arthur* (1485). This effort to render the tales of King Arthur and the Knights of the Round Table in blank verse was part of a larger project that occupied Wright throughout much of his life; not long after he completed it, however, the manuscript was destroyed during World War II. Also in 1919, he remarried; he and his second wife, Truda Hancock, had one son and three daughters, bringing the number of children Wright supported to ten.

Another demand on his time, in addition to his family responsibilities, was that Wright assumed editorial duties for the publishing enterprises of the Empire Poetry League, both for its book division, the Merton Press, and for its journal, *Poetry* (later retitled *Poetry and the Play*), which he edited from 1920 to 1932. In addition, throughout the 1920s Wright edited several volumes of regional British poetry. When the Merton Press foundered, he started his own publishing line, Fowler Wright Books, which published his science-fiction novel *Deluge: A Romance* in 1927, and he began translating Dante's *Divine Comedy* (circa 1310–1314).

Also in the 1920s Wright tried his hand at novels, publishing the first through the Merton Press. *The Amphibians: A Romance of 500,000 Years Hence* (1925) shows the legacy of Wells, in particular *The Time Machine* (1895), in its ideas; but this volume and its sequel, *The World Below* (1929), also reveal some of Wright's own concerns. In addition, the two books were intended to form the first two parts of a trilogy, decades before trilogies became commonplace in science fiction and especially fantasy thanks to the success of J. R. R. Tolkien's three-volume novel *The Lord of the Rings* (1954–1955). More than likely Wright's inspiration for this abandoned project was his ongoing work of translating Dante's tripartite masterpiece.

The Wellsian character of *The Amphibians* lies in its setting (half a million years into the future, as indicated by the subtitle) and in the evolutionary changes that have taken place over such a long span of time, as well as its mode, the romance—or, to be more accurate, the scientific romance. As Brian M. Stableford has argued in his *Scientific Romance in Britain, 1890–1950* (1985), Wells, though he called his classic science-fiction novels "scientific romances," did not invent either the mode or the name. Instead, Stableford claims, the scientific romance developed toward the end of the nineteenth century as a subcategory of the romance, a fictional work that included an exotic setting and/or nonrealistic elements and that was therefore distinct from the novel or the realistic short story. For this subcategory the nonrealistic element was generally a speculative use of science, and while the setting may be the contemporary world, it could also include other

THE
NEW GODS LEAD

BY
S. FOWLER WRIGHT

JARROLDS *Publishers* LONDON
Limited 34 Paternoster Row E.C.4

*Title page for Wright's first collection of short stories, several of which are
cautionary science-fiction tales about the abuse of technology
(Bruccoli Clark Layman Collection)*

worlds, either in space or in time. According to Stableford, the British scientific romance eventually became indistinguishable from the more American form that was labeled "science fiction," but from the 1890s to roughly the 1950s it is possible to talk of the scientific romance as a separate mode.

Wright was clearly operating within the conventions of this mode in *The Amphibians,* writing about an Earth 500,000 years in the future contested by three intelligent species, none of them human. Like Wells, Wright extrapolates about the far future from an evolutionary viewpoint; he speculates about the possibility of human extinction and the idea of more than one powerful species in conflict; and he does so for more than mere entertainment. As indicated by the title of Mary S. Weinkauf's study *Sermons in Science Fiction: The Novels of S. Fowler Wright* (1994), he often wrote science fiction to examine certain ideas in a critical light.

The narrator of *The Amphibians,* who has been projected into the future to rescue two explorers who preceded him in a scientific experiment, discovers three intelligent species: the telepathic, highly intellectual creatures of the title; the reptilian Killers; and the giant, scientific Dwellers. The story describes how the narrator tries to aid the hermaphroditic Amphibians, who are not aggressive by nature. Even though he helps them, the narrator realizes that he repulses the Amphibians—precisely because he has so much in common with the violent Killers. As with Gulliver's encounters with the Houyhnhnms in Jonathan Swift's *Gulliver's Travels* (1726) and as with much science fiction, human pride is taken down a few steps by means of contact with a morally superior race.

Wright also critiques other aspects of humanity indirectly. For instance, the huge, literally thick-skinned Dwellers, with their cold devotion to science, are obviously a metaphor for the modern scientific worldview that Wright so detested and feared. Moreover, as is shown in the expanded material on the Dwellers in *The World Below* (1929), their dominance over this future world is no indication of their superiority, as they are slowly becoming extinct.

Wright's financial and critical breakthrough as a writer came in 1927–1928 with the publication of *Deluge,* a science-fiction work about a great flood in modern times. The novel had been rejected by publishers in 1920, but Wright published it himself seven years later through his own newly formed publishing house, Fowler Wright Ltd. (One of his sons later took over the company and focused its energies on religious books.) *Deluge* became one of the largest successes for any self-published book when the New York firm Cosmopolitan bought the American rights and it became a best-seller in the United States in 1928. Its sales and acclaim finally launched Wright, at age fifty-three, on a full-time career as a writer, although he did not retire from his accounting job until 1933. That same year, a somewhat melodramatic movie adaptation, also called *Deluge,* was released. As in some later Wells adaptations, the action is transferred to the United States. In particular, many viewers have been impressed by the special-effects scenes showing the destruction of New York City in a massive tidal wave—some six and a half decades before a similar scene in the comet-catastrophe movie *Deep Impact* (1998).

The disaster novel has long been a mainstay in British speculative fiction, and in this case the disaster is an immense flood, caused by abrupt geological transformations, that overtakes a substantial portion of England and most of the world. The biblical story of Noah is an obvious parallel, but there are significant differences. First, the story in Genesis glosses over the many deaths caused by the Flood, while *Deluge* realistically relates how most of England drowns, often person by person. While Wright addresses social issues in the novel, he treats many of the characters as individuals.

Nor are those who survive blessed with a miraculous salvation; their survival is difficult and uncertain. The narrative focuses upon three survivors in particular, one man and two women. Martin Webster, separated from his wife and children in a storm, manages to survive. Believing his family to be dead, he becomes involved with another survivor, a woman whom he "marries" even though the institutions of society have been destroyed and the world has been returned to a primal state. They are among a handful of survivors in a part of England now cut off by water from the rest of the world. Readers might expect Webster to give up one of his wives when his first wife turns up alive–but Webster is such a natural leader that the community of survivors makes an exception to traditional social norms in his case. Under his leadership, they then proceed to establish a new society.

Reviewers of the time noted the key elements of the book: its detailed, realistic treatment of its fantastic premise; its social commentary; and its entertainment value as a well-told story. One critic for *The New York Times* (4 March 1928) even called it "vastly amusing." Critics were generally less approving of Wright's treatment of broader social concerns, such as his criticism of modern industrial society; but such concerns are integrally related to the major themes of *Deluge*. The flood kills thousands of people, but in some ways it serves a function similar to the biblical Flood–the destruction of a corrupt society to provide for the possibility of a better one. In this way the focus on the three survivors becomes central to the novel. Their efforts to remake their world offer at least a glimmer of hope for better things. Nor, argues Stableford, does the threesome represent, as some contemporary critics claimed, "a shocking victory of immorality" but rather a statement on Wright's part about the significance of the social contract: "Martin's acceptance of his two wives is not a manifestation of sexual greed but a recognition of the vital necessity of honouring contracts which he had made in good faith."

Following the success of *Deluge,* Wright rapidly began producing more works in a science-fiction or fantasy vein, and his new status allowed him to publish his next novel, *The Island of Captain Sparrow* (1928), with the established London firm Gollancz. *The Island of Captain Sparrow,* like its predecessors, draws on more than one source for inspiration. Like some of the best-known works of writers such as Sir Arthur Conan Doyle and H. Rider Haggard, it involves a story about a lost race of human-like beings; like

Wells's *The Island of Doctor Moreau* (1896), it includes the protagonist's discovery of an island of creatures that are half human, half beast. Again, however, the approach is distinctly Wright's own.

There is nothing in Wright's book similar to the moral questions posed by Moreau and his dreadful efforts at playing God. Instead, Wright's novel is a briskly paced adventure, the crux of which involves protagonist Charlton Foyle's rescue of a young woman, Marcelle, who has been stranded on the island for two years. Still, Wright was incapable of simply churning out a straightforward tale of adventure (although the island also includes an Atlantean race and mutated pirates). For instance, the fact that one group of creatures on the island are part human and part satyr is surely a comment on mixed human nature, echoed to a lesser extent in the young woman's French-English ancestry. Likewise, the man and woman who find love on a deserted island that includes a garden evoke parallels to the Garden of Eden–except that this garden is tended by giant birds.

Once more, Wright in *The Island of Captain Sparrow* critiques modern "civilization" by contrasting it with a world far removed from what he considered its corrupting influences. While the island on which Foyle is shipwrecked is no paradise, Wright presents it as certainly preferable to the outside world. Thus, readers are not surprised when, rather than removing Marcelle from the island, Foyle stays with her there.

The Island of Captain Sparrow, like *Deluge,* received generally good reviews, which are also of interest for what they reveal about how such novels were taken at the time. Some reviewers, for instance, praised it simply as an exciting adventure; others had mixed feelings about its use of fantasy elements; and some said the book was well written. The fact that the book was reviewed at all is noteworthy, in contrast to the indifference shown by the mainstream American press to most works of fantasy or science fiction for much of the twentieth century. These reviews reinforce Stableford's claim that British writers of speculative fiction in the first half of the twentieth century were not marginalized in the same fashion as their American counterparts, and that their work typically resided in the middlebrow stratum of literary effort.

Dawn, Wright's sequel to *Deluge,* was published in 1929. In plot, however, it is less a sequel than a companion, as much of the action parallels the story in *Deluge.* In addition, the part of the novel set beyond the ending of the first book is extremely similar in the crisis it presents. *Dawn* was less critically successful than its predecessor, in large part because there is less action and more philosophical discussion on the part of the characters. For instance, the main conflict of the novel,

Martin Webster's efforts to navigate between economic and social interests, is depicted mainly as a clash of ideas via personalities. However, some critics admired how Wright used fiction in exploring particular themes.

The World Below, a sequel to *The Amphibians,* was also published in 1929, in one volume with *The Amphibians.* However, it is also less a sequel than a blending of its predecessor with other material, possibly written earlier, related to the story and the world in which it is set. The additional material focuses more on the subterranean Dwellers, who occupied an important though not central role in *The Amphibians.* This material, however, is less fully developed than the first part of the narrative about the Amphibians.

In the following year Wright published two novels that foreshadowed the direction for much of his later work: *The King Against Anne Bickerton* (1930), his first foray into another genre, mystery fiction, which occupied a considerable portion of his creative energies for most of his literary career; and *Elfwin* (1930), an historical novel. Nonetheless, he continued writing works of fantasy or science fiction, although these were outnumbered by his crime fiction and historical novels. Most of the crime novels were published under the pseudonym Sydney Fowler, and most are considered second-rate by critics.

Occasionally Wright combined his crime stories with his interest in science fiction. The first such example is *The Bell Street Murders* (1931), which involves a fantastic invention that allows a screen to record its surroundings, a replay of which can be recalled under certain circumstances. This screen records the murder of its inventor, and the plot then is dominated by the mystery element. The science-fiction or fantasy element is missing from the two sequels, *The Secret of the Screen* (1933) and *Who Murdered Reynard?* (1947).

Wright's next fantastic novel, *Dream; or, The Simian Maid* (1931), is the first in another planned trilogy, completed by *Vengeance of Gwa* (1935) and, finally, *Spiders' War* (1954). The protagonist of *Dream,* Marguerite Leinster, travels into the past via dreams in an effort to cure her depression. After visiting various sites of antiquity and legend, she is sent by her experimental psychologist to prehistoric times, where she assumes a human-like primate form. Nor is she the only visitor from the future at this point, as she is followed by a man who wants to marry her, Stephen Cranleigh, and his sister. They take form in this prehistoric past as cave dwellers. Complicating matters further is a third primate race, the Ogpurs, who may be the forebears of humanity–a notion in keeping with Wright's earlier depictions of human savagery. The three main characters experience assorted adventures, culminating in a conflict with giant rats. Clearly,

Wright did not limit himself to known facts or commonly accepted theories of prehuman life, but accuracy was less his objective than the ideas his fictional worlds allowed him to examine.

In 1932 Wright published a collection of stories, *The New Gods Lead.* The new gods, he suggested, were science and technology, and the best stories in the volume, Stableford suggests, "constitute what is perhaps the most vitriolic vision of the future ever produced; they have an imaginative savagery of tone and content that is quite unparalleled." Many people unfamiliar with the genre assume that science-fiction writers are uniformly unabashed enthusiasts for science and technology, but in fact many writers of science fiction are among the harshest critics. Wright falls into this camp, and *The New Gods Lead* includes many stories critical of the dehumanizing effects of "progress."

For example, "Justice" is set in a future in which birth control has substantially reduced the size of younger generations, and the consequently large numbers of elderly people become subject to legally sanctioned murder. In "Automata," a sequence of vignettes shows machines taking over not only human tasks but also sometimes human beings themselves, as in a scene in which two women discuss their mechanical children. Another futuristic story, "Brain," is emblematic of several of the concerns that Wright embodied in his science fiction. Aided by superior technology, scientists take over the world, which is then ruled by a set of twenty-one self-appointed philosopher kings. While some of the scientists believe in science as a means of improving the lot of humanity, some desire knowledge for its own sake (one even wants to try switching the brains of babies and dogs to see how they fare in different bodies), and all are depicted as heartless, power-hungry men. (Apparently, in 1932 Wright could not foresee women in such roles; moreover, in much of his fiction women are shown as more closely connected to nature, freer than men from societal corruptions.) The quest for knowledge and power, as is often the case in cautionary science fiction, leads to the scientists' destruction, aided by their own Machiavellian manipulations.

These three stories are grouped with four others in *The New Gods Lead* under the collective heading "Where the New Gods Lead," and all constitute a type of future history. The other three stories in the book are grouped as "Also," which includes one of Wright's best-known stories, "The Rat." A country doctor discovers a serum that will grant immortality, as he proves by testing it on an old rat. He considers using it on humans but feels that to do so he would have to give immortality to everyone, good and bad alike. Moreover, as he contemplates the prospect of immortality he

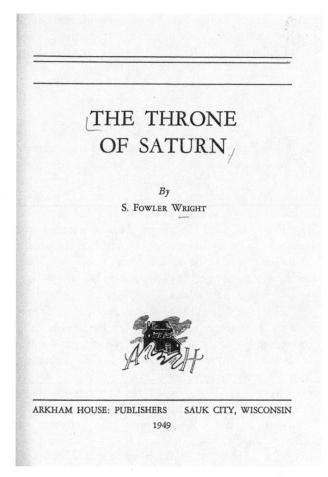

THE THRONE
OF SATURN

By

S. Fowler Wright

ARKHAM HOUSE: PUBLISHERS   SAUK CITY, WISCONSIN
1949

Title page for a collection of Wright's short fiction that includes the stories from The New Gods Lead *and other pieces (Thomas Cooper Library, University of South Carolina)*

comes to believe that it might not be such a good thing after all.

Thematically "The Rat," first published in the March 1929 issue of the renowned American horror pulp magazine *Weird Tales,* is related to another story in the "Also" section of *The New Gods Lead,* "Choice." After many trials and tribulations, a man and a woman are reunited in heaven. They find paradise too dull, however, and ask God to be returned to earth. Even though they have no guarantee that they will ever meet again if they do so, they decide that the struggles of a familiar earthly existence are preferable to the eternal peace of paradise.

Wright attempted another variation on the lost-race motif in another work published in 1932, *Beyond the Rim.* A group of Antarctic explorers comes across an isolated valley much warmer than the rest of the continent. Even more surprising is that it is inhabited—by, as they learn, the descendants of a Puritan group that tried to reach the Americas from England centuries ago. After such a long time away from the rest

of humanity, they have developed some peculiar notions about the nature of their world, which are disturbed by the sudden appearance of the explorers. The novel, though it touches on various ideas, is straightforward adventure.

Wright's next science-fiction novel was *Power* (1933). Unlike his other efforts to that point, however, *Power* was set neither in the distant past nor the far future but rather the near future—undoubtedly a concern, given the volatile political changes of the early 1930s. One man, Stanley Maitland, has the opportunity to govern Britain temporarily, giving Wright ample space to vent his social and political ideas. At the same time, Wright realistically depicts how an ordinary person might respond when thrust into a position of such great responsibility, even though the plotting of the novel is closer to popular formulas than to the novel of ideas or of character.

Wright published *Vengeance of Gwa,* the first sequel to *Dream,* in 1935 under the pseudonym Anthony Wingrave. Again a female protagonist travels into the far past and finds herself in the midst of another massive conflict between competing species. Rather than coming from the contemporary world, she is from a futuristic city, and Wright contrasts the two worlds without making either seem ideal.

Also in 1935 Wright began publishing another fantastic trilogy, set, like *Power,* in the near future. The year after his retirement from accounting in 1933 Wright traveled to Nazi Germany on a newspaper assignment. Seeing the Nazi regime as the fulfillment of many of his worst fears about the future of society, he wrote a series of highly critical reports. His experiences also inspired him to write *Prelude in Prague: A Story of the War of 1938* (1935), serialized in the *Daily Mail* as "1938"; *Four Days War* (1936); and *Megiddo's Ridge* (1937). In these works Wright speculated about what might occur over the next few years as a result of the rise of fascist power. While Wright was ultimately correct that it would lead to world war, reviewers of the time were generally unconvinced. In retrospect the prediction of war—accurately beginning with the German invasion of Czechoslovakia, continuing in *Four Days War* with a German air attack on Britain, and concluding in *Megiddo's Ridge* with America becoming involved—is the only prophetic thing about the trilogy, which has more in common with the tradition of future-war stories than with most of the actual events of World War II.

Wright's short story "Original Sin" was rejected repeatedly after he wrote it in the late 1930s; it was finally placed in his collection *The Witchfinder* (1946), which, despite the title, includes only one other work of fantastic fiction. Nonetheless, the story provided the basis for his novel *The Adventure of Wyndham Smith* (1938), about a future society that, despite its utopian life of leisure, has come to adhere to a belief called the Doctrine of Futility. As in "Choice," a life of troubles and conflict is depicted as preferable to a seemingly perfect yet static existence. In the novel humanity chooses mass suicide, although a man and a woman attempt to preserve the human race and create a new, and hopefully better, society. The novel goes beyond the story in detailing the nature of the future society and the couple's struggles for survival in an already hostile world made more dangerous by the menacing machines left behind by the rest of the human race.

In the years before and during World War II, Wright devoted his efforts mostly toward mystery fiction rather than science fiction or fantasy, and, as always, he wrote quickly and prolifically. Neither his reputation nor the quality of his work benefited from this speed, and he never regained the level of popularity or critical acclaim that he enjoyed in the late 1920s. While he kept trying different types of writing, he did not abandon fantastic fiction, as is attested by the publication in 1945 of *The Adventure of the Blue Room,* the second of his crime novels that borders on the scientific romance. It is essentially a thriller with a futuristic setting.

In 1947, when he was in his early seventies, Wright became editor of a magazine called *Books of Today.* His position allowed him to circumvent his difficulties in finding a publisher for some of his books by publishing through its book division. This position, however, was short-lived.

In 1949 the well-known American fantasy publisher Arkham House published Wright's collection *The Throne of Saturn,* which includes all of the material from *The New Gods Lead,* as well as other short works. This collection—along with the inclusion of his story "Brain" in the landmark Modern Library anthology *Famous Science-Fiction Stories: Adventures in Time and Space* (1946), edited by Raymond J. Healy and J. Francis McComus, and the republication of other works in such venues as the *Avon Fantasy Reader* and the reprint pulp magazine *Famous Fantastic Mysteries*—helped to bring Wright's work to the attention of American readers of science fiction and fantasy.

Wright's last novel, the final installment of the trilogy begun with *Dream* in 1931 and continuing with *Vengeance of Gwa* in 1935, appeared in 1954, when he was eighty years old. Like the first volume, *Spiders' War* concerns the struggles of humanoid beings against fearsome creatures, in this case monstrous spiders. Unlike the other two books in the trilogy, however, this novel is set in the future—although in its level of civilization this future is not all that different from the past depicted in the other novels. Like the others, *Spiders' War* also serves as a forum for discussions about what civilization actually might mean.

In the last ten years of his life Wright, often living with his children and carrying his manuscripts around with him, continued to write; but his publishing days were all but over by the mid 1950s. He left many unpublished works that may yet appear as historians return to his work. One of his last published stories, "The Better Choice" (1955), is about a scientist who changes his wife into a cat, only to find that she prefers a feline existence to being a scientist's wife and abandons him—a two-page encapsulation, in other words, of a few of Wright's pet ideas.

Although Wright's literary career did not really begin until his forties and he did not begin publishing fiction until his fifties, he produced dozens of noteworthy stories and novels in the half of his life remaining. He may have written too quickly, hurting the quality of his work as a result—and he was never much of a stylist, even at his best. His death on 25 February 1965 was unnoticed in the national press. Nevertheless, as Anthony Boucher put it in a review of *The Throne of Saturn* for the 3 February 1950 *Chicago Sun,* Wright's work in the fantastic constitutes a "deft and delightful assortment of previews, often chilling in their implications, of the aseptic and rational world of tomorrow."

References:

E. F. Bleiler, "S. Fowler Wright," in *Science Fiction Writers: Critical Studies of the Major Authors from the Early Nineteenth Century to the Present Day,* edited by Bleiler (New York: Scribners, 1982), pp. 83–89;

Sam Moskowitz, "Birth Control: Better the World Below Than the World Above," in his *Strange Horizons: The Spectrum of Science Fiction* (New York: Scribners, 1976), pp. 92–106;

Brian Stableford, "Against the New Gods: The Speculative Fiction of S. Fowler Wright," *Foundation,* 29 (November 1983): 10–52;

Stableford, *Scientific Romance in Britain, 1890–1950* (London: Fourth Estate; 1985; New York: St. Martin's Press, 1985);

Mary S. Weinkauf, *Sermons in Science Fiction: The Novels of S. Fowler Wright* (San Bernardino, Cal.: Borgo, 1994).

John Wyndham
(John Wyndham Parkes Lucas Beynon Harris)
(10 July 1903 – 10 March 1969)

Robert Carrick

BOOKS: *The Secret People,* as John Beynon (London: Newnes, 1935); as John Beynon Harris (New York: Lancer, 1964);

Foul Play Suspected, as Beynon (London: Newnes, 1935);

Planet Plane, as Beynon (London: Newnes, 1936); abridged as *Stowaway to Mars,* as Beynon (London: Nova, 1953); restored and republished as *Stowaway to Mars,* as by Wyndham writing as Beynon (Greenwich, Conn.: Fawcett, 1972; London: Coronet, 1972);

The Day of the Triffids (Garden City, N.Y.: Doubleday, 1951; London: Joseph, 1951);

The Kraken Wakes (London: Joseph, 1953); republished as *Out of the Deeps* (New York: Ballantine, 1953);

Jizzle (London: Dobson, 1954);

Re-Birth (New York: Ballantine, 1955); republished as *The Chrysalids* (London: Joseph, 1955);

The Seeds of Time (London: Joseph, 1956);

Tales of Gooseflesh and Laughter (New York: Ballantine, 1956);

The Midwich Cuckoos (London: Joseph, 1957; New York: Ballantine, 1958);

The Outward Urge, as by Wyndham and Lucas Parkes (London: Joseph, 1959; New York: Ballantine, 1959);

Trouble with Lichen (London: Joseph, 1960; New York: Ballantine, 1960);

Consider Her Ways and Others (London: Joseph, 1961);

The Infinite Moment (New York: Ballantine, 1961);

The John Wyndham Omnibus (London: Joseph, 1964; New York: Simon & Schuster, 1966)—comprises *The Day of the Triffids, The Kraken Wakes,* and *The Chrysalids;*

Chocky (New York: Ballantine, 1968; London: Joseph, 1968);

Sleepers of Mars, as by Wyndham writing as Harris (London: Coronet, 1973);

Wanderers of Time, as by Wyndham writing as Harris (London: Coronet, 1973);

John Wyndham

Exiles on Asperus, as by Wyndham writing as Beynon (London: Coronet, 1979);

Web (London: Joseph, 1979).

Collections: *The Best of John Wyndham,* edited by Angus Wells (London: Sphere, 1973);

John Wyndham (London: Heinemann/Octopus, 1980)—comprises *The Day of the Triffids, The Kraken Wakes, The Chrysalids, The Seeds of Time, Trouble with Lichen,* and *The Midwich Cuckoos.*

PRODUCED SCRIPTS: "Dumb Martian," television, *Out of This World,* ITV, 24 June 1962;

"No Place Like Earth," by Wyndham and Stanley Miller, television, *Out of the Unknown,* BBC, 1965.

OTHER: "The Cathedral Crypt," as John Beynon Harris, in *Marvel Tales* (1935); republished in *The Unspeakable People,* edited by Peter Haining (London: Everest Books, 1975), pp. 118–124;

"Never on Mars," in *Fantastic Universe* (January 1954): 62–80; republished in *Gateway to the Stars,* edited by John Carnell (London: Museum Press, 1955);

"Consider Her Ways," in *Sometime, Never: Three Tales of Imagination,* by Wyndham, William Golding, and Mervyn Peake (London: Eyre & Spottiswoode, 1956; New York: Ballantine, 1957);

"Wise Child," as "It's a Wise Child," in *Argosy* (November 1962); republished in *Playboy's Stories of the Sinister and Strange* (Chicago: Playboy Press, 1969), pp. 120–136;

"Exiles on Asperus," in *Three Stories,* by Wyndham, Murray Leinster, and Jack Williamson, edited by Sam Moskowitz (Garden City, N.Y.: Doubleday, 1967); volume republished as *A Sense of Wonder: Three Science Fiction Stories* (London: Sidgwick & Jackson, 1967);

Out of the Deeps, in *Alfred Hitchcock Presents Stories That Scared Even Me* (New York: Random House, 1967), pp. 309–463.

SELECTED PERIODICAL PUBLICATIONS–UNCOLLECTED: "Beyond the Screen," as John Beynon, *Fantasy* (August 1938); republished as "Judson's Annihilator," as Beynon, *Fantastic* (March 1967): 57–99;

"In Outer Space There Shone a Star," *T.V. Times Xmas Extra* (December 1965): 6–8, 58–59.

For most of the 1950s and into the early 1960s, John Wyndham was one of the most widely read English writers of speculative fiction. His books were reviewed not only by the science-fiction publications of the time but by such periodicals as *Kirkus Reviews, The New Statesman, The New York Times, Library Journal, The Times Literary Supplement (TLS),* and *The New York Herald Tribune Book Review.* Two of his novels were made into well-received feature-length movies, two others into BBC radio plays, and two of his shorter pieces into episodes of television series. More than twenty-five years after his death, new editions or reprints of his novels and short-fiction collections still appeared regularly. Certain of his works were still to be found on the recommended reading lists or syllabi of many British schools. The message repeated in his most important books—that humanity's continued viability as a species is a never-ending and arduous struggle demanding

adaptation and evolution—continues to be presented to new generations of Wyndham readers. It is impossible to say how many speculative-fiction writers have been influenced by Wyndham, but certainly J. G. Ballard and John Christopher are among them.

John Wyndham Parkes Lucas Beynon Harris—he used all of these names in various combinations on his novels and short fiction—was born in Knowle, Warwickshire, on 10 July 1903. He was the first of two children of George Beynon Harris, a barrister of Welsh descent, and Gertrude Parkes Harris, daughter of a Birmingham ironmaster. His brother, Vivian, born two and a half years later, became a true friend and companion during a somewhat unsettled and peripatetic childhood.

His parents separated when Wyndham was eight, and his mother, for whatever reasons, changed residences frequently, with the result that Wyndham attended several grammar schools. He did, however, manage to spend the last three years of his formal education, from 1918 to 1921, at Bedales School, a progressive coeducational public school in Hampshire. His intention to follow his father in the study and practice of law was frustrated when he failed the entrance examination for Oxford University.

Neither Wyndham nor anyone else recorded much about his private life, but it is generally known that after leaving school he became an apprentice farmer and was later involved in advertising and commercial art. In *Seekers of Tomorrow: Masters of Modern Science Fiction* (1966) Sam Moskowitz says that Wyndham's work in advertising "helped develop some of his writing skills," which suggests he was a copywriter.

Wyndham became a professional writer at age twenty-eight. His first sale, to Hugo Gernsback's *Wonder Stories,* was "Worlds to Barter" (1931), a time-travel novelette remarkable for several things, one of which was not, however, the high quality of the writing. The most notable thing about this story was that something in it captured the interest of either Gernsback or his managing editor at *Wonder Stories,* David Lasser. For the next three and a half years Wyndham sold all of his output, except for one story, to *Wonder Stories* under the name John Beynon Harris. The one exception was sold to *Amazing Stories,* also founded by Gernsback. The quality of these stories was not high, and without the support of these magazines Wyndham was a doubtful starter in the tenuous science-fiction market.

Although "Worlds to Barter" puts a severe strain upon the willing suspension of disbelief, two important indicators of Wyndham's future work emerge. The first is a Wellsian bent; not only is the title character of H. G. Wells's novel *When the Sleeper Wakes* (1899) mentioned in the text, but Wyndham's time-travel apparatus also

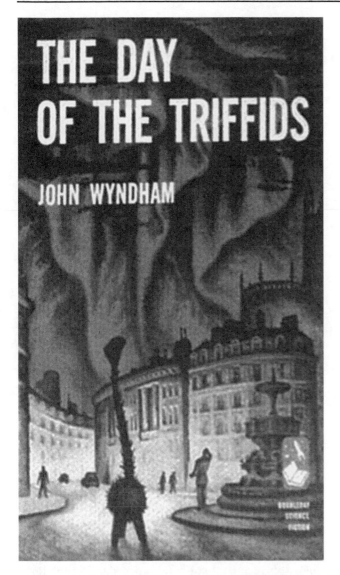
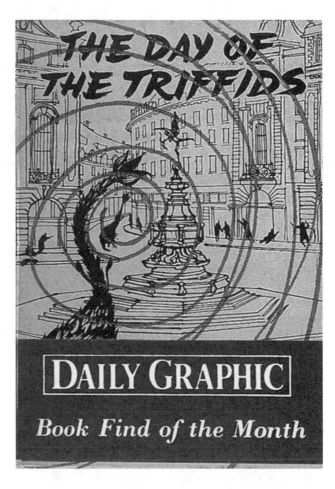

Dust jackets for the U.S. and British editions of Wyndham's 1951 novel about giant carnivorous plants and worldwide blindness
*(*Modern First Editions *auction catalogue/* Between the Covers *auction catalogue)*

bears a close resemblance to the one employed by Wells in *The Time Machine* (1895). Most critics familiar with the work of the two writers have noted Wyndham's indebtedness to Wells. The second hint of Wyndham's work to come is the theme of humanity poised on the brink of destruction. This theme plays a part in many of the writer's most important works.

The final noteworthy aspect of Wyndham's first published story is that it includes what appears to be the kernel of Isaac Asimov's well-known story "Nightfall" (1941) ten years before Asimov wrote it. To anyone familiar with the Asimov piece, about the panic created on a planet with more than one sun when darkness falls every two thousand years, these lines from the Wyndham story will seem eerily familiar: "it was the darkness which caused the panic. Across the world, in

the sunlight, they cannot have had that catastrophic madness in which crowds rushed, milled and swirled without reason, without object."

The ten stories Wyndham sold in this first period of his writing career are of little interest to modern readers. They range from inept to pedestrian space operettas, time-travel adventures, and eve-of-destruction pieces. Five are interplanetary stories, three with Martian settings and two with Venusian. Mostly because of Wyndham's ignorance, at that time, of the basic physics, mechanics, and mathematics of space travel, these are among the worst of this initial group of stories. Wyndham's interplanetary vessels are like Cunard ocean liners in space: they have plenty of room and no gravity problems and are capable of horizontal landings with no need for wheels.

A perusal of early pulp magazines, however, will unearth stories that are worse—even much worse. But nowhere in these early Wyndham narratives is there a hint of the skill he later displayed in "Jizzle" (1949), "And the Walls Came Tumbling Down . . . " (1951), "Perfect Creature/Una" (1953), or other short pieces Wyndham eventually wrote.

Individually, there are noteworthy aspects to some of the stories. His second sale, "The Lost Machine" (1932), an unconvincing sentient robot story, was the basis for his second science-fiction novel, *Planet Plane* (1936), originally serialized in *Passing Show* in 1936 under the better-known title *Stowaway to Mars*. "The Lost Machine," while not wonderful, was good enough to consolidate his position as an adequate producer of juvenile science fiction and popular enough to warrant a reprint in less than two years. His sixth published piece, the novelette "Spheres of Hell" (1933), showed considerable all-around improvement—though there are some flaws in the logic of the characters' actions—but more important, it includes the basic plot idea of *Revolt of the Triffids* (later, much better known as *The Day of the Triffids*), his huge breakthrough novel, not written until eighteen years later (1951).

In all of these early pieces for *Wonder Stories* Wyndham had problems with credibility; too many of his stories asked the reader to accept the unbelievable—and that included readers usually willing to suspend disbelief in almost any situation. In his next story, however, "The Cathedral Crypt" (1935), published in *Marvel Tales* just six months after his final *Wonder Stories* piece appeared, Wyndham achieved a chilling realism. It is his first horror story, a short piece (around 2,300 words) recounting the simple plot of a British tourist couple witnessing a religious ritual murder in Spain and then being themselves murdered to maintain the secrecy of the event. Well-known British anthologist Peter Haining, who reprinted the story in *The Unspeakable People* (1975), commented in a foreword to the story, "I still remember the chill it sent up my spine . . . I can still experience the gnawing effect of John Wyndham's sparse, dramatic prose."

Wyndham's first novel, serialized in the British weekly magazine *Passing Show* from 20 July to 14 September 1935 and published in a hardback edition almost immediately thereafter by George Newnes, was *The Secret People*. This adventure fantasy was based upon an idea being bruited about at the time, primarily in popular-science magazines and newspaper columns: the flooding of desert areas to restore fertility to the soil. *Passing Show* was a general-interest family magazine, but *The Secret People* can only be considered as a novel for juvenile readers. As such, it has held up remarkably well, with ten editions or reprints through 1987. One of

the principal characters brings up some controversial theories related to the evolution of humanity in general and to that of the subterranean-dwelling villains of the book in particular. This material may be considered to presage a principal Wyndham theme in most of his later, more important novels: the existence and inevitability of social Darwinism. This book was published under the name John Beynon. The John Beynon pen name was also used on a detective novel, *Foul Play Suspected,* also published by Newnes in 1935, which appears to have vanished without trace or critical comment.

Wyndham continued to write in the longer form by next expanding his 1932 story "The Lost Machine" to a novel. The history of this book is rather confusing, as it was published by three separate publishers with three different titles and with substantive differences in one of the magazine versions. *Passing Show* serialized the novel as *Stowaway to Mars* in eight episodes from 2 May to 20 June 1936. George Newnes published it as a hardback immediately thereafter as *Planet Plane* by John Beynon. *Modern Wonder,* basically a boys' magazine, published it as *The Space Machine* (as by John Beynon) in ten episodes from 22 May to 24 July 1937 but insisted on drastic revisions by Wyndham to eliminate a female character (who became impregnated by a Martian without benefit of clergy—bold stuff for 1930s England) and thematic philosophizing. Readers should also be aware that in subsequent book editions the title and authorship were changed to *Stowaway to Mars* by John Wyndham. According to Phil Stephensen-Payne's bibliography of Wyndham's complete works, *John Wyndham: Creator of the Cosy Catastrophe* (1989), the 1953 Nova SF Novels edition should be avoided, as it is a clumsy abridgment by a hand other than Wyndham's, but "The later editions of *Stowaway to Mars* (in the 1970's) use the original George Newnes text."

Except for the unwed mother, *Stowaway to Mars* is rather routine juvenile space opera and in no way comparable to Wyndham's later and better-known novels. To begin with, this novel is based on the novelette that was only Wyndham's second sale, the work of an inexperienced writer. Given that fact, it is not surprising that the sentient-robot element of the plot is no more credible in the novel than it was in "The Lost Machine." Wyndham's main theme, developed through conversations among his principal characters, is a warning-cum-prediction that humanity on Earth faces potential problems with the machinery it has produced, which could result in the disappearance of the former and the evolution of the latter. In the book, that is precisely what is happening on Mars at the time. Vaygan, a Martian, says in a long speech of warning to his Terran lover, "Man's rise and his survival depend on his adaptability." Even early in his career and in a minor work, Wyndham expressed his commitment to the theory that humanity must strive for—indeed, must insist upon—adaptability. Wyndham's recurrent message was that the human species must not only accept Charles Darwin's theories of evolution and the survival of the fittest but also must realize that without vigilance and adaptability, the fittest will not necessarily be human.

Wyndham's apparent easy acquiescence to editorial requests for alterations of previously published material can lead to confusion for readers and scholars. In addition to those in *Stowaway to Mars,* textual variations are to be found in some of the editions of *The Secret People, Revolt of the Triffids/The Day of the Triffids, The Kraken Wakes/Out of the Deeps* (1953), *Re-Birth/The Chrysalids* (1955), *The Midwich Cuckoos/Village of the Damned* (1957), and *Trouble with Lichen* (1960). Most of the variations—not all of them made or agreed to by Wyndham—such as the title changes, occurred when the American version of the British book was published and, occasionally, vice versa. Apart from minor changes in spelling (such as "colour" to "color") or words (such as "lift" to "elevator"), this revision happened less frequently to Wyndham's shorter pieces, although "The Perfect Creature" (title later changed to "Una," by which it is probably best known) is a notable exception.

Stowaway to Mars was Wyndham's sole literary production for 1936, and after its publication his output began to decline. After having three novels published in little more than a year, he published one short story in 1937, a novella and a short story in 1938, three novelettes in 1939, one short story in 1940, and another in 1941; then nothing until 1946. Surely World War II was largely responsible for the declining number of Wyndham's publications in the early 1940s.

"The Perfect Creature," the 1937 short story, is important for bringing together Wyndham and a man who claims to have had a vital impact on his career. The story appeared in the first issue of *Tales of Wonder,* "the first adult UK sf magazine" according to Peter Nicholls in *The Encyclopedia of Science Fiction* (1993). The editor of the relatively short-lived *Tales of Wonder* (sixteen issues) was Walter Gillings, who became one of Wyndham's most enthusiastic eulogizers after the writer's death, writing several fanzine articles praising Wyndham's work and introductions to many of the Coronet paperback editions of Wyndham novels. Most important, in the eighth issue of the British fanzine *Cypher* (September 1972) Gillings also claimed to have been Wyndham's literary agent when the writer produced *Revolt of the Triffids,* at which time Wyndham "entrusted the manuscript to me expressing some doubt

Janette Scott and Kieron Moore in a scene from the 1962 movie version of The Day of the Triffids *(Security Pictures Inc.)*

if it would prove successful." Gillings is clearly implying that he was responsible for the sale and publication of the novel that gave readers the essential John Wyndham. However, this account is contradicted by Sir Robert Lusty, Wyndham's publisher, in his memoir *Bound to Be Read* (1975). "The Perfect Creature," a take on Mary Shelley's *Frankenstein* (1818), was unremarkable and was never reprinted. However, the basic plot idea seems to have stuck with Wyndham, because more than fifteen years later he redid it as "Perfect Creature" (later retitled "Una").

The only positive aspect to Wyndham's decline in productivity was that the stories were getting better. The last two to be written before the author went off to serve in World War II were harbingers of possible things to come.

"Vengeance by Proxy" appeared in *Strange Stories* under the name John Beynon in February 1940. It was only his second attempt at pure horror fiction, but he makes it work despite having to convince readers of the possibility of the basically implausible transference of personality from one human body to another. He does so first by setting the scene in the rural Balkans—Transylvania will immediately come to many minds—and then by introducing gypsy vendettas, hex marks, and the evil eye. Obviously, anything could happen, in the purview of devotees of the occult. In this story he does effectively what he often fails to do in his space stories: make the incredible credible. Like Wells, whose work he so much admired, he sometimes, and inexplicably, goes too far and adds that final straw that renders the tale impossible to believe. Readers will believe in a state of suspended animation, but not one that lasts millions of years. They will believe in robots from Mars, but not ones that commit suicide because they are depressed. In this story, however, disbelief is suspended because the reader has been carefully set up to suspend it. Wyndham wrote only one other straight horror piece, much later, the substandard "Close Behind Him" (1953).

Amazing Stories published the last Wyndham story to appear before the five-year wartime hiatus, "Phoney Meteor" (better known as "Meteor," since most of its reprints were under the latter title), as by John Beynon. This story is remarkable in more ways than one. Of foremost importance is the style, much more relaxed than in his previous stories. "Meteor" is perhaps the pivotal Wyndham story, as it shows that he was capable of creating more sympathetic characters, alien as well as human, than the usually stiff and unrealistic ones of his heroic adventures. After the unexpected event–the arrival of the "meteor"–the story moves forward with increasing drama and complexity, with excerpts from the journal of one of the aliens alternating with actions of the humans. At last one sees the polish of Wyndham's novels to come and such short pieces as "Jizzle," "Technical Slip" (1949), "Operation Peep" (1951; also known as "Pawley's Peepholes"), and "Esmerelda" (1954). "Meteor" is also an important story because it clearly inspired what is possibly the best of Wyndham's short pieces, "And the Walls Came Tumbling Down . . . ," ten years later. In terms of editors' interest, "Meteor" was one of Wyndham's most popular pieces, sharing with "Pawley's Peepholes" the Wyndham short-fiction record of nine reprints.

During the early part of World War II, Wyndham worked as a censor in the British civil service, then served in the Royal Signal Corps and took part in the Normandy invasion. In *Seekers of Tomorrow* Moskowitz quotes Wyndham as saying, "I took to writing sonnets because you can't carry a lot of paper on a campaign," but if any of these survived, they never found their way into print.

Released from the army in 1946, Wyndham, writing as John Beynon, sold one story that year, "The Living Lies," published in *New Worlds*. Apart from an admirable statement on the iniquity of color prejudice, the story, set on a Venus where the Terran-descended Venusians stroll about as unencumbered as if they were on Earth, is absurd.

In *Seekers of Tomorrow* Moskowitz alleges that while in military service Wyndham made the decision to write nothing but fantasy when he returned to civilian life and gave himself two years to become established in that field. What happened, according to Moskowitz, was that "the rejection slips mounted uninterruptedly" during those two years. Whatever the reason, it is a fact that Wyndham did not sell a single piece of fiction in 1947 or in 1948.

Still writing as John Beynon, he returned with one of his most artful stories, "Jizzle," which was published by the American family magazine *Collier's* in January 1949. The title character, whose name is a corruption of the French name Giselle, is a talented and wicked little monkey with a demonic disposition and a jealous streak. Jizzle, acquired by the narrator from a sailor during a drinking session, is an accomplished artist. She destroys the narrator's marriage, then the man himself, through innuendo in her drawings. The story proceeds logically from scene to scene, with nothing needful missing, with no extraneous material crammed in, and with a masterful surprise ending. It was revised for *Fantasy and Science Fiction* (February 1952). Wyndham's second, and much more illustrious, career can be said to have begun with this short story.

Wyndham sold only four more stories in 1949 and 1950, with mixed results. A Mars story, "Adaptation" (1949), was unbelievable, and a Venus story, "The Eternal Eve" (1950), was both unbelievable and poorly written. However, the other Mars story, "Time to Rest" (1949), was the first of his planetary stories that could be called a sensitive piece. The remaining story, "Technical Slip," was an above-average deal-with-the-devil piece with a dash of time travel thrown in.

The year 1951 began more auspiciously than any other in Wyndham's career to that point. In five episodes, beginning on 6 January and finishing on 3 February, *Collier's* serialized his novel *Revolt of the Triffids*. It was a huge, instant, and enduring success. Almost immediately Doubleday published a hardback edition in the United States, and in August of the same year Michael Joseph brought out a hardback edition in England. In both of these editions, and in most subsequent ones, the title is given as *The Day of the Triffids*. It has probably been Wyndham's most popular book, with many editions and reprints; the Stephensen-Payne bibliography lists seventy-eight, including more than forty Penguin paperback editions or reprints alone. The book was also probably the most widely reviewed Wyndham novel in book-review periodicals, library journals, and newspapers as well as in science-fiction publications. It was dramatized as a BBC radio play in 1957 and made into a well-received movie in 1963.

The story line follows a double disaster: first, the proliferation of triffids, dangerous plants raised for their oil; second, the simultaneous loss of sight afflicting most of the residents of Great Britain—and, the reader is informed, much of the rest of humanity. The triffids, seven to ten feet tall at maturity, are mobile, carnivorous, and armed with whip-like stingers capable of injecting a poison lethal to people. In the British version of the book the triffids were developed in Russia; hence, this disaster is man-made. In the *Collier's* version the origin of the plants was given as Venus, but it is clear that Wyndham intended for humanity to take the blame, and since he was a well-known Russia-basher, it was logical that he point to that country. The blindness is attributed to the near-universal observation of a mysterious meteor display, but near the end of the book the decent, middle-class protagonist (typical in Wyndham novels to come), William Masen, expresses his suspicion that the mass blindings were caused by the accidental firing of one of the many satellite weapons—some of them bacterial—put into orbit by the Eastern and Western superpowers. Therefore, this disaster also seems to be man-made. Whether Wyndham intended it as a warning or was simply introducing an element of irony into the plot structure, this scenario was published some thirty-five years before American president Ronald Reagan and his administration advisers approved what detractors dubbed the "Star Wars" armament systems, borrowing the term from the 1977 George Lucas movie.

The narrative hook is set in the opening chapter, when Wyndham's hero, his eyes bandaged after a minor encounter with a triffid, awakens in the hospital to an uncanny silence on a working day in central London. From that point, Wyndham takes the reader on a quick, brutal tour of London, where almost everyone is blind (the bandages preserved Masen's sight). Even without the triffids, the city will soon become a charnel house. For the blind, finding a sighted person is the only hope for survival. Masen encounters a young woman, Josella Playton, who has escaped blindness by sleeping through the nocturnal display. Masen and Josella team up, ostensibly for mutual protection, but clearly also to provide romantic interest for the story.

The couple meet a sighted group whose intention is to establish a rural retreat and find a way to defeat the triffids, who have grown in numbers and become vastly more dangerous since most people became easy targets because of their blindness. Thus the principal moral issue of the book arises: what are the minority of those with sight to do about the vast majority who have lost it? To his credit, the author resists maudlinness in addressing the issue. He has his characters do what real people would almost certainly do in the same circumstances: leave the blind behind, except for a few healthy blind women of childbearing age. In what is probably the most quoted passage in the book, a minor, avuncular character advises the group that "*the race is worth preserving.* To that consideration all else will, for a time at least, be subordinate." That is Wyndham's recurrent message: adapt and survive.

The romance proceeds, but in an attack by sighted dissidents who want the blind cared for, Masen and Josella become separated, and he spends much of the rest of the novel trying to find her, getting into and out of awkward or dangerous situations. Another of the messages in the book concerns British pluck. In an unpromising situation, one of Wyndham's characters says, "The way I see it, we've been given a flying start in a new kind of world." This sentiment is expressed again in later books.

Near the end of the book, with the self-married lovers reunited and living on a farm on the Sussex Downs with their adopted family, the author compresses six years into a few pages. The reader learns that the triffids have multiplied, improved their rudimentary communications skills, and begun acting in concert, rendering them infinitely more dangerous than before. The humans, however, have persevered and have managed to keep the monsters at bay. The humans have been communicating also, and one group has managed to clear the Isle of Wight of triffids and is experimenting with methods of eradicating them from the mainland as well. This attitude is another Wyndham trademark: a "we will fight on the beaches" determination to overcome calamity, no matter how pervasive it may be. The family has one final adventure—outwitting a large group of neo-Nazis intent on establishing a new feudal system—before they escape to the Isle of Wight, aware of the difficulties ahead but optimistic about the future.

For the most part, Wyndham tells his story in the spare, stark terms appropriate to the dismal scenes and desperate situations he creates, but he can be effectively eloquent when the occasion calls for it, as in his description of Westminster Abbey in a nearly deserted London: "Marvellously clear-fretted in the unsmoked air, the Abbey rose, silver-grey. It stood detached by the serenity of age from the ephemeral growths around it. It was solid on a foundation of centuries, destined, perhaps, for centuries yet to preserve within it the monuments to those whose work was now all destroyed."

In his introduction to the 1969 Easton Press edition of *The Day of the Triffids* Marshall B. Tymn summarizes the impact of the work in its various presentations: "In terms of popularity, *The Day of the Triffids* stands as one of the most successful science fiction novels of the twentieth century; it helped create a broader audience for science fiction by its publication as a serial in *Collier's,* as a best-selling novel for Doubleday, and as a film in 1963." The other thing it did, rightly or wrongly, was to bestow an enduring label upon its author. In a consideration of this novel in *Billion Year Spree* (1973), Brian W. Aldiss commented that in the writing of it, Wyndham "embarked on the course that was to make him master of the cosy catastrophe."

The year continued to be a good one for Wyndham with the sale of six short pieces in addition to the novel. One of them, "And the Walls Came Tumbling Down . . . ," published in *Startling Stories* in May 1951, is built upon one of the author's most clever concepts: aliens who are composed almost entirely of silicates and, because they are in effect made of glass, are never seen by the humans who inadvertently destroy them with sound waves. As in "Meteor," the author treats his unaggressive aliens sympathetically and renders anything said or written by them in a stylized English just different enough from the language of Wyndham's time and place to make it intriguing.

The considerable humor of this piece results from the aliens' baffled examination of first a lizard, then the body of a man who is killed when his car runs into their (glass) redoubt, then his surviving female companion. After the man's body has been dissected, one of the aliens wonders, "How . . . can any form of intelligence recognizable as such be expected from a sloppy collection of innumerable tubes slung on a hardened lime framework?"

A second notable story sold in 1951, to the American multigenre magazine *Suspense* (summer issue), was "Operation Peep" (more often known, in its many reprints, as "Pawley's Peepholes," but once run in *Argosy* under the title "A New Kind of Pink Elephant"). A lighthearted piece that Wyndham (in the introduction to the Michael Joseph edition of *The Seeds of Time,* 1956) characterized as "satirical farce," this story of people popping back in time some forty-five or fifty years, on organized sightseeing tours, was one of Wyndham's most popular. The busloads of time tourists do their traveling by some sort of astral projection and soon become a severe annoyance to the locals, appearing out of walls, emerging into bedrooms, and so on. The thrust of the story then becomes how to get rid of them, a matter resolved somewhat differently, but more or less equally satisfactorily, in the American and British versions of the story. An editorial blurb in *Suspense* said,

> Unlike so many writers who approach the future with a stiff neck and deadly seriousness, John Wyndham allows a bit of lightness, even fun, to leaven his tales, writing in an easy, unforced fashion which not only

grips but entertains. One result is that the general reader and the dyed-in-the-wool science aficionado equally enjoy him. Another is that he can plumb to the full the matchless potentialities of the medium for ironic comment on our own times without becoming didactic or irascible.

These observations are true of much of Wyndham's work. The version of the story published in *The Seeds of Time,* while adhering fairly closely to the original story line, is a complete rewrite. The events now take place in England rather than America and, unsurprisingly, all the American colloquialisms and usages have been changed to British. More significantly, however, there are substantive textual changes on almost every page; the manner in which the unwanted visitors are gotten rid of is different; and the story has been lengthened by several hundred words. The British text reads better after Wyndham's changes.

During this period science-fiction scholar E. F. Bleiler met Wyndham for the first time at the White Horse pub in London, well known in science-fiction circles. The pub at that time was a rather scruffy watering hole where such British science-fiction luminaries as Arthur C. Clarke, John Carnell, Edmund Cooper, and William F. Temple met every fortnight or so to discuss the state of the genre. Bleiler's nostalgic reminiscence, "Luncheon with John Wyndham" (*Extrapolation,* Winter 1984), describes the writer as "of medium height (perhaps 5'9" or so), with a long, very mobile British Celtic face something like Robert Graves." The luncheon took place a few months after their first meeting, and the article says much about Wyndham's character and personality. Bleiler recalls:

> Somehow or other we got onto traditional mainstream standards as applied to science fiction, at which time I made a gaff that embarrassed me for a long time. I lamented the fact that too many writers did not have a feeling for form, and as an example cited a story (author and title of which escaped me) that I had read a year or two earlier when I was working on one of the *Best Science Fiction* volumes. I pontificated away, telling Harris how the author could have done this and that instead of these and those, but had really botched things up. Harris listened courteously and agreed in a soft way saying that the story demonstrated "bad craftsmanship." I noted a certain diffidence in his manner, but we went on to something else. When I got back to Leiden, memories suddenly clicked. It had been a story of Harris' that I had been knocking! I would guess that it was "Technical Slip," but I am not sure.

Concluding the article, Bleiler writes, "For me Harris created the impression of a highly intelligent, cultured, tolerant, genial but rather shy man, and as such I still interpret him."

The first of the three excellent stories Wyndham wrote in 1952 was "The Wheel," a short parable of self-sacrifice published in the January issue of *Startling Stories*. Next was the serious and chilling novelette "Survival," published in *Thrilling Wonder Stories* in February, which dealt with the problem of a spaceship crew and passengers starving to death and of the classic solution to that problem. A good hard-hitting story that has been anthologized at least six times, it ventures some interesting opinions regarding the strength and ferocity of maternal instincts. The final story was the equally popular "Dumb Martian," a novelette originally published in the July issue of *Galaxy,* anthologized at least five times, and televised on 24 June 1962 as an episode of the *Out of This World* series on Independent Television (ITV). In this piece Wyndham creates memorable, complex protagonists: a kind of good-old-boy space bum who cracks under the assorted stresses of isolation, a basic inferiority complex, and cohabiting with an alien; and the Martian of the title, who turns out to be far from dumb. It is not a pretty story, involving as it does conjugal brutality, murder, and retribution, but it makes positive statements regarding the rights of minorities and women long before such issues were commonly raised in science fiction. In fact, Wyndham's mistreated female Martian character specifically questions the meaning of "female emancipation."

Originally published as a serial in the British magazine *Everybody's,* Wyndham's fifth novel appeared in 1952. In that version it was titled *The Things from the Deep.* Michael Joseph put out a hardback edition in England in July 1953, changing the title to *The Kraken Wakes,* and in November of the same year Ballantine published it as *Out of the Deeps,* also in hardback. This midcareer novel, written during a productive decade both for science fiction and for Wyndham, was and remains another popular seller (at least fifty editions or printings).

The influence of Wells, and of *The War of the Worlds* (1898) in particular, is apparent in this novel. Early in the narrative, after the consensus opinion is reached that the submerged visitors are hostile invaders, the Wells novel is even specifically referred to by Wyndham's pessimistic scientist character, and the possible similarity between the two situations is noted. Wyndham is considerably ahead of his time in not describing the aliens per se, but only their vessels, the modern theory of effective horror writing being that the suggestion of the atrocious is usually more gripping than a photographic depiction.

Like many of Wyndham's most effective stories, this novel is a first-person narrative, and, like most of

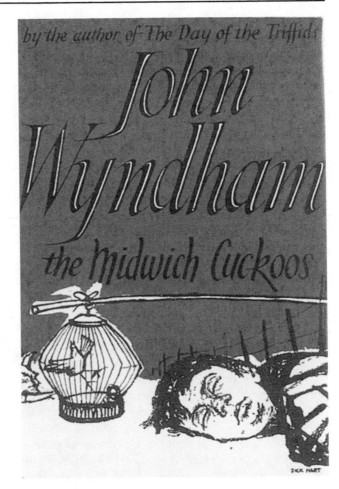

*Dust jacket for Wyndham's 1957 novel, about an English village in which the women give birth to the offspring of space aliens (*Modern First Editions *auction catalogue)*

Wyndham's narrators, this one is a common man—adequately educated, intelligent, employed in interesting work, but just an ordinary chap. He is the sort of individual one trusts, whose word the reader is unlikely to doubt. The utilization of this sort of storyteller is certainly a major factor in the popularity of the sort of drama for which Wyndham is most likely to be remembered: the eventual triumph of the decent right-thinking but tough-minded British citizen over evil intruders, be they the product of human miscalculation or the agents of alien aggression.

Most critics agree that *The Kraken Wakes* is an important part of Wyndham's work; even the staid *New York Times Book Review* praised it. In his *In Search of Wonder* (1967) Damon Knight commented, "keeping his focus sharply on the human figures in the foreground, Wyndham works a curious household magic: You have to believe in the monstrous events of the story, because they're happening to people you know." Many students of science fiction have noted the influence of Wyndham on Ballard, especially in Ballard's early work. His second novel, *The Drowned World* (1962), is set in an inundated London quite similar to the soggy British capital portrayed in *The Kraken Wakes*.

In January 1953 one of Wyndham's best pieces of short fiction was published by *Fantasy and Science Fiction* as "Perfect Creature." It was a rewrite of "The Perfect Creature" published by *Tales of Wonder* in 1937. The second version was reprinted by the British magazine *Argosy* as "Female of the Species," and this version has been reprinted in several anthologies and Wyndham collections, usually as "Una," the name of its leading character/creature. It is important to distinguish between the *Tales of Wonder* version and all the others, because in the rewrite the gender of the laboratory-made creature was changed from male to female and its motivation from anger to lust, thus producing an entirely different impact on the reader than the original version. As rewritten, the story is a classic of science-fiction humor. The contrast between the monstrous female creation, enormously oversexed as a result of an error in the laboratory, and the short, bespectacled object of her affection is a basic comic juxtaposition. When Wyndham adds his descriptions of the horny horror stamping her elephantine foot, rattling the bars of her cage, and bellowing "Gimme! Gimme!" as she stares fixedly at young Albert, it is about as funny as speculative fiction gets. This story is one of perhaps a dozen less-than-novel-length pieces that demonstrate that Wyndham was more than "the master of the cosy catastrophe" novel; when he finally got it right, he was a superb short-fiction writer.

The novelette "Chinese Puzzle," published in the British *Argosy* in February 1953, was a venture into pure fantasy and was Wyndham's only dragon story. The charming fable was set in Wales and exhibited not only the author's continued expansion of the droll side of his writing but also his skill in accurately portraying regional characteristics, speech patterns, and syntax.

Of the seven additional stories Wyndham produced in 1953, only one, "The Chronoclasm," purchased by Frederik Pohl for the first volume of the *Star Science Fiction Stories* series, is of more than routine interest. Despite his awareness of the possible paradoxes to be found in time-travel stories, Wyndham allows his characters to commit what appear to be several of them. They are, in fact, the "chronoclasms" (a word apparently coined by Wyndham) of the title. The most flagrant of these occurs when the girl from the twenty-second century marries the man from the twentieth and, based on the text, presumably has his baby when she is forced to return to her own time. In his foreword to *The Seeds of Time* Wyndham says, "The intention of 'Chronoclasm,' in the comedy-romantic, was to entertain the general reader and break away from the

science-fiction enthusiast." His point seems to be that the occurrence of such paradoxes, or "chronoclasms," is not only possible but is indeed a fact. He cites several examples, such as Leonardo da Vinci's invention of the parachute, an apparatus for which there could have been no conceivable use in his day. The implication is, of course, that da Vinci picked up the idea from a time traveler. The primary plot device for this story (the accessibility of time machines to highly qualified historians in order to visit their periods of specialization) is almost precisely the same as in Connie Willis's Nebula and Hugo Award–winning novel *Doomsday Book* (1992).

Another of Wyndham's best stories, "Esmerelda," first appeared in the collection *Jizzle,* published in England by Dobson in April 1954. Like the title story, it is set in the rather seamy atmosphere of a circus sideshow. The characters are a step—perhaps several steps—down the social ladder from the heroes of Wyndham's novels, but they are no less skillfully or sympathetically portrayed. Superficially about the wondrously strong title character, the story is really a well-crafted example of the eternal triangle plot, with one lady imaginatively getting the better of the other. It is entirely convincing, down to the detailed methods of training fleas to perform. A conceivable reason why this story was never anthologized, while some of the author's lesser pieces were, is that it is perhaps the only Wyndham story that cannot be classified as some form of speculative fiction.

Another 1954 Wyndham story that enjoyed great popularity and received the wide exposure of publication in a Sunday newspaper was "Compassion Circuit," first published by *Fantastic Universe* in December of that year. Its publication in the *Sunday Chronicle* was also in December. Such well-known anthologists as John Carnell, Groff Conklin, and Kingsley Amis and Robert Conquest reprinted the story over the years. This short story features Wyndham's only Terran robot, and she/it is far more believable than the coffin-shaped Martian ones of his earliest stories, even if her/its idea of compassion is a bit skewed.

Re-Birth, originally published in the United States by Ballantine in May 1955 in both hardback and paperback editions, was released in England by Michael Joseph in a hardback edition in September of that same year as *The Chrysalids,* the title by which it is better known. Immediately and enduringly popular, this novel had run to more than fifty editions or reprints by 1983. It also generated an audiotape recording and a rock album using portions of the text as lyrics ("Crown of Creation" by Jefferson Airplane, 1968). Many readers and critics consider it Wyndham's most important novel.

Wyndham again breaks new ground in his full-length works with this postcataclysm story of genetic

Scene from The Village of the Damned, *the 1960 motion picture based on*
The Midwich Cuckoos *(© 1960 Metro-Goldwyn-Mayer, Inc.)*

mutation. While both the British and American titles make it plain that Wyndham's primary focus is upon some form of regeneration—from what disaster is quickly revealed—he raises questions of human behavior that do not admit definitive answers. Arguably more thought-provoking than any of his other novels, *The Chrysalids* not only decries bigotry, it also reiterates one of his favorite themes, the desirable inevitability of social Darwinism. Far from suggesting that this ongoing evolution will be a panacea for humanity's ills, however, Wyndham predicts that even a superman will likely make the same sorts of errors, commit the same types of atrocities, and face the same relentless struggle for existence as his predecessors.

The story is told by young David Strorm, a telepathic mutant whose character is sympathetically developed through several metamorphoses, from age ten at the beginning of the novel to age twenty at the end. Wyndham's hard-earned skill in character delineation is displayed; readers learn about each player, major or minor, what they need to know.

The Labrador setting is described as somewhat austere—rather like a Pennsylvania Dutch farm—but not unpleasant. Thirty miles south, however, the dangerous areas begin: the "Wild Country," a ten-to-twenty-mile-deep band, where the chance of breeding mutants is greater than 50 percent; the "Fringes," where "nothing was dependable"; and the "Badlands," usually fatal to visitors.

The two themes—the postholocaust survival through persecution of deviants and evolution through mutation—are dealt with both concurrently and separately. The primary feature of the survivors' society is the code that mutations—plant, animal, or human—must be destroyed without exception. Later, however, Wyndham provides the reader with a plethora of possible interpretations when he introduces the controversy of the "great horses": animals identical to normal horses but half again the size. These horses are obviously mutations, but since they can do more than twice the work of normal horses while consuming less than twice the feed, and since the nonmechanized society (no fuel for machinery) is desperate for any kind of horse-power, the government declares that the great horses are not mutants, despite a division of public opinion over the issue. Human babies with six toes, however, or even the slightest blemish, are put to death. When the telepathic powers of some mutated children are discovered, they are pursued by a veritable army determined to destroy them. One thing that Wyndham is certainly doing is deploring the persecution of humans because they differ from the majority. (Presumably, if they were dangerously different—mutated to homicidal maniacs, for example—his attitude would be different.) But there is more than that on the author's mind, or there would be no point in bringing the great horses into the narrative. He could be commenting upon the conveniently elastic morals of the government; he could also be warning against throwing the baby out with the bath water. Certainly, he intended the reader to notice the irony of the great horses being the means of the children's escape.

Probably the most important comments on *The Chrysalids* by a Wyndham contemporary were those made by the dean of North American science-fiction critics at the time, Knight, and reprinted in his *In Search of Wonder*. An admirer of Wyndham's previous work, with high praise for *The Day of the Triffids* and *The Kraken Wakes,* Knight lauded Wyndham's "unflagging expert writing all the way through" this book; however, he felt that the original theme of persecution of those who are different should have been the author's sole focus and that when he introduced the telepathic element, he "hauled the whole plot away from his carefully built background, into just one more damned chase with a rousing cliché at the end of it." Not everyone felt that way. Aldiss, one of Britain's foremost science-fiction critics, noted in *Billion Year Spree* that in this book "the characters and settings are beautifully realised" and stated that *The Chrysalids* is Wyndham's "best novel."

In a 1979 critique in *Survey of Science Fiction Literature,* Gary K. Wolfe, a Wyndham specialist, considered *The Chrysalids* "a stylistically superior novel" and "perhaps the most successful of John Wyndham's novels, in terms of characterization and setting." He compared Wyndham favorably with Wells and noted that "Wyndham's skill in constructing an engrossing narrative is also in evidence throughout." Wolfe's only adverse criticism is the comment, "The novel's chief weakness stems from Wyndham's difficulty in integrating his two major science fiction concepts and the thematic ideas that are associated with each."

British university lecturer Rowland Wymer wrote what is probably the most thorough critical examination of *The Chrysalids*. In the Summer 1992 issue of *Foundation,* generally considered the most prestigious academic journal devoted to science fiction in the United Kingdom, Wymer characterized the book as "Wyndham's most interesting and complex novel."

Attacking Knight's "just one more damned chase" condemnation, Wymer countered that "the ostensible moral basis of the story is interestingly challenged and subverted as the narrative develops." Referring to the gradual shift of emphasis in the book from a liberal concern about persecution of those who are different to a "Nietzschean celebration of the superman," Wymer concludes that it is "a particularly interesting manifestation of what is Wyndham's most permanent and obsessive concern—the conflict between decent, liberal, 'English' social values and the harsher, more radical forms of thinking compelled by the recognition that life is a ceaseless and merciless struggle for survival."

During 1956 Wyndham made only one sale, of a relatively short novella (about twenty-four thousand words), but it was an important contribution to the author's body of work. "Consider Her Ways" was first published in a three-story anthology titled *Sometime, Never* (1956) and was reprinted seven times. Such well-known anthologists as Knight, Edmund Crispin, and Robert Silverberg liked it well enough to include it in books they edited. It has received more critical commentary than any of Wyndham's other short works.

A young physician and recent widow, Jane, volunteers to participate in an experiment involving a hallucinogenic narcotic and either finds herself or imagines herself in an all-female near future, where she is one of the revered "Mother" caste in a logically organized, four-tiered, ant-like, human society. Indeed, the title is derived from the Bible (Prov. 6:6): "Go to the ant, thou sluggard; consider her ways, and be wise." In the early part of the story, the young woman is convinced that she is having an incredibly detailed dream, as her situation and surroundings are so bizarre and yet so real. In the end, however, after her return to the present (or to reality), she decides that she has been permitted a glimpse of a possible and—to her—horrific future. In an attempt to prevent that future from taking place, she murders the scientist she believes will be responsible for the eradication of the men and burns his laboratory to wipe out his work. Whether she succeeds or not Wyndham leaves tantalizingly ambiguous, when in the denouement we learn that the scientist has a biochemist son who "appears to have taken quite a close interest in his father's work, and is determined that it shan't be wasted."

Wyndham successfully establishes the dream-like, almost nightmarish setting, which at first reminds one of the work of Franz Kafka and, later, of George Orwell. The characters—almost all female—are skillfully realized, despite the fact that Wyndham, although having previously expressed various female points of view, had never used a female protagonist. In this novel there are two.

The heart of the story, taking up about a third of its length, is the discussion between Jane and Laura, the chief historian of the female society and one of its few members to have knowledge of the now-disappeared male gender. (All the males, it is explained, died when attacked by a virus created to eliminate rats.) Basically, their conversation is a debate on the subject of whether the single-gender society is a utopia (Laura's view) or a dystopia (Jane's view). Laura makes various telling points relating to the second-class citizenship of women in Jane's time and concludes that, logically, women are better off without men. Jane counters with her belief that without romantic love for a man, a woman's life is pointless. Wymer commented, "The ant's-nest society of *Consider Her Ways* has a feminist dimension which complicates interpretation but . . . the dominant effect is frighteningly alien rather than Utopian." In his acclaimed 1960 book *New Maps of Hell* author and critic Amis, in a two-page evaluation of the story, took the opposite view: "Laura is not only a thoughtful and intelligent person but gets the best of the argument." The sexual urge is never mentioned, but it is reasonable to assume that, with no need for such an urge in a system of reproduction akin to that of bees, it would atrophy or be transmuted into platonic affection. With that assumption, the question of whether or not Wyndham would have been willing to venture into the subject of lesbianism in 1956 England does not become an issue.

In a review of *Sometime, Never* printed shortly after its publication and printed in *In Search of Wonder*, Knight wrote, "the story is beautifully written, fully realized in a way that few s.f. stories have been." In his introduction to the volume Arthur C. Clarke comments, "Wyndham's story has a nightmare quality and a psychological intensity which makes it quite different from anything else he's ever written. It's a new Wyndham which makes one sit up and think. I tried to forget this story—and I know perfectly well I won't succeed."

In 1957, after selling an odd little story called "But a Kind of Ghost," which raised no great clamor of approval, Wyndham turned out another good and popular novel (more than fifty editions or reprints) that meshed nicely with his other mature novels, dealing with the desperate measures sometimes necessary to ensure the continuation of the human race. Published as a hardback in Britain by Michael Joseph as *The Midwich Cuckoos* in September, it was brought out in the United States the following year, also in hardback, by Ballantine. In a paperback Ballantine edition in 1960 the title was changed to *The Village of the Damned,* the title of a feature-length movie version released the same year. The movie was well reviewed and is still occasionally seen on late-night television or Saturday "creature features."

In this novel Wyndham appears to present the reverse argument of one of the themes of *The Chrysalids,* that persecution of those who differ from others in some way is inherently wrong. In *The Midwich Cuckoos* he argues, with equal vigor, that the different minority must be destroyed if humanity is to survive. The distinction between the two situations, however, is that in *The Chrysalids* the minority is composed of human beings, who are sympathetically portrayed, while in *The Midwich Cuckoos* the minority is made up of aliens for whom no sympathy is ever developed.

The title derives from the habit of cuckoo birds of depositing their eggs in the nests of other birds and thus avoiding the difficulties of raising their own young. The cuckoos of the title are aliens—the reader is told nothing about them—who, during a day lost to the memory of all residents, impregnate all sixty-two women of childbearing age in an English village. In due course the babies are born and soon begin to exert control over the humans, forcing them, for example, to keep all the children in the village. When they feel they are being threatened, the alien children are capable of committing atrocious acts, reminiscent of the monstrous child in Jerome Bixby's classic story "It's a *Good* Life" (1953). The aliens do not have a hive mentality but rather a group awareness: what is taught to one is learned by all. It seems probable that this linked-mind concept influenced Wyndham's thinking in the plotting of his final, posthumously published novel, *Web* (1979).

There are the same underlying messages of social Darwinism found in all of Wyndham's novels going back to *The Day of the Triffids.* Wyndham's authoritative figure, author/philosopher/teacher Gordon Zellaby, the man who ultimately sacrifices himself to remove the peril represented by the changeling children, sums up the message when he says, "there is no conception more fallacious than the sense of cosiness implied by 'Mother Nature.' Each species must strive to survive, and that it will do, by every means in its power, however foul—unless the instinct to survive is weakened by conflict with another instinct."

Most reviewers seemed to feel that *The Midwich Cuckoos* displays Wyndham's continued excellence as a speculative-fiction writer during the early and mid 1950s, when he was a dominant force in the genre in England. P. Schuyler Miller, in the September 1958 issue of *Astounding Science-Fiction,* remarked, "It's beginning to look as if 'John Wyndham' can do no wrong. By mid-February he had already given us what may very well be voted the best SF novel of '58." Gary K. Wolfe, in *Survey of Science Fiction Literature* (1979), edited by Frank N. Magill, wrote, "Superior in plotting, style, and characterization, *The Midwich Cuckoos* is only slightly short of being a science fiction masterpiece."

In 1958, apparently with a commission from John Carnell, then editor of *New Worlds,* Wyndham wrote a series of novelettes set in various places in the solar system. Four linked stories, occurring fifty years apart, concern the adventures of space pioneer George Montgomery "Ticker" Troon and various of his descendants. The stories—"The Space-Station: A.D. 1994," "The Moon: A.D. 2044," "Mars A.D. 2094," and "Venus A.D. 2144"—appeared in almost-successive issues of the magazine between April and September. A final story in the series appeared in *New Worlds* in November 1960.

This series is unusual in several respects: the astronaut dynasty concept; the even, fifty-year spacing of the episodes; and the emergence of Brazil as the unlikely superpower in space. Wyndham's apparent intention was to put the stories together eventually as a saga in novel form. All the stories carried the byline John Wyndham, but when they were published together as a Michael Joseph hardback, *The Outward Urge,* in 1959, the byline was John Wyndham and Lucas Parkes. The latter was another of Wyndham's pseudonyms; speculating on the reason for crediting a fake collaborator, David Pringle suggests in *The Ultimate Guide to Science Fiction* (1990) that "the use of this name perhaps indicated the author's unease (or his publisher's) with this material." Others have guessed that it was to set the "novel" apart from the catastrophic/Darwinistic books he had been producing since *The Day of the Triffids.*

These stories were all competitive with most of the space operettas being published at the time. The final one, "The Emptiness of Space," about the last of the Troons, who literally loses his soul in space, has an ethereal quality that is reminiscent of the best of Gerald Kersh's short fiction. Anthologized by editors such as Mike Ashley and Judith Merril, it was reprinted seven times.

Wyndham's production fell off sharply following the fourth Troon episode for *New Worlds.* His entire output between September 1958 and September 1960 was "Brief to Counsel," a strange, never-reprinted mixture of crime and fantasy that, at 1,100 words, was little more than a vignette. It was published in the British *Argosy* in February 1959. His byline was not seen again until September 1960, when *Suspense* published his tongue-in-cheek deal-with-the-devil story "A Long Spoon."

That same month Wyndham got back into the novel business. First published in hardback by Michael Joseph and a few months later by Ballantine in paperback, *Trouble with Lichen* was not quite the smash hit that some of Wyndham's previous novels were with either the publishers or the critics. Still, with more than thirty editions or reprints, it must have had some popular appeal. Some students of Wyndham's work have nothing but praise for it. In *Science Fiction Monthly* Walter Gillings considered it "Wyndham at his most Wellsian—and at his best." In *Anatomy of Wonder,* edited by Neil Barron (third edition, 1987), Joe De Bolt and John R. Pfeiffer judged it "Good social psychology. Fine Wyndham story, as usual." Many speculative-fiction historians, however, have ignored the book or given it superficial consideration.

Trouble with Lichen is relatively free of the violent action of most of his previous novels. Wyndham's characters are fully formed and true to life; his settings are realistic and appropriate; and his narrative and dialogue are effective, urbane, and frequently witty. The satiric treatment of politicians, newspapermen, the advertising industry, the filthy rich, and other segments of the society of Wyndham's day is on target and amusing. Most essential, though, is the credibility of his plotline, which concerns the discovery of a substance that can delay the aging process. All of his other novels required anywhere from a little to a great deal of suspension of disbelief, but it is not needed for this novel—at least not in the modern world.

In the years since Wyndham developed this idea, scientific knowledge, particularly that related to biochemistry, has increased greatly. It is now conceivable—indeed, it seems almost inevitable—that a life-prolonging substance will eventually be synthesized. Once that premise is accepted, all of Wyndham's hypotheses in the novel fall into place. In real life the majority of people probably would act and react just as Wyndham's characters do, and things would happen more or less as they happen in the book: the discoverers are in a quandary of indecision; they eventually treat themselves and a few, select others; the secret is uncovered; people take extreme actions of various kinds; and so on. Because it foresees an increasingly likely scenario, *Trouble with Lichen* may one day become Wyndham's best-known work.

The author only produced a few short pieces in 1961, the most remarkable of which was "Random Quest," an alternate-universe novelette (almost a novella) written specifically for inclusion in his six-story collection, *Consider Her Ways and Others.* It was reprinted three times, made into a BBC teleplay in 1969, and filmed in 1971 as *Quest for Love.* The characterization, the plotting, and the attention to nuance and detail are all excellent.

"Chocky," a novelette, was Wyndham's only published work in 1963. *Amazing* published it in March, and *Good Housekeeping* reprinted it in April. It is a low-key story, with more cerebration than action, depicting an alien scout who becomes friendly with a twelve-year-old English boy, the only human who can see or hear him. There is a simple plot in which the alien is responsible for saving the boy's sister from drowning before returning to wherever he came from (deeming Earth unsuitable for colonization), but the piece is really a vehicle for considering some ways that Wyndham thought the world could be improved. These ruminations all come from the alien in the form of puzzlements. Why do humans not have a more logical calendar? Why do they not have land vehicles that are incapable of running into each other? Why do they not live to the much more sensible age of two-hundred-plus years (consistent with Wyndham's thinking in *Trouble with Lichen*)?

It was almost three years before another Wyndham piece appeared, and it did not rank among his best. There is no way of estimating how many people read this Christmas story, but since "In Outer Space There Shone a Star" was published in the magazine *T.V. Times Xmas Extra* in December 1965, the potential readership must have been considerable. Wyndham's spaced-out astronaut delivers this coda to those assembled: "Go away, and learn humility . . . learn that god is not only the God of Earth. He is the God of the Universe—God of *all* the planets." The story was never reprinted.

By the time Wyndham wrote *Chocky* (1968), his last "finished" novel, he was either almost out of inspiration or almost out of energy. The short novel (not much more than fifty thousand words) was first published as a Ballantine paperback in 1968 and quickly followed by a Michael Joseph hardback edition. The book was an expansion of Wyndham's 1963 novelette, and although he was somewhat more optimistic about humanity's prospects in the novel than in the shorter piece, the story and the message were to all intents and purposes the same.

The book was virtually ignored by reviewers and has rarely been mentioned in considerations of Wyndham's work. Critical disdain notwithstanding, book sales ran to twenty-five editions (including a Science Fiction Book Club edition) or reprints. Interest was sufficient to engender a BBC radio play and an ITV serial and two sequels.

A bachelor for sixty years, Wyndham married schoolteacher Grace Wilson (with whom he had been friends since 1932) and moved out of London to Petersfield in Hampshire in 1963. He died there on 10 March 1969, peacefully, of heart failure. The short novel *Web* (about fifty thousand words) was published more than ten years later. Sparsely reviewed (Stephensen-Payne lists only three reviews—two of those in fanzines—as compared to the ten to twenty that attended each of his previous catastrophe novels), the book was not nearly

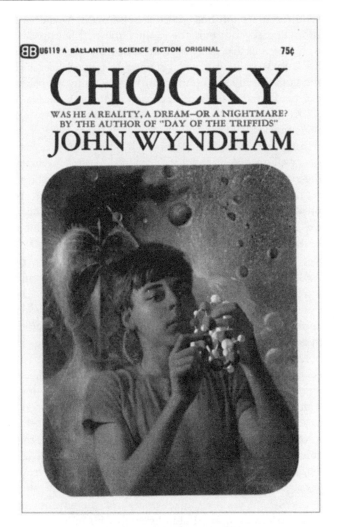

Cover for Wyndham's 1968 novel, about the friendship of an Earth boy and an alien

as popular as his others, with only three editions and half a dozen reprints. Part of this decline in interest was because Wyndham was ten years dead. Part of it was because of the proliferation of new writers of speculative fiction, as well as new themes and directions, that appeared in the 1970s. And part of it was because of the subject matter. People have traditionally feared and hated spiders and, despite the current popularity of "creepy-crawly" horror stories, many did not want to read about them, particularly when an entirely plausible case was made for the possibility of those particular arachnids becoming the dominant species on the planet and eliminating Homo sapiens in the process.

The book was still under revision at the time of Wyndham's death; it had not yet been accepted by his regular hardcover publisher, Michael Joseph. In *The Ultimate Guide to Science Fiction* Pringle says that the book "was published in unfinished form," which is debatable since Wyndham's brother, Vivian, seems to have been responsible for the published version. Supposedly Wyndham submitted several revisions to the publisher, but his editors there felt that none of them raised the quality of the book to Wyndham's usual standard of excellence, and the house declined to publish it. Yet, the same publisher accepted it ten years later; the Science Fiction Book Club (U.K.) put out a hardback edition that same year; and Penguin Books printed a paperback edition in 1980, with reprints in 1982, 1983, 1984, 1987, and 1988. If it did that well after Wyndham was relatively long gone from the scene, one can only surmise how it might have been received when he was still alive and so popular that his previous novel, *Chocky,* a lightweight novel of ideas expanded from a five-year-old novelette, went through several editions and reprints in a year or so.

Despite critical indifference and editorial stubbornness, this novel is entirely consistent with Wyndham's repeated themes and ongoing philosophy expressed in his other major works: the preservation of any species is a difficult, ruthless, and endless struggle; any species must continuously evolve to survive; and humanity is not necessarily the culmination of the evolutionary process. Wyndham's authoritative figure, conspicuously named Cogent, sums up much of the Wyndham doctrine economically when she says, "Nature is a process, not a state—a continuous process. A striving to keep alive. No species has a right to exist; it simply has the ability or the inability. It survives by matching its fecundity against the forces which threaten it with destruction."

Also, Wyndham again points out the advantages that a society composed of individuals with some kind of group consciousness would have over one without such a symbiotic connection. He illustrated this idea first in the just-hinted-at mental blanket beginning to be shared by the triffids, restated it with the telepathic powers of the mutant human children in *The Chrysalids,* reiterated it in the hive behavior in "Consider Her Ways," and made it frighteningly inimical to human survival in the mental osmosis of the alien children in *The Midwich Cuckoos.* In *Web* the spiders, while retaining their individuality, attack in concert, making them deadly. Cogent remarks, "Becoming social may have implications we haven't seen yet. It has had immense implications with the ants and the bees. They are now the original spiders plus something, as I said. It remains to be discovered just what that plus is."

The premise is the believable one of a rich man, Lord Foxfield, seeking "a medium that would express—and, incidentally, be seen to express—his desire to benefit mankind by tidying up some neglected corner of its feckless world." What that medium turns out to be is the establishment of a utopian colony on a small Pacific island. He finds as his project manager an idealistic architect who "was almost constantly in a state of inky vendetta with other correspondents upon one or other of our social inadequacies." Readers are briefly introduced to the members of the colony (including a farmer, a carpenter, an engineer, and a biologist), and Lord Foxfield sees them off with William Ernest Henley's well-known line, "I am the master of my fate; I am the captain of my soul."

In the long second chapter Wyndham gives the reader a condensed version of the history of the fictional island of Tanakuatua, the chosen spot, from the days of Captain James Cook to approximately 1968. Important in that history is the fact that the island was evacuated a few years after World War II for fear of radioactive fallout from a distant atomic bomb test. Refusing to leave, the head medicine man placed a terrible curse of destruction on all who attempt to live on the island and killed himself to bind the taboo. As he had often done before, Wyndham holds humanity at least partly responsible for the ensuing catastrophe.

About the project readers learn little, because there is only time to set the scene and philosophize a bit about the inevitability of the survival of the fittest before disaster strikes. What appears, through binoculars, to be mist hanging over the far end of the island turns out to be an enormous web. In investigating the phenomenon, a member of the party is attacked and killed by spiders that individually are neither particularly large nor particularly menacing but whose developed "corporate sensitivity" renders them nightmarishly horrific. After that there is considerable Grand Guignol horror as other members of the colony succumb. In between the colonists' various attempted defenses against the now-voracious arachnids, Wyndham hypothesizes all sorts of gruesome evolutionary possibilities for the spiders—including transportation on thermal currents to other lands—any one of which could end with the spiders the dominant, if not the only, species left on Earth. Eventually just two survivors, Cogent and the narrator, are rescued. The island is nuked, but at the end of the book the narrator receives a pickled specimen of island spider sent to him by Cogent—from Peru.

In an otherwise perceptive review of the book in *Foundation,* Ashley Rock characterized the first and closing chapters of the novel as "pedestrian," but concluded, "if the episode on the island falls short of being a masterpiece, it is only by the breadth of a silken thread."

During the 1950s and for a few years beyond, a period when speculative-fiction stories and novels were being written by giants of the genre, John Wyndham dominated the field in Great Britain and more than held his own against American writers when his work was published in the United States. He did not hesitate to express his principles in what he wrote. He was against what he believed to be wrong–discrimination or bigotry of any kind, greed and self-aggrandizement, military expansionism–and said so. He supported the commitment of humanity to whatever adaptation and evolutionary growth was necessary to ensure the continued viability of the human race. And he could deliver these messages in different but always entrancing formats. His books, translated into dozens of languages, sold in the hundreds of thousands, and they are still selling.

Bibliography:

Phil Stephensen-Payne, *John Wyndham: Creator of the Cosy Catastrophe,* second revised edition (Leeds: Galactic Central, 1989).

References:

Brian W. Aldiss, *Billion Year Spree* (London: Weidenfeld & Nicolson, 1973, pp. 290–291, 293–294);

Kingsley Amis, *New Maps of Hell* (New York: Harcourt, Brace, 1960);

Neil Barron, ed., *Anatomy of Wonder,* third edition (New York: R. R. Bowker, 1987);

E. F. Bleiler, "Luncheon with John Wyndham," *Extrapolation,* 24 (Winter 1984): 314–317;

Thomas D. Clareson and Alice Clareson, "The Neglected Fiction of John Wyndham: 'Consider Her Ways,' *The Trouble with Lichen* and *Web,*" in *Science Fiction Roots and Branches: Contemporary Critical Approaches,* edited by Rhys Garnett and R. J. Ellis (London: Macmillan, 1990; New York: St. Martin's Press, 1990), pp. 88–103;

Walter Gillings, "In The Days Before the Triffids," *Cypher,* no. 8 (September 1972): 46–49;

Gillings, "John Wyndham," *Science Fiction Monthly,* 1, no. 9 (1974): 6–9;

Vivian Beynon Harris, "John Wyndham, a Memoir," edited by David Ketterer, *Foundation,* 75 (Spring 1999): 5–50;

L. J. Hurst, "Remembrance of Things to Come? *Nineteen Eighty-Four* and *The Day of the Triffids* Again," *Vector,* 201 (September/October 1998): 15–17;

Hurst, "*We Are the Dead': The Day of the Triffids* and *Nineteen Eighty-Four,*" *Vector,* 133 (August/September 1986): 4–5;

David Ketterer, "John Wyndham and 'the Searing Anguishes of Childhood': From 'Fairy Story' to *Chocky,*" *Extrapolation,* 41 (Summer 2000): 87–103;

Ketterer, "*Plan for Chaos/Fury of Creation*: An Unpublished Science Fiction Novel by John Beynon," *Foundation,* 74 (Autumn 1998): 8–25;

Ketterer, "'Vivisection': Schoolboy 'John Wyndham's' First Publication," *Foundation,* 79 (Summer 2000): 70–84;

Damon Knight, *In Search of Wonder* (Chicago: Advent, 1967), pp. 178–179, 245–246, 252–254;

P. Schuyler Miller, "The Reference Library," *Astounding Science Fiction,* British edition (September 1958): 151–152;

Sam Moskowitz, *Seekers of Tomorrow: Masters of Modern Science Fiction* (Cleveland: World, 1966), pp. 118–132;

David Pringle, *The Ultimate Guide to Science Fiction* (New York: Pharos Books, 1990);

Ashley Rock, "*Web* by John Wyndham," *Foundation,* 17 (September 1979): 81–83;

Marshall B. Tymn, Introduction to *The Day of the Triffids,* by John Wyndham (Norwalk, Conn.: Easton Press, 1969);

Gary K. Wolfe, "*Re-Birth,*" in *Survey of Science Fiction Literature,* volume 4, edited by Frank N. Magill (Englewood Cliffs, N.J.: Salem Press, 1979), 1394, pp. 1755–1758;

Rowland Wymer, "How 'Safe' is John Wyndham? A Close Look at His Work, with Particular Reference to *The Chrysalids,*" *Foundation,* 55 (Summer 1992): 25–34.

Papers:

An almost complete archive of John Wyndham's manuscripts, typescripts (including unpublished works), proofs, and correspondence is held by the Sydney Jones Library at the University of Liverpool.

Books for Further Reading

Aldiss, Brian W., and David Wingrove. *Trillion Year Spree: The History of Science Fiction.* London: Gollancz, 1986; New York: Atheneum, 1986.

Amis, Kingsley. *New Maps of Hell: A Survey of Science Fiction.* New York: Harcourt, Brace, 1960; London: Gollancz, 1961.

Ashley, Mike. *The Time Machines: The Story of the Science-Fiction Pulp Magazines from the Beginning to 1950,* 3 volumes. Liverpool: Liverpool University Press, 2000.

Ashley. *Who's Who in Horror and Fantasy Fiction.* London: Elm Tree, 1977; New York: Taplinger, 1978.

Attebury, Brian. *Strategies of Fantasy.* Bloomington: Indiana University Press, 1992.

Bailey, J. O. *Pilgrims through Space and Time: Trends and Patterns in Scientific and Utopian Fiction.* New York: Argus, 1947.

Barron, Neil, ed. *Anatomy of Wonder: A Critical Guide to Science Fiction,* fourth edition. New Providence, N.J.: Bowker, 1995.

Barron, ed. *Fantasy and Horror: A Critical and Historical Guide to Literature, Illustration, Film, TV, Radio, and the Internet.* Lanham, Md.: Scarecrow Press, 1999.

Becker, Allienne R. *The Lost Worlds Romance: From Dawn Till Dusk.* Westport, Conn.: Greenwood Press, 1992.

Bleiler, Everett F. *The Guide to Supernatural Fiction.* Kent, Ohio: Kent State University Press, 1983.

Bleiler, ed. *Supernatural Fiction Writers: Fantasy and Horror,* 2 volumes. New York: Scribners, 1985.

Bleiler, Richard, ed. *Science Fiction Writers: Critical Studies of the Major Authors from the Early Nineteenth Century to the Present Day,* second edition. New York: Scribners, 1998.

Bloom, Clive, ed. *Creepers: British Horror and Fantasy in the Twentieth Century.* London & Boulder, Colo.: Pluto, 1993.

Boyer, Robert H., and Kenneth J. Zahorski, eds. *Fantasists on Fantasy: A Collection of Critical Reflections.* New York: Avon, 1984.

Briggs, Julia. *Night Visitors: The Rise and Fall of the English Ghost Story.* London: Faber & Faber, 1977.

Carpenter, Humphrey. *The Inklings: C. S. Lewis, J. R. R. Tolkien, Charles Williams, and Their Friends.* London: Allen & Unwin, 1978; Boston: Houghton Mifflin, 1979.

Carter, Lin. *Imaginary Worlds: The Art of Fantasy.* New York: Ballantine, 1973.

Carter, Paul A. *The Creation of Tomorrow: Fifty Years of Magazine Science Fiction.* New York: Columbia University Press, 1977.

Cavaliero, Glen. *The Supernatural and English Fiction.* Oxford & New York: Oxford University Press, 1995.

Cawthorn, James, and Michael Moorcock. *Fantasy: The 100 Best Books*. London: Xanadu, 1988; New York: Carroll & Graf, 1988.

Clarke, I. F. *The Pattern of Expectation, 1644–2001*. London: Cape, 1979; New York: Basic Books, 1979.

Clute, John, and John Grant, eds. *The Encyclopedia of Fantasy*. London: Orbit, 1997; New York: St. Martin's Press, 1997.

Clute and Peter Nicholls, eds. *The Encyclopedia of Science Fiction*. New York: St. Martin's Press, 1993.

Cooper, Susan. *Dreams and Wishes: Essays on Writing for Children*. New York: Margaret K. McElderry Books, 1996.

Daniels, Les. *Living in Fear: A History of Horror in the Mass Media*. New York: Scribners, 1975.

de Camp, L. Sprague. *Literary Swordsmen and Sorcerers: The Makers of Heroic Fantasy*. Sauk City, Wis.: Arkham House, 1976.

Ferns, Chris. *Narrating Utopia: Ideology, Gender, Form in Utopian Literature*. Liverpool: Liverpool University Press, 1999.

Gose, Elliott B. *Mere Creatures: A Study of Modern Fantasy Tales for Children*. Toronto & Buffalo, N.Y.: University of Toronto Press, 1988.

Green, Roger Lancelyn. *Into Other Worlds: Space-Flight in Fiction, from Lucian to Lewis*. London & New York: Abelard-Schuman, 1958.

Gunn, James, ed. *The New Encyclopedia of Science Fiction*. New York: Viking, 1988.

Heller, Terry. *The Delights of Terror: An Aesthetics of the Tale of Terror*. Urbana: University of Illinois Press, 1987.

Hillegas, Mark R. *The Future as Nightmare: H. G. Wells and the Anti-Utopians*. New York: Oxford University Press, 1967.

Hume, Kathryn. *Fantasy and Mimesis: Responses to Reality in Western Literature*. London: Methuen, 1984.

Irwin, W. R. *The Game of the Impossible: A Rhetoric of Fantasy*. Urbana: University of Illinois Press, 1976.

Jackson, Rosemary. *Fantasy: The Literature of Subversion*. London & New York: Methuen, 1981.

James, Edward. *Science Fiction in the 20th Century*. Oxford & New York: Oxford University Press, 1994.

Jones, Stephen, and Kim Newman, eds. *Horror: 100 Best Books*. London: Xanadu, 1988; New York: Carroll & Graf, 1988.

Joshi, S. T. *The Weird Tale: Arthur Machen, Lord Dunsany, Algernon Blackwood, M. R. James, Ambrose Bierce, H. P. Lovecraft*. Austin: University of Texas Press, 1990.

Kroeber, Karl. *Romantic Fantasy and Science Fiction*. New Haven: Yale University Press, 1988.

Le Guin, Ursula K. *The Language of the Night: Essays on Fantasy and Science Fiction,* edited by Susan Wood. Revised edition. New York: HarperCollins, 1992.

Lewis, C. S. *An Experiment in Criticism*. Cambridge: Cambridge University Press, 1961.

Lewis. *Of Other Worlds: Essays and Stories,* edited by Walter Hooper. London: Bles, 1966; New York: Harcourt, Brace & World, 1967.

Lewis. *On Stories, and Other Essays on Literature*. New York: Harcourt Brace Jovanovich, 1982.

Little, T. E. *The Fantasts: Studies in J. R. R. Tolkien, Lewis Carroll, Mervyn Peake, Nikolay Gogol, and Kenneth Grahame*. Amersham, U.K.: Avebury, 1984.

Lochhead, Marion. *The Renaissance of Wonder in Children's Literature*. Edinburgh: Canongate, 1977. Republished as *Renaissance of Wonder: The Fantasy Worlds of J. R. R. Tolkien, C. S. Lewis, George MacDonald, E. Nesbit and Others*. San Francisco: Harper & Row, 1980.

MacRae, Cathi Dunn. *Presenting Young Adult Fantasy Fiction*. New York: Twayne, 1998.

Magill, Frank N., ed. *Survey of Modern Fantasy Literature,* 5 volumes. Englewood Cliffs, N.J.: Salem Press, 1983.

Magill, ed. *Survey of Science Fiction and Fantasy Literature,* 4 volumes. Pasadena: Salem Press, 1996.

Magill, ed. *Survey of Science Fiction Literature,* 5 volumes. Englewood Cliffs, N.J.: Salem Press, 1979.

Manlove, C. N. *Christian Fantasy: From 1200 to the Present*. London: Macmillan, 1992; Notre Dame, Ind.: University of Notre Dame Press, 1992.

Manlove. *The Impulse of Fantasy Literature*. Kent, Ohio: Kent State University Press, 1983.

Manlove. *Modern Fantasy: Five Studies*. Cambridge & New York: Cambridge University Press, 1975.

Manlove. *Scottish Fantasy Literature: A Critical Survey*. Edinburgh: Canongate, 1994.

Moorcock, Michael. *Wizardry and Wild Romance: A Study of Epic Fantasy*. London: Gollancz, 1987.

Parrinder, Patrick. *Science Fiction: Its Criticism and Teaching*. London & New York: Methuen, 1980.

Parrinder, ed. *Science Fiction: A Critical Guide*. London & New York: Longman, 1979.

Penzoldt, Peter. *The Supernatural in Fiction*. New York: Nevill, 1952.

Pringle, David. *Modern Fantasy: The Hundred Best Novels, an English-Language Selection, 1946–1987*. London: Grafton, 1988; New York: Bedrick, 1989.

Punter, David. *The Literature of Terror: A History of Gothic Fictions from 1765 to the Present Day*. London & New York: Longman, 1980.

Rabkin, Eric S. *The Fantastic in Literature*. Princeton: Princeton University Press, 1976.

Rabkin, Martin H. Greenberg, and Joseph D. Olander, eds. *No Place Else: Explorations in Utopian and Dystopian Fiction*. Carbondale: Southern Illinois University Press, 1983.

Ruddick, Nicholas. *British Science Fiction: A Chronology, 1478–1990*. New York, Westport, Conn. & London: Greenwood Press, 1992.

Ruddick. *Ultimate Island: On the Nature of British Science Fiction*. Westport, Conn. & London: Greenwood Press, 1993.

Sammons, Martha C. *"A Better Country": The Worlds of Religious Fantasy and Science Fiction*. Westport, Conn.: Greenwood Press, 1988.

Schlobin, Roger C. *The Literature of Fantasy: A Comprehensive, Annotated Bibliography of Modern Fantasy Fiction*. New York: Garland, 1979.

Scholes, Robert, and Rabkin. *Science Fiction: History, Science, Vision.* New York: Oxford University Press, 1977.

Schweitzer, Darrell, ed. *Discovering Classic Fantasy Fiction: Essays on the Antecedents of Fantastic Literature.* San Bernardino, Cal.: Borgo Press, 1996.

Searles, Baird, Martin Last, Beth Meacham, and Michael Franklin. *A Reader's Guide to Science Fiction.* New York: Avon, 1979.

Searles, Meacham, and Franklin. *A Reader's Guide to Fantasy.* New York: Avon, 1982.

Smith, Curtis C., ed. *Twentieth-Century Science-Fiction Writers,* second edition. Chicago: St. James Press, 1986.

Smith, Karen Patricia. *The Fabulous Realm: A Literary-Historical Approach to British Fantasy, 1780–1990.* Metuchen, N.J.: Scarecrow Press, 1993.

Stableford, Brian. *Algebraic Fantasies and Realistic Romances: More Masters of Science Fiction.* San Bernardino, Cal.: Borgo Press, 1995.

Stableford. *Scientific Romance in Britain, 1890–1950.* London: Fourth Estate, 1985; New York: St. Martin's Press, 1985.

Sullivan, Jack. *Elegant Nightmares: The English Ghost Story from Le Fanu to Blackwood.* Athens: Ohio University Press, 1978.

Sullivan, ed. *The Penguin Encyclopedia of Horror and the Supernatural.* New York: Viking, 1986.

Suvin, Darko. *Metamorphoses of Science Fiction: On the Poetics and History of a Literary Genre.* New Haven & London: Yale University Press, 1979.

Swinfen, Ann. *In Defence of Fantasy: A Study of the Genre in English and American Literature Since 1945.* London & Boston: Routledge & Kegan Paul, 1984.

Thompson, Raymond H. *The Return from Avalon: A Study of the Arthurian Legend in Modern Fiction.* Westport, Conn.: Greenwood Press, 1985.

Tuck, Donald H., ed. *The Encyclopedia of Science Fiction and Fantasy through 1968,* 3 volumes. Chicago: Advent, 1974–1982.

Tymn, Marshall B., and Ashley, eds. *Science Fiction, Fantasy, and Weird Fiction Magazines.* Westport, Conn.: Greenwood Press, 1985.

Wagar, W. Warren. *Terminal Visions: The Literature of Last Things.* Bloomington: Indiana University Press, 1982.

Wagenknecht, Edward. *Seven Masters of Supernatural Fiction.* New York: Greenwood Press, 1991.

Waggoner, Diana. *The Hills of Faraway: A Guide to Fantasy.* New York: Atheneum, 1978.

Wilson, Colin. *The Strength to Dream: Literature and the Imagination.* London: Gollancz, 1962; Boston: Houghton Mifflin, 1962.

Wolfe, Gary K. *Critical Terms for Science Fiction and Fantasy: A Glossary and Guide to Scholarship.* Westport, Conn.: Greenwood Press, 1986.

Yoke, Carl B., and Donald M. Hassler, eds. *Death and the Serpent: Immortality in Science Fiction and Fantasy.* Westport, Conn.: Greenwood Press, 1985.

Contributors

Walter Albert . . . . *Pittsburgh, Pennsylvania*

Bernadette Lynn Bosky . . . . *Yonkers, New York*

Corbin S. Carnell . . . . *University of Florida*

Robert Carrick . . . . *Málaga, Spain*

Edgar L. Chapman . . . . *Bradley University*

Steve Eng . . . . *Nashville, Tennessee*

Tanya Gardiner-Scott . . . . *Mount Ida College*

Michael W. George . . . . *Ohio Northern University*

Darren Harris-Fain . . . . *Shawnee State University*

Johan Heje . . . . *Greve Gymnasium, Denmark*

Maureen F. Moran . . . . *Brunel University, London*

Marie Nelson . . . . *University of Florida*

Daphne Patai . . . . *University of Massachusetts Amherst*

Salvatore Proietti . . . . *Università di Roma "La Sapienza"*

John R. Pfeiffer . . . . *Central Michigan University*

Betty Richardson . . . . *Southern Illinois University at Edwardsville*

Amelia A. Rutledge . . . . *George Mason University*

Joe Sanders . . . . *Mentor, Ohio*

William F. Touponce . . . . *Indiana University–Purdue University at Indianapolis*

Cumulative Index

Dictionary of Literary Biography, Volumes 1-255
Dictionary of Literary Biography Yearbook, 1980-2000
Dictionary of Literary Biography Documentary Series, Volumes 1-19
Concise Dictionary of American Literary Biography, Volumes 1-7
Concise Dictionary of British Literary Biography, Volumes 1-8
Concise Dictionary of World Literary Biography, Volumes 1-4

Cumulative Index

DLB before number: *Dictionary of Literary Biography,* Volumes 1-254
Y before number: *Dictionary of Literary Biography Yearbook,* 1980-2000
DS before number: *Dictionary of Literary Biography Documentary Series,* Volumes 1-19
CDALB before number: *Concise Dictionary of American Literary Biography,* Volumes 1-7
CDBLB before number: *Concise Dictionary of British Literary Biography,* Volumes 1-8
CDWLB before number: *Concise Dictionary of World Literary Biography,* Volumes 1-4

C

J

L

O

ISBN 0-7876-5249-0

90000